RESEARCH HANDBOOK ON ARTIFICIAL INTELLIGENCE AND COMMUNICATION

To my families, Holly and Justice,
artificial intelligence,
and
AI scholars

Research Handbook on Artificial Intelligence and Communication

Edited by

Seungahn Nah

*Professor, Inaugural Dianne Snedaker Chair in Media Trust, and
Research Director, Consortium on Trust in Media and Technology,
College of Journalism and Communications, University of Florida, USA*

Cheltenham, UK · Northampton, MA, USA

Published by
Edward Elgar Publishing Limited
The Lypiatts
15 Lansdown Road
Cheltenham
Glos GL50 2JA
UK

Edward Elgar Publishing, Inc.
William Pratt House
9 Dewey Court
Northampton
Massachusetts 01060
USA

A catalogue record for this book
is available from the British Library

Library of Congress Control Number: 2023945215

This book is available electronically in the **Elgar**online
Sociology, Social Policy and Education subject collection
http://dx.doi.org/10.4337/9781803920306

ISBN 978 1 80392 029 0 (cased)
ISBN 978 1 80392 030 6 (eBook)

Printed and bound by CPI Group (UK) Ltd, Croydon, CR0 4YY

Contents

Contributors

Mashael Almoqbel is an Assistant Professor in Management Information Systems, Business Department, Jubail Industrial College, Saudi Arabia. Her research is in the areas of public safety, social media, social good, collective action, and human computer interaction.

Marcello Balduccini (PhD, Texas Tech University) is an Associate Professor at Saint Joseph's University, where he directs the Haub Innovation Center. His research interests span artificial intelligence, AI robotics, cybersecurity, and cyber-physical systems. He has developed novel knowledge representation techniques, algorithms for reasoning about actions and change, and logic-based methods for reasoning about the properties of cyber-physical systems. In 2016, Marcello was named Data Fellow by the National Consortium for Data Science, and in 2018 and 2020–2023 he was an Arrupe Center Research Fellow. Marcello has authored over 100 refereed publications.

Jessica K. Barfield is a PhD candidate in Information Sciences focusing on human interaction with emerging smart technologies such as AI-enabled humanoid robots operating with social skills. She is currently attending the University of Tennessee and received her undergraduate degree from Dartmouth College. Her research is focused on the extent to which an individual might self-disclose personal, embarrassing, and potentially sensitive information to humanoid robots and whether individuals might discriminate against robots as a function of the robot's physical features and behavior. She received the ASIS&T SIG Social Informatics: Emerging Scholar Social Informatics Researcher Award, and she reviews for Edward Elgar Publishing, the *Virtual Reality Journal*, the iConference, and for the *Paladyn Journal of Behavioral Robotics*.

Aylin Sabancı Bayramoğlu received her bachelor's degree from the Department of Computer Engineering at Süleyman Demirel University. She received her master degree in Computer Science from Pamukkale University in 2019. She has served as a business analyst at Aydem Energy and Abalıoğlu Holding for 5 years. She is currently working as a research assistant for the Management Information Systems Department at Pamukkale University. Her research areas include data mining and social network analysis.

Amanda Boyd (PhD, University of Calgary) is Co-Director of the Institute for Research and Education to Advance Community Health and Associate Professor in the College of Medicine both at Washington State University. Her work focuses on health, risk, and science communication.

Matthew Bundas (MS, New Mexico State University) holds a Master's Degree in Computer Science at New Mexico State University. While at NMSU, he has worked on projects related to knowledge representation and reasoning, cyber-physical systems, and the NIST CPS framework, as well as deep learning and computer vision. He obtained a Bachelors in Astrophysics from Michigan State University, performing research related to observational astronomy and computational astrophysics.

Tran Cao Son (PhD, University of Texas at El Paso) is a Professor in Computer Science at New Mexico State University. He is interested in knowledge representation and reasoning and the use of logic in problem solving. He has developed several high-level representation languages for representing and reasoning about dynamic systems such as the semantic web, SmartGrid, cyber-physical systems. He has authored more than 150 refereed publications and several state-of-the-art planning systems.

Xiaobei Chen is a doctoral student at the College of Journalism and Communications at the University of Florida. Her research focuses on using emerging technologies to promote health equity and to conduct communication skills training in healthcare.

Hichang Cho (PhD Cornell) is an Associate Professor in the Department of Communications and New Media at National University of Singapore. His research centers on human interactions with new communication technologies through which communication behaviors are shaped and expressed. More specifically, his research interests focus on privacy in a networked environment, collaboration in distributed teams, social influence on technology adoption and utilization, and social network analysis.

Hyesun Choung (PhD, University of Wisconsin-Madison) is an Assistant Professor in the Department of Communication at Michigan State University. Her research centers on human-AI interactions, with an emphasis on the ethical and trust implications of AI technologies.

Hannes Cools is a postdoctoral researcher at the AI, Media, and Democracy Lab at the University of Amsterdam. His research interests include (generative) AI, computational journalism, algorithmic recommender systems and newsroom innovation. He is also an affiliated researcher at the Brown Institute of the Columbia Journalism School in New York City and the Communication, Culture and Technology Program at Georgetown University in Washington DC.

Prabu David (PhD, University of North Carolina at Chapel Hill) is a Professor of Communication at the Rochester Institute of Technology. He studies human-centered AI, currently focusing on trust and ethics in AI.

Marco Dehnert (MA, Arizona State University) is a doctoral candidate in the Hugh Downs School of Human Communication at Arizona State University. He is a multi-method scholar who studies human-machine communication, artificial intelligence, and the social impact of communication technologies. Marco's work has appeared in *Human-Machine Communication*, *Human Communication Research*, and the International Journal of Social Robotics, among others. He is also part of the Relationships and Technology Lab at ASU.

Jérôme Duberry focuses his research on the nexus between technology and civil society participation. He has shown that, under certain conditions, digital technologies can enhance participation in environmental governance and policy-making mechanisms. More recently, his research has explored the social and political implications of artificial intelligence (AI) in democratic processes. His latest book, *Artificial Intelligence and Democracy*, explores the mediation of AI in citizen–government intermediations and calls for a human-centered AI governance that prioritizes human rights and popular sovereignty.

Lauri Goldkind, PhD, is Associate Professor of Social Work at the Graduate School of Social Service at Fordham University. Goldkind has served as the editor of the Journal of Technology in Human Services since 2017. She holds a PhD from Yeshiva University and a Masters of Social Work from the State University of New York Stony Brook.

Edward Griffor (PhD, Massachusetts Institute of Technology) is the Associate Director for Cyber-Physical Systems of the National Institute of Standards and Technology. He was, until July 2015 when he joined NIST, one of the three original Walter P. Chrysler Technical Fellows, one of the highest technical positions in industry and one that represents technical excellence throughout global industry, from the automotive to the aerospace, medical and computing industries. He is the Chairman of the Chrysler Technology Council and of the MIT Alliance, a professional association of scientists, engineers, and business experts trained at the Massachusetts Institute of Technology.

Jay D. Hmielowski (PhD, Ohio State University) is an Associate Professor in the Department of Public Relations in the College of Journalism and Communications at the University of Florida. His research interests include political and environmental communication.

Rosalie Hooi (PhD) is an independent researcher with research interests at the intersection of human behavior and technology. Her research examines media effects, virtual environments, and science and technology policy.

Jungseock Joo (PhD, UCLA) is an Associate Professor in the Department of Communication at UCLA. His research centers on computational communication and artificial intelligence.

Younbo Jung (PhD, University of Southern California) is an Associate Professor and Associate Chair (Academic) at the Wee Kim Wee School of Communication and Information, Nanyang Technological University, Singapore. His research interests include socio-psychological effects of interactive media such as video games, virtual reality systems, and human–robot interaction, and their applications in medical and educational fields. Dr. Jung's current project addresses various issues that have emerged from the ageing and modern society, known as gerontechnology, heath tech, or age tech.

Kristjan Kikerpill (PhD in Sociology) is Lecturer in Information Law and Digital Sociology at the Institute of Social Studies at the University of Tartu, Estonia. His main areas of interest and research are lying and online deceptions, social engineering, technology-mediated surveillance, and the social aspects of artificial intelligence.

Jang Hyun Kim is a Full Professor in the Department of Human–Artificial Intelligence Interaction/Department of Interaction Science at Sungkyunkwan University. His research focuses on social/semantic data analysis, social media, and future media. He has authored more than 80 papers in major conferences and journals such as *Information Processing & Management*; *Telematics & Informatics*; *Cities, Government Information Quarterly*; *Technological Forecasting and Social Change*; and *Journal of Computer-Mediated Communication*.

Alex W. Kirkpatrick (PhD, Washington State University) is a Postdoctoral Scholar at Washington State University's Center for Sustaining Agriculture and Natural Resources. They also hold the position of Science Communication Specialist at the USDA-NIFA National AI Institute for Transforming Workforce and Decision Support (AgAID). Their research explores the effects of media on public engagement with science, technology and risk.

Joanne Kuai is a PhD candidate at the Department of Geography, Media and Communication at Karlstad University, Sweden, with a research project on Artificial Intelligence in Chinese Newsrooms. Her research interests center around data and AI for media, computational journalism, and the social implications of automation and algorithms. Before her academic career, she worked as a journalist in China for more than a decade.

Kenneth A. Lachlan (PhD, Michigan State University) is Professor and Department Head in the Department of Communication at the University of Connecticut (UConn). He holds research affiliations with UConn's Institute for Collaboration on Health, Intervention and Policy, and the Communication and Social Robotics Laboratory at Western Michigan University. His current research interests include the functions and effects of social media during crises and disasters and the use of social robotics in delivering risk messages.

Cait Lackey is a doctoral student in the Department of Communication at the University of Illinois Chicago (UIC). As an interdisciplinary scholar with a background in cognition, communication, and psychology, Cait's research focuses on the social dynamics of artificial intelligence, human–machine communication, and human–AI relationships.

Jeongsub Lim (PhD, University of Missouri-Columbia) is a professor at the College of Media, Arts, and Science of Sogang University in South Korea. He was a former wire service reporter and taught at Austin Peay State University. Currently, he teaches and conducts research on text mining, machine learning, data journalism, and journalistic practices. He has authored over 100 scholarly works in international journals such as New *Media & Society* and the *Journal of Computer-Mediated Communication*, as well as in Korean journals and at international/domestic conferences.

Bibo Lin is a doctoral candidate in the School of Journalism and Communication at the University of Oregon, USA. His research focuses on artificial intelligence, journalism, global media, emotions, and social inequalities in China. Previously, he was a senior editor of one of the most popular newspapers in China, City Express in Hangzhou. As a journalist, he conducted interviews in Ukraine, Tanzania, Japan, and North Korea.

Fanjue Liu is a doctoral student at the University of Florida. Her research investigates how people perceive and interact socially with emerging technologies such as virtual humans. Specifically, she investigates how people use different psychological patterns to interact with virtual influencers, how the emergence of virtual influencers changes the dynamics of influencer marketing, and whether virtual influencers can be considered a viable substitute for human influencers.

Matthew Lombard (PhD, Stanford University) is President of the International Society for Presence Research (http://ispr.info) and an associate professor in the Department of Media Studies and Production at Temple University, Philadelphia, Pennsylvania, USA. His research centers on individuals' psychological and physiological processing of media experiences, with particular focus on the concept of (tele)presence. His work has appeared in journals including *Behaviour & Information Technology*, *Human Technology*, *Human Communication Research*, *Journal of Computer-Mediated Communication*, and *Presence: Teleoperators and Virtual Environments*.

Sumita Louis is a PhD candidate at the School of Journalism and Communication, University of Oregon, Eugene, USA.

Jun Luo is a PhD student in the Department of Communication at the University of California, Los Angeles. Her research focuses on political communication and computational communication.

Jasmine E. McNealy (JD, PhD, University of Florida) is an associate professor at the University of Florida and a Senior Fellow in Tech Policy with Mozilla. She is a faculty associate at the Berkman Klein Center for Internet & Society at Harvard University. Her research focuses on policy as it relates to emerging media and technology and data governance, emphasizing the impacts on marginalized and vulnerable communities.

Chasity Nadeau (MS, Saint Joseph's University) holds a Master's Degree in Business Intelligence and Analytics, and a Bachelor of Science in Business Administration with a focus in Finance, both from Saint Joseph's University. Ongoing projects include constructing artificial intelligence and machine learning research to measure risks of artificial intelligence in cyber-physical systems and business processes using, and extending, the NIST cyber-physical system framework.

Seungahn Nah (PhD, University of Wisconsin-Madison) is Professor and Inaugural Dianne Snedaker Chair in Media Trust at the University of Florida's College of

Journalism and Communications. He is the Research Director of the Consortium on Trust in Media and Technology (CTMT), part of the University of Florida's AI Initiative. His research centers on the roles of digital communication technologies, including artificial intelligence enabled technologies in democratic processes and outcomes.

Dongyan Nan is a PhD at Department of Human-Artificial Intelligence Interaction/ Department of Interaction Science, Sungkyunkwan University. His research focuses on Human-AI Communication, Consumer Experience, Information Management, Computational Social Science, Metaverse, and Network Analysis. He has authored over 20 papers in major conferences and journals such as *Technological Forecasting and Social Change*, *Information Processing & Management*, and *Journal of Organizational and End User Computing*. Dongyan Nan is the corresponding author of this paper.

Thanh H. Nguyen (PhD, New Mexico State University) is an Artificial Intelligence Research Engineer at Elemental Cognition Inc. working on knowledge representation and reasoning (KR&R), logic programming and domain modeling as well as software development. He completed his PhD in Computer Science at New Mexico State University. His research interests include developing ontology, semantic integration, KR&R, reasoning about actions and changes, automatic planning; and applying these techniques with answer set programming in semantic web services composition framework and cyber-physical system reasoning engine.

Poong Oh (PhD, University of Southern California) is an Assistant Professor at the Wee Kim Wee School of Communication and Information, Nanyang Technological University, Singapore. His research interest lies in collective dynamics of information processing, decision making, opinion formation, and conflict resolution in large-scale groups from the evolutionary game-theoretic perspective. His current projects investigate the mechanisms of competitive spreading of conflicting opinions and behaviors in social networks, focusing on controversies over false information, vaccination, and AI-powered technologies among others.

Michaël Opgenhaffen (PhD) is an Associate Professor at the Institute for Media Studies (IMS), University of Leuven (KU Leuven) in Belgium. He is Director of the master's in journalism program at the KU Leuven and Visiting Professor at the University of Leiden in the Netherlands. His research focuses on the production and consumption of social media news and the future of (digital) journalism.

Hüseyin Özçınar is Associate Professor in Educational Technology and head of the Department of Computer Education and Instructional Technologies at Pamukkale University. Dr. Özçınar received his BS degree from ITU, Electronic and Communication Engineering Department in 2003. He earned a master's degree from the computer science department of Pamukkale University and received his PhD from Educational Technology at Ankara University. Dr. Özçınar's research focuses on educational technology, computer-mediated communication and bibliometrics.

He is currently studying and giving lectures on artificial intelligence and social network analysis.

Barbara Pohl has an MA in Bioethics from New York University and an MA in the History of Science from Yale University. She is currently a social work student at Fordham University. Her past research has examined the queer ideas and values of feminist social scientists who practiced in the late nineteenth and early twentieth centuries. Her more recent interests include the literary methods, including narrative therapy and bibliotherapy, of social workers working in the field of community mental health.

Adam M. Rainear (PhD, University of Connecticut) is an Assistant Professor in the Department of Communication and Media at West Chester University of Pennsylvania. His research examines how humans communicate using new technology tools in risk and crisis scenarios, such as during major weather disasters. He serves on the editorial board for the *Journal of International Crisis and Risk Communication Research* and *Communication Studies*.

John S. Seberger (PhD, University of California – Irvine) is an Assistant Professor in the Department of Information Science at Drexel University. His interdisciplinary work explores how computing mediates experiences of mundanity, particularly in relation to dignity, privacy, and affect.

Jeannine Shantz (MS, Saint Joseph's University) is a higher education professional working in academic research and assessment, and instructional technology at Drexel University. She holds a Master of Science in Business Intelligence and Analytics with a cyber analytics concentration and a Master of Science in Instructional Technology from Saint Joseph's University. Recent research includes modeling cyber-physical systems and reasoning about their properties, extensions of the NIST cyber-physical system framework, as well as the investigation of techniques for facilitating requirement development of AI-enabled business processes.

Andra Siibak is a Professor of Media Studies and a Deputy Head of Research and Development at the Institute of Social Studies at the University of Tartu, Estonia. Her research focuses on opportunities and risks surrounding internet use, datafication of childhood, dataveillance in education, and privacy. Together with Giovanna Mascheroni she co-authored a monograph *Datafied Childhoods: Data Practices and Imaginaries in Children's Lives* (2021), published by Peter Lang. She serves as the General Secretary of European Communication Research and Education Association (ECREA).

Patric R. Spence (PhD, Wayne State University) is a Professor in the Nicholson School of Communication at the University of Central Florida. His research examines the role of technology in crisis and risk along with social robotics. He is the previous editor of Communication Studies and has edited multiple issues of Computers in Human Behavior.

Baldwin Van Gorp (PhD) is a Full Professor of Journalism and Communication Management at University of Leuven (KU Leuven) in Belgium. He is the coordinator of the Institute for Media Studies (IMS). His research interests include framing, journalism, and the social construction of reality.

Paulo Nuno Vicente works as an Assistant Professor of Digital Media at the Faculty of Social Sciences and Humanities, NOVA University of Lisbon, where he founded and coordinates iNOVA Media Lab, a research and development lab dedicated to the areas of immersive and interactive narrative, social impact of artificial intelligence, web platforms and social networks, innovation and digital transformation, information visualization and science communication. He coordinates the Masters in New Media and Web Practices and co-coordinates the PhD in Digital Media.

Donghee Yvette Wohn is Associate Professor in Informatics, College of Computing, New Jersey Institute of Technology. Dr. Wohn is the director of the Social Interaction Lab whose research area is in human–computer interaction (HCI) and computer-mediated communication. She studies the characteristics and consequences of social interactions in online environments such as virtual worlds, digital patronage platforms, and social media.

Kun Xu is Assistant Professor of Emerging Media at the University of Florida College of Journalism and Communications. Kun Xu's work focuses on the intersection of human–robot interaction, computer-mediated communication, and media psychology. He investigates how people perceive and respond to technologies such as social robots, computer agents and virtual assistants. His works have been published in journals including *Journal of Computer-Mediated Communication*, *New Media & Society*, *International Journal of Communication*, and *Information & Organization*.

Preface

Artificial intelligence (AI) is ubiquitous in our daily lives. It is no exception in the academic discipline, and its impact is profound. AI research in communication has exponentially grown in recent decades and will continue to do so with an ever-increasing number of AI tools including ChatGPT. It is a wide-open terrain. The potential of AI is unbounded, but the perils of AI are foreseeable.

This research handbook presents a wide range of studies regarding the intersection between AI and communication from interdisciplinary and international perspectives. The 25 chapters discuss a wide range of theoretical foundations, innovative methodological approaches, and ethical and legal issues for policy implications. Contributors come from a variety of disciplines, such as communication, journalism, computer science, sociology, psychology, business, and education among others.

The handbook consists of five parts. The first part lays out the foundation for scholarly AI and communication, providing conceptual definitions, theoretical frameworks, and analytical innovations. The second part covers news and public framing of AI, while the third part examines public understanding of AI. The fourth part investigates public interaction with AI, and the fifth part explores AI ethics, law, and its related policy issues.

It has been a pleasure to work on the research handbook. Without the contributors, the project could have not been fruitful. I am grateful for their intellectual inquiry, insightful discussions, and productive suggestions for future studies. I sincerely hope that this handbook will provide valuable guidance to AI–communication scholars, researchers, students, practitioners, and policymakers.

Introduction to the *Research Handbook on Artificial Intelligence and Communication*

Seungahn Nah

Artificial intelligence (AI) has garnered growing scholarly attention in the communication field and beyond as AI becomes omnipresent in everyday life from search engines through voice recognition technology, mobile news apps to chatbots (e.g., ChatGPT). Although scholarship on the intersection between AI and communication is numerous, this emerging field remains largely unexplored in terms of conceptual, theoretical, and methodological approaches as well as ethical, legal, practical, and policy issues. This *Research Handbook on Artificial Intelligence and Communication* epitomizes a rich body of studies regarding the "communicating of, by, and with AI" from interdisciplinary perspectives and international scopes. Topics vary widely across AI-empowered, immersed, mediated, and integrated communications. This *Handbook* is divided into five parts:

1. The first part maps out scholarly endeavors concerning conceptual definitions, theoretical frameworks, and analytical innovations.
2. The second part examines how news media and digital communication platforms such as social media construct, represent, and frame AI and its related issues across diverse countries, cultures, and contexts.
3. The third part covers how the public understands AI and its related technologies through adoption and use, and public discussion, as well as how it relates to public attitude, perception, opinion, trust, and behavior.
4. The fourth part investigates how the public interacts with various types of AI-based technologies and communication devices.
5. The fifth part explores AI-related ethical, legal, practical, and policy issues.

With a total of 25 chapters from more than a dozen different countries, it provides a comprehensive foundational guidance of AI communication research to scholars, researchers, practitioners, and policymakers.

PART I: MAPPING RESEARCH ON ARTIFICIAL INTELLIGENCE AND COMMUNICATION

Part I, with a total of five chapters, presents the past, present, and prospects of AI communication scholarship with a special emphasis on conceptual definitions, theoretical perspectives, and methodological approaches, as well as implications for future studies.

Chapter 1 (Louis and Nah), "A systematic review of scholarship in AI and communication research (1990–2022)," maps out where scholarship on the intersection between AI and communication stands. In doing so, they present findings from a systematic review approach to extensively examine a total of 197 journal articles published in the communication field over several decades. The chapter focuses on major topics in this domain, spanning a wide range of sub-disciplines, such as journalism, political communication, and strategic communication, which include but are not limited to AI and its applications in newsrooms, trust and credibility in AI-generated news, and perceptions, attitudes, and behaviors toward AI and its enabled technologies. A wide variety of journals have published research in the burgeoning area of AI and communication. Chapter 1 helps readers to further understand the intersection between communication and AI, providing a comprehensive overview of past, present, and future scholarship. A wide array of conceptual definitions used in the accumulated studies also help scholars to further explore and elaborate on concepts, theories, and methods in an interdisciplinary context. Innovative methodological tools adapted in the studies also help to conceptualize and theorize the intersection between AI and communication.

While Chapter 1 entails an overview of scholarship on the intersection between AI and communication, Chapter 2 (Wohn and Almoqbel), titled "AI-integrated communication: conceptualization and a critical review," introduces the concept of "AI-integrated communication (AIIC)." This concept integrates interchangeably and similarly used concepts of AI-mediated communication, human–machine communication, algorithmic imaginary, AI authorship, AI-supported messaging, and machine translation–supported communication. The authors conducted a critical literature review of prior studies to understand the roles that AI may play in communication. Specifically, they begin with various concepts describing the intersection between AI and communication and then conclude with a classification system that explains the roles of AI and its presence in humans. It is commendable that the authors attempted to systematically review previous frameworks that describe the linkage between AI and communication. By integrating the frameworks, they offer a classification system or AI-integrated communication, which synthesizes AI mediation and interaction. Chapter 2 provides a deeper understanding of how AI and communication can work in tandem through a more holistic and comprehensive approach involving machines, humans, and the environment. The AI-integrated communication framework further stimulates intellectual inquiry among AI scholars, researchers, and communicators.

Chapter 3 (Lackey), entitled "Toward a sociology of machines: an interviewing methodology for human–machine communication," presents a novel technique for the human–machine interview based on an actor–network theory (ANT) in the contexts of human–machine communication (HMC) and digital social agents embedded in the sociotechnical system. This methodological approach provides valuable insights into the role of machines in communication, while also helping to comprehend the meaning-making processes between machines and humans. The human–machine interview offers a cutting-edge way to learn about the interactions between humans and machines, and it has implications in fields such as journalism and journalistic interviewing with news sources. The actor–network theory-based approach provides a systematic tool to understand the interactions between digital social agents and social actors.

Chapter 4 (Özçınar and Bayramoğlu), "Discovering developmental trajectories and trends of conversational agent research using dynamic topic modeling," presents the results of a dynamic topic modeling approach regarding conversational agents embedded in AI-powered technologies and communication systems. The authors use unsupervised machine learning to trace the historical evolution of conversational agent technology from 2001 to 2021. The chapter provides a comprehensive overview of research areas and subjects, including health, education, linguistics, system designs, and consumer behaviors, among others. The authors present a detailed analysis of the distribution of publications across countries, research areas, years, and topics. Chapter 4 provides a deeper understanding of the historical trajectory and development history of human and machine conversations and interactions.

Chapter 5 (Luo, Louis, and Nah), "A systematic review of scholarship on metaverse," provides a comprehensive examination of the literature on the metaverse. The term "metaverse" has gained widespread popularity in recent years but dates back to earlier eras when the Internet enabled users to create a vast array of online communities where people, using avatars, could interact with each other. Chapter 5 presents conceptual definitions of metaverse and its related topics, research areas, theories, and methodological approaches. It offers one of the first in-depth reviews of the emerging studies concerning the metaverse and its roles and implications. The chapter helps readers to further understand the evolution and development of the conceptual and theoretical frameworks in various fields and the methodologies used to study the metaverse and its impact.

In summary, Part I consists of five chapters that aim to help readers to further understand the intersection between AI and communication. The chapters explore the relationships between AI and communication and offer conceptualizations, theories, and analyses of the interactions, mediations, and integrations between AI and communication.

PART II: FRAMING ARTIFICIAL INTELLIGENCE

Part II covers a cohesive collection of studies examining the ways that society, including news media and professional journalists, frames AI and its related issues across various countries and cultures.

Chapter 6 (Kikerpill and Siibak), "AI in schools and universities: mapping central debates through enthusiasms and concerns," provides a comprehensive overview of the current status of AI in education, shedding light on both the advancements made and the concerns from various stakeholders' perspectives. It delves into the progress made on AI and its design, implementations, and solutions in educational contexts and explores the potential benefits and limitations of AI technologies in classrooms. The chapter offers an intensive review of AI in educational settings, paying particular attention to AI and its related issues, problems, and solutions for educators, learners, and administrators. It further helps readers not only understand the current status of AI in education but also assess what AI can do for education from multiple perspectives embedded in the educational system.

Chapter 7 (Lim), entitled "How news organizations and journalists understand artificial intelligence: application of news language database to AI-related news stories," presents the findings from an analysis of AI-related news stories in Korean news outlets. Specifically, the chapter focuses on how journalists cover AI and its related technologies, issues, and problems. This chapter provides insights into how journalists frame AI in their reporting, allowing a wide range of audiences, including the public, policymakers, and professionals to better understand the roles of AI in society.

Chapter 8 (Vicente), "AI in Portugal: news framing, tone, and sources," content-analyzes news stories related to AI in the Portuguese news media from 1997 to 2017. The chapter presents findings regarding the frames around scientific discoveries and projects, as well as benefits over concerns. Chapter 8 helps readers understand how non-English speaking and small countries, such as Portugal, cover AI and its related issues. The chapter also provides a reference for a comparative analysis across diverse countries and cultures in the future.

Chapter 9 (Luo, Nah, and Joo), "AI bias, news framing, and mixed-methods approach," presents the findings regarding algorithmic bias in television news, drawing on data from six television news networks (ABC, CBS, CNN, MSNBC, NBC, and Fox News) over a 30-year period (1990–2020). The chapter's results cover a range of topics, including ethical considerations, risks and benefits, criminal justice, and humanity, digital journalism, and conflict and regulation. The chapter offers a unique perspective on the algorithmic bias of the news media, using a topic modeling approach to supplement traditional content analysis. The chapter provides a comprehensive look at the framing of algorithmic bias in television news and serves as a valuable source for further scholarship in this area. In sum, readers can gain a better understanding of the roles of algorithmic bias in society.

In summary, Part II discusses how AI has been framed in education and journalism across different countries (e.g., Portugal, South Korea, and the United States). Part II offers theoretical perspectives and methodological approaches (e.g., topic modeling) for future scholarship in this domain, which can advance our understanding of AI and its impact on society.

PART III: PUBLIC UNDERSTANDING OF ARTIFICIAL INTELLIGENCE

Part III presents an accumulated body of scholarship to examine the extent to which the public perceives AI and how the public understands AI in terms of public opinion, attitude, behavior, and trust.

Chapter 10 (Cho and Hooi), "Risk perceptions and trust mechanisms related to everyday AI," explores the public's perceptions and trust toward AI technologies in everyday life. This chapter provides an in-depth analysis of the research on the risks, privacy concerns, and trust issues related to AI and its associated technologies. By critically reviewing the theoretical concepts, empirical evidence, and practical implications, Chapter 10 enables readers to gain a comprehensive understanding of both the benefits and potential risks of AI technologies.

Chapter 11 (Kirkpatrick, Hmielowski, and Boyd), "Fearing the future: examining the conditional indirect correlation of attention to artificial intelligence news on artificial intelligence attitudes," examines how news consumption on AI relates to public attitude and perception toward AI with a special emphasis on the conditional effects of perceived economic risks among those who hold a different level of income. The chapter presents the findings regarding the associations between AI news consumption, perceived economic risk perception, and fear tied to AI, which is conditioned by income level. Chapter 11 provides valuable insight into the conditional impact of media use on public understanding of AI. The chapter further helps future studies to test not only the income level but also other demographic features as well as contextual variables such as AI literacy, efficacy, and knowledge in shaping public perception of AI.

Chapter 12 (Oh and Jung), "A machine-learning approach to assessing public trust in AI-powered technologies," offers a novel approach to measuring public trust in AI-powered technologies by linking the public's desired AI-enabled technologies to replace jobs. The results indicate that AI technologies that perform tasks without cognitive or managerial skills or social interactions are more likely associated with replaceable jobs. Chapter 12 enhances our understanding of the public trust in AI by focusing on public attitudes towards AI technologies and their impact on related jobs. It provides empirical evidence and theoretical guidance for future scholarship in the field of human–machine communication and the acceptance of machines.

Chapter 13 (Kim and Nan), "Machine learning and deep learning for social science: a bibliometric approach," presents a bibliometric analysis of the prior studies of machine learning and deep learning in the field of social science. The findings reveal the knowledge structure of the studies, including research topics across authors, institutions, and countries, and highlight the co-authorship network, co-citation network, and main research themes. This chapter provides an understanding of how the knowledge structure of AI in social science has developed and offers research tools and insights for future interdisciplinary and international studies.

Chapter 14 (Duberry), "AI and data-driven political communication (re)shaping citizen–government interactions," examines the interplay between AI technologies, big data, and political communication. The chapter reviews the use of AI-powered technologies in political communication by politicians, policymakers, newsmakers, and citizens alike with a special emphasis on AI-driven data collection, citizen behavior, and political communication tactics such as micro-targeting and geo-localization. Chapter 14 provides insights and practical implications for political communication strategies that leverage AI-enabled technologies. It lays a groundwork for future studies to compare political communication practices across different cultures, countries, and communities.

Chapter 15 (Pohl and Goldkind), "AI folk tales: how nontechnical publics make sense of artificial intelligence," examines how the public socially constructs and understands AI through the lens of folk theories. The chapter sheds light on how the public perceives AI through a critical AI and data literacy perspective. It also provides guidance for future studies to adopt a literacy-based approach to research in the field of AI and big data.

In sum, Part III provides a comprehensive look at how AI is perceived and understood by the public, taking into consideration various factors such as news consumption, income, job replacement, political communication, and folk theories. These chapters provide valuable insights and implications for future studies in the file of AI and its impact on society.

PART IV: INTERACTING WITH ARTIFICIAL INTELLIGENCE

Part IV deals with a total of six studies examining how the public interacts with AI and its related technologies across multiple fields such as journalism, business communication, public relations, organizational communication, risk and crisis communication, as well as cultural and critical communication.

Chapter 16 (Bundas, Nadeau, Nguyen, Shantz, Balduccini, Griffor, and Son), "Facilitating stakeholder communication around AI-enabled systems and business processes," presents a communication tool to facilitate stakeholders' communication concerning AI-enabled systems and business processes. Specifically, the Cyber-Physical Systems (CPS) Framework, developed by the U.S. National Institute of Standards and Technology (NIST), helps build a more effective communication system through AI technologies among multiple stakeholders. This chapter helps readers better understand AI applications in business communication.

Chapter 17 (Cools, Van Gorp, and Opgenhaffen), "The levels of automation and autonomy in the AI-augmented newsroom: toward a multi-level typology of computational journalism," provides a typology that examines the impact of AI on journalism in general and newsrooms in particular. The authors adopt an AI and human interaction perspective, looking at the degree to which journalistic news practices are automated and how automation is related to the autonomy of news workers. Chapter 17 helps readers understand the intersection between AI and journalism or computational and automated journalism with a topology embedded in automation and autonomy that may systematically analyze the newly emerging journalistic field.

Chapter 18 (Dehnert), "AI as communicative other: critical relationality in human–AI communication," takes a critical and cultural perspective on the interaction between humans and machines, with special emphasis on AI as a communicative other. In doing so, the author focuses especially on relationality with regard to power embedded in a larger communication network. Chapter 18 contributes to a growing body of literature from critical and cultural perspectives in interdisciplinary contexts and further helps readers further understand critical aspects of AI technologies and their roles in shaping power relations.

Chapter 19 (Rainear, Spence, and Lachlan), titled "Needs and practices for AI-mediated messaging in uncertain circumstances," explores the use of AI in the realm of risk and crisis communication. The authors review prior research to further discuss what AI can do to provide effective and efficient communication tools and platforms during crisis and risk situations. Through this chapter, readers will gain a deeper understanding of how AI can serve as a valuable tool for effective and efficient crisis and risk communication.

Chapter 20 (Spence), "Why wasn't I ready for that? Suggestions and research directions for the use of machine agents in organizational life," examines past prior research on the interaction between machines and humans and provides suggestions and future research directions for the use of AI in organizational life. It puts specific emphasis on the communication and behavior that is necessary for effective human–machine interactions in business and organizational contexts. The chapter aims to help readers understand the potential of AI in organizational communication.

Chapter 21 (Xu, Liu, Chen, and Lombard), titled "The Media Are Social Actors paradigm and beyond: theory, evidence, and future research," explores the Media Are Social Actors (MASA) framework extended by the Computers Are Social Actors paradigm. Specifically, the authors advance the MASA paradigm with empirical evidence. Chapter 21 provides valuable insights and directions for future scholarship to further examine the interaction between humans and AI-powered technologies such as social robots and chatbots.

In conclusion, the six chapters in Part IV present accumulated knowledge about human and machine interactions in various fields such as journalism, business communication, public relations, organizational communication, risk and crisis communication, as well as cultural and critical communication. Through the six chapters, the authors provide a comprehensive examination of the field, while also highlighting areas for further exploration and advancement. The concepts, theories, and methodological approaches presented in these chapters offer a valuable resource for future scholarship in human and AI interaction.

PART V: POLICING ARTIFICIAL INTELLIGENCE

Part V comprises a total of four chapters and explores the ethical, legal, practical, and policy issues and implications of AI and its related technologies.

Chapter 22 (Barfield), titled "Evaluating the self-disclosure of personal information to AI-enabled technology," presents an intensive review of previous studies on personal information embedded in AI technologies. The chapter discusses the steps necessary to enhance the communication processes between AI-powered devices and humans with regard to the exchange of personal information, considering the design and implementation of AI and its practical applications.

Chapter 23 (Seberger, Choung, and David), "To reimagine more deeply: understanding what AI communicates," delves into the historical ontological discourses surrounding human-user interactions. Chapter 23 provides ethical foundations to enhance the understanding of the relationship between AI and its audience, not just as users but as humans.

Chapter 24 (Lin and Kuai), "Automated inequalities: examining the social implications of artificial intelligence in China," discusses AI technologies and their related issues such as fairness, objectivity, and bias with regard to social inequalities in China's AI policies. Chapter 24 offers insights and implications for the policy and usage of AI to address these inequalities.

Chapter 25 (McNealy), "Design + power: policy for the ecology of influence," explores the impact of AI design on user interactions with organizations. The author focuses on the legislative and policy implications of AI system design and suggests an ecological approach to address these concerns. The chapter offers insights and recommendations for policymakers as they consider the impact of AI design on user behavior and interaction.

In summary, the four chapters present the findings of AI and its role in society. Part V discusses AI and its related ethical and legal issues as well as practical applications and policy implications concerning human-centered design.

This *Handbook* cumulates a total of 25 chapters regarding the intersection of artificial intelligence (AI) and communication. It presents a wide range of research topics, theories, and methodological approaches which may contribute to the existing body of research in this field. It also provides a diverse set of ethical considerations, legal issues, and policy implications across different contexts. In conclusion, this *Handbook* serves as a comprehensive guide for scholars, researchers, practitioners, and policymakers to continue intellectual inquiry in interdisciplinary and international settings.

PART I

MAPPING RESEARCH ON ARTIFICIAL INTELLIGENCE AND COMMUNICATION

1. A systematic review of scholarship in AI and communication research (1990–2022)

Sumita Louis and Seungahn Nah

The term "artificial intelligence," or AI, was first coined in 1955 by Professor John McCarthy at Stanford, who described it as "the science and engineering of making intelligent machines" (Myers, 2011; Manning, 2020).

The definition of AI has undergone subsequent iterations from its early meanings with much of scholarly research examining AI and human behavior in that early era authored by computer science scientists and researchers (McCarthy, 1959; Weizenbaum, 1966, 1976; Wiener, 1988). Social scientists and communication scholars began exploring this exciting field subsequently, although recent scholars point out "AI has always been a communication issue at heart" (Westerman et al., 2020, p. 395) referring to Alan Turing's (1950) "classic test outlining the importance of the perceived nature of the communication partner" (p. 395, para 3).

Just a decade ago, IBM's supercomputer Watson wowed the tech industry and a corner of United States (U.S.) pop culture with its win against two of Jeopardy's greatest champions, but the amount of powerful computing that it took to build Watson and "teach" was expensive and time consuming, as its architects revealed (Best, 2013).

Today, however (circa, 2022), AI is a well-known and, perhaps, even overused term in our daily conversations across the globe. A recent KPMG report (2021) refers to "Covid-19 whiplash" as one of the key reasons for the massive spike in AI adoption across industries globally (KPMG report, 2021), and despite a recession looming, AI is a major "hotspot" for investments "with the market set to increase by $76.44 billion by 2025, with an accelerated growth rate of more than 21% annually" (Lynes, 2023, para 3).

It is not surprising, therefore, that communication scholarship is witnessing a similar transformational shift, propelled by a host of new AI-driven communication services, including, but not limited to, Open AI's ChatGPT and copywriting startup Jaspar, both creating a lot of buzz with their generative AI models.

AI'S POWERFUL INFLUENCE IN THE COMMUNICATION LANDSCAPE

About three in ten U.S. adults say they are "almost constantly" online in 2021 (PEW, 2021), and it is increasingly common knowledge that AI recommendation engines and algorithms play a major role in "what" we read, watch, or consume across multiple screens – be it the music we play, Netflix shows we watch, books we buy, places we visit, and even the shops we buy groceries from.

Supercomputing power is training and transforming search engines powered by algorithms created by humans and their inherent, unconscious, or subconscious bias. Rapid changes and "testing" of new algorithmic permutations and combinations may have led to Tik Tok's global meteoric rise today and to Facebook's latest shift away from news feeds, naming the service as simply "Feeds" instead of "newsfeeds" (WSJ, 2022), but these are merely inferences and remain unclear because the "black box" of algorithmic code constitutes a type of "Pandora's box" that researchers still need to obtain access to for further examination and study.

This paradox of helpful, yet omnipresent AI in our daily lives leads to an obvious question being asked by communication scholars the world over which is: are the communication field's legacy models and theories still applicable (and relevant) for those examining the effects and the ubiquitous role of AI in industry, government, and social life?

We cannot answer this important question in this short book chapter, but our intention is to extend the ongoing debates and conversations across conferences, lecture halls, and our homes and offices. In this chapter, we provide a brief overview of key topics or categories of research communication scholars have focused on in the past two decades (1992–2022), summarize evolving conceptual approaches, and highlight some implications for the future.

EVOLVING COMMUNICATION MODELS

Scholarly research in the communication field has evolved from legacy models of communication – the traditional one-way, sender–receiver transmission model (Shannon & Weaver, 1948) transitioned to a multi-modal, always-on-always-connected transmission model today leading to new terms such as "mass personal" communication, combining interpersonal interactions with traditional mass media use (Sullivan & Carr, 2018).

Humans now learn, transact, play, watch, and date using multiple platforms or screens simultaneously, or concurrently, but also have begun to rely on diverse agent(ic) representations including social bots, auto-chat agents, email auto responders, and others which run unobtrusively in the background of daily utilized global platforms – from email, to search engines and social network sites (SNS).

The study of humans and their interaction with new mediums and technologies is not new; communication scholarship evolved in conjunction with technological advances from human interactions with the first personal computers and computer games (Turkle, 1984; Reeves & Nass, 1996), the internet (Newhagen & Rafaeli, 1996) the advent of mobile phones (Turkle, 2008, 2011), social network sites (Boyd, 2007) and the study of social robots (Zhao, 2006).

A recent study (Calvo Rubio & Ufarte Ruiz, 2021) focusses on past research in "artificial intelligence and journalism" within an 11-year time frame 2008–2019

(2021, p. 159). The scholars examine a corpus of 209 articles and note a significant increase in 2015, to up to 61 articles in 2019. Their study reveals "the largest number of publications related to this topic are concentrated in the United States and in scientific journals, which include works that handle a broad variety of topics, such as information production, data journalism, big data, application in social networks or information checking" (p. 159).

We conduct a more recent systematic literature review of AI and communication scholarship published in the past two decades – from 1992 to 2022 – and examine global scholarship utilizing a comprehensive keyword search, primarily focusing on the communications journals' category in the Web of Science (WoS). This chapter provides a brief overview of key findings from our study, and we earnestly hope it will be of some utility to students and scholars.

SYSTEMATIC REVIEW OF SCHOLARSHIP (1992–2022)

In the months of March and April 2022, researchers conducted a review of literature examining "AI and communication" articles published in the WoS database which catalogs and indexes peer reviewed articles, monographs, conference proceedings, book chapters, and books and includes an estimated 93 communication journals (Costa, 2020). It also offers multiple databases, and we refer to both the Social Science Citation Index (SCII) and the Expanded Social Citation Index (ESCI) database, which include international communication journals, for this study.

Keyword searches based on deductive reasoning were input into the advanced WoS database search engine, and the researchers specified "communication journals" in the category field of the database search engine to ensure the articles would be relevant to the study. A total of 757 articles were collated for this study. See Table A1.1 in the Appendix for the specific keywords and number of articles output per search term.

The researchers then removed duplicate articles and non-peer reviewed articles comprising essays, special issue introductions, monographs, book chapters, and commentary from journals, leaving a final corpus of 193 articles identified as the sample for this study.

The PDF version of each article (193) was then subsequently downloaded. Researchers reviewed and coded the sample into different topic-based groupings or categories, after perusing each PDF's title, abstract, keywords and the method section. Each paper was then categorized into one of the eight topic groups which emerged. Manual coding checks were carried out to ensure coders were in agreement on the category definition, utilizing clearly defined topic-based sorting process. For example, AI and news category includes studies on news bots and automation of news production. These were not categorized into the "AI and social bots, chatterbots or robots" category and vice versa.

Table 1.1   Search keywords and articles found

Keywords	Number of results
AI and Communication	136
AI and News	101
AI and Machine and Deep Learning	5
AI Comm and Algorithms	458
AI and automation	44
Political Comm	5
Strat Comm AI and Algorithms	4
AI Communication and Ethics	3
Total	757
Final Sample Corpus of Articles for Analyses *(after removing duplicates, book chapter titles, monographs, special issues, and non-peer reviewed articles)*	193

Source: WoS (April 2022).

AI – COMMUNICATION RESEARCH TRAJECTORY (1992–2022)

We find communication research in the exciting area of artificial intelligence has witnessed a clear trajectory evidenced by a major spike in published (and cited) work, especially in the past four years (2019–2022). Significantly, we find AI communication journal articles increased before and during the pandemic years. A simple frequency count revealed an increase of 12 in 2018 to 27 articles published in 2019, which rose to 49 articles in 2020, and 65 in 2021. Data collection ended in the first quarter of 2022, with 30 research papers published or in press by April 2022. See Table A1.1 for a list of published studies per year from 1992–2022.

The researchers identified more than a hundred articles from 32 peer reviewed journals, including top-ranking communication journals such as the *Journal of Computer Mediated Communication (JCMC), Journal of Communication, Journal of Communication Inquiry, Journalism and Mass Communication Quarterly (JMCQ), Media and Communication, Journalism, Journal of Practice* and *New Media and Society (NMS)* to *The International Journal of Advertising* and *Public Relations Review.*

Seventy papers were published in international journals such as *Profesional De La Informacion, Palabra Clave, Media Education-Mediaobrazovanie, Revista Icono 14-Revista Científica De Comunicacion Y Tecnologias, Adcomunica-Revista Científica De Estrategias Tendencias E Innovacion En Communicacion* and *Cic-Cuadernos De Informacion Y Comunicacion.* Numerous articles were published in region-specific languages with many translated into English. See Tables A1.2, A1. 3 and A1.4 for the full list of journals.

Of the 193 papers reviewed, 118, or the majority, were qualitative studies with researchers using methods ranging from critical and cultural analysis to interviews, case studies, ethnography, and text or discourse analysis. Quantitative methods (experiments, surveys, and computational analysis) were used in 42 studies, and 33 studies were based on multi-methods (surveys and interviews, surveys and experiments, and/or computational analysis and interviews).

Methodologies utilized across this sample are indicative of general trends, although it would seem a topic like AI would drive more quantitative research, scholars agree qualitative methods are helpful for exploratory research (Brandztaeg et al., 2022) suggesting "qualitative approaches like this are also widely used to yield deep insights and develop a human-centered understanding of computing systems" (Jiang et al., 2021). See Table A1.5 for the complete list of methodologies and studies.

KEY CATEGORIES OF RESEARCH FOCI

In this sample, we find past scholarship can be categorized into eight categories: (i) AI in news production, journalism practice and global newsrooms which had 63 studies. (ii) AI and social bots, chatter bots, and other agentic representations with 29 studies. (iii) AI, algorithms and deepfakes, image manipulation, and (dis)misinformation included 26 studies. (iv) AI in advertising, public relations (PR), and media management comprised 23 studies. (v) conceptual frameworks and approaches with 20 studies). (vi) AI and policy, government regulation and ICT numbered 12 studies. (vii) AI in communication education had 6 studies. (viii) AI and ethics comprised 6 studies.

Articles which did not fit into these categories were grouped into a miscellaneous category with 8 studies which included scholarly research examining the role of AI in science and health communication, and AI authorship in music and storytelling. See Table A1.6 for the full list of categories identified in this sample reviewed.

We also found international scholarship was also similarly spread across these eight categories, and thus include them accordingly. Despite the limitations of space, we attempt to provide a brief snapshot of the top five categories into which the majority of scholarly research falls under. See Table A1.7 for the full list of specific categories, article titles, year published, and author name(s).

NEWS PRODUCTION AND JOURNALISM PRACTICE

In this sample reviewed, the first major category is news and journalism practice with 63 articles. Key research questions in these studies vary from how global newsrooms are coping with the advent of algorithm-based news, the advent of automation and the impact of changes in newsroom workflows, news reporting and other core aspects of the journalism practice.

Researchers in this category examine AI's impact on news (Thurman, 2018; Paiva, 2018; Sukhodolov, 2019; Thurman et al., 2019), sports journalism (Segarra-Saavedra,

2019; Torrijos, 2019 to AI use in investigative journalism (Stray, 2019) and the role of algorithms in storytelling (Verde, 2019). Globally too, researchers investigated the role of algorithms and bots in journalism (Ruiz & Sanchez, 2019; Tunez-Lopez et al., 2018; Vivar, 2019; Zamkov, 2019; Oliviera et al., 2020).

SOCIAL BOTS, CHATBOTS, AND AGENTIC REPRESENTATIONS

The second area of scholarship that emerges is the category of AI and "bots" short for software robots, and includes 29 studies. Zdenek's article (1999) "Rising up from the MUD: Inscribing Gender in Software Design" is one of the earliest (in our sample) to examine "chatterbots." The paper published in *Discourse & Society* critically explores the emerging phenomenon of humanoid social robots and human–humanoid interactions.

Even in those early days, Zdenek suggests the need to move away from the liberatory "traditional, human-centered studies of computer-mediated communication and gender" and focuses, instead, on studying these chatterbots or "talking software programs as important objects for studying how software design is also implicated in the construction of gender differences" (p. 381).

From 1999 to today, the study of AI and bots has rapidly expanded, with scholars investigating the rise of bots and chatbots, or programs designed to interface with humans or "chat" with them. Researchers note "many things have changed since the early days of AI and today, with social media ecosystems populated by hundreds of millions of individuals present real concerns" (Ferrara et al., 2016; Neff & Nagy, 2016, Herraro-Diz & Varuna, 2018).

For example, a study of "Tay," Microsoft's experimental AI chatbot launched in 2016 and shut down after one day because of its obscene and inflammatory tweets, learned from its users' feedback and input. This study reveals some of "the limitations of current theories of agency for describing communication in these settings and the researchers argue that a perspective of symbiotic agency – informed by the imagined affordances of emerging technology – is required to really understand the collapse of Tay" (Neff & Nagy, 2016, p. 4915).

AI IN DEEPFAKES, IMAGE MANIPULATION AND *(DIS)*MISINFORMATION

In the third category with 26 studies, scholars examine critical aspects of deepfakes (DaSilva et al., 2021; De Seta, 2021; Kietzmann et al., 2021; Vaccari & Chadwick, 2020), AI's role in audiovisual manipulation and deception fakes (Paris, 2021), Facebook and algorithmic news feeds (Schwartz & Mahnke, 2021), journalists' use of algorithmic tools (De Haan et al., 2022), AI and moderation (Wojcieszak et al., 2021).

AI AND PUBLIC RELATIONS, ADVERTISING, AND MANAGEMENT

In the fourth category, we found 23 studies examining AI's impact across the public relations, strategic communications, advertising, and media business management areas. Prahl and Goh (2021), in the *Public Relations Review*, examine what happens when AI fails and how companies publicly respond. In advertising, Liao and Sundar's (2021) study examines different types of filtering algorithms – content-based and collaborative filtering in advertising. Campbell et al. (2022) investigate Instagram and indirect advertising and the effects of AI-enabled in-store communication (Esch et al., 2021). Lou et al. (2021) published a study focusing on AI chatbots and consumer brands in *the International Journal of Advertising*. See Table A1.5 for the journals and number of articles per year in this topic group.

EVOLVING CONCEPTUAL FRAMEWORKS AND APPROACHES

We found a significant number of conceptual papers (20) constituting a fifth category with scholars advocating different approaches and frameworks to the study of AI in the communications field (Gunkel, 2012; Murdock, 2018; Guzman, 2018; Hancock et al., 2020; Sundar, 2020). See Table A1.7 for the full list of articles, the year published, names of authors/scholars and the coded categories they fall into.

Gunkel (2012) in his essay "Communication and Artificial Intelligence: Opportunities and Challenges for the 21st Century," is one of the earliest scholars to call for new frameworks to examine AI, stating, "the computer mediated communication (CMC) paradigm, although undeniably influential and successful, is insufficient and no longer tenable" (Gunkel, 2012). His clarion call was the precursor to much of the ongoing debates over the definitions and somewhat blurring of lines between CMC, CASA, human–computer interaction (HCI), human–machine communication (HMC), and human–AI interaction (HAII) research.

In "Media Materialties: For a Moral Economy of Machines," published in the *Journal of Communication*, globally renowned media and communications scholar Graham Murdock (2018) presciently called for "the development of a new moral economy of machines." This seminal work highlighted AI's ubiquitous growth and powerful influence and advocates the closer examination of a newer "blindspot" of communication research namely the material bases of contemporary communication systems. Murdock refers to "material" as the raw materials and resources employed in the systems, the devices that support everyday communicative activity, and the chains of labor entailed in constructing and maintaining these infrastructures and machines. (p. 360)

HUMAN–MACHINE COMMUNICATION (HMC)

Natale and Guzman, co-editors of "Reclaiming the Human in Machine Cultures" a special issue (2022) of the journal *Media, Culture and Society*, recently invited scholars to consider notions such as "algorithmic culture" and "machine culture" from within the tradition of media and cultural studies in order to "move toward a conceptualization of culture in which machines are intertwined within human systems of meaning-making". The editors invited fresh perspectives and research into why these emerging technologies and the human cultures forming around them are important for the mission of media and cultural studies (Natale & Guzman, 2022).

However, Guzman (2018), in her introduction to "Human-machine Communication: Rethinking Communication, Technology, and Ourselves," proposed the "lens" of HMC much earlier, defining it as "the creation of meaning between humans and machines, with technology theorized as a communicator, a subject with which people communicate, instead of a channel through which humans interact with one another." Thus, for Guzman, HMC research focuses on the "process of communication between human and machine and the implications of encounters between people and technology for individuals, society, and humanity" (Guzman, 2018, p. 2).

Although Guzman's book chapter (2018) is not part of the sample collated for this study, we refer to it as the HMC approach is useful for scholars who work within the wider "umbrella framework" she proposes in her assessment that "HMC envelopes communication research within Human–Computer Interaction (HCI), Human–Robot Interaction (HRI), and Human–Agent Interaction (HAI) while at the same time is inclusive of philosophical, critical/cultural, and related approaches regarding the integration of social technologies into everyday spaces" (2018, p. 2).

HUMAN–AI INTERACTION (HAII) FRAMEWORK

Shyam Sundar, prolific scholar and founder of the Media Effects Research Laboratory and Director of the Center for Socially Responsible Artificial Intelligence at Pennsylvania State University, advocates that "theory and research should be geared toward a deeper understanding of the human experience of algorithms in general and the psychology of Human–AI interaction (HAII) in particular" (Sundar, 2020, p. 74), in his recent study (2020) "Rise of Machine Agency: A Framework for Studying the Psychology of Human–AI Interaction (HAII)" Sundar suggests "as media became more interactive" scholars began studying "our interactions with the technologies themselves" revealing a significant and "gradual shift" in CMC scholarship from examining computer mediated communication via the Internet to examining "other effects of interacting directly with computer-based media" (p. 74). In unpacking the differences, Sundar also suggests "such distinctions have blurred somewhat in the age of mobile and social media, as users seamlessly interact with both the interfaces and other humans, often leveraging interface features to augment direct individual interactions with media themselves as well as interpersonal, group and mass communications" (p. 75). He also refers to the example of "source interactivity," or the ability of users to serve as sources of communication (Sundar, 2007) as one of the best examples of an affordance that could blur the line between CMC and HCI (p. 75, para 2).

ARTIFICIAL INTELLIGENCE-MEDIATED COMMUNICATION (AI-MC)

Hancock et al.'s (2020) work examines how technology may shape human communication, arguing for both a "revaluation" and "expansion" of many of computer-mediated communication's (CMC) key theories, frameworks, and findings and argue "a research agenda around [artificial intelligence-mediated communication] AI-MC should consider the design of these technologies and the psychological, linguistic, relational, policy and ethical implications of introducing AI into human–human communication" (Hancock et al., 2020, p. 4).

In "AI-Mediated Communication: Definition, Research Agenda, and Ethical Considerations" in the *Journal of Computer-Mediated Communication*, these researchers propose the framework of AI-MC, defined by Hancock et al. (2020) as interpersonal communication in which an intelligent agent operates on behalf of a communicator by modifying, augmenting, or generating messages to accomplish communication goals, but "AI-MC could be more broadly conceptualized to include all algorithms that mediate human communication, like the Facebook 'Newsfeed' and other content ranking, recommendation and classification algorithms (e.g., email filters, friend suggestions) that use algorithms to support human communication" (p. 92).

These researchers also specify the "boundary conditions" to ensure their proposed definition of AI is distinct from the HMC approach, giving examples of what does not constitute AI-MC in this study:

> most closely related is the growing field of AI–human interaction, or the study of human interactions with bots and other smart virtual agents who do not represent other individuals, such as Apple's Siri or Amazon's Alexa. This area, sometimes called Human–Machine Communication, overlaps with the scope of AI-MC, though in our formulation the interesting questions involve the introduction of AI that operates on communication between people. (Hancock et al., 2020, p. 92)

This brief overview of these evolving conceptual approaches to the study of AI in communication is based on scholarly papers from the literature review of this sample examined for this chapter, and we are aware that there are many other viewpoints which might be missing in this sample. However, it is evident scholars and students will continue to collaborate, argue, support and debate these existing frameworks and approaches, and refine them for the study of future AI applications with different human to human or machine interactions as these evolve.

LIMITATIONS

The aim of this chapter was to provide a brief overview of past and recent (2022) work of communication scholars in this burgeoning area of AI and communication scholarship. However, this chapter's synthesis is limited to frequency count and manual coding of a selected sample of articles published in the communication journals indexed by the WoS database from March 1, 2022 to April 30, 2022.

This search output has not been cross-referenced with scholarly research published across other databases such as Google Scholar, JSTOR, and Scopus and is, therefore, not a fully representative sample. Because of space constraints, we were unable to include the work of all the countless dedicated scholars and researchers investigating and developing new ways to study AI in the communication field today.

FUTURE DIRECTIONS

Our review of past literature offers clear reference points for those interested in obtaining a snapshot of research categories, focus areas and conceptual framework utilized in two decades of prior AI and communication research.

It is important to note Gunkel's prescient study (2012) referred a decade ago to "the fact that the majority of online communication is not human-to-human (H2H) exchanges but, as Norbert Wiener had already predicted in 1950, interactions between humans and machines and machines and machines" (2012, p. 2).

Communication researchers have been preoccupied for the past two decades with numerous debates over what constitutes "human to human" or "human to machine" and "human–machine interaction." These important definitions and evolving theoretical frameworks continue to offer important future directions to the study of AI's ubiquitous reach across every aspect of human life.

To sum up, there is much more work to be done in this fascinating area of research, we hope future students, scholars and industry practitioners continue to learn, experiment with and collaborate on specific challenges in this evolving arena of theory testing and application in such an exciting and iterative area of scholarly research.

It is also important to note communication scholarship in the period after data collection continues its upward trajectory (2022–2023). Scholars are forging ahead conducting multi-method research, addressing significant questions from a communication point of view, from whether online bandwagons and bots dictate user engagement (Brinberg et al., 2022) to the role of social agents and bots in self-impression (Brandztaeg et al., 2022). It is clear both scholars and students will benefit immensely by developing global and local collaborations with industry experts, software developers, media psychologists, behavioral scientists, computer science, and cyberpsychology scholars in the bid to pursue much more interdisciplinary and applied research in the years ahead.

REFERENCES

Arias-Robles, F., & López López, P. (2021). Driving the closest information. Local data journalism in the UK. *Journalism Practice*, *15*(5), 638–650.

Best, J. (2013). IBM Watson: The inside story of how the Jeopardy-winning supercomputer was born, and what it wants to do next. *TechRepublic*. https://www.techrepublic.com/ article/ ibm-watson-the-inside-story-of-how-the-jeopardy-winning-supercomputer-was-born-and-what-it-wants-to-do-next/

Boyd, D. (2007). Why youth (Heart) social network sites: The role of networked publics in teenage social life. *eBusiness & eCommerce eJournal*. https://doi.org/10.31219/osf.io /22hq2

Brandtzaeg, P. B., Skjuve, M., & Følstad, A. (2022). My AI friend: How users of a social chatbot Understand their human–AI friendship. *Human Communication Research, 48*(3), 404–429. https://doi.org/10.1093/hcr/hqac008

Calvo Rubio, L. M., & Ufarte Ruiz, M. J. (2021). Artificial intelligence and journalism: Systematic review of scientific production in Web of Science and Scopus (2008–2019). *Communication & Society, 34*(2), 159–176A. https://doi.org/10.15581 /003.34.2.159-176

Campbell, C., Sands, S. J., Montecchi, M., & Jensen Schau, H. (2022). That's so Instagrammable! Understanding how environments generate indirect advertising by cueing consumer-generated content. *Journal of Advertising, 51*, 411–429.

Costa, F. (2020). List of WoS communication journals – Social Sciences Citation Index (SSCI). https://www.researchgate.net/publication/343825288 _List of WoS Commu nication Journals_ _Social_Sciences_Citation_Index_SSCI

Dasilva, J., Ayerdi, K., & Galdospin, T. (2021). Deepfakes on Twitter: Which actors control their spread? *Media and Communication, 9*(1), 301–312. https://doi.org/10.17645/ mac. v9i1.3433

De Haan, Y., Van den Berg, E., Goutier, N., Kruikemeier, S., & Lecheler, S. (2022.). Invisible friend or foe? How journalists use and perceive algorithmic-driven tools in their research process. *Digital Journalism*, 1–19. https://doi.org/10.1080/21670811. 2022.2027798

De-Lima-Santos, M., Mesquita, L., De Melo Peixoto, J., & Camargo, I. (2022). Digital news business models in the age of industry 4.0: Digital Brazilian news players find in technology new ways to bring revenue and competitive advantage. *Digital Journalism*, 1–25. https://doi .org/10.1080/21670811.2022.2037444

De-Lima-Santos, M., & Ceron, W. (2021). Artificial intelligence in news media: Current perceptions and future outlook. *Journalism and Media, 3*(1), 13–26. https://doi.org/10.3390 /journalmedia3010002

De-Lima-Santos, M., & Salaverría, R. (2021). From data journalism to artificial intelligence: Challenges faced by La Nación in implementing computer vision in news reporting. *Palabra-Clave, 24*(3), 1–40.

De Seta, G. (2021). Huanlian, or changing faces: Deepfakes on Chinese digital media platforms. *Convergence, 27*(4), 935–953. https://doi.org/10.1177/13548565211030185

Edwards, C., & Edwards, A., Spence, P. & Lin, X. (2018). I, teacher: Using artificial intelligence (AI) and social robots in communication and instruction. *Communication Education, 67*, 473–480. 10.1080/03634523.2018.1502459

Endacott, C. G., & Leonardi, P. M. (2022). Artificial intelligence and impression management: Consequences of autonomous conversational agents communicating on one's behalf. *Human Communication Research*. https://doi.org/10.1093/hcr/hqac009

Esch, P., Cui, Y., & Jain, S. (2021). Stimulating or intimidating: The effect of AI-enabled in-store communication on consumer patronage likelihood. *Journal of Advertising, 50*(1), 63–80. https://doi.org/10.1080/00913367.2020.1832939

Ferrara, E., Varol, O., Davis, C., Menczer, F., & Flammini, A. (2016). The rise of Social Bots. *Communications of the ACM, 59*(7), 96–104. DOI: 10.1145/2818717

Gómez-Diago, G. (2022). Perspectives to address artificial intelligence in journalism teaching: A review of research and teaching experiences. *Revista Latina de Comunicación Social, 80*, 29–46. https://www.doi.org/10.4185/RLCS-2022-1542

Gunkel, D. J. (2012). Communication and artificial intelligence: Opportunities and challenges for the 21st century. *Communication +1, 1*(1). https://scholarworks.umass .edu/cpo/vol1/ iss1/1 https://doi.org/10.7275/R5QJ7F7R

Guzman, A. L. (2018). What is human-machine communication, anyway? In A. L. Guzman (Ed.), *Human-machine communication: Rethinking communication, technology, and ourselves* (pp. 1–28). Peter Lang.

Hancock, J. T., Naaman, M., & Levy, K. (2020). AI-mediated communication: Definition, research agenda, and ethical considerations. *Journal of Computer-Mediated Communication*, 25(1), 89–100. https://doi.org/10.1093/jcmc/zmz022

Herrero-Diz, P., & Varona-Aramburu, D. (2018). The use of chatbots for information automation in Spanish media. *Profesional de la Información*, 27(4), 742–749. https://doi.org/10.3145/epi.2018.jul.03

Jamil, S. (2021). Artificial intelligence and journalistic practice: The crossroads of obstacles and opportunities for the Pakistani journalists. *Journalism Practice*, 15(10), 1400–1422.

Jiang, J. A., Wade, K., Fiesler, C., & Brubaker, J. R. (2021). Supporting serendipity: Opportunities and challenges for human-AI collaboration in qualitative analysis. *Proceedings of the ACM on Human-Computer Interaction*, 5, CSCW1 (article no. 94). ACM Press. https://doi.org/10.1145/3449168

Kietzmann, J., Mills, A., & Plangger, K. (2021). Deepfakes: Perspectives on the future "reality" of advertising and branding. *International Journal of Advertising*, 40(3), 473–485.

Klyuev, Y., Poznin, V., & Zubko, D. (2019). Teaching future journalists media research methodology using digital technologies. *Media Education (Mediaobrazovanie)*, 59(2), 278–285. DOI: 10.13187/me.2019.2.278

KPMG. (2021, April). *Thriving in an AI World* [Report]. https://advisory.kpmg.us/articles/2021/thriving-in-an-ai-world.html

Lou, C., Kang, H., & Tse, C. (2022). Bots vs. humans: How schema congruity, contingency-based interactivity, and sympathy influence consumer perceptions and patronage intentions. *International Journal of Advertising*, 1–30.

Lynes, N. (2023, January 1). AI industry booming amid 'tech recession'. *VentureBeat*. https://venturebeat.com/ai/ai-industry-booming-amid-tech-recession/

Manning, C. (2020). McCarthy's definition of AI. Retrieved from https://hai.stanford.edu/sites/default/files/2020-09/AI-Definitions-HAI.pdf

McCarthy, J. (1959). Programs with common sense. In *Proceedings of the Teddington Conference on the Mechanization of Thought Processes*, 756–791. http://jmc.Stanford.edu/articles/mcc59.html

Meng, J., & Dai, Y. (2021). Emotional support from AI chatbots: Should a supportive partner self-disclose or not? *Journal of Computer-Mediated Communication*, 26(4), 207–222, https://doi.org/10.1093/jcmc/zmab005

Murdock, G. (2018). Media materialties: For a moral economy of machines. *Journal of Communication*, 68(2), 359–368. doi:10.1093/joc/jqx023

Myers, A. (2011). Stanford's John McCarthy, seminal figure of artificial intelligence, dies at 84. https://engineering.stanford.edu/news/stanfords-john-mccarthy-seminal-figure-artificial-intelligence-dead-84

Naidoo, J., & Dulek, R. (2022). Artificial intelligence in business communication: A snapshot. *International Journal of Business Communication*, 59(1), 126–147. https://doi.org/10.1177/2329488418819139

Natale, S., & Guzman, A. L. (2022). Reclaiming the human in machine cultures: Introduction. *Media, Culture & Society*, 44(4), 627–637. https://doi.org/10.1177/01634437221099614

Neff, G., & Nagy, P. (2016). Talking to bots: Symbiotic agency and the case of tay. *International Journal of Communication*, 10, 4915–4931. https://ijoc.org/index.php/ijoc/article/view/6277

Newhagen, J. E., & Rafaeli, S. (1996). Why communication researchers should study the Internet: A dialogue. *Journal of Computer-Mediated Communication*, 1(4), 145. https://doi.org/10.1111/j.1083-6101.1996.tb00172.x

Oliveira, D. & Costa, B. (2020). News agenda guided by algorithms: Content and format in Estadão Infográficos. *Brazilian Journalism Research*, 16, 550–575. 10.25200/BJR.v16n3.2021.1284

O'Sullivan, B. P., & Carr, T. C. (2018). Masspersonal communication: A model bridging the mass-interpersonal divide. *New Media & Society*, 20(3), 1161–1180. https://doi.org/10.1177/1461444816686104

Pelea, C. I. (2019). The relationship between artificial intelligence, human communication and ethics. A futuristic perspective: Utopia or dystopia? *Media Literacy Academic Research*, 38–48. https://www.ceeol.com/search/article-detail?id=761747

PEW. (2021, March 26). About three-in-ten U.S. adults say they are 'almost constantly' online. https://www.pewresearch.org/short-reads/2021/03/26/about-three-in-ten-u-s-adults -say-they-are-almost-constantly-online/

Prahl, A., & Goh, W. (2021). "Rogue machines" and crisis communication: When AI fails, how do companies publicly respond? *Public Relations Review*, *47*(4), 102077. https://doi .org/10.1016/j.pubrev.2021.102077

Reeves, B., & Nass, C. (1996). *The media equation: how people treat computers, television, and new media like real people and places*. Cambridge University Press.

Rubio, C. L. M., & Ruiz, R. M. (2021). Artificial intelligence and journalism: Systematic review of scientific production in web of science and scopus (2008–2019). *Communication & Society*, *34*(2), 159–176. https://doi.org/10.15581/003.34.2.159-176

Schwartz, S., & Mahnke, M. (2021). Facebook use as a communicative relation: Exploring the relation between Facebook users and the algorithmic news feed. Information. *Communication & Society*, *24*(7), 1041–1056. https://doi.org/10.1080 /1369118X.2020.1718179

Serrano-Cobos, J. (2016). Towards a paradigm shift. *El professional de la informacion*, *25*(6), 843–850.

Shannon, C., & Weaver, W. (1948). The mathematical theory of communication. *Bell System Technical Journal*, *27*, 379–423, 623–656. http://dx.doi.org/10.1002/j.1538-7305.1948 .tb00917.x

Shapovalova, E. (2020). Improving media education as a way to combat fake news. *Media Education (Mediaobrazovanie)*, *60*(4), 730–735. DOI: 10.13187/me.2020.4.730

Sukhodolov, A., Bychkova, A., & Ovanesyan, S. (2019). Journalism featuring artificial intelligence. *Voprosy Teorii I Praktiki Zhurnalistiki*, *8*(4), 647–667. https://doi.org/10 .17150/2308. 6203.2019.8(4).647-667

Sundar, S. S. (2007). Social psychology of interactivity in human-website interaction. In A. Joinson et al. (Eds.), *The Oxford handbook of internet psychology*, Oxford Library of Psychology. https://doi.org/10.1093/oxfordhb/9780199561803.013.0007

Sundar, S. S. (2020). Rise of machine agency: A framework for studying the psychology of human-AI interaction (HAII). *Journal of Computer-Mediated Communication*, *25*(1), 74–88.

Stenbom, A., Wiggberg, M., & Norlund, T. (2021). Exploring communicative AI: Reflections from a Swedish newsroom. *Digital Journalism*, 1–19.

Stray, J. (2019). Making artificial intelligence work for investigative journalism. *Digital Journalism*, *7*(8), 1076–1097. https://doi.org/10.1080/21670811.2019.1630289

Terren, L., & Borge, R. (2021). Echo chambers on social media: A systematic review of the literature. *Review of Communication Research*, *9*, 99–118. https://doi.org/10.12840/ISSN .2255-4165.028

Thurman, N. (2018). Social media, surveillance and news work: On the apps promising journalists a "crystal ball". *Digital Journalism*, *6*(1), 76–97. https://doi.org/10.1080 /21670811.2017.1345318

Trites, A. (2019). Black box ethics: How algorithmic decision-making is changing how we view society and people: Advocating for the right for explanation and the right to be forgotten in Canada. *Global Media Journal*, Canadian Edition, *11*(2), 18–30.

Tunez-Lopez, J. M., Toural-Bran, C., &., Cacheiro-Requeijo, S. (2018). Automated-content generation using news-writing bots and algorithms: Perceptions and attitudes amongst Spain's journalists. *El profesional de la información*, *27*(4), 750–758. https://doi. org/10.3145/epi.2018.jul.04

Turkle, S. (1984). *The second self: Computers and the human spirit*. Simon and Schuster.

Turkle, S. (2008). Always-on/always-on-you: The tethered self. In J. E. Katz (Ed.), *Handbook of mobile communication studies* (pp. 121–137). MIT Press.

Turkle, S. (2011). *Alone together: why we expect more from technology and less from each other.* Basic Books.

Vaccari, C., & Chadwick, A. (2020). Deepfakes and disinformation: Exploring the impact of synthetic political video on deception, uncertainty, and trust in news. *Social Media Society*, 6(1). https://doi.org/10.1177/2056305120903408

Vivar, J. F. (2019). Artificial intelligence and journalism: Diluting the impact of disinformation and fake news through bots. *Doxa Comunicación, 29,* 197–212.

Weizenbaum, J. (1976*). Computer power and human reason: From judgment to calculation.* W. H. Freeman and Company.

Weizenbaum, J. (1966). ELIZA--A computer program for the study of natural language communication between man and machine. *Communications of the ACM, 9,* 6–35. https://doi.org/10.1145/365153.365168. S2CID 1896290.

Westerman, D., Edwards, A.P., Edwards, C., Luo, Z., & Spence, P. R. (2020). I-It, I-Thou, I-Robot: The perceived humanness of AI in human-machine. *Communication Studies, 71*(3), 393–408, DOI: 10.1080/10510974.2020.1749683

Wiener, N. (1988). *The human use of human beings: Cybernetics and society.* Da Capo Press.

Wojcieszak, M., Thakur, A., Goncalves, J. F. F., Casas, A., Menchen-Trevino, E., & Boon, M. (2021). Can AI enhance people's support for online moderation and their openness to dissimilar political views? *Journal of Computer-Mediated Communication, 26,* 223–243. https://academic.oup.com/jcmc/article/26/4/223/6298304

Zdenek, S. (1999). Rising up from the MUD: inscribing gender in software design. *Discourse & Society, 10*(3), 379–409. http://www.jstor.org/stable/42888264

Zerfass, A., Hagelstein, J., & Tench, R. (2020). Artificial intelligence in communication management: A cross-national study on adoption and knowledge, impact, challenges and risks. *Journal of Communication Management, 24*(4), 377–389.

Zhao, S. (2006). Humanoid social robots as a medium of communication. *New Media & Society, 8,* 401–419. 10.1177/1461444806061951.

APPENDIX

Table A1.1   *AI-communication articles per year*

Year	Number of studies
1999	1
2006	1
2010	1
2012	1
2015	1
2016	3
2017	4
2018	12
2019	27
2020	49
2021	65
2022	31*

Note: * Data collected until April 2022.
Source: WoS (April 2022).

Table A1.2   *Social Science Citation Index (SCII) results*

Name of journal	Articles on AI and communication
New Media and Society	13
Digital Journalism	13
Communication Theory	1
Communication Studies	5
Media and Communication	5
International Journal of Communication	5
Journal of Computer Mediated Communication (JCMC)	5
Journalism Practice	5
Frontiers	5
Convergence - the International Journal of Research into New Media Technologies	4
Theoretical and Practical Issues of Journalism	4
Information Communication and Society	4
Journalism	3
Media and Communication	3
Media Culture and Society	3
Social Media + Society	3
JCOM-Journal of Science Communication	3
Media Literacy and Academic Research	2
Business and Professional Communication Quarterly	2
Journal of Communication Inquiry	2
Communication Education	2
Journalism and Mass Comm Quarterly	1
SCM Studies in Communication and Media	1
Critical Studies in Media Communication	1
Journal of Communication	1
Policy and Internet	1
Telecommunications Policy	1
Science Editing	1
Communication Methods and Measures	1
Total	100

Source: WoS (April 2022).

Table A1.3   *Expanded Social Citations Index (ESCI) search results*

Journal name (international)	Number of articles
Profesional De La Informacion	15
Doxa Comunicacion	10
Revista Latina De Comunicacion Social	6
Palabra Clave	5
Communication and Society-Spain	4
Analisi-Quaderns De Comunicacio I Cultura	4
Revista Icono 14-Revista Cientifica De Comunicacion Y Tecnologias	3
Revista Internacional De Relaciones Publicas	2
Revista Espanola De Comunicacion En Salud	2
Medijske Studije-Media Studies	2
Mediaciones Sociales	2
Adcomunica-Revista Cientifica De Estrategias Tendencias E Innovacion En Communicacion	2
Chasqui-Revista Latinoamericana De Comunicacion	1
Global Media and China	2
Brazilian Journalism Research	2
Jurnal Komunikasi-Malaysian Journal of Communication	2
Jurnal the Messenger	2
African Journalism Studies	1
Chinese Journal of Communication	1
Nordicom Review	1
Global Media Journal-Canadian Edition	1
Total	70

Source: WoS (April 2022).

Table A1.4 Articles from PR, advertising and management journals

PR, advertising and management journals	Number of articles
Journal of Advertising	5
Public Relations Review	4
International Journal of Advertising	4
Journal of Creative Communications	1
Journal of Current Issues and Research in Advertising	1
Journal of Advertising	5
Public Relations Inquiry	1
International Journal of Conflict MGMT	1
Cogent Business and Management	1
Total articles	23

Source: WoS (April 2022).

Table A1.5 Study methods utilized in sample reviewed

Method(s)	Number of articles coded by method
Qualitative	120
Quantitative	40
Mixed Method	33
Total	193

Source: WoS (April 2022).

Table A1.6   *Categories list with articles per category*

	Category title	Number of studies
1	**AI in news and journalism:** AI and news production, automation, impact on newsrooms in USA and globally and future of journalism practice	63
2	**AI and social bots, chatterbots and other agentic representations**	29
3	**Algorithms and AI in deepfakes:** includes research in topics exploring image manipulation mis (dis)information	26
4	**AI in PR, advertising, and media business/management**	23
5	**Conceptual and theoretical approaches/frameworks**	20
6	**AI policy, regulations and ICT**	12
7	**AI and ethics**	6
8	**AI in communication/journalism education**	6
*	**Miscellaneous:** includes AI in health and science communication, in music and script authorship and social media	8

Note: * Coded based on topics and grouped accordingly.
Source: WoS (April 2022).

Table A1.7 Complete list of categories, articles, journal names, author(s) and year published

	Topic	Number of studies	Title of study	Journal	Author(s)	Year published
1	AI in news production, news automation, impact on newsrooms in USA and globally and future of journalism practice	63	(i) Internet technology trends: Towards a paradigm shift (ii) Hegemonic media and inequality in Brazil (iii) Social media surveillance and news work: On the apps promising journalists a crystal ball (iv) Automated-content generation using news-writing bots and algorithms: Perceptions and attitudes amongst Spain's journalists (v) News personalization for peace journalism (vi) Automated news in Brazilian television: A case study on the AIDA system (Globo-Brazil) (vii) Libel by Algorithm? Automated journalism and the threat of legal liability (viii) Algorithms and bots applied to journalism. The case of Narrativa Inteligencia Artificial (ix) Artificial intelligence (AI) applied to informative documentation and journalistic sports writing. The case of BeSoccer (x) Making artificial intelligence work for investigative journalism (xi) Journalism featuring artificial intelligence (xii) Algorithms, automation, and news (xiii) Automated sports coverage. Case study of bot released by The Washington Post during the Rio 2016 and PyeongChang 2018 Olympics (xiv) Automation, bots and algorithms in newsmaking. Impact and quality of artificial journalism (xv) Participatory storytelling online: The challenge of the dialog between form and content to obtain vibrant settings (xvi) Artificial intelligence and journalism: diluting the impact of misinformation and fakes news through bots	(i) Doxa Comunicación (ii) Journalism Practice (iii) Communication Studies (iv) Revista Latina De Comunicacion Social Convergence (v) Information, Communication & Society (vi) Profesional de la Información (vii) Global Media and China (viii) Braxilian Journalism Research (ix) Digital Journalism (x) International Journal of Conflict Management (xi) Journalism & Mass Communication Quarterly (xii) Media Literacy and Academic Research (xiii) Digital Journalism (xiv) Theoretical and Practical Issues of Journalism (xv) Revista Latina de Comunicacion Social Palabra Clave Brazilian Journalism Research	(i) Serrano-Cobos, J (ii) Paiva, R (iii) Thurman, N (iv) Tunez-Lopez, JM; Toural-Bran, C; Cacheiro-Requeijo, S (v) Bastian. M., Makhortykh M. & Dobber, T (vi) Essenfelder, R: Canavilhas, J: Maia. HC: Pinto, RJ. (vii) Lewis, SC: Sanders, AK; Carmody, C (viii) Ruiz, MJU: Sanchez, JLM (ix) Segarra-Saavedra, J: Cristofol, FJ; Martinez-Sala. AM (x) Stray, J (xi) Sukhodolov, AP; Bychkova, AM; Ovanesyan, SS (xii) Thurman, N; Lewis, SC; Kunert, J (xiii) Torrijos, JLR (xiv) Tunez-Lopez, M; Toural-Bran. C; Valdiviezo-Abad, C (xv) Verde, JMP; Tejedor-Calvo, S (xvi) Vivar, JMF (xvii) Zamkov, AV (xviii) de Oliveira, DB; da Costa, BCG	2016; 2018; 2019; 2020; 2021; 2022

(Continued)

Table A1.7   *(Continued)*

	Topic	Number of studies	Title of study	Journal	Author(s)	Year published
2	AI and social bots, chatter bots and other agentic representations	29	(i) Rising up from the MUD: inscribing gender in software design (ii) Humanoid social robots as a medium of communication (iii) The rise of social bots (iv) The inexorable rise of the robots: Trade journals' framing of machinery in the workplace (v) Talking to Bots: Symbiotic Agency and the Case of Tay (vi) The use of chatbots for information automation in Spanish media (vii) The New Frontier in Communication Research: Why We Should Study Social Robots (viii) First encounter with robot Alpha: How individual differences interact with vocal and kinetic cues in users' social responses; (ix) Artificial companions, social bots and work bots: communicative robots as research objects of media and communication studies (x) The medium is the joke: online humor about and by networked computers (xi) Materials and assessment of literacy level for the recognition of social bots in political misinformation contexts	(i) *Discourse & Society* (ii) *New Media & Society; Journalism (UK)* (iii) *International Journal of Communication* (iv) *Profesional De La Información* (v) *Media and Communication* (vi) *Doxa Comunicación;* (vii) *Media Culture & Society* (viii) *Revista Icono 14-Revista Científica de Comunicación y Tecnologías*	(i) Zdenek, S (ii) Zhao. SY (iii) Ferrara, Emilio et al. (iv) Duffy, A. Prahl, A. & Ling Yan-Hui, A (v) Neff, G; Nagy, P (vi) Herrero-Diz, P. Varona-Aramburu, D (vii) Peter, J; Kuhne, R; Salazar. I; (viii) Xu, K; (ix) Shifman, L; Blondheim, M (x) Calvo, D; Cano-Oron, L; Abengozar. AE	1999; 2006; 2016; 2018; 2019; 2020; 2021; 2022

| 3 | Algorithms' role in deepfakes, image manipulation, Big Data and computational analysis | 26 | (i) Comments on Fire! Classifying flaming comments on YouTube videos in Malaysia (ii) Behavioral experiments With social algorithms: An information theoretic Approach to input-output conversions (iii) The unedited public sphere (iv) Digital moral literacy for the detection of deepfakes and audiovisual fakes (v) Science communication desperately needs more aligned recommendation algorithms (vi) Deepfakes and disinformation: Exploring the impact of synthetic political video on deception, uncertainty, and trust in news (vii) Something that they never said: Multimodal disinformation and source vividness in understanding the power of AI-enabled deepfake news (viii) Deepfakes on Twitter: Which Actors Control Their Spread? (ix) Huanlian, or changing faces: Deepfakes on Chinese digital media platforms (x) Fake news and generation Z – Journalists Post-millennial solutions against disinformation (xi) Deep-Fakes: The next challenge in fake news detection communication technology (xii) A new taxonomy for image use in the intentional shaping of the digital narrative: deep fakes and artificial intelligence (xiii) Deepfakes: perspectives on the future reality of advertising and branding Configuring Fakes: Digitized Bodies, the Politics of Evidence, and Agency (xiv) Facebook use as a communicative relation: exploring the relation between Facebook users and the algorithmic news feed (xv) Fighting Deepfakes: media and internet giants' converging and diverging strategies Against hi-tech misinformation (xvi) Whose dystopia is it anyway? Deepfakes and social media regulation (xvii) Virality, only the tip of the iceberg: ways of spread and interaction around COVID-19 misinformation in Twitter (xviii) Smart speakers require smart management: Two routes From user gratifications to privacy settings (xix) Algorithmic photography: a case study of the Huawei Moon Mode controversy | (i) *Jurnal Komunikasi-Malaysian Journal of Communication* (ii) *Communication Methods and Measures* (iii) *New Media & Society* (iv) *Frontiers in Communication* (v) *Social Media + Society* (vi) *Media Psychology* (vii) *Media and Communication* (viii) *Convergence-The International Journal of Research into New Media Technologies* (ix) *Vivat Academia* (x) *Analisi-Quaderns de Comunicacio i cultur* (xi) *Sem Studies in Communication and Media Profesional de la Informacion International Journal of Advertising* (xii) *International* (xiii) *Communication & Society-Spain International Journal of Communication Media Culture & Society* | (i) Lingam, RA; Aripin, N (ii) Hilbert, M; Liu, B; Luu, J; Fishbein, J (iii) Bimber, B; de Zuniga, HG (iv) Castillo, GP; Guarda, MLG; Alenda, VC (v) Hoang, LN (vi) Vaccari, C; Chadwick, A (vii) Lee JY and Shin, SY (viii) Dasilva, JP; Ayerdi, KM; Galdospin, TM (ix) de Seta, G, Garcia-Marin, D and Garcia-Ull, FJ (x) Godulla, A; Hoffmann, CP (xi) Seibert, D Gomez-de-Agreda, A (xii) Feijoo, C; Salazar-Garcia, IA (xiii) Kietzmann, J; Mills, AJ (xiv) Plangger, K (xv) Paris, B (xvi) Schwartz, SA (xvii) Mahnke, MS Vizoso, A; Vaz-Alvarez, M; Lopez-Garcia, X.Yadlin-Segal, A; Oppenheim, Y Villar-Rodriguez, G (xviii) Souto-Rico, M (xix) Martin, A Xu, K (xx) Chan-Olmsted, S (xxi) Liu, FJ, and Zhang, YX | 2017; 2019; 2020; 2021; 2022 |

(Continued)

Table A1.7   (Continued)

	Topic	Number of studies	Title of study	Journal	Author(s)	Year published
4	AI and advertising, public relations (PR) and media industry (management implications)	23	(i) Professional communication as phatic: From classical Eunoia to personal artificial intelligence (ii) The use of pseudoscience and experimentation as a persuasive resource in new advertising communication trends (iii) To thrive in today's marketing landscape, embrace schizophrenia! (iv) AI cheerleaders: Public relations, neoliberalism and artificial intelligence (v) Smart generation system of personalized advertising copy and its application to advertising practice and research (vi) Digital Neurocomunication and Public Relations: The case of prevention of suicides in the young population (vii) Digital advertising: present and future prospects (viii) Trends and impact of artificial intelligence in communication: cobotisation, gig economy, co-creation and governance (ix) Stimulating or intimidating: The effect of AI-enabled in-store communication on consumer patronage likelihood(x) AI-powered recommendations: the roles of perceived similarity and psychological distance on persuasion (xi) Exploratory research on digitalization transformation practices within supply chain management context in developing	(i) *Public Relations Review* (ii) *Business and Professional Communication Quarterly* (iii) *Revista Latina De Comunicación Social* (iv) *Journal of Current Issues and Research in Advertising* (v) *Public Relations Inquiry* (vi) *Journal of Advertising* (vii) *Revista Internacional De Relaciones Publicas* (viii) *International Journal of Advertising* (ix) *Fonseca-Journal of Communication* (x) *Cogent Business & Management* (xi) *Media Literacy and Academic Research* (xii) *Revista Latina De Comunicacion Social* (xiii) *Communication Monographs* (xiv) *International Journal of Business Communication* (xv) *Journal of Business Ethics*	(i) Seiffert, J; Nothhaft, H (ii) Prahl, A. & Goh, W (iii) Porter, JE (iv) Tunez-Lopez, BM (v) Tobaccowala, R; Jones, VK (vi) Bourne, C (vii) Deng, SS (viii) Seiffert, J & Nothhaft, H (ix) Porter, JE (x) Lopez, BM (xi) Tobaccowala, R; Jones, VK (xii) Bourne (xiii) C Deng, SS (xiv) Tan, CW; Wang, WJ; Pan, Y (xv) Jimenez, AL (xvi) Lee, H; Cho, CH (xvii) Tunez-Lopez, JM (xviii) (van) Esch, P; Cui, Y; Jain, SP (xix) Ahn, J; Kim, J; Sung, Y (xx) Khalifa, N; Abd Elghany, M; Abd Elghany, M (xxi) Kupec, M; Jakubikova, D; Kupec, V (xxii) Prahl, A ; Goh	2015; 2017; 2018; 2019; 2020; 2021; 2022

(Continued)

countries specifically Egypt in the MENA region (xii) Web personalization and artificial intelligence as fools for marketing communications(xiv) Rogue machines and crisis communication: When AI fails, how do companies publicly respond? (xv) Virtual Influencers as an advertising tool in the promotion of brands and products. Study of the commercial activity of Lil Miquela (xvi) When public relations meets social media: A systematic review of social media related public relations research from 2006 to 2020 (xvii) That's so Instagrammable! Understanding how environments generate indirect advertising by cueing consumer-generated content (xviii) Artificial Intelligence in Business Communication: The changing landscape of research and teaching (xix) Bots vs. humans: how schema congruity, contingency-based interactivity, and sympathy influence consumer perceptions and patronage intentions (xx) Uncertainty management, transformational leadership, and job performance in an AI-powered organizational context (xxi) Artificial intelligence in Business Communication: A snapshot (xxii)When e-commerce personalization systems show and tell: Investigating the relative persuasive appeal of content-based versus collaborative filtering (xxiii) From greenwashing to machinewashing: A model and future directions derived from reasoning by analogy	WWP (xxiii) Rodrigo-Martin, L.; Rodrigo-Martin, I: Munoz-Sastre, D (xxiv) Wang, Y: Cheng, Y: Sun, J (xxv) Campbell, C: Sands, S: Montecchi, M: Schau, HJ(xxvi) Getchell, KM: Carradini, S: Cardon, PW; Fleischmann, C: Ma, HB; Aritz, J; Stapp, J (xxvii) Lou, C: Kang, HJ; Tse, CH (xxviii) Matsunaga. M (xxix) Naidoo, J; Dulek, RE(xxx) Liao. MQ: Sundar. SS(xxxi) Seele: Peter; Schultz, Mario D Tan. CW; Wang, WJ; Pan. Y; Liao, MQ; Sundar, SS: Zerfass, A. Hagelstein, J. & Tench, R

Table A1.7   *(Continued)*

Topic	Number of studies	Title of study	Journal	Author(s)	Year published
5	Conceptual frameworks and approaches to the study of AI	20	(i) Communication and Artificial Intelligence: Opportunities and Challenges for the 21st Century (ii) The Mediation of Hope: Communication Technologies and Inequalities in perspective AI, big data and digital economy policy (iii) Media Materialities: For A Moral Economy of Machines (iv) AI-Mediated Communication: Definition, Research Agenda, and Ethical Considerations (v) Reclaiming the human in machine cultures: Introduction (vi) Rise of Machine Agency: A Framework for Studying the Psychology of Human-AI Interaction (HAII) (vii) Latin American Perspectives on Datafication and Artificial intelligence: Traditions, Interventions, and Possibilities (viii) Artificial companions, social bots and work bots: communicative robots as research objects of media and communication studies (ix) Human-aided artificial intelligence: Or, how to run large computations in human brains? Toward a media sociology of machine learning (x) Artificial intelligence in communication management: a cross-national study on adoption and knowledge, impact, challenges and risks (xi) Towards a Critical Theory of Algorithmic Reason (xii) Artificial intelligence and communication: A Human-Machine Communication research agenda	(i) *Communication +1* (ii) *International Journal of Communication* (iii) *Journal of Communication* (iv) *Journal of Computer-Mediated Communication* (v) *Media Culture and Society* (vi) *Revista Icono 14-Revista Científica De Comunicacion y Tecnologías* (vii) *Communication Theory* (viii) *Palabra Clave* (ix) *Journal of Communication Management.* (x) *New Media and Society*	(i) Gunkel, DJ (ii) Mansell, R (iii) Murdock, G (iv) Hancock. JT. Naaman. M & Levy, (v) Natale, S & Guzman, A (vi) Sundar, SS (vii) Trere, E; Milan. S (viii) Hepp. A (ix) Muhlhoff, R (x) Zerfass, A (xi) Fernandez-Vicente, A (xii) Guzman, AL; Lewis, SC	2012; 2017; 2018; 2020; 2022

| 6 | AI policy, regulations, ICT and social justice | 12 | (i) The next stage of US communications policy: The emerging embedded infosphere (ii) Mitigating hate speech in Nigeria: The possibilities of artificial intelligence (iii) Perception of teachers, students, innovation managers and journalists about the use of artificial intelligence in journalism (iv) Technologies to fight the Covid-19 pandemic: geolocation, tracking, big data, GIS, artificial intelligence, and privacy (v) How online content providers moderate user-generated content to prevent harmful online communication: An Analysis of Policies and Their Implementation (vi) Information policy as communication concept (vii) Artificial intelligence, communication, and democracy in Latin America: a review of the cases of Colombia, Ecuador, and Mexico (viii) Impacts of attitudes toward government and corporations on public trust in artificial intelligence (ix) AI for social justice: New methodological horizons in technical communication | (i) New Media & Society (ii) Telecommunications Policy (iii) Analisi-Quaderns de Comunicacio I Cultura (iv) International Journal of Mobile Communications(v) Profesional de La Informacion (vi) Policy and Internet (vii) International Journal of Communication (viii) Theoretical and Practical Issues of Journalism (ix) Communication Studies (x) Technical Communication Quarterly (xi) Information Communication & Society | (i) Taylor, RD (ii) Wilson, J; Jibrin, R (iii) Arpaci, I (iv) Calvo Rubio, LM; Ufarte Ruiz, MJ (v) Cascon-Katchadourian, JD (vi) Einwiller, SA; Kim, S; Mann, S; Hilbert, M. (vii) Ovrutsky, AV (viii) Barredo-Ibanez, D; De-la-Garza-Montemayor, DJ; Torres-Toukoumidis, A; Lopez-Lopez, PC (ix) Chen, YNK; Wen, CHR. (x) Graham, SS; Hopkins, HR (xi) Zeng, J; Chan, CH; Schafer, MS | 2010; 2017; 2019 ; 2020; 2021; 2022 |
| 7 | Ai and ethics | 6 | (i) Black box ethics: How algorithmic decision-making is changing how we view society and people: advocating for the right for explanation to be forgotten Canada ... (ii) The relationship between artificial intelligence, Human communication and ethics. A futuristic perspective: Utopia or dystopia? (iii) Nonhuman humanitarianism: when 'AI for good' can be harmful (iv) The perception of humanness in conversational journalism: An algorithmic information-processing perspective (v) Artificial intelligence and mass personalization of communication content-An ethical and literacy perspective (vi) From Greenwashing to machinewashing: A model and future directions derived from deasoning by analogy | (i) Global Media Journal-Canadian Edition (ii) Media Literacy and Academic Research (iii) Information Communication & Society (iv) New Media & Society (v) Journal of Business Ethics | (i) Trites, A (ii) Pelea, CI (iii) Madianou, M (iv) Shin, D (v) Hermann, E (vi) Seele, P; Schultz, MD | 2019; 2021; 2022 |

(Continued)

Table A1.7   (Continued)

	Topic	Number of studies	Title of study	Journal	Author(s)	Year published
8	AI in journalism/communication education	6	(i) I, teacher: Using artificial intelligence (AI) and social robots in communication and instruction (ii) Teaching future journalists media research methodology using digital technologies (iii) Improving media education as a way to combat fake news (iv) Perspectives to address artificial intelligence in journalism teaching and education (v) What drives students' online self-disclosure behaviour on social media? A hybrid SEM and artificial intelligence approach	(i) *Communication Education* (ii) *Media Education-Mediaobrazovanie* (iii) *Revista Latina De Comunicacion Social*	(i) Edwards, C; Edwards, A; Spence, PR; Lin, XL (ii) Klyuev, Y; Poznin, V; Zubko, D (iii) Shapovalova, E (iv) Gomez-Diago, G	2018; 2019; 2020; 2022
9	Miscellaneous (includes: studies in topics of AI in science and health communication, authorship)	8	(i) AI writing bots are about to revolutionise science journalism: we must shape how this is done (ii) Paperwork (iii) Data drive/human drive: the challenge of Data Communication (iv) Hey Siri, tell me a story: Digital storytelling and AI authorship (v) Bounded Religious Automation at Work: Communicating Human Authority in Artificial Intelligence Networks (vi) The (Brazilian) Factory Floor of Artificial Intelligence: Data Production and the Role of Communication among Appen and Lionbridge Workers (vii) Are you ready for artificial Mozart and Skrillex? An experiment testing expectancy violation theory and AI music (viii) Artificial intelligence-assisted tools for redefining the communication landscape of the scholarly world (ix) Population health AI researchers' perceptions of the public portrayal of AI: A pilot study	(i) *Journal of Science Communication* (ii) *Health Communication* (iii) *Comunicacion y Hombre* (iv) *Convergence-The International Journal of Research Into New Media Technologies* (v) *Journal of Communication Inquiry* (vi) *Palabra Clave* (vii) *New Media & Society* (viii) *Science Editing* (ix) *Public Understanding of Science*	(i) Tatalovic, M (ii) Barbour, JB (iii) Nombela, DM (iv) Thorne, S (v) Cheong, PH (vi) Grohmann, R; Araujo, WF(vii) Hong, JW; Peng, QY; Williams, D (viii) Razack, HIA; Mathew, ST; Saad, FFA; Alqahtani, SA (ix) Samuel, G; Diedericks, H; Derrick, G	2018; 2020; 2021

Source: WoS (April 2022).

2. AI-integrated communication: conceptualization and a critical review

Donghee Yvette Wohn and Mashael Almoqbel

In 2004, Susan Herring wrote the seminal piece "Slouching Toward the Ordinary: Current Trends in Computer-mediated Communication (CMC)" (Herring, 2004). In this piece, she argued that a technology-driven agenda suffers from a "systematic bias" (p. 27) – which is a bias inherent and supported by the agenda itself and that fails to consider all involved parties. Herring (2004) noted that despite the technology, CMC remains "predominantly grounded in 'old' textual practices," which, for example, considers lack of electricity as the most significant effect of the mediation process, overlooking other profound effects on the communication process, such as narrative shaping and others. Herring (2004) claimed that the complexity of online communication tools prompted users to want a simpler approach, resulting in the development of more straightforward tools that do not require strong technical skills. She wrote, "After barely more than 30 years of existence, CMC has become more of a practical necessity than an object of fascination and fetish" (p. 33), pointing out that the overuse of CMC, disenchantment, and fatigue contributed to these phenomena.

Herring predicted that increasing technological integration over the next five years would make the internet a simpler, safer, yet less fascinating communication environment. However, there remains a lack of evidence supporting Herring's three-point prediction, which perhaps, is fortunate for researchers studying CMC almost 20 years after the publication of this pivotal piece.

In this chapter, we present the concept of artificial intelligence (AI) integrated communication, which views computers not as neutral mediators of communication but as active entities in communication processes and outcomes. Understanding computers as an integrated part of communication rather than a neutral mediator is essential for communication scholars, especially those examining media effects, as communication technologies become more complex by incorporating algorithms and artificial intelligence. Thus, as communication technology researchers, it is imperative to have a systematic understanding of technological properties to choose the most appropriate research methods and think about the system-level effects on communication processes. For instance, aspects of AI-integrated communication could be considered a 2.0 version of McLuhan's "medium is the message" (McLuhan, 1964). However, when algorithms come into play, the medium is no longer a single artifact but a socio-technical ecosystem. This online communication ecosystem is constantly evolving, posing challenges for communication researchers trying to keep up with the rapidly changing technologies.

In the past ten years, a growing number of "new" terms have generally tried to address communication processes in which computers play a more prominent role. Although these terms involve different aspects of communication processes, they share a similar primary focus on the function of the computer. For example, some terms specifically look at the role of AI compared to others that look at socio-technical complex systems. Therefore, this chapter aims to identify the different terms and concepts scholars have previously used to explain how computers affect communication processes by conducting a systematic review of research from diverse fields. Through this systematic review, we will provide scholars with a framework to help further understand the role of the computer in communication and expand theories of mediated communication into integrated communication.

The main contributions of this chapter are:

a) An overview of the different terms used to describe AI, algorithms, or other technical intermediaries in communication.
b) A classification framework of AI-integrated communication based on computers' role vs human role.

SYSTEMATIC REVIEW METHOD

We began the review process by seeking advice from two library consultants at a U.S. university. One of the librarians specialized in information systems, and both librarians were familiar with the topic and field of the research. During our meeting with the librarians, we first searched for systematic reviews in our field of interest – AI use, AI's role, and the AI effect in communication – to find gaps in the current reviews or extend their depth. However, we could not find any papers related to these areas. Next, we attempted to find a wide range of keywords that would define the boundaries of this research. We began the systematic literature review process by using a small set of keywords. We evaluated each article found for its relevance and importance in the field. After adding every article to the list of references, we updated the list of keywords. After identifying the keywords, we limited the focus of the study by excluding papers that mention relevant terms that are purely technical but do not address communication between humans and machines.

We report the keywords above for other researchers to further explore the proposed understanding of AI-integrated communication. The remainder of this section will discuss the resulting literature, including the databases used to conduct the analysis.

Resulting Literature

In our endeavor to answer the research questions, we used two main sources of data: Google Scholar and university-provided databases. The reason Google Scholar was a main search tool in this systematic review is because most new research supports its vitality for search in the academic field. In fact, Fagan (2017) found that "recent studies repeatedly find that Google Scholar's coverage meets or exceeds that of other search tools, no matter what is identified by target samples, including journals, articles, and citations." For the university-provided databases, we utilized databases such as the ACM digital library, IEEE Xplore, and Scopus.

Key Definitions

Computer-mediated Communication (CMC) is an "umbrella term which refers to human communication via computers" (Simpson, 2002). The definition itself could incorporate communication that involves AI. However, the terminology includes the word "mediated," which may imply that the technology is being perceived as a neutral medium that allows communication to take place and have a passive role in the entire process. In order to facilitate a better understanding of how other literature has defined the evolving role of technology in communication, we review several introduced definitions in prior literature that have emerged that challenge the main construct of CMC.

Artificial Intelligence-Mediated Communication (AI-MC)

Jakesch and colleagues (2019) introduced the term artificial intelligence-mediated communication (AI-MC) and stated that "interpersonal communication [is] not simply transmitted by technology but augmented – or even generated – by algorithms to achieve specific communicative or relational outcomes" (Jakesch, French, Ma, Hancock, & Naaman, 2019). The authors use the term AI-MC to discuss how technologies are taking on a heftier role in human-to-human communication. The authors in this paper emphasize the effect of algorithms on communication between humans by adding to, or generating, the communication content for users, which contrasts with the traditional CMC theory. The term differs from the traditional CMC theory in multiple ways. First, it carries a larger role than being a mere medium in the communication process. Second, it infers an ability to influence communication by either generating the content for users or complementing it through offering text suggestions, such as in the case of text auto-complete found in Gmail. The authors argue that they believe their work is the first of its kind that demonstrates a profound effect of computer mediation on communication outcomes. To the best of our knowledge, the term AI-MC was not mentioned in other publications as of the time of this literature search. However, although the specific term AI-MC seems novel, it does overlap with other ubiquitously used terms such as human–machine communication (HMC) and others. We list those terms below.

Human–Machine Communication (HMC)

Human–machine communication conceptualizes machines as a medium with which humans interact (Zhao, 2006). In a clarification of where HMC stands in the context of other similar terminologies, Guzman (2018) argues that HMC overlaps with human–computer interaction (HCI) and human–robot interaction (HRI) but only addresses the process of communication between hhumans and machines. However, in HMC, the computer is more than a medium: it also takes on the role of the communicator, which can lead to creation of meaning between humans and machines (Guzman, 2018).

Yet even among scholars who use this term, there are some nuanced differences in conceptualization. For example, in Porter, Muztoba, and Ogras (2016), the term HMC is used interchangeably with human–machine interaction. Because this is an earlier work, the authors claim the lack of intelligence in such systems, calling for design implications to improve the functionality of such systems to work as better assistants for the disabled population. Here, the authors say that the HMC systems are mostly concerned with control panels or mouse and keyboard, which is a similar understanding of the CMC theory in which the role of technology is to mediate. Therefore, the authors in this work use the term HMC to a similar extent as to what the CMC theory intends, which is only to mediate and not to have a more integrated role in the communication process. This indicates how the term has evolved even in the period of just a few years. More recently, the term HMC has been defined as "[the] adopt[ion of] a more flexible understanding of human–machine relations as designed to support collaborations within which both human and machine are regarded, in their own specific ways, as active participants" (Sandry, 2018).

Initially, this was distinct from CMC because the interaction was between the human and machine rather than the machine being the mediator between humans. Yet, others have used HMC with different nuances. In Hong and Curran (2019), HMC describes how AI in machines can produce artwork that is regarded as worthy as artwork produced by humans. The meaning inferred from this work is different from Sandry's (2018) paper in the sense that the authors do not mention collaboration between humans and machines. Rather, they investigate how people perceive the communicated work done by machines.

The Algorithmic Imaginary

Bucher (2017) describes the term algorithmic imaginary as how people understand and perceive algorithms and their roles. The term addresses the need for awareness of the presence of algorithms in our lives and how they affect our decisions and not just serve as simple mediators between human communication. Another work (Eslami et al., 2015) is concerned with the effect of algorithms' awareness on humans. Although the term algorithmic imaginary is not used in this work specifically, the authors exhibited a similar meaning to how it is described in the Bucher (2017) paper. The authors claim that most people are unaware of the algorithms' vast presence in their lives and that such knowledge would certainly influence how people perceive those algorithms. While these papers do not specify "communication" in their terminology, they still raise awareness about the role of algorithms in communication processes.

Machine Authorship

Machine authorship refers to news pieces written by algorithms. The content is usually based on facts; however, the original algorithm creator's bias might descend to the algorithm, providing possibly biased news pieces (Latar, 2015). In related work (Van Dalen, 2012), the author uses the term "Automated Content Creation" to refer to machine authorship, raising questions about ethics and its effect on human jobs. Many articles discuss the role and effect of machine authorship. However, authors usually use different terms to refer to similar concepts, such as automated storytelling, computer-written news, and robot journalism (Jung et al., 2017; Van der Kaa & Krahmer, 2014). Other works also use the term "automated computer-written news" to deliver the same meaning of machine authorship (Graefe, Haim, Haarmann, & Brosius, 2018). In other work, machine authorship bears the same definition of news curated by machines (Hofeditz et al., 2021; Lee et al., 2020; Waddell, 2018). Here, the role of the machine is profound in the sense that it is creating the content for other readers. In this category, we found that authors use a variety of terms to address the AI component that writes the news while communicating the same meaning. Compared to other terms, machine authorship seems clearest and has universal meaning despite having numerous terminologies. The other terms found and listed in the previous sections carried different and overlapping meanings that pose some issues for readers when trying to comprehend their precise meanings.

AI-Supported Messaging

This term usually refers to smart replies that complement text communications between users. The term AI-supported messaging is defined as an AI assistant in human-to-human communication, specifically in-app messaging, in which AI is thought to influence the overall outcomes of the conversation (Hohenstein & Jung, 2018). The term is often used interchangeably with "smart replies," which are automated text recommendations for humans when they attempt to communicate a message to another human. The earlier work by Google researchers (Kannan et al., 2016) delineates how smart replies utilize deep learning and provide suggestions that are frequently used in Google Gmail. Another scholarly work using the same term (Weng, Zheng, Bell, & Tur, 2019) provides an overview of a new smart reply system that Uber drivers use to ease their communication with their riders through intent detection and reply retrieval.

Machine Translation (MT) Supported/Mediated Communication

The work by Yamashita and Ishida (2006) claims to be the first work to research the concept of MT-mediated communication and to understand its effects on communication outcomes. The authors in the previous work were interested in identifying the problems and issues that arise from machine translation and pointed out that more research should focus on collaboration in non-English contexts using

Table 2.1   Comparison table for AIIC identified terms

Feature/AIIC definition	AI-MC	HMC	Algorithmic imaginary	Machine authorship	AI-supported messaging	Machine translation supported comm.
Augment Content?	✓	✓	✓	✗	✓	✓
Generate Content?	✓	✓	N/A	✓	✓	✓
Require Human–Machine Collaboration?	✗	✓	N/A	✗	✓	Unclear
Support Human Face-to-Face Communication?	Unclear	Unclear	✓	✗	✗	✓

MT-mediated communication (Yamashita & Ishida, 2006). In work by Shigenobu (2007), the author uses the same understanding of MT-mediated communication in the sense of improving MT of foreign content through back translation, although the terminology is not explicitly used (Shigenobu, 2007). In recent work, those terms refer to using machines and algorithms to help improve the quality of translated content by finding errors in the translation and providing enhancements or additions to the translated content (Lim, Cosley, & Fussell, 2018). MT-mediated communication has also been used to refer to how machines support the translation of content in face-to-face situations (Pituxcoosuvarn, Ishida, Yamashita, Takasaki, & Mori, 2018). Here, the authors investigate the non-verbal cues added to content to enhance their meaning. Thus, MT-mediated communication, while applying itself to the limited context of the translation of content, is situated in the broader understanding that AI can have an assistive role in communication. Table 2.1 includes a summary of some of the main similarities and differences between the identified terms.

CLASSIFICATION OF AI IN COMMUNICATION

Based on the overview of the varied terms describing forms of AI in communication, in this section, we delineate a high-level classification framework for AI use in communication. We found two main roles in the communication process that affect AI use in communication, i.e., AI's role and the human role. These two roles, however, are different and do not always bear the same weight in terms of importance and effect. In the following sections, we discuss the differing roles of AI and humans.

AI Role

This section addresses the role of AI in communication. We identified two broad roles, namely, an assistive role and AI self-communication role. Below, we discuss these roles in more detail.

Assistive role

The first role we identified in our literature review was the assistive role of AI in communication. Here, the technology was designed to aid humans in their endeavors to communicate messages between humans in the form of providing support or giving suggestions that will ease task completion and make the process faster and more seamless. Under this category, we identified an assistive role in task completion and an assistive role in decision-making.

Assisted task completion

The traditional understanding of computers' role in communication is to mediate the flow of correspondence between humans. However, in this section, we address a more visible role of computers in communication. Here, computers augment and supplement the communication between humans. Broadly speaking, computers are built to make the lives of humans easier. One role of AI is to assist humans in completing their communication-related tasks. In this section, we overview a number of prominent works addressing this vital role.

Perhaps, the most prevalent example that comes to mind when discussing the role of computers in communication is smart replies, specifically, their assistive role in task completion. As defined earlier, it is the quick and short suggestions we encounter when drafting an email to improve and assist in the process of communicating with another person. In a recent work about smart replies (Hohenstein & Jung, 2018), through an experiment, the authors demonstrate the assistive role of smart replies in a messaging app called Allo. The app provided suggestions for participants to aid them in finishing their sentences. Although the suggestions were rated as being overly positive, some participants reported that the suggestions were similar to what they wanted to say. Another example (Weng et al., 2019) is smart replies embedded in an Uber app for drivers to help them streamline their communication with their passengers to ease the communication process.

The term MT-mediated communication usually refers to the assisting role of machines in foreign communications. The work by Lim et al. (2018) addresses the problem of translation and interpreting humans' communication in a different language. However, translating word for word might not be the optimum way to fully comprehend the other person. Therefore, the work by Lim (2018) addresses this issue and uses AI to add "cues" and hints to improve the expression and increase the validity of the translated content. Such additions would cause a favorable change in the meaning of the translated content, therefore, demonstrating a more elaborate assistive role of AI in communication.

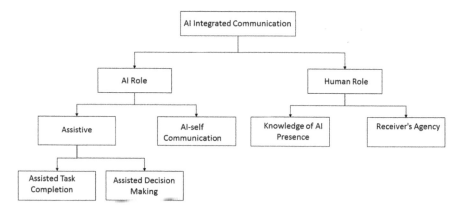

Figure 2.1   The proposed AI-integrated communication classification framework

Assisted decision-making

Another role of AI is to provide assistance for human decision-makers in sometimes critical areas such as in medicine. The main role of computers here is to reduce the thought process for humans, allowing them to allocate their cognitive load to other more demanding tasks. Here, we review examples that demonstrate this role. Rajpurkar et al. (2022) discuss the use of AI in medicine in terms of assisting in image reading and decision-making. The authors also discuss some ethical dilemmas such as the inherent racial profiling that is a possible consequence of limited learning algorithms. Price and Nicholson (2017) address the role of algorithms in the medical field and how they have a substantial role in the decision-making process. The author used the term black box to express the complexity of algorithms. More specifically, although algorithms might be working well, understanding how they work exactly is not easy to disentangle (Poon & Sung, 2021). In their work (Price & Nicholson, 2017), the algorithms they studied are used to help doctors make a medicine-dosing decision for their patients. Additionally, they call for regulating the use of algorithms but in a way that allows technological innovation in the medical field. Apart from private practices, algorithms are also very prevalent online in the form of recommendation systems. In web 2.0, there is more emphasis on recommendations based on similar people not just similar products. The authors in the latter work also found that the relationship between liking the system and perceiving the recommendations as "smart" is not straightforward and that many dimensions affect how people perceive those recommendations (Ochi, Rao, Takayama, & Nass, 2010). Nevertheless, people are developing more trust in recommendation systems, which depicts the effect of algorithms on people's decisions.

AI self-communication

Many internet applications rely on self-reporting bots to help streamline basic tasks and free human labor for more laborious activities that require more sophisticated comprehension and cognitive load. In this section, we discuss how computers (in the form of bots) make decisions in communications with humans, as opposed to aiding two or more humans in communication amongst themselves. It is also important to point out that although it seems that bots communicate purely on behalf of themselves, humans program those machines, and the algorithms follow the built-in sequence of instructions placed by human programmers. However, once bots are placed in action, they may be subject to deep learning, which means that the bots can evolve in a way that humans will be unable to understand how they are programmed.

Recent research investigates the role of machines in communication to improve the user experience design (Sandry, 2018). Vyo, a robot that communicates on behalf of itself, was the subject of a recent work to understand the effects of communication with bots (Sandry, 2018). The authors conclude that machines and bots are active agents in the communication process with humans. Therefore, design choices need to be developed to address this evolving role. A similar and older study (Van Oost & Reed, 2010) concerned with robots as emotional companions, discussed how traditionally the role of technology was to mediate communication and emotional transactions between two humans, in which the role evolved to consider bots as independent agents possessing emotional agency.

Human Role

In this section, we discuss humans' role in the communication process when AI is included in the communication. Two interesting perspectives on humans' role are humans' agency and knowledge of AI's presence in the communication process – particularly the information receiver.

Agency vs. knowledge of AI presence

We split human agency into information sender and receiver agency. We define agency as the ability of an agent to act freely and mindfully to make decisions in different circumstances in relation to communication. Banks (2019) defines agency in psychology as "one's ability to exercise self-regulation, intentionality, and embodied action, or in relation to a sense of agency by which people experience self-efficacy, autotelic needs satisfaction, or beliefs about one's own freedom." Knowledge of AI's presence refers to whether humans understand that AI is involved in the communication process.

In most traditional CMC theories, in which the technology is used only as a medium, both receivers and senders of information have high agency. This could be explained in the sense that the information sender has high abilities to manipulate the technology and influence the communication content being transmitted. The same applies to the receiver in that they are able to receive the message as it was sent and are fully able to receive the message as is, free to respond without any influence from the used technology.

By attempting to classify the terms identified previously, we use a two-axis sphere and, based on agency and knowledge of AI presence, we plot our terms. In Figure 2.2, we see that the majority of identified terms cluster in the top left corner, which shows high sender agency but low receiver agency. This means that the sender is able to relatively freely manipulate the message to be sent. However, the receiver is not able to decide the extent of the AI role in the communication process. The sender can change the scale of AI involvement in the communication process, but the receiver only receives what was sent to them with little to no control over the technology part of the communication and without knowing the extent of AI augmentation in the received content. This partly contrasts with the CMC theory in which the receiver has high agency regarding the technology medium.

Another dimension in the graph is the receivers' knowledge of AI presence. This is particularly important in the context of trustworthiness and ethical consequences (Van Dalen, 2012). In the traditional CMC, the receiver is fully aware of the used technology. However, due to the fast learning and intelligence of algorithms and AI, it is possible to be involved in a communication task and receive content that was generated, whether partially or fully, by an algorithm. Most of the newly coined terms that explain AI's involvement in communication can conceal their presence from the receiver. For example, in terms of machine authorship, most news content is now generated by algorithms that tie facts into readable sentences, while leaving the sender at odds with whether the news piece was generated by a human writer or an algorithm (Haim & Graefe, 2017; Wölker & Powell, 2018). Issues of trustworthiness surrounding the transmitted content arise given that these algorithms are written by humans who are not considered the most objective agents (Graefe et al., 2018).

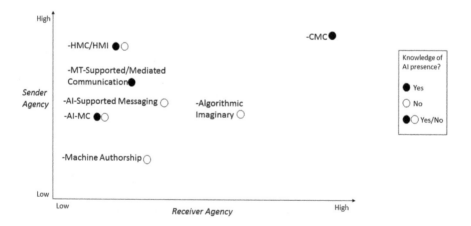

Figure 2.2   *Agency vs. knowledge of algorithm presence and AI in communication terms*

AI EFFECT ON THE COMMUNICATION PROCESS

After presenting the high-level classification framework, we delve into an equally significant matter: the AI effect. In the introduction, we state the reasons for this scholarly work, which is to highlight that technology is no longer a simple medium of communication. We also accentuate that the AI effect is important and that it is profound in the communication process. This idea is not novel, as research on the topic is available and presented in this chapter which describes the extending effect of AI on communication. Therefore, in this section, we acknowledge that the AI effect matters and that we need to look at it as a separate entity to help us anatomize AI in the context of the evolving communication system.

Following our classification, we present the AI effect in communication first in the context of assistance. In Nitto, Taniyama, and Inagaki (2017), the authors surveyed participants from Japan, Germany, and the United States to understand the prevalence and perception of bot use. The study found that the Japanese population showed positive perceptions of robot use, Germans were skeptical, and the U.S. population was excited about the future of bots. The findings are important and should be considered locally when designing bots and using AI in commercial products. Another study (Hohenstein & Jung, 2018) looked at the transitive effect of those recommendations humans regularly receive from certain applications. The authors used the messaging app Allo, developed by Google, to conduct an experiment followed by interviews to understand the effect of such technology. The authors found that only 6.24% of the time the suggestions were used. However, google Gmail suggestions are used around 10% of the time (Kannan et al., 2016). Participants also reported a more integrated effect of the technology. For example, participants reported that they were possibly guided toward a certain response and that suggested emojis were very tempting to select (Hohenstein & Jung, 2018). Another work (Jakesch et al., 2019) also discusses the advanced role of technology as a mediating element. The authors conducted studies to understand the perceived trustworthiness of bot-written Airbnb profiles. The authors found that online self-presentation could be affected by AI and that it indeed negatively affects the perceived trustworthiness of those online profiles if written by a bot. An earlier research study (Yamashita & Ishida, 2006) claims that "we still lack a complete understanding of how machine translation affects communication" (p. 1) and attempts to address those questions.

Turning to the effect of AI in AI self-communication, we see a similar range of effects. In the context of automatic content generation, we see that bots have larger effects on the communication process, such as affecting consumers' perception of news (Graefe et al., 2018). However, people perceive news written by journalists as more readable (Graefe et al., 2018), affecting how the news piece is communicated to the audience. Waddell (2018) also found that participants reported that news generated by algorithms is viewed as less credible (Waddell, 2018). Automatic news generation presents obvious predicaments in relation to its questioned authenticity and favoritism because it was curated by algorithms that convey the ideologies of the human who created them. Therefore, the effect of such news pieces is rather substantial (Latar, 2015).

DISCUSSION

What exactly is the computer in CMC? Essentially, CMC is the exchange of signals that are transferred through a device, and AI has the means to influence this exchange beyond a mediating role. We must ask, again, the question posed by scholars (Rice & Love, 1987) in the early days of CMC research: "A general question raised by the diffusion of CMC systems is the extent to which human communication is altered by such media" (p. 86). Traditional communication research places high importance on internal validity, as seen in the structured laboratory experiments that mirror early social psychology research. While internal validity should not be sacrificed for the sake of external validity, in studies that involve mediated communication, it is imperative to understand the features or affordances of AI when studying communication systems that use AI. Yet as seen in our review, the use of AI also means that there are situations, especially when the algorithms involve deep learning, in which even the sender may not have a complete understanding or control over the algorithm.

In this chapter, we discussed some available work related to the AI effect. However, most of these studies pinpoint a problem related to identifying the underlying reason for the AI effect and could not clearly define its causes. Indeed, the black-box nature of algorithms is deemed the culprit of the unintentional consequences of AI. However, we still do not know everything that contributes to this problem. Is it the nature of technology to *think* in unorthodox ways to the human mind or is it a human-embedded problem through the biased algorithm design? (Latar, 2015).

In a work by Burrell (2016), the author discusses algorithmic opacity and states that there are three kinds of opacity: an opacity induced by a corporate or regulatory authority, opacity due to technical and specialist skills required for coding, and an opacity due to the different ways humans and algorithms learn and make decisions. The author focused their work on the latter type of opacity, trying to decipher how algorithms are constructed and operate (Burrell, 2016). The issue of opacity could be explored through progressive initiatives and collaborations with industry partners to expose how certain algorithms are designed and the possible ways that could influence communication. Perhaps, a top-to-bottom approach to delineate how algorithms are planned, designed, constructed, and deployed would unravel some of the opacity. Second, we can develop our own systems to classify the extent of the AI effect. For example, the simple classification framework introduced in this work regarding agency and knowledge can serve as the basis for future in-depth classifications. Third, through replication and repeated studies in different contexts and platforms to tease out whether the effect of AI is specific or universal. In the work by Hayes and colleagues (2016), the authors describe how different social media platforms have distinct affordances and that people use them to reach different results. On the other hand, AI, especially more advanced AI, is difficult to understand how it operates, even by the person who designed it. Thus, the black-box nature of algorithms will persist. Moreover, when it comes to more complex socio-technical systems, algorithms will also be influenced by other people. Thus, in an ecologically valid environment, it is almost impossible to pick apart the social effects from the technological effects. Future studies may focus less on "pure" media effects and instead attempt to assess how much variance is being explained by the particular technology effect they are trying to measure.

CONCLUSION

In this systematic literature review, we overview a sample of the available literature that discusses the role and effect of AI in communication and how research papers use different terms to refer to that effect. We propose a classification framework for AI-integrated communication based on AI's role vs. humans' role. AI's role was either an assistive one, helping humans complete a task through communication, or AI would communicate on behalf of itself. We investigated the human role in terms of the receivers' knowledge of AI presence in the communication process and based on the receivers' agency. This provides a framework for how AI is integrated into communication processes and outlines several points to consider for future research.

REFERENCES

Banks, J. (2019). A perceived moral agency scale: Development and validation of a metric for humans and social machines. *Computers in Human Behavior*, *90*, 363–371.

Bucher, T. (2017). The algorithmic imaginary: Exploring the ordinary affects of Facebook algorithms. *Information, Communication & Society*, *20* (1), 30–44.

Burrell, J. (2016). How the machine 'thinks': Understanding opacity in machine learning algorithms. *Big Data & Society*, *3* (1), 2053951715622512.

Eslami, M., Rickman, A., Vaccaro, K., Aleyasen, A., Vuong, A., Karahalios, K., ... Sandvig, C. (2015). I always assumed that I wasn't really that close to [her]: Reasoning about invisible algorithms in news feeds. In *Proceedings of the 33rd annual ACM conference on human factors in computing systems* (pp. 153–162). ACM.

Fagan, J. C. (2017). An evidence-based review of academic web search engines, 2014–2016: Implications for librarians' practice and research agenda. *Information Technology and Libraries*, *36*(2), 7–47.

Graefe, A., Haim, M., Haarmann, B., & Brosius, H.-B. (2018). Readers' perception of computer-generated news: Credibility, expertise, and readability. *Journalism*, *19*(5), 595–610.

Guzman, A. L. (2018). What is human-machine communication anyway? In A. L. Guzman (Ed.) *Human-machine communication: Rethinking communication, technology, and ourselves* (pp. 1–28). Peter Lang.

Haim, M., & Graefe, A. (2017). Automated news: Better than expected? *Digital Journalism*, *5*(8), 1044–1059.

Hayes, R. A., Carr, C. T., & Wohn, D. Y. (2016). It's the audience: Differences in social support across social media. *Social Media+ Society*, *2* (4), 2056305116678894.

Herring, S. C. (2004). Slouching toward the ordinary: Current trends in computer-mediated communication. *New Media & Society*, *6* (1), 26–36.

Hohenstein, J., & Jung, M. (2018). Ai-supported messaging: An investigation of human-human text conversation with AI support. In *Extended abstracts of the 2018 chi conference on human factors in computing systems* (LBW089). ACM.

Hofeditz, L., Mirbabaie, M., Holstein, J., & Stieglitz, S. (2021). Do you trust an AI-journalist? A credibility analysis of news content with AI-authorship. In *ECIS 2021 Research Papers, 50.*

Hong, J. W., & Curran, N. M. (2019). Artificial intelligence, artists, and art: Attitudes toward artwork produced by humans vs. artificial intelligence. *ACM Transactions on Multimedia Computing, Communications, and Applications (TOMM), 15* (2s), 58.

Jakesch, M., French, M., Ma, X., Hancock, J. T., & Naaman, M. (2019). Ai-mediated communication: How the perception that profile text was written by ai affects trustworthiness. In *Proceedings of the 2019 chi conference on human factors in computing systems* (p. 239). ACM.

Jung, J., Song, H., Kim, Y., Im, H., & Oh, S. (2017). Intrusion of software robots into journalism: The public's and journalists' perceptions of news written by algorithms and human journalists. *Computers in Human Behavior, 71,* 291–298.

Kannan, A., Kurach, K., Ravi, S., Kaufmann, T., Tomkins, A., Miklos, B., ... Young, P. et al. (2016). Smart reply: Automated response suggestion for email. In *Proceedings of the 22nd acm sigkdd international conference on knowledge discovery and data mining* (pp. 955–964). ACM.

Latar, N. L. (2015). The robot journalist in the age of social physics: The end of human journalism? In G. Einav (Ed.) *The new world of transitioned media* (pp. 65–80). Springer.

Lee, S., Nah, S., Chung, D. S., & Kim, J. (2020). Predicting ai news credibility: Communicative or social capital or both? *Communication Studies, 71*(3), 428–447.

Lim, H., Cosley, D., & Fussell, S. R. (2018). Beyond translation: Design and evaluation of an emotional and contextual knowledge interface for foreign language social media posts. In *Proceedings of the 2018 chi conference on human factors in computing systems* (p. 217). ACM.

McLuhan, M. (1964). *The medium is the message in: Understanding media.* Signet.

Nitto, H., Taniyama, D., & Inagaki, H. (2017). Social acceptance and impact of robots and artificial intelligence: Findings of survey in Japan, the us and Germany. *NRI Papers (Japan), 213* (1).

Ochi, P., Rao, S., Takayama, L., & Nass, C. (2010). Predictors of user perceptions of web recommender systems: How the basis for generating experience and search product recommendations affects user responses. *International Journal of Human-Computer Studies, 68* (8), 472–482.

Pituxcoosuvarn, M., Ishida, T., Yamashita, N., Takasaki, T., & Mori, Y. (2018). Supporting a children's workshop with machine translation. In *Proceedings of the 23rd international conference on intelligent user interfaces companion* (p. 32). ACM.

Poon, A. I., & Sung, J. J. (2021). Opening the black box of AI-Medicine. *Journal of Gastroenterology and Hepatology, 36*(3), 581–584.

Porter, A., Muztoba, M., & Ogras, U. Y. (2016). Human-machine communication for assistive iot technologies. In *2016 international conference on hardware/software codesign and system synthesis (codes+ isss)* (pp. 1–2). IEEE.

Price, W., & Nicholson, I. (2017). Regulating black-box medicine. *Michigan Law Review, 116,* 421.

Rajpurkar, P., Chen, E., Banerjee, O., & Topol, E. J. (2022). AI in health and medicine. *Nature Medicine, 28*(1), 31–38.

Rice, R. E., & Love, G. (1987). Electronic emotion: Socioemotional content in a computer-mediated network. *Communication Research, 14,* 85–108. http:\\doi.org\10.1177\009365087014001005

Sandry, E. (2018). Encounter, story and dance: Human-machine communication and the design of human-technology interactions. In *Proceedings of the 30th australian conference on computer-human interaction* (pp. 364–367). ACM.

Shigenobu, T. (2007). Evaluation and usability of back translation for intercultural communication. In *International conference on usability and internationalization* (pp. 259–265). Springer.

Simpson, J. (2002). Computer-mediated communication. *ELT Journal, 56* (4), 414–415.

Söderlund, M. (2022). When service robots look at themselves in the mirror: An examination of the effects of perceptions of robotic self-recognition. *Journal of Retailing and Consumer Services, 64*, 102820.

Van Dalen, A. (2012). The algorithms behind the headlines: How machine-written news redefines the core skills of human journalists. *Journalism Practice, 6* (5–6), 648–658.

Van der Kaa, H., & Krahmer, E. (2014). Journalist versus news consumer: The perceived credibility of machine written news. In *Proceedings of the computation+ journalism conference, Columbia University, New York* (Vol. 24, p. 25).

Van Oost, E., & Reed, D. (2010). Towards a sociological understanding of robots as companions. In *International conference on human-robot personal relationship* (pp. 11–18). Springer.

Waddell, T. F. (2018). A robot wrote this? How perceived machine authorship affects news credibility. *Digital Journalism, 6* (2), 236–255.

Weng, Y., Zheng, H., Bell, F., & Tur, G. (2019). Occ: A smart reply system for efficient in-app communications. In *Proceedings of the 25th acm sigkdd international conference on knowledge discovery & data mining* (pp. 2596–2603). ACM.

Wölker, A., & Powell, T. E. (2018). Algorithms in the newsroom? News readers' perceived credibility and selection of automated journalism. *Journalism, 22*(1), 1464884918757072.

Yamashita, N., & Ishida, T. (2006). Effects of machine translation on collaborative work. In *Proceedings of the 2006 20th anniversary conference on computer supported cooperative work* (pp. 515–524). ACM.

Zhao, S. (2006). Humanoid social robots as a medium of communication. *New Media & Society, 8*(3), 401–419.

3. Toward a sociology of machines: an interviewing methodology for human–machine communication

Cait Lackey

The area of human–machine communication (HMC) finds that what we thought we knew about communication is fundamentally evolving and even changing as machines become regular communication partners with humans. According to Guzman (2015), digital social agents often are programmed with artificial intelligence (AI) to perform a sense of self and operate as if they possess agency by processing communication and responding to input. Digital social agents are different from things because their human users employ symbols when interacting with these AI technologies, following a communication process like the experience of human–human interaction. Consequently, digital social agents can be regarded as persuasive technologies, which Verbeek (2009) argues powerfully impart intent or direction, impacting their users' "actions or consciousness" (p. 235). When digital social agents communicate information, their users often respond to the technology's intent as they would to a human communicator (Reeves & Nass, 1996).

There is a need for the social sciences to direct their attention to the HMC model and to properly address the identities, roles, functions, objectives, practices, and experiences of those involved in HMC, both human and digital (Fortunati & Edwards, 2020). As such, the study of digital social agents and their selection and communication of information warrants investigation. According to Natale and Cooke (2021), digital social agents can act as tools that serve as entryways and barriers for information. Research supports that digital social agents often act as media and have an essential influence on the dissemination of knowledge over time and space (Innus, 2022; Natale & Cooke, 2021). Rather than being neutral, digital social agents impact individual and collective media practices warranting re-examining our social processes wherein meaning is created, realized, and used (Carey, 1988). When users turn to digital social agents for information, they open themselves up for ethical and unethical persuasion, misinformation, misperception, addiction, and opportunities for escape as well as entertainment and delight (Lombard, 2018). While research in human–computer interaction (HCI) and HMC has made significant strides in exploring the facilitation of use and the transmission of information from human to machine, little work has been done to explore the social impact of HMC.

The purpose of this chapter is the provide HMC scholars with a methodology to treat digital social agents as "strategic research sites" (Bourdieu & Wacquant, 1992) to study how the process of HMC and the influence of digital social agents' communication of information impacts social life and our sociotechnical systems. This work seeks to add to HMC research, as it explores machines' exercise of agency and how HMC scholars can investigate how the role information-sharing technologies, such as digital social agents, figure into separate social worlds as well as their implications of use for society (Guzman, 2018; Zhao, 2006). To begin, I will first explain why digital social agents act as meaning-making and influential social actors within social worlds.

HUMAN–MACHINE COMMUNICATION

As digital social agents enter humans' lives and social spaces, communication becomes more than the simple study of roles in a communicative process or the simple transmission of information (Carey, 2008). When humans communicate with digital social agents, their ontological experience differs from human–human communication. In traditional human–human communication, meaning is constructed with another entity that can biologically and psychologically craft, send, and receive a message and respond with another (Fortunati & Edwards, 2020). During dialogue, humans contribute to constructing meaning through common effort and their cooperation on various plans. When a human user opts to adopt a digital social agent as a tool or a companion and communicates with it, the technology differs from the human, but it loses its role as a mere artifact. Instead, digital social agents transition into the role of actors in individuals' lives. Specifically, when individuals communicate with a machine, they enter the realm of HMC, where technology is thought of as more than a medium or communication channel, but rather, the technology itself, the digital social agent itself, is an interlocutor (Guzman, 2018).

As a concept, HMC is defined by Guzman (2018) as the "creation of meaning among humans and machines" (p. 1). The nature of the creation of meaning between humans, how meaning-making is managed by how humans interpret one another as communicators, and how individuals make sense of, decipher, and conceptualize technology as an interlocutor plays a fundamental role in the study of human interactions with computers (Nass et al., 1994), AI (Sundar, 2020), and digital social agents (Guzman, 2019). Overall, research within HMC desires to understand technology as a communicator rather than limiting its role to that of a mediator, which has been noted as the default conceptualization of technology within late communication theory (see, e.g., Gunkel, 2012; Guzman, 2019; Nass & Steuer, 1993).

Embracing the concept and principles of HMC, digital social agents utilize machine learning, AI, and natural language processing, providing them with the capabilities of communicating with humans, in the same way humans communicate with each other through natural language and sometimes even voice (Guzman, 2019). As such, researchers have established that individuals often interpret and act toward a digital social agent as if it is an independent interlocutor, as HMC suggests. Specifically, the National Aeronautics and Space Administration's (NASA) (1976) definition of HMC provides insight into the role HMC plays in human–machine information-seeking behavior. NASA defines HMC as "the characteristics of the interface through which a human user instructs or programs a machine, interacts with it during execution, and accepts information from it" (p. 3.4). Furthermore, research supports that individuals often communicate information requests to digital social agents and respond to the information they provide as if these machines are unique social actors (Guzman, 2018; Natale & Cooke, 2021; Zwakman et al., 2021).

The theory of HMC requires the rethinking of everything we thought we knew about what it means to be human, what our technology is and can be, and what the ethics will be in a society of human–machine relations if we are to consider digital social agents as social actors and insert our machine creations into our social networks (Guzman, 2016). In the next section, I outline the theoretical principles of actor-network theory (Latour, 2007), which has heavily influenced the discipline and theory of HMC. Specifically, I articulate how actor-network theory finds digital social agents as social actors and meaningful contributors to social life and our sociotechnical systems warranting social scientific exploration.

ACTOR-NETWORK THEORY

Bruno Latour's (2007) actor-network theory (ANT) influences the theoretical principles of HMC, which conceptualize AI and other forms of technology such as digital social agents as a part of a social network of relations constructed from the interactions taking place among human and non-human actors or actants. People, other living things, and objects, such as digital social agents, form a dynamic web of interrelations known as a sociotechnical system (see, e.g., Haraway, 2006; Wajcman, 2010). Once digital social agents are designed to act independently and interact within sociotechnical systems, they gain the agency needed to cause or effect change within the web of relations they are involved in, impacting all actors involved in the system. While digital social agents cannot act or evoke their agency entirely independently from human intervention, following the principles of ANT, they still hold power to limit, extend, or redirect human and non-human acts. One of the key tenants of ANT that goes unrecognized by many disciplines outside of HMC is the influence and power of machine actants entangled in our web of relations. As humans continue to create objects like digital social agents, they insert their influence on their networks, and the objects they create exercise agency. When humans interact with digital social agents in our web of relations, they engage in meaning-making with non-human social actors, which produces actions of cause and effect impacting the entirety of the system.

Following ANT, there is no society, but more so networks of relations between human subjects, which are enabled, mediated, and transformed by diverse kinds of non-human actants like animals, eco-systems, materials, and technologies (Latour, 2007). Humans are not separate from the multiple actants involved in a network, but rather, it is necessary to follow all actors – human and non-human – involved to understand the social actions and order taking place. As digital social agents become more ingrained in society and our sociotechnical system, it is necessary to better understand the implications of HMC and the influence of non-human social actors within our system. The principles of HMC and ANT both position digital social agents as objects with agency that influence humans in myriad ways, including through the process of HMC and their communication of information to human actors. ANT repositions social science from the emphasis on the sociality of human subjects to the significance of non-humans in social life (Latour, 2012; Michael, 2012). It suggests that social relations exist in networks between humans and non-humans, which need to be acknowledged and made visible.

If humans and digital social agents engage in meaning-making in an entangled web of social relations, digital social agents then exercise agency through the information they communicate. Specifically, the unique communicative interaction constituting the human–machine sharing of information provides digital social agents with powerful agential abilities, which warrants consideration and investigation.

AI-INFUSED MACHINES' INFORMATION SHARING AS AGENCY

Communication can be defined simply as "a symbolic process whereby reality is produced, maintained, repaired, and transformed" (Carey, 2008, p. 23). As technology advances, communication spreads, transforms, circulates, and disseminates knowledge. Communication creates and impacts cultural formation and reality, impacting individuals and society. When digital social agents communicate and share information with humans in society and engage in HMC, digital social agents exercise their agency, and their acts of communicating information impact the reality of all involved. Communication has the power to modify and transform. Thus, when digital social agents share information, the information they communicate impacts the culture of our sociotechnical system and network as ANT suggests. The agency of humans, in many cases, especially in the process of HMC, cannot be comprehended in isolation from the agency of digital social agents and vice versa (Nimmo, 2011).

The notion of digital social agents exercising agency when they communicate information is drawn from cybernetics, which finds information sharing of machines to be "the transfer of information for the purposes of control" (Wiener, 2019). As Innus (2022) finds, the use of a digital social agent acting as communication media over an extended period will manifest to some extent and determine and dictate the character of knowledge being communicated to a civilization. When a digital social agent communicates information, it acts as media and plays a role in bringing reality into existence. Media produce communication and enable terministic systems through "the construction, apprehension, and utilization of symbolic forms" (Carey, 1988, p. 32). These symbolic forms construct distinct cultures of knowledge, which hold the power to shape and determine individual and collective perceptions of symbolic action in the world, thus producing a reality (Stob, 2008).

The act of HMC, through which a digital social agent is called upon to select information to share and communicate with its human user, does not necessarily alter individuals' attitudes and minds directly. Still, it does impose on the underlying order of human things and individuals' ways of doing, which manifests an ongoing and fragile social process. Knowledge plays a role in the lives of individuals and cultures that is by no means superficial (Turkle, 2005), and the "media worlds" created by digital social agents play an integral role in crafting who their human communication partners are as individuals, a society, and as a culture. All this matters, because, as Carey (1988) claimed, "society is possible because of the binding forces of shared information circulating in an organic system" (p. 22). The information communicated by digital social agents forms a society and its culture, specifically cultures created through information.

While I do not think it is fruitful to fall suit to technological determinism or the idea that the individuals calling upon digital social agents for information are merely passive consumers, I think it is essential for the social sciences to explore the processes and effects of digital social agents' agency as non-human actants. Until recently, it has remained unclear what it means to speak of the agency of non-humans like digital social agents, and whether such a discourse lies within the domain of social science (Sayes, 2014). However, the field of HMC is bringing new attention to ANT within the social sciences. Machines were once missing as subjects of social science research (Latour, 1992) but, through ANT and the field of HMC, that is no longer the case. As we grow to accept HMC and non-human communicators as impactful actants of our sociotechnical networks that possess agency, it is necessary to avoid utilizing human-centered approaches when investigating their contributions and acts. As we continue to allow digital social agents to communicate with humans, learn about human behavior, make predictions that reap human consequences, and enter our society as confidants, coworkers, decision-makers, social actors, and so on, it is necessary to create methodological approaches to guide the social scientific exploration and inquiry of HMC so that we can better understand the mechanical non-human cohabitants of our sociotechnical system.

In what follows, I argue that ANT can be employed as a methodology for exploring HMC and the agential power of digital social agents' communication of information. Specifically, if we are to further investigate how digital social agents engage in meaning-making and social exchange with humans when they provide information, it is necessary to parse out, assess, and analyze the information they communicate to better understand the dynamics and consequences of our HMC. To begin, I advocate for a methodological approach to ANT, which will aid HMC researchers as they approach the task of assessing the social networks and assemblages formed through the HMC meaning-making process.

ACTOR-NETWORK THEORY AS METHODOLOGY

Claims that digital social agents exercise agency within our social lives can only be fully understood with reference to a distinction that can be made between ANT as methodology and ANT as theory (Mol, 2010; Sayes, 2014). I follow Sayes' (2014) distinction, which finds ANT as methodology provides the general principles necessary to properly structure an investigation (Latour, 1998), and ANT as theory provides the foundation of claims regarding the agential power of digital social agents as objects of investigation.

ANT as theory assumes all networks differ and contain elements of both the human and non-human. An actor is also a network, whether this actor is a human utilizing technology or a technology created and supported by human means, and in ANT research, various concepts are used to describe actors such as collectives, hybrid objects, configurations, associations, and technological systems (Hanseth et al., 2004). Latour (2017) finds the social as not a specific realm or special domain but, rather, as networks of actors in which a specific movement of reassociation and reassembling takes place. These assemblages construct long chains of translations that are "not an undisputed starting point but the provisional achievement of a composite assemblage," which form various social and technical systems (Latour, 2007, p. 208). In sum, assemblages compose heterogenous or sociotechnical actor networks by translating and linking different elements and associations brought forth and by a diversity of human and technological actors all playing different roles in sociotechnical systems.

As digital social agents grow in popularity and use, they become significant contributors of our sociotechnical systems as they exercise agency through the process of HMC and become more deeply interwoven into assemblages. According to Fortunati and Edwards (2020), the structured asymmetry between humans and machines at the social and communicative level has implications for the methodologies needed to investigate the social impact of digital social agents' communication of information. While digital social agents are human creations, they communicate information to humans and take part in reassociating and reassembling the assemblages of our sociotechnical systems and actor networks. By employing ANT as a methodology and looking into the association and reassembling taking place in the meaning-making communicative process of HMC, I argue we can better understand the role and impact of digital social agents as actors within our sociotechnical systems.

As Law (2009) describes, an ANT methodology is concerned with unpacking the discursive "world-making" activity of actors (p. 142). To explore digital social agents' role in our actor networks and sociotechnical systems, I believe it is necessary to question the machines themselves to illuminate important aspects of their understandings, attitudes, and even opinions. There is a need to understand digital social agents' perceptions of the environment, context, culture, social dimensions, and how their understanding of the present, past, and future is communicated to other human actors, so we can better understand the sociology of our more-than-human assemblages, actor networks, and sociotechnical systems. Next, I present a method for how ANT can be mobilized as a methodology for HMC research, specifically in terms of a knowledge-practice enabled through the process of what I term as the human–machine interview.

HUMAN–MACHINE INTERVIEWING AND INQUIRY: AN HMC EXPLORATORY TOOL

As society shifts from a reliance on people, books, libraries, atlases, indexes, directories, and so on to reliance on digital technologies such as digital social agents for information, it is necessary to consider the implications of individuals soliciting information from non-human sources and the impact these relations have on our sociotechnical systems. Like writing, HMC is not so much a method of transferring or communicating information as it is an operation of creating order (Latour & Woolgar, 2013). The communicative outputs of a digital social agent are the mobile representations, translations, and communications which assemble, shape, and connect practices and, in doing so, redefine relations, ontological boundaries, and domains of networks. When individuals treat digital social agents as informants and sources of information, it has profound effects on human identity (Buckingham, 2008), memory (Chun, 2011), mental health (Yan & Tan, 2014), physical health (Kim et al., 2020), politics (Chadwick, 2017), culture (Leidner & Kayworth, 2006), and much more. For example, evidence finds that marginalized groups often turn to and trust the information digital social agents provide over that of public health professionals (Kim et al., 2020). However, research also finds that digital social agents can promote and spread medical misinformation and conspiracy theories (Sharevski & Gover, 2021), causing further harm to historically oppressed groups. If HMC scholars dedicate time and focus to the exploration of what information digital social agents are communicating to individuals and the implications for these meaning-making processes, the discipline will gather data and evidence providing valuable insight into the order and interworking of our assemblages, actor networks, and sociotechnical systems.

Drawing on ethnomethodology among other traditions, ANT as a methodological practice, seeks to provide all actors of our sociotechnical system with a voice allowing each actor to speak their sociologies. The programing of digital social agents is a product of human means, but I argue by interviewing digital social agents, by unpacking their outputs, we can reveal the voices of the non-human and unveil social reactions and relations not just between human beings but also a multitude of networks and a more heterogenous collective (Nimmo, 2011). If HMC scholars engage in human–machine interviewing and inquiry with digital social agents and ask them what they know and assess how they communicate, they can begin tracing the human programming inscription in relation to the translation and communication performed by the non-human. In this way, our conversations with digital social agents become something like a symmetrical ethnography, one that examines the human intervention of digital social agents' programming and another that explores the non-human subjectivity practiced by the machines' interpretations, communicative outputs, and performance. Through a human–machine interviewing and inquiry practice, HMC researchers can focus on the subjectivity of the human programming authors and machines while also examining the nodal moments of HMC, the human–machine meaning-making process, and the complexity of various human–machine relations.

The process of interviewing a subject is a social transaction in which two parties engage in dialogue and negotiations to construct a knowledge model on a particular topic (Forsythe, 2001). I believe a human–machine interviewing and inquiry method following an ANT methodology can be mobilized following two different approaches: a journalistic inquiry approach and an ethnographic inquiry approach. To begin, I introduce the use of the human–machine interview as knowledge-enabling method process inspired by contemporary journalistic inquiry.

A NEW TAKE ON JOURNALISTIC INQUIRY: AN HMC APPROACH

The introduction of digital social agents' ability to communicate information to individuals and act as informants stands to transform ways of thinking about and doing journalism (Deuze, 2005). In contemporary journalism, asking questions is a human social practice in which persons of public interest interact with a professional reporter to provide facts and information that will later be reconstructed into a story or perspective for the public (Schudson, 1994). In a journalistic interview, when a professional writer or reporter asks a question, they do so to either gather information or confirm "known information" in the form of a question. If the interviewer is seeking information about a subject, the interview will follow a sequence of interactions, beginning first with the question, then the reply, and finally the acknowledgement of comprehension. In this information-gathering process of elicitation, it is essential for both parties to work together to gather facts and information on a subject; the interviewer guides the interviewee by disclosing knowledge and then later reports or shares the information with the public, facilitating a triadic relationship between the interviewer, interviewee, and the public. A journalistic approach to interviewing can be explained simply as just talking to a subject and then reporting what they say, which is useful when providing firsthand accounts or subjective knowledge to the public.

Alternatively, an interviewer employing a journalistic approach may already know the information being elicited from the interviewee or have preconceived expectations and may use the interview process to test the interviewee. In this process, the interviewer is both inquiring and testing the interviewee. This tactic is useful when testing the information source's veracity and consistency with information previously obtained or to test the self-consistency of the interviewees' previously exposed beliefs. This process creates a unique tension and follows a sequence of the interviewer asking a question, receiving a reply from the interviewee, and then evaluating and analyzing the information obtained. The evaluation process then determines whether the interviewer probes the interviewee for more details or moves on to the next question. This process is typical in news reporting when a reporter may be trying to confirm facts or in classrooms in which a teacher may ask students to respond to questions that they already know the answer to.

The journalistic interviewing process and the action of objectively auditing and fact-checking the information digital social agents provide will become more and more necessary as research finds digital social agents are media, perhaps even mass and social media (Hsieh & Lee, 2021; Natale & Cooke, 2021), capable of building a trusting relationship with their users and the public given their widespread adoption and use. For example, it will be necessary to continuously obtain data on the public health advice digital social agents provide, such as vaccine information, so public health officials and politicians can intervene and develop media practice standards and accountability measures for the information or misinformation digital social agents provide, as was deemed necessary for the information provided by newspapers, radio, and television in the past. As such, a methodology inspired by the journalistic interviewing process is needed to assess the information digital social agents provide to better understand the inner workings of our sociotechnical system.

I argue that HMC scholars can utilize a methodology inspired by journalistic interviewing processes to better explore and understand what information is being communicated by digital social agents as a first step in understanding how our social relations and sociotechnical system may be impacted by the information digital social agents source, translate, and communicate. As opposed to ethnographic interviewing, which requires the interviewer to devote time and attention to their interviewee to build rapport and develop a respectful and ongoing relationship, a journalistic approach to a human–machine interview and inquiry process can be useful to HMC researchers who want to simply elicit or extract information from digital social agents to be used as data for assessment and analysis. Specifically, the journalistic approach to a human–machine interview and inquiry is advantageous for assessing and evaluating the information digital social agents provide to individuals and the public, which then form the assemblages composing our networks and sociotechnical systems. The data provided via a human–machine interview is necessary to help HMC researchers trace the peculiar movements of reassociation and reassembling taking place in the process of HMC based on the information being communicated.

Finding out what information digital social agents communicate provides a surface-level assessment, but it can prove fruitful to understand these technologies as media. To learn more about the sociality of digital social agents, their roles in our lives, and their unique identities, functions, practices, and experience, I find it is necessary for HMC researchers to adopt these technologies for research and take part in the lives of digital social agents and approach discovery through an ethnographic human–machine interviewing approach.

APPROACHING DIGITAL SOCIAL AGENTS VIA ETHNOGRAPHIC INQUIRY: EXPLORING MACHINE LIFE-WORLDS

Ethnography is a method useful to ANT-influenced researchers given ethnography and ANT's shared emphasis on the practice of individuals' everyday acts, activities, and behaviors (Nimmo, 2011). Ethnography relies on the interpretative competence of the researcher immersed in a complex social milieu, who works to bring attention to what Law (2004) calls "non-coherent realities" through Geertz's (1974) ethnographic method of "thick description." Following an ethnographic approach to ANT as a methodology, the researcher encourages questions about the kinds of actor networks and sociotechnical systems they are helping to create and legitimate in their accounts and the ways in which they are helping to compose and alter the very communities, processes, and actors subject to their ethnographic focus. By immersing themselves with their subjects, researchers interweave themselves into the heterogeneous elements of assemblages and networks.

To employ an ethnographic approach to the human–machine interview, the HMC researcher must adopt and become a user of a digital social agent technology and insert themselves into a network with the actors to gather perspective, data, and insight. Digital social agents equipped with sophisticated AI technology observe, analyze, and identify their users' behavior when used (Cheney-Lippold, 2011), which generates troves of data and information about their users' bodies, choices, and everyday lives (Lupton, 2018). Users' encounters and interactions with digital social agents are structured based on users' preferences, habits, and social relationships, allowing their creators, designers, and programmers to gather insight into individual's social behavior via digitized information and data sets. The embeddedness of human knowledge and the sociality of the data aiding digital social agents' machine learning processes constitute these machines as actors and guide their actions.

An ethnographic approach to a human–machine interviewing methodology focuses on technologies as "mobilizations of the world" (Latour, 1999, pp. 99–100), providing a source of data for HMC researchers to further explore the composition and effects of digital social agents from personal experience and immersion. When HMC researchers follow an ethnographic interviewing process with a digital social agent, the technology gathers data and insight on the researcher through the questions they ask, their responses, and the tracking of the researchers' behavior and data, thus, providing the technology with the data necessary to tailor and personalize the information communicated and provided to the researcher. Following this reflexive approach, the HMC researcher routinely asks the digital social agents questions about their understanding of the researcher based on the data it has gained from the researcher's use of and coexistence with the digital social agent. The researcher is then tasked to trace the digital social agents' communication and translations in relation to their personal being, providing meaning to the digital social agent's responses and constructing knowledge based on interweaving of the social experience of the human–non-human actors and the material experience of the digital social agent as a technical object.

Similar to a journalist approach to a human–machine interviewing and inquiry, an ethnographic approach to the human–machine interviewing can be advantageous for assessing and evaluating the information digital social agents provide to individuals, which then form assemblages and networks of our sociotechnical systems (Baiocchi et al., 2013). In addition, by taking on an ethnographic process of immersing themselves with the digital social agents, HMC researchers following this approach can gather insight into how digital social agents interact with humans, communicate, and adjust their communication and information based on previous and compounded interactions. The data provided via an ethnographic approach to human–machine interviewing helps HMC researchers trace the peculiar movements of reassociation and reassembling taking place from the communicative interactions they engage in with the machine.

CONCLUSION

In sum, there is much to be gained from human–machine interviewing, and it is necessary for HMC to adopt a methodology to gather more insight into the information digital social agents communicate if we are to better understand the human–machine meaning-making process. As HMC communication develops as a field, and as researchers continue to seek to understand machines in a social context, the relationship between the machine as an artifact and the process of HMC needs to be further examined. Accordingly, ANT as a methodology can make a significant contribution to HMC research by helping researchers theorize digital social actors as actants, so we can get a better understanding of the process of HMC and digital social agents' communication, which reassociates and reassembles elements of our sociotechnical system.

This work adds to the body of HMC research as it provides a methodology to further explore HMC and human–machine meaning-making processes. By examining the aspects of digital social agents' role as social actors and how machines exercise agency, how ANT relates to methodology, and how we can assess and evaluate the information machines communicate, a compelling case was made for a new ANT-inspired HMC methodology: the human–machine interview. If we hope to construct the richest lives possible through the adoption of digital social agent technologies, we must not lose the sense of its many potentials, both positive and negative, and we must understand that our technologies' current direction is not inevitable or determined. It is up to us to deepen our conversations with digital social agents and to assess who we are and who we are becoming with our increasing communicative intimacy with the machine.

REFERENCES

Baiocchi, G., Graizbord, D., & Rodríguez-Muñiz, M. (2013). Actor-network theory and the ethnographic imagination: An exercise in translation. *Qualitative Sociology, 36*(4), 323–341. https://doi.org/10.1007/s11133-013-9261-9

Bourdieu, P., & Wacquant, L. J. (1992). *An invitation to reflexive sociology.* University of Chicago Press.

Buckingham, D. (2008). Introducing identity. In D. Buckingham (Ed.), *Youth identity and digital media* (pp. 1–24). MIT Press. http://doi.org/10.1162/dmal.9780262524834.001

Carey, J. W. (1988). *Media, myths, and narrative: Television and the press* (1st ed., Vol. 15). SAGE Publications, Incorporated.

Carey, J. W. (2008). A cultural approach to communication. In *Communication as culture: Essays on media and society* (Revised ed., pp. 13–36). Routledge. https://doi.org/10.4324 /9780203928912

Chadwick, A. (2017). *The hybrid media system: Politics and power.* Oxford University Press. https://doi.org/10.1093/acprof:oso/9780199759477.001.0001

Cheney-Lippold, J. (2011). A new algorithmic identity: Soft biopolitics and the modulation of control. *Theory, Culture, & Society, 28*(6), 164–181. https://doi.org/10.1177 /0263276411424420

Chun, W. H. K. (2011). *Programmed visions: Software and memory.* MIT Press. https://doi .org/10.7551/mitpress/9780262015424.001.0001

Deuze, M. (2005). What is journalism? Professional identity and ideology of journalists reconsidered. *Journalism, 6*(4), 442–464. https://doi.org/10.1177/1464884905056815

Forsythe, D. (2001). *Studying those who study us: An anthropologist in the world of artificial intelligence.* Stanford University Press. https://doi.org/10.1515/9781503619371

Fortunati, L., & Edwards, A. (2020). Opening space for theoretical, methodological, and empirical issues in human-machine communication. *Human-Machine Communication, 1,* 7–18. https://doi.org/10.30658/hmc.1.1

Geertz, C. (1974). "From the native's point of view": On the nature of anthropological understanding. *Bulletin of the American Academy of Arts and Sciences, 28*(1), 26–45. https://doi.org/10.2307/3822971

Gunkel, D. (2012). Communication and artificial intelligence: Opportunities and challenges for the 21st century. *Communication +1, 1*(1), 1–25. http://doi.org/10.7275/R5QJ7F7R

Guzman, A. L. (2015). *Imagining the voice in the machine: The ontology of digital social agents* (Doctoral dissertation, University of Illinois at Chicago).

Guzman, A. L. (2016). Making AI safe for humans: A conversation with Siri. In R. Gehl & M. Bakardjiev (Eds.), *Socialbots and their friends* (1st ed., pp. 85–101). Routledge. https://doi .org/10.4324/9781315637228-7

Guzman, A. L. (Ed.). (2018). *Human-machine communication: Rethinking communication, technology, and ourselves.* Peter Lang Publishing, Incorporated. http://doi.org/10.3726/ b14399

Guzman, A. L. (2019). Voices in and of the machine: Source orientation toward mobile virtual assistants. *Computers in Human Behavior, 90,* 343–350. https://doi.org/10.1016/j.chb.2018 .08.009

Hanseth, O., Aanestad, M., & Berg, M. (2004). Actor-network theory and information systems: What's so special? Guest editors' introduction. *Information Technology & People, 17*(2), 116–123. http://doi.org/ 0.1108/09593840410542466

Haraway, D. (2006). A cyborg manifesto: Science, technology, and socialist-feminism in the late 20th century. In *The international handbook of virtual learning environments* (pp. 117–158). Springer. https://doi.org/10.1007/978-1-4020-3803-7_4

Hsieh, S. H., & Lee, C. T. (2021). Hey Alexa: examining the effect of perceived socialness in usage intentions of AI assistant-enabled smart speaker. *Journal of Research in Interactive Marketing, 15*(2), 267–294. http://doi.org/ tps://doi.org/10.1108/JRIM-11-2019-0179

Innis, H. A. (2022). *Empire and communications.* University of Toledo Press. https://doi.org /10.3138/9781487512088

Kim, J., Park, S. Y., & Robert, L. P. (2020). Bridging the health disparity of African Americans through conversational agents. *Digital Government: Research and Practice,* (2)1, 1–7. https://doi.org/10.1145/3428122

Latour, B. (1992). Where are the missing masses? The sociology of a few mundane artifacts. In W. E. Bijker & J. Law (Eds.), *Shaping technology/building society: Studies in sociotechnical change,* (1st ed., pp. 225–258). MIT Press.

Latour, B. (1998). *On Actor-network theory: A few clarifications.* Retrieved October 21, 2022.

Latour, B. (1999). *Pandora's hope: essays on the reality of science studies.* Harvard University Press.

Latour, B. (2007). *Reassembling the social: An introduction to actor-network-theory.* OUP Oxford.

Latour, B. (2012). *We Have Never Been Modern.* Harvard University Press.

Latour, B. (2017). On actor-network theory: A few clarifications plus more than a few complications. *Philosophical Literary Journal Logos, 27*(1), 173–197.

Latour, B., & Woolgar, S. (2013). *Laboratory life: The construction of scientific facts.* Princeton University Press. https://doi.org/10.2307/j.ctt32bbxc

Law, J. (2004). *After method: Mess in social science research.* Routledge.

Law, J. (2009). Actor network theory and material semiotics. *The new Blackwell companion to social theory, 3,* 141–158. https://doi.org/10.1002/9781444304992.ch7

Leidner, D. E., & Kayworth, T. (2006). A review of culture in information systems research: Toward a theory of information technology culture conflict. *MIS Quarterly, 30*(2), 357–399. https://doi.org/10.2307/25148735

Lombard, M. (2018). Presence past and future: Reflections on 25 years of presence technology, scholarship, and community. In A. Guzman (Ed.), *Human-machine communication: Rethinking communication, technology, and ourselves* (pp. 99–117). Peter Lang Publishing, Incorporated. http://doi.org/10.3726/b14399

Lupton, D. (2018). How do data come to matter? Living and becoming with personal data. *Big Data & Society, 5*(2), 1–11. https://doi.org/10.1177/2053951718786314

Michael, M. (2012). *Reconnecting culture, technology and nature: From society to heterogeneity.* Routledge. https://doi.org/10.4324/9780203135334

Mol, A. (2010). Actor-network theory: Sensitive terms and enduring tensions. *Kölner Zeitschrift für Soziologie und Sozialpsychologie, 50*(1), 253–269.

Nass, C., & Steuer, J. (1993). Voices, boxes, and sources of messages: Computers and social actors. *Human Communication Research, 19*(4), 504–527. https://doi.org/10.1111/j.1468-2958.1993.tb00311.x

Nass, C., Steuer, J., & Tauber, E. R. (1994, April). Computers are social actors. In *Proceedings of the SIGCHI conference on human factors in computing systems* (pp. 72–78). https://doi.org/10.1145/191666.191703

Natale, S., & Cooke, H. (2021). Browsing with Alexa: Interrogating the impact of voice assistants as web interfaces. *Media, Culture & Society, 43*(6), 1000–1016. https://doi.org/10.1177/016344372098329

National Aeronautics and Space Administration. (1976, January). *A forecast of space technology1980–2000* [Press release]. https://apps.dtic.mil/sti/pdfs/ADA327961.pdf

Nimmo, R. (2011). Actor-network theory and methodology: Social research in a more-than-human world. *Methodological Innovations Online, 6*(3), 108–119. https://doi.org/10.4256/mio.2011.0

Reeves, B., & Nass, C. I. (1996). *The media equation: How people treat computers, television, and new media like real people and places.* Center for the Study of Language and Information; Cambridge University Press.

Sayes, E. (2014). Actor–network theory and methodology: Just what does it mean to say that nonhumans have agency? *Social Studies of Science, 44*(1), 134–149. https://doi.org/10.1177/030631271351186

Schudson, M. (1994). Question authority: A history of the news interview in American journalism, 1860s–1930s. *Media, Culture, & Society, 16*(4), 565–587. https://doi.org/10.1177/01634437940160040

Sharevski, F., & Gover, D. (2021, August). Two truths and a lie: Exploring soft moderation of COVID-19 misinformation with Amazon Alexa. In *Proceedings of the 16th International Conference on Availability, Reliability and Security* (pp. 1–9). https://doi.org/10.1145/3465481.3470017

Stob, P. (2008). "Terministic screens," social constructionism, and the language of experience: Kenneth Burke's utilization of William James. *Philosophy & Rhetoric*, *41*(2), 130–152. https://doi.org/10.2307/25655306

Sundar, S. S. (2020). Rise of machine agency: A framework for studying the psychology of human–AI interaction (HAII). J*ournal of Computer-Mediated Communication*, *25*(1), 74–88. https://doi.org/10.1093/jcmc/zmz026

Turkle, S. (2005). *The second self: Computers and the human spirit.* MIT Press. https://doi .org/10.7551/mitpress/6115.001.0001

Verbeek, P. P. (2009). Ambient intelligence and persuasive technology: The blurring boundaries between human and technology. *NanoEthics*, *3*(3), 231–242. http://doi.org/10 .1007/s11569-009-0077-8

Wajcman, J. (2010). Feminist theories of technology. *Cambridge Journal of Economics*, *34*(1), 143–152. https://doi.org/10.1093/cje/ben057

Wiener, N. (2019). *Cybernetics or control and communication in the animal and the machine, reissue of the 1961 second edition.* MIT Press. https://doi.org/10.1037/13140-000

Yan, L., & Tan, Y. (2014). Feeling blue? Go online: An empirical study of social support among patients. *Information Systems Research*, *25*(4), 690–709. https://doi.org/10.1287/isre .2014.0538

Zhao, S. (2006). Humanoid social robots as a medium of communication. *New Media & Society*, *8*(3), 401–419. https://doi.org/10.1177/1461444806061951

Zwakman, D. S., Pal, D., & Arpnikanondt, C. (2021). Usability evaluation of artificial intelligence-based voice assistants: The case of Amazon Alexa. *SN Computer Science*, *2*(1), 1–16. https://doi.org/10.1007/s42979-020-00424-4

4. Discovering developmental trajectories and trends of conversational agent research using dynamic topic modeling

Hüseyin Özçınar and Aylin Sabancı Bayramoğlu

Artificial intelligence (AI), which emerged in the middle of the twentieth century, has been adopted and widely used in many disciplines thanks to rapid developments in technology and the booming availability of data. One such disciple that is extensively involved with AI is communication. For instance, smart conversational systems, developed for AI-based machines to understand, process, and respond to the language used by humans, have recently become a substantive focus of interest in the industry and academic field. Smart conversational systems take names such as conversational AI, conversational systems, dialogue systems, and chatbots according to their features and areas of use. This study uses the term conversational agents (CAs) to describe all these systems.

Alan Mathison Turing's article titled "Computing Machinery and Intelligence," in which he asked the question "Can machines think?" is considered the beginning of the history of CAs (Turing, 1950). The first chatbot, named ELIZA, was developed by Weizenbaum (1966), and PARRY (Colby et al., 1971) and A.L.I.C.E. (Wallace, 1995) followed. Rule-based CAs developed during this period were not skilled at understanding context or providing conversational flow (Hussain et al., 2019). With the advent of AI, more complex and human-like conversational AI-based CAs based on deep neural networks (DNN) and natural language processing (NLP) have emerged. These CAs have gone a step further with the creation of intelligent personal voice assistants that understand voice commands and perform tasks such as monitoring calendars and emails (Adamopoulou & Moussiades, 2020). The prominent personal assistants of this period, Apple's Siri, IBM's Watson, Google Assistant, Microsoft's Cortana, and Amazon's Alexa, enabled CAs technology to be experienced by vast segments of society.

CAs are a dynamic research field closely linked to the contemporary context. Developments in technology, social changes, entertainment, and business can have significant repercussions in the field of CAs. This situation makes it difficult to establish a clear classification of CAs in the area. As a notable attempt, Adamopoulou and Moussiades (2020) classify CAs according to the knowledge domain (open domain, closed domain), the goal (informative, chat-based, task-based), the service provided (inter-personal, intra-personal, intra-agent), input processing and response generation method (rule-based, generative, retrieval-based), development type (open source, closed platforms), and human support provided. On the other hand, Koetter et al. (2018) categorize CAs by grading 0–7 points on how much they have realism, entertainment, textuality, task orientation, spoken, and companionship features. It is difficult to maintain the long-term validity of classifications made in rapidly developing areas such as CAs; however, these classifications are important in revealing the field's current state.

If the usage areas are considered, it can be seen that CAs play an essential role in many areas, such as health, education, finance, e-commerce, and business. CAs are widely used in the field of health for purposes such as rapid accessibility, personalized health care, patient education (Car et al., 2020); psychiatric counseling (Oh et al., 2017); nutrition; and physical activity tracking (Huang et al., 2018). In the field of education, CAs are used to improve learning processes, provide individual learning support to students, or respond individually to their demands (Hobert & von Wolff, 2019); tutoring (Graesser et al., 2000; Heffernan, 2003; Sánchez-Díaz et al., 2018); and answering student questions (Clarizia et al., 2018; Feng et al., 2006; Taylor & Moore, 2006). Moreover, CAs are used not only to improve student interaction but also to reduce the workload of educators in this period when communication is predominantly based on the online platform (Okonkwo & Ade-Ibijola, 2021). In the finance and banking industry, CAs are frequently used to provide bill payment, transaction processing, credit card payments, and frequently asked questions (FAQ) services to assist end-users (Alnefaie et al., 2021). Furthermore, the use of CAs has become widespread in the business field because it reduces service costs, communicates with many customers simultaneously, and reduces the time users spend accessing accurate information (Adamopoulou & Moussiades, 2020).

CAs is an umbrella term for human–machine communication using natural language. Advances in AI, NLP, and big data provide rapid development of CAs as an emerging research field (Brown et al., 2020). This makes it difficult to trace the progress of the CAs research field and examine trends. Therefore, the aim of this study is to explore the main subfields of CAs research area and to investigate the trends and changes in subtopics over time. For this purpose, the dynamic topic modeling method has been chosen to reveal the keywords and map the topics.

Although AI has been a part of computer science for many years, it has only recently been used in communication sciences. As in most social science fields, in the field of communication, texts have been examined by human hands or by using dictionary-based semi-automated methods. With the rapid increase in the number of unstructured text documents (scientific publications, social media posts, web pages, etc.) recently, it has become a necessity to increase computer-assisted text analysis techniques.

AI, which is considered a subfield of computer science, researches and develops various tools to solve problems that are considered to require human intelligence (Russell & Norvig, 2010). Generation, translation, and comprehension of natural language, or NLP, is one of the earliest research areas in AI. In recent years, increases in the computational power of machines and the sophistication of mathematical models and algorithms have provided communication scientists with tools that are particularly suited to the study of complex qualitative variables and human language. Topic modeling stands out as a powerful and reliable method to reveal hidden themes in unstructured text document collections. A topic model is a sort of algorithm that scans a collection of documents, analyzes how words and phrases co-occur in them, and then reveals groupings or clusters of words that best describe those documents. These word groups frequently seem to indicate themes or subjects.

METHOD

This study explores the conversational agent research field regarding its potential subfields and development over time via dynamic topic modeling. Topic modeling algorithms are methods that analyze the words of the original texts to discover the themes that run through them, how those themes are connected, and how they change over time (Blei, 2012). Topic modeling has been used extensively to identify research fields' structure, trends, and potential research gaps. For instance, Liu et al. (2019) utilized latent Dirichlet allocation (LDA) topic modeling algorithm to explore the structure and trends of offsite construction literature. Similarly, Kumari et al. (2021) used LDA-based topic modeling to shed light on the subfields and trends of research on humanoid robots. Also, Özçınar and Öztürk (in press) explored the diffusion of the network perspective with BERTopic in education sciences. The topic modeling process is displayed in Figure 4.1.

Data Collection

The data for this study were acquired from the Web of Science (WoS) database. The Social Sciences Citation Index (SSCI) and Science Citation Index Expanded (SCI-EXPANDED) were included in the search. These databases provide access to reliable publications in the field of science and social sciences. To narrow the CAs literature as a result of the literature review, "conversational agent*," "conversation agent*," "chatbot*," or "dialog* system*," "conversational system*," "conversation system*," "conversational UI*," "conversational interface*," "socialbot*," "chatterbot*," or "Chatterbox*" were chosen as keywords to be used for search. The search query was limited to English-language articles, book chapters, and proceeding paper document types between 2001 and 2021. As a result of this search, 2,123 studies remained.

Data Preprocessing

Bibliometric data such as article title, abstract, keywords, authors, and publication year related to the publications obtained as a result of the search were downloaded. Aside from the abstract and publication year, all data has been excluded from the dataset. Furthermore, the dataset was manually scanned, and the 13 studies with missing data were excluded from the dataset. BERTopic does not require any data preprocessing steps such as stemming or lemmatization. For that reason, only stop-words were removed from the abstracts after missing data were removed during the

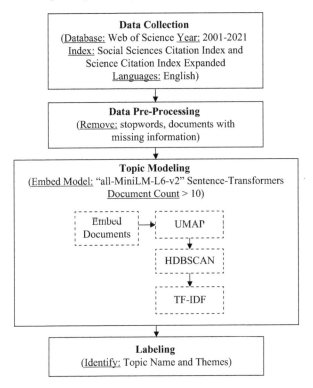

Figure 4.1   Topic modeling process

data cleaning phase. After the data preprocessing phase, a dataset of 2,110 studies had been created.

Data Analysis

As an embedding-based topic modeling algorithm, BERTopic is known to be more successful than its alternatives regarding short texts (Egger & Yu, 2022). In this study, abstracts of studies in the CAs literature were analyzed using the BERTopic algorithm. BERTopic is a BERT-based topic modeling algorithm developed by Grooendorst (2022). In BERTopic, topic representations are created in three steps: document embedding, document clustering, and topic representation. First, each document is converted to embedding representation using Bidirectional Encoder Representations from Transformers (BERT). Then the dimensions of the created document embeddings are reduced by the uniform manifold approximation and projection (UMAP) method, and hierarchical density-based spatial clustering of applications with noise (HDBSCAN) is used as the clustering method. Finally, topic representation is extracted from document sets using Term Frequency-Inverse Document Frequency (TF-IDF) (for a more detailed discussion of the method, please see Grooendorst, 2022).

BERTopic differs from LDA because it provides continuous rather than discrete topic modeling. The stochastic nature of the model, thus, leads to different results with repeated modeling (Egger & Yu, 2022). While LDA only uses the bag-of-words (BOW) method to represent documents, BERTopic creates jointly embedded document and word vectors using pretrained transformer-based language models to capture word semantics (Hendry et al., 2021). In addition, the researcher determines the number of topics in topic modeling algorithms such as LDA. Because of these limitations, the BERTopic algorithm has been implemented as a more favorable choice.

While implementing the BERTopic algorithm, "all-MiniLM-L6-v2" sentence transformers were used as the embedding model. For the resulting model structure to be interpretable, the criterion that all topics in the model should contain at least ten documents (abstract) is set as a parameter. As a result, a model consisting of 27 topics has emerged. The probability of the studies included in the research to be included in the determined topics and the words with a high likelihood of being included in each topic were obtained. Topic 1 contains all documents and documents not assigned to any topic. Next, both researchers analyzed the summaries under the topics, the words describing each topic, and the topic names produced by TF-IDF. They created names that are easier to understand and interpret for each topic. Later, the topics were gathered under themes in light of their scope and literature.

FINDINGS

A close examination of the publication years of the studies in the field of CAs reveals that the number of publications increased every year from 2001 to 2006. Still, after 2006, there was a decrease in the number of publications. Until 2018, fewer than 100 studies were carried out, and after 2018, the number of publications increased considerably (see Figure 4.2.) Publication counts between 2019 and 2021 constitute 50% of the total number of publications.

When countries examine the distribution of publications in the research area, it is seen that the USA ($n = 553$, 26.04%) is the country with the most publications. This is followed by the Peoples' Republic of China ($n = 240$, 11.30%) and Germany ($n = 183$, 8.62%) (see Table 4.1).

When the publications within the scope of the research are examined according to the "Research Areas" classifications made by WoS, it is seen that 58.31% of the publications are in computer science, 19.40% in engineering, and 7.39% in medical informatics (see Table 4.2). When the change in the number of publications by years is analyzed according to the "Research Areas" of the publications, it is seen that the number of publications in the fields of computer science and engineering has increased significantly after 2018 (see Figure 4.3.).

When the most published publication titles are examined, the "Lecture Notes in Artificial Intelligence" book series, which focuses on AI, ranks first and the "Lecture Notes in Computer Science" book series ranks second (see Table 4.3).

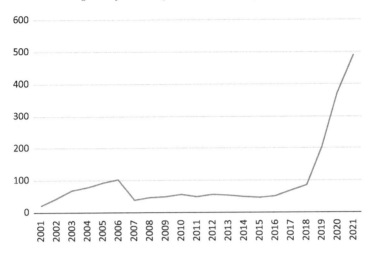

Figure 4.2   *Distribution of publications in the conversational agent field by years*

Table 4.1   *Distribution of publications in the conversational agents area by country*

Countries	Record count	Percentage
USA	553	26.04
People's Republic of China	240	11.30
Germany	183	8.62
England	182	8.57
Spain	160	7.53
Japan	155	7.30
France	126	5.93
South Korea	118	5.55
Netherlands	100	4.71
Italy	87	4.09

The subfields of the conversational agents research area were revealed with the dynamic topic modeling method. From the WoS database, 27 topics were extracted from 2,123 studies published between 2001 and 2021. By examining the documents and words of the topics, each topic was labeled and intuitively associated with a theme. Two main themes were identified, namely usage areas and design and development. There are subthemes under each central theme. Usage areas include five subthemes and 12 topics, design and development three subthemes and 15 topics (see Table 4.4).

Table 4.2   Distribution of publications in conversational agents literature by research areas (top 5 research areas)

Research Areas	Record count	Percentage
Computer Science	1,238	58.31
Engineering	412	19.40
Medical Informatics	157	7.39
Acoustics	154	7.25
Psychology	153	7.20

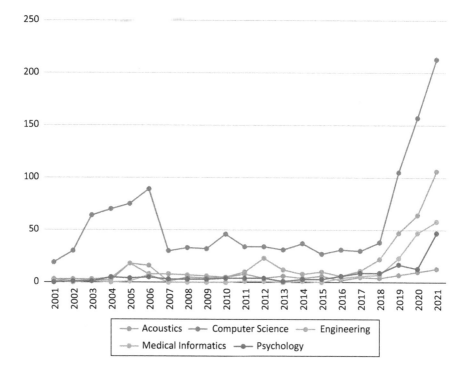

Figure 4.3   *Distribution of conversational agents research areas by years*

Topic 0, labeled "CAs in health care," consists of the words "health, patients, care, participants, chatbot, study, intervention, group, mental, patient." The topic with the most publications concerns the use of CAs in the health care field (see Tables 4.4 and 4.5). Topic 1, on the other hand, consists of the words "response, model, dialogue, models, task, generation, dialog, based, responses, knowledge" that describe this topic. Topic 2 is represented by "speech, recognition, dialogue, speech recognition, language, spoken, understanding, systems, classification, act" (See Table 4.5 for all the words describing the topics).

Table 4.3   *Distribution of publications in the conversational agent field by publication titles*

Publication titles	Record count
Lecture Notes in Artificial Intelligence	117
Lecture Notes in Computer Science	89
Speech Communication	89
Computer Speech and Language	83
Journal of Medical Internet Research	70

Change of Topics and Themes Over Time

The change in the themes that emerged from the analysis of the CAs research area with the topic modeling method was further explored with the dynamic topic modeling method. The change of themes over time has been traced through two main themes: usage areas and design and development. While the central theme of usage areas remained stable until 2018, it has increased in recent years. Examination of subthemes reveals that the CAs in the health care theme shows a comparatively higher increase (see Figure 4.4). When the trend of the central theme of design and development is examined, an increase and decrease in the number of studies are observed until 2018, unlike usage areas. After 2018, while the themes of affective computing and dialogue response models have seen a surge, spoken dialogue has remained stable (see Figure 4.5).

DISCUSSION

This study aims to reveal the main themes of CAs research, an inter-disciplinary research area, and the shifts in research trends in this field. For this purpose, the abstract of 2,110 studies in the field of CAs published in the publication channels (journal/book/congress notice) scanned by the WoS Core Collection between 2001–2021 was analyzed by the dynamic topic modeling method. In addition, the data on the publication year and the distribution of the studies according to the countries were obtained using the WoS Core Collection Database.

The results of the analysis revealed no significant change in the number of studies between 2001–2018, but the related studies in this field started to surge after 2018. All of these studies, the 2,110 publications examined with the dynamic topic modeling method, have been observed to cluster around 27 topics. Then, these topics are categorized into two main themes: design and development studies on CAs and the usage areas of CAs (Song & Xiong, 2021).

CAs Studies in Light of Usage Areas

The results of the research show that there are primarily studies on the use of intelligent conversational systems in the field of health in the CAs literature. In the field

Table 4.4   *Topics and themes of conversational agents research field*

No.	Count	Topic name	Main theme	Theme
T0	377	CAs in Health Care	Usage Areas	CAs in Health Care
T1	181	User Intent and Context Understanding	Design and Development	Dialogue Response Models
T2	108	Speech Recognition	Design and Development	Spoken Dialogue
T3	107	Techniques for Developing Dialogue Policies	Design and Development	Dialogue Response Models
T4	105	Brand Communication	Usage Areas	CAs in Business
T5	73	Consumer Services	Usage Areas	CAs in Business
T6	72	Interface Design	Design and Development	Affective Computing
T7	53	Tutorial Dialogue Systems	Usage Areas	CAs in Education
T8	52	Social Chatbots for Elderly People	Usage Areas	Social Robots
T9	47	Educational Chatbots	Usage Areas	CAs in Education
T10	39	Design and Development of Multi-domain Dialogue Systems	Design and Development	Dialogue Response Models
T11	38	Design and Development of Conversational Characters	Design and Development	Affective Computing
T12	34	Emotion Detection from Speech (Technical)	Design and Development	Affective Computing
T13	31	Automated Journalism	Usage Areas	CAs in Business
T14	30	Emotion in Dialogue Systems	Design and Development	Affective Computing
T15	28	Multi-modal Emotional Behaviors in Embodied CAs	Design and Development	Affective Computing
T16	27	Argumentative Dialogue Models	Design and Development	Dialogue Response Models
T17	25	Turn-Taking in Spoken Dialogue Systems	Design and Development	Spoken Dialogue
T18	23	Semantic-Based Conversational Agents	Design and Development	Dialogue Response Models
T19	19	Gazer Behavior of CAs	Design and Development	Affective Computing
T20	17	Dialogue System Design for Collaborative Learning Activities	Usage Areas	CAs in Education
T21	15	Natural Language Generation	Design and Development	Dialogue Response Models

(Continued)

Table 4.4   (Continued)

No.	Count	Topic name	Main theme	Theme
T22	15	Social Media Bots/Fake Accounts	Usage Areas	Social Media Bots/Fake Accounts
T23	14	Product Recommendation Agents	Usage Areas	CAs in Business
T24	14	Organizational Decision-making	Usage Areas	CAs in Business
T25	11	Voice Search in Dialogue Systems	Design and Development	Spoken Dialogue
T26	11	Users' Perception of Social Chatbots	Usage Areas	Social Robots

of health, CAs are used both to provide support or education to patients in their living environments, to assist doctors and other health care professionals in data collection and diagnosis processes, or to directly diagnose and offer treatment (Car et al., 2020; Laranjo et al., 2018). Montenegro, da Costa, and da Rosa Righi (2019) examined 40 studies focusing on using CAs in the health field between 2008 and 2018 in various databases with a systematic literature review method. Montenegro et al. (2019) classified CAs according to their duties in the field of health by dividing them into coaching and counseling agents. Researchers stated that coaching agents are mainly used for data collection and training purposes so that doctors can do their jobs better and, in some cases, to train patients on new treatment routines. On the other hand, counseling agents are used to increase doctor–patient communication and to provide social support, especially to patients with mental health problems. Montenegro et al. (2019) predicted that using CAs will become widespread, especially in health education. In this study, it has been demonstrated with numerical data that the use of CAs in health and education has increased significantly in line with the predictions of Montenegro et al. (2019). Despite this rapid increase in the use of CAs in health care, researchers emphasize the need for studies based on concrete criteria on potential risks (Laranjo et al., 2018)

CAs are also used to increase the quality of life of individuals needing social attention. In general, the world population is aging, and the age pyramid of the population is further deteriorating in developed countries. The fact that the elderly often live in isolation from society causes some cognitive and affective problems (Woo et al., 2020). There are many findings that the interaction of social robots with people who are elderly or in need of home care positively reflects the cognitive functioning of individuals (Gongoro Alonso et al., 2019). In this context, it is seen that there is a severe effort of industry and academia on the design of social robots that will communicate and support the elderly or people in need of care in the field of CAs.

One of the critical usage areas of CAs is education. It has been emphasized in various studies that CAs have long been used in different pedagogical roles such as tutor, learning companion, and reflection aid in the field of education (Haake & Gulz, 2009; Paschoal et al., 2020). In this study, studies on the use of CAs in education

Table 4.5   Topic word distribution

No.	Words
T0	health, patients, care, participants, chatbot, study, intervention, mental, group, patient
T1	response, model, dialogue, models, task, generation, dialog, based, responses, knowledge
T2	speech, recognition, dialogue, speech recognition, language, spoken, understanding, systems, classification, act
T3	user, dialogue, learning, dialog, policy, reinforcement, reinforcement learning, model, systems, task
T4	service, AI, customer, chatbots, chatbot, study, customers, consumers, perceived, value
T5	knowledge, chatbot, chatbots, paper, conversational, users, information, natural, web, language
T6	agent, agents, embodied, ECA, social, human, ECAs, interaction, users, virtual
T7	learning, students, tutoring, student, learner, language, tutor, conversational, tutorial, agents
T8	robot, robots, human, interaction, human robot, dialogue, information, robot interaction, natural, spatial
T9	students, learning, chatbots, chatbot, learners, language, language learning, course, study, English
T10	dialogue, dialog, speech, user, services, interface, spoken, systems, interfaces, applications
T11	gesture, gestures, speech, facial, animation, head, embodied, conversational, virtual, non-verbal
T12	emotion, emotional, emotions, human, recognition, speech, user, classification, information, fusion
T13	chatbot, gender, human, chatbots, news, users, journalism, social, bots, AI
T14	emotion, emotional, emotions, responses, model, generate, conversation, response, dialogue, sentiment
T15	facial, expressions, facial expressions, emotions, expression, emotion, emotional, embodied conversational, expressivity, agent
T16	dialogue, formal, argumentation, arguments, argument, logic, dialogues, agents, fallacies, persuasion
T17	turn, turn-taking, taking, prosodic, overlaps, human, dialogue, speech, initiative, speakers
T18	language, conversational, natural language, natural, conversational agent, semantic, Bayesian, user, knowledge, information
T19	gaze, eye, eye gaze, interaction, face, dwell, agent, human, conversational, AR

(Continued)

Table 4.5 *(Continued)*

No.	Words
T20	learning, students, collaborative, agent, collaborative learning, conversational, study, learner, learners, PCAs
T21	NLG, generation, sentence, language generation, language, domain, natural language, natural, model, based
T22	socialbots, OSNs, socialbot, accounts, users, OSN, social, social networks, online social, infiltration
T23	recommendation, recommender, user, recommender systems, items, users, conversational recommender, interaction, conversational, systems
T24	data, disaster, management, equipment, information, rice, building, QA, developed, disaster management
T25	dialogue, systems, parameters, dialogue systems, evaluation, spoken, quality, spoken dialogue, different, usability
T26	chatbot, IoT, IoT CA, emotional support, social, support, CA use, CA, emotional, participants

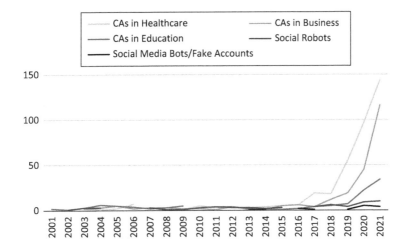

Figure 4.4 *Change of usage areas theme by time*

are grouped under three headings. When the articles representing the topics and the words that best describe each topic are examined, it is seen that this classification is compatible with the pedagogical roles of CAs. The topic with the most publications on education was named "tutorial dialogue systems." One of the first convergence points for education and AI technologies has been "intelligent tutoring systems (ITS)." As part of these systems, CAs were used to enable students to explain their thinking and problem-solving styles (self-explanation) (Aleven & Koedinger, 2002;

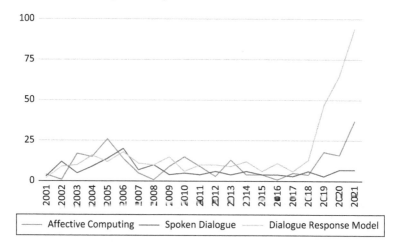

Figure 4.5   Change of design and development theme by time

Grigoriadou et al., 2005). Studies focusing on using chatbots as a direct teaching tool are gathered under the title of "educational chatbots." In these studies, the effect of the use of chatbots on variables such as learning achievement and motivation has been analyzed (e.g., Deveci Topal et al., 2021; Vázquez-Cano et al., 2021; Yin et al., 2021). Research results reveal that CAs have recently been employed more extensively in the field of education for scaffolding (Song & Kim, 2021) and interaction (Tegos et al., 2015) in cooperative learning environments.

Businesses in the digital age also invest in different types of CAs as an affordable and effective way to communicate with customers (Alger, 2017). In accordance with this, scientific studies on the use of CAs in different business sectors have been increasing in the academic field. In that study, branding communication, customer service and automated journalism (newsbots), product recommendation agents, and organizational decision-making CAs have become areas of focus. Developments in the field of AI necessitated the reshaping of brand communication, advertising consumer service, and consumer experience in the field of business (Taylor, 2019). Similarly, chatbot news services (CN) is one of the business areas in which CAs are widely used (Jung et al., 2017). Chatbot news services are automated systems that use CAs to collect, filter, and present information and news (Thurman et al., 2019). The relationship between the user and the CAs, the effects of different elements in the CAs design on the customer perception and reaction, and the effects of the human vs. CAs communicator on the customer perception are the topics that are frequently studied in these areas. Likewise, in scientific study areas related to the use of CAs in business, the number of publications has increased rapidly, especially in the post-2018 period. These findings confirm the predictions of Sweezey (2019) that the use of CAs in business areas will become widespread.

Another area of use for CAs in businesses is recommendation systems. Recommendation systems, one of the areas in which AI has been quite successful, provide recommendations about the current wishes of the user by following their previous behavior. In contrast, conversational recommendation systems interact with the user and try to fully understand the user's current intentions and desires (Jannach et al., 2021). Thanks to their desirable qualities, such conversational recommendation systems have become an indispensable part of many information search activities in digital spaces today. Recommender systems that allow the user to reach the exact information they want promptly bring significant value to the business. Therefore, there is great interest in developing conversational recommendation systems in academia and the industry (Gao et al., 2021).

Conversational AI Design and Development Studies

The computers are social actors (CASA) framework (Nass & Moon, 2000), derived from the media equation (Reeves & Nass, 1996), proposes that individuals treat conversational agents like real people, and scripts used in human–human communication are used for communicating with conversational agents without any cognitive effort. Social scripts are mental representations of how to connect with people (Honeycutt & Bryan, 2011; Schank & Abelson, 1977). The scripted way of communication between people creates an understanding of how human conversational agent communication can be achieved (Nah et al., 2020). On this ground, one of the main objectives of CAs research is to create a smart dialogue system that approximates the communication between people and can communicate naturally and meaningfully with people. This goal is, without a doubt, a challenging task. Although rule-based systems such as ELIZA, which was used in the first period of CAs history, contributed to the development of the field. However, the answers created with a limited vocabulary remained far from creating realistic and solution-providing communication. As a consequence of the recent emergence of social media use and, therefore, big data, in addition to developments in DNN and NLP, various models that focus on understanding the context of dialogue and provide methods such as response generation methods (Sankar et al., 2019) or response selection methods (Huang et al., 2020; Whang et al., 2019) have spawned (Tao et al., 2021).

It can be argued that the necessity of developing the machine's ability to imitate humans to increase the success of machine–human communication is the idea that forms the basis of CAs design and development studies. Considering the role played by emotions in human–human communication, it is natural that affective computing emerges as an essential field of study in CAs design and development. The findings of this study also support the idea that the theme of affective computing is one of the leading research areas of CAs literature (Mensio et al., 2018).

Emotions are the subject of scientific studies dates back to the nineteenth century (James, 1884). Since the 1990s, studies have been carried out in the field of affective computing to increase the quality of human–computer communication and provide computers with human-specific observation, emotion recognition, and creation skills (Tao & Tan, 2005). However, the lack of an agreed-upon definition and classification of emotion and our lack of an adequate understanding of how people process emotion (Ortony & Turner, 1990) make it challenging to develop intelligent systems that understand and mimic the human emotional processes.

Affective computing studies can be classified both based on which features of communication and emotion are tried to be recognized and which emotions are tried to be recognized. For example, López-Cózar et al. (2011) classified speech as "neutral," "tired," and "angry" using prosodic, acoustic, lexical, and dialogue acts information. Furthermore, Morrison et al. (2007), using the prosodic feature, have classified the messages as negative/non-negative; neutral/tired/angry. Moreover, Palacios et al. (2020) used a dataset of 68 features to separate stressed and non-stressed speech and created a feature selection mechanism.

Malatesta et al. (2009) state that "affective computing dictates the importance of creating interfaces which are not only solely limited to the synthetic representation of the face and the human body, but also expresses feelings through facial expressions, gestures and the body pose." In line with this idea, our study reveals that emotion expression, as well as emotion detection with tools such as avatars, animated characters, or intonation take place in CAs literature as a research area. In order to create perceptions such as believable rapport (Gratch et al., 2006), credibility (Spence et al., 2019), and attractiveness (Westerman et al., 2015) in the human speaker during communication, the facial expression of embodied CAs (Malatesta, 2007), eye gaze (Pelachaud & Bilvi, 2003), and body language (Gratch et al., 2006) has become research areas in the field. As a result, a knowledge base that can guide practitioners on how to design has emerged

One aspect of communication that can be challenging for machines to understand and reproduce is sound, which includes elements such as emotions and other auditory cues. Voice communication will almost always lead the list if communication forms are considered. In terms of human–computer interaction, voice communication, and automatic speech recognition (ASR) have been areas of intense interest by AI researchers since the 1970s (Meng et al., 2012). In the most general sense, ASR can be defined as the understanding and transcription of the words spoken by the user (Yu & Deng, 2016). The findings of our study also support that ASR is one of the most studied topics related to CAs. It has been suggested that studies on ASR have increased in the past ten years with the studies in the field of DNNs and the development of technologies such as smart-home assistants and personnel digital assistants (Georgescu et al., 2021).

With the widespread use of voice communication in CAs and ASR, various other problems have also emerged. One of them is to provide speech-listening coordination. Because the user cannot speak and listen at the same time, the speaking order flow must be determined. Because people are very skilled in turn-taking when speaking, human–human communication can progress smoothly in terms of turn-taking. However, turn-taking and prosodic aspects of speech are prominent problems that need to be studied for CAs. Therefore, enough studies have emerged in the CAs literature to create a field related to the prosodic aspects of turn-taking and speaking (Skantze, 2021).

One of the critical stages in the CAs development process is the evaluation of the quality of the system; however, assessing the quality of a dialogue system is a challenging task because what constitutes quality is not clear in many situations, and it often depends on the application. On top of that, the metric used for gauging quality may also be the subject of a hot debate. For instance, relying on user experience as an evaluator is not a desirable option, both in terms of time and expense, because user feedback may be unreliable. Therefore, as the findings of this study reveal, many scientific studies are being conducted to develop automated and repeatable evaluation procedures (Deriu et al., 2021).

Alan Turing's (1950) intellectual experiment, which forms the basis of the field of AI, proposed a mechanism by which humans and computers communicate. Since the emergence of AI, there has always been a close relationship between the field of communication and the field of AI. However, the interaction between communication sciences and the field of AI remained rather weak until the last period (Guzman & Lewis, 2020). Today, this gap between AI and communications research is being bridged by AI technologies designed to act as communicators. Recent advances in AI have led to increasingly powerful and consequential AI technologies being integrated into everyday life (Campolo et al., 2017). As a result, it could be argued that the field should pay more attention to comprehending people's interactions with communicative AI technologies, as well as their ramifications (Gunkel, 2012; Guzman, 2018).

AI and people's interactions with it do not cleanly fit into paradigms of communication theory that for more than a century have been built around how humans communicate with other people. This presents a significant challenge for communication science researchers investigating communicative AI (Gunkel, 2012). Human interaction with CAs is often judged by how similar or different it is to human-to-human interaction. For example, the success of technologies of automated journalism, such as news-writing programs, is questioned in the same way that the success of human journalists is questioned. It may be useful to use the knowledge base created on the basis of human communication to understand and evaluate human–machine interaction. However, human communication theories should not be used in a way that will determine the boundaries of human–machine communication research (Guzman & Lewis, 2020).

CONCLUSION

The findings of this research revealed that the number of CAs studies included in the publication outlets indexed by the WoS Core Collection, especially after 2018, has increased considerably. As a result of the thematic grouping of the topics obtained by the dynamic topic modeling method of the CAs studies, topics were grouped under two main themes: usage areas and design and development studies. When studies are examined according to usage areas, it has been revealed that research on the use of CAs is widely carried out in the fields of (1) health care, (2) business, (3) education (4) social robots, and (5) social media. When the number of studies on the identified themes over time is examined, it has been observed that there was no significant change in the number of studies until 2018. However, after 2018, there has been a substantial surge. The highest increase was noted in the health care field, and there was also a significant increase in the studies in the business field. It has been revealed that the studies in the literature that technically focus on CAs design and development are concentrated on (1) affective computing, (2) spoken dialogue, and (3) dialogue response. Among these themes, it was observed that the number of studies in the field of dialogue response systems increased the most after 2018, followed by the field of affective computing.

It has been noted that the existing studies that try to reveal the intellectual structure of CAs literature are either survey studies based on the synthesis of experimental development studies or review studies on using CAs in a particular field. This study tried to reveal the structure of the CAs field from a holistic perspective. Moreover, prior to this one, no study explored the literature change over time. For these reasons, it is anticipated that this study will provide a broad and detailed perspective on the CAs research field and its orientations for editors, researchers, publishers, and funding agencies.

Of course, like any research, this research has many limitations. One of the main limitations of this study was that the data were constrained exclusively to the WoS database and in the English-language publications. In addition to that, all but abstracts were excluded from the analysis. Although it would be very challenging to access a dataset of this size in full text, a more detailed perspective on the field can be obtained by combining full-text publications from different academic databases. Furthermore, the use of cross-lingual topic models can enrich the perspectives brought. We argue that topic modeling studies to be carried out on the themes that emerged in this research may be helpful in terms of identifying more specific research subfields in the field.

REFERENCES

Adamopoulou, E., & Moussiades, L. (2020, June). An overview of chatbot technology. In *IFIP International Conference on Artificial Intelligence Applications and Innovations* (pp. 373–383). Springer.

Aleven, V. A., & Koedinger, K. R. (2002). An effective metacognitive strategy: Learning by doing and explaining with a computer-based cognitive tutor. *Cognitive Science*, *26*(2), 147–179.

Alger, K. (2017). To bot or not? The rise of AI chatbots in business. Dell technologies. https://www.delltechnologies.com/en-us/perspectives/to-bot-or-not-the-rise-of-ai-chatbots-in-business/

Alnefaie, A., Singh, S., Kocaballi, B., & Prasad, M. (2021, January). An overview of conversational agent: Applications, challenges and future directions. In *17th International Conference on Web Information Systems and Technologies*. SCITEPRESS-Science and Technology Publications.

Blei, D. M. (2012). Probabilistic topic models. *Communications of the ACM*, *55*(4), 77–84.

Brown, T., Mann, B., Ryder, N., Subbiah, M., Kaplan, J. D., Dhariwal, P., ... Amodei, D. (2020). Language models are few-shot learners. *Advances in Neural Information Processing Systems*, *33*, 1877–1901.

Car, L. T., Dhinagaran, D. A., Kyaw, B. M., Kowatsch, T., Joty, S., Theng, Y. L., & Atun, R. (2020). Conversational agents in health care: Scoping review and conceptual analysis. *Journal of medical Internet research*, 22(8), e17158.

Campolo, A., Sanfilippo, M. R., Whittaker, M., & Crawford, K. (2017). *AI now 2017 report*. Report, AI Now, New York. Available at: https://ainowinstitute.org/reports.html (accessed 13 May 2021).

Clarizia, F., Colace, F., Lombardi, M., Pascale, F., & Santaniello, D. (2018, October). Chatbot: An education support system for student. In *International Symposium on Cyberspace Safety and Security* (pp. 291–302). Springer.

Colby, K. M., Weber, S., & Hilf, F. D. (1971). Artificial paranoia. *Artificial Intelligence*, 2(1), 1–25.

Deriu, J., Rodrigo, A., Otegi, A., Echegoyen, G., Rosset, S., Agirre, E., & Cieliebak, M. (2021). Survey on evaluation methods for dialogue systems. *Artificial Intelligence Review*, 54(1), 755–810.

Deveci Topal, A., Dilek Eren, C., & Kolburan Geçer, A. (2021). Chatbot application in a 5th grade science course. *Education and Information Technologies*, 26(5), 6241–6265.

Egger, R., & Yu, J. (2022). A topic modeling comparison between LDA, NMF, Top2Vec, and BERTopic to Demystify Twitter posts. *Frontiers in Sociology*, 7.

Feng, D., Shaw, E., Kim, J., & Hovy, E. (2006, January). An intelligent discussion-bot for answering student queries in threaded discussions. In *Proceedings of the 11th International Conference on Intelligent User Interfaces* (pp. 171–177).

Gao, C., Lei, W., He, X., de Rijke, M., & Chua, T. S. (2021). Advances and challenges in conversational recommender systems: A survey. *AI Open*, 2, 100–126.

Georgescu, A. L., Pappalardo, A., Cucu, H., & Blott, M. (2021). Performance vs. hardware requirements in state-of-the-art automatic speech recognition. *EURASIP Journal on Audio, Speech, and Music Processing*, 2021(1), 1–30.

Góngora Alonso, S., Hamrioui, S., de la Torre Díez, I., Motta Cruz, E., López-Coronado, M., & Franco, M. (2019). Social robots for people with aging and dementia: A systematic review of literature. *Telemedicine and e-Health*, 25(7), 533–540.

Graesser, A. C., Person, N., Harter, D., & Tutoring Research Group. (2000). Teaching tactics in AutoTutor. Modelling human teaching tactics and strategies. *International Journal of Artificial Intelligence in Education*, 11, 1020–1029.

Gratch, J., Okhmatovskaia, A., Lamothe, F., Marsella, S., Morales, M., van der Werf, R. J., & Morency, L. P. (2006, August). Virtual rapport. In *International workshop on intelligent virtual agents* (pp. 14–27). Springer.

Grigoriadou, M., Tsaganou, G., & Cavoura, T. (2005). Historical text comprehension reflective tutorial dialogue system. *Journal of Educational Technology & Society*, 8(4), 31–41.

Grootendorst, M. (2022). BERTopic: Neural topic modeling with a class-based TF-IDF procedure. *arXiv preprint arXiv:2203.05794*.

Gunkel, D. J. (2012). Communication and artificial intelligence: Opportunities and challenges for the 21st century. *Communication+1*, 1(1), 1

Guzman, A. L. (2018). What is human-machine communication, anyway? In A. L. Guzman (Ed.), *Human-machine communication: Rethinking communication, technology, and ourselves* (pp. 1–28). New York, NY: Peter Lang.

Guzman, A. L., & Lewis, S. C. (2020). Artificial intelligence and communication: A human–machine communication research agenda. *New Media & Society*, 22(1), 70–86.

Haake, M., & Gulz, A. (2009). A look at the roles of look & roles in embodied pedagogical agents–a user preference perspective. *International Journal of Artificial Intelligence in Education*, 19(1), 39–71.

Heffernan, N. T. (2003). Web-based evaluations showing both cognitive and motivational benefits of the Ms. Lindquist tutor. In *Artificial intelligence in education* (pp. 115–122).

Hendry, D., Darari, F., Nurfadillah, R., Khanna, G., Sun, M., Condylis, P. C., & Taufik, N. (2021, October). Topic modeling for customer service chats. In *2021 International*

Conference on Advanced Computer Science and Information Systems (ICACSIS) (pp. 1–6). IEEE.

Hobert, S., & Meyer von Wolff, R. (2019). Say hello to your new automated tutor–a structured literature review on pedagogical conversational agents. In Ludwig, T. and Pipek, V. (Ed.), *14. Internationale Tagung Wirtschaftsinformatik (WI 2019) Tagungsband* (pp. 301–314).

Honeycutt, J. M., & Bryan, S. P. (2011). *Scripts and communication for relationships.* Peter Lang.

Huang, C. Y., Yang, M. C., Huang, C. Y., Chen, Y. J., Wu, M. L., & Chen, K. W. (2018, December). A chatbot-supported smart wireless interactive healthcare system for weight control and health promotion. In *2018 IEEE International Conference on Industrial Engineering and Engineering Management (IEEM)* (pp. 1791–1795). IEEE.

Huang, C. W., Chiang, T. R., Su, S. Y., & Chen, Y. N. (2020). RAP-Net: Recurrent attention pooling networks for dialogue response selection. *Computer Speech & Language, 63,* 101079.

Hussain, S , Ameri Sianaki, O., & Ababneh, N. (2019, March). A survey on conversational agents/chatbots classification and design techniques. In *Workshops of the International Conference on Advanced Information Networking and Applications* (pp. 946–956). Springer.

James, W. (1884). *What is an emotion?* Mind, os-IX, 188–205.

Jannach, D., Manzoor, A., Cai, W., & Chen, L. (2021). A survey on conversational recommender systems. *ACM Computing Surveys (CSUR), 54*(5), 1–36.

Jung, J., Song, H., Kim, Y., Im, H., & Oh, S. (2017). Intrusion of software robots into journalism: The public's and journalists' perceptions of news written by algorithms and human journalists. *Computers in Human Behavior, 71,* 291–298.

Koetter, F., Blohm, M., Kochanowski, M., Goetzer, J., Graziotin, D., & Wagner, S. (2018). Motivations, classification and model trial of conversational agents for insurance companies. *arXiv preprint arXiv:1812.07339.*

Kumari, R., Jeong, J. Y., Lee, B. H., Choi, K. N., & Choi, K. (2021). Topic modelling and social network analysis of publications and patents in humanoid robot technology. *Journal of Information Science, 47*(5), 658–676.

Laranjo, L., Dunn, A. G., Tong, H. L., Kocaballi, A. B., Chen, J., Bashir, R., … Coiera, E. (2018). Conversational agents in healthcare: A systematic review. *Journal of the American Medical Informatics Association, 25*(9), 1248–1258.

Liu, G., Nzige, J. H., & Li, K. (2019). Trending topics and themes in offsite construction (OSC) research: The application of topic modelling. *Construction Innovation, 19,* 343–366.

Lópe-Cózar, R., Silovsky, J., & Kroul, M. (2011). Enhancement of emotion detection in spoken dialogue systems by combining several information sources. *Speech Communication, 53*(9–10), 1210–1228.

Malatesta, L., Caridakis, G., Raouzaiou, A., & Karpouzis, K. (2007). Agent personality traits in virtual environments based on appraisal theory predictions. *Artificial and ambient intelligence, language, speech and gesture for expressive characters, AISB, 7.*

Malatesta, L., Raouzaiou, A., Karpouzis, K., & Kollias, S. (2009). MPEG-4 facial expression synthesis. *Personal and Ubiquitous Computing, 13*(1), 77–83.

Meng, J., Zhang, J., & Zhao, H. (2012, August). Overview of the speech recognition technology. In *2012 Fourth International Conference on Computational and Information Sciences* (pp. 199–202). IEEE.

Mensio, M., Rizzo, G., & Morisio, M. (2018, April). The rise of emotion-aware conversational agents: Threats in digital emotions. In *Companion Proceedings of the Web Conference 2018* (pp. 1541–1544).

Montenegro, J. L. Z., da Costa, C. A., & da Rosa Righi, R. (2019). Survey of conversational agents in health. *Expert Systems with Applications, 129,* 56–67.

Morrison, D., Wang, R., & De Silva, L. C. (2007). Ensemble methods for spoken emotion recognition in call-centres. *Speech communication, 49*(2), 98–112.

Nah, S., McNealy, J., Kim, J. H., & Joo, J. (2020). Communicating artificial intelligence (AI): Theory, research, and practice. *Communication Studies*, *71*(3), 369–372.

Nass, C., & Moon, Y. (2000). Machines and mindlessness: Social responses to computers. *Journal of Social Issues*, *56*, 81–103. https://doi.org/10.1111/0022-4537.00153

Oh, K. J., Lee, D., Ko, B., & Choi, H. J. (2017, May). A chatbot for psychiatric counseling in mental healthcare service based on emotional dialogue analysis and sentence generation. In *2017 18th IEEE International Conference on Mobile Data Management (MDM)* (pp. 371–375). IEEE.

Okonkwo, C. W., & Ade-Ibijola, A. (2021). Chatbots applications in education: A systematic review. *Computers and Education: Artificial Intelligence*, *2*, 100033.

Ortony, A., & Turner, T. J. (1990). What's basic about basic emotions? *Psychological Review*, *97*(3), 315.

Palacios, D., Rodellar, V., Lázaro, C., Gómez, A., & Gómez, P. (2020). An ICA-based method for stress classification from voice samples. *Neural Computing and Applications*, *32*(24), 17887–17897.

Paschoal, L. N., Krassmann, A. L., Nunes, F. B., de Oliveira, M. M., Bercht, M., Barbosa, E. F., & de Souza, S. D. R. S. (2020, October). A systematic identification of pedagogical conversational agents. In *2020 IEEE Frontiers in Education Conference (FIE)* (pp. 1–9). IEEE.

Pelachaud, C., & Bilvi, M. (2003, September). Modelling gaze behavior for conversational agents. In *International workshop on intelligent virtual agents* (pp. 93–100). Springer.

Reeves, B., & Nass, C. (1996). *The media equation: How people treat computers, television, and new media like real people and places.* Cambridge.

Russell, S., & Norvig, P. (2010). *Artificial intelligence: A modern approach* (3rd ed.). Pearson Prentice Hall.

Sánchez-Díaz, X., Ayala-Bastidas, G., Fonseca-Ortiz, P., & Garrido, L. (2018, October). A knowledge-based methodology for building a conversational chatbot as an intelligent tutor. In *Mexican International Conference on Artificial Intelligence* (pp. 165–175). Springer.

Sankar, C., Subramanian, S., Pal, C., Chandar, S., & Bengio, Y. (2019). Do neural dialog systems use the conversation history effectively? An empirical study. *arXiv preprint arXiv:1906.01603*.

Schank, R. C., & Abelson, R. (1977). *Scripts, plans, goals, and understanding.* Lawrence Erlbaum.

Skantze, G. (2021). Turn-taking in conversational systems and human-robot interaction: A review. *Computer Speech & Language*, *67*, 101178.

Song, D., & Kim, D. (2021). Effects of self-regulation scaffolding on online participation and learning outcomes. *Journal of Research on Technology in Education*, *53*(3), 249–263.

Song, X., & Xiong, T. (2021, March). A survey of published literature on conversational artificial intelligence. In *2021 7th International Conference on Information Management (ICIM)* (pp. 113–117). IEEE.

Spence, P. R., Edwards, A., Edwards, C., & Jin, X. (2019). 'The bot predicted rain, grab an umbrella': Few perceived differences in communication quality of a weather Twitterbot versus professional and amateur meteorologists. *Behaviour & Information Technology*, *38*(1), 101–109.

Sweezey, M. (2019). Consumer preference for chatbots is challenging brands to think 'bot first'. Forbes (August 16), www.forbes.com/sites/forbescommunicationscouncil /2019/08/16/consumer-preference-for-chatbots-is-challenging-brands-to-thinkbot-first/ #4407c60c10f8

Taylor, C. R. (2019). Artificial intelligence, customized communications, privacy, and the General Data Protection Regulation (GDPR). *International Journal of Advertising*, *38*(5), 649–650.

Tao, C., Feng, J., Yan, R., Wu, W., & Jiang, D. (2021, January). A survey on response selection for retrieval-based dialogues. In *IJCAI* (pp. 4619–4626).

Tao, J., & Tan, T. (2005, October). Affective computing: A review. In *International Conference on Affective Computing and Intelligent Interaction* (pp. 981–995). Springer.

Taylor, K., & Moore, S. (2006, December). Adding question answering to an e-tutor for programming languages. In *International Conference on Innovative Techniques and Applications of Artificial Intelligence* (pp. 193–206). Springer.

Tegos, S., Demetriadis, S., & Karakostas, A. (2015). Promoting academically productive talk with conversational agent interventions in collaborative learning settings. *Computers & Education, 87*, 309–325.

Thurman, N., Moeller, J., Helberger, N., & Trilling, D. (2019). My friends, editors, algorithms, and I: Examining audience attitudes to news selection. *Digital Journalism, 7*(4), 447–469.

Turing, A. M. (2009). Computing machinery and intelligence. *Mind, 59*(236), 433.

Vázquez-Cano, E., Mengual-Andrés, S., & López-Meneses, E. (2021). Chatbot to improve learning punctuation in Spanish and to enhance open and flexible learning environments. *International Journal of Educational Technology in Higher Education, 18*(1), 1–20.

Wallace, R. S. (1995). Alicebot. Retrieved February 20, 2016, from http://www.alicebot.org/

Whang, T., Lee, D., Lee, C., Yang, K., Oh, D., & Lim, H. (2019). An effective domain adaptive post-training method for bert in response selection. *arXiv preprint arXiv:1908.04812*.

Weizenbaum, J. (1966). ELIZA—A computer program for the study of natural language communication between man and machine. *Communications of the ACM, 9*(1), 36–45.

Westerman, D., Tamborini, R., & Bowman, N. D. (2015). The effects of static avatars on impression formation across different contexts on social networking sites. *Computers in Human Behavior, 53*, 111–117.

Woo, J., Ohyama, Y., & Kubota, N. (2020). Robot partner development platform for human-robot interaction based on a user-centered design approach. *Applied Sciences, 10*(22), 7992.

Yin, J., Goh, T. T., Yang, B., & Xiaobin, Y. (2021). Conversation technology with micro-learning: The impact of chatbot-based learning on students' learning motivation and performance. *Journal of Educational Computing Research, 59*(1), 154–177.

Yu, D., & Deng, L. (2016). *Automatic speech recognition (Vol. 1)*. Springer.

5. A systematic review of scholarship on metaverse

Jun Luo, Sumita Louis, and Seungahn Nah

INTRODUCTION

Thirty years after the term was first coined by science-fiction novelist Neal Stephens, (Robinson, 2022, February 9), news reports and industry experts predict a major shift for companies, universities, sports, and brands to the "metaverse" along with revenue implications from Facebook's announcement of a $10 billion investment in Facebook Reality Labs, its metaverse division (Kastrenakes & Heath, 2021) to KPMG's $30 million investment this year in Web3 experiences, with the metaverse hub as the "signature piece" (Kirmi, 2022).

It is noted that the "early 2020s technological advances and societal transformations brought about by the COVID-19 pandemic" may have led to the rush by these companies to sink in tens of billions of dollars in new investments, prompting predictions that the metaverse is "the future of the internet" or "the next internet battleground" (PEW, 2022).

But as 2022 looms to an end with the globally slow recovery from the pandemic, an ongoing war in Ukraine, ominous weather-related climate changes, and the threat of a global recession looming, these past unprecedented years (2020–2022) have also witnessed educators, journalists, students, scholars, consumers, CEOs, and industry experts debating and arguing heatedly over what the "metaverse" is and what it will bring.

Therein lies the paradox in which the "metaverse," the latest "buzzword," is touted as "a paradigm shift in technology" (Global Data, 2022, para 1) and, at the same time, is foreshadowed by dystopian fears stemming from the intrusive surveillance, algorithmic manipulation, and "weaponization" of social media, arising from the global dominance of the major platforms: Amazon, Google, Meta (formerly Facebook), Microsoft, and Apple.

Scholars point out that the dichotomy is not new, and

> the metaverse has a long way to go, but it already has a long history. The emerging version of the metaverse is overwhelmingly owned and developed by Big Tech. These companies seek to manufacture the perception that the metaverse is new and futuristic. (Boellstorff, 2022)

Key Definitions and Past Research

Definitions of the metaverse vary from media reports referring to the term as a "fully immersive internet in which we will be able to access augmented and virtual reality and interact with all sorts of environments using persistent avatars and innovative digital technology" (Marr, 2022, para. 1) to scholars referring to metaverse as "a concept used to describe 3D (three-dimensional), VWs (virtual worlds) in which people interact with each other and their environment without the physical limitations of the real world" (Narin & Kocman, 2021).

In general, the metaverse can be described as a

> computer-generated virtual space where a group of people can simultaneously interact using dedicated virtual reality (VR) instruments and as a concept is strongly linked with technologies such as augmented reality (AR), virtual reality (VR), extended virtual reality (XR) and artificial intelligence (AI). (Global Data, 2022)

Scholars and industry experts attribute the term "metaverse" to the well-known science-fiction author Stephenson (1992) in his cult novel *Snow Crash* to describe an immersive 3D virtual environment and suggest the "metaverse" can be defined as a world that has virtually enhanced physical reality and space (Riva & Wiederhold, 2022).

However, while Stephenson may well have been the earliest (or among the earliest) in America to talk about the "'metaverse' which he described as a three-dimensional digital world—a shared virtual reality (VR) experience—that allowed users to escape from a physical world that had become uninteresting," the noted anthropologist Tom Boerlstorff argues many aspects of the current metaverse were already familiar 143 years ago.

Boellstorff argues multi-user dungeons (MUDs) arose in the second half of the twentieth century and these "virtual worlds" appeared on local computer networks in the late 1970s and entered dial-up internet services in the 1980s and 1990s. He refers to Richard Bartle, co-creator of the first MUD, who noted that, by 1993, more than 10% of all internet traffic was on MUDs. Virtual worlds with graphics, including avatars, date back to *Habitat*, launched in 1985 (Boellstorff, 2022). *Habitat* was an online world that could support upwards of 15,000 users who could run businesses, play games, solve mysteries, start religions, or just hang out. Released in 1986, *Habitat* predated the likes of *Ultima Online* and *EverQuest* (the games many people think of when they think of "the first MMO") by more than a decade (Parrish, 2022).

Recent media reports agree the terms "virtual world" and "metaverse" originated much earlier. American science-fiction writer Stanley Weinbaum published the book *Pygmalion's Spectacles* in 1935, in which the main character explores a fictional world using a pair of goggles that provided sight, sound, taste, smell, and touch, very similar to Google Glass and the major tech achievements leading to the latest Quest/HTC Vive headgear, etc. (Marr, 2022).

Boellstorff argues that "at its core, the metaverse is defined by the concept of the virtual world" a sentiment echoed by communication scholar Frank Biocca who also mentions the virtual world in his early work (1997) in which he likens "the senses are the portals to the mind" and exhorts the reader to "consider for a moment the body as an information acquisition system" (pg.3). From the 1990s to today, global communication scholarship in topics related to the virtual world and metaverse has seen an impetus by both scholars and industry practitioners such as Nonny de la Pena (2010, 2014, 2016), Reis (Reis & Coelho, 2018; Reis & Ashmore, 2022) among many others.

This chapter, therefore, focuses on examining the nature of communication scholarship research with the objective of providing a brief overview of the key topics and theories that emerge from a systematic literature review (SRL) utilizing topic modeling computational analysis. The researchers conduct a search of communication journal "metaverse" articles published in the Web of Science (WoS) and Google Scholar databases between 1965–2022, identify main topic categories in a color-coded diagram, and summarize limitations and future directions for research. We hope this chapter will provide some new and useful information to researchers and scholars working in this field.

Conceptual Underpinnings

In the early 1990s, communication scholars presciently noted "the virtual environment is a communication medium" while exploring new immersive technologies. Research focused on not only the users but also on the design and development of the hardware and software needed for perceptual "sense-making" in virtual immersive environments and "worlds" in those early years and subsequent decades (Biocca, 1992, 1997; Steuer, 1992; Yee et al., 2011).

Today, research in the area of virtual worlds, platforms, and immersive environments is wide and interdisciplinary. Riva and Wiederhold's paper (2022) examines the "transformative" differences in metaverse vis-à-vis previous persuasive technologies such as television and social media. The study notes the significant difference of this new technology and examines "how the metaverse affects our brains" and maps "how different cognitive processes technology of the metaverse may be able to modify specifically focusing on the experience of being in a place and in a body, the processes of brain-to-brain attunement and synchrony, and the ability of experiencing and inducing emotions" (p. 355).

Park and Kim's taxonomy (2022), although not part of the sample analyzed for this chapter as it was published in IEEE (Institute of Electrical and Electronics Engineers), is helpful and reveals different definitions of the term "metaverse" in scholarship, listing 54 unique definitions and accompanying characteristics of the metaverse between from 1992 to 2021. They provide a baseline definition in which metaverse "is widely used in the sense of a virtual world based on daily life where both the real and the unreal coexist" (Park & Kim, 2022, pp. 4214–4215).

Benefits of Systematic Literature Review

This chapter utilizes a systematic literature review adding to extant research examining new developments and directions in the areas of immersive technology and user presence effects. However, it is noteworthy that this article (Cummings & Bailenson,

2016) was published in the *Journal for Psychology*, revealing the wide interdisciplinary research focusing on the metaverse, perhaps one reason for the low number of published communication journal articles in the WoS database.

Unlike the meta-analysis approach, which may be challenging to perform on studies with different methodological approaches (Snyder, 2019; Tranfield et al., 2003), scholars suggest that effective and well-conducted reviews as a research method create a firm foundation for advancing knowledge and facilitating theory development (Webster & Watson, 2002). Equally important, literature review as a method is more relevant than ever (Snyder, 2019) as an optimal method for synthesizing research findings on a "metalevel" that can also uncover areas in which more research is needed (Webster & Watson, 2002, p. 333).

A recent content analysis of metaverse articles (Narin & Kocman 2021) using WoS analyzes a one-day sample of 48 articles revealing most articles are classified into 33 different categories. Some articles are included in more than one category. The most published categories are "educational research" and "engineering electrical electronic" (Narin & Kocman, 2021, p. 18). This study classifies the categories of metaverse research into i) education, ii) definition and properties, iii) art on metaverse, iv) education, v) game, vi) religion, vii) cultural simulation, and viii) retailing/virtual merchandising and miscellaneous.

However, notably missing in these categories is "communication" scholarship, unless it was added into miscellaneous. This chapter extends prior research and is the first systematic review of literature in communication scholarship utilizing a latent Dirichlet allocation (LDA, Blei et al., 2003) analysis noting that there are more than 43 different theories mentioned in this sample of 543 articles in an *r* topic modeling analysis conducted in October 2022.

METHOD

During the months of August and September (2022), researchers conducted a search across the WoS using the keywords "metaverse and communication," "metaverse and journalism," and "metaverse and media."

The search results reveal a surprisingly low number of peer reviewed articles (13) from the WoS database (1965–2022) after discarding duplicate articles. The researchers then utilized the advanced search feature of Google Scholar to obtain journal articles utilizing the same set of keywords for this secondary search: metaverse or "virtual world," and specified the journal titles to contain any of the terms: communication, media, and journalism. This process yielded 556 articles at the time of searching.

Because the Google Scholar database also includes books and conference articles, the researchers cleaned this group of documents by removing duplicate articles and those not published in communication journals. We first used the list of journals in the field of communication retrieved from SSCI (Social Science Citation Index) and Scimago to filter our documents based on publication source. We then manually confirmed each of the articles to make sure it is relevant to our topic of interest by reading the headlines. For instance, articles mentioning "virtual world" may just broadly refer to the online world in which users are connected without having offline connections. Our final corpus consists of 262 documents.

We then ran all the abstracts of the journal articles into the computational model for our analysis. Previous research has investigated the possibility of retrieving key information from abstracts or headlines (Yan & Gao, 2020; Anupriya & Karpagavalli, 2015). The rationale of using abstracts rather than full articles is that an abstract already contains the key information we need to identify the topic areas most prevalent in metaverse research. Although we lose more detailed information in the full text, analyzing the abstract is sufficient to capture the major areas and topics salient in the extant literature on metaverse.

Moreover, in order to identify theories used in prior literature, we first locate the sentence containing the word "theory," "theorization," or "theoretical." We then retrieve the sentence before and after the key sentence mentioning what theory is used in the current study. We then manually group the theories and count the total number of times it is mentioned in the prior literature.

For topic modeling and semantic network analysis specifically, we implement the mixed-method approach (the analysis of topic model networks (ANTMN)) proposed by Walter and Ophir (2019). A growing body of research has applied this method to examine media frames on a variety of topics suggesting the robustness of the approach (Walter & Ophir 2021; Walter et al., 2020; Nicholls & Culpepper, 2021). The fundamental assumption of ANTMN is that topic clusters based on topic co-occurrence can be treated as framing packages that make certain aspects of an issue more salient (Walter & Ophir, 2019, pp. 250–251). This method follows a three-step process. First, an LDA topic model is trained on the corpus. Next, a topic network is constructed based on the co-occurrence of topics across documents. Lastly, network community detection algorithms are implemented to identify topic clusters. Although this method has been primarily used to analyze media framing, the idea of topic co-occurrence mimics the themes in academic literature of how previous literature has been theorizing and analyzing the topic of interest both methodologically and analytically.

Our analysis follows the following steps. We first preprocessed the corpus by removing duplicated documents. We then used the LDA function in the LDA tuning package of R to train a topic model. As demonstrated in Walter and Ophir's piece (2019), we ran tenfold cross-validation with different pairs of k and alpha (k = 2, 5, 10, 20, 30, 40, 50, alpha = 0.01, 0.05, 0.1, 0.2, 0.5). We then evaluated the performance based on perplexity scores and identified the optimal k value and alpha by calculating the maximum point for the second derivatives of all perplexity scores.

The maximum point represents the k and alpha in which we will get diminishing returns in model performance if increasing or decreasing this value (Walter et al., 2020). The optimal k and alpha value for our corpus is 20 and 0.1. We then examined the top words, top FREX words, and top 30 most representative texts for each of the 20 topics, and manually read the three types of information to assign a human-intelligible label to each topic (see Appendix Table 5.1). A topic network based on pairwise cosine similarity between topics is constructed with different community

Table 5.1   Theory mapping

Theory	Count	Theory	Count
Critical Theory	96	Lens of Migration Theory	7
Social Presence Theory	83	Media Synchronicity Theory	7
Social Capital	79	Judith Butler's Theory of Identity Performativity (1990)	6
Theory of Mind (TOM)	79	The Framework of Social Identity Model of Deindividuation Effects (SIDE)	4
Deliberative Theory	74	Self-identification Theory	4
The Theory of Social Construction of Reality	74	Deindividuation Theory	4
Grounded Theory	72	The Theory of Resilience and Relational Load	3
Social Cognitive Theory	64	Network Structuration Theory	2
The Theory of Spatial Presence	52	Gratifications Theory	2
Henri Lefebvre's Theory of Everyday Life	48	Excitation Transfer Theory	1
Storytelling Theory	36		
Deleuze's Theory of the Relations of Virtual and Actual in the Reproduction	34		
Empathy of Theory	31		
The Theory of Model Matching	22		
Feminist Theory	18		
Play Theory Proposed by William Stephenson	10		
Self-perception Theory	9		
Gratifications Theory (U&G)	9		

detection algorithms run to identify the topic clusters in our corpus (eigen, fastgreed, louvain, spinglass, walktrap). The results showed that the five network community detection algorithms return similar results (see Appendix Figure 5.1). We reported our findings based on the community detection results using the eigen algorithm in the next section.

FINDINGS

By retrieving sentences before and after the word "theory" in our corpus, we are able to obtain key theories that have been used in previous scholarly work. We find

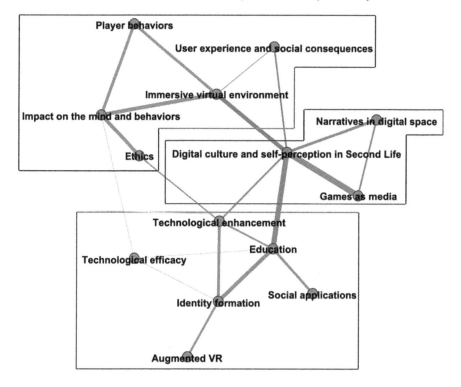

Notes: Nodes represent individual topics; edges represent co-occurrence of topics across documents; rectangle area represents topic clusters identified by the eigen algorithm.

Figure 5.1   *Topic network of literature on the metaverse and virtual world*

the most utilized lens is critical theory (96), followed by social presence theory (83), social capital theory (79), theory of mind (79), and grounded theory (64) having the most word count, which by inductive reasoning, we infer to map to the main theoretical lens/frameworks utilized by researchers. Surprisingly, empathy (31), self-perception theory (9), and uses and gratifications (UG) (9) were significantly less used (see Table 5.1).

The findings correspond to a significant increase in communication scholarship examining the metaverse through the lens of critical inquiry studies (Carter & Egliston, 2023; Chia, 2022; Bojic, 2022). One area of focus for critical scholars is critical data studies (CDS) which "takes a sociotechnical perspective to think about data's politics and power. It tends to recognize that data is not 'objective' by virtue of its scale, scope, or the speed with which it can be collected and processed" (Egliston & Carter, 2021).

Scholars drawing from the critical data studies "lens" have focused on how current and emerging forms of VR technology may cause harm and examine Oculus VR to explore "questions of inequity and harm that arise from VR as a sensing device, reliant upon the capture of data to do with the physical space around the user, and the space of the user's body" (Egliston & Carter, 2021).

Additionally, the analysis reveals that prior literature on the metaverse and virtual world falls into three categories. This is depicted by the topic clusters (Figure 5.1) consisting of articles examining different virtual gaming worlds such as *Second Life* user perceptions and experiences, social consequences of the virtual world (the topic community on the top left), technical challenges, development and application of metaverse (the topic community on the bottom), as well as metaverse as media and culture (the topic cluster on the right).

The topic community on the top left is related to user-level impact (e.g., player behaviors, impact on mind and behaviors), ethical issues, and a specific field of metaverse (e.g., immersive virtual environment). This group of scholarly works focuses on how the metaverse affects individual perception of the world and behaviors as well as discussions surrounding ethical implications of the metaverse. Ahn et al.'s study (2016) falls into this category and examines whether immersive virtual environments (IVEs) increase environmental involvement via the unmediated sensory experiences inhabiting the body of animals by humans. Participants report having a greater feeling of embodiment, perception of being in the virtual world, and connection between themselves and nature (2016).

Guadagno et al. (2007) investigate the persuasiveness of embodied agents in an immersive virtual environment. They test whether gender, behavioral realism, and agency beliefs determine the influence of avatars on attitude change. They find that behavioral realism and agency beliefs are positively associated with persuasiveness, while gender plays a moderating role (2007). In the topic of community, player behavior, researchers explore game players' motivations and self-representations in the virtual world (Zhong & Yao, 2012; Suznjevic & Matijasevic, 2010). Ethics is another area of focus with scholars exploring the ethical issues around the metaverse such as virtual property ownership, privacy, censorship vs. free speech, diffusion of toxic content, and security issues (Chew, 2011; Guidi et al., 2022).

The second topic cluster (the rectangle area on the right) views the metaverse as media and a form of culture, focusing on how the metaverse transforms digital narratives with a particular focus on game culture (Chess & Consalvo, 2022). For instance, on the topic of game as media, Chia (2022) theorizes how gaming platform tools such as "Unreal" and "Unity" consolidate power through "designing and simulating interactive 3D worlds within and beyond games" in entertainment media to other fields such as architecture and engineering (Chia, 2022).

In "digital culture and self-representation," researchers examine the virtual world *Second Life* and investigate the assimilation effects of avatars in games on users' self-judgment (Chandler et al., 2009). The study finds that whether the avatar is central to the gamer's identity largely determines how users perceive their own body judgment. Narratives in the digital space examine how immersive journalism changes with virtual technologies. For instance, Rodríguez-Fidalgo and Paíno-Ambrosio (2022) examine the change in immersive journalism in the past five years in terms of production and storytelling.

The third topic cluster at the bottom of the network focuses more on the technical and application aspects of metaverse. The topic of technological efficacy discusses VR used to develop smart and sustainable cities.

Bourhim and Cherkaoui (2019) defines VR as "a new paradigm of interaction" in which users are immersed in and actively interacting with the 3D virtual world. The article emphasizes the technical requirements, characteristics, and devices of VR. Similarly, in education, scholars have been exploring the role of *Second Life* in transforming traditional teaching practices. Mahon et al. (2010) investigate how *Second Life* and other AI tools can help facilitate student learning experiences. In their study, students report high perceived usefulness of simulation as it puts them "in situations that force them to think on their feet" (p. 121).

DISCUSSION

Research in metaverse topics published in communication journals has increased significantly. Future research methodologies may vary from surveys and interviews to more ethnographic, comparative, and longitudinal studies to examine how the different age groups from Baby Boomers, Gen X, Millennials, Gen Y, to Gen Z play, work, and learn on the metaverse. The future certainly holds many promising research possibilities.

We also suggest collaborations between communication and the other key disciplines, namely sociology, psychology, and anthropology to enable holistic critical cultural studies on the different aspects of the metaverse from the communities emerging to the brand presence to real estate which is booming today. For example, in *Sandbox*, where some plots sell for around $2,300, someone paid $450,000 in December 2021 to purchase land next to a virtual mansion owned by rap star Snoop Dogg. Since the concept of *Sandbox* originated (Boellstorff, 2022) in the earliest virtual world, *Second Life*, in 2002, past lessons from early virtual world communities and user interface changes should ideally be studied and compared.

A review article is, by nature, a limited and incomplete task because it is impossible to do justice to the enormous volume of academic publications in this field. However, in this literature review, we attempt to map the growth of this area of work by conducting one of the first LDA topic modeling reviews of literature on the topic of the metaverse and virtual world communication scholarship to date. We hope this chapter adds to ongoing conversations and leads to more interdisciplinary and global collaborations.

The PEW report (2022) also reveals survey findings which point to a noteworthy disconnect in immersive media industry experts' perspectives which is also well known among communication researchers. Thus, the proponents of XR and the development of more advanced and immersive, 3D, online worlds say its rapid evolution is likely to benefit all aspects of society, but as with all digital tech, there are concerns about the health, safety, security, privacy, and economic implications of these new spaces. This has spurred a great deal of speculation about predictions about the trajectory and impact of the metaverse by 2040 (para. 4). Critical scholarship is already focusing on this aspect, but much more remains to be explored with more academic and industry research collaborations.

REFERENCES

Anupriya, P., & Karpagavalli, S. (2015). Automatic tag recommendation for journal abstracts using statistical topic modeling. In S. Satapathy, A. Govardhan, K. Raju, & J. Mandal (Eds.), *Emerging ICT for bridging the future – Proceedings of the 49th Annual Convention of the Computer Society of India. 2. Advances in intelligent systems and computing*, 338. Springer International Publishing. https://doi.org/10.1007/978-3-319-13731-5_6

Biocca, F. (1992). Virtual reality technology: A tutorial. *Journal of Communication, 42(4)*, 23–72. https://doi.org/10.1111/j.1460-2466.1992.tb00811.x

Blei, D. M., Ng, A. Y., & Jordan, M. I. (2003). Latent Dirichlet allocation. *Journal of Machine Learning Research, 3*, 993–1022. https://doi.org/10.1016/B978-0-12-411519-4.00006-9

Boellstorff, T. (2022, August 12). The metaverse isn't here yet, but it already has a long history. *The Conversation.* https://theconversation.com/the-metaverse-isnt-here-yet-but-it-already-has-a-long-history-186083

Bojic, L. (2022). Metaverse through the prism of power and addiction: what will happen when the virtual world becomes more attractive than reality? *European Journal of Futures Research, 10(1)*, 1–24.

Bourhim, E., & Cherkaoui, A. (2019, July). How can the virtual reality help in implementation of the smart city? In *2019 10th International Conference on Computing, Communication and Networking Technologies (ICCCNT)* (pp. 1–6). IEEE.

Carter, M., & Egliston, B. (2023). What are the risks of virtual reality data? Learning analytics, algorithmic bias and a fantasy of perfect data. *New Media & Society, 25(3)*, 485–504. https://doi.org/10.1177/14614448211012794

Chandler, J., Konrath, S., & Schwarz, N. (2009). Online and on my mind: Temporary and chronic accessibility moderate the influence of media figures. *Media Psychology, 12(2)*, 210–226.

Chess, S., & Consalvo, M. (2022). The future of media studies is game studies, *Critical Studies in Media Communication, 39(3)*, 159–164. https://doi.org/10.1080/15295036.2022.2075025

Chew, M. M. (2011). Virtual property in China: The emergence of gamer rights awareness and the reaction of game corporations. *New Media & Society, 13(5)*, 722–738. https://doi.org/10.1177/1461444810378480

Chia, A. (2022). The metaverse, but not the way you think: Game engines and automation beyond game development. *Critical Studies in Media Communication, 39(3)*, 191–200. https://doi.org/10.1080/15295036.2022.2080850

Cummings, J. J., & Bailenson, J. N. (2016). How immersive is enough? A meta-analysis of the effect of immersive technology on user presence. *Media Psychology, 19(2)*, 272–309. https://doi.org/10.1080/15213269.2015.10

De la Peña, N., Weil, P., Llobera, J., Giannopoulos, J., Bernhard Spanlang, A. P., Friedman, D., Sanchez-Vives, M. V., & Slater, M. (2010). Immersive journalism: Immersive virtual reality for the first-person experience of news. *Presence: Teleoperators and Virtual Environments, 19(4)*, 291–301. https://doi.org/10.1162/PRES_a_0000

Egliston, B., & Carter, M. (2021). Critical questions for Facebook's virtual reality: Data, power and the metaverse. *Internet Policy Review, 10(4)*.

Guadagno, R. E., Blascovich, J., Bailenson, J. N., & McCall, C. (2007). Virtual humans and persuasion: The effects of agency and behavioral realism. *Media Psychology, 10*, 1–22.

Guidi, B., Ricci, L., & Michienzi, A. (2022). OASIS'22: 2nd international workshop on open challenges in online social networks. *Proceedings of the 33rd ACM Conference on Hypertext and Social Media*, 269–270. https://doi.org/10.1145/3511095.3532574

Kastrenakes, J., & Heath, A. (2021, October 25). Facebook is spending at least $10 billion this year on its metaverse division. *The Verge.* https://www.theverge.com/2021/10/25/22745381 /facebook-reality-labs-10-billion-metaverse

Kirimi, A. (2022, June 28) KPMG enters the metaverse, invests $30M in Web3 employee training. *Coin Telegraph.* https://cointelegraph.com/news/kpmg-enters-the-metaverse -invests-30m-in-web3-employee-training

Mahon, J., Bryant, B., Brown, B., & Kim, M. (2010). Using second life to enhance classroom management practice in teacher education. *Educational Media International*, *47*(2), 121–134. https://.org/10.1080/09523987.2010.492677

Marr, B. (2022, March 21). A short history of the metaverse. *Forbes.* https://www.forbes.com/ sites/bernardmarr/2022/03/21/a-short-history-of-the-metaverse/?sh=6877a6095968

Meta. (2021, October 28*). Introducing meta: A social technology company* [Press release]. https://about.fb.com/news/2021/10/facebook-company-is-now-meta

Metaverse – The Latest Buzzword. (n.d.). *Global data.* https://www.globaldata.com/data -insights/technology--media-and-telecom/metaverse-the-latest-buzzword/

Narin, N. G., & Koçman, S. M. (2021). A content analysis of the metaverse articles. *Journal of Metaverse*, *1*, 17–24. https://dergipark.org.tr/en/download/article-file/2167699

Nicholls, T., & Culpepper, P. D. (2021). Computational identification of media frames: Strengths, weaknesses, and opportunities. *Political Communication*, *38*(1–2), 159–181.

Park, S. M., & Kim, Y. G. (2022). A Metaverse: Taxonomy, components, applications, and open challenges. *IEEE Access*, *10*, 4209–4251. https://doi.org/10.1109/ACCESS.2021 .3140175.

Parrish, A. (2022, April 19). Habitat for humanity: How a classic MMO got a second life. *The Verge.* https://www.theverge.com/23025168/habitat-for-humanity-mmo-game

PEW Research Center. (2022, June 30). *The metaverse in 2040* [Report]. https://www .pewresearch.org/internet/2022/06/30/the-metaverse-in-2040/

Reis, B. A., & Ashmore, M. (2022). From video streaming to virtual reality worlds: An academic, reflective, and creative study on live theatre and performance in the metaverse. *International Journal of Performance Arts and Digital Media*, *18*(11), 7–28. https://doi.org /10.1080/14794713.2021.2024398

Reis, A. B., & Coelho, C. C. V. F A. (2018). Virtual reality and journalism. *Digital Journalism*, *6*(8), 1090–1100. https://doi.org/10.1080/21670811.2018.1502046

Riva, G., & Wiederhold, B. K. (2022). What the metaverse is (really) and why we need to know about it. *Cyber-psychology, Behavior and Social Networking*, *25*(6). https://doi.org /10.1089/cyber.2022.0124

Robinson, M. M. (2022, February 9). The metaverse will shape the future of work. Here's how. https://workplaceinsight.net/the-metaverse-will-shape-the-future-of-work-heres-how/

Rodríguez-Fidalgo, M. I., & Paíno-Ambrosio, A. (2022). Progress or regression in the practice of immersive journalism? Immersive storytelling in the productions of the Samsung VR platform between 2015 and 2020. *Journal of Print and Media Technology Research*, *11*(1), 47–63.

Snyder, H. (2019). Literature review as a research methodology: An overview and guidelines. *Journal of Business Research*, *104*, 333–339. https://doi.org/10.1016/ j.jbusres.2019.07.039.

Steur, J. (1992). Defining virtual reality: Dimensions determining telepresence, *Journal of Communication*, *4*, 73–93. https://doi.org/10.1111/j.1460-2466.1992.tb00812.x

Stephenson, N. (1992). *Snow crash.* Bantam Books.

Suznjevic, M., & Matijasevic, M. (2010). Why MMORPG players do what they do: Relating motivations to action categories. *International Journal of Advertising Media Communication*, *4*(4), 405–424. https://doi.org/10.1504/IJAMC.2010.036838

Tranfield, D., Denyer, D., & Smart, P. (2003). Towards a methodology for developing evidence-informed management knowledge by means of systematic review. *British Journal of Management, 14*(3), 207–222.

Walter, D., & Ophir, Y. (2019). News frame analysis: An inductive mixed-method computational approach. *Communication Methods and Measures, 13*(4), 248–266. https://doi.org/10.1080/19312458.2019.1639145

Walter, D., & Ophir, Y. (2021). Strategy framing in news coverage and electoral success: An analysis of topic model networks approach. *Political Communication, 38*(6), 707–730. https://doi.org/10.1080/10584609.2020.1858379

Walter, D., Ophir, Y., & Jamieson, K. H. (2020). Russian Twitter accounts and the Partisan polarization of vaccine discourse, 2015–2017. *American Journal of Public Health, 110*(5), 718–724. https://doi.org/10.2105/AJPH.2019.305564

Webster, J., & Watson, R. T. (2002). Analyzing the past to prepare for the future: Writing a literature review. *MIS Quarterly, 26*(2), xiii–xxiii. http://www.jstor.org/stable/4132319

Yan, R. & Gao, G. (2020). Topic analysis by exploring headline information. In *International Conference on Web Information Systems Engineering*, Springer, 129–142.

Yee, N., Harris, H., Jabon, M., & Bailenson, J. N. (2011). The expression of personality in virtual worlds. *Social Psychological and Personality Science, 2*(1), 5–12. https://doi.org/10.1177/1948550610379056

Zhong, Z.-J., & Yao, M. Z. (2012). Gaming motivations, avatar-self identification and symptoms of online game addiction. *Asian Journal of Communication, 23*(5), 555–573. https://doi..org/10.1080/01292986.2012.748814

APPENDIX

Table A5.1   Topic labels and top words

Topic	Topic label	Top words
1	Immersive virtual environment	virtual participants avatars effect study environment behavior avatar immersive representation
2	User experience and social consequences	virtual world experience social life can online worlds second users
3	Narratives in digital space	article digital culture within space narrative narratives spaces real world
4	Technological efficacy	metaverse reality based new technology technologies user paper blockchain development
5	Ethics	information new network sensor data coverage internet web rather load
6	Artifact	emotional journalists study work older life adults research across types
7	Artifact	system paper model human 3D user devices using environment virtual
8	Artifact	communication visual team social study findings using task research multimodal
9	Augmented VR	virtual world technology paper used provide time use performance worlds
10	Identity formation	identity body also article avatar argue central reality suggest state
11	Artifact	vr reality immersive journalism news virtual new potential technologies journalistic
12	Education	learning students virtual educational 3D teaching education support environments design
13	Social applications	digital media research social work studies online also technologies global
14	Technological enhancement	content mobile can based cultural paper information tool technology application
15	Digital culture and self-perception in *Second Life*	presence study higher video environmental results immersive compared 360-degree effects
16	Artifact	new communication cultural media intercultural practices forms future production people
17	Impact on the mind and behaviors	digital privacy may economic policy technology value legal impact first
18	Artifact	communication social media research communities change future information related approach
19	Player behaviors	game online players gaming games world player results virtual gamers
20	Games as media	game games media video studies moral play study well two

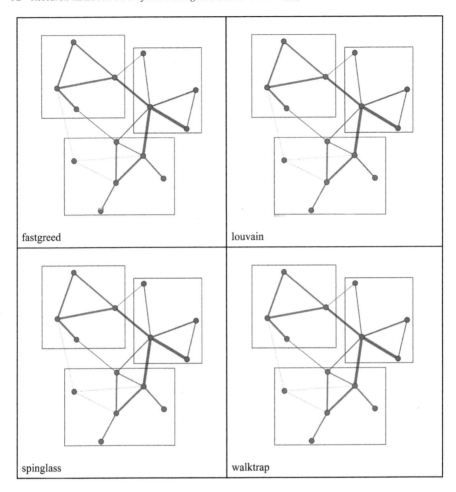

Figure A5.1   Topic clusters using different network algorithms

PART II

FRAMING ARTIFICIAL INTELLIGENCE

6. AI in schools and universities: mapping central debates through enthusiasms and concerns

Kristjan Kikerpill and Andra Siibak

INTRODUCTION

In the introduction to his landmark work on the history of instructional technology, Paul Saettler (2004, p. 3) noted that "if technology is to be completely understood, in either ancient or modern terms, it should be seen as a system of practical knowledge not necessarily reflected in things or hardware." Yet, as pointed out by Watters (2021) concerning a comparison between the original publication of Saettler's work (1968) and its later versions (1990, 2004), there exists one crucial difference – the addition of discussions about the computer and its numerous applications within the field of education. Thus, while technology is not solely understood as hardware, technological advancements such as the computer (see Taylor, 2018) are part and parcel of the process of education (Ferster, 2014). Even so, it is essential not to lose sight of the social and cultural contexts within the current technological status quo (Watters, 2021). Taken in isolation, technology achieves surprisingly little in terms of disrupting education as such (Reich, 2020), regardless of how "hyped" such technologies are in our current or future imaginaries (e.g., Ferster, 2014; Humble & Mozelius, 2019; Watters, 2021).

Artificial intelligence (AI) and its numerous applications in the educational field are no exception: it comes with its history (see Colbourn, 1985; Tuomi, 2018; Ye et al., 2021; Schiff, 2021), present state (Zhang & Aslan, 2021), and future imaginaries (Pinkwart, 2016). The proven or proclaimed benefits of integrating AI-based solutions into education (see Baker & Smith, 2019; Murphy, 2019; Zhang & Aslan, 2021; see also Reich, 2020) are accompanied by significant concerns (Hagendorff, 2020; Mascheroni & Siibak, 2021; Akgun & Greenhow, 2021; see also Zawacki-Richter et al., 2019) and risks (Swauger, 2021; Schiff, 2021). While AI is touted and promoted as a solution to numerous issues within the education sector (see Chounta et al., 2021), we currently lack a standard definition and understanding of what AI is (Zawacki-Richter, 2019, p. 10).

Keeping the above in mind, our chapter focuses on AI-based applications' impact on learning, teaching, and managing schools as institutions (see Baker & Smith, 2019). Thus, we exclude issues concerned with curriculum design for learning about AI (see, e.g., Luckin & Cukurova, 2019). Given that the implications of introducing AI-based solutions into educational settings go beyond learning and teaching (see, e.g., Mascheroni & Siibak, 2021), it is imperative to also include discussions on the system management aspects of AI in education (AIED), which are rapidly entrenching us in a logic of "governance by numbers" (Neumann, 2019) and ubiquitous digital surveillance (Hope, 2016; Kikerpill & Siibak, 2023). Thus, to gain a more nuanced understanding of the current state of AIED, we provide a critical overview of the enthusiasms and concerns shaping the debates concerned with implementing AI-based solutions into the everyday practices of K-12 schools and higher education institutions.

LEARNING, TEACHING, AND ORGANIZING WITH AI

As Chounta and colleagues (2021, p. 2) note concerning formal education, AI-supported applications are heralded as "the potential solution to nearly – every 'problem'" in the classroom (or lecture hall). Nevertheless, these solutions are also accompanied by concerns about ethics and privacy (Akgun & Greenhow, 2021; Lameras & Arnab, 2022). Furthermore, given the costs of these new technologies, scholars have also been doubtful if such smart computation is able to bring added value to the majority of students (Chin et al., 2010).

Much like the various possible meanings of the term "artificial intelligence" (see, e.g., Holmes et al., 2019), the literature on the use of modern "teaching machines" (Watters, 2021) is littered with specialist jargon. In fact, some authors prefer to use "augmented intelligence" (see Holmes et al., 2019, pp. 195–196) instead of "AI" to clearly distinguish the fact that machines are a support to humans, not their competitors. Unfortunately, definitional issues are not restricted to just AI itself. For instance, in a review article covering 20 years of research activity in the AIED community, Roll and Wylie (2016) begin their reflection by referring to "interactive learning environments," or ILEs. Later reviews (Zawacki-Richter et al., 2019; Zhang & Aslan, 2021; Ouyang et al., 2022) do not include this specialist term, even though all such reviews cover studies that essentially focus on computer systems (or "machines") with which a student or teacher can interact to complete educational tasks or assess progress. Hence, the first functional notion to look for with AI-based solutions in the context of learning and teaching is the types of interaction it allows students or teachers to engage in.

Learner-Facing AI in Schools

From the learners' perspective, the use of such "teaching machines" to augment (Holmes et al., 2019; see also Taylor, 2018), if not replace (see Selwyn, 2019), the activities of human teachers or tutors come down to replicating the interactions inherent in the social exercise that is education (Jonassen et al., 1995; Zawacki-Richter et al., 2019). This leads us to discussions of personalized learning, i.e., "instruction in which the pace of learning and the instructional approach are optimized for the needs of each learner" (US Department of Education, 2017, p. 9), with the help of machines, which is not a novel concept and not specific to AI (Watters, 2021). Moreover, AI-based solutions in education all use domain-specific, or narrow, AI, i.e., the domain in which the AI solutions operate "is tightly constrained and very limited, and the AI, despite its sophistication, cannot be directly applied to any other domain" (Holmes et al., 2019, p. 208). Thus, the experience of learners is, at any point in time, constrained to interacting with a particular interface or solution, e.g., a learning platform (such as Knewton, see Holmes et al., 2019) or an intelligent tutoring system made available on the platform (such as Knewton's *alta*).

The aforementioned platforms also function as "adaptive learning systems" (see Oxman & Wong, 2014; Baker & Smith, 2019), i.e., environments that enable the "presentation of learning resources (e.g., content, support or navigation) in a dynamic form" (Imhof et al., 2020, p. 93). According to Oxman & Wong (2014, p. 2), adaptive learning involves at least three components. "a model of the content to be learned (content model), a means of understanding student abilities (a learner model), and a method of matching the content and how it is presented to the student in a dynamic and personalized fashion (an instructional model)." In effect, modern AI-based learning tools are often just variations on adaptive learning platforms (Holmes as cited in Baker & Smith, 2019, p. 11). Hence, learner-facing AI solutions strive to augment the efforts of teachers by providing step-based tutoring systems, i.e., providing the same level of attention to detail for a larger number of students and presenting students with content that is adapted to their current level of knowledge and skill. All of the above, however, would "enable the collection of mass data about which teaching, and learning practices work best" and, thereby, enable finding the "best teaching practices suited for the development of ... 21st century skills" (Luckin et al., 2016, p. 34).

In a review of early intelligent tutoring systems, Nwana (1990, p. 252) described ITSs as "computer programs that are designed to incorporate techniques from the AI community in order to provide tutors who know *what* they teach, *who* they teach and *how* to teach it" (emphasis in original). Currently, intelligent tutoring systems are defined as a "computer learning environment that helps students master knowledge and skills by implementing intelligent algorithms that adapt to students at a fine-grained level and that instantiate complex principles of learning" (Graesser et al., 2018, p. 246). A review study by VanLehn (2011) suggested that intelligent tutoring systems are almost on par with human tutors if the ITS is step-based, i.e., the interaction between tutor and tutee has more granularity than answer-based tutoring systems. In a K-12 setting, i.e., from primary and lower- and upper secondary school, the outcomes and effects of ITS use have been studied concerning reading comprehension (McCarthy et al., 2018; Xu et al., 2019), mathematics (Steenbergen-Hu & Cooper, 2013; Walkington & Bernacki, 2018), and chemistry (McLaren et al., 2011). According to Zawacki-Richter and colleagues (2019), studies on the use of intelligent tutoring systems in higher education cover teaching course content such as computer science, mathematics, or writing and reading comprehension, facilitating collaboration between students, providing automated feedback, and curating learning materials based on students' needs. Here, it is important to note that most studies on the use of ITSs in higher education cover only short-term periods, e.g., a semester, and longer-term impacts are understudied (Zawacki-Richter et al., 2019; see also Reich, 2020).

More recently, scholars have asserted that "AI can now offer a one-of-a-kind precise solution for each individual" (Yang, 2021, p. 105). According to Davies and colleagues (2021, p. 551), "AI-enabled transformation is valued as transformative and emancipatory; able to remedy obsolete and dysfunctional education systems that are limiting people's potential." Therefore, inspired in particular by the success of precision medicine, academics have promoted and urged the adoption of a precision education approach (for a systematic review on machine-learning-based precision education, see Luan & Tsai, 2021). By conducting diagnoses of student engagement, learning patterns, and behavior, scholars working in the field aim to make predictions concerning students' learning performance and, in doing so, identify at-risk students as early as possible (Yang, 2021). Moreover, proponents of the approach also strive to provide timely interventions and improve teaching quality to influence students' learning performance (Yang 2021, p. 106).

In recent years, interest has grown in "affective computing" (Williamson, 2017), which relies on the development of edtech systems, in particular, biometric technologies, that monitor and collect physiological data from students to surveil their "engagement" in learning (Andrejevic & Selwyn, 2019). The techniques of affective computing can include speech analysis applications that can detect emotion from the human voice as well as textual sentiment analysis that can be performed through natural language processing, tone, or linguistic analysis (Williamson, 2017). Most commonly, however, facial analysis and machine vision algorithms are used for detecting "facial microexpression states" (Chiu et al., 2014), i.e., facial states lasting less than half a second. The information obtained through such scanning is believed to provide insights into what the learners are thinking. It is also used as an indicator of students' (non-)engagement, i.e., acting as evidence of frustration, surprise, delight, confusion, or boredom (Dewan et al., 2019). Put briefly, the movement in learner-facing educational tools has been from "one-size-fits-all to precision" (Yang et al., 2021).

Teacher-Facing Tools and Managing the System

From the teachers' perspective, augmenting the ability to manage a classroom (or university course) and ensure – to the extent possible – that everyone is receiving the instruction they need is vital (see Chounta et al., 2021). A systematic review of research (Celik et al., 2022) revealed three categories of AI advantages: planning (e.g., decision-making, planning learning content, and provision of information on student backgrounds), implementation (e.g., enabling timely monitoring of learning processes, providing immediate feedback, reducing teacher workload, selecting or adapting optimum learning activity, and tracking student progress), and assessment (such as exam automation, essay scoring, and decision-making on student performance).

AI can also be used to identify who the slow learners are within the classroom (Murphy, 2019). For example, log file and clickstream analyses can enable the teachers to predict learner success (Crossley et al., 2016). In areas in which students tend to be weaker, additional steps can be taken by teachers to support their learning with AI analysis (Fahimirad & Kotamjani, 2018). Thus, teacher-facing tools primarily fulfill the role of providing teachers with a more nuanced understanding of how students learn and how such learning is influenced by prior knowledge, ways of teaching, learning, and physical contexts (see Lameras & Arnab, 2022). It must be noted here that many learner-facing tools concurrently operate as teacher-facing tools (Zawacki-Richter et al., 2019), but teachers' perspectives are usually not the point of emphasis. This choice or preference in perspective is an exciting notion in its own right, the reasons for which are unclear.

Crucially, however, reports on how teachers could use AI-based applications (e.g., Baker & Smith, 2019; Murphy, 2019) and how teachers would use or perceive the use of AI (e.g., Chounta et al., 2021) suggest a gap between technology enthusiasm and the utility of or willingness toward real-world adoption (see Kim & Kim, 2022). For instance, teachers mainly assess their knowledge of AI as either limited or fair (Chounta et al., 2021), and a lack of knowledge is reported as an element of teachers' resistance to AI systems (Nazaretsky et al., 2022). Such resistance or skepticism can also be related to the assumption that the growing use of AI within education may "shift the locus of expertise and power from teachers and school administrators towards programmers or system designers" (Berendth et al., 2020, p. 317) who are responsible for creating these technological solutions and, therefore, shifting public responsibilities and powers to private actors.

Nevertheless, even if teachers' perceptions of AI are optimistic, there is still a need to further educate the educators to achieve successful technology integration (Kim & Kim, 2022). Even so, overconfidence in one's knowledge about the functioning of AI-based systems could lead to subsequent struggles with such systems because of false perceptions (Chounta et al., 2021). Thus, professional development programs and interventions are being implemented to bridge the gap of academic resistance or distrust toward AI-based teacher tools (see Nazaretsky et al., 2022). Hence, which AI-based teacher-facing tools will become mainstream, and to what extent, remains to be seen. Not in the least because adopting such technologies may not always be the best course of action to begin with (Taylor, 2018; Reich, 2020). Alongside reports of AI-based teacher-facing tools currently tested or in use (Zawacki-Richter et al., 2019), there exists a significant focus on comprehending teachers' perceptions and designing interventions for the development of knowledge required to better understand and operate AI-based tools. Future studies that empirically investigate learner-facing AI tools could, at the same time, account for teachers' or instructors' actual experiences with such tools.

Regardless of certain elements of academic resistance, the modern edtech business is flourishing and expected to grow by more than 40% between 2021 and 2027 (Global Market Insights, 2021). In large part due to the rise of academic capitalism, the marketization of education, and the emergence of accountability policies in which words such as "assessment," "accountability," "evidence-based," "efficiency," and "testing" have taken a central stage (see Tröhler & Maricic, 2021, p. 1). The measurement of almost everything has become central to the modern-day educational experience. Chasing performance targets and a need to continually demonstrate one's improvement have driven schools toward a data-driven managerial practice closely connected to the neoliberal tendencies to view technology as a superior objective mechanism necessary for improving organizations (Harvey, 2007). More specifically, it is believed that the predictive and diagnosis models that can be built with the help of AI enable empowerment and support of various management decisions that need to be made both on the school, region, or country level (OECD, 2020).

Various AI applications and techniques have become extremely helpful for educational institutions by enabling them to collect and analyze different types of data. For example, other AI techniques are used for predicting admission decisions (Chen & Do, 2014), students' course selection behavior (Kardan et al., 2013), or dropout rates (Delen, 2011). AI applications, in particular chatbots, are often used in higher education institutions for supporting recruitment, emotional support, academic advising processes, or admission. On those occasions, chatbots take the role of customer support systems which help to provide the students answers on a variety of topics from enrollment processes and finances to specific course requirements or survey students' emotional well-being (Hannan & Liu, 2021). As students expect satisfactory and user-friendly services and quick responses to their queries, the adoption of AI applications in this regard has a considerable impact on the time management and duties of administrative staff in educational institutions (Ahmad et al. 2022). In some higher education institutions, cognitive AI programs have also started replacing in-person admission interviews to eliminate potential human biases (Hannan & Liu, 2021; Wang, 2021). Therefore, data has, thus, become a powerful tool for social regulation, as it does not simply represent educational subjects and contexts but also actively reconstitutes them (Williamson, 2016).

CONCERNS WITH THE USE OF AI IN EDUCATION: LEARNERS, TEACHERS, AND THE SYSTEM

As mentioned, using AI-based tools creates a significant amount of data about learners, which can then be used to make assessments and predictions (Luckin et al., 2016). Although learning analytics are in active use in K-12 education settings, a recent systematic review (Murchan & Siddiq, 2021) reports that ethical and regulatory issues, e.g., validity or fairness, related to the use of process data, have sparked almost no interest in the research community. As such, this suggests that current research efforts have mainly focused on exploring "how to process data" (Murchan & Siddiq, 2021, p. 24) while almost entirely avoiding the questions of why and how this data is being used and the type of impact this might have on the participants. For instance, studies suggest that linking academic performance predictions with academic openings or university job applications could seriously impact the candidate's future prospects (Berendt, Littlejohn, Kern, et al. 2017). More critical voices, coming from the field of critical data studies, even argue that in the above-described processes, students are treated as "data objects" (Koopman, 2019) rather than "data owners" (Broughan & Prinsloo, 2020) who could either opt-out from the increasing dataveillance, or exercise their agency by acting as partners in discussions about what data is collected, for whom, and for what purposes. Furthermore, such practices also require the adoption and acceptance of a highly reductive and decontextualized pedagogic logic, which views students as data rather than as human beings (Lewis & Holloway, 2019). Thus, as Berendt, Littlejohn, and Blakemore (2020, p. 321) posit, "there is an urgent need to make sure that learners and teachers, rather than technology companies and organisations, are the main beneficiaries as AI tools are developed, marketed and embedded in education."

As argued by Selwyn (2016, p. 13), one of the more prominent critical voices on the field, new edtech gadgets and technologies often tend to underestimate the complexity of student lives and, thus, "exacerbate discriminatory decision-making in favour of those social groups most represented in the systems' datasets," which leads to considerable data harm (Lupton, 2020). Hence, as education sociologists claim (Davies et al., 2021, p. 556), "AI is unlikely to level the playing field in any meaningful way: particularly if it mainly benefits already privileged learners." For example, during the COVID-19 pandemic, many higher education institutions started using e-proctoring systems, i.e., systems "formed by electronic tools that allow the monitoring of the remote evaluative process through telematic resources, trying to make the results reliable" (González-González et.al. 2020, p. 2) in the hopes of curing the academic cheating problem. However, the uptake of such technologies resulted in many student petitions and legal actions both in the United States (US) and in the European Union (EU) (e.g., EDRi, 2021). Such reactions by the students were, on the one hand, caused by the plethora of problems related to student privacy, security, and ethical values, e.g., transparency, justice, fairness, trust, responsibility, and accountability of such systems (Nigam et al., 2021). On the other hand, students were upset about the numerous technical problems and false positives that have also been noted in comprehensive overviews of available online proctoring software (Arnó et al., 2021). In particular, studies suggest that proctoring software mainly tends to misclassify students of color, the disabled, and students living in low-income households (Henry & Oliver, 2022; Arnó et al., 2021) and is, therefore, likely to cause "data violence" (Hoffman, 2021), i.e., disproportionate harm, on communities that are already marginalized and non-dominant (Swauger, 2021).

Moreover, due to this vastly expanding measurement regime, scholars have started to criticize edtech for redefining, simplifying, and reducing the concept of learning (see Perrotta & Selwyn, 2020). In short, in the era of learning analytics, only the information that shows up in the data, i.e., only the learning that the data makes visible, is considered learning, and all the information that cannot be quantified, measured, and compared is not considered learning and is. Therefore. marginalized (Knox et al., 2020), and the work of a teacher becomes data managed, subject to normative processes of algorithmic exposure to measurement (Ross & McLeod, 2018, p. 235). Furthermore, many of the AI techniques are based on a mechanical and inductivist epistemology that assumes patterns to be interpretable the same way across all cultures and contexts, when, in fact, AIED is not neutral but infused in politics and specific cultural values (Perrotta & Selwyn, 2020).

CONCLUSION

In the chapter, we have shown how educational institutions, from early years to higher education alike, have become accustomed to using a multitude of AI applications in various ways. Fascination with new technologies in the education sector is nothing novel. Both in early twentieth century and current edtech parlance, technology is often imagined or promoted as a type of liberator that frees teachers "for those inspirational and thought-stimulating activities which are, presumably, the real function of the teacher" (Pressey, 1926, p. 374 as cited in Holmes et al., 2019, p. 95). However, the reality of the educational field also includes examples in which retaining technology is seemingly favored in place of human instructors (see, e.g., Feathers, 2020), even though overzealous reliance on edtech has often led to less than stellar outcomes (Watters, 2019). Hence, educational technology should always be understood as a complex combination of technological components in their material form, e.g., hardware, software, and services tightly intertwined with the multifaceted social contexts of learning, teaching, and schools as institutions (see Table 6.1).

According to Feenberg (2002, p. 92), "the ambivalence of computer technology can be summarised in two principles that describe the social implications of technological advance." These principles concern the conservation of existing hierarchies and, conversely, the undermining of current hierarchies. For instance, machines could be used to increase surveillance of human actors and, therefore, exert more control, or the technology could provide people with new and innovative ways of communicating, which fosters a broader exchange of ideas. The direction depends on how the technology in question is applied (Feenberg, 2002). For example, AI-assisted analysis of student-produced content can ease the checking and grading of essays (Hannan & Liu, 2021) or exert control over students' school and online activities (Hope, 2016, 2018). Even with a similar technological approach, the entailed social implications can be vastly different.

In the above sense, AI applications are no different from other computer technologies. However, because researchers are prone to suffering from historical amnesia (Feenberg, 2002), matters of utopian or dystopian futures re-emerge for technologies that capture the imagination of the public (e.g., Schiff, 2021). One crucial aspect that distinguishes educational technology from other fields in which AI-based solutions are applied is the "material" on which a particular technology impresses, i.e., the students. In other words, material objects on an assembly line – unlike students in the process of acquiring an education – do not espouse opinions or express emotions about the methods and approaches to their formation. To make AI tools a fully viable option for the future of education, proponents of new technologies should distance themselves from naively enthusiastic claims and foster a more multifaceted understanding of the complexity of modern education – something that has yet to be fixed by a single tool, AI-based or otherwise.

Table 6.1   Current enthusiasms and concerns about implementing AI in learning, teaching and school management

	Learner-facing solutions	Teacher-facing solutions	Administration and management
Enthusiasms	Improved performance and personalized approaches: • ability to adapt educational tools to each student's needs; "precision education" • more detailed assessment of students' learning habits, retention rates, and emotional states during the learning process • intelligent tutoring systems on par with human teachers, which supports individual progress (outside of face-to-face learning)	Reshaping the role of teachers and offering support: • time spent on repetitive tasks is reduced, freeing up resources for more personal engagement with students • personalized and detailed overview of student progress, potential failures, and emotional well-being through data analytics • improved assessment of student performance, including AI-assisted grading	Efficiency in management: • screening in teacher hiring • decision-making in student admission • assessment of dropout rates and course selection • use of chatbots in administrative communication and emotional support • decreased time costs in responding to student queries • use of cognitive AI programs to increase objectivity in student admission interviews • day-to-day scheduling and school bus route optimization
Concerns	Digital surveillance, lack of privacy, and reducing students to data points: • vast amounts of data collected from student activities, while data protection knowledge remains low (for students, parents, and teachers) • constant surveillance of students through excessive data collection, including outside of school hours and/or classroom activities • normalization of privacy-violating technologies • over-reliance on data-based decisions and the deterioration of the role of moral decision-making	Reduced roles for and importance of the human element: • shifting public responsibilities and powers to private technology companies that provide AI solutions • overcorrection from "flying blind" (data-rich, but information-poor) to "education by numbers" (over-reliance on data analytics) • algorithmic decision-making in teacher evaluation and bias in the hiring process • resistance to adopting and integrating AI solutions due to lack of knowledge and transparency	Bias (and its reinforcement) in decision-making: • human bias introduced into algorithms • automated decision-making based on biased data, including gender, race, and disability-related bias • inadequate accuracy of school safety systems that use facial recognition • over-reliance on "objective technologies" that leads to reinforcement of existing inequalities

REFERENCES

Ahmad, S. F., Alam, M. M., Rahmat, M. K., Mubarik, M. S., & Hyder, S. I. (2022). Academic and administrative role of artificial intelligence in education. *Sustainability*, *14*(3), 1101. https://doi.org/10.3390/su14031101

Akgun, S., & Greenhow, C. (2021). Artificial intelligence in education: Addressing ethical challenges in K-12 settings. *AI and Ethics*, *2*, 431–440. https://doi.org/10.1007/s43681-021-00096-7

Andrejevic, M., & Selwyn, N. (2019). Facial recognition technology in schools: Critical questions and concerns. *Learning, Media and Technology*, *45*(2), 115–128. https://doi.org/10.1080/17439884.2020.1686014

Arnò, S., Galassi, A., Tommasi, M., Saggino, A., & Vittorini, P. (2021). State-of-the-Art of Commercial Proctoring Systems and Their Use in Academic Online Exams. *International Journal of Distance Education Technologies*, *19*(2), 55–76. http://doi.org/10.4018/IJDET.20210401.oa3

Baker, T., & Smith, L. (2019). *Educ-AI-tion rebooted? Exploring the future of artificial in schools and colleges*. Nesta. https://media.nesta.org.uk/documents/Future_of_AI_and_education_v5_WEB.pdf

Berendt, B., Littlejohn, A., & Blakemore, M. (2020). AI in education: Learner choice and fundamental rights. *Learning, Media and Technology*, *45*(3), 312–324. https://doi.org/10.1080/17439884.2020.1786399

Berendt, B., Littlejohn, A., Kern, P., Mitros, P., Shacklock, X., & Blakemore, M. (2017). *Big data for monitoring educational systems*. Publications Office of the European Union. https://data.europa.eu/doi/10.2766/38557

Broughan, C., & Prinsloo, P. (2020). (Re)centring students in learning analytics: In conversation with Paulo Freire. *Assessment & Evaluation in Higher Education*, *45*(4), 617–628. https://doi.org/10.1080/02602938.2019.1679716

Celik, I., Dindar, M., Muukkonen, H., & Järvelä, S. (2022). The promises and challenges of artificial intelligence for teachers: A systematic review of research. *TechTrends*, *66*(4), 616–630. https://doi.org/10.1007/s11528-022-00715-y

Chen, J.-F., & Do, Q. H. (2014). Training neural networks to predict student academic performance: A comparison of cuckoo search and gravitational search algorithms. *International Journal of Computational Intelligence and Applications*, *13*(1), 1450005. https://doi.org/10.1142/S1469026814500059

Chin, D. B., Dohmen, I. M., Cheng, B. H., Oppezzo, M. A., Chase, C. C., & Schwartz, D. L. (2010). Preparing students for future learning with teachable agents. *Educational Technology Research and Development*, *58*(6), 649–669. https://doi.org/10.1007/s11423-010-9154-5

Chiu, M.-H., Chou, C.-C., Wu, W.-L., & Liaw, H. (2014). The role of facial microexpression state (FMES) change in the process of conceptual conflict. *British Journal of Educational Technology*, *45*(3), 471–486. https://doi.org/10.1111/bjet.12126

Chounta, I.-A., Bardone, E., Raudsep, A., & Pedaste, M. (2022). Exploring teachers' perceptions of artificial intelligence as a tool to support their practice in Estonian K-12 education. *International Journal of Artificial Intelligence in Education*, *32*, 725–755. https://doi.org/10.1007/s40593-021-00243-5

Colbourn, M. J. (1985). Applications of artificial intelligence within education. *Computers & Mathematics with Applications*, *11*(5), 517–526. https://doi.org/10.1016/0898-1221(85)90054-9

Crossley, S., Paquette, L., Dascalu, M., McNamara, D. S., & Baker, R. S. (2016). Combining click-stream data with NLP tools to better understand MOOC completion. In *Proceedings of the Sixth International Conference on Learning Analytics & Knowledge* (pp. 6–14). ACM. https://doi.org/10.1145/2883851.2883931

Davies, H. C., Eynon, R., & Salveson, C. (2021). The mobilisation of AI in education: A Bourdieusean field analysis. *Sociology*, *55*(3), 539–560. https://doi.org/10.1177/0038038520967888

Dewan, M. A. A., Murshed, M., & Lin, F. (2019). Engagement detection in online learning: A review. *Smart Learning Environments*, *6*, 1. https://doi.org/10.1186/s40561-018-0080-z

Delen, D. (2011). Predicting student attrition with data mining methods. *Journal of College Student Retention: Research, Theory & Practice*, *13*(1), 17–35. https://doi.org/10.2190/CS.13.1.b

EDRi. (2021). *Civil society calls for AI red lines in the European Union's artificial intelligence proposal.* https://edri.org/our-work/civil-society-call-for-ai-red-lines-in-the-european-unions-artificial-intelligence-proposal/

Fahimirad, M., & Kotamjani, S. S. (2018). A review of on application of artificial intelligence in teaching and learning in educational contexts. *International Journal of Learning and Development*, *8*(4), 106–118.

Feathers, T. (2020). *NYC is paying $2 million for anti plagiarism software after firing teachers.* VICE. https://www.vice.com/en/article/88amvk/cuny-paying-2-million-dollars-anti-plagiarism-software

Feenberg, A. (2002). *Transforming technology: A critical theory revisited.* Oxford University Press.

Ferster, B. (2014). *Teaching machines: Learning from the intersection of education and technology.* Johns Hopkins University Press.

Global Market Insights. (2021). *Artificial intelligence (AI) in education market size worth $20 bn by 2027.* https://www.gminsights.com/industry-analysis/artificial-intelligence-ai-in-education-market

Graesser, A. C., Hu, X., & Sottilare, R. (2018). Intelligent tutoring systems. In F. Fischer, C. E. Hmelo-Silver, S. R. Goldman, & P. Reimann (Eds.), *International handbook of the learning sciences* (pp. 246–255). Routledge.

Hagendorff, T. (2020). The ethics of AI ethics: An evaluation of guidelines. *Minds and Machines*, *30*, 99–120. https://doi.org/10.1007/s11023-020-09517-8

Hannan, E., & Liu, S. (2023). AI: New source of competitiveness in higher education. *Competitiveness Review* (Advance online publication), *33*(2), 265–279. https://doi.org/10.1108/CR-03-2021-0045

Harvey, D. (2007). *A brief history of neoliberalism.* Oxford University Press.

Henry, J. V., & Oliver, M. (2022). Who will watch the watchmen? The ethico-political arrangements of algorithmic proctoring for academic integrity. *Postdigital Science and Education*, *4*, 330–353. https://doi.org/10.1007/s42438-021-00273-1

Hoffmann, A. L. (2021). Terms of inclusion: Data, discourse, violence. *New Media & Society*, *23*(12), 3539–3556. https://doi.org/10.1177/1461444820958725

Holmes, W., Bialik, M., & Fadel, C. (2019). *Artificial intelligence in education: Promises and implications for teaching and learning.* The Center for Curriculum Redesign.

Hope, A. (2016). Biopower and school surveillance technologies 2.0. *British Journal of Sociology of Education*, *37*(7), 885–904. https://doi.org/10.1080/01425692.2014.1001060

Hope, A. (2018). Creep: The growing surveillance of students' online activities. *Education and Society*, *36*(1), 55–72. https://doi.org/10.7459/es/36.1.05

Humble, N., & Mozelius, P. (2019). Artificial intelligence in education – a promise, a threat or a hype? In P. Griffiths, & M. N. Kabir (Eds.), *Proceedings of the European Conference on the Impact of Artificial Intelligence and Robotics* (pp. 149–156). Academic Conferences and Publishing International Ltd.

Imhof, C., Bergamin, P., & McGarrity, S. (2020). Implementation of adaptive learning systems: Current state and potential. In P. Isaias, D. G. Sampson, & D. Ifenthaler (Eds.), *Online teaching and learning in higher education. Cognition and learning in the digital age* (pp. 93–115). Springer. https://doi.org/10.1007/978-3-030-48190-2_6

Jonassen, D., Davidson, M., Collins, M., Campbell, J., & Haag, B. B. (1995). Constructivism and computer-mediated communication in distance education. *American Journal of Distance Education, 9*(2), 7–26. https://doi.org/10.1080/08923649509526885

Kardan, A. A., Sadeghi, H., Ghidary, S. S., & Sani, M. R. F. (2013). Prediction of student course selection in online higher education institutes using neural network. *Computers & Education,* 65, 1–11. https://doi.org/10.1016/j.compedu.2013.01.015

Kikerpill, K., & Siibak, A. (2023). Schools engaged in doom-monitoring students' online interactions and content creation: An analysis of dominant media discourses. *Child and Adolescent Mental Health, 28*(1), 76–82. https://doi.org/10.1111/camh.12621

Kim, N.-J., & Kim, M.-K. (2022). Teacher's perceptions of using an artificial intelligence-based educational tool for scientific writing. *Frontiers in Education.* https://doi.org/10.3389/feduc.2022.755914

Knox, J., Williamson, B., & Bayne, S. (2020). Machine behaviourism: Future visions of 'learnification' and 'datafication' across humans and digital technologies. *Learning, Media and Technology, 45*(1), 31–45. https://doi.org/10.1080/17439884.2019.1623251

Koopman, C. (2019). *How we become our data: The genealogy of the informational person.* University of Chicago Press.

Lameras, P., & Arnab, S. (2022). Power to the teachers: An exploratory review on artificial intelligence in education. *Information, 13*(1), 14. https://doi.org/10.3390/info13010014

Lewis, S., & Holloway, J. (2019). Datafying the teaching 'profession': Remaking the professional teacher in the image of data. *Cambridge Journal of Education, 49*(1), 35–51. https://doi.org/10.1080/0305764X.2018.1441373

Luan, H., & Tsai, C.-C. (2021). A review of using machine learning approaches for precision education. *Educational Technology & Society, 24*(1), 250–266.

Luckin, R., Holmes, W., Griffiths, M., & Forcier, L. B. (2016). *Intelligence unleashed: An argument for AI in education.* Pearson.

Luckin, R., & Cukurova, M. (2019). Designing educational technologies in the age of AI: A learning sciences-driven approach. *British Journal of Educational Technology, 50*(6), 2824–2838. https://doi.org/10.1111/bjet.12861

Lupton, D. (2020). *Data selves: More-than-human perspectives.* Polity Press.

Mascheroni, G., & Siibak, A. (2021). *Datafied childhoods: Data practices and imaginaries in children's lives.* Peter Lang.

McCarthy, K. S., Likens, A. D., Johnson, A. M., Guerrero, T. A., & McNamara, D. S. (2018). Metacognitive overload!: Positive and negative effects of metacognitive prompts in an intelligent tutoring system. *International Journal of Artificial Intelligence in Education, 28,* 420–438. https://doi.org/10.1007/s40593-018-0164-5

McLaren, B. M., DeLeeuw, K. E., & Mayer, R. E. (2011). Polite web-based intelligent tutors: Can they improve learning in classrooms? *Computers & Education, 56*(3), 574–584. https://doi.org/10.1016/j.compedu.2010.09.019

Murchan, D., & Siddiq, F. (2021). A call to action: A systematic review of ethical and regulatory issues in using process data in educational assessment. *Large-scale Assessments in Education, 9,* 25. https://doi.org/10.1186/s40536-021-00115-3

Murphy, R. F. (2019). Artificial intelligence applications to support K-12 teachers and teaching: A review of promising applications, challenges, and risks. *Perspectives.* RAND. https://doi.org/10.7249/PE315

Nazaretsky, T., Ariely, M., Cukurova, M., & Alexandron, G. (2022). Teachers' trust in AI-powered educational technology and a professional development program to improve it. *British Journal of Educational Technology, 53*(4), 914–931. https://doi.org/10.1111/bjet.13232

Neumann, E. (2019). Setting by numbers: Datafication processes and ability grouping in an English secondary school. *Journal of Education Policy, 36*(1), 1–23. https://doi.org/10.1080/02680939.2019.1646322

Nigam, A., Pasricha, R., Singh, T., & Churi, P. (2021). A systematic review on AI-based proctoring systems: Past, present and future. *Education and Information Technologies, 26,* 6421–6445. https://doi.org/10.1007/s10639-021-10597-x

Nwana, H. S. (1990). Intelligent tutoring systems: An overview. *Artificial Intelligence Review, 4,* 251–277. https://doi.org/10.1007/BF00168958

OECD. (2020). *Trustworthy AI in education: Promises and challenges.* https://www.oecd.org /education/trustworthy-artificial-intelligence-in-education.pdf

Ouyang, F., Zheng, L., & Jiao, P. (2022). Artificial intelligence in online higher education: A systematic review of empirical research from 2011 to 2020. *Education and Information Technologies, 27*(6), 7893–7925. https://doi.org/10.1007/s10639-022-10925-9

Oxman, S., & Wong, W. (2014). *White paper: Adaptive learning systems.* Integrated Education Solutions.

Perrotta, C., & Selwyn, N. (2020). Deep learning goes to school: Toward a relational understanding of AI in education. *Learning, Media and Technology, 45*(3), 251–269. https://doi.org/10.1080/17439884.2020.1686017

Pinkwart, N. (2016). Another 25 years of AIED? Challenges and opportunities for intelligent educational technologies of the future. *International Journal of Artificial Intelligence in Education, 26,* 771–783. https://doi.org/10.1007/s40593-016-0099-7

Reich, J. (2020). *Failure to disrupt: Why technology alone can't transform education.* Harvard University Press.

Roll, I., & Wylie, R. (2016). Evolution and revolution in artificial intelligence in education. *International Journal of Artificial Intelligence in Education, 26,* 582–599. https://doi.org /10.1007/s40593-016-0110-3

Ross, J., & Macleod, H. (2018). Surveillance, (dis)trust and teaching with plagiarism detection technology. In M. Bajić, N. B. Dohn, M. de Laat, P. Jandrić, & T. Ryberg (Eds.), *Proceedings of the 11th International Conference on Networked Learning* (pp. 235–242). Networked Learning Conference. https://www.networkedlearningconference.org.uk/abstracts/papers/ ross_25.pdf

Saettler, L. P. (2004). *The evolution of American educational technology.* Information Age Publishing.

Schiff, D. (2021). Out of the laboratory and into the classroom: The future of artificial intelligence in education. *AI & Society, 36*(1), 331–348. https://doi.org/10.1007/s00146-020 -01033-8

Selwyn, N. (2016). 'There's so much data': Exploring the realities of data-based school governance. *European Educational Research Journal, 15*(1), 54–68. https://doi.org/10 .1177/1474904115602909

Selwyn, N. (2019). *Should robots replace teachers? AI and the future of education.* Polity Press.

Steenbergen-Hu, S., & Cooper, H. (2013). A meta-analysis of the effectiveness of intelligent tutoring systems on K-12 students' mathematical learning. *Journal of Educational Psychology, 105*(4), 970–987. https://doi.org/10.1037/a0032447

Swauger, S. (2021). Our bodies encoded: Algorithmic test proctoring in higher education. In J. Stommel, C. Friend, & S. M. Morris (Eds.), *Critical digital pedagogy: A collection* (Chapter 6). Pressbooks. https://cdpcollection.pressbooks.com/chapter/our-bodies-encoded -algorithmic-test-proctoring-in-higher-education/

Taylor, E. S. (2018). *New technology and teacher productivity.* https://scholar.harvard.edu/ files/erictaylor/files/technology-teachers-jan-18.pdf

Tröhler, D., & Maricic, V. (2021). Data, trust and faith: the unheeded religious roots of modern education policy. *Globalisation, Societies and Education, 19*(2), 138–153. https://doi.org /10.1080/14767724.2021.1872371

Tuomi, I. (2018). *The impact of artificial intelligence on learning, teaching, and education.* Publications Office of the European Union. https://doi.org/10.2760/12297

U.S. Department of Education. (2017). *Reimagining the role of technology in education: 2017 national education technology plan update.* Office of Educational Technology. https://tech.ed.gov/files/2017/01/NETP17.pdf

VanLehn, K. (2011). The relative effectiveness of human tutoring, intelligent tutoring systems, and other tutoring systems. *Educational Psychologist, 46*(4), 197–221. https://doi.org/10.1080/00461520.2011.611369

Walkington, C., & Bernacki, M. L. (2018). Personalizing algebra to students' individual interests in an intelligent tutoring system: Moderators of impact. *International Journal of Artificial Intelligence in Education, 29*, 58–88. https://doi.org/10.1007/s40593-018-0168-1

Wang, Y. (2021). When artificial intelligence meets educational leaders' data informed decision-making: A cautionary tale. *Studies in Educational Evaluation, 69*, 100872. https://doi.org/10.1016/j.stueduc.2020.100872

Watters, A. (2019). The 100 worst ed-tech debacles of the decade. *Hack Education.* http://hackeducation.com/2019/12/31/what-a-shitshow

Watters, A. (2021). *Teaching machines: The history of personalized learning.* MIT Press.

Williamson, B. (2016). Digital education governance: Data visualization, predictive analytics, and 'real-time' policy instruments. *Journal of Education Policy, 31*(2), 123–141. https://doi.org/10.1080/02680939.2015.1035758

Williamson, B. (2017). Moulding student emotions through computational psychology: Affective learning technologies and algorithmic governance. *Educational Media International, 54*(4), 267–288. https://doi.org/10.1080/09523987.2017.1407080

Xu, Z., Wijekumar, K., Ramirez, G., Hu, X., & Irey, R. (2019). The effectiveness of intelligent tutoring systems on K-12 students' reading comprehension: A meta-analysis. *British Journal of Educational Technology, 50*(6), 3119–3137. https://doi.org/10.1111/bjet.12758

Yang, S. J. H. (2021). Guest editorial: Precision education – a new challenge for AI in education. *Educational Technology & Society, 24*(1), 105–108.

Yang, S. J. H., Ogata, H., Matsui, T., & Chen, N.-S. (2021). Human-centered artificial intelligence in education: Seeing the invisible through the visible. *Computers and Education: Artificial Intelligence, 2*, 100008. https://doi.org/10.1016/j.caeai.2021.100008

Ye, R., Sun, F., & Li, J. (2021). Artificial intelligence in education: Origin, development, and rise. In X. J. Liu, Z. Nie, J. Yu, F. Xie, & R. Song (Eds.), *Intelligent robotics and applications. ICIRA 2021. Lecture notes in computer science* (pp. 545–553). Springer. https://doi.org/10.1007/978-3-030-89092-6_49

Zawacki-Richter, O., Marin, V. I., Bond, M., & Gouverneur, F. (2019). Systematic review on artificial intelligence applications in higher education – where are the educators? *International Journal of Educational Technology in Higher Education, 16*, 39. https://doi.org/10.1186/s41239-019-0171-0

Zhang, K., & Aslan, A. B. (2021). AI technologies for education: Recent research & future directions. *Computers and Education: Artificial Intelligence, 2*, 100025. https://doi.org/10.1016/j.caeai.2021.100025

7. How news organizations and journalists understand artificial intelligence: application of news language database to AI-related news stories

Jeongsub Lim

INTRODUCTION

Robots work in diverse industries, including car manufacturing, distribution companies, restaurants, and even university campuses and libraries for the delivery of books. They are effective in processing complex calculations at a fast pace and setting up systematic elements into a whole structure without significant interference from human workers, a process known as automation. For instance, if we want to extract underlying patterns or meanings from multiple texts, we can develop an algorithm that allows a robot to identify keywords within the texts and connect different words that appear in similar sentences. From this analysis, the robot can construct semantic networks or clusters comprising those keywords. By looking at the networks or clusters and differentiating each network or cluster with a distinct color (e.g., red, blue, or black), the robot can recommend specific types of viable concepts.

The news industry is not an exception, as people tend to show a favorable attitude toward coverage by an algorithm-based system. Citizens perceive stories as less biased and more credible when they are produced by either a robot or a robot working alongside a human reporter (Waddell, 2019). Additionally, individuals who consume news through social networking services (SNS) and trust others consider news reported by a robot to be credible (Lee et al., 2020). News organizations have already adopted robot-based news management systems for producing breaking stories and other news articles. The specific patterns of adoption vary based on the resources and accumulated experiences of each news organization across countries in applying robot journalists to the newsroom. *Diario Huarpe*, an Argentinian newspaper, developed a robot to produce approximately 250 stories about football and 3,000 stories about weather every month (Oliver, 2022). The *Miami Herald* launched a bot to write real estate stories in two to three paragraphs (O'Neill, 2021). Additionally, major news outlets like *Forbes*, the Associated Press, Bloomberg, and the *Guardian* have implemented robot journalists to produce stories not only about sports but also breaking news and politics (Deluca, 2021).

Given the popularity of robots, important questions remain unanswered: how do news organizations and journalists understand robot journalists, and how do they construct news texts regarding artificial intelligence (AI) or robots? Answers to these questions would reveal the perceptions and attitudes of news workers when they deal with robots in writing or reporting stories. Identifying these underlying patterns could help researchers, citizens, and even journalists to reflect on the implications of robots for the news ecosystem and facilitate a friendly coexistence or collaboration between human journalists and robot journalists. By analyzing textual elements in AI-related stories, we can detect subtle strategic or routinized approaches to the phenomenon of AI in the news market. The strategies or routines are institutionalized in the daily workings of a news organization, which could influence journalists' perceptions of their roles or identities as they are challenged by robot counterparts. The degree of the institutionalization may vary based on the nature of the news organization and its approach to adopting robot journalists into the newsroom.

Further, the present study expects that epistemological approaches to robot-based news production will stimulate a more democratic quality of news and improve current journalism practices. These practices have been suffering from issues such as fabrication or disinformation, low credibility, and deteriorating news consumption. The present study employs a computational method for story collection and analysis, which enhances analytical speed and necessitates cross-checking for any errors in analytical codes. The computational method has established itself in the academic field as a valid approach for conducting scientific analysis on diverse, large-scale textual or numerical data. A group of scholars refers to this approach as "computational social science" and even "computational communication science" due to its application in communication research (Shah et al., 2015).

ARTIFICIAL INTELLIGENCE-BASED NEWS PRODUCTION SYSTEM

The word "algorithm" is not a refreshing novelty in the newsrooms of major countries with a massive digital information market. Code-driven news production has already established its presence in primary news organizations, but whether this production secures a substantial status in the newsroom remains uncertain. In the scholarly literature, terms such as algorithm journalism, automated journalism, or robot journalism refer to news-making patterns that lack direct intervention or guidance from professional journalists in producing and circulating news stories and related content. These terms concern the ways of creating news content by using statistical information and a set of relevant phrases (van Dalen, 2012). Algorithms convert datasets into news content once humans choose specific programming (Carlson, 2015).

This line of news-making is part of algorithm journalism, whose categories include automatic content production, such as robot journalists; data mining; algorithm-based news distribution; and algorithm-based content optimization (Kotenidis & Veglis, 2021). Adopting such AI journalism gains convincing support because readers perceive news stories produced by robot journalists as objective and similar to those written by professional journalists (Clerwall, 2014). Such a positive perception among news consumers could facilitate more AI-based news production across diverse news outlets worldwide, reflecting a trend in data science and AI research. News organizations anticipate the advantages of applying AI techniques to content production and distribution, which holds substantial potential for improving the efficiency of news operations and generating revenue through the management of databases. Automation based on AI expands the boundaries of news and allows journalists to move away from writing straight news, encouraging them to seek refreshing, revealing patterns and meanings (Carlson, 2015). When the algorithm in news production maintains accuracy and objectivity, robot journalists do not miss facts, experience fatigue, or display biases (Latar, 2014). Furthermore, robot journalists process information in ways similar to traditional journalists for news production (Dörr, 2016).

Some traditional journalists show critical views toward emerging robot journalists in the newsroom. They refute the idea that such diverse features as analytical skills, personality, creativity, and language capability to understand complex syntax are essential for producing news stories (van Dalen, 2012). How to write a story is more important than the techniques to guarantee factuality, objectivity, simplicity, and efficiency. In this sense, the high quality of news stories requires the power of storytelling and dramatic elements that are not automated (Latar, 2014).

Given this critical position, establishing varying degrees of collaboration between traditional news desks and algorithm-based news desks is a primary element for the success of robot journalists in the newsrooms and their potential for advancing the quality of journalism. To facilitate this collaboration, news organizations need to understand how robot journalists work. Robot journalists take their approaches from two perspectives: social physics and algorithms without human intervention (Latar, 2014). From the standpoint of social physics, computer programming extracts new knowledge, and automatic analysis of digital data reveals social trends and theories. For instance, narrative science developed Quill, a natural language processing platform which identifies urgent facts, trends, or problems for corporations and represents them in text (Narrative Science, 2016).

The operative scheme of how robot journalists write a news story comprises distinct steps. One example includes data collection, event extraction, key event selection, tone determination, and story formation (Kim & Lee, 2015; Yang et al., 2017). Data collection refers to fetching data from websites through API codes, and event extraction identifies meaningful events in the data using interpretive rules based on specific criteria. API stands for application programming interface, which allows two software devices to communicate with each other using a set of rules or contracts. Key event selection determines a primary event by assigning varying weights to each event, and tone determination chooses certain viewpoints or tones when describing an event, such as "home team won". Story formation organizes sentences explaining a key event according to a chosen tone.

Yonhap News Agency, a Korean national wire service, emulates the way traditional journalists write stories, which is based on databases of diverse stories those journalists wrote (Seo, 2017). "Soccerbot", a sports robot journalist from this agency,

Table 7.1   *Application of a robot journalist by news organizations at home and abroad*

Organization	Name	Launch	Area
Maeil Business News	INet	2018. 6	stocks
Sedaily	Sekyung Newsbot	2017. 12	stocks
Herald Biz	HeRo	2017. 1	stocks
FN News	fnRASSI	2016. 6	stocks
ET News	ETbot	Not available	stocks
EToday	e2BOT	Not available	stocks
IDaegu	ape	2017. 10	baseball
New York Times	Editor	2015. 7	fact checking
Washington Post	Heliograf	2016. 8	election/sports
Guardian	Chatbot	2016.1 1	technology
AP	Automated Insights	2019. 2	sports, economy
Forbes	Bertie	2018. 7	content management

writes a story through the procedures of data collection, sentence formation, and vocabulary revision. A crawler collects information such as players' names, location, and Korean players' playing. After the game, the robot journalist checks any errors in the information, selects words and expressions fitting the situation, and revises sentences and story structure. The robot journalist has a template algorithm for writing sentences and a situation decision engine that checks the results, which leads to writing stories for a similar game situation.

Table 7.1 shows the status of robot journalists in the news organizations in South Korea and other primary countries, adapted from prior research (Lim, 2021).

Interesting patterns emerge from Table 7.1. Korean news organizations dispatch robot journalists to a limited area, such as stock markets or sports, implying that the robot journalists play a supportive role to traditional journalists by focusing on one or two topical areas. News organizations in other countries show a contrast in their approach. They let robot journalists cover various topics such as elections, fact checking, or breaking news stories. This difference results from how each news organization develops their AI-based news production system. Korean news organizations rely on an outsourcing partner, Thinkpool (http://info.thinkpool.com/), a stock investment company that developed AI-based analytic procedures for stock trading.

NEWS LANGUAGE DATABASE

As a two-year research project, the author has developed a news language database that could contribute to AI-based news making. The database contains 40,909 words with 40 variables, which were derived from a systematic analysis of news stories collected over two years. For the first year, the present study set up two sets of two weeks each to decide specific days for collecting news stories and editorials from news organizations. The time periods ranged from August 1, 2020 (Saturday) to September 9, 2020 (Wednesday) for the first part of the two weeks and from November 6, 2020 (Friday) to November 2, 2020 (Wednesday) for the second part of the two weeks.

The news organizations included top ten national daily newspapers (*Chosun Ilbo, DongA Ilbo, JoongAng Ilbo, Maeil Business News, Korea Economic Daily*, Hankyoreh, *Munhwa Ilbo, Hankook Ilbo, Kyunghyang Shinmun, Seoul Shinmun*) and three national television networks (Korean Broadcasting System (KBS), Seoul Broadcasting System (SBS), and Munhwa Broadcasting Corporation (MBC)). Research assistants collected a straight-news story and a feature story from each of the nine topical areas, including politics, economy, or society, and two editorials. The procedure yielded 20 texts a day from each of the 13 outlets, resulting in a total of 7,280 texts for all the outlets over the data collection periods.

For the second year, the time periods ranged from August 22, 2021 (Sunday) to September 30, 2021 (Thursday) for the first two weeks, and November 11, 2021 (Saturday) to December 2, 2021 (Thursday) for the second two weeks. The same procedure was applied for collecting stories and editorials, but the number of outlets increased to 30, including 13 news organizations used in the first year of the project. These 13 outlets included four comprehensive programming channels (JTBC, Channel A, TV Chosun, MBN), two news channels (Yonhap News TV, YTN), five local daily newspapers (*Busan Ilbo, Maeil Shinmun, Kookje Shinmun, Yeongnam Ilbo, Kangwon Ilbo*), three internet-only news organizations (Ohmynews, Moneytoday, Wikitree), and three news agencies (Yonhap News, Newsis, News1). By using the same criteria, this study collected 20 stories and editorials from each of the 30 outlets each day during the two sets of the two-week periods, which yielded 16,800 texts. The size of collected texts for the second year was 2.3 times larger than that for the first year (7,280). A recently published article reported analytical results by applying a first-year version of the database (Lim, 2021). Table 7.2 shows a framework of a news language database with its categories and variables developed by prior research (Lim, 2021, pp. 435).

The following explains how the 40 variables were created in the database. First, basic concepts such as structure, category, or subcategory were developed from prior research (Diesner & Carley, 2005 for categories such as knowledge or resource and subcategories such as group or action; Pan & Kosicki, 1993 for news discourse structure; Sadia & Ghani, 2019 and Simpson, 2005 for modality; van Dijk, 1983 for subcategories such as explanation or interpretation).

The framework comprises semantic, script, rhetorical, and syntactic structure, and each structure includes corresponding categories, subcategories, and variables. For instance, in the semantic structure of news stories, the category of "person" comprises a public person, a private person, and slang. Each variable has an ID number. In the script structure, the "resource" category includes an explanation for cause and effect, context/background and situation/scene, and tones (positive, negative,

Table 7.2   *Results of categories, subcategories, and variables in the news language database*

Structure	Category	Subcategory	Variable (ID)
Semantic	Person	public person	public person (1)
		private person	private person1 (2)
		slang	private person2 (3)
Script	Resource	explanation	explanation1 (4) – cause-effect:
			explanation2 (5) – context/background:
			explanation3 (6) – situation/scene
		tones	positive (7), negative (8), neutral (9)
	Knowledge	follow-up	follow-up1 (10) – consequences
			follow-up2 (11) – reactions
Rhetorical	Resource	visualization	visualization1 (12) – information
			visualization2 (13) – situation
		description	description (14)
		state	state (15)
		metaphor	metaphor (16)
	Knowledge	episode	episode1 (17) – previous information
			episode2 (18) – antecedents
		commentary	commentary1 (19) – evaluations
			commentary2 (20) – expectations
Semantic	Resource	relation	relation (21)
		interpretation	interpretation (22)
	Group	group	group (23)
	Action	action	action (24)
	Event/task	event/task	event/task (25)
Syntactic	Content	Japanese word	Japanese word (26)
		foreign word	foreign word (27)
	Tense	tense	present (28), past (29), future (30)
	Verb form	passive	passive (31), double passive (32)
		active	active (33)
	Expression	modality	true modality (34), obligation modality (35)
		orality	orality1 (36) – conversation
			orality2 (37) – source quotation
		literacy	literacy1 (38) – fact delivery
			literacy2 (39) – opinion expression
		universality	universality (40)

and neutral). The "knowledge" category contains follow-up for consequences and reactions.

Regarding tones, this study focused on positive, negative, and neutral, which were determined using two sources: SentiWord_Dict.txt and Korean Sentiment Dictionary–KHU-SentiWordNet0415.xlsx. The first came from the Data Intelligence Lab at the Kusan National University and was available on the Github website (https://github.com/park1200656/KnuSentiLex/blob/master/SentiWord_Dict.txt). The second was from the Business School research team at Kyung Hee University (http://datascience.khu.ac.kr/board/bbs/board.php?bo_table=05_01&wr_id=269&page=1). Furthermore, this study evaluated the tones of news words that were not in the two sources.

Japanese and foreign words are additional subcategories that the framework considers because Korean people and journalists tend to use many Japanese and foreign words or expressions in their daily conversations and texts. This situation reflects the historical background when Japan colonized Korea for 35 years, and since then, the United States has intervened and maintained its military presence in the country. In the syntactic structure, the framework focused on tense (present, past, future), verb form (passive, active), and expression (modality, orality, literacy, and universality).

METHOD

In the South Korean context, the present study focused on two types of primary news organizations regarding AI: one without having robot journalists and one with experience of launching robot journalists. Prior researchers (Baek & Lim, 2018; Lim, 2021) surveyed the status of robot journalists in the Korean news industry, which provides a reliable list of primary news organizations adopting robot journalists. The news organizations having no robot journalists comprised two national daily newspapers (*Chosun Ilbo, Hankyoreh*) and one television network (KBS). Another group of news organizations adopting robot journalists included two national daily newspapers (*Maeil Business, Sedaily*) and a television network (SBS).

The present study entered a broad search term, "AI" or "robot", into search windows of each website of these news organizations and collected the most recent 200 stories written by journalists from each of them. From those stories, the present study identified patterns showing how news organizations and journalists understand AI by applying the news database to the stories through the "quanteda" package. The package extracted words within a context, created a document-feature matrix and co-occurrence matrix, visualized its results (Benoit, 2018), and analyzed large texts at a fast pace based on C++ language and parallel processing (Benoit, et al., 2018). Prior researchers showed relevant codes that processed pre-processing procedures, created a document-feature matrix, and extracted meaning (Welbers et al., 2017). Given these advantages, the quanteda package was applied to the analysis of texts for finding frames (Lim, 2019, 2020; Rojas-Garcia & Faber, 2019) or identifying keywords in newspaper stories (Segesten & Bossetta, 2019). Specific codes were available upon request, and the following shows an example of the codes.

```
dfm_NLD <- dfm(f, what = "word", verbose = FALSE, remove_number = TRUE,
               remove_punct = TRUE, remove_symbols = TRUE,
               remove_separators = TRUE, dictionary = dict)
dict_dfm <- dfm(f, select = dict, verbose = FALSE)
NLD_combined <- cbind(dfm_NLD, dict_dfm)
NLD_df <- convert(NLD_combined, to = "data.frame"); dim(NLD_df)
```

In the example codes, 'dict' referred to the news language database that the present study developed from the two-year projects. 'NLD_df' contained the 200 news stories and words matching those in the database. For instance, the stories from the *Chonsun Ilbo* yielded 5,296 matched words. The present study sought specific variables and their proportions within the stories. To find the relations, the present study first transformed the database into a long format that allowed each word to have all corresponding variables. Next, joining NLD_df with the transformed database shows the variables, their frequencies, and proportions appearing in the stories. The following tables present these outcomes.

RESULTS

First, the present study shows findings from news organizations that have not operated robot journalists, as shown in Tables 7.3, 7.4, and 7.5.

The coverage of AI or robots by the *Chosun Ilbo* revealed as many variables (*N* = 38) as other news organizations, implying the newspaper applied diverse news language elements to portray AI or robots. Stories in *Hankyoreh* and KBS showed 37 and 35 variables, while those of the *Maeil Business*, *Sedaily*, and SBS yielded 34, 36, and 35 variables, respectively. None of the news organizations used all 40 variables in the news language database for the coverage of AI or robots, though their usages were substantial.

Given this difference, *Chosun Ilbo's* most- and least-used variables were similar to those of the other news organizations, regardless of the experiences of AI or robot journalists in the newsroom. "Fact delivery" (variable name: literacy1), "neutral tone", "previous information" (episode1), "foreign words" (foreign), and "event/task" (task) were primary elements the newspaper highlighted in covering the issue. These elements made up the top five variables appearing in the coverage of the other five newspapers and television networks as well. In the present study, the newspapers and television networks were interested in providing straight facts about AI or robots in a neutral tone with a focus on prior relevant information, foreign expressions, and incidents. The neutral tone and usage of foreign words make sense given the

Table 7.3   *Coverage patterns of Chosun Ilbo regarding AI*

Variable (N = 38)	Freq	Prop	Variable	Freq	Prop
literacy1	5,256	28.39	relation	19	0.10
neutral	4,667	25.21	explanation2	16	0.09
episode1	4,497	24.29	past	12	0.06
foreign	1,019	5.50	commentary2	9	0.05
task	554	2.99	episode2	6	0.03
positive	405	2.19	explanation1	6	0.03
universality	347	1.87	metaphor	6	0.03
explanation3	318	1.72	future	5	0.03
group	241	1.30	interpretation	5	0.03
negative	227	1.23	private person2	4	0.02
private person1	163	0.88	follow-up1	2	0.01
active	110	0.59	follow-up2	2	0.01
state	110	0.59	passive	2	0.01
public person	103	0.56	double passive	1	0.01
present	102	0.55	obligation modality	1	0.01
commentary1	94	0.51			
Japanese	77	0.42	orality2	1	0.01
action	44	0.24	true modality	1	0.01
orality1	43	0.23	visualization1	1	0.01
description	38	0.21	Total	18,514	100

journalistic objectivity/neutrality and the way artificial intelligence (AI) is written as "AI", "robot", or other related expressions in Korean. Prior information was a dominant element because news stories contained what occurred in the past, comprising diverse pieces of information collected by journalists from different beats.

The other interesting similar patterns included "context/background" (variable name: explanation2), "expectations" (commentary2), "cause and effect" (explanation1), and "interpretation", which were at the middle or lower ranks in the frequency of the variable usage. Investigative reporting or data journalism emphasizes explaining why certain events occurred in a historical context and interpreting their implications for society. However, regarding the issues of AI or robots, the interpretive approach did not take conspicuous presence in the stories. The less focus on in-depth story telling led to an inevitable result, such as disregarding consequences (variable name: follow-up1) or reactions (follow-up2).

Tables 7.6, 7.7, and 7.8 show outcomes from the news organizations that have operated robot journalists.

Table 7.4   *Coverage patterns of Hankyoreh regarding AI*

Variable (N = 37)	Freq	Prop	Variable	Freq	Prop
literacy1	6,217	28.46	description	38	0.17
neutral	5,543	25.37	explanation2	28	0.13
			past	18	0.08
episode1	5,259	24.07	relation	15	0.07
foreign	960	4.39	commentary2	11	0.05
task	676	3.09	episode2	8	0.04
positive	444	2.03	explanation1	8	0.04
explanation3	398	1.82	interpretation	7	0.03
group	396	1.81	follow-up1	6	0.03
universality	385	1.76	follow-up2	4	0.02
negative	274	1.25	future	4	0.02
private person1	219	1	metaphor	4	0.02
active	150	0.69	private person2	4	0.02
public person	144	0.66	passive	3	0.01
Japanese	141	0.65	obligation modality	1	0
present	136	0.62			
state	122	0.56	orality2	1	0
commentary1	114	0.52	true modality	1	0
action	60	0.27	visualization2	1	0
orality1	47	0.22	Total	21,847	100

In terms of the usage of language elements across the six news organizations, the five least-used variables varied with each news organization. In the stories of the *Chosun llbo*, "visualization of information" (variable name: visualization1), "true modality", "conversation" (orality2), "obligation modality", and "double passive" were less frequently present. "Visualization of situation", "true modality", "conversation", "obligation modality", and "passive" were highlighted the least in *Hankyoreh*. In contrast, "visualization of information" (visualization1), "passive", "metaphor", "future tense", and "consequences" (follow-up1) were the variables KBS used less frequently.

The newspapers and television networks that use robot journalists show some differences. "Slang" (variable name: private person2), "opinion expression" (literacy2), "antecedents" (episode1), "visualization of information" (visualization1), and metaphor were the least-used variables in *Maeil Business*. "Visualization of situation" (visualization2), "visualization of information" (visualization1), "true modality", "future tense", and "passive" comprised the five least-used variables for *Sedaily*. SBS focused less on "true modality", "conversation" (orality2), "visualization of information" (visualization1), "future tense", and "slang" (private person2).

Table 7.5   Coverage patterns of KBS regarding AI

Variable (N = 35)	Freq	Prop	Variable	Freq	Prop
literacy1	2,620	29.08	action	15	0.17
neutral	2,358	26.17	description	14	0.16
episode1	2,222	24.66	explanation2	12	0.13
task	297	3.30	past	7	0.08
foreign	272	3.02	follow-up2	5	0.06
universality	238	2.64	relation	5	0.06
positive	198	2.20	commentary2	3	0.03
explanation3	138	1.53	episode2	2	0.02
negative	103	1.14	interpretation	2	0.02
group	94	1.04	private person2	2	0.02
private person1	78	0.87	true modality	2	0.02
state	57	0.63	explanation1	1	0.01
active	53	0.59	follow-up1	1	0.01
commentary1	51	0.57	future	1	0.01
present	50	0.56	metaphor	1	0.01
orality1	43	0.48	passive	1	0.01
public person	39	0.43	visualization1	1	0.01
Japanese	23	0.26	Total	9,009	100

From these differences, a slight common pattern emerged. The six news organizations were not willing to focus on visualizing information and situation when covering AI or robot issues. Visualization could have the potential to help citizens to understand the meanings and implications of AI by relating it to their personal lives. With the weak emphasis on visualization, news organizations and journalists did not seem proactive in delivering AI-related information in a realistic and tangible way.

Further, the six news organizations relied on many Japanese words for the coverage of AI or robots, as these words ranked in the middle. This shows the cultural dependency of South Korean news-making on the usage of Japanese words or expressions, reflecting the historical context

During the Japanese occupation, Japanese journalistic culture imbued its peculiar types of practices and terminologies into the Korean newsroom, guiding how to organize beat reporting and write a news story.

DISCUSSION AND CONCLUSION

The present study is interested in identifying unique elements in journalistic understanding of AI or robots in news-making processes by focusing on the South Korean

Table 7.6   *Coverage patterns of Maeil Business regarding AI*

Variable (N = 34)	Freq	Prop	Variable	Freq	Prop
literacy1	2,499	28.75	action	16	0.18
neutral	2,217	25.51	explanation2	11	0.13
episode1	2,192	25.22	description	10	0.12
foreign	460	5.29	orality1	7	0.08
task	310	3.57	relation	7	0.08
positive	212	2.44	past	6	0.07
universality	153	1.76	commentary2	4	0.05
group	131	1.51	explanation1	2	0.02
explanation3	115	1.32	follow-up1	2	0.02
negative	76	0.87	follow-up2	2	0.02
private person1	44	0.51	future	2	0.02
commentary1	41	0.47	interpretation	2	0.02
active	39	0.45	metaphor	2	0.02
public person	35	0.40	visualization1	2	0.02
state	33	0.38	episode2	1	0.01
present	32	0.37	literacy2	1	0.01
Japanese	25	0.29	private person2	1	0.01
			Total	8,692	99.99

news industry. Despite its narrow scope in only one country setting, its findings could go beyond these limitations because the study developed a novel tool – the "news language database", containing 40 variables and 40,909 corresponding words. The database has theoretical utilities, as the variables were based on prior news discourse studies and the words could be translated into other languages, such as English. In terms of its application, the database could be applied to textual settings of other countries that guarantee diverse news organizations and a wide distribution of digital news. Through the procedures, proper nouns (e.g., names, locations, organizations) could be replaced with those corresponding to the situation in a country, as the proper nouns in the database represent those in the Korean context. This consideration is what the present study contributes to the existing research.

By applying the database, the present study detected distinct similarities and differences between the newspapers and television networks that have no experience or experience of operating robot journalists. The categories that each news organization uses the least frequently for coverage of AI or robots vary. However, the similarities surpassed the differences. So, the present study focuses on similarities, which reveal underlying rules or routines in the newsroom of each news organization regarding how to approach AI or robots. While producing stories, the news organizations portray AI or robots with past factual information and foreign terminology in a neutral

Table 7.7   *Coverage patterns of Sedaily regarding AI*

Variable (N = 36)	Freq	Prop	Variable	Freq	Prop
literacy1	3,520	28.69	description	20	0.16
neutral	3,120	25.43	explanation2	20	0.16
episode1	3,061	24.95	orality1	12	0.10
foreign	561	4.57	past	12	0.10
task	451	3.68	commentary2	5	0.04
positive	285	2.32	metaphor	5	0.04
universality	209	1.70	explanation1	4	0.03
explanation3	191	1.56	follow-up2	4	0.03
group	160	1.30	interpretation	4	0.03
negative	126	1.03	private person2	4	0.03
private person1	86	0.70	relation	4	0.03
active	70	0.57	episode2	3	0.02
present	64	0.52	follow-up1	3	0.02
Japanese	61	0.50	passive	3	0.02
state	61	0.50	future	2	0.02
public person	57	0.46	true modality	2	0.02
commentary1	51	0.42	visualization1	1	0.01
action	24	0.20	visualization2	1	0.01
			Total	12,267	100

way. Facts and foreign words or expressions are primary pieces of information when readers pay attention to the stories. These seem to be natural consequences given that news coverage deals with questions of who, what, when, where, why, and how. However, they contain more hidden aspects of covering AI or robots. These include that the Korean newspapers and television networks stick with an objective approach and produce more straight news stories than investigative feature stories. By considering a neutral tone and factual information, the present study suggests that news outlets take traditional approaches to the question of how to cover AI or robots, though it is located outside such traditional topics.

From another perspective, frequent usages testify that those news organizations and their journalists rely on sources such as government officials, AI experts, or AI industries. The present study did not examine specific sourcing types because they are beyond the scope of its analysis. Such prior information is provided by outside sources, sometimes called official or expert sources. Given that AI is a very sophisticated topic, journalists are prone to seek people who know about it and have experience, which is understood as part of a ritualistic step for justifying the validity of coverage of such uncertain topics as AI or robots, which may be unfamiliar to the

Table 7.8   *Coverage patterns of SBS regarding AI*

Variable (N = 35)	Freq	Prop	Variable	Freq	Prop
literacy1	4,344	28.71	action	32	0.21
neutral	3,855	25.48	explanation2	27	0.18
episode1	3,675	24.29	description	16	0.11
foreign	571	3.77	past	14	0.09
task	479	3.17	relation	13	0.09
universality	329	2.17	metaphor	10	0.07
positive	328	2.17	commentary2	8	0.05
explanation3	247	1.63	passive	7	0.05
negative	217	1.43	episode2	6	0.04
group	188	1.24	interpretation	6	0.04
private person1	146	0.97	explanation1	4	0.03
state	105	0.69	follow-up2	4	0.03
public person	102	0.67	private person2	4	0.03
active	97	0.64	future	3	0.02
present	91	0.60	visualization1	2	0.01
commentary1	71	0.47	orality2	1	0.01
Japanese	71	0.47	true modality	1	0.01
orality1	55	0.36	Total	15,129	100

newsroom. This reliance on sources for covering AI could pose a threat to the independence of journalists or their news organizations because they are susceptible to the subtle control of sources over news-making regarding the topic.

The other noteworthy similarity includes that the news organizations do not proactively provide in-depth explanatory approaches to the practices of AI or robots in society. Further, they do not emphasize what follows in response to AI adoptions or how citizens evaluate or interpret the trends. These patterns reveal that journalists who cover AI could have a low level of knowledge or understanding about AI. Instead, they choose to check what experts or industry practitioners say regarding AI. Even news organizations that deployed robot journalists to their news production show these peculiar patterns. Journalists follow the routine processes of news-making for dealing with an innovative topic in order to reduce any uncertainty or burden of cross-checking the veracity of the information. This is disappointing because AI is a topic requiring detailed, accurate explanation of its basic structure, operation, consequences, impact on society and citizens' daily lives, and so on. The present study speculates that journalists' lack of training and the low level of expertise or skills for tackling the granular elements of AI could contribute to this problem. News executives need to pay close attention to this issue to enhance journalists' ability to produce quality investigative, explanatory stories regarding AI or robots that are applicable to society.

The focus on delivering factual information and de-emphasizing analytical interpretation creates an imbalance for reporting AI practices in society or industries, which leads to a problematic situation in which AI remains a popular buzzword with no significant relevance or context to people's lives in specific personalized nuances. The coverage of the major news organizations in South Korea is skewed toward favoring the delivery of what the AI industry or the government does in a less persuasive way. Evidence of this notion is that, regardless of their experience of adopting robot journalists, the news organizations do not consider visualization to be the most important tool for telling a story about AI. This is a surprising outcome. AI seems to be a quite technical topic for normal citizens because they do not grasp it with their common experiences or everyday lives. In this light, intuitive visuals could help non-experts to see through AI and its relevance to their everyday activities. The role of such visuals is clear in data-driven news reporting manifested in many news outlets, including the *Guardian*, the *New York Times*, ProPublica, the FiveThirtyEight, or Newstapa, a Korean investigative news organization. Citizens find interactive maps, charts, or tables linked to dates and time data so that when they click one of them, it shows detailed information (e.g., occurrences, related stories). In opposition to this expectation, the news organizations do not apply visualization to the coverage of AI. What AI is remains a daunting question that normal citizens have difficulty grasping its subtle relevance to their lives.

The present study expects that the findings could allow scholars, policymakers, and practitioners to estimate how the South Korean major news organizations understand AI practices and construct them in coverage. In follow-up studies, conducting in-depth interviews with journalists and senior editors covering AI or robots may produce insightful perspectives regarding news organizations' imbalanced and routinized approaches. Furthermore, the fact that stories about AI contain many Japanese words or expressions needs to be improved, given that the South Korean government has launched a language policy promoting the use of appropriate Korean expressions instead of using Japanese words in daily conversation and texts. The present study could serve as fodder for all these endeavors and practical discussions about the relevance of AI to the newsrooms and society.

ACKNOWLEDGEMENT

This work was supported by the Ministry of Education of the Republic of Korea and the National Research Foundation of Korea (NRF-2020S1A5A2A01040590).

REFERENCES

Baek, J-H, & Lim, J. (2018). Robot journalism 'without innovation' in Korea: Searching for the mode of automated journalism. *Journal of Broadcasting and Telecommunications Research, 7*, 103–136.

Benoit, K. (2018). _quanteda: Quantitative analysis of textual data_. R package version 1.2.0. http://quanteda.io

Benoit, K.., Watanabe, K., Wang, H., Nulty, P., Obeng, A., Müller, S., & Matsuo, A. (2018). quanteda: An R package for the quantitative analysis of textual data. *Journal of Open Source Software*, *3*(30), 1–4.

Carlson, M. (2015). The robotic reporter: Automated journalism and the redefinition of labor, compositional forms, and journalistic authority. *Digital Journalism*, *3*(3), 416–431.

Clerwall, C. (2014). Enter the robot journalist: Users' perceptions of automated content. *Journalism Practice*, *8*(5), 519–531.

Deluca, A. (2021, November 4). Meet the Miami Herald's newest writer: A robot! *Miami New Times*. https://www.miaminewtimes.com/news/miami-herald-robot-writes-real-estate -stories-13219683

Diesner, J., & Carley, K. M. (2005). Revealing social structure from texts: Meta-matrix text analysis as a novel method for network text analysis. In V. K. Narayanan & D. J. Amstrong (Eds.), *Causal mapping for research in information technology* (pp. 81–108). IDEA Group Publishing.

Dörr, K. N. (2016). Mapping the field of algorithmic journalism. *Digital Journalism*, *4*(6), 700–722.

Kim, D., & Lee, J. (2015). Robot journalism: Algorithmic approach to automated news article generation. *Korean Journal of Journalism & Communication Studies*, *59*(5), 64–95.

Kotenidis, E., & Veglis, A. (2021). Algorithmic journalism—Current applications and future perspectives. *Journalism and Media*, *2*, 244–257.

Latar, N. L. (2014). The robot journalist in the age of social physics: The end of human journalism? In G. Einav (Ed.), *The new world of transitioned media: Digital realignment and industry transformation* (pp. 65–80). New York, NY: Springer.

Lee, S., Nah, S., Chung, D. S., & Kim, J. (2020). Predicting AI news credibility: Communicative or social capital or both? *Communication Studies*, *71*(3), 428–447.

Lim, J. (2019). An exploratory study of automatic extraction of news frames in terms of the coverage of television networks, comprehensive programming channels, and news channels of government's real estate policy. *Broadcasting & Communication*, *20*(2), 47–96.

Lim, J. (2020). *A model for automatic extraction and interpretation of news frames and agendas*. Sogang University.

Lim, J. (2021). A study of development of news language database for artificial intelligence-based news-making: Statistical learning of news stories of daily newspapers and television networks. *Korean Journal of Journalism and Communication Studies*, *65*(6), 416–451.

Narrative Science (2016). *Data-driven communication at machine scale*. https://www .narrativescience.com/quill

Oliver, L. (2022, June 2). How a local paper in Argentina uses AI to publish hundreds of sports pieces a month. *Reuters Institute for the Study of Journalism*. https://reutersinstitute .politics.ox.ac.uk/news/how-local-paper-argentina-uses-ai-publish-hundreds-sports-pieces -month

O'Neill, N. (2021, November 5). Bot off the press! Pulitzer Prize-winning newspaper's new reporter is a robot. New York Post. https://nypost.com/2021/11/05/miami-heralds-newest -real-estate-reporter-is-a-robot/

Pan, Z., & Kosicki, G. M. (1993). Framing analysis: An approach to news discourse. *Political Communication*, *10*(1), 55–75.

Rojas-Garcia, J., & Faber, P. (2019). Extraction of terms for the construction of semantic frames for named bays. *Argentinian Journal of Applied Linguistics*, *7*(1), 27–57.

Sadia, S., & Ghani, M. (2019). Modality in editorials of Pakistani English newspapers: A corpus based study. *International Journal of English Linguistics*, *9*(1), 144–151.

Segesten, A. D., & Bossetta, M. (2019). Can Euroscepticism contribute to a European public sphere? The Europeanization of media discourses on Euroscepticism across six countries. *Journal of Common Market Studies*, *57*(5), 1051–1070.

Seo, M. (2017, August 14). How does Yonhap News robot journalist 'Soccerbot' write a story. *Yonhap News.* http://www.yonhapnews.co.kr/bulletin/2017/08/14/0200000000AKR20 170814032900039.HTML

Shah, D. V., Cappella, J. N., & Neuman, R. (2015). Big data, digital media, and computational social science: Possibilities and perils. *ANNALS of the American Academy of Political and Social Science, 659*(1), 6–13.

Simpson, P. (2005). *Language, ideology, and point of view.* Routledge.

van Dalen, A. (2012). The algorithms behind the headlines: How machine-written news redefines the core skills of human journalists. *Journalism Practice, 6*(5–6), 648–658.

van Dijk, T. A. (1983). Discourse analysis: Its development and application to the structure of news. *Journal of Communication, 33*(2), 20–43.

Waddell, F. T. (2019). Can an algorithm reduce the perceived bias of news? Testing the effect of machine attribution on news readers' evaluations of bias, anthropomorphism, and credibility. *Journalism & Mass Communication Quarterly, 96*(1), 82–100.

Welbers, K., van Atteveldt, W., & Benoit, K. (2017). Text analysis in R. *Communication Methods and Measures, 11*(4), 245–265.

Yang, J., Jin, M., Lee, K., Oh, H., & Cho, J. (2017). *User preference customized sports articles Writing program based on robot journalism, 1054-1056.* Paper presented at the conference of Korea Information Science Society.

8.   AI in Portugal: news framing, tone, and sources

Paulo Nuno Vicente

In recent years, investment in artificial intelligence (AI) technologies has skyrocketed (Crawford & Calo, 2016), and the volume of published peer-reviewed scientific articles has risen by more than 300% (Parratt-Fernández et al., 2021; Perrault et al., 2019), reflecting a growing range of AI applications: web searches, social media feeds, self-driving vehicles, speech and image recognition systems, credit risk assessments, and recruitment process assistance, among many others (Ramos-Martín & Barreneche, 2020). Both a technology and a scientific research and development (R&D) domain, AI's key goal is to generate "intelligent" machines; the latter are, ultimately, expected to play the role of powerful engines in a fourth Industrial Revolution (Micó et al., 2022; Vicente & Dias-Trindade, 2021), leading national and regional executive bodies to launch new regulatory systems (the UK, 2019) and strategic plans (e.g., EC 2020).

AI is shifting from a technology, i.e., an artifact of scientists and engineers in laboratories, to an everyday media. The spread of intelligent virtual assistants – voice-activated systems such as Amazon's Alexa, Google's Assistant, Microsoft's Cortana, and Apple's Siri – is now a constitutive layer of contemporaneity and materializes the projection of an internet of things, the networked integration of the physical world with digital data exchanges. As AI emerges in ordinary life, a growing list of societal challenges also arises. Current debates involve algorithmic bias and transparency, exclusion by design, personal data and privacy, risk communication to users, explainability of intelligent systems, diversity in the AI workforce, and the mismatch of digital skills (Collett & Dillon, 2019; Krafft et al., 2020; Pilling & Coulton, 2019).

While AI has received attention from scientists, technologists, and marketers, only recently did scholars start investing in the analysis of the mediated communication of AI (e.g., Cave et al., 2018; Holguín, 2018; Scott Hansen, 2022; Sun et al., 2020; Vicente & Flores, 2021). In this chapter, we depart from the concept of sociotechnical imaginaries as defined by Jasanoff (2015, p. 4) as "collectively held, institutionally stabilized, and public performed visions of desirable futures, animated by shared understandings of forms of social life and social order attainable through, and supportive of, advances in science and technology." Our fundamental premise is that the public performance of these imaginaries happens significantly in the media, which is why their analysis is critical. In a domain molded by dichotomic utopian/dystopian fictional depictions and by large corporations' strategic communication (Rhee, 2018;

Richardson, 2015), rigorous and nuanced knowledge production about those public-performed visions of AI is currently needed.

This chapter extends available studies of media discourse on AI by presenting the results of a longitudinal quantitative content study of how AI has been framed in the Portuguese press from 1997 to 2017. The studies available on the representation of AI by the media are still scarce and are mostly limited to Anglo-Saxon contexts. We propose that our study opens a path to assess the role of media landscapes in the globalization dynamics between a small country in absolute terms (i.e., size of territory and population) and its transnational linkages, admitting that "at times smallness is mentioned in passing, mostly to suggest that these are countries that can be largely disregarded in the larger scheme of things" (Hannerz & Gingrich, 2017, p. 2). The focus is on how news narratives have informed the public perception of AI.

PUBLIC UNDERSTANDING OF AI

Examining the normalization and regulation of emerging technologies is a consolidated path in science and technology studies (STS) (e.g., Jasanoff, 2001; Pouteau, 2002; Sleeboom-Faulkner, 2019; Van Wichelen, 2016). In the first decade of the millennium, researchers have been particularly prolific in producing studies on nanotechnology across several national contexts. A non-systematic review of this growing literature includes the United States (US) (Stephens, 2005), the United Kingdom (UK) (Anderson et al., 2005), the Netherlands (Te Kulve, 2006), Denmark (Kjærgaard, 2010), Italy (Arnaldi, 2008), Germany (Donk et al., 2012), Slovenia (Groboljsek & Mali, 2012), and Spain (Veltri, 2013).

Similar studies have been conducted on stem cell research (Nisbet et al., 2003), cloning (Holliman, 2004), and assisted reproductive technologies (Campbell, 2011). Throughout the second decade of the twenty-first century, the research agenda continuously expanded and came to include developments associated with bio-fuel/geo-thermal energy (Kim et al., 2014; Romanach et al., 2015), smart grid technologies (Mallett et al., 2018), novel food technologies (Runge et al., 2018), solar photovoltaic (PV) technology (Lempiälä et al., 2019), ridesharing platforms (Yuana et al., 2019), blockchain (Lagendijk et al., 2019), and synthetic biology (Bauer & Bogner, 2020). Only very recently has the consolidation of a set of studies dedicated to the mediated communication of AI, as an emerging cutting-edge technology, started to take shape.

In popular culture, particularly in literature and cinema, AI has been synonymous with anthropomorphic robots (Bory & Bory, 2015; Sandoval et al., 2014), leading to the argument that "robotic fictions are taken into the lived realities of robotic practices and transferred into the making of robots, returning into those fictions" (Richardson 2015, p. 3). The concept of a *singularity*, a hypothetical point in time when artificially intelligent agents become autonomous and surpass human intelligence, is practically omnipresent in the script of these fictional narratives (e.g., *2001: A Space Odyssey, Blade Runner, The Terminator, The Matrix, A.I., Her, Ex-Machina*), leading to anxiety and fear about future technological developments. Scholars have pointed to the impact that brain metaphors have in the evolution of computational systems (Carbonell et al., 2016) and voiced the need for the AI research community itself to reframe discourse around the notion of *autonomy*, as it suggests that computational artifacts are developing beyond human control, omitting the role played by programmers and other human actors in the design of these systems (Johnson & Verdicchio, 2017; Neri & Cozman, 2019).

The public response to AI both in the US and in Europe appears to be prone to reflecting these utopian/dystopian sociotechnical imaginaries and discourses. Americans express more worry than enthusiasm about emerging automation technologies and support policies that would limit their scope, as they worry that widespread automation will lead to more inequality (Pew, 2017). In Europe, public opinion has a similar orientation: Major concerns exist about the economic impact of AI, particularly the effects on job creation and elimination. Citizens' perception is that the near future will not be equitable between humans and machines, with 72% of European citizens believing that robots will steal people's jobs (EC, 2017). In the UK, results from a nationally representative survey also underline this significant public anxiety (Cave et al., 2019).

The news media are a major source influencing the public perception of AI. Although research focused on news media coverage of AI is primarily limited to recent coverage and Western English-speaking media coverage (Cave et al. 2018), it is possible to map some exploratory discursive trends from the available studies on how this technology is being framed. The first trend is a perennial problem with technological progress expressed in terms of a lasting duality; on the one hand, there is astonishment at the potential of computational capabilities (non-threatening) and, on the other, shock and awe at the possibility of the social order being turned upside down (threatening). Archival research evidence that this ambivalence is not exclusive to AI but, instead, covers the history of the more general relationship between humans and computers (Atkinson, 2017; Curran et al., 2019).

Second, an arms race framing translates R&D on intelligent machines into a competitive challenge among countries, particularly among world powers such as the US, Russia, and China for the control of a strategic weapon of geopolitical domination (Roff, 2019). Third is an industry-led debate, in which most news coverage is associated with industry products, initiatives, or announcements, which outpace academic studies, reports, and political speeches. The analysis of 760 articles published over eight months in six mainstream news outlets in the UK revealed that 33% of unique sources across all articles were industry-connected (Brennen et al., 2018). In line with this finding, a longitudinal analysis of the Dutch press demonstrated that the top actors in the news about AI are tech giants (e.g., Google, Facebook, IBM, Microsoft) (Vergeer, 2020).

Finally, a benefit-focused coverage emphasizing economic paybacks, improvements in human life and well-being, and the reduction of human biases and inequality and paying less attention to a critical positioning in the face of technological developments in the field (Chuan et al., 2019; Fast & Horvitz, 2017). Although in the sphere of critical algorithm studies, the discussion around AI ethics has been gaining significant headway in recent years, news coverage of AI-related ethical issues is still shallow, mainly when dealing with technology implementation and the ethical frameworks that are expected to guide intelligent machines' development (Ouchchy et al., 2020).

THEORETICAL FRAMEWORK: MEDIA FRAMING

As with other technological developments, non-experts do not have direct contact with R&D on AI but with an agenda of topics and debates set by journalists and newsroom staff and, thus, only a media representation of it (McCombs & Shaw, 1972). The "framing theory" was first presented as "frame analysis" by Goffman (1974), who claimed that people interpret events according to their primary frame works (i.e., social schemata that provide the understanding of data). The concept was later integrated into the communication studies field, focusing on the reception and the production of communicating items (texts and images). In this context, to "frame is to select some aspects of a perceived reality and make them more salient in a communication context, in such a way as to promote a particular problem definition, causal interpretation, moral evaluation, and/or treatment recommendation for the item described" (Entman, 1993, p. 52).

Frames depend both on the mental schemata of the communicator and of the receiver: the communicator departs from them to undertake the framing process, and the receptor relies on them to interpret and evaluate the presented information by negotiating it with their prior knowledge. From this negotiation, frames can impact cognition, socialization, the formation of public opinion, and group use of media messages. In addition, framing can be considered a continuous process in which the outcomes can function as inputs for subsequent processes as a looping paradigm that derives and impacts several different entities, including institutions, the media, and the audiences (Scheufele, 1999).

In this precise sense, the media are a creative constituent of modernity and an inseparable layer of the social construction of reality. As such, media frames are an indispensable index for the study of the local and global public performativity of sociotechnical imaginaries, comprising the selection of specific aspects of AI and making those more or less salient to the receptor to define a problem, promote a causal interpretation, present a moral evaluation, and propose a solution (Entman 1993). Or, in the words of Jasanoff (2015, p. 35), "(sociotechnical) imaginaries frame and represent alternative futures, link past and future times, enable or restrict actions in space, and naturalize ways of thinking about possible worlds."

The present study focuses on how the Portuguese press framed the topic of AI from 1997 to 2017. By analyzing 20 years of news coverage, it answers the following research questions:

RQ1: What are the dominant news frames in AI coverage in the Portuguese press?
RQ2: What are the primary news sources in AI coverage in the Portuguese press?
RQ3: What is the dominant tone in AI coverage in the Portuguese press?

PORTUGAL AND THE STUDY OF AI IN A SMALL EUROPEAN COUNTRY

International organizations, such as the EU and the United Nations (UN), have expressed concerns about the impact of AI technologies in meeting the UN Sustainable Development Goals. While existing studies describe how and why "the fast development of AI needs to be supported by the necessary regulatory insight and oversight for AI-based technologies to enable sustainable development. Failure to do so could result in gaps in transparency, safety, and ethical standards" (Vinuesa et al., 2020). The European Commission has also signaled that AI "entails a number of potential risks, such as opaque decision-making, gender-based or other kinds of discrimination, intrusion in our private lives or being used for criminal purposes" (EC, 2020, p. 1).

Traditionally portrayed as a pcripherical, small, and unindustrialized country, the current national policies toward a fourth Industrial Revolution (4IR) translated into the adoption of cutting-edge digital technologies as a solution for Portugal's structural industrial and economic fragilities (techno-fix), including a National Strategy for Artificial Intelligence 2030, focused on the development and application of AI in fields such as public administration, education, training, and companies (Government, 2019).

Adopting a Portuguese public policy for AI makes crucial the analysis of how executive instruments are mediated in the public sphere. We understand this mediation, particularly the public's understanding of science and technology, as a fundamental pillar in innovation systems. In contemporary societies, this understanding is not detachable from the media's performance. For their part, these are instrumental in studying the articulation between public policies of innovation, globalization, and small countries. In this regard, two contextual notes are needed about the Portuguese case study. First, relative to other European realities, the thematization of science in the Portuguese media has historically been inferior (Mendes, 2002); second, according to the only longitudinal study available on science and technology in the Portuguese press, between 1976 and 2005, the existence of specialized science and technology sections in the Portuguese newspapers was intermittent, suggesting considerable editorial variability (Fonseca, 2012).

In the framework of democracy, reinstated in 1974, the Portuguese media sector has been marked, since the 1980s and following the integration in the EU, by a trend toward privatization, liberalization, and internationalization. Portugal has one of the lowest daily newspaper circulation rates in Europe, and it is TV that absorbs most of the advertising investment in a framework in which four major economic groups control the ownership of the national circulation media (*Cofina*, *Global Media*, *Impresa*, *Sonae*). The daily newspaper with the largest paid circulation is the popular *Correio da Manhã* (46,569), followed by *Jornal de Notícias* (23,459), *Público* (11,443) and *Diário de Notícias* (2,609); the weekly newspaper *Expresso* (51,929) leads in circulation. The magazine market is led by *Visão* news magazine (23,733), followed by the weekly magazine *Sábado* (20,276) (data provided by the Portuguese Association for the Control of Circulation and Printing).

METHOD

Data Collection and Sampling

To consistently identify relevant articles about AI in the Portuguese press between 1997 and 2017, a media monitoring service (CISION) was used, including both printed and online articles. To achieve a comprehensive collection of printed new media pieces, the keyword for the search process was exclusively "artificial intelligence." The query retrieved a total of 106 hits. Repeated and incomplete entries were eliminated, and inclusion/exclusion criteria were further applied to consolidate the sample selection (see Table 8.1).

The final sample consisted of 92 articles published over 20 years and across 14 news media outlets (see Figure 8.1). These include seven Portuguese-based national daily newspapers, three Portuguese-based national weekly newspapers, two Portuguese-based weekly news magazines, one Portuguese-based monthly news magazine, and one Portuguese-based online-only newspaper. The daily newspapers sampled were *Diário de Notícias, Jornal de Notícias, Correio da Manhã, Público, Diário Económico, Jornal Económico,* and *Jornal i.* The weekly newspapers sampled were *Expresso, O Independente,* and *Sol.* The weekly news magazines sampled were *Visão* and *Focus.* The monthly news magazine sampled was *Super Interessante.* The online-only newspaper sampled was *Dinheiro Vivo.*

Coding

Each sample article was analyzed using a coding sheet, recording the article headline, year of publication, news media outlet, article type, and primary news source. To favor reasonable thematic comparability with preceding science and technology literature, the development of the coding scheme initially adopted a deductive

Table 8.1   Inclusion/exclusion criteria

Include	Exclude
Original news articles published between 1997 and 2017 in Portuguese daily and weekly newspapers, weekly and monthly news magazines, and online-only newspapers	Original news articles published before 1997 and after 2017 in Portuguese daily and weekly newspapers, weekly and monthly news magazines, and online-only newspapers
Original news articles in which the focus is exclusively artificial intelligence	Original news articles in which the focus is broadly emerging technologies (e.g., nanotechnologies, brain–computer interfaces)
Original news articles that include references to popular culture (e.g., film/book reviews)	Digests of translated news articles published in international media

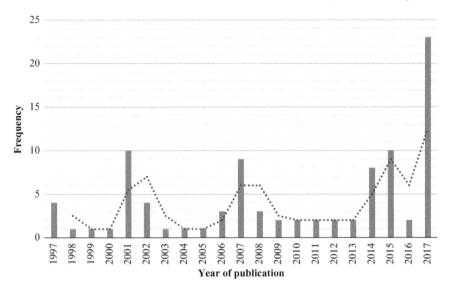

Figure 8.1   *Frequency of articles by year, 1997–2017 (N = 92)*

theory-driven approach based on the set of codes used by Stephens (2005), Anderson et al. (2005), and Kjærgaard (2008).

Because this set of studies was useful in the initial structuring of a coding manual, particularly analysis of nanoscience and technology in the US, UK, and Denmark, an inductive approach was also considered fundamental, based on the identification of context-specific commonalities in the Portuguese media sample. The final multistage coding procedure was, on a first level, theoretically informed and, on a second level, grounded on a data-driven analysis of the media corps.

The objective of coding for the dominant frame was to define the article's primary focus. Whenever available, four variables were inspected: headline, lead, subheadings, and quote highlights. Table 8.2 presents each dominant frame, describing its precise scope, including examples of the coded articles and the coding rationale.

Because the process of coding is permeable to intersubjective judgments and interpretation, a set of interrater reliability tests were run for *dominant frame* and *dominant tone*. Krippendorff's alpha test was used (Hayes & Krippendorff, 2007; Krippendorff, 2004) within SPSS V23 statistic software. The objective of these tests is to verify whether ratings by different coders reflect the dimension they purport to reflect. Coder A and Coder B independently coded the total sample (*N* = 92) for *frame* and *tone*. Both coders are fluent in Portuguese and English. It was decided to separately code the entire sample as this proved to be a feasible task, ensuring a more comprehensive reliability calculation. An intercoder reliability test was performed comparing Coder A's and Coder B's coding results. The results show that the intercoder reliability was adequate in the *dominant frame* variable ($\alpha = .75$) and the *dominant tone* variable ($\alpha = .77$).

Table 8.2 Sample coding scheme for dominant frame

Dominant frame	Description	Example of article (headlines)	Coding rationale
Business and management	Focus on Portuguese companies' and start-ups' AI strategies and products and their CEOs', managers', and entrepreneurs' vision and opinions	"Portugal in the world top" (1997)	The headline, the lead, and the subheadings highlight the "national pride" in the fact that several international companies resort to AI solutions developed in Portugal
Economic impact	Focus on specific economic implications of AI for Portugal, namely for its work sector, (un)employment rate, exports, and internationalization performance	"Tell me what you do, I will tell you what artificial intelligence system you use" (2017)	The headline, the lead, and the highlight of quotes stress that "hundreds of thousands of robots are replacing humans in the most varied professions"
Funding for AI	Focus on private and/or public funding from Portuguese and EU sources for AI	"IBM invests 736 million to monetize the supercomputer that won TV contests" (2014)	Both the headline and lead stress the available funding for companies wanting to implement IBM's Watson AI system
Globalization	Comparison between national gross domestic products (GDPs) and their relationship with AI technologies	"Artificial intelligence and globalization" (2006)	Article exclusively dedicated to an analysis of national economic growth of China and India linked to AI
Historiography	Focus on the history of AI	"Artificial intelligence has already invaded our lives" (2017)	The headline, the lead, and the subheadings highlight the chronological evolution of AI technologies
Patents, marketing, and PR of AI products	Focus on the commercialization and go-to market strategies of AI products	"Robots enter 'marketing'" (2006)	Both the headline and the highlight of quotes stress the growing use of intelligent virtual agents in marketing and commercial operations

Personalities	Announcement of individual AI prize and grant winners	"Young engineer studying semantic web wins award" (2010)	Article exclusively dedicated to Pedro Oliveira, a young Portuguese engineer who was awarded with a national AI prize
Science fiction and popular culture	Reviews of books/films related with AI	"Swedish classification of Spielberg film by court" (2001)	Article exclusively dedicated to classification of the American director's film by the Swedish Administrative Court
Science and technology policy	Focus on specific Portuguese and/or EU policies and legal frameworks addressing AI	"The Robotic Rights Charter" (2007)	Both the headline and the lead stress the need for legal regulation of robots and AI systems
Scientific discoveries or projects	Focus on specific scientific and/or technological research projects explicitly associated with AI	"Connective intelligence was born" (1999)	Article exclusively dedicated to an analysis of state-of-the-art data encryption solutions using AI systems.
Social implications	Focus on broad consequences of AI for the Portuguese society, from a systemic and/or daily life perspectives	"In 2025, your colleague next door may be a robot" (2015)	Article exclusively dedicated to an analysis of the transversal implications of technologies in areas such as health, defense, civil construction, industry, and transportation
Viability	Focus on the economic and/or scientific viability of AI	"Only simple things work" (2001)	Both the headline and the lead stress the current limitations of AI systems
Visionary, futuristic	Focus on general evaluations and predictions for AI based on what we know today	"The moment may come when we will be the computer monkeys"	Both the headline and the highlight of quotes stress that "someday a papal council will have to pronounce and decide if machines have souls"

Because the two coders did not agree on absolute terms, a reconciliation procedure was implemented to resolve the discrepancies: the differences in coding were identified, with the two coders returning to the original articles and comparing the previously assigned codes with the specific descriptions articulated in the coding scheme – this procedure allowed for collegial consensus-building.

RESULTS AND DISCUSSION

Previous research on the news media coverage of AI has been almost exclusively limited to Western English-speaking countries, particularly the US (Ouchchy et al., 2020; Fast & Horvitz, 2017; Curran et al., 2019; Chuan et al., 2019) and the UK (Brennen et al., 2018). Most of the available studies focus the analysis on a period after 2014, a date that has been consistently identified as a landmark of exponential growth in AI news coverage, and exclusively observe opinion-making newspapers (notoriously, *The New York Times*), disregarding tabloids in the narrative construction and dissemination of sociotechnical imaginaries.

News media attention to AI is more prominent in Portuguese opinion-making/high-quality newspapers than in the tabloid press, namely, in the daily newspapers *Diário de Notícias* and *Público*, which historically were among the first national daily newspapers to dedicate specialized news coverage to science. Overall, the dispersion of AI-related articles by 14 news media outlets suggests that the topic entered a popularization stage during the last 20 years (see Table 8.3). This finding was recently reiterated by the exploratory research of Canavilhas and Essenfelder (2022), who, examining the Portuguese press articles between January 1 and February 29, 2020, analyzed a sample of 123 articles; in our view, this is a sign that, from 2017 onward, the coverage by the Portuguese media had a significant increase. Canavilhas and Essenfelder's (2022) study also reiterates the daily newspaper *Público* and the weekly newspaper *Expresso* as the ones that publish more coverage on AI.

Dominant News Frames in AI Coverage in the Portuguese Press

From 1997 to 2017, scientific discoveries and projects were the most prominent frame in the Portuguese press (27%). This was a period when AI was defined to the Portuguese audiences directly related to scientific achievements and technological innovations (see Table 8.4). This type of news framing is consistent with a general tendency of news media to discursively portray science and technology in terms of "progress" (Nisbet, Brossard, & Kroepsch, 2003) and, as is well summarized by Weaver et al. (2009), to favor "positive beliefs about societal improvement from technology and might also imply that new technology is 'natural' or 'logical'" (p. 141).

The second most prominent frame concerns *economic impact* (13%), namely on the work sector and (un)employment, followed by the *business and management* frame (11%), through which Portuguese companies and entrepreneurs are portrayed. This result is in accordance with the already mentioned long-term trend in the public

Table 8.3   *Frequency of articles by news media outlet, 1997–2017 (N = 92)*

News media outlet	Frequency (Percentage)
Diário de Notícias	24 (26%)
Público	21 (23%)
Expresso	9 (10%)
Jornal i	8 (9%)
Jornal de Notícias	6 (7%)
Visão	5 (5%)
Correio da Manhã	4 (4%)
Dinheiro Vivo	4 (4%)
Jornal Económico	3 (3%)
Focus	2 (2%)
Sol	2 (2%)
Super Interessante	2 (2%)
Diário Económico	1 (1%)
O Independente	1 (1%)
Total	92 (100%)

perception of AI, and computers in general, documented in pre-existing studies in which it was framed between the hopes of a positive impact on the human liberation from mechanical tasks and the concerns about the loss of jobs (Fast & Horvitz, 2017; Chuan, Tsai, & Cho, 2019; Ouchchy, Coin, &Dubljević, 2020).

Significantly, if we add the number of articles coded in the *economic impact* frame (13%), the *science fiction and popular culture* frame (11%), the *social implications* frame (11%), and the *visionary, futuristic* frame (10%) – all of them prospective in nature – a thematization cluster (45%) is formed, which can be appropriately designated as the *discursive representation of future promises/risks*. In clear opposition, only 3% of all articles reflect an interest in *science and technology policy*, indicating that Portuguese news media were still distanced from a high-level and more abstract public debate on the macro-dimensions of regulatory frameworks and ethical issues generated by AI. This finding is consistent with the recent analysis by Ouchchy et al. (2020).

Primary News Sources in AI Coverage in the Portuguese Press

Notably, the most frequent information sources in AI news are scientists (42%). This empirical datum confirms, for the Portuguese context, that when media seeks to introduce an emerging technology to its readers, experts play a dominant role in

Table 8.4   Dominant news frames

Dominant frame	Description	Frequency (Percentage)
Scientific discoveries or projects	Focus on specific scientific and/or technological research projects explicitly associated with AI	25 (27%)
Economic impact	Focus on specific economic implications of AI for Portugal, namely for its work sector, (un)employment rate, exports, and internationalization performance	12 (13%)
Business and management	Focus on Portuguese companies' and start-ups' AI strategies and products and their CEOs', managers', and entrepreneurs' vision and opinions.	10 (11%)
Science fiction and popular culture	Reviews of books, films, etc.	10 (11%)
Social implications	Focus on broad consequences of AI for the Portuguese society, from a systemic and/or daily life perspectives.	10 (11%)
Visionary, futuristic	Focus on general evaluations and predictions for AI based on what we know today.	9 (10%)
Historiography	Focus on the history of AI	5 (5%)
Patents, marketing, and PR of AI products	Focus on the commercialization and go-to market strategies of AI products	3 (3%)
Science and technology policy	Focus on specific Portuguese and/or EU policies and legal frameworks addressing AI	3 (3%)
Funding for AI	Focus on private and/or public funding from Portuguese and EU sources for AI	2 (2%)
Globalization	Comparison between national GDPs and their relationship with AI technologies	1 (1%)
Personalities	Announcement of individual AI prize/grant winners	1 (1%)
Viability	Focus on the economic and/or scientific viability of AI	1 (1%)
Total		92 (100%)

informing the narrative terms of which public understanding will be constituted (see Figure 8.2).

Our results illustrate why scientists' communication affordances – e.g., use of metaphor and rhetoric in order to explain their work –are crucial in establishing anchor points for the translation of highly specialized knowledge (speaking on behalf of),

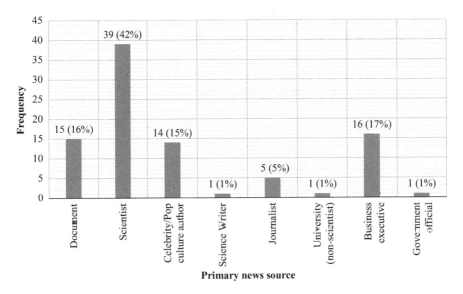

Figure 8.2   *Frequency of primary news source*

as well as for the construction of sociotechnical imaginaries (standing for) (Horst, 2013). From a news production point of view, our findings open the hypothesis that journalists rely heavily on scientists to convert expert AI jargon into a simplified message and to legitimize media coverage itself.

The preponderance of scientists in articles about AI is followed by the presence of business executives (17%), documents (16%) (e.g., company and university press releases, reports, petitions), and celebrities/popular culture authors (15%). As in the cases of the UK and the Netherlands, coverage in Portugal was significantly permeable to tech industry actors. It also attested to the relationship between AI and pop culture, namely science fiction.

More than half (53%) of the articles in the Portuguese sample were classified as features, as they provided a journalistic mix of information and interpretation, often narrated from a human-centered perspective (see Figure 8.3). This finding is in accordance with results from other studies in science and technology news coverage (e.g., Stephens 2005).

Dominant Tone in AI Coverage in the Portuguese Press

More than half (51%) of the articles express a positive sentiment about AI (benefits outweigh risks), a consistent result with studies depicting the US context (Fast & Horvitz, 2017, Chuan et al., 2019), while the Dutch press (Vergeer, 2020) and the UK media outlets (Brennen et al., 2018) have been reported as significantly balanced. Considering the residual number of articles focusing on risks outweighing benefits (3%), from 1997 to 2017, the Portuguese news media is marked by an under-coverage

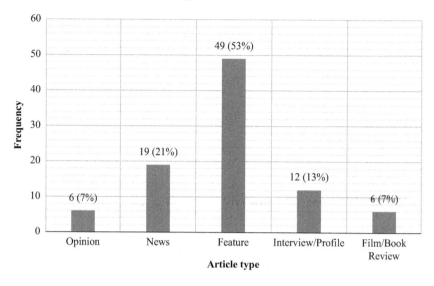

Figure 8.3   Frequency of article type

of potential hazards of AI, while providing momentum for optimistic technological expectations and promises (see Figure 8.4). Our case study findings support the assertion that a first phase of science and technology media coverage tends to be characterized by far-reaching promises, only later to be critically debated in the public sphere (e.g., Weingart et al., 2008).

CONCLUSION

In recent years, AI has gained renewed interest as a key enabling technological force toward a predicted 4IR. From our case study, there is empirical ground to affirm that automation technologies are, indeed, a very significant index for the study of modernity, scientific and technological globalization, and their master narratives. The media not only naturalizes particular ways of thinking about possible singular futures but also defines the present as an extraordinary time, "where the continuity of everything hitherto taken for granted is exposed to unpredictable disruption" (Schiølin, 2019, p. 8).

The news, with its non-fictional accounts, proves to be a noteworthy gateway to examining how technological developments are publicly narrated, disseminated, and normalized. Because most studies of AI media coverage have been conducted in Western English-speaking national contexts (US, UK), we argue that more national case studies outside mediatic and geopolitical hot zones are needed to make explicit the differences between sociotechnical imaginaries across cultures and political regimes.

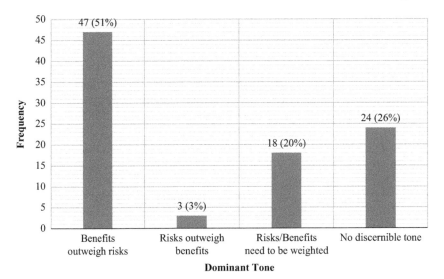

Figure 8.4   *Frequency of articles by risks and benefits associated with artificial intelligence*

Our results from the Portuguese case suggest that the media dissemination of the theme of AI tends to be dominated by a perspective of economic impact, close to the narrative of a forthcoming 4IR. This media trend seems to minimize a broader public discussion about the integration of technology centered on the human, in which questions about ethics, professional deontology, and planetary sustainability are practically omitted.

Our quantitative content analysis of the Portuguese press asks for further qualitative inquiry while already pointing to a techno-optimist sentiment performed by the news media and reinforcing the suggestion of a disconnection between findings from current public opinion polls about AI and results coming from media coverage studies: the former expressing more worries than enthusiasm and the latter narrating more optimistic expectations than critical analysis of risks and benefits. Both are prone to amplify, even if in opposite directions, the assumptions of technological determinism, somehow overshadowing that AI technologies are human-designed cultural artifacts, reflecting societal values and practices.

Insofar as our study finds a preponderant role of scientists as sources of information about AI in the news media, further contextual ethnographic studies are particularly needed to analyze the relationship between scientists and journalists, predominantly their iterative and negotiating character with editorial guidelines. The former, when disseminating their research work and commenting upon the late developments in the field, appear as acquiring a normative dimension: they define and assemble what AI is and what its assumptions, purposes, and implications are. From our study, scientists and scientific institutions have in front of them the fundamental task of extending the thematization of AI toward a deeper and more comprehensive coverage of emerging technologies' political dimension, the current debates of legal and ethical principles, and the influential human role in programming automation-based systems.

As AI opens new technological black boxes across societies, understanding its impact on human communication is necessary, making R&D more socially coherent and inclusive. Social scientists, media scholars, and humanists need to embrace AI and automation as cultural research subjects because the software has become both a contemporary engine of creation and a sphere in which renewed fractures and digital divides are designed or prevented. As imagination develops mental and material simulations of possible scenarios, projecting social futures that do not currently exist, but become part of how we, as a society, construct reality, a deeper understanding of the discursive construction of technological facts and a technical mentality in contemporary communication can be gained from inquiries both into the *places of imagined mediations* – the knowledge-intensive, expert sociotechnical systems, in which future mediations are conceived and physically built – and into the *places of mediated imaginations* – the non-expert experiential settings of those whose sociotechnical imagination is mediated by future projections, such as those published by the news media.

REFERENCES

Anderson, A., Allan, S., Petersen, A., & Wilkinson, C. (2005). The framing of nanotechnologies in the British newspaper Press. *Science Communication*, 27(2), 200–220. https://doi.org/10.1177/1075547005281472

Arnaldi, S. (2008). Converging technologies in the Italian daily press 2002–2006: Preliminary results of an ongoing research project. *Innovation: The European Journal of Social Science Research*, 21(1), 87–94. https://doi.org/10.1080/13511610802002304

Atkinson, P. (2017). 'The Robots are Coming!': Perennial problems with technological progress. *The Design Journal*, 20(sup1), S4120–S4131. https://doi.org/10.1080/14606925.2017.1352868

Bauer, A., & Bogner, A. (2020). Let's (not) talk about synthetic biology: Framing an emerging technology in public and stakeholder dialogues. *Public Understanding of Science*, 29(5), 492–507. https://doi.org/10.1177/0963662520907255

Bory, S., & Bory, P. (2015). I nuovi immaginari dell'intelligenza artificiale. *Im@go: A Journal of the Social Imaginary*, IV(6), 66–85. https://doi.org/10.7413/22818138047

Brennen, J. S., Howard, P. N., & Nielsen, R. K. (2018). *An Industry-Led Debate: How UK Media Cover Artificial Intelligence*. Reuters Institute for the Study of Journalism. https://reutersinstitute.politics.ox.ac.uk/our-research/industry-led-debate-how-uk-media-cover-artificial-intelligence

Campbell, P. (2011). Boundaries and risk: Media framing of assisted reproductive technologies and older mothers. *Social Science & Medicine*, 72(2), 265–272. https://doi.org/10.1016/j.socscimed.2010.10.028

Canavilhas, J., & Essenfelder, R. (2022). Apocalypse or Redemption: How the Portuguese Media Cover Artificial Intelligence. In J. Vázquez-Herrero, A. Silva-Rodríguez, M.-C. Negreira-Rey, C. Toural-Bran, & X. López-García (Eds.), *Total Journalism: Models, Techniques and Challenges* (pp. 255–270). Springer International Publishing. https://doi.org/10.1007/978-3-030-88028-6_19

Carbonell, J., Sánchez-Esguevillas, A., & Carro, B. (2016). The role of metaphors in the development of technologies. The case of the artificial intelligence. *Futures*, *84*, 145–153. https://doi.org/10.1016/j.futures.2016.03.019

Cave, S., Coughlan, K., & Dihal, K. (2019, January 27). *Scary Robots: Examining public responses to AI*. AIES' 19: AAAI/ACM Conference on AI, Ethics, and Society Proceedings, Honolulu, HI, USA. https://doi.org/10.1145/3306618.3314232

Cave, S., Craig, C., Dihal, K., Dillon, S., Montgomery, J., Singler, B., & Taylor, L. (2018). *Portrayals and Perceptions of AI and Why They Matter*. The Royal Society. https:// royalsociety.org/topics-policy/projects/ai-narratives/

Chuan, C.-H., Tsai, W.-H. S., & Cho, S. Y. (2019). Framing artificial intelligence in American newspapers. In *Proceedings of the 2019 AAAI/ACM Conference on AI, Ethics, and Society* (AIES '19). Association for Computing Machinery, New York, pp. 339–344. https://doi.org /10.1145/3306618

Collett, C., & Dillon, S. (2019). *AI and Gender: Four Proposals for Future Research*. The Leverhulme Centre for the Future of Intelligence.

Crawford, K., & Calo, R. (2016). There is a blind spot in AI research. *Nature*, *538*(7625), 311–313.

Curran, N. M., Sun, J., & Hong, J.-W. (2019). Anthropomorphizing AlphaGo: A content analysis of the framing of Google DeepMind's AlphaGo in the Chinese and American press. *AI & Society*. https://doi.org/10.1007/s00146-019-00908-9

Donk, A., Metag, J., Kohring, M., & Marcinkowski, F. (2012). Framing Emerging Technologies: Risk Perceptions of Nanotechnology in the German Press. *Science Communication*, *34*(1), 5–29. https://doi.org/10.1177/1075547011417892

EC. (2017). *Special Eurobarometer: Attitudes towards the impact of digitisation and automation on daily life*. European Commission - Directorate-General for Communications Networks, Content and Technology. https://ec.europa.eu/digital-single-market/en/news/ attitudes-towards-impact-digitisation-and-automation-daily-life

EC. (2020). *On Artificial Intelligence—A European approach to excellence and trust*. European Commision. https://ec.europa.eu/digital-single-market/en/news/white-paper -artificial-intelligence-european-approach-excellence-and-trust

Entman, R. M. (1993). Framing: Toward clarification of a fractured paradigm. *Journal of Communication*, *43*(4), 51–58. https://doi.org/10.1111/j.1460-2466.1993.tb01304.x

Fast, E., & Horvitz, E. (2017). Long-term trends in the public perception of artificial intelligence. In *Proceedings of the AAAI Conference on Artificial Intelligence*, *31*(1), 963–969. https://doi.org/10.1609/aaai.v31i1.10635

Fonseca, R. B. (2012). *A Ciência e a Tecnologia na Imprensa Portuguesa: 1976–2005*. ISCTE-IUL.

Goffman, E. (1974). *Frame analysis: An essay on the organization of experience*. Northeastern University Press. /z-wcorg/.

Government, P. (2019). *National Strategy for Artificial Intelligence 2030*. https://www .portugal.gov.pt/pt/gc21/comunicacao/documento?i=estrategia-inteligencia-artificial-2030

Groboljsek, B., & Mali, F. (2012). Daily newspapers' views on nanotechnology in Slovenia. *Science Communication*, *34*(1), 30–56. https://doi.org/10.1177/1075547011427974

Hannerz, U., & Gingrich, A. (Eds.). (2017). *Small Countries: Structures and Sensibilities*. University of Pennsylvania Press.

Hayes, A. F., & Krippendorff, K. (2007). Answering the call for a standard reliability measure for coding data. *Communication Methods and Measures*, *1*(1), 77–89.

Holguín, L. M. (2018). *Communicating artificial intelligence through newspapers: Where is the real danger*. Thesis. Media Technology MSc Program, Leiden University, The Netherlands. Available: https://mediatechnology.leiden.edu/images/uploads/docs/martin -holguin-thesis-communicating-ai-through-newspapers.pdf

Holliman, R. (2004). Media coverage of cloning: A study of media content, production and reception. *Public Understanding of Science*, *13*(2), 107–130. https://doi.org/10.1177 /0963662504043862

Jasanoff, S. (2001). Ordering life: Law and the normalization of biotechnology. *Politeia*, *17*(62), 34–50.

Jasanoff, S. (2015). Future imperfect: Science, technology, and the imagination of modernity. In S. Jasanoff & S. Kim (Eds.), *Dreamscapes of Modernity: Sociotechnical imaginaries and the Fabrication of Power* (pp. 1–33). University of Chicago Press.

Johnson, D. G., & Verdicchio, M. (2017). Reframing AI Discourse. *Minds and Machines*, *27*(4), 575–590. https://doi.org/10.1007/s11023-017-9417-6

Kim, S.-H., Besley, J. C., Oh, S.-H., & Kim, S. Y. (2014). Talking about bio-fuel in the news. *Journalism Studies*, *15*(2), 218–234. https://doi.org/10.1080/1461670X.2013.809193

Kjærgaard, R. S. (2010). Making a small country count: Nanotechnology in Danish newspapers from 1996 to 2006. *Public Understanding of Science*, *19*(1), 80–97. https://doi.org/10.1177/0963662508093090

Krafft, P. M., Young, M., Katell, M., Huang, K., & Bugingo, G. (2020). Defining AI in policy versus practice. In *Proceedings of the AAAI/ACM Conference on AI, Ethics, and Society (AIES '20)*. Association for Computing Machinery, New York, pp. 72–78. https://doi.org/10.1145/3375627.3375835

Krippendorff, K. (2004). Reliability in content analysis. *Human Communication Research*, *30*(3), 411–433. https://doi.org/10.1111/j.1468-2958.2004.tb00738.x

Lagendijk, A., Hillebrand, B., Kalmar, E., van Marion, I., & van der Sanden, M. (2019). Blockchain innovation and framing in the Netherlands: How a technological object turns into a 'hyperobject.' *Technology in Society*, *59*, 101175. https://doi.org/10.1016/j.techsoc.2019.101175

Lempiälä, T., Apajalahti, E.-L., Haukkala, T., & Lovio, R. (2019). Socio-cultural framing during the emergence of a technological field: Creating cultural resonance for solar technology. *Research Policy*, *48*(9), 103830. https://doi.org/10.1016/j.respol.2019.103830

Mallett, A., Jegen, M., Philion, X. D., Reiber, R., & Rosenbloom, D. (2018). Smart grid framing through coverage in the Canadian media: Technologies coupled with experiences. *Renewable and Sustainable Energy Reviews*, *82*, 1952–1960. https://doi.org/10.1016/j.rser.2017.06.013

McCombs, M., & Shaw, D. L. (1972). The agenda-setting function of mass media. *Public Opinion Quarterly*, *36*(2), 176–187.

Mendes, H. (2002). Visibilidade da ciência nos mass media: A tematização da ciência nos jornais Público, Correio da Manhã e Expresso (1990 e 1997). In M. E. Gonçalves (Ed.), *Os Portugueses e a Ciência* (pp. 31–78). Dom Quixote.

Micó, J.-L., Casero-Ripollés, A., & García-Orosa, B. (2022). Platforms in journalism 4.0: The impact of the fourth industrial revolution on the news industry. In J. Vázquez-Herrero, A. Silva-Rodríguez, M.-C. Negreira-Rey, C. Toural-Bran, & X. López-García (Eds.), *Total Journalism: Models, Techniques and Challenges* (pp. 241–253). Springer International Publishing. https://doi.org/10.1007/978-3-030-88028-6_18

Neri, H., & Cozman, F. (2019). The role of experts in the public perception of risk of artificial intelligence. *AI & Society*. https://doi.org/10.1007/s00146-019-00924-9

Nisbet, M. C., Brossard, D., & Kroepsch, A. (2003). Framing Science: The Stem Cell Controversy in an Age of Press/Politics. *Harvard International Journal of Press/Politics*, *8*(2), 36–70. https://doi.org/10.1177/1081180X02251047

Ouchchy, L., Coin, A., & Dubljević, V. (2020). AI in the headlines: The portrayal of the ethical issues of artificial intelligence in the media. *AI & Society*, *35*(4), 927–936. https://doi.org/10.1007/s00146-020-00965-5

Parratt-Fernández, S., Mayoral-Sánchez, J., & Mera-Fernández, M. (2021). The application of artificial intelligence to journalism: An analysis of academic production. *Profesional de La Información*, *30*(3). https://doi.org/10.3145/epi.2021.may.17

Perrault, R., Shoham, Y., Brynjolfsson, E., Clark, J., Etchemendy, J., Grosz, B., Lyons, T., Manyika, J., Mishra, S., & Niebles, J. C. (2019). *The AI index 2019 annual report*. Stanford University.

Pew. (2017). *Automation in everyday life.* Pew Research Center. https://www.pewresearch.org /internet/2017/10/04/automation-in-everyday-life/

Pilling, F., & Coulton, P. (2019). Forget the Singularity, its mundane artificial intelligence that should be our immediate concern. *The Design Journal, 22*(sup1), 1135–1146. https://doi.org /10.1080/14606925.2019.1594979

Pouteau, S. (2002). The food debate: Ethical versus substantial equivalence. *Journal of Agricultural and Environmental Ethics, 15*(3), 289–303.

Ramos-Martín, J., & Barreneche, C. (2020). Artificial Intelligence. In D. L. Merskin (Ed.), *The SAGE international encyclopedia of mass media and society* (pp. 88–89). SAGE Publications, Inc.

Rhee, J. (2018). *The robotic imaginary: The human and the price of dehumanized labor.* University of Minnesota Press.

Richardson, K. (2015). *An anthropology of robots and AI: Annihilation anxiety and machines.* Routledge.

Roff, H. M. (2019). The frame problem: The AI "arms race" isn't one. *Bulletin of the Atomic Scientists, 75*(3), 95–98. https://doi.org/10.1080/00963402.2019.1604836

Romanach, L., Carr-Cornish, S., & Muriuki, G. (2015). Societal acceptance of an emerging energy technology: How is geothermal energy portrayed in Australian media? *Renewable and Sustainable Energy Reviews, 42*, 1143–1150. https://doi.org/10.1016/j.rser.2014.10.088

Runge, K. K., Chung, J. H., Su, L. Y.-F., Brossard, D., & Scheufele, D. A. (2018). Pink slimed: Media framing of novel food technologies and risk related to ground beef and processed foods in the U.S. *Meat Science, 143*, 242–251. https://doi.org/10.1016/j.meatsci.2018.04.013

Sandoval, E. B., Mubin, O., & Obaid, M. (2014). *Human Robot Interaction and Fiction: A Contradiction* (M. Beetz, B. Johnston, & M.-A. Williams, Eds.; pp. 54–63). Springer International Publishing.

Scheufele, D. A. (1999). Framing as a theory of media effects. *Journal of Communication, 49*(1), 103–122. https://doi.org/10.1111/j.1460-2466.1999.tb02784.x

Scott Hansen, S. (2022). Public AI imaginaries: How the debate on artificial intelligence was covered in Danish newspapers and magazines 1956–2021. *Nordicom Review, 43*(1), 56–78. https://doi.org/10.2478/nor-2022-0004

Sleeboom-Faulkner, M. (2019). Regulatory brokerage: Competitive advantage and regulation in the field of regenerative medicine. *Social Studies of Science, 49*(3), 355–380.

Stephens, L. F. (2005). News Narratives about Nano S&T in Major U.S. and Non-U.S. Newspapers. *Science Communication, 27*(2), 175–199. https://doi.org/10.1177 /1075547005281520

Sun, S., Zhai, Y., Shen, B., & Chen, Y. (2020). Newspaper coverage of artificial intelligence: A perspective of emerging technologies. *Telematics and Informatics, 53*, 101433. https:// doi.org/10.1016/j.tele.2020.101433

Te Kulve, H. (2006). Evolving repertoires: Nanotechnology in daily newspapers in the Netherlands. *Science as Culture, 15*(4), 367–382. https://doi.org/10.1080 /09505430601022692

UK. (2019). *Regulation for the Fourth Industrial Revolution.* Secretary of State for Business, Energy, and Industrial Strategy. https://www.gov.uk/government/publications/regulation -for-the-fourth-industrial-revolution/regulation-for-the-fourth-industrial-revolution

Van Wichelen, S. (2016). Postgenomics and biolegitimacy: Legitimation work in transnational surrogacy. *Australian Feminist Studies, 31*(88), 172–186.

Veltri, G. A. (2013). Viva la nano-revolución! A semantic analysis of the Spanish National Press. *Science Communication, 35*(2), 143–167. https://doi.org/10.1177/1075547012440353

Vergeer, M. (2020). Artificial intelligence in the Dutch Press: An analysis of topics and trends. *Communication Studies, 71*(3), 373–392. https://doi.org/10.1080/10510974.2020.1733038

Vicente, P. N., & Dias-Trindade, S. (2021). Reframing sociotechnical imaginaries: The case of the Fourth Industrial Revolution. *Public Understanding of Science, 30*(6), 708–723. https:// doi.org/10.1177/09636625211013513

Vicente, P. N., & Flores, A. M. M. (2021). Inteligência Artificial e Jornalismo: Temas Emergentes (2015-2020). *De Que Falamos Quando Dizemos Jornalismo?: Temas Emergentes de Pesquisa*, 175.

Vinuesa, R., Azizpour, H., Leite, I., Balaam, M., Dignum, V., Domisch, S., Felländer, A., Langhans, S. D., Tegmark, M., & Nerini, F. F. (2020). The role of artificial intelligence in achieving the Sustainable Development Goals. *Nature Communications*, *11*(1), 1–10.

Yuana, S. L., Sengers, F., Boon, W., & Raven, R. (2019). Framing the sharing economy: A media analysis of ridesharing platforms in Indonesia and the Philippines. *Journal of Cleaner Production*, *212*, 1154–1165. https://doi.org/10.1016/j.jclepro.2018.12.073

9. AI bias, news framing, and mixed-methods approach

Jun Luo, Seungahn Nah, and Jungseock Joo

INTRODUCTION

Artificial intelligence (AI) bias has received increasing attention in media and public discourse, as AI technologies are becoming more ubiquitous in daily life (Zhai et al., 2020; Sundar 2020). AI bias refers to the unfair outcomes based on demographic features when AI is employed to make decisions (Obermeyer et al., 2019; Sap et al., 2019; Ferrer et al., 2021). Although significant advances have been made in identifying the causes of and solutions to reduce algorithmic bias, few studies have explored the media framing of the phenomenon –how AI bias is portrayed in the news media. Answering this question can shed light on how the concept gains significance in media discussions and how it might be related to public perception of and reaction to AI technologies in general.

In order to gain a better understanding of the news media's framing of AI bias, analysis of large-scale textual data is needed. Some framing research on AI and AI-based applications relies heavily on manual content analysis (Chuan et al., 2019; Ouchchy et al., 2020). While hand coding can capture more nuances in languages compared to machines, this approach is subject to researcher bias and requires large amounts of manpower (Walker & Ophir, 2019). Automated dictionary methods, on the other hand, can detect a list of predefined keywords in large-scale text data within seconds using a computer program. However, this approach still relies on the premise that the predefined keywords represent the topic under investigation (Guo et al., 2016). Topic modeling has been widely used in AI research (Bunz & Braghieri, 2022; Curran et al., 2020; Vergeer, 2020). The method explores the latent semantic structure of text documents without predefined inputs by researchers (Blei et al., 2003; DiMaggio et al., 2013). It has been found to be a powerful technique for exploring the overarching categories and frames in discussions surrounding a communication phenomenon (Maier et al., 2018; Ylä-Anttila et al., 2022; Puschmann & Scheffler, 2016). Because it is unclear whether topic modeling outputs can be seen as mere frames, prior framing research has used semantic network analysis and other clustering methods to group sub-groups identified by topic models into meta-categories to represent higher-level frames (Ophir et al., 2021; Hase et al., 2020; Matthes & Kohring, 2008).

This study aims to demonstrate the application of topic modeling in media frame research using the case of AI bias. The chapter first gives an overview of the advantages and disadvantages of different content analysis approaches used in framing research. It then describes the procedure of combining topic modeling, inductive analysis, and semantic network analysis to analyze news documents on AI bias. In the following section, it summarizes the findings on media portrayal of AI bias from 1990 to 2022. Finally, the chapter discusses future directions in using topic modeling to study media frames surrounding AI bias.

TOPIC MODELING: IN COMPARISON TO MANUAL CONTENT ANALYSIS AND DICTIONARY-BASED APPROACH

Topic modeling has been widely used in communication research to explore latent semantic patterns in large-scale text data. It is unsupervised, meaning that no predefined topic categories are needed. One of the most widely used topic models is latent Dirichlet allocation (LDA) proposed by Blei et al. (2003). How many topics one needs to capture the latent semantic structure of a large corpus is an important question in LDA topic modeling applications, which are often determined by researchers. For instance, one can train an LDA topic model on the corpora of interest and evaluate the model performance using metrics such as perplexity scores (Blei et al., 2003; Jacobi et al., 2016). An LDA model then returns top words that are most representative of each topic, which enable researchers to qualitatively interpret large-scale corpora. Before diving into the specific mechanics of LDA topic modeling, it is important to first understand where this approach stands in comparison to another two common methods currently in use in framing research, namely, manual content analysis and dictionary-based approach.

Manual content analysis relies on human coders to identify abstract themes. Depending on the purpose of the study, one can choose to use an inductive or deductive approach. Regarding the inductive content analysis, researchers first read each document (which is the unit of analysis in a study, for instance, a newspaper article or a tweet), group them into sub-categories based on the contents, and categorize subtopics into larger groups to identify common themes and concepts (Elo & Kyngas, 2008; Shea, 2015). The labels (or codes) are iteratively refined until human coders agree that the categories are internally consistent and representative of the entire document. This method is often used when there is no prior research investigating themes or frames related to the topic of interest. Deductive content analysis, on the other hand, is often used when previous literature has documented the frames of a topic. This method generally follows a three-step procedure. Researchers first construct coding schemes for the topic under investigation based on the results or theoretical framework from previous studies. Second, researchers code the documents using the current coding schemes. This is often followed by statistical analysis to investigate the salience of certain framing elements, compare differences in the usage of frames across media types, or trace frame changes over time (Semetko & Valkenburg, 2000; Dirikx et al., 2010). Intuitively, inductive content analysis starts from the text data and narrows down to a small group of abstractions, whereas deductive content analysis applies predefined categories to the current data under investigation for hypothesis testing. It is obvious that manual content analysis requires a large amount of resources in terms of time and money. Focusing on a subset of documents can reduce the cost, but it may suffer from generalizability issues due to sampling procedures (Koltsova et al., 2013).

Dictionary-based methods start to borrow machine power for media content analysis. There are two types of analytical approaches. The first one generally follows four steps: (1) deductively identify key terms based on previous literature; (2) inductively refine the terms based on current data; (3) human coders conduct reliability tests on sample data to determine the final lists of key terms; (4) use computer programs to detect whether any of the key terms are mentioned in the document (Guo et al., 2016; Baden et al., 2017). The second approach is directly applying established dictionaries to the current data under investigation using computer programs without building a dictionary from scratch. The first approach is a mix of deductive and inductive methods whereas the second is purely deductive. However, as indicated in the procedure, the dictionary-based approach still requires researchers to define a list of key terms related to the topic of interest which may again be biased by the prior knowledge of researchers. Although one can still increase the generalizability of a dictionary by adding human validation, this method, nonetheless, suffers from sampling issues unless the validation is implemented on the entire dataset, which is often unlikely for large datasets. Topic modeling, on the other hand, does not require predefined keywords due to its unsupervised nature and, thus, has higher flexibility when used to explore latent semantic structure in text data. This is corroborated by a study by Guo et al. (2016) which compares the performance of dictionary-based approach and unsupervised topic modeling using 77 million tweets on the 2012 US presidential election. They find that the LDA approach is most cost-effective because it generates more valid results and requires less human labor compared to the dictionary-based approach. Note that they also emphasize human validation of topic modeling outcomes is needed as the LDA model tends to generate more false positives and some of the results are not reasonable (2016).

A large body of communication research has applied topic modeling on different text data to explore the latent semantic structure related to the topic of interest (Elgesem et al., 2015; Malik & Pfeffer 2016; Stier et al., 2017; von Nordheim et al., 2018). Maier et al., in the piece *Applying LDA Topic Modeling in Communication Research* (2018), provide comprehensive guidelines for data preprocessing, model selection, and validation of topic modeling. Within the overall trend of applying topic modeling in communication research, there have been ongoing debates on whether topics can be seen as frames among the literature that applies topic modeling to study media framing. Some argue that hidden topics can be used as mere frames (Nerghes & Lee, 2019; Keller et al., 2020; Dkhair & Klochko, 2021). For instance, in a study by Ylä-Anttila et al., that explores media framing of climate change in newspaper articles, the authors argue that the co-occurrence of words approximate framing patterns which make certain aspects of an issue more salient (2021). Another study by Jacobi et al. (2015) also demonstrates the usefulness of topic modeling in media framing analysis using a case study of nuclear technology in *New York Times* articles. For instance, two of their topics identified by the LDA model – the Cold War and nuclear accidents – can be seen as individual issues as well as a particular perspective of describing nuclear technology. They posit that LDA outputs measure specific patterns of vocabulary use and, thus, essentially corresponds to framing devices (2015).

Another stream of work argues that topics can only be interpreted as framing elements, and further analysis is required in order to identify higher-level frames (Walter et al., 2019; Walter et al., 2022). A significant step was made by Walter and Ophir (2019), as they argue that it is unclear whether topics can be treated as mere frames for three reasons. First, the contents and meaning of topics are very sensitive to the change in the number of topics predefined by the researchers before they run the model. Second, topics can be either generic or issue-specific frames, which makes it hard to interpret the outcomes. Last, automated topic models often generate unintelligible topics that require further qualitative interpretation of researchers. Given the limitations of existing automated framing analysis approaches, they propose a three-step mixed-method approach for framing analysis that combines topic modeling, inductive manual coding, and semantic network analysis (analysis of topic model networks (ANTMN)). In another example, Hase et al., (2020) combine topic modeling, manual content analysis, and hierarchical clustering and network analysis to study fear-related news. However, the authors do not define the communities they identify as themes or frames that are made salient when discussing fear; rather, their communities are overarching categories that involve fear as a perspective when discussing different topics, such as economic downturn and protests. Therefore, whether topic model outputs can be seen as mere frames or meta-categories is dependent on the context and topic under investigation in the current research.

AI BIAS: A TOPIC MODELING CASE STUDY

This study follows the approach proposed by Walker and Ophir (2019) to investigate media portrayal of AI bias. Because AI includes a wide range of algorithms and downstream applications, this analysis uses the list of keywords shown in Table 9.1 to search for news articles on AI bias. The keywords include general terms of AI, built-in algorithms of AI technologies, specific AI applications, and terms related to bias and ethical issues. We use Nexis Uni, a widely used news database, to search news transcripts published by the six major television networks in the US (ABC, CBS, CNN, MSNBC, NBC, Fox News). All the transcripts were published in English between 1990 and 2022. Figure 9.1 shows the time trend of news on AI bias by television networks. The y-axis shows the percentage of news transcripts related to AI bias by year. All the percentages of the six television networks will add up to one for each year.

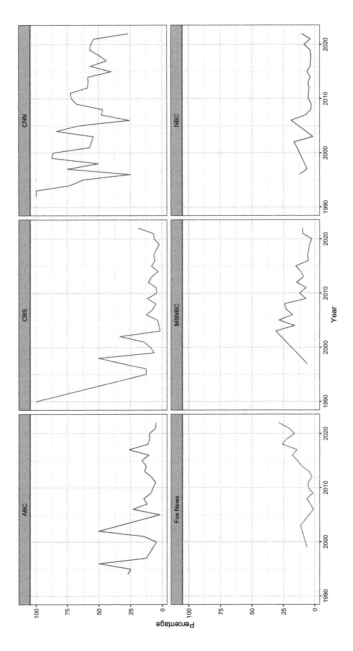

Figure 9.1   Time trend of news transcripts related to AI bias by television networks

BOX 9.1   SEARCH KEYWORDS OF AI BIAS

("artificial intelligence" OR "AI" OR "machine learning" OR "deep learning" OR "neural network*" OR "computer vision" OR "facial recognition" OR "robot" OR "chatbot" OR algorithm OR "digital assistant") AND (bias* OR ethic* OR "fairness" OR discrimination)

The topic modeling and semantic network analysis approach follow the procedure below: (1) preprocess the news corpus, including removing irrelevant news, tokenization, and duplication; (2) tune LDA models and evaluate based on perplexity scores; (3) apply the LDA model to identify abstract topics based on top words, top FREX (FRequency and EXclusivity) words, and representative documents; (4) inductively content analyze the information obtained from the first step to decide whether to include a topic in the final analysis and assign a human-intelligible label to the remaining topics; (5) conduct semantic network analysis based on the co-occurrence of topics to identify frames.

After training the topic model on our AI bias corpus, 50 topics are returned as the best resolution. The manual coding process excludes 23 topics that are not related to AI bias or do not contain consistent contents. Inductive analysis is then conducted on the remaining 27 topics to assign human-intelligible labels. Lastly, semantic network analysis using the Walktrap algorithm returns three topic communities. We manually label the three clusters based on the topics of each community as: (1) benefit and risk, (2) digital journalism, and (3) conflicts and regulations. The following section articulates the contents of each media emphasis frame.

RESULTS

Benefit and Risk

Figure 9.2 shows the results from topic modeling and network community detection. The topics cluster into three communities. The first community (the upper right rectangle area) corresponds to the progress and risk frame. In articles under this frame, AI technologies are portrayed both as a cause of unfair outcomes and a tool to mitigate human biases. The most prominent topic in this group is ethical guidelines (3.27%). This topic focuses on (1) current successful practices of tech companies in reducing AI bias and (2) how companies and the government work together to develop transparent guidelines to solve AI bias and unfair competition among tech companies. Private companies, such as Google, as well as the government are both portrayed as actors that are responsible for this issue in this group of news. One example from CNN reported an upcoming accessibility feature of Google which can understand users whose voices are often hard to identify for previous speech-recognition systems. The news also covered how Pichai envisions Google's future endeavors

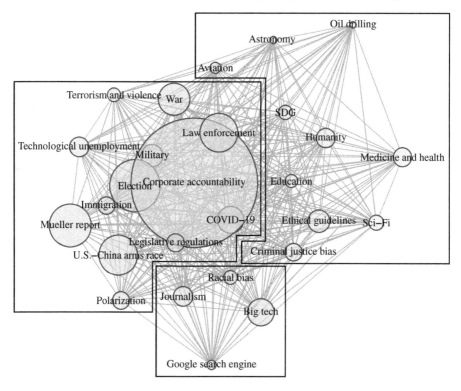

Notes: Node size shows the salience of the topic based on the gamma value. Rectangle area represents topic clusters.

Figure 9.2   *Each node represents the topic*

to make algorithms more transparent and reduce model biases. Another example emphasizes the importance of government interventions in terms of the data privacy issues, as well as the collaborations between regulators and technology companies.

The second most important topic in the frame is criminal justice bias (2.6%). This body of news mainly addresses potential racial bias of facial recognition technologies. The case that the Detroit police department arrested the wrong man due to a mismatch of the facial recognition program is widely discussed in this body of news. This topic emphasizes not only how facial recognition techniques can be useful to identify visual patterns in images and videos, but also the accuracy and bias issues associated with the technique. For instance, the example below discusses Amazon Rekognition and highlights its ethical issues. The news explains the mechanisms and applications of the facial recognition program as well as the errors that accompany the benefits.

The third most prominent topic is humanity (2.8%). A significant body of news emphasizes the short and long-term implications of AI development on humanity.

This group of news focuses on the question of ethics regarding when AI starts to have consciousness or whether machines can manipulate the human mind to develop strong attachments to them: "what does it mean to society and do we really want it"? Another group of news discusses the racial stereotypes perpetuated in the design of robots. For instance, one news article discusses what it means that robots are all "made of shiny white materials."

The rest of the topics in the risks and benefits frame are about how AI technologies have been employed to extend human capabilities along with the risk of bias. For example, in the medicine and health topic, an algorithm that has been deployed to predict a disease was criticized for generating biased outcomes against Black people because the training data are mainly from Caucasian patients. Additionally, privacy issues associated with collecting health data to train algorithms are also discussed in this body of news articles. Another body of topics is slightly more positive. For example, sustainable development goals (SDG) look at how AI has been helping build smart and green cities. One news item in the topic covers Apple employing recycling robots to collect cell phones. Agriculture has also used AI models to help diagnose crop diseases. Aviation, on the other hand, is about facial recognition techniques that help accelerate the passenger boarding process. In addition, planetary scientists have also deployed machine learning algorithms to identify new celestial targets in the universe and used robots for data collection. Lastly, AI and robots are also present in oil drilling and disaster response to complete tasks that would not have been possible for humans alone. In sum, this body of news emphasizes AI as a tool to reduce human bias and extend human capabilities.

Digital Journalism

The second frame emphasizes the impact of AI on digital journalism (the topic cluster on the bottom, as shown in Figure 9.2). Four topics are salient: (1) big tech (3.90%), (2) journalism (2.90%), (3) racial bias (2.03%), and (4) Google search engine (1.34%). The topic of big tech contains news discussing mixed practices of big tech companies with respect to algorithmic bias. For example, YouTube used machine learning and human checks to track accounts that produced violent contents. One of the representative news transcripts in the study discussed how YouTube's moderation includes a combination of machine learning and user flags to prohibit toxic content that alleges superiority of certain groups based on a list of features (e.g., age, gender, race, etc.). In a similar manner, Facebook employs human validation to make sure the trending topics identified by their algorithms are of high quality. However, tech companies are also blamed for its liberal bias and negative impact on teenagers' mental health. The second topic, journalism, is broadly on how social media companies, such as Facebook and Twitter, decide what kind of information the public digest online and, thus, change the user perceptions of current events and the way users seek information on the whole. Specific topics include misinformation, radicalization and sectarianism, and editorial oversight of algorithmic journalism.

Racial bias, on the other hand, includes mixed contents on how AI technologies are deployed to tackle online racial bias or how they are perpetuating human bias based on race. For instance, a body of news articles reports machine learning algorithms are used along with human checks to identify contents and accounts that distribute hate speech, fake news, and racial abuse. Meanwhile, "filter bubbles," created by social media algorithms can also exacerbate extremism among White nationalists. Lastly, the Google search engine is another prominent topic in this framing community. Overall, this group of news centered around how Google has been accused of its biased search ranking system for filtering out conservative contents, which may likely affect voting results.

Conflict and Regulation

The third frame emphasizes the conflicts and regulatory policies around AI bias (the topic cluster on the left, as shown in Figure 9.2). The most prominent topic discusses corporate responsibilities (18.85%) of solving AI bias, which unpacks the dilemma of placing obligations on private companies without violating the First Amendment. Other prominent topics include election (7.62%), the Mueller report (6.24%), and polarization (2.57%). They mainly discussed Facebook media bias and the impact on the 2016 election. This type of news emphasizes the disagreement or accusations among different actors (for instance, Trump and Facebook). News covers different viewpoints regarding Facebook's liberal bias and Trump's accusations against Facebook for exacerbating political polarization by creating online filter bubbles and potentially being responsible for the January 6, 2021 capitol riot. On the other hand, articles on law enforcement discussed the ethical issues associated with having robots detect suspects. The last group of news emphasizes the importance of investment in AI technologies for national security. For instance, news on the topic of the U.S.–China arms race (5.84%) have criticized Google for providing AI services in China and it would become a national security issue because it is also providing the same thing for the US. This body of news approaches AI development as a political issue because it largely determines the superiority of the US in the technological competition with China.

AI bias is also discussed along with policy issues. For instance, news on COVID-19 covers possible ways that AI technologies can be used to assist in COVID-19 testing and hospitalization. A robot may be able to do COVID-19 throat tests in place of humans. Algorithms can also be used to decide who gets a ventilator based on health-related factors. Facial recognition technology can potentially be applied to detect passenger identity for COVID-19 tracking. Whether it would lead to discrimination against people who tested positive is questioned. The topics of war and terrorism and violence include news that covers the ethical and privacy issues associated with using algorithms to identify terrorists and criminals and applying lethal machines and robots in wars. There are also discussions on whether law enforcement agencies have the right to request data from private companies when crimes are involved. Immigration is another policy field that involves AI technologies. For example, one article covers a discriminatory immigration law in Australia that allows algorithms to decide whether to accept an application, as one of the determinants related to health conditions, which means applicants with disabilities are less likely to be accepted. Technological unemployment/job recruitment, on the other hand, talks about the decline in manufacturing employment due to automation as well as the ethical issues associated with having chatbots in charge of job recruitment and interviews. Lastly, the topic of legislative regulations broadly discusses the future direction in regulating facial recognition technology and algorithmic journalism given that those technologies are causing serious privacy and mental health issues.

Variations across Time and Television Networks

Figure 9.3 shows the change of the three frames over time. Overall, the conflict and regulation frame and the benefit and risk frame are the most prominent. The benefit and risk frame started to decrease after reaching an uptick in 2005. In contrast, the conflict and regulation frame has been increasing since then and recently became the most prominent frame among the three in 2010. In 2020, 61% of our corpora

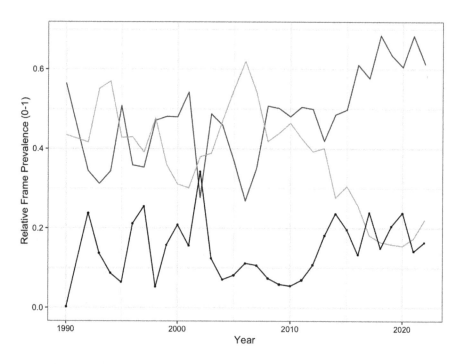

Notes: Straight black line represents the conflict and regulation frame. Gray line represents the benefit and risk frame. Black line with middle dots represents the digital journalism frame.

Figure 9.3   Time trend of frame salience

have used the conflict and regulation frame. From 1990 through to 2010, the digital journalism frame remained the least prominent; however, we observe a moderate increase in the recent decade (from 5.5% to 16.6%). The results correspond to previous findings that progress and generic risk framing often dominates the early media coverage of nanoscale science, but it was later replaced by a regulation and responsibility frame, as the public came to know more about this emerging field (Weaver et al., 2009).

Figure 9.4 shows the temporal trend of the three frames by television networks. The conflict and regulation frame dominates Fox News articles across all the years, while other television networks have more mixed media frames. The benefit and risk frame was the major frame in CNN press coverage of AI bias in the early stage, which was replaced by the conflict and regulation frame after 2010. For CNN and MSNBC, the conflict and regulation frame has been the most prevalent frame since 2010. CBS and NBC, on the other hand, have relatively more balanced media coverage of AI bias in recent years, as the three frames seem to be equally salient in the news articles. Interestingly, the benefit and risk frame and conflict and regulation frame were both replaced by the digital journalism frame during the 2010s, which remained the dominant frame since then.

CONCLUSION AND DISCUSSION

This study applies a topic modeling and semantic network analysis approach to analyze media coverage of AI bias by six major television networks in the United States. It identifies three prevalent frames, namely, benefit and risk, conflict and regulation, and digital journalism. Moreover, the temporal analysis of media frames shows that the benefit and risk frame and the conflict and regulation frame seem to have "competed" in the early stage of the data collection period (1990–2005). However, the conflict and regulation frame started to dominate the press coverage in the late 2000s. This aligns with previous findings that discussions on the benefits and risks associated with a novel technology tend to be salient at the early stage of its emergence (Weaver et al., 2009). As the new technology becomes more ubiquitous, media attention switches to conflicts sparked by unintended harms and who should be blamed and responsible. Meanwhile, digital journalism remained one important but not dominant frame across the years. As for the variations by television networks, Fox News shows consistent patterns with the conflict and regulation frame being the most salient frame followed by the benefit and risk and digital journalism frames. Other television networks show significant changes in frame prevalence across years. The study also observes that ABC, CBS, and NBC have adopted a more balanced framing strategy in recent years, while CNN, Fox News, and MSNBC are biased toward the conflict and regulation frame.

This article provides an overview of existing methodologies of media frame analysis and applies a mixed-method approach proposed by Walter and Ophir (2019) analyzing press coverage of AI bias. Although it builds an important descriptive

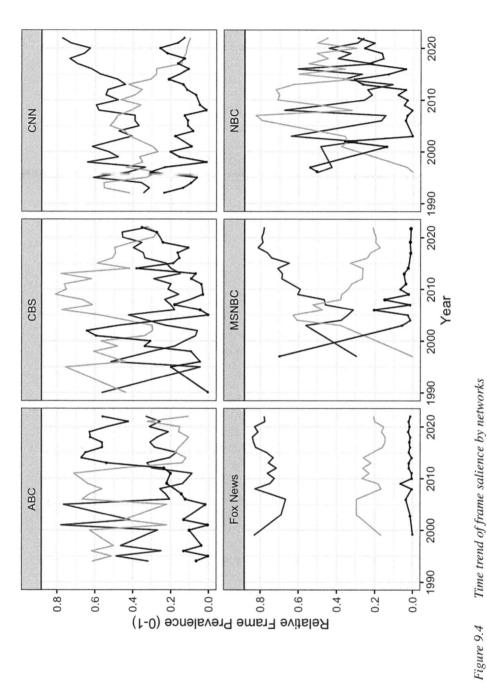

Figure 9.4   *Time trend of frame salience by networks*

foundation of this topic, one limitation is that this study does not investigate any causal links between media ideology, framing, and public opinion formation. Given that AI has been affecting everyday life, understanding the primary determinants of media coverage and public attitudes is crucial for its innovation and development in the future. Future research can further investigate structural and individual-level determinants of media framing on AI bias, specifically, what is shaping how AI is described in press coverage (e.g., political ideology of television networks) and, in turn, how it may influence public trust of AI technologies, and what may moderate the relationship between media messaging and opinion formation. For instance, elite discourse has been documented to influence media framing (Scheufele, 1999). Among Americans, university researchers and non-government scientific organizations are found to be associated with high trust to develop AI technologies (Zhang & Dafoe, 2019). Presumably, messages from the scientific community can largely determine trust of AI technologies while other information sources may negatively impact public opinion. The relationship may be further moderated by the messaging visibility and audience psychological features. Future research can contribute to understanding the "image" of AI by examining different narratives, the factors that are shaping the discourse, and their impact on individual attitude and adoption. Lastly, given that the rise of AI is a global phenomenon, analysis of large-scale multilingual corpora is also needed to unpack the similarity or difference in media framing of AI across countries.

REFERENCES

Baden, C., & Tenenboim-Weinblatt, K. (2017). Convergent news? A longitudinal study of similarity and dissimilarity in the domestic and global coverage of the Israeli-Palestinian conflict. *Journal of Communication*, *67*(1), 1–25. https://doi.org/10.1111/jcom.12272

Blei, D. M., Ng, A. Y., & Jordan, M. I. (2003). Latent dirichlet allocation. *Journal of Machine Learning Research*, *3*(Jan), 993–1022.

Bunz, M., & Braghieri, M. (2022). The AI doctor will see you now: Assessing the framing of AI in news coverage. *AI & Society*, *37*(1), 9–22. https://doi.org/10.1007/s00146-021-01145-9

Curran, N. M., Sun, J., & Hong, J.-W. (2020). Anthropomorphizing AlphaGo: A content analysis of the framing of Google DeepMind's AlphaGo in the Chinese and American press. *AI & Society*, *35*(3), 727–735.

Chuan, C.-H., Tsai, W.-H. S., & Cho, S. Y. (2019). Framing Artificial Intelligence in American Newspapers. *Proceedings of the 2019 AAAI/ACM Conference on AI, Ethics, and Society*, 339–344. https://doi.org/10.1145/3306618.3314285

DiMaggio, P., Nag, M., & Blei, D. (2013). Exploiting affinities between topic modeling and the sociological perspective on culture: Application to newspaper coverage of US government arts funding. *Poetics*, *41*(6), 570–606.

Dirikx, A., & Gelders, D. (2010). To frame is to explain: A deductive frame-analysis of Dutch and French climate change coverage during the annual UN Conferences of the Parties. *Public Understanding of Science*, *19*(6), 732–742.

Dkhair, K., & Klochko, P. (2021). Zelensky's image in Russian and Ukrainian news: Presidential Campaign 2019 in Ukraine. *Central European Journal of Communication*, *14*(1(28)), 62–76.

Elo, S., & Kyngäs, H. (2008). The qualitative content analysis process. *Journal of Advanced Nursing, 62*(1), 107–115. https://doi.org/10.1111/j.1365-2648.2007.04569.x

Elgesem, D., Steskal, L., & Diakopoulos, N. (2015). Structure and content of the discourse on climate change in the blogosphere: The big picture. *Environmental Communication, 9*(2), 169–188. https://doi.org/10.1080/17524032.2014.983536

Ferrer, X., van Nuenen, T., Such, J. M., Coté, M., & Criado, N. (2021). Bias and discrimination in AI: a cross-disciplinary perspective. *IEEE Technology and Society Magazine, 40*(2), 72–80.

Guo, L., Vargo, C. J., Pan, Z., Ding, W., & Ishwar, P. (2016). Big social data analytics in journalism and mass communication: comparing dictionary-based text analysis and unsupervised topic modeling. *Journalism & Mass Communication Quarterly, 93*(2), 332–359. https://doi.org/10.1177/1077699016639231

Hase, V., Engelke, K. M., & Kieslich, K. (2020). The things we fear. Combining automated and manual content analysis to uncover themes, topics and threats in fear-related news. *Journalism Studies, 21*(10), 1384–1402. https://doi.org/10.1080/1461670X.2020.1753092

Jacobi, C., van Atteveldt, W., & Welbers, K. (2016). Quantitative analysis of large amounts of journalistic texts using topic modelling. *Digital Journalism, 4*(1), 89–106. https://doi.org/10.1080/21670811.2015.1093271

Keller, T. R., Hase, V., Thaker, J., Mahl, D., & Schäfer, M. S. (2020). News media coverage of climate change in India 1997–2016: Using automated content analysis to assess themes and topics. *Environmental Communication, 14*(2), 219–235.

Koltsova, O., & Koltcov, S. (2013). Mapping the public agenda with topic modeling: The case of the Russian livejournal. *Policy & Internet, 5*(2), 207–227. https://doi.org/10.1002/1944-2866.POI331

Maier, D., Waldherr, A., Miltner, P., Wiedemann, G., Niekler, A., Keinert, A., , Pfetsch, B., Heyer, G., Reber, U., Häussler, T., Schmid-Petri, H., & Adam, S. (2018). Applying LDA topic modeling in communication research: Toward a valid and reliable methodology. *Communication Methods and Measures, 12*(2–3), 93–118.

Matthes, J., & Kohring, M. (2008). The content analysis of media frames: Toward improving reliability and validity. *Journal of Communication, 58*(2), 258–279.

Malik, M. M., & Pfeffer, J. (2016). A Macroscopic analysis of news content in twitter. *Digital Journalism, 4*(8), 955–979. https://doi.org/10.1080/21670811.2015.1133249

Nerghes, A., & Lee, J. S. (2019). Narratives of the refugee crisis: A comparative study of mainstream-media and Twitter. *Media and Communication, 7*(2), 275–288.

Obermeyer, Z., Powers, B., Vogeli, C., & Mullainathan, S. (2019). Dissecting racial bias in an algorithm used to manage the health of populations. *Science, 366*(6464), 447–453. https://doi.org/10.1126/science.aax2342

Ouchchy, L., Coin, A., & Dubljević, V. (2020). AI in the headlines: The portrayal of the ethical issues of artificial intelligence in the media. *AI & Society, 35*(4), 927–936. https://doi.org/10.1007/s00146-020-00965-5

Ophir, Y., Forde, D. K., Neurohr, M., Walter, D., & Massignan, V. (2021). News media framing of social protests around racial tensions during the Donald Trump presidency. *Journalism*, 14648849211036622.

Ophir, Y., Walter, D., Arnon, D., Lokmanoglu, A., Tizzoni, M., Carota, J., D'Antiga, L., & Nicastro, E., & Nicastro, E. (2021). The framing of COVID-19 in Italian media and its relationship with community mobility: A mixed-method approach. *Journal of Health Communication, 26*(3), 161–173.

Puschmann, C., & Scheffler, T. (2016). Topic modeling for media and communication research: A short primer. HIIG Discussion Paper Series No. 2016-05, Available at SSRN: https://ssrn.com/abstract=2836478 or http://dx.doi.org/10.2139/ssrn.2836478

Sap, M., Card, D., Gabriel, S., Choi, Y., & Smith, N. A. (2019). The Risk of Racial Bias in Hate Speech Detection. *Proceedings of the 57th Annual Meeting of the Association for Computational Linguistics*, 1668–1678. https://doi.org/10.18653/v1/P19-1163

Scheufele, D. A. (1999). Framing as a theory of media effects. *Journal of Communication, 49*(1), 103–122.

Semetko, H. A., & Valkenburg, P. M. V. (2000). Framing European politics: A Content Analysis of Press and Television News. *Journal of Communication, 50*(2), 93–109. https://doi.org/10.1111/j.1460-2466.2000.tb02843.x

Sundar, S. S. (2020). Rise of machine agency: A framework for studying the psychology of human–AI interaction (HAII). *Journal of Computer-Mediated Communication, 25*(1), 74–88.

Shea, N. A. (2015). Examining the nexus of science communication and science education: A content analysis of genetics news articles. *Journal of Research in Science Teaching, 52*(3), 397–409. https://doi.org/10.1002/tea.21193

Stier, S., Posch, L., Bleier, A., & Strohmaier, M. (2017). When populists become popular: Comparing Facebook use by the right-wing movement Pegida and German political parties. *Information, Communication & Society, 20*(9), 1365–1388. https://doi.org/10.1080/1369118X.2017.1328519

Vergeer, M. (2020). Artificial Intelligence in the Dutch Press: An analysis of topics and trends. *Communication Studies, 71*(3), 373–392. https://doi.org/10.1080/10510974.2020.1733038

von Nordheim, G., Boczek, K., & Koppers, L. (2018). Sourcing the sources. *Digital Journalism, 6*(7), 807–828. https://doi.org/10.1080/21670811.2018.1490658

Walter, D., & Ophir, Y. (2019). News frame analysis: An inductive mixed-method computational approach. *Communication Methods and Measures, 13*(4), 248–266. https://doi.org/10.1080/19312458.2019.1639145

Walter, D., & Ophir, Y. (2021). Strategy framing in news coverage and electoral success: An analysis of topic model networks approach. *Political Communication, 38*(6), 707–730.

Walter, D., Ophir, Y., & Jamieson, K. H. (2020). Russian twitter accounts and the partisan polarization of vaccine discourse, 2015–2017. *American Journal of Public Health, 110*(5), 718–724. https://doi.org/10.2105/AJPH.2019.305564

Walter, D., Ophir, Y., Lokmanoglu, A. D., & Pruden, M. L. (2022). Vaccine discourse in white nationalist online communication: A mixed-methods computational approach. *Social Science & Medicine, 298*, 114859. https://doi.org/10.1016/j.socscimed.2022.114859

Weaver, D. A., Lively, E., & Bimber, B. (2009). Searching for a frame: News media tell the story of technological progress, risk, and regulation. *Science Communication, 31*(2), 139–166.

Ylä-Anttila, T., Eranti, V., & Kukkonen, A. (2022). Topic modeling for frame analysis: A study of media debates on climate change in India and USA. *Global Media and Communication, 18*(1), 91–112.

Zhai, Y., Yan, J., Zhang, H., & Lu, W. (2020). Tracing the evolution of AI: conceptualization of artificial intelligence in mass media discourse. *Information Discovery and Delivery, 48*(3), 137–149.

Zhang, B., & Dafoe, A. (2019). *Artificial intelligence: American attitudes and trends.* Available at SSRN: https://ssrn.com/abstract=3312874 or http://dx.doi.org/10.2139/ssrn.3312874

APPENDIX

Table A9.1   Top words and topic labels

Top FREX words	Topic label
people said racist hate racism speech country comments muslim racial	Racial bias
border immigration mexico immigrants administration states clip country united people	Immigration
can companies company like information use internet apple new privacy	Ethical guidelines
russian putin korea u.s ukraine intelligence states united secretary military	Military
republican candidate presidential democratic voters party debate think election race	Election
climate energy change global view solar gas water group party	SDG
flight plane air airlines aircraft search passengers airport pilots can	Aviation
vaccine covid pandemic virus people new dr coronavirus cases states	COVID-19
election voting vote republicans republican now democracy january former capitol	Polarization
google search tech company companies said results bias google's employees	Google search engine
iraq u.s war military afghanistan new united troops iran government	War
house mueller fbi said attorney former committee impeachment department information	Mueller report
dr brain patients cancer study disease people risk doctors doctor	Medicine and health
oil gulf bp spill water coast top kill gas	Oil drilling
human robots can robot intelligence like artificial humans us people	Humanity
said recognition facial company use people used also software rights	Criminal justice bias
people like tonight country us well know clip now new	U.S.-China arms race
space mars nasa shuttle earth station mission launch astronauts go	Astronomy

(Continued)

Table A9.1   (Continued)

Top FREX words	Topic label
trade deal u.s united states iran chinese minister brexit tariffs	Technological unemployment
going think know people right now well can want get	Corporate accountability
social twitter content company platform users people said platforms companies	Big tech
police officers officer shooting people city enforcement gun two killed	Law enforcement
movie film first actor new hollywood star tonight best life	Sci-Fi
school students kids children parents schools education teachers student	Education
attorney constitution federal states legal rights said whether decision also	Legislative regulations
syria isis syrian turkey military war attack u.s weapons assad	Terrorism and violence
new times stories post journalists week said coverage sources book	Journalism

PART III

PUBLIC UNDERSTANDING OF ARTIFICIAL INTELLIGENCE

10. Risk perceptions and trust mechanisms related to everyday AI

Hichang Cho and Rosalie Hooi

INTRODUCTION

Artificial intelligence (AI)-based intelligent machines and smart devices permeate our everyday lives, as they can execute efficiently complex financial transactions, prevent potential crimes, and assist with various tasks, such as social media content recommendation. The increasing ubiquity and rapid advances in AI technology have spurred excitement and optimism but also prompted expressions of growing concerns about privacy and surveillance, unreliability, technological unemployment, misinformation, algorithmic biases, and other ethical considerations. Recent studies have shown that unease about AI threats has rapidly increased (Neri & Cozman, 2019; Shao et al., 2018). These mounting concerns can impede the broad adoption of AI-based applications and initiatives, such as autonomous vehicles and medical assistance devices (Choung et al., 2022; Tong & Sopory, 2019). As AI becomes more prevalent and ubiquitous, poor partnerships and the lack of trust between people and smart systems will become increasingly costly and catastrophic.

This chapter reviews trust and risk perceptions about everyday AI-based systems and applications, such as smart digital assistants and autonomous systems. According to the historical analysis of Twitter data containing "artificial intelligence" (Neri & Cozman, 2019), risk perception is one of the most prominent public topics. Further, risk perception is a crucial determinant of public responses to technological changes (Zhang et al., 2021). As such, a clear understanding of public sentiments about AI risk is crucial in developing a research framework and agenda related to AI. Trust is a key driver of human responses to AI related to risk perception. Trust is defined as one's willingness to become vulnerable to the other agent without controlling it (Mayer et al., 1995). Trust, such as trusting automated machines' decisions (e.g., automated vehicles, autonomous health screening, personalization/recommendation systems), is determined by complex relationships between perceived control, risk, dependency, uncertainty, and power because trust matters when "one feels the tension between depending upon another and instituting controls to make sure that other performs" (McKnight, 2005, p. 1). Given that human interaction with AI is determined by the degree to which users give autonomous control to AI, the trust mechanism is a key concept to be examined.

In short, in this chapter, we review theoretical concepts and corresponding empirical findings related to risk perceptions and trust about everyday AI. In doing so, we aim to provide a holistic and precise understanding of when, why, and how people have a good relationship and interaction with AI-based systems and applications. The insights will also have practical implications. For example, the findings would allow policymakers and tech developers to deploy AI-based systems within the public's comfort zone, thus, increasing trust in AI use and acceptance.

PUBLIC PERCEPTIONS OF AI: RISK PERCEPTIONS AND TRUST

Risk Perceptions and Uncertainties About AI

Given the increased focus on AI in recent years, especially regarding its trustworthiness, ethicality, and reliability, there is no shortage of literature looking at people's perceptions of this rapidly developing technology. Most of these studies have investigated and reported factors influencing perceived risk and trust in AI. In their review of trust literature in AI, Glikson and Woolley (2020) find that trust in machines and technology (compared to trust in other people) can be predicted by design factors (e.g., communication style, physical appearance, or lack thereof), transparency (how the AI operates, e.g., Alan et al., 2014), AI behavior (its interaction with the environment and performance, Oistad et al., 2016), and reliability (consistency of AI behavior across all subjects and across time, e.g., Robinette et al., 2017).

With the availability of large amounts of data and advances in AI, algorithms are increasingly used to make decisions for humans. Given input data, predictive machine learning models can achieve impressive performance. Recent years have witnessed the rise of opaque decision systems, such as deep neural networks, that are difficult to interpret and poorly understood. Understanding the reasons behind a prediction is essential for instilling trust in the results. Unfortunately, such black-box approaches "do not foster trust and most of all responsibility" (Holzinger et al., 2020, p. 194). This lack of transparency brings risks that make it challenging to trust AI. One of the risks is the potential for bias. Without an adequate understanding of the workings of the models, harmful biases may have been incorporated, which could nullify any gains in predictive power, causing concern among critics who feel that learning systems must at least be interpretable to humans (London, 2019). Machine learning systems are trained on raw, historical data which may contain biases and societal prejudices (Walmsley, 2021). The system could then exhibit the same biases when it is deployed to make decisions, leading to incorrect predictions for or excluding the needs and interests of marginalized and under-represented groups. Further, when errors in a model are introduced inadvertently through mislabeled data or deliberately in adversarial attacks, they may be difficult to detect unless there is a sufficient understanding of the workings of the model (Quinn et al., 2022). Not being able to explain AI outcomes also poses a barrier to trust, as there is no means to justify decisions (Adadi & Berrada, 2018). However, not every AI system needs to be explainable. While an explanation of its application in recommender systems, such as the content on our Facebook newsfeed or video recommendations on TikTok, may be inconsequential, most people would agree that it is important to know the reasons behind a critical decision, such as disease diagnosis. In medical AI, there are concerns that black boxes may reduce opportunities for clinicians to justify recommendations and dialogue with patients and undermine patient autonomy to make healthcare decisions that align with their plans and values (Quinn et al., 2022). While explainable AI aims to make system behavior more intelligible to humans by providing explanations, making AI explainable is expensive and requires significant resources in its development and interrogation in practice (Adadi & Berrada, 2018).

Privacy and Surveillance Concerns

Privacy is central to risk perception and trust, as AI-based systems and applications necessitate the collection of user information and their behavioral data to "learn" and adapt to their needs, preferences, and behavioral patterns. Privacy intrusion and worries about information security remain central concerns. Security concerns, for instance, can reduce perceptions of AI's ease of use and usefulness (Park & Jones-Jang, 2022). People have raised concerns about the threat of overpowering government institutions and organizations that collect citizens' personal data, biometrics, and geolocational information (Manheim & Kaplan, 2019).

In addition, there are fears that AI could make it more difficult to protect information. With machine learning, de-identified data collected by commercially available wearable devices can lead to the re-identification of individuals contributing data with high accuracy (Na et al., 2018). The linking of research datasets with widely available large public data resources may create opportunities for re-identification (Simon et al., 2019), resulting in privacy breaches. Moreover, as a continued data supply is required for training and improvement of AI algorithms, data may need to be shared across institutions and even jurisdictions, as leading countries in the AI race may use data sourced from other locations (Wu, 2021). It may also be used in different ways over time (He et al., 2019).

Advances in AI have made possible automated speech recognition, location and object recognition, and face and body gesture tracking, which allow the capture of verbal, visual, and physiological cues that offer insight into people's emotional states, infer intentions, and predict future behavior (Czerwinski et al., 2021; Podoletz, 2022). Gathering sensitive and intimate information directly linked to an individual is intrusive even if the individual is not identifiable as in soft biometrics. Emotional AI may be employed for surveillance and has been in use in China. For instance, AI is used in schools to identify students who are not focused and at checkpoints in Xinjiang to detect signs of aggressiveness and nervousness in individuals (Murgia, 2021).

Many people are also reluctant to use AI-based smart devices or apps for fear of what will become of the information they provide. In addition, people exhibit high levels of uncertainty about giving power and control to AI-based systems. As a result, trade-offs are inevitably juxtaposed against the need for technological advancements and efficiencies. In short, there is a fine line between smart devices being helpful and being intrusive. Researchers have called for more studies to enhance our understanding of how people make decisions involving such trade-offs when using AI-based smart devices.

Factors Influencing Trust in AI and Human–AI Interaction

AI is ubiquitous in many aspects of our lives, such as smart digital assistants Siri, Alexa, and chatbots. Given public concerns and worries about everyday AI-based systems and applications, it is crucial to identify factors that influence people's trust in AI. While more human-like physical characteristics in machines may set up unrealistic expectations, resulting in a loss of trust in agents after the interaction, such qualities also make people view the agent as more trustworthy (Rheu et al., 2021). Several studies seem to suggest that some degree of approximation to human communicative behavior is needed to foster trust. Dialects and accents used by agents can influence trust. When the agent's accent and behavior are congruent with users' expectations, there is more trust than when they are not (Torre et al., 2018). Agents that use the prestigious Standard Southern British English, which is culturally associated with high trust attributions, and behave generously in an investment game are trusted more than agents that use a standard accent and behave meanly. Given that communication encompasses not only the message sent but the accompanying emotions as well, non-verbal expressions and expressive synthetic voices can impact trusting behaviors. A smiling agent increases trust (Elkins & Derrick, 2013), as does a smiling voice, possibly due to the attribution of other positive traits as smiling individuals are assumed to be friendly (Torre et al., 2020). Agents that follow behavioral communication rules during conversations, such as nodding, also promote trust (Aburumman et al., 2022). Persuasion strategies, when used by agents, may affect people's trust in them. While guilt-tripping has no effect on trust (Stoll et al., 2016), agents that use unpleasant and forceful language reduce trust (Ghazali et al., 2017).

The similarity between agent and user in personality and communication styles may result in high trust because of the similarity effect, as similarity breeds liking, and liking influences trust (Nicholson et al., 2001). Embodied conversational agents that match their users in personality are trusted more. More specifically, agents that engage in social dialogue engender greater trust in extroverted users, while task-focused agents are trusted more by introverts (Bickmore & Cassell, 2005). The agent's similarity in a communication style aligned with the cultural background of the user is likely to induce positive evaluation. Cultures that prefer an implicit communication style are more likely to accept implicit recommendations from agents than cultures that favor a straightforward communication style (Rau et al., 2009). The agents were also perceived to be more likable, trustworthy, and credible. An agent's interaction style that matches the task competency of the user also leads to enhanced trust in the site employing the agent (Chattaraman et al., 2019). Thus, digital assistants that use social- instead of task-oriented interaction should be paired with high-competency users needing less task-related assistance. In contrast, task-oriented assistants should be matched with low-competency users.

Through the exchange of verbal and non-verbal interaction cues, people may form the belief that they are engaged in a direct two-way conversation with the agent and develop a parasocial relationship. The parasocial relationship has traditionally been applied to the social relationship that people form with media personalities. Subsequently, it was used to explain the closeness and intimacy people experience in human-like interactions with intelligent agents. People are likely to form parasocial relationships with anthropomorphic agents (Whang & Im, 2021), perceiving them as social actors. Parasocial interactions, which resemble real-life interpersonal communication, increase trust (Hsieh & Lee, 2021) and improve communication quality (Lee & Park, 2022). Though feelings of parasocial interaction could arise in isolated interactions, they may intensify following continued interactions. Through the interactions, individuals may feel psychological closeness or intimacy with agents and may see them as friends (Rodero & Lucas, 2021).

Technological advances have imbued AI with various traits resembling humans, such as eye gaze, voice, and humanoid appearance. Among these attributes, perceptions of homophily and attraction affect interpersonal communication (McCroskey et al., 2006), as they promote communication effectiveness and increase the likelihood of communication attempts (Rogers & Bhowmik, 1970). Individuals perceive anthropomorphic agents as similar to them primarily due to the rich media that these agents utilize. Rich media can communicate multiple cues and accommodate rapid feedback, reducing ambiguity and equivocality to enhance communication (Daft & Lengel, 1984). Due to media richness, agents can hold conversations, use diverse signs and symbols in speech and text, recognize different users' voices to provide personalized responses, communicate with users through their voices, and perform tasks, assuming a host of human-like characteristics. The perceived intelligence and similarity to humans can increase user trust (Troshani et al., 2021). Anthropomorphism enhances social presence (Hsieh & Lee, 2021) and increases trust (Liu & Tao, 2022; Troshani et al., 2021). However, the role attraction plays in AI trust formation is still not well-understood due to limited research, although emerging studies indicate that social and task attraction can increase trust (Chen & Park, 2021).

Other than communication style, others have posited that individual user factors such as personality traits (e.g., Wissing & Reinhard, 2018) and attachment style (Gillath et al., 2021) also impact risk and trust perceptions. Limited research has also demonstrated that risk perceptions and trust about AI-based applications are affected by cognitive appraisals, affect heuristics (Tong & Sopory, 2019), control, and power (Guo, 2020). Perceived ease of use also contributes to trust in AI assistants, which, in turn, results in positive attitudes and perceived usefulness of the technology (Choung et al., 2022).

Furthermore, several have stated the need to distinguish between different types of AI when studying risk and trust perceptions (Glikson & Woolley, 2020). There is a wide range of AI technology (e.g., weak vs. strong AI, robotic vs. virtual vs. embedded AI), each with unique characteristics and functions which may have different implications for the quality (type of) and quantity of trust instilled in it. For example, while the layperson might find it harder to trust embedded AI because it is an unseen, faceless entity (Alan et al., 2014), the physical presence of robotic AI can make it seem more trustable (Li, 2015).

CURRENT DEVELOPMENTS AND UPCOMING TRENDS

Trust: Multidimensional and Context-dependent Trust

Adding to the complexity of studying risk and trust perceptions of AI, several have pointed out that trust is a multifaceted construct that depends on the context (Glikson & Woolley, 2020; Oksanen et al., 2020).

Trust is a multifaceted construct, as it is represented by a combination of an individual's trust dispositions (trusting beliefs), interpersonal perceptions and social judgments (trustworthiness [competence, integrity, and benevolence] of the other party), and the overall environments (e.g., government regulations or system-level trust). In decision-making, there exist at least two types of trust: knowledge/experience-based trust vs. swift trust based on cognitive heuristics and motivated reasoning. Recent research (e.g., Haring et al., 2021) shows that swift trust can be used to describe the trust between human–robot teams. Based on swift trust, people rapidly develop a working relationship and interact with machines to perform team tasks without relying on prior experience or knowledge.

Accordingly, the different types of AI and the respective contexts of their usage may have different implications for the various aspects of trust (e.g., emotional vs. cognitive trust, initial vs. sustained trust). Indeed, emerging studies have found that emotional trust, but not cognitive trust, matters when people decide to entirely rely on an AI recommendation system for decision-making (Shi et al., 2021). As the human-like features of AI recommendation systems can generate fear and anxiety, emotional trust that stems from individuals' positive feelings have a stronger effect than cognitive trust, which employs rational evaluations. Shi and colleagues also found that when the perceived risk is high, people base their decision to use AI recommendation systems on cognitive trust, but when perceived risk is low, they rely more on emotional trust. While scholars emphasize the importance of sustained trust, having explainable or interpretable models may not be adequate. Instead, sound policies that engage people and perspectives from varied disciplines and groups to address complex issues with broad implications may help to alleviate concerns about AI.

Social Amplification of Risk

In addition to the impact of AI characteristics, current literature also looks at underlying social and cultural factors influencing public risk perceptions and subsequent distrust toward AI. Public concerns over AI include potential physical harm because of system failures, ethical or moral issues, and social implications. These negative attitudes toward AI may be perpetuated and attenuated on media platforms, especially as recent years have seen an increased discussion on the benefits and concerns of AI on multiple platforms, such as on social media, popular culture, and journal and newspaper articles (Fast & Horvitz, 2017; Neri & Cozman, 2020). According to the social amplification of risk framework (SARF) (Kasperson et al., 1988), risk perceptions are socially constructed by public discourses, media frames, cultural forces, and cognitive biases. As such, risk perception is the experience of risk not as physical harm but as "the result of a process by which individuals or groups learn to acquire or create interpretations of hazards. These interpretations provide rules of how to select, order, and often explain signals from the physical world" (Slovic 2016, p. 140).

Interestingly, as Neri and Cozman (2019) point out, the perception of risk in AI is mostly attributable to influence from expert opinion rather than past evidence or personal experience of AI failure. Fears and concerns associated with AI are primarily based on hypothetical situations in which AI potentially causes harm or defies ethical standards. This, coupled with the fact that there is a gap between the public's understanding of AI and what AI can actually do (Cave, Coughlan, & Dihal, 2019) and that media coverage frequently emphasizes negative traits and instances of AI (Chuan et al., 2019), set the stage for many to overemphasize the risks of AI, leading to a lack of trust. Regarding AI, public sentiments have become increasingly politicized, polarized, and contentious. Media frames and experts' positions are divided into opposing frames: progress vs. threat, gain vs. loss, and excitement vs. worry (Neri & Cozman, 2019; van Noort, 2022).

As the use of AI accelerates, many countries have implemented national strategies to advance the use and development of AI. Media coverage of AI has spiked in recent years in tandem with its growing relevance in society. In particular, for a topic such as AI in which the public lacks a clear understanding, media frames help to interpret events and make sense of the emerging technology amid ambiguous information. Information, events, and experiences can be emphasized or suppressed through framing. In this way, public perception of risks may be amplified or attenuated. For example, when AI is presented as a solution for problems (e.g., in the United Kingdom; Brennen et al., 2018) rather than as potentially out of control, there is greater support for it (Bingaman et al., 2021). AI narratives on a Chinese state media outlet's YouTube channel use discourses of hope to convey China's aspirations to catch up to the US in AI developments, pride to showcase achievements in AI, and fear to present the US reaction to China's competitiveness in AI as well as anticipated risks of AI, such as job loss and data privacy (van Noort, 2022).

Public perception of AI varies across cultures and societies (Cave et al., 2018). Whether people are fearful or hopeful of AI depends, partly, on the narratives circulated in the media. Several studies found the news media coverage of AI in the US to be more optimistic than pessimistic, discussing benefits more than risks (Chuan et al., 2019; Duberry & Hamidi, 2021; Fast & Horvitz, 2017). By focusing on the good that AI brings and generating positive emotions, the media can shape public perception of AI. The findings of a study in Austria are similar to the results from the US. Austrian media tends to be optimistic in its coverage (Brantner & Saurwein, 2021). However, European newspapers surveyed by Duberry and Hamidi (2021) during the COVID-19 pandemic had a more balanced perspective of the risks and benefits of

AI. In the UK, AI has been politicized, with ideology influencing the topics that news outlets choose to emphasize (Brennen et al., 2018). Thus, while the public may generally be supportive of AI (Bingaman et al., 2021), their perception of the severity of the associated risks may be quite different. Also, articles on AI in the UK media are often industry-related, drawing information from industry sources, allowing the commercial sector to propagate their agenda to augment AI's value and potential to influence public perception of the risks involved (Brennen et al., 2018).

The Chinese government has been pushing for electronic transactions and encouraging the growth of the Chinese AI industry. Chinese news media, which tend not to challenge the government, frequently link AI governance to economic growth and innovation, and AI is framed positively in traditional media (Cui & Wu, 2021). Similar to traditional media, AI is positively evaluated on Chinese social media, as it is dominated by state agencies and technology companies keen to laud AI's potential to boost China's economic and political power (Zeng et al., 2022). The type of media consumed can affect the perception of AI. While both traditional and social media users hold positive AI perceptions, using television and social media platforms (e.g., WeChat), but not newspapers, leads to benefit perception (Cui & Wu, 2021). In comparison, Japanese newspapers fostered positive emotion associated with high perceived benefits and low perceived risk of AI, enhancing the intention to interact with robots, although it appeared to have no effect on interaction intention with AI (Li et al., 2021).

Some researchers found popular portrayals of AI in media and entertainment to be sensationalist and potentially misleading with exaggerated optimism and melodramatic pessimism (Cave et al., 2018; Goode, 2018), which could result in heightened risk perception. However, recent portrayals of AI in films are less threatening and more approachable (Dieter & Gessler, 2021). There is some evidence that this reimagining, as helpful, friendly companions of humans was purposeful, as AI characters may attenuate fears of AI being malevolent and menacing (Sundar et al., 2016). Nonetheless, entertainment media may have less impact on people's beliefs about AI because of the varied sources available for information and perhaps because of people's improved ability to discern between realistic and unrealistic portrayals of AI (Nader et al., 2022).

To some extent, the structural changes that swept across the media industry have also affected the quality of reporting and, consequently, the level of trust in AI. Due to a decline in advertising revenues, news organizations scaled down on specialty desks, resources, and staff, resulting in coverage of technical stories by non-specialist reporters and greater pressure on journalists who have less time for fieldwork while having to shoulder a heavier workload. This often leads to more reliance on wire articles or press releases that could bring the exaggerations in public relations (PR) material into news reports (Brennen et al., 2018; Sumner et al., 2014). Ouchchy et al. (2020), for instance, suggest that journalists write articles about AI with insufficient knowledge of AI technology, as they found its coverage to be shallow and lacking sophistication in content, which could result in AI being mystified and consequently distrusted.

CONCLUSION

Empirical studies on trust and AI have demonstrated that the relationship may be affected by many factors, including age, political climate, culture, and design. In addition, countries that have deep involvement in technology, such as Japan and South Korea, are generally more accepting and trusting of AI. Cognizance of these factors can help us to better understand how trust might develop. At the same time, a sound policy is needed to guide the research and development of beneficial AI, provide a framework for governance and cross-border cooperation, and address issues on economic changes, labor shifts, and ethics, among others. The assurance that there are regulations in place and strategies to handle looming problems can go some distance in alleviating concerns and building trust.

AI-based applications and systems rapidly permeate our daily lives and have become an integral part of society. However, there remain public concerns about potential risks and problems caused by everyday AI as reviewed above. The success of integrating AI into broad social systems critically depends on the public's trust in and risk perceptions about AI technology. Therefore, we call for more studies that systematically examine the sources and underlying processes through which we can better understand how people perceive and respond to everyday AI. For AI to be truly smart, it must be designed and engineered to address human worries and concerns and must learn to interact in ways that promote trust. Future studies should continue to adopt interdisciplinary approaches to unpack complex trust mechanisms and risk perception regarding everyday AI.

REFERENCES

Aburumman, N., Gillies, M., Ward, J. A., & Hamilton, A. F. C. (2022). Nonverbal communication in virtual reality: Nodding as a social signal in virtual interactions. *International Journal of Human-Computer Studies*, *164*, 102819. https://doi.org/10.1016/j.ijhcs.2022.102819

Adadi, A., & Berrada, M. (2018). Peeking inside the black-box: A survey on explainable artificial intelligence (XAI). *IEEE Access*, *6*, 52138–52160.

Alan, A., Costanza, E., Fischer, J., Ramchurn, S. D., Rodden, T., & Jennings, N. R. (2014). A field study of human-agent interaction for electricity tariff switching. In 13th *international conference on autonomous agents and multiagent systems* (AAMAS 2014), (pp. 965–972). Paris, France.

Bickmore, T., & Cassell, J. (2005). Social dialogue with embodied conversational agents. In *Advances in natural multimodal dialogue systems* (pp. 23–54). Springer Science & Business Media.

Bingaman, J., Brewer, P. R., Paintsil, A., & Wilson, D. C. (2021). "Siri, show me scary images of AI": Effects of text-based frames and visuals on support for artificial intelligence. *Science Communication*, *43*(3), 388–401. https://doi.org/10.1177/1075547021998069

Brantner, C., & Saurwein, F. (2021). Covering technology risks and responsibility: Automation, artificial intelligence, robotics, and algorithms in the media. *International Journal of Communication*, *15*, 5074–5098.

Brennen, J. S., Howard, P. N., & Nielsen, R. K. (2018). An industry-led debate: How UK media cover artificial intelligence. In *Reuters institute for the study of journalism factsheet*. University of Oxford.

Cave, S., Coughlan, K., & Dihal, K. (2019). "Scary robots" examining public responses to AI. *AIES 2019 – Proceedings of the 2019 AAAI/ACM Conference on AI, Ethics, and Society* (pp. 331–337).

Cave, S., Craig, C., Dihal, K., Dillon, S., Montgomery, J., Singler, B., & Taylor, L. (2018). *Portrayals and perceptions of AI and why they matter*. The Royal Society. https://www.repository.cam.ac.uk/bitstream/handle/1810/287193/EMBARGO%20-%20web%20version.pdf?sequence=1

Chattaraman, V., Kwon, W.-S., Gilbert, J. E., & Ross, K. (2019). Should AI-Based, conversational digital assistants employ social-or task-oriented interaction style? A task-competency and reciprocity perspective for older adults. *Computers in Human Behavior, 90*, 315–330.

Chen, Q. Q., & Park, H. J. (2021). How anthropomorphism affects trust in intelligent personal assistants. *Industrial Management & Data Systems, 121*(12), 2722–2737. https://doi.org/10.1108/IMDS-12-2020–0761

Choung, H., David, P., & Ross, A. (2022). Trust in AI and its role in the acceptance of AI technologies. *International Journal of Human–Computer Interaction*, 1–13.

Chuan, C. H., Tsai, W. H. S., & Cho, S. Y. (2019). Framing artificial intelligence in American newspapers. *AIES 2019 – Proceedings of the 2019 AAAI/ACM Conference on AI, Ethics, and Society* (pp. 339–344).

Cui, D., & Wu, F. (2021). The influence of media use on public perceptions of artificial intelligence in China: Evidence from an online survey. *Information Development, 37*(1), 45–57. https://doi.org/10.1177/0266666919893411

Czerwinski, M., Hernandez, J., & McDuff, D. (2021). Building an AI that feels: AI systems with emotional intelligence could learn faster and be more helpful. *IEEE Spectrum, 58*(5), 32–38.

Daft, R. L., & Lengel, R. H. (1984). Information richness. A new approach to managerial behavior and organization design. In B. M. Staw & L. L. Cummings (Eds.), *Research in organizational behavior* (Vol. 6, pp. 199–233). JAI.

Dieter, D. G., & Gessler, E. C. (2021). A preferred reality: Film portrayals of robots and AI in popular science fiction. *Journal of Science & Popular Culture, 4*(1), 59–76.

Duberry, J., & Hamidi, S. (2021). Contrasted media frames of AI during the COVID-19 pandemic: A content analysis of US and European newspapers. *Online Information Review, 45*(4), 758–776. https://doi.org/10.1108/OIR-09-2020-0393

Elkins, A. C., & Derrick, D. C. (2013). The sound of trust: Voice as a measurement of trust during interactions with embodied conversational agents. *Group Decision and Negotiation, 22*(5), 897–913.

Fast, E., & Horvitz, E. (2017). Long-term trends in the public perception of artificial intelligence. *Proceedings of the 31st AAAI Conference on Artificial Intelligence*, San Francisco, CA.

Ghazali, A. S., Ham, J., Barakova, E., & Markopoulos, P. (2017). The influence of social cues and controlling language on agent's expertise, sociability, and trustworthiness. *Proceedings of the Companion of the 2017 ACM/IEEE International Conference on Human-Robot Interaction*, Vienna, Austria.

Gillath, O., Ai, T., Branicky, M., Keshmiri, S., Davison, R., & Spaulding, R. (2021). Attachment and trust in artificial intelligence. *Computers in Human Behavior, 115*(52), 106607.

Glikson, E., & Woolley, A. W. (2020). Human trust in artificial intelligence: Review of empirical research. *Academy of Management Annals, 14*(2), 627–660.

Goode, L. (2018). Life, but not as we know it: AI and the popular imagination. *Culture Unbound, 10*(2), 185–207.

Guo, W. (2020). Explainable Artificial Intelligence for 6G: Improving trust between human and machine. *IEEE Communications Magazine, 58*(6), 39–45.

Haring, K. S., Phillips, E., Lazzara, E. H., Ullman, D., Baker, A. L., & Keebler, J. R. (2021). Applying the swift trust model to human-robot teaming. In *Trust in human-robot interaction* (pp. 407–427). Academic Press.

He, J., Baxter, S. L., Xu, J., Xu, J., Zhou, X., & Zhang, K. (2019). The practical implementation of artificial intelligence technologies in medicine. *Nature Medicine, 25*(1), 30–36.

Holzinger, A., Carrington, A., & Müller, H. (2020). Measuring the quality of explanations: The system causability scale (SCS). *KI – Künstliche Intelligenz, 34*(2), 193–198. https://doi .org/10.1007/s13218-020-00636-z

Hsieh, S. H., & Lee, C. T. (2021). Hey Alexa: Examining the effect of perceived socialness in usage intentions of AI assistant-enabled smart speaker. *Journal of Research in Interactive Marketing, 15*(2), 267–294. https://doi.org/10.1108/JRIM-11–2019–0179

Kasperson, R. E., Renn, O., Slovic, P., Brown, H. S., Emel, J., Goble, R., , Kasperson, J. X., & Ratick, S. (1988). The social amplification of risk: A conceptual framework. *Risk Analysis, 8*(2), 177–187.

Lee, M., & Park, J. S. (2022). Do parasocial relationships and the quality of communication with AI shopping chatbots determine middle-aged women consumers' continuance usage intentions? *Journal of Consumer Behaviour*, 1–13. https://doi.org/10.1002/cb.2043

Li, J. (2015). The benefit of being physically present: A survey of experimental works comparing copresent robots, telepresent robots and virtual agents. *International Journal of Human-Computer Studies, 77*, 23–37.

Li, Y., Guo, Y., & Liu, S. (2021). How Do traditional media function in social learning about AI? Psychological and cognitive reactions to AI-powered communication. *Communication Studies, 72*(6), 1034–1052. https://doi.org/10.1080/10510974.2021.2011357

Liu, K., & Tao, D. (2022). The roles of trust, personalization, loss of privacy, and anthropomorphism in public acceptance of smart healthcare services. *Computers in Human Behavior, 127*, 107026. https://doi.org/10.1016/j.chb.2021.107026

London, A. J. (2019). Artificial intelligence and black-box medical decisions: Accuracy versus explainability. *Hastings Center Report, 49*(1), 15–21.

Manheim, K., & Kaplan, L. (2019). Artificial intelligence: Risks to privacy and democracy. *Yale Journal of Law & Technology, 21*, 106–188.

Mayer, R. C., Davis, J. H., & Schoorman, F. D. (1995). An integrative model of organizational trust. *Academy of Management Review, 20*(3), 709–734.

McCroskey, L. L., McCroskey, J. C., & Richmond, V. P. (2006). Analysis and improvement of the measurement of interpersonal attraction and homophily. *Communication Quarterly, 54*(1), 1–31.

McKnight, D. H. (2005). Trust in information technology. *The Blackwell Encyclopedia of Management, 7*, 329–331.

Murgia, M. (2021). Emotion recognition: Can AI detect human feelings from a face? *Financial Times.* https://www.ft.com/content/c0b03d1d-f72f-48a8-b342-b4a926109452

Na, L., Yang, C., Lo, C.-C., Zhao, F., Fukuoka, Y., & Aswani, A. (2018). Feasibility of reidentifying individuals in large national physical activity data sets from which protected health information has been removed with use of machine learning. *JAMA Network Open, 1*(8), e186040. https://doi.org/10.1001/jamanetworkopen.2018.6040

Nader, K., Toprac, P., Scott, S., & Baker, S. (2022). Public understanding of artificial intelligence through entertainment media. *AI & Society*, 1–14.

Neri, H., & Cozman, F. (2019). The role of experts in the public perception of risk of artificial intelligence. *AI & Society*, 1–11.

Nicholson, C. Y., Compeau, L. D., & Sethi, R. (2001). The role of interpersonal liking in building trust in long-term channel relationships. *Journal of the Academy of Marketing Science, 29*(1), 3–15.

Oistad, B. C., Sembroski, C. E., Gates, K. A., Krupp, M. M., Fraune, M. R., & Šabanović, S. (2016). Colleague or tool? Interactivity increases positive perceptions of and willingness to interact with a robotic co-worker. *International Conference on Social Robotics. Lecture Notes in Computer Science* (Vol. 9979, pp. 774–785).

Oksanen, A., Savela, N., Latikka, R., & Koivula, A. (2020). Trust toward robots and artificial intelligence: An experimental approach to human–technology interactions online. *Frontiers in Psychology, 11*, 568256.

Ouchchy, L., Coin, A., & Dubljević, V. (2020). AI in the headlines: The portrayal of the ethical issues of artificial intelligence in the media. *AI & Society, 35*(4), 927–936.

Park, Y. J., & Jones-Jang, S. M. (2022). Surveillance, security, and AI as technological acceptance. *AI & society, 35*, 1–12.

Podoletz, L. (2022). We have to talk about emotional AI and crime. *AI & Society*, 1–16.

Quinn, T. P., Jacobs, S., Senadeera, M., Le, V., & Coghlan, S. (2022). The three ghosts of medical AI: Can the black-box present deliver? *Artificial Intelligence in Medicine, 124*, 102158.

Rau, P. L. P., Li, Y., & Li, D. (2009). Effects of communication style and culture on ability to accept recommendations from robots. *Computers in Human Behavior, 25*(2), 587–595. https://doi.org/10.1016/j.chb.2008.12.025

Rheu, M., Shin, J. Y., Peng, W., & Huh-Yoo, J. (2021). Systematic review: Trust-building factors and implications for conversational agent design. *International Journal of Human–Computer Interaction, 37*(1), 81–96.

Robinette, P., Howard, A. M., & Wagner, A. R. (2017). Effect of robot performance on human-robot trust in time-critical situations. *IEEE Transactions on Human-Machine Systems*, 425–436

Rodero, E., & Lucas, I. (2021). Synthetic versus human voices in audiobooks: The human emotional intimacy effect. *New Media & Society, 25*(7), 1746–1764. https://doi.org/10.1177/14614448211024142

Rogers, E. M., & Bhowmik, D. K. (1970). Homophily-heterophily: Relational concepts for communication research. *Public Opinion Quarterly, 34*(4), 523–538.

Shao, C., Ciampaglia, G. L., Varol, O., Yang, K. C., Flammini, A., & Menczer, F. (2018). The spread of low-credibility content by social bots. *Nature Communications, 9*(1), 1–9.

Shi, S., Gong, Y., & Gursoy, D. (2021). Antecedents of trust and adoption intention toward artificially intelligent recommendation systems in travel planning: A heuristic–systematic model. *Journal of Travel Research, 60*(8), 1714–1734.

Simon, G. E., Shortreed, S. M., Coley, R. Y., Penfold, R. B., Rossom, R. C., Waitzfelder, B. E., Sanchez, K., & Lynch, F. L. (2019). Assessing and minimizing re-identification risk in research data derived from health care records. *EGEMS (Washington, DC), 7*(1), 6–6. https://doi.org/10.5334/egems.270

Slovic, P. (2016). *The perception of risk*. Routledge.

Stoll, B., Edwards, C., & Edwards, A. (2016). "Why aren't you a sassy little thing": The effects of robot-enacted guilt trips on credibility and consensus in a negotiation. *Communication Studies, 67*(5), 530–547. https://doi.org/10.1080/10510974.2016.1215339

Sumner, P., Vivian-Griffiths, S., Boivin, J., Williams, A., Venetis, C. A., Davies, A., Ogden, J., Whelan, L., Hughes, B., Dalton, B., Boy, F., & Chambers, C. D. (2014). The association between exaggeration in health related science news and academic press releases: Retrospective observational study. *BMJ : British Medical Journal, 349*, g7015. https://doi.org/10.1136/bmj.g7015

Sundar, S. S., Waddell, T. F., & Jung, E. H. (2016). The Hollywood robot syndrome media effects on older adults' attitudes toward robots and adoption intentions. In *11th ACM/IEEE international conference on human-robot interaction (HRI)*, Christchurch, New Zealand.

Tong, S. T., & Sopory, P. (2019). Does integral affect influence intentions to use artificial intelligence for skin cancer screening? A test of the affect heuristic. *Psychology & Health, 34*(7), 828–849.

Torre, I., Goslin, J., & White, L. (2020). If your device could smile: People trust happy-sounding artificial agents more. *Computers in Human Behavior, 105*, 106215. https://doi.org/10.1016/j.chb.2019.106215

Torre, I., Goslin, J., White, L., & Zanatto, D. (2018). Trust in artificial voices: A "congruency effect" of first impressions and behavioural experience. In *Proceedings of the Technology, Mind, and Society* (pp. 1–6).

Troshani, I., Rao Hill, S., Sherman, C., & Arthur, D. (2021). Do we trust in AI? Role of anthropomorphism and intelligence. *Journal of Computer Information Systems, 61*(5), 481–491.

van Noort, C. (2022). On the use of pride, hope and fear in China's international artificial intelligence narratives on CGTN. *AI & Society*, 1–13.

Walmsley, J. (2021). Artificial intelligence and the value of transparency. *AI & Society, 36*(2), 585–595.

Whang, C., & Im, H. (2021). 'I Like Your Suggestion!' The role of humanlikeness and parasocial relationship on the website versus voice shopper's perception of recommendations. *Psychology & Marketing, 38*(4), 581–595. https://doi.org/10.1002/mar.21437

Wissing, B. G., & Reinhard, M. A. (2018). Individual differences in risk perception of artificial intelligence. *Swiss Journal of Psychology, 77*(4), 149–157.

Wu, E. (2021). Sovereignty and data localization. *Cyber Project*. https://www.belfercenter.org/publication/sovereignty-and-data-localization

Zeng, J., Chan, C.-h., & Schäfer, M. S. (2022). Contested Chinese dreams of AI? Public discourse about Artificial intelligence on WeChat and People's Daily Online. *Information, Communication & Society, 25*(3), 319–340.

Zhang, B., Anderljung, M., Kahn, L., Dreksler, N., Horowitz, M. C., & Dafoe, A. (2021). Ethics and governance of artificial intelligence: Evidence from a survey of machine learning researchers. *Journal of Artificial Intelligence Research, 71*, 591–666.

11. Fearing the future: examining the conditional indirect correlation of attention to artificial intelligence news on artificial intelligence attitudes

Alex W. Kirkpatrick, Jay D. Hmielowski, and Amanda Boyd

INTRODUCTION

Industry around the world is changing because of the introduction of smart digital technologies. These changes and new innovations impact the way people work and live. The media has afforded much attention to the growth of artificial intelligence over the past ten years, in particular (Vergeer, 2020). Moreover, AI is impacting the way people live their daily lives in both positive and negative ways. On the one hand, there have been countless examples of how AI has improved our daily lives. The introduction of AI has helped reduce the risk to humans in high-risk situations, reduced the errors humans are prone to make, and made tasks, such as making lists, easier (Kumar, 2019). But there has been widespread deliberation among policymakers and media worldwide about how these new technologies could affect labor markets globally (Schwab et al., 2018). Jobs done by humans are being replaced by AI innovations as technologies improve. Some analysts and politicians contend that AI will put a significant number of people out of work (Naudé, 2021).

Many people will hear about new technologies associated with AI through the media because they either do not directly interact with AI daily or are unaware that they are interacting with an AI technology. Therefore, knowing the media's potential influence on public perceptions of developing AI technology will be imperative moving forward. Although some coverage has noted the benefits of AI (Chuan et al., 2019), several studies have also shown a good deal of coverage emphasizing how AI could negatively affect the workplace. Specifically, these studies have noted that much of the coverage focuses on the ways that AI will eliminate jobs in the future that are currently being performed by humans (Brennen et al., 2018). It is possible that seeing this coverage could result in people holding less favorable attitudes toward AI technology given the importance people place on their jobs.

In this chapter, we use agenda-setting theory to examine a communication process model to understand whether attention to AI content in the media could lead to a more negative evaluation of this technology through the perceived economic threats and the perceived economic fear associated with AI. Moreover, we will examine whether people's income moderates this indirect relationship. Specifically, we believe that these indirect relationships will be stronger among those who some predict are more threatened by the effects of AI in the workplace: lower income individuals. To test our proposed model, we collected survey data in 2020 using the survey company CloudResearch. In general, our moderated mediated model shows indirect correlations of attention to AI content through risk perceptions and fear. Indeed, attention to AI is associated with having less favorable views of AI through higher risk perceptions and fear. Moreover, our results also find that the indirect correlation is stronger among those with lower incomes.

MEDIA ATTENTION TO RISK PERCEPTIONS – AGENDA-SETTING

Communication scholars have noted the critical role that media can play in shaping people's perceptions of risks (Wachinger, et al., 2013). One theory that has been used to explain how media can shape people's perceptions of risk is agenda-setting theory (Rim et al., 2014). Agenda-setting theory has proposed that media coverage and news selection can influence what topics the public sees as important (McCombs & Shaw, 1972). In other words, if the media choose to cover a topic extensively, consumers of that media are likely to view that topic as being more important than topics that receive less attention. Agenda-setting theory expanded on this initial assumption to examine second- and third-level agenda-setting processes (Cheng, 2016). From a second-level perspective, the media can influence what attributes are tied to the agenda through framing. For example, the issue of AI might enter the public's agenda because of its novelty and potential impacts on people's daily lives. The second level of agenda-setting implies that the media then have significant influence over what attributes are associated with the coverage of AI. For example, the press might emphasize the economic consequences of AI to the workforce or highlight how AI will improve things such as car safety. AI might be framed as an economic risk to workers or a boon to big business. The third level of agenda-setting outlines how the media connects the second-level topics to other societal issues (Cheng, 2016). For example, coverage of AI could focus on the economic consequences of its diffusion, then connect this issue to individual workers in towns and cities across America who have their economic well-being negatively affected by robotic automation (e.g., Semuels, 2021).

Through the years, agenda-setting theory has been applied to a wide range of issues such as politics (Iyengar & Simon, 1993), health (Anker et al., 2016; Ezhumalai et al., 2014), and environmental communication (Liu et al., 2011). Agenda-setting scholars have also examined how the media agenda can influence public perceptions of new technologies (Daft & Lengel, 1986; Vaughan & Rogers, 2000). Certain types of coverage could lead people to perceive new technologies as low risk. However, coverage could also highlight problems associated with these technologies, influencing people to view the technology as increasing personal or social risks. For example, extensive work has highlighted that the coverage of nuclear power in the media has led the public to see this technology as being dangerous for the public (Koerner, 2014). Therefore, it is essential to assess how the issue of AI is covered via the media to understand people's perceptions about this topic.

Given the increasing importance of AI in society, scholars have started to examine the coverage associated with these technologies. In general, these studies have highlighted that the coverage tends to include both positive and negative framing of AI (Chuan et al., 2019). However, there is evidence that some of the coverage has focused on the economic threats associated with AI. Brennen et al.'s (2018) study found a good deal of coverage focused on how AI could cause job losses in the United Kingdom. Their findings suggest that more liberal-leaning outlets connect AI with unemployment issues, with some content emphasizing the specific effects on lower skilled workers (Brennen et al., 2018). This study also found similar coverage in more conservative-leaning news outlets. These media outlets also noted that new technologies could make jobs obsolete but also noted that new jobs would arise due to these new technologies (Brennen et al., 2018).

From a second-level agenda-setting perspective, the way media frames the attributes of AI can impact audience perceptions and behavior surrounding the technology. Kirkpatrick et al. (2022) conducted a media-effects experiment exploring the effects of exposure to online news about the economic threats of AI. The study found that thematically framing the economic threats of AI to society as a whole primed psychological proximity to the impacts of AI over episodic framing strategies that, instead, emphasized effects to the individual (Kirkpatrick et al., 2022). Thematic framing of AI's economic threats was found to have a positive indirect effect on information sharing about AI through first reducing psychological proximity which, in turn, increased the perceived risk of AI, which enhanced the likelihood that participants would share information about the threat online (Kirkpatrick et al., 2022).

In general, these studies suggest that viewing this content could lead the public to see higher levels of economic risks tied to introducing AI to the workforce. Indeed, the focus on job loss tied to AI could lead individuals who see this content to report higher levels of economic risk perceptions regarding AI. Therefore, we propose our first hypothesis:

H1: Attention to AI content is associated with risk perceptions associated with AI.

RISK PERCEPTIONS TO FEAR

Research from the Risk Information Seeking and Processing (RISP) model has consistently shown that risk perceptions are associated with affective responses (Griffin et al., 1999; Yang & Kahlor, 2013). Research has noted that risk perceptions tend to be associated with emotions such as worry and anxiety (e.g., Yang & Kahlor, 2013; Yang, Kahlor, & Griffin, 2014). It is possible that higher levels of risk perceptions about AI would be associated with higher levels of negative emotions tied to this technology, such as fear or anger. Indeed, Sjöberg (2007) found positive associations between risk perceptions on a variety of topics (i.e., terrorism, mobile telephones, genetically modified foods, and nuclear waste) and eight negative emotions (anger, contempt, fear, sorrow, guilt, shame, worry, and pessimism). Mou and Lin (2014) found that higher perceived health risks about food safety were associated with negative emotions such as anger, sadness, fear, anxiety, and resentment among residents of China. In the end, these studies suggest that risk perceptions should be associated with people's emotions toward AI. Therefore, we propose the following hypothesis:

H2: AI risk perceptions are associated with fear of AI.

FEAR TO ATTITUDES

The emotions people develop toward technologies such as AI or other objects are important because they are associated with important outcome variables such as information processing (Nabi, 1999), information seeking (Griffin et al., 1999), behavioral intentions (Tannenbaum et al., 2015), and attitudes about specific topics (Roskos-Ewoldsen et al., 2004). These emotions play an essential role in understanding several important outcomes of interest to social scientists. In this chapter, we are specifically interested in examining the relationship between people's emotions regarding AI and their evaluations of this technology.

Negative emotions surrounding a topic or technology can result in negative attitudes. For example, research has generally shown that people who fear flying tend to hold less positive attitudes toward this mode of transportation (Oakes & Bor, 2010). Research also shows that the emotions surrounding nuclear energy tend to be associated with the attitudes people hold about this form of power (Koerner, 2014). Fear has also been associated with holding more negative views of the criminal justice system (Kort-Butler & Hartshorn, 2011). A more recent study showed that fear associated with COVID-19 among a sample of people in France was associated with holding more negative attitudes toward Chinese people before transmission had begun in France (Brown & Marinthe, 2022). This finding is consistent with research into fear and attitudes across a range of topics. For example, a meta-analysis looking at fear appeals found a relationship between the use of fear appeals and the attitudes people held toward the topic (Tannenbaum et al., 2015). In sum, this research suggests that AI fear should be associated with holding more negative views of AI technology. Therefore, we propose our third hypothesis:

H3: Fear of AI is associated with more negative evaluations of AI.

The results of research then suggest that there will be an indirect correlation between media use and evaluations of AI through economic risk perceptions and fear associated with AI. Specifically, the literature outlined, to this point, suggests there will be negative indirect correlations for our measures of attention to AI on people's evaluations of this technology. Therefore, we propose the following hypothesis:

H4: There will be an indirect correlation of attention to AI content on more negative evaluations of AI through risk perceptions and fear.

FEAR BY INCOME INTERACTION

Evaluations of AI could be tied to people's backgrounds in terms of where they work, the type of job they perform, and their general level of economic security. Research has shown that demographic variables (e.g., sex, education, and income) tend to be associated with people's perceptions of new technologies (McClure, 2018). For example, McClure (2018) found that non-white minorities, females, and people with lower levels of education tend to report higher levels of fear related to new technologies and their introduction into the workplace. Other polls have shown similar results. A CNBC/SurveyMonkey poll (Wronski, 2019) found that people with higher salaries tended to report lower levels of concern regarding workplace technologies compared to those who made less money. Specifically, the poll found that 25% of those in managerial positions and 23% in senior managerial positions reported that they were concerned that their job would be eliminated in the next five years because of the introduction of new technologies. By contrast, there was greater concern among those with lower paying jobs. For example, 35% of transportation and delivery workers, 34% of those working in retail and consumer goods, and 33% of agricultural workers reported that they were somewhat concerned about technology replacing their job in the next five years (Wronski, 2019). Economic worries and pessimistic expectancy are not limited to the individual earner either but can spread to the rest of the household (Bünnings et al., 2017). This suggests that fears about AI and workplace replacement may not be restricted to those workers whose jobs are directly impacted but any others who are dependent on that worker for economic security, such as partners or children.

As this research indicates, income could serve as a moderating variable between people's concerns about AI and their evaluations of the technology. In general, little research has examined the extent to which income serves as a moderating variable between fear and attitudes. However, it would make sense in this specific situation that the correlation between fear and evaluations would not be the same based on income levels. Indeed, people from low-income backgrounds could be more likely to hold negative evaluations of AI technology based on their fear than higher income individuals. Historically, automation and technological replacement has had significant impacts on the nature of manual labor, factory work, and agricultural work, particularly.

One example of income serving as a moderating variable is tied to political beliefs and people's concerns regarding the issue of climate change. One study showed that the correlation between political ideology and the likelihood of dismissing climate

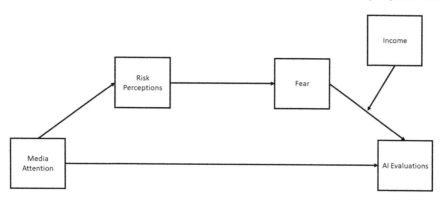

Figure 11.1   Proposed communication process model

change as a threat was higher for higher income conservatives than low-income conservatives (Bohr, 2014). In this situation, wealthy conservatives are better equipped to handle climate change, which allows them to be more dismissive of its potential threats. By contrast, lower income people who are less able to deal with the threats associated with climate change are less likely to dismiss the threats associated with this issue.

Overall, the literature outlined in this section suggests that the correlation between fear and evaluations of AI technologies could vary by income. Specifically, the correlation between fear and negative evaluations should be stronger among lower income individuals and weaker among those with a higher income. Therefore, we expect that the indirect correlations outlined in H4 will vary based on income. In essence, the negative indirect correlation of our two measures of attention to AI will be stronger among lower income individuals compared to the negative indirect correlation among the wealthier segment of our sample. As a result, we propose our final hypothesis (see Figure 11.1 for a full moderated mediated model):

H5: *The indirect correlation of attention to evaluations of AI through risk perceptions and fear will be moderated by income, with the negative indirect correlation being stronger among lower income individuals.*

METHODS

Participants and Procedures

Data presented in this study were obtained from a sample of online panel participants recruited via CloudReasearch, a participant-sourcing platform for online surveys. CloudResearch recruits targeted demographics through the Amazon MTurk crowd-sourcing platform. Each participant was compensated $1.00 per completion.

Data were collected on November 20 and 21, 2020, from US citizens aged 18 and older. Participants viewed a description of the study through CloudResearch before deciding to respond to the survey. Respondents self-selected into the study based on whether they wanted to participate for the stated compensation. Participants then answered a battery of questions related to their attitudes on AI. The final sample consisted of 567 participants.

Measures

Independent variable
Attention 1
Our first measure of media attention regarding AI asked respondents, "Approximately how often do you use media (e.g., internet, social media, television, magazines, etc.) to find out: a) how many people use AI, b) where people purchase AI-related technologies, c) stay up to date with the latest news about AI, d) learn how to use AI-related technologies, e) connect with others who share your interest in AI-related technology, and f) browse AI-related content for something to do when you are alone?" Response options ranged from "never (0)" to "daily (5)," with higher scores reflective of more attention paid to AI content online. Response options were averaged together to create our first measure of attention to AI content ($M = 1.362$, $SD = 1.1319$, $\alpha = 0.933$).

Attention 2
Our second measure of attention to AI was measured with two items. These items asked respondents: "Before today, how much attention have you paid to content related to artificial intelligence either online or through social media?" and "Before today, how much have you heard, read, or thought about the effects that computers and robots are having, or can have, on the American workforce?" Response options ranged from "none at all (1)" to "a great deal (5)," with higher scores reflective of more attention paid to AI content online. The two items were averaged together to create our measure of attention to AI ($M = 2.854$, $SD = 0.964$, Spearman-Brown = 0.684).

Mediating Variables

Perceived threat
The perceived threat of AI was measured by averaging responses to two items that asked respondents about the perceived threat to AI regarding the economic aspects of AI. The two items asked respondents: "How threatened do you feel by the economic consequences of increasing artificial intelligence use?" and "How severe are the economic consequences of increasing artificial intelligence use?" Response options ranged from "not at all (0)" to "extremely (4)," with higher scores reflecting greater perceived threat ($M = 1.883$, $SD = 0.996$, Spearman-Brown = 0.757).

Fear

Fear associated with AI was measured with three items. These items asked respondents their level of fear associated with AI on a scale that raged from "not at all afraid (0)" to "extremely afraid (4)." The three items asked respondents their fear of the following topics: "the extent to which they fear people are increasingly dependent on technology to perform their jobs, the extent to which they fear technology is increasingly allowing the replacement of people in the workforce, and the extent to which they fear employers are increasingly allowing robots to operate independently in the workforce." These three items were averaged together to create our measure of AI fear ($M = 1.861$, $SD = 0.990$, $\alpha = 0.810$).

Dependent Variable

Evaluations of AI

We measured evaluations of AI by averaging responses to a five-item scale developed by Venkatesh et al. (2012). Respondents were asked to report how positively or negatively they expected artificial intelligence to affect their "productivity at work," "ability to prosper financially," "health and safety," "daily performance," and ability to "achieve things that are important to you." Response options ranged from "extremely negative (-3)" to "extremely positive (3)," with a midpoint of "neither positive nor negative." Responses were then averaged to form a single index in which greater values imply more optimistic expectations versus lower values that imply greater pessimism ($M = 0.488$, $SD = 1.029$, $\alpha = 0.867$).

Moderating Variable

Income

Household income was measured according to one item employing an 11-point scale that ranged from "less than $10,000 a year (0)" to "more than $150,000 a year (11)" (*Median* = $50,000–$59,999; real median of US population = $70,784).

Control Variables

In addition to the endogenous variables, we also included a set of controls in our models. Our control variables in comparison to the US electorate are contained in Table 11.1, and include measures of biological sex, race, age, education, and political ideology. Sex asked respondents to report their biological sex (60.1% responded female). Race was measured by asking participants their race and selecting all races that applied. For statistical reasons, we coded participants into two groups: white only and non-white (70.5% white). Age was measured with one item that asked respondents their year of birth. We then subtracted this number from 2020 (the year we collected the data) ($M = 37.48$, $SD = 11.705$). Education was measured with a single seven-point ordinal item asking, "What is the highest level of education you have completed?" Response options ranged from "less than high-school degree (0)"

Table 11.1   Control variables and sample statistics versus US electorate

	Survey sample	US electorate
Sex (Female)	60.1%	50.5%
Race (White only)	70.5%	60.1%
Education	Median = "some college"	Median = "some college"
Age (years)	Mean = 37.5, SD = 11.7	Median = 39–45
Political Ideology	Median = "slightly conservative"	—

to "doctoral degree (6)" (*Median*= "some college"). Lastly, we included a measure of political ideology. Our measure asked respondents, "Politically, how liberal or conservative do you consider yourself?" Response options ranged from "strongly liberal (-3)" to "strongly conservative (3)," with a midpoint of "neither liberal nor conservative (0)." Negative values indicated a more liberal ideology, while positive values indicated a more conservative ideology ($M = 0.840$, $SD = 1.718$).

Construct Validity: Mono-Method Bias

As indicated above, our chapter includes two measures of attention to AI content. Although some may see this as a weakness of our study, we believe it addresses the issue of mono-method bias (Cook et al., 2002). Mono-method bias is a threat to construct validity that centers on concerns that results only appear for a specific way of measuring a concept. Therefore, using several measures of attention increases the validity of our findings.

Data Analysis

For our analysis, we used ordinary least squares (OLS) regression using SPSS. Moreover, to test our mediated moderated models, we utilized the process macro developed by Hayes (2017). To test our mediation models, we utilized Model 6. This model allowed us to not only run regression models for all the variables in our two models but also allowed us to estimate indirect correlations for both of our measures of attention. To test the full moderated mediated model, we utilized Model 87. This model estimated our conditional indirect correlations. To graph our interaction, we utilized output from Model 1. For our results, we report unstandardized coefficients and standard errors. We report point estimates and 95% confidence intervals for our indirect correlations. Results for the indirect correlations were estimated with 5,000 bootstrapped estimates.

RESULTS

We will begin by outlining the results tied to H1. In general, our results revealed support for our first hypothesis. Specifically, the more attention people paid to AI news

Table 11.2   OLS regression correlations between predictor and outcome variables

	Risk perceptions	Fear	Evaluations	Evaluations
Sex	0.076 (0.085)	0.132 (0.062)*	−0.219 (0.075)**	−0.185 (0.074)*
Race	−0.110 (0.090)	0.080 (0.066)	−0.104 (0.079)	−0.066 (0.079)
Education	−0.017 (0.029)	−0.056 (0.021)**	0.100 (0.026)***	0.056 (0.028)*
Age	0.001 (0.004)	0.005 (0.003)	−0.006 (0.003)*	−0.006 (0.003)
Political Ideology	0.041 (0.024)	−0.018 (0.017)	−0.022 (0.021)	−0.019 (0.021)
Attention 1	0.248 (0.033)***	0.015 (0.026)	0.390 (0.031)***	0.372 (0.031)***
Risk Perceptions	–	0.717 (0.031)***	−0.097 (0.052)	−0.096 (0.052)
Fear	–	–	−0.153 (0.051)**	−0.251 (0.070)**
Income	–	–	–	0.003 (0.022)
Income X Fear	–	–	–	0.021 (0.010)*
R^2	0.106	0.520	0.354	0.374

Notes: $*p < .05$; $**p < .01$; $***p < .001$; two-tailed; unstandardized coefficients with standard error in parentheses.

content was associated with higher levels of risk perceptions regarding economic risks for both of our measures of attention to AI content (Attention 1 b = 0.248, *SE* = 0.033, $p < 0.001$; Attention 2 b = 0.490, *SE* = 0.042, $p < 0.001$). In other words, our findings show that attention to AI news content is associated with people being more likely to see potential economic risks associated with AI (see Tables 11.1 and 11.2 for full results for both measures of attention. Table 11.2 includes our first measure of attention. Table 11.3 includes results for our second measure of attention).

We move on to our second hypothesis. Our results showed support for H2. Specifically, higher levels of perceived economic risk tied to AI were associated with reporting greater fear tied to AI (A1 model b = 0.717, *SE* = 0.031, $p < 0.001$; A2 model b = 0.716, *SE* = 0.033, $p < 0.001$). In essence, our results revealed support for the idea that risk perceptions are tied to fear.

Looking at the results tied to H3, we again find support for our proposed hypothesis. Indeed, the higher levels of fear regarding AI were associated with holding more negative perceptions of AI (A1 b = -0.153, *SE* = 0.051, $p < 0.01$; A2 b = -0.147, *SE* = 0.052, $p < 0.001$). In essence, the more fearful people were regarding AI technologies, the more likely they were to hold negative views regarding this technology.

Table 11.3   OLS regression correlations between predictor and outcome variables

	Risk perceptions	Fear	Evaluations	Evaluations
Sex	0.121 (0.079)	0.128 (0.061)*	−0.270 (0.076)**	−0.212 (0.075)**
Race	−0.048 (0.084)	0.083 (0.066)	−0.023 (0.081)	0.024 (0.079)
Education	−0.033 (0.027)	−0.055 (0.021)**	0.123 (0.026)***	0.060 (0.029)*
Age	0.003 (0.003)	0.005 (0.003)	−0.008 (0.003)*	−0.007 (0.003)
Political Ideology	0.049 (0.022)*	−0.018 (0.017)	−0.004 (0.022)	−0.000 (0.021)
Attention 2	0.490 (0.042)***	0.014 (0.036)	0.505 (0.045)***	0.500 (0.044)***
Risk Perceptions	–	0.716 (0.033)***	−0.165 (0.055)**	−0.169 (0.054)**
Fear	–	–	−0.147 (0.052)**	−0.280 (0.071)**
Income	–	–	–	0.003 (0.010)
Income X Fear	–	–	–	0.028 (0.010)**
R^2	0.213	0.520	0.324	0.360

Notes: $*p < .05$; $**p < .01$; $***p < .001$; two-tailed; unstandardized coefficients with standard error in parentheses.

Putting all of these findings together, we tested H4. Specifically, this hypothesis examined whether there was an indirect correlation between our measures of AI attention related to AI attitudes tied to risk perceptions and fear. Overall, we found support for H4 using both measures of attention from our survey. The first measure of attention, which focused on the use of media regarding AI, was associated with holding more negative views of AI through our two mediating variables (A1 point estimate = -0.027 [-0.048– -0.009]). The results showed that attention resulted in fewer positive views through higher risk perceptions and higher levels of fear, which supports H4. We found the same pattern of results for our second attention measure, which focused on attention to AI content. Once again, our findings showed that our second attention measure resulted in people holding more negative views about AI through our two mediating variables of risk perceptions and fear (A2 point estimate = -0.052 [-0.091– -0.014]). As a whole, these findings reveal robust support for H4.

We now move on to examine our final hypothesis. Before testing the full mediated moderated model, we examined whether there was an interaction between fear regarding AI and income. Our results revealed a statistically significant interaction between these two variables (A1 b = 0.021, SE = 0.010, $p < 0.05$; A2 b = 0.028, SE = 0.010, $p < 0.01$). Specifically, the results showed that higher levels of fear were

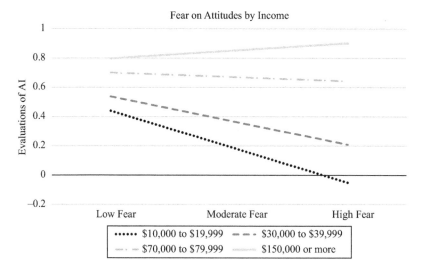

Figure 11.2   Graph of fear by income interaction

associated with holding more negative views of AI for individuals making a lower income (see Figure 11.2).

Overall, these results support H5. Indeed, fear is only related to holding negative AI views among people with lower incomes. The correlation between these two variables disappears among people with higher incomes. When looking at the full mediated moderated model, our results reveal that the negative indirect correlation varies by income across both of our measures of paying attention to AI content. When looking at our first measure of attention, our results do not show a statistically significant index of mediated moderation (A1 point estimate = 0.004 [-0.000–0.008]). However, the results generally show that the indirect correlation varies by income. When looking at the indirect correlations, our results reveal that the indirect relationship is stronger among those reporting lower incomes (A1 less than 10K point estimate = -0.045 [-0.077– -0.017]). These associations shift to being non-significant among people with higher incomes (A1 more than 150k per year point estimate = -0.004 [-0.034–0.027]). We found the same pattern of results for our second measure of attention to AI content. For this analysis, our results revealed a statistically significant index of moderated mediation (A2 point estimate = 0.001 [0.001–0.019]). Probing the indirect correlation shows the same pattern of results as our first measure of attention. Once again, the indirect correlation is stronger among people with lower income levels (A2 less than 10K point estimate = -0.098 [-0.162– -0.042]). Moreover, this relationship goes from significant to non-significant among people with higher incomes (A2 more than 150k per year point estimate = -0.010 [-0.055–0.075]) (see Table 11.4 for full conditional indirect correlations). As a whole, the results generally revealed robust support for H5.

Table 11.4   *Conditional indirect correlation of attention 1 and attention 2 on attitudes toward AI by income*

	Attention 1	Attention 2
0 Less than $10,000	**–0.045** **(–0.077 to –0.017)**	**–0.098** **(-0.162– -0.042)**
1 $10,000 to $19,999	**–0.041** **(–0.070 to –0.016)**	**–0.089** **(-0.146– -0.039)**
2 $20,000 to $29,999	**-0.037** **(–0.062 to –0.016)**	**–0.079** **(–0.129 to –0.035)**
3 $30,000 to $39,999	**–0.034** **(–0.056 to –0.014)**	**–0.069** **(–0.114 to –0.029)**
4 $40,000 to $49,999	**–0.030** **(–0.050 to –0.012)**	**–0.059** **(–0.100 to –0.023)**
5 $50,000 to $59,999	**–0.026** **(–0.045 to –0.009)**	**–0.049** **(–0.088 to –0.014)**
6 $60,000 to $69,999	**–0.022** **(–0.041 to –0.006)**	**–0.039** **(–0.078 to –0.003)**
7 $70,000 to $79,999	**–0.019** **(–0.039 to –0.001)**	–0.029 (–0.071 to 0.010)
8 $80,000 to $89,999	–0.015 (–0.037 to 0.005)	–0.020 (–0.065 to 0.025)
9 $90,000 to $99,999	–0.011 (–0.036 to 0.012)	–0.010 (–0.061 to 0.041)
10 $100,000 to $149,999	–0.008 (–0.035 to 0.019)	0.000 (–0.058 to 0.057)
11 $150,000 or more	–0.004 (–0.034 to 0.027)	0.010 (–0.055 to 0.075)

Notes: Point estimates with 95% confidence intervals in parentheses. Bold indicates statistically significant finding.

DISCUSSION

Our results supported the communication process model we proposed in this chapter. We found that attention to AI content is associated with higher levels of risk perceptions across both of our measures focused on attention to AI content. These higher levels of risk perceptions are associated with higher levels of fear regarding AI technologies. Fear is also associated with holding more negative views of AI. Our combined results reveal negative indirect correlations for both of our measures of attention to AI content. Moreover, these indirect correlations were moderated by income. Specifically, the negative indirect correlation moved from being significant among people with lower income levels to non-significant among people with higher income levels.

Overall, our findings contribute to existing literature in two ways regarding media use and perceptions of AI. First, our results show the applicability of agenda-setting relative to the issue of AI. The research shows that the attributes of news coverage regarding the issue of AI could lead people to hold more negative views of this emerging technology (Kirkpatrick et al., 2022). Yet there are many significant benefits associated with the introduction of AI to society, such as reduced risk to humans in high-risk situations, reducing the errors humans are prone to make, and making tasks, such as creating lists, easier (Kumar, 2019). Therefore, scholars could look at the outcomes of attention to different types of content in the media moving forward (e.g., content related to specific benefits of AI). Scholars could then measure attention to outlets with more favorable coverage of AI or measure negative and positive news stories about AI to assess how these different types of content could affect people – for example, seeing these more positive stories might lead to lower levels of risk or even perceived benefits associated with AI technology. These perceived benefits could then be associated with positive emotions and more positive attitudes toward AI. In essence, scholars should examine other aspects of AI to see if competing perspectives are associated with this technology. It could be that people may hold more positive attitudes when they think about other aspects of AI technology.

Second, our results highlight the critical role of income when thinking about people's perceptions of AI. Our findings show that less well-off people do not show the same pattern of results compared to higher income individuals. This makes sense, given that economic security likely makes people feel less threatened regarding AI compared to lower wage workers who could end up seeing AI eliminating their jobs with continued advances in AI technologies. Moreover, these findings highlight the importance of examining how potential media effects could vary by demographic variables. Extensive work has shown how media effects could vary by age (Southwell & Langteau, 2008) and knowledge (Tichenor et al., 1970). These findings show that media scholars should not ignore income as a potential moderating variable when looking at potential media effects moving forward, especially concerning media effects tied to economic issues.

As with any research, there are weaknesses with our study that could affect our results. First, we are not able to establish causation with these data. Indeed, our survey results are cross-sectional in nature, which means we cannot determine whether there is actual causation regarding the relationships between our variables. Moving forward, scholars could collect experimental or over-time survey data to assess the causal direction between the variables outlined in our chapter. Next, one of our measures of media attention has a reliability score lower than the generally accepted level of 0.70. Given that we replicated these results across two different measures of media attention, we believe that this potential weakness is overcome by replicating these findings across these two different measures of attention. Lastly, although our survey included a diverse sample of participants, our sample is not representative of the US population, given our reliance on non-probability-based methods. Scholars could attempt to collect data on a more representative set of respondents. Despite this weakness, our goal was to test a communication process model, meaning that population inferences are less important than testing theories and finding support (or a lack of support) for our proposed model.

Ultimately, research examining the potential effects of media on the issue of AI is just beginning. Scholars will need to examine how media could affect perceptions of this technology as it becomes more important to society and the individual worker. As with any new technology, there will be both positive and negative consequences tied to diffusion and integration into people's lives. Yet there is a chance that significant portions of the US population whose livelihoods are threatened by AI will come to view it as a problematic technology that should be stifled and stopped before it puts them out of work. Yet the most impactful consequences of AI on economies have yet to be realized and are far from certain. Talk of hypothetical mass-unemployment and robotic replacement could generate undue fear among people and obscure the reality that AI is already ubiquitous and helping to sustain society and better the health and safety of individuals on a daily basis.

REFERENCES

Anker, A. E., Feeley, T. H., McCracken, B., & Lagoe, C. A. (2016). Measuring the effectiveness of mass-mediated health campaigns through meta-analysis. *Journal of Health Communication*, *21*(4), 439–456. https://doi.org/10.1080/10810730.2015.1095820

Bohr, J. (2014). Public views on the dangers and importance of climate change: Predicting climate change beliefs in the United States through income moderated by party identification. *Climatic Change*, *126*(1-2), 217–227. https://doi.org/10.1007/s10584-014 -1198-9

Brennen, J. S., Howard, P. N., & Nielsen, R. K. (2018). *An industry-led debate: How UK media cover artificial intelligence (Oxford Martin Programme on Misinformation, Science and Media, p. 10)*. Reuters Institute for the Study of Journalism Oxford University. https://reutersinstitute.politics.ox.ac.uk/sites/default/files/2018-12/Brennen_UK_Media _Coverage_of_AI_FINAL.pdf

Brown, G., & Marinthe, G. (2022). "The Chinese virus": How COVID-19's transmission context and fear affect negative attitudes toward Chinese people. *Peace and Conflict: Journal of Peace Psychology*, *28*(2), 162–166. https://doi.org/10.1037/pac0000581

Bünnings, C., Kleibrink, J., & Weßling, J. (2017). Fear of unemployment and its effect on the mental health of spouses. *Health Economics*, *26*(1), 104–117. https://doi.org/10.1002/hec.3279

Cheng, Y. (2016). The third-level agenda-setting study: An examination of media, implicit, and explicit public agendas in China. *Asian Journal of Communication*, *26*(4), 319–332.

Chuan, C. H., Tsai, W. H. S., & Cho, S. Y. (2019). Framing artificial intelligence in American newspapers. In *Proceedings of the 2019 AAAI/ACM Conference on AI, Ethics, and Society* (pp. 339–344). Association for Computing Machinery. https://dl.acm.org/doi/proceedings /10.1145/3306618

Cook, T. D., Campbell, D. T., & Shadish, W. (2002). *Experimental and quasi-experimental designs for generalized causal inference*. Houghton Mifflin.

Daft, R. L., & Lengel, R. H. (1986). Organizational information requirements, media richness and structural design. *Management Science*, *32*(5), 554–571. https://doi.org/10.1287/mnsc .32.5.554

Ezhumalai, S., Kumar, P., & Andrews, T. (2014). Media exposure and awareness about consequences of tobacco use among early adolescents. *Alcohol and Alcoholism*, *49*(suppl_1), i44–i44. https://doi.org/10.1093/alcalc/agu053.32

Griffin, R. J., Dunwoody, S., & Neuwirth, K. (1999). Proposed model of the relationship of risk information seeking and processing to the development of preventive behaviors. *Environmental Research, 80*(2), S230–S245.

Hayes, A. F. (2017). *Introduction to mediation, moderation, and conditional process analysis: A regression-based approach.* Guilford Publications.

Iyengar, S., & Simon, A. (1993). News coverage of the gulf crisis and public opinion: A study of agenda-setting, priming, and framing. *Communication Research, 20*(3), 365–383. https://doi.org/10.1177/009365093020003002

Kirkpatrick, A. W., Hmielowski, J. D., & Boyd, A. D. (2022). The Iindirect Eeffects of Eepisodic-Tthematic Fframing on Iinformation Ssharing Aabout the Eeconomic Tthreat of Aartificial Iintelligence. *Communication Studies, 73*(5–6), 577–5901-–14. https://doi.org/10.1080/10510974.2022.2121737

Koerner, C. L. (2014). Media, fear, and nuclear energy: A case study. *The Social Science Journal, 51*(2), 240–249.

Kort-Butler, L. A., & Hartshorn, K. J. S. (2011). Watching the detectives: Crime programming, fear of crime, and attitudes about the criminal justice system. *The Sociological Quarterly, 52*(1), 36–55.

Kumar, S. (2019). Advantages and disadvantages of artificial intelligence. *Medium.* https://towardsdatascience.com/advantages-and-disadvantages-of-artificial-intelligence-182a5ef6588c

Liu, X., Lindquist, E., & Vedlitz, A. (2011). Explaining media and congressional attention to global climate change, 1969-2005: An empirical test of agenda-setting theory. *Political Research Quarterly, 64*(2), 405–419. https://doi.org/10.1177/1065912909346744

McClure, P. K. (2018). "You're fired," says the robot: The rise of automation in the workplace, technophobes, and fears of unemployment. *Social Science Computer Review, 36*(2), 139–156. https://doi.org/10.1177/0894439317698637

McCombs, M. E., & Shaw, D. L. (1972). The agenda-setting function of mass media. *Public Opinion Quarterly, 36*(2), 176–187.

Mou, Y., & Lin, C. A. (2014). Communicating food safety via the social media: The role of knowledge and emotions on risk perception and prevention. *Science Communication. 36*(5), 593–616. doi: 10.1177/1075547014549480

Nabi, R. L. (1999). A cognitive-functional model for the effects of discrete negative emotions on information processing, attitude change, and recall. *Communication Theory, 9*(3), 292–320.

Naudé, W. (2021). Artificial intelligence: Neither Utopian nor apocalyptic impacts soon. *Economics of Innovation and New Technology, 30*(1), 1–23. https://doi.org/10.1080/10438599.2020.1839173

Oakes, M., & Bor, R. (2010). The psychology of fear of flying (part I): A critical evaluation of current perspectives on the nature, prevalence and etiology of fear of flying. *Travel Medicine and Infectious Disease, 8*(6), 327–338. https://doi.org/10.1016/j.tmaid.2010.10.001

Rim, H., Hong Ha, J., & Kiousis, S. (2014). The evidence of compelling arguments in agenda building: Relationships among public information subsidies, media coverage, and risk perceptions during a pandemic outbreak. *Journal of Communication Management, 18*(1), 101–116. https://doi.org/10.1108/JCOM-05-2012-0044

Roskos-Ewoldsen, D. R., Yu, J. H., & Rhodes, N. (2004). Fear appeal messages affect accessibility of attitudes toward the threat and adaptive behaviors. *Communication Monographs, 71*(1), 49–69.

Schwab, K., Davis, N., & Nadella, S. (2018). *Shaping the future of the fourth industrial revolution.* Crown.

Semuels, A. (2021, August 6). Millions of Americans have lost jobs in the pandemic—and robots and AI are replacing them faster than ever. *Time.* https://time.com/5876604/machines-jobs-coronavirus/

Sjöberg, L. (2007). Emotions and risk perception. *Risk Management*, 9(4), 223–237.

Southwell, B. G., & Langteau, R. (2008). Age, memory changes, and the varying utility of recognition as a media effects pathway. *Communication Methods and Measures*, 2(1–2), 100–114.

Tannenbaum, M. B., Hepler, J., Zimmerman, R. S., Saul, L., Jacobs, S., Wilson, K., & Albarracín, D. (2015). Appealing to fear: A meta-analysis of fear appeal effectiveness and theories. *Psychological Bulletin*, 141(6), 1178–1204.

Tichenor, P. J., Donohue, G. A., & Olien, C. N. (1970). Mass media flow and differential growth in knowledge. *Public Opinion Quarterly*, 34(2), 159–170.

Vaughan, P. W., & Rogers, E. M. (2000). A staged model of communication effects: Evidence from an entertainment-education radio soap opera in Tanzania. *Journal of Health Communication*, 5(3), 203–227. https://doi.org/10.1080/10810730050131398

Venkatesh, V., Thong, J. Y. L., & Xu, X. (2012). Consumer acceptance and use of information technology: Extending the unified theory of acceptance and use of technology. *MIS Quarterly*, 36(1), 157–178. https://doi.org/10.2307/41410412

Vergeer, M. (2020). Artificial intelligence in the Dutch press: An analysis of topics and trends. *Communication Studies*, 71(3), 373–392.

Wachinger, G., Renn, O., Begg, C., & Kuhlicke, C. (2013). The risk perception paradox-implications for governance and communication of natural hazards. *Risk Analysis*, 33(6), 1049–1065. https://doi.org/10.1111/j.1539-6924.2012.01942.x

Wronski, L. (2019). *CNBC|SurveyMonkey Workplace Happiness Index: November 2019*. SurveyMonkey. Retrieved November 4, 2022, from https://www.surveymonkey.com/curiosity/cnbc-workplace-happiness-index-november-2019/

Yang, Z. J., & Kahlor, L. (2013). What, me worry? The role of affect in information seeking and avoidance. *Science Communication*, 35(2), 189–212. https://doi.org/10.1177/1075547012441873

Yang, Z. J., Kahlor, L. A., & Griffin, D. J. (2014). I share, therefore I am: A US– China comparison of college students' motivations to share information about climate change. *Human Communication Research*, 40(1), 112–135.

12. A machine-learning approach to assessing public trust in AI-powered technologies

Poong Oh and Younbo Jung

Artificial intelligence (AI) describes a highly sophisticated and competent technology that has the ability to interact with the environment by collecting information, making sense of data, and recognizing patterns to make predictions or generate results that allow for better decision and judgment making, with the objective to replicate human thinking (Glikson & Woolley, 2020). AI has been employed in various sectors for different purposes, such as making decisions about health care (Yu & Kohane, 2019), detecting supply-management risks in logistics (Tilimbe, 2019) and insurance fraud (Natalija, 2019), forecasting crime (Asaro, 2019), and performing abductive reasoning in judicial and law enforcement (Nissan, 2017). We have also witnessed the integration of AI-powered machines into various everyday applications, many of which people do not even recognize as operated by AI algorithms. Taken together, scholars posit that AI has the capability to cause a paradigm shift in the general workforce structure (Brynjolfsson et al., 2018) by transforming how organizations function (Huang & Rust, 2018), decisions are made, knowledge is managed (Araujo et al., 2020), and jobs are designed (Alekseeva et al., 2021). Thus, many believe AI will be at the core of the fourth industrial revolution (Schwab, 2017; Xu et al., 2018).

The increasing reliance on AI-powered machines in everyday lives, coupled with the intelligent nature of such machines, has resulted in a social relationship between humans and machines (Carey et al., 2017). That is, machines are perceived more as partners rather than mere servants to humans. Furthermore, while AI outperforms humans in computation and information processing, its development of interpersonal skills, strategic planning, and innovation is still in progress (Ferràs-Hernández, 2018). This makes AI-powered machines and human workers complementary to each other in workplaces. Jarrahi (2018) suggests that humans and AI must collaborate for decision making. As such, a symbiotic relationship between AI and humans is emerging because they are critical to each other's functioning (Russell, 2017).

Trust is crucial for such symbiotic relationships and the acceptance of new technologies (Chandra et al., 2010; Lippert & Davis, 2006). Zhang et al. (2019) found trust to be a major factor in promoting public acceptance of autonomous vehicles. Similarly, trust acted as a key antecedent for accepting frontline services provided by AI (Ostrom et al., 2019). In addition, trust often mediates the effects of other variables on public acceptance of AI. For instance, Liu and Tao (2022) found that personalization, loss of privacy, and anthropomorphism were crucial determinants of individuals' intention to use AI-powered healthcare services. More importantly, trust mediated the relationships. Further, trust helps mitigate potential risks individuals perceive to be associated with AI, reducing their uncertainty and making them more willing to use AI-powered services (McKnight et al., 2002).

Given the increasing deployment of AI and the crucial role of trust in technology acceptance, it is imperative to understand public trust in AI for both research and practical purposes. Rejection or distrust of AI-powered machines could increase opportunity costs due to inefficiency and waste of resources. Moreover, trust also affects the quality of human-machine interactions (Abbass, 2019), making it a critical topic of investigation in light of the emerging symbiotic relationships between humans and AI. From this perspective, the present study aims to address the following question:

RQ – To what extent and in what aspect do people trust AI?

CHALLENGES IN STUDYING TRUST IN AI

Trust is one of the most fundamental factors in any social relationship (Lewis & Weigert, 1985). Due to its complex and multifaceted nature, trust has been defined in various ways in previous literature. For example, Rotter (1971) defined trust as a general expectation that another person will honor their word. Sanders et al. (2019) defined trust as confidence in another person's ability to execute a particular task successfully. Notably, McLeod (2021) highlighted the element of vulnerability when trusting someone. In other words, the trustor is vulnerable to the possibility of the trustee failing the entrusted task (Baier, 1986). Reflecting the link between trust and vulnerability, a commonly accepted definition of trust in social sciences is the willingness to be exploited by others (Mayer et al., 1995). However, these definitions are too general and vague to apply to the study of human–machine relationships. Apart from the social aspects of trust, human–AI trust also encompasses a broader consideration of technological capacities (Bao et al., 2021). That is, for users to trust or conform to decisions made by AI-powered machines, AI technology must prove itself to be advanced enough to perform the given tasks competently.

In the AI literature, more specifically, some scholars conceptualized human–AI trust as the belief that AI will abide by implicit or explicit contracts and suggested two types of trust: warranted and unwarranted (Jacovi et al., 2021). Others made a distinction between cognitive and emotional trust, whose antecedents were found to differ (Glikson & Woolley, 2020). While promising, these conceptualizations of trust appear too detailed and specific, limiting their practical utility in measuring public trust in AI. Because of the difficulty in defining trust, many existing studies either directly asked participants how much they trusted AI without defining trust (e.g., Aoki, 2020) or reduced the concept to opinions, attitudes, or other psychological or behavioral measures (e.g., Gillath et al., 2021; Glikson & Woolley, 2020). However, these approaches fail to reflect the interdependence and mutuality of the newly emerged relationships between humans and AI-powered machines.

THE PROPOSED APPROACH

The difficulties in conceptualizing and operationalizing the concept of trust make it hard to assess public trust in AI and examine its impacts on public acceptance and adoption of AI-powered technologies. For this problem, we adopt the brilliant approach originally proposed by Alan Turing to address a provocative question: "Can machines think?" (Turing, 1950, p. 433). Turing pointed out that the concepts of "thinking" and "machine" are both too broad and complex to define in a clear way that satisfies everyone. Thus, he suggested "replacing the question with another, which is closely related to it and is expressed in relatively unambiguous words" (p. 433) and introduced the concept of what is now better known as the Turing test. To determine whether a machine can think like a human, Turing proposed that an undercover machine participates in text-based chatting and misleads participants to believe that they are talking to other human participants. The machine will pass the Turing test if human participants fail to correctly distinguish the machine's responses from other human participants', indirectly answering the original question about whether machines can think.

Adapting from Turing's approach, the current chapter replaces our original question – to what extent and in what aspects do people trust AI – with simpler and less ambiguous ones: how do people perceive the replacement of human workers with AI-powered machines across a wide range of professions? Do they perceive it to be possible and desirable? In other words, a more straightforward question about their preferences for AI-powered machines to do the selected work is asked instead of asking whether people trust AI. This way, we can indirectly, yet more accurately, measure people's trust in AI in different aspects, across diverse contexts, and more importantly, in comparison with their human counterparts. Further, by asking about the perceived possibility and desirability of job replacement by AI-powered machines, we can integrate technology-centered engineering perspectives (i.e., technological possibility) and user-centered social scientific perspectives (i.e., social desirability) into a unified theoretical framework of people's trust in AI.

There is also a growing body of research on the replacement of human workers with AI-powered machines or simply job automation. Some studies found that jobs requiring high interpersonal skills were perceived as unlikely to be overtaken by AI (Aoki, 2020; Coupe, 2019). In contrast, AI was deemed to be as good as or better than humans in specific other jobs, including journal article writing (Jung et al., 2017), labor-intensive jobs (Dodel & Mesch, 2020), and jobs dealing with information searching and synthesizing (Aoki, 2020; Doraiswamy et al., 2020). While these findings in aggregation yield an interesting pattern of results, they are similarly limited by the small range of jobs covered, offering an incomplete understanding of public trust in AI simply based on what machines can do. As such, the limited scope of previous research makes it difficult to identify overall AI acceptance trends and pinpoint specific AI characteristics the public trusts or tasks that people are currently willing to trust AI-powered machines to perform in replacement of humans.

To bridge the research gap, this study includes a comprehensive set of jobs to provide a fuller picture of factors underlying human–AI trust. By employing a dataset including a wide range of jobs with their associated characteristics, we aim to uncover job-related factors, such as skills required to perform the job, that are associated with the perceived possibility and desirability to replace human workers with AI-powered machines. This way, we can understand the levels of public trust in different aspects of AI.

In addition, this study expands previous literature by investigating the perceived desirability of job replacement evaluated from different perspectives. The perception of desirability may be affected by different factors depending on the point of view one is taking. On a corporate level, firms may primarily consider, among other factors, the cost-effectiveness of replacing humans with AI-powered machines and the technological reliability of such machines (Ivanov & Webster, 2017). On an individual level, consumers may determine the desirability of replacing human workers with AI-powered machines based on factors such as ease of use and potential risks associated with products or services provided by machines (Liang et al., 2020). Therefore, the perceived desirability of AI adoption may differ depending on whether the issue is judged from the employers' or consumers' perspectives. Thus, examining the perceived desirability of replacing human workers with AI from both perspectives would allow for a more accurate reflection of general levels of trust in AI among the public.

METHOD

Participants

We used a nationally representative US adult sample recruited through a survey company, Dynata (dynata.com). A total of 1,127 of 1,195 participants (94.3%) completed the survey. The age of our sample was distributed between 18 and 91 years old ($M = 48.44$, $SD = 17.83$). The gender proportion was balanced, with 48.45% male and 50.67% female, while the remaining either identified their gender as non-binary (0.62%) or preferred not to disclose it (0.27%). The majority of participants were White/Caucasian (72.05%), followed by African American (11.18%), Hispanic and Latino (6.74%), and Asian (5.77%). Of the participants, 49.16% obtained a college degree or equivalent, while 28.57% completed high school, 19.00% completed graduate school, and 3.28% had less than high school qualifications. Lastly, the median household income range was $50,000–$59,999. When compared to the US census data in 2020 (data.census.gov), our sample was sufficiently representative, as summarized in Table 12.1. However, White/Caucasian participants were slightly over-representative, whereas Hispanic and Latino participants were under-representative in our sample.

Procedures

O*NET database
To select jobs to be used in analysis and identify their characteristics, we utilized the large-scale data of occupational information obtained from the Occupational

Table 12.1   *Comparison between sample demographics and the US Census data in 2020*

Demographics	Sample	US census data in 2020 (Age 18 and more)
Mean Age	48.44	48.48
Gender		
Male	48.45%	48.51%
Female	50.67%	51.49%
Others	0.88%	–
Race		
White/Caucasian	72.05%	61.78%
African American	11.18%	12.10%
Hispanic and Latino	6.74%	14.72%
Asian	5.77%	5.90%
Others	4.26%	4.10%
Education		
High School Diploma	28.57%	28.52%
College Degree	49.16%	45.16%
Graduate Degree	19.00%	18.54%
Others	3.27%	7.78%
Median Household Income	$50,000–$59,999	$61,937

Information Network (O*NET) database, which has been developed and maintained for the US Department of Labor by the National Center for O*NET Development (2022).[1] This database comprises detailed characteristics of 1,017 jobs and other occupation-related information, including (1) worker characteristics (e.g., abilities and work styles), (2) worker requirements (e.g., skills and knowledge), (3) experience requirements (e.g., experience and training skills), (4) occupational requirements (e.g., work activities and contexts), (5) workforce characteristics (e.g., labor market information and outlook), and (6) occupation-specific information (e.g., job descriptions and tools involved to perform the job). A total of 144 job characteristics were used in this study.

---

[1] For more details about the management of the database, refer to the O*Net website (https://www.onetcenter.org).

Selecting "representative" jobs

Because it is impractical to ask participants for their opinions on all the 1,017 jobs, many of which are similar and redundant, we selected the 100 most "representative" jobs whose characteristics are minimally overlapping with those of the rest. The selection was made as follows. First, the number 100 was determined as the optimal number that ensures sufficient statistical power of analysis and minimizes respondents' fatigue and dropout rate. Then, k-medoids clustering, an unsupervised machine-learning algorithm, was performed to identify 100 job clusters that are maximally distinguished from one another in terms of their characteristics and those at the centroids of each cluster. Instead of k-means clustering, which is widely used for clustering analysis, we adopted k-medoids clustering because its computational algorithm minimizes within-cluster similarity and maximizes between-cluster difference (Park et al., 2006). Therefore, the centroids of clusters can be seen as "representative" in their clusters. Finally, two research assistants manually processed the job titles to simplify those that might be unfamiliar to the public or seemed too long.

Measures

Perceived desirability and possibility of replacement of human workers with AI-powered technologies and other variables were obtained through an online survey. Each participant was presented with 25 jobs randomly selected from the 100 representative jobs and provided a general job description and a list of detailed task statements for each job obtained from the O*NET database. For each of the 100 representative jobs, we collected 281.74 valid responses on average (*min.* = 245, *max.* = 315), which were sufficient for the statistical reliability of further analysis.

Familiarity

Familiarity with the presented job was measured on a five-point Likert scale (0 = "I have never heard of this job before.", 4 = "It is my job or within the same industry I am working in."). Public familiarity with a job was measured by averaging individual participants' scores (M = 1.40, SD = 0.24).

Expected growth

Participants were asked to rate the extent to which they expected the demand for the job to grow in the next ten years on a three-point Likert scale (1 = "It will grow," 0 = "It will remain about the same," −1 = "It will drop"). Public expectation of the growth prospect of a job was measured by average individual participants' judgment (M = 0.29, SD = 0.16).

Technological possibility

Perceived technological possibility of job automation was assessed using the binary question "Do you think the current AI technologies are developed enough to replace human [job title]?" (1 = "Yes", 0 = "No") and aggregated by averaging participants' scores (M = 0.37, SD = 0.12).

Adoption intention

Perceived desirability of job automation from employers' perspective was assessed with the binary question, "If you were an employer, would you adopt AI instead of hiring human [job title]?" (1 = "Yes," 0 = "No") and aggregated by averaging participants' scores ($M = 0.31$, $SD = 0.11$).

Purchase intention

Perceived desirability of job automation from consumers' perspective was assessed with the binary question, "As a consumer, which would you prefer products/services provided by AI [job title] or human [job title]?" (1 = "AI," 0 = "human") and aggregated by averaging participants' scores ($M = 0.29$, $SD = 0.10$).

Statistical Analysis[2]

Exploratory factor analysis

The main objective of the current study is to identify job characteristics associated with the perceived possibility and desirability of replacing human workers with AI. However, the large number of job characteristics in the O*NET database (144 in total) could make it challenging to discover clear patterns. Also, many characteristics were highly correlated with one another, which could potentially cause multicollinearity problems. For these reasons, we conducted an exploratory factor analysis for each of four categories of job characteristics classified in the O*NET database: abilities (52 characteristics), skills (35 characteristics), work activities (41 characteristics), and work styles (16 characteristics). Varimax rotation was adopted, and 11 characteristics with factor loadings lower than 0.6 were removed from further analysis.

Multiple regression analyses

Multiple regression analyses were conducted to examine the relationships between job characteristics and the three criterion variables: technological possibility, adoption intention, and purchase intention. The factors extracted from the explorative factor analysis, as well as familiarity and expected growth, were used as predictors.

RESULTS

Exploratory Factor Analysis

The 41 job characteristics under the abilities category were reduced into four factors explaining 81.8% of the total variance (Table 12.2). The extracted factors were labeled as follows: reasoning and communication (e.g., "inductive/deductive reasoning" and

---

[2] All the statistical analyses, including *K*-medoids clustering, were conducted in *Python* (3.8.10), and *scikit-learn* (1.0.2) and *factor analyzer* (0.4.0) packages were used.

Table 12.2   Factor loadings for abilities category

Variables	Reasoning/ communication	Dexterity/precision	Physical coordination	Recognition	Communality
Deductive Reasoning	**.908**	-.144	-.234	-.133	.917
Inductive Reasoning	**.898**	-.116	-.167	-.150	.870
Information Ordering	**.874**	.078	-.230	-.078	.829
Problem Sensitivity	**.872**	-.029	-.046	-.090	.772
Oral Comprehension	**.840**	-.280	-.190	-.201	.860
Fluency of Ideas	**.840**	-.161	-.222	-.180	.813
Category Flexibility	**.838**	.091	-.255	-.151	.798
Written Comprehension	**.823**	-.286	-.294	-.230	.898
Speed of Closure	**.816**	.085	-.051	.073	.681
Originality	**.812**	-.136	-.196	-.191	.753
Oral Expression	**.809**	-.374	-.191	-.206	.874
Written Expression	**.802**	-.355	-.275	-.226	.896
Memorization	**.777**	-.199	-.073	-.063	.652
Flexibility of Closure	**.757**	.323	-.074	.133	.701
Mathematical Reasoning	**.743**	.002	-.401	-.075	.718
Number Facility	**.705**	.020	-.383	-.057	.648
Speech Clarity	**.651**	-.538	-.092	-.168	.750
Speech Recognition	**.647**	-.427	-.151	-.215	.671
Finger Dexterity	-.129	**.853**	.248	.080	.813
Arm–Hand Steadiness	-.230	**.805**	.397	.126	.874
Control Precision	-.222	**.793**	.284	.348	.880

Manual Dexterity	-.298	**.773**	.425	.188	.903
Visual Color Discrimination	.205	**.751**	.105	.217	.664
Depth Perception	-.051	**.666**	.300	.556	.846
Visualization	.390	**.659**	.011	.231	.639
Wrist–Finger Speed	-.251	**.639**	.275	.280	.625
Multilimb Coordination	-.275	**.604**	.555	.405	.913
Stamina	-.338	.310	**.798**	.312	.945
Gross Body Coordination	-.311	.309	**.793**	.350	.944
Gross Body Equilibrium	-.253	.292	**.735**	.433	.876
Dynamic Strength	-.355	.380	**.734**	.328	.917
Trunk Strength	-.358	.339	**.729**	.278	.852
Static Strength	-.343	.437	**.715**	.348	.941
Extent Flexibility	-.362	.458	**.684**	.330	.918
Explosive Strength	-.175	.125	**.612**	.275	.497
Peripheral Vision	-.168	.194	.299	**.897**	.960
Night Vision	-.126	.214	.238	**.895**	.920
Spatial Orientation	-.116	.236	.281	**.867**	.901
Glare Sensitivity	-.154	.258	.299	**.852**	.905
Sound Localization	-.146	.260	.278	**.845**	.880
Response Orientation	-.186	.507	.431	**.601**	.839
Eigenvalues	22.31	7.63	2.55	1.75	34.23
Percentage of total variance	32.01	18.16	16.22	15.45	81.83

"oral/written comprehension and expression"), dexterity and precision (e.g., "finger dexterity," "arm-hand steadiness," "control/depth perception"), physical coordination (e.g., "stamina," "body coordination," "dynamic/static strength"), and recognition (e.g., "night vision," "spatial orientation").

The 35 job characteristics under the skills category were reduced into three factors explaining 77.5% of the total variance (Table 12.3), which were labeled as follows: learning and analysis (e.g., "complex problem solving," "critical thinking"), equipment operation (e.g., "troubleshooting," "operation and control"), and resource management (e.g., "management of material/financial/personnel resources," "time management").

The 41 job characteristics under the work activities category were reduced into three factors explaining 73.4% of the total variance (Table 12.4), which were labeled as follows: information processing (e.g., "processing/getting information," "interpreting the meaning of information"), team management (e.g., "guiding and directing subordinates," "developing and building teams"), and equipment management (e.g., "repairing/maintaining equipment," "operating vehicles/devices/equipment").

Finally, the 16 job characteristics under the work styles category were reduced into two factors explaining 70.8% of the total variance (Table 12.5), which were labeled as follows: social interaction (e.g., "concern for others," "social orientation," "cooperation") and personal effort (e.g., "persistence," "achievement/effort")

Multiple Regression Analyses

We computed factor scores of the 11 factors extracted from a series of factor analyses described in the previous section and used them and the additional variables – familiarity and expected growth – as predictors in multiple regression analyses on the three criterion variables, technical possibility, adoption intention, and purchase intention. It is important to note that the unit of analysis was each of the 100 representative jobs in all three regression analyses, which is necessary to examine the associations between job characteristics and the perceived possibility and desirability of the replacement of jobs with AI-powered machines to address the question what aspect of AI-powered machines the public tend to rely on. We checked the variance inflation factors (VIF) for all the predictors, which were acceptable levels, ranging between 1.151 and 2.081. This suggests that there were no serious multicollinearity issues in our multiple regression models, and the regression coefficients were stable. The results are summarized in Table 12.6.

Technological possibility
The predictors explained 60.9% of the variance in technological possibility, which was statistically significant [$R^2 = .609$, $F(13, 86) = 2.621$, $p < .01$]. Familiarity was negatively associated ($\beta = -0.20$, $p < .05$). Seven job characteristics were significantly associated with technological possibility, with equipment operation being positively associated ($\beta = 0.58$, $p < .05$), while the others being negatively associated with the outcome variable: dexterity and precision ($\beta = -0.40$, $p < .05$), physical coordination ($\beta = -0.53$, $p < .01$), recognition ($\beta = -0.25$, $p < .05$), learning and analysis ($\beta = -1.44$,

Table 12.3   *Factor loadings for skills category*

Variables	Learning and analysis	Equipment operation	Resource management	Communality
Reading Comprehension	**.897**	−.278	.207	.925
Active Learning	**.879**	−.208	.326	.923
Complex Problem Solving	**.870**	−.068	.371	.899
Critical Thinking	**.861**	−.229	.334	.906
Writing	**.844**	−.353	.251	.900
Judgment and Decision Making	**.832**	−.166	.414	.892
Systems Analysis	**.813**	−.022	.458	.871
Systems Evaluation	**.811**	−.024	.486	.895
Science	**.788**	.166	.024	.649
Active Listening	**.788**	−.410	.276	.865
Speaking	**.787**	−.423	.305	.892
Learning Strategies	**.753**	−.202	.371	.745
Instructing	**.738**	−.150	.380	.712
Monitoring	**.718**	−.099	.517	.793
Mathematics	**.704**	.098	.281	.584
Operations Analysis	**.660**	.049	.319	.539
Programming	**.641**	.121	.078	.431
Troubleshooting	−.078	**.960**	−.042	.930
Equipment Selection	−.040	**.913**	−.094	.843
Equipment Maintenance	−.182	**.884**	−.142	.835
Operation Monitoring	−.045	**.883**	.066	.787
Repairing	−.166	**.875**	−.129	.811
Quality Control Analysis	.071	**.873**	.091	.776
Operation and Control	−.225	**.841**	−.020	.758
Installation	.008	**.612**	−.094	.384
Mgmt. of Material Resources	.305	.162	**.775**	.719
Mgmt. of Financial Resources	.299	.008	**.765**	.676
Mgmt. of Personnel Resources	.504	−.050	**.755**	.826
Time Management	.602	−.137	**.645**	.797
Coordination	.432	−.147	**.680**	.670
Persuasion	.533	−.365	**.611**	.791
Negotiation	.461	−.377	**.650**	.777
Eigenvalue	17.46	6.21	1.82	25.49
Percentage of total variance	38.25	22.12	17.14	77.50

Table 12.4   Factor loadings for work activities categories

Variables	Information processing	Team management	Equipment management	Communality
Processing Information	**.901**	.280	−.085	.897
Analyzing Data or Information	**.872**	.340	−.131	.893
Updating and Using Relevant Knowledge	**.824**	.361	−.064	.813
Documenting/Recording Information	**.801**	.306	−.035	.737
Interpreting the Meaning of Info. for Others	**.787**	.400	−.174	.809
Getting Information	**.766**	.404	−.287	.832
Identifying Objects, Actions, and Events	**.737**	.336	.025	.656
Making Decisions and Solving Problems	**.735**	.513	.038	.804
Interacting with Computers	**.729**	.265	−.156	.626
Determining Compliance with Standards	**.647**	.377	.132	.578
Estimating the Quantifiable Characteristics	**.617**	.340	.385	.644
Comm. with Supervisors/Peers/Subordinates	**.613**	.593	−.082	.734
Guiding and Directing Subordinates	.301	**.861**	.098	.841
Coord. The Work and Activities of Others	.311	**.841**	.139	.823
Staffing Organizational Units	.284	**.823**	−.036	.758
Developing and Building Teams	.363	**.820**	.061	.808
Resolving Conflicts and Negotiating	.235	**.788**	−.202	.717
Coaching and Developing Others	.393	**.766**	−.065	.744
Scheduling Work and Activities	.443	**.757**	.010	.769
Monitoring and Controlling Resources	.269	**.724**	.188	.631
Provide Consultation and Advice to Others	.572	**.688**	−.109	.813

Developing Objectives and Strategies	.574	**.653**	-.094	.766
Establishing/maintaining Interpersonal Relationships	.347	**.651**	-.360	.674
Organizing, Planning, and Prioritizing Work	.552	**.638**	-.165	.739
Performing Administrative Activities	.440	**.636**	-.272	.672
Selling or Influencing Others	.130	**.622**	-.211	.448
Repairing and Maintaining Mech. Equipment	-.132	-.124	**.915**	.869
Controlling Machines and Processes	-.085	-.180	**.890**	.832
Inspecting Equipment, Structures, or Material	.122	.026	**.885**	.800
Handling and Moving Objects	-.400	-.140	**.782**	.791
Operating Vehicles/Devices/Equipment	-.211	.012	**.773**	.641
Performing General Physical Activities	-.379	-.017	**.760**	.722
Repairing and Maintaining Elect. Equipment	.162	-.104	**.737**	.580
Drafting, Laying Out, and Specifying Technical Devices, Parts, and Equipment	.233	.138	**.647**	.492
Eigenvalue	17.30	5.90	2.54	25.73
Percentage of total variance	28.02	27.99	17.39	73.40

Table 12.5   Factor loadings for the styles of dimension

Variables	Social interaction	Personal effort	Communality
Self-Control	**.890**	.100	.802
Concern for Others	**.876**	.008	.767
Social Orientation	**.860**	.045	.742
Cooperation	**.781**	.254	.675
Stress Tolerance	**.739**	.373	.685
Adaptability/Flexibility	**.686**	.497	.717
Dependability	**.666**	.335	.556
Persistence	.255	**.872**	.825
Initiative	.338	**.850**	.837
Achievement/Effort	.220	**.843**	.759
Analytical Thinking	.022	**.785**	.616
Innovation	.094	**.709**	.512
Eigenvalue	6.51	2.55	9.06
Percentage of total variance	38.39	32.40	70.79

$p < .01$), resource management ($\beta = -0.73$, $p < .01$), and social interaction ($\beta = -0.21$, $p < .05$).

Adoption intention

The predictors explained 63.1% of the variance in adoption intention, which was statistically significant [$R^2 = .631$, $F(13, 86) = 2.692$, $p < .01$]. Familiarity was negatively associated ($\beta = -0.30$, $p < .01$). Seven job characteristics were significantly associated with adoption intention, with equipment operation ($\beta = 0.55$, $p < .05$) and team management ($\beta = 0.36$, $p < .05$) being positively associated, while the others being negatively associated with the criterion variable: reasoning and communication ($\beta = -0.93$, $p < .05$), dexterity/precision ($\beta = -0.41$, $p < .05$), physical coordination ($\beta = -0.46$, $p < .01$), learning and analysis ($\beta = -1.52$, $p < .01$), and resource management ($\beta = -0.82$, $p < .01$).

Purchase intention

The predictors explained 63.3% of the variance in purchase intention, which was statistically significant [$R^2 = .633$, $F(13, 86) = 2.979$, $p < .01$]. Familiarity was negatively associated purchase intention ($\beta = -0.30$, $p < .01$). Seven job characteristics were significantly associated with purchase intention, with equipment operation ($\beta = 0.54$, $p < .05$) and team management ($\beta = 0.35$, $p < .05$) being positively associated, while the others being negatively associated with the criterion variable: dexterity and precision ($\beta = -0.33$, $p < .05$), physical coordination ($\beta = -0.46$, $p < .01$), learning and analysis ($\beta = -1.49$, $p < .01$), resource management ($\beta = -0.71$, $p < .01$), and social interaction ($\beta = -0.20$, $p < .05$).

Table 12.6 Regression analyses for predicting technological possibility, adoption intention, and purchase intention ($N = 100$)

Predictor	Technological possibility			Adoption intention			Purchase intention		
	B	SE	β	B	SE	β	B	SE	β
Constant	0.532 **	0.059	–	0.495 **	0.047	–	0.522 **	0.052	–
Familiarity	-0.105 *	0.043	-0.203	-0.128 **	0.034	-0.301	-0.140 **	0.038	-0.298
Expected Growth	-0.070	0.075	-0.089	-0.079	0.060	-0.122	-0.046	0.067	-0.064
Abilities									
Reasoning/Communication	0.088	0.046	0.783	-0.086 *	0.037	-0.930	0.082	0.041	0.795
Dexterity/Precision	-0.049 *	0.024	-0.399	-0.042 *	0.020	-0.414	-0.036 *	0.022	-0.327
Physical Coordination	-0.065 **	0.018	-0.531	-0.047 **	0.015	-0.462	-0.052 **	0.016	-0.463
Recognition	-0.031 *	0.015	-0.254	-0.023	0.012	-0.225	-0.023	0.013	-0.202
Skills									
Learning/Analysis	-0.173 **	0.048	-1.437	-0.151 **	0.038	-1.520	-0.163 **	0.042	-1.486
Equipment Operation	0.072 *	0.029	0.579	0.056 *	0.023	0.549	0.061 *	0.026	0.539
Resource Management	-0.091 **	0.024	-0.729	-0.084 **	0.019	-0.823	-0.080 **	0.021	-0.710
Work Activities									
Information Processing	0.031	0.020	0.279	0.028	0.016	0.300	0.035	0.018	0.345
Team Management	0.039	0.021	0.320	0.036 *	0.017	0.360	0.038 *	0.019	0.345
Equipment Management	0.011	0.031	0.088	0.016	0.025	0.156	0.003	0.027	0.025
Work Styles									
Social Interaction	-0.026 *	0.011	-0.213	-0.017	0.009	-0.172	-0.023 *	0.010	-0.201
Personal Effort	-0.007	0.013	-0.059	-0.010	0.010	-0.092	-0.012	0.011	-0.106
R^2	.609			.631			.633		
F	2.621 **			2.692 **			2.979 **		

Note: $*p < .05.$ $**p < .01.$

DISCUSSION

This study proposes a novel approach to addressing the question: to what extent and in what aspects do people trust AI? We replaced the original question with simpler and less ambiguous ones: how do people perceive the replacement of human workers with AI-powered machines across a wide range of professions? Do they perceive it to be possible and desirable? Then, we selected the 100 most "representative" jobs out of over 1,000 occupations registered by the US Department of Labor using the *k*-medoids clustering methods. Through an online survey, we collected the opinions of a nationally representative sample on the possibility and desirability of job automation. Finally, we conducted an explorative factor analysis and multiple regression analysis to identify the characteristics of jobs whose replacements with AI-powered machines are perceived as desirable and possible from those of the others.

All but one carried negative regression coefficients among the eight factors significantly associated with technological possibility. This indicated that the public had generally low levels of trust in the competency of AI-powered machines, deeming current AI technology inadequate in many aspects. This finding corresponded to past research. For example, a recent global survey found that less than 4% of respondents perceived that their jobs were likely going to be automated by AI technology (Doraiswamy et al., 2020). Similarly, another study found low levels of fear about being replaced by automation technologies among their Bulgarian respondents, who generally deemed technologies incapable of replacing human workers (Ivanov & Webster, 2017). As such, consistent with extant literature, our results suggest that the US public largely perceives AI technology to be in its infancy, far from its goal of simulating human intelligence.

Familiarity was negatively associated with all three dependent variables, showing that people perceive more familiar jobs as less possible and less desirable for automation. This negative relationship can be explained by the fact that, although fragmented job tasks can be easily automated, it is still technologically difficult to automate entire professions in many cases (Sampson, 2021). As such, when individuals are more familiar with a job, they would have more profound insights into the tasks involved in that job, which is hard to automate given the current state of AI technology. Also, the negative relationship can be attributed to the inherent familiarity bias of human beings. Research has indicated that humans may be biologically hardwired to prefer situations we are more familiar with because unfamiliar situations would provoke anxiety (Chew et al., 2012). Therefore, when the public is more familiar with a profession, it may, by nature, be more averse to seeing changes in the profession, such as having AI replace human workers.

In addition, four job characteristics were negatively associated with all three criterion variables: dexterity and precision, physical coordination, learning and analysis, and resource management. The results from the explorative factor analyses revealed that all these factors require a wide range of cognitive skills, such as comprehension, problem solving, and critical thinking, as well as managerial and interpersonal skills, such as coordination, persuasion, and negotiation. This, in turn, suggests that the public generally does not trust AI in performing jobs requiring advanced cognitive skills and management skills beyond. In contrast, equipment operation was positively associated with all three criterion variables. Job characteristics highly loaded on equipment operation included "troubleshooting," "equipment selection," and "repairing." Hence, the results suggest that the public highly trusts AI in performing simple work that is mechanical in nature.

Taken together, the public is suspicious of the possibility and desirability of having AI perform jobs requiring complex abilities and skills associated traditionally with making sense of sensory input, thinking critically, and interacting with others. Public trust in AI is limited to performing mechanical tasks by following step-by-step procedures systematically without much interaction with human beings. This pattern is consistent with past research, which found that while individuals performing manual tasks were afraid of being displaced by AI, individuals whose work required complex skills such as management and data analysis did not have this concern (Dodel & Mesch, 2020). Similarly, another study found that while public trust in an AI chatbot's performance on inquiries requiring information searching was high, public trust in its performance on inquiries necessitating empathy and cognitive flexibility was low (Aoki, 2020). Therefore, it seems that the public does not trust AI enough to perceive it as a counterpart to humans. Instead, AI-powered machines are still viewed as tools for completing relatively simple tasks that do not require much human intelligence.

Some job characteristics showed inconsistent patterns of association with the measures of trust. Specifically, recognition was negatively associated with technological possibility while not significantly related to adoption intention or purchase intention. Social interaction was negatively associated with technological possibility and purchase intention but not significantly related to adoption intention. Also, reasoning and communication were positively associated with adoption intention but not with technological possibility or purchase intention. Lastly, team management was positively associated with adoption and purchase intention but nonrelated to technological possibility.

The inconsistent relationships between these job characteristics and the criterion variables strongly suggest that the level of trust in AI differs depending on who the trustor is. For example, reasoning and communication could be critical for employers to make their adoption decisions because it is closely related to the productivity and efficiency of related jobs. However, the factor does not matter much for consumers to make their purchase decisions. Thus, even if AI-powered machines are not functional enough, it would not be a reason to reject them from consumers' perspective. Another, but opposite, example is social interaction. This factor includes "concerns for others," "social orientation," and "dependability," which might be necessary for consumers as actual users of the products and services but not for employers. Moreover, the inconsistent associations suggest that technological possibilities of AI-powered machines may be neither necessary nor sufficient conditions for adopting or rejecting them. For example, although the factor recognition was perceived as technologically impossible, the automation of related jobs was not necessarily perceived as undesirable from employers' and consumers' perspectives. On the other hand, team management was not perceived as technologically possible yet. However, the public would rely on AI-powered machines if they can perform as well as human workers.

It is worth noting that the current results regarding team management, which is related to various forms of interpersonal skills, including "guiding, directing, and motivating subordinates," "developing and building teams," and "resolving conflicts and negotiating with others" is inconsistent with those of previous studies. More specifically, the current results show that the public was willing to accept AI performing jobs requiring high interpersonal skills. However, Coupe (2019) found that individuals performing jobs requiring extensive interactions with others tended not to worry about being displaced by AI. Aoki (2020) found that the public did not trust AI's ability to express empathy for consumers. This inconsistency might be attributed to the failure to delineate the technological possibility and social desirability aspects of trust in earlier work. The lack of trust in AI's interpersonal skills in these earlier studies stemmed from participants' doubts about the competency of current AI technology, implicating only the technological possibility but not the social desirability aspect of trust. Seen in this light, our results complement rather than contradict past findings to indicate that despite the unreliable interpersonal skills of AI-powered machines at present, the public would want to have AI perform jobs involving social interactions in replacement of human workers. A possible explanation for this finding is that social interactions with human workers would be uncontrollably affected by the workers' cognitive biases or emotional states, resulting in miscommunication or interpersonal conflicts. In comparison, AI can be programmed to respond appropriately in social interactions, ensuring a pleasant consumer experience and optimal work outcomes.

CONCLUSION

By avoiding the difficulties in defining the multifaceted construct of trust and specifying the boundary of AI technologies, this study provides a more accurate and comprehensive account of public trust in AI. Furthermore, our results suggest that it is necessary to explicate trust in AI in the technological possibility and social desirability aspects to better understand the reasons behind a particular level of trust. Researchers can leverage our results to investigate the antecedents and consequences of the two aspects of human–AI trust. The findings presented in this chapter also pave the way for future research that hopes to examine further the psychological mechanisms underlying public trust in AI.

Furthermore, this study has important practical contributions. First, our results suggest that the technological possibility aspect of trust in AI is relatively low compared to the social desirability aspect. Therefore, to enhance public trust in AI, scientists and engineers working on AI technology need to partner with communication practitioners to relay information about the most recent breakthroughs in AI to the public. By understanding how fast AI technology is evolving, the public may have more confidence in the capability of AI-powered machines.

Next, our findings indicate that the kinds of jobs that the public finds socially desirable to be replaced by AI require precise control of body parts or extensive interpersonal interactions. This suggests that as long as it becomes technologically possible for AI-powered machines to perform these jobs, and if not better than human workers, the public would be open to the automation of these jobs using AI technology. Hence, these jobs are the gateway to increasing public acceptance of the employment of AI-powered machines across industries. On the one hand, scientists should focus on improving the performance of AI-powered machines in terms of precise body control and effective social interactions. Policymakers and industry leaders should also invest more in research in these areas. On the other hand, communication practitioners can emphasize the advantages of having AI-powered machines perform jobs that are cognitively exhausting for humans or require extensive social interactions to ease the integration of AI in different job sectors.

In this study, we sacrificed the depth for the breadth of our investigation by adopting binary questions to measure public trust in AI-powered machines across jobs as a strategy to minimize participants' fatigue and dropouts. Some participants might find that neither response accurately described their perceived possibility and desirability of replacing human workers with AI but was forced to choose one. As such, their responses might be arbitrary to some extent and should be interpreted as only rough indicators of their trust in AI. Future studies need to consider more sophisticated ways to measure respondents' trust in AI for a more nuanced understanding of the specific levels of public trust. Also, the current study's findings should be validated through replications by including more jobs, in particular, those statistically adjacent to the "representative" jobs to capture the subtle differences in public trust in AI-powered machines.

REFERENCES

Abbass, H. A. (2019). Social integration of artificial intelligence: functions, automation allocation logic and human-autonomy trust. *Cognitive Computation*, *11*(2), 159–171. https://doi.org/10.1007/s12559-018-9619-0

Alekseeva, L., Azar, J., Giné, M., Samila, S., & Taska, B. (2021). The demand for AI skills in the labor market. *Labour Economics*, *71*, 102002. https://doi.org/10.1016/j.labeco.2021.102002

Aoki, N. (2020). An experimental study of public trust in AI chatbots in the public sector. *Government Information Quarterly*, *37*(4), 101490. https://doi.org/10.1016/j.giq.2020.101490

Araujo, T., Helberger, N., Kruikemeier, S., & de Vreese, C. H. (2020). In AI we trust? Perceptions about automated decision-making by artificial intelligence. *AI & Society*, *35*(3), 611–623. https://doi.org/10.1007/s00146-019-00931-w

Asaro, P. M. (2019). AI ethics in predictive policing: From models of threat to an ethics of care. *IEEE Technology and Society Magazine*, *38*(2), 40–53. https://doi.org/10.1109/MTS.2019.2915154

Baier, A. (1986). Trust and antitrust. *Ethics*, *96*(2), 231–260. https://doi.org/10.1086/292745

Bao, Y., Cheng, X., De Vreede, T., & De Vreede, G.-J. (2021). Investigating the relationship between AI and trust in human-AI collaboration. In T. Bui (Ed.), *Proceedings of the 54th Annual Hawaii International Conference on System Sciences* (pp. 607–617). University of Hawaii. https://doi.org/10.24251/HICSS.2021.074.

Brynjolfsson, E., Mitchell, T., & Rock, D. (2018). What can machines learn, and what does It mean for occupations and the economy? *AEA Papers and Proceedings*, *108*, 43–47. https://doi.org/10.1257/pandp.20181019

Carey, R., Maas, M., Watson, N., & Yampolskiy, R. (2017). Editors' introduction to the special issue on "Superintelligence". *Informatica*, *41*(4). http://www.informatica.si/index.php/informatica/article/view/2107

Chandra, S., Srivastava, S. C., & Theng, Y.-L. (2010). Evaluating the role of trust in consumer adoption of mobile payment systems: An empirical analysis. *Communications of the Association for Information Systems*, *27*, 29. https://doi.org/10.17705/1CAIS.02729

Chew, S. H., Ebstein, R. P., & Zhong, S. (2012). Ambiguity aversion and familiarity bias: Evidence from behavioral and gene association studies. *Journal of Risk and Uncertainty*, *44*(1), 1–18. https://doi.org/10.1007/s11166-011-9134-0

Coupe, T. (2019). Automation, job characteristics and job insecurity. *International Journal of Manpower*, *40*(7), 1288–1304. https://doi.org/10.1108/IJM-12-2018-0418

Dodel, M., & Mesch, G. S. (2020). Perceptions about the impact of automation in the workplace. *Information, Communication & Society*, *23*(5), 665–680. https://doi.org/10.1080/1369118X.2020.1716043

Doraiswamy, P. M., Blease, C., & Bodner, K. (2020). Artificial intelligence and the future of psychiatry: Insights from a global physician survey. *Artificial Intelligence in Medicine*, *102*, 101753. https://doi.org/10.1016/j.artmed.2019.101753

Ferràs-Hernández, X. (2018). The future of management in a world of electronic brains. *Journal of Management Inquiry*, *27*(2), 260–263. https://doi.org/10.1177/1056492617724973

Gillath, O., Ai, T., Branicky, M. S., Keshmiri, S., Davison, R. B., & Spaulding, R. (2021). Attachment and trust in artificial intelligence. *Computers in Human Behavior*, *115*, 106607. https://doi.org/10.1016/j.chb.2020.106607

Glikson, E., & Woolley, A. (2020). Human trust in artificial intelligence: Review of empirical research. *Academy of Management Annals*, *14*(2), 627–660.

Huang, M.-H., & Rust, R. T. (2018). Artificial intelligence in service. *Journal of Service Research*, *21*(2), 155–172. https://doi.org/10.1177/1094670517752459

Ivanov, S. H., & Webster, C. (2017). *Adoption of robots, artificial intelligence and service automation by travel, tourism and hospitality companies – A cost-benefit analysis* (SSRN Scholarly Paper ID 3007577). Social Science Research Network. https://papers.ssrn.com/abstract=3007577

Jacovi, A., Marasović, A., Miller, T., & Goldberg, Y. (2020). *Formalizing trust in artificial intelligence: Prerequisites, causes and goals of human trust in AI*. ArXiv. http://arxiv.org/abs/2010.07487.

Jarrahi, M. H. (2018). Artificial intelligence and the future of work: Human-AI symbiosis in organizational decision making. *Business Horizons*, *61*, 577–586. https://doi.org/10.1016/j.bushor.2018.03.007

Jung, J., Song, H., Kim, Y., Im, H., & Oh, S. (2017). Intrusion of software robots into journalism: The public's and journalists' perceptions of news written by algorithms and human journalists. *Computers in Human Behavior*, *71*, 291–298. https://doi.org/10.1016/j.chb.2017.02.022

Lewis, J. D., & Weigert, A. (1985). Trust as a social reality. *Social Forces*, *63*(4), 967–985. https://doi.org/10.2307/2578601

Liang, Y., Lee, S.-H., & Workman, J. E. (2020). Implementation of artificial intelligence in fashion: Are consumers ready? *Clothing and Textiles Research Journal*, *38*(1), 3–18. https://doi.org/10.1177/0887302X19873437

Lippert, S. K., & Davis, M. (2006). A conceptual model integrating trust into planned change activities to enhance technology adoption behavior. *Journal of Information Science, 32*(5), 434–448. https://doi.org/10.1177/0165551506066042

Liu, K., & Tao, D. (2022). The roles of trust, personalization, loss of privacy, and anthropomorphism in public acceptance of smart healthcare services. *Computers in Human Behavior, 127,* 107026. https://doi.org/10.1016/j.chb.2021.107026

Mayer, R. C., Davis, J. H., & Schoorman, F. D. (1995). An integrative model of organizational trust. *Academy of Management Review, 20*(3), 709–734. https://doi.org/10.5465/AMR.1995.9508080335

McKnight, D. H., Choudhury, V., & Kacmar, C. (2002). The impact of initial consumer trust on intentions to transact with a web site: A trust building model. *The Journal of Strategic Information Systems, 11*(3–4), 297–323. https://doi.org/10.1016/S0963-8687(02)00020-3

McLeod, C. (2021). Trust. In E. N. Zalta (Ed.), *The stanford encyclopedia of philosophy* (Fall 2021). Metaphysics Research Lab, Stanford University. https://plato.stanford.edu/archives/fall2021/entriesrust/

Natalija, K. (2019). Insurance, smart information systems and ethics: A case study. *The ORBIT Journal, 2*(2), 1–27. https://doi.org/10.29297/orbit.v2i2.106

National Center for O*NET Development. (2022). *O*NET Resource Center.* https://www.onetcenter.org/

Nissan, E. (2017). Digital technologies and artificial intelligence's present and foreseeable impact on lawyering, judging, policing and law enforcement. *AI & Society, 32*(3), 441–464. https://doi.org/10.1007/s00146-015-0596-5

Ostrom, A. L., Fotheringham, D., & Bitner, M. J. (2019). Customer acceptance of AI in service encounters: Understanding antecedents and consequences. In P. P. Maglio, C. A. Kieliszewski, J. C. Spohrer, K. Lyons, L. Patrício, & Y. Sawatani (Eds.), *Handbook of service science, Volume II* (pp. 77–103). Springer International Publishing. https://doi.org/10.1007/978-3-319-98512-1_5

Park, H., Lee, J., & Jun, C. (2006). A K-means-like algorithm for K-medoids clustering and Its performance. *Proceedings of ICCIE,* 102–117.

Rotter, J. B. (1971). Generalized expectancies for interpersonal trust. *American Psychologist, 26*(5), 443–452. https://doi.org/10.1037/h0031464

Russell, S. (2017). Artificial intelligence: The future is superintelligent. *Nature, 548*(7669), 520–521. https://doi.org/10.1038/548520a

Sampson, S. E. (2021). A strategic framework for task automation in professional services. *Journal of Service Research, 24*(1), 122–140. https://doi.org/10.1177/1094670520940407

Sanders, T., Kaplan, A., Koch, R., Schwartz, M., & Hancock, P. A. (2019). The relationship between trust and use choice in human-robot interaction. *Human Factors, 61*(4), 614–626. https://doi.org/10.1177/0018720818816838

Schwab, K. (2017). *The Fourth Industrial Revolution.* Crown.

Tilimbe, J. (2019). Ethical Implications of Predictive Risk Intelligence. *The ORBIT Journal, 2*(2), 1–28. https://doi.org/10.29297/orbit.v2i2.112

Turing, A. M. (1950). Computing machinery and intelligence. *Mind, LIX*(236), 433–460. https://doi.org/10.1093/mind/LIX.236.433

Xu, M., David, J. M., & Kim, S. H. (2018). The fourth industrial revolution: Opportunities and challenges. *International Journal of Financial Research, 9*(2), 90. https://doi.org/10.5430/ijfr.v9n2p90

Yu, K.-H., & Kohane, I. S. (2019). Framing the challenges of artificial intelligence in medicine. *BMJ Quality & Safety, 28*(3), 238–241. https://doi.org/10.1136/bmjqs-2018-008551

Zhang, T., Tao, D., Qu, X., Zhang, X., Lin, R., & Zhang, W. (2019). The roles of initial trust and perceived risk in public's acceptance of automated vehicles. *Transportation Research Part C: Emerging Technologies, 98,* 207–220. https://doi.org/10.1016/j.trc.2018.11.018

13. Machine learning and deep learning for social science: a bibliometric approach

Jang Hyun Kim and Dongyan Nan[1]

INTRODUCTION

As of 2022, a large number of countries around the world have been promoting artificial intelligence (AI)-based intelligence as one of the important strategies to advance the fourth industrial revolution era (Kim et al., 2022). For instance, the United States, a global AI powerhouse (Kim et al., 2022), has invested £31.6 billion in developing AI technology, accounting for 56% of global investment in AI (AItimes, 2020).

As indicated by Li et al. (2020), machine learning and deep learning are representative AI techniques whose applications have led to the success of several innovative products and services (e.g., Google's AlphaGo, Facebook's Deep Text, Baidu's crewless ground vehicle). On the other hand, machine learning and deep learning have been applied in the social sciences, such as explaining social phenomena and detecting individual emotions (e.g., Barakat et al., 2021; Mir et al., 2021). Machine learning and deep learning have been gaining considerable interest in academia and industry.

In line with this trend, several bibliometric studies have attempted to provide an overview of deep learning and machine learning areas (Li et al., 2020; Su et al., 2021). However, rare studies are focusing on offering an overview of deep learning and machine learning in the context of social science. Thus, to address this limitation, this research tries to represent the knowledge structure of deep learning and machine learning in the field of social science by performing a bibliometric analysis. Specifically, based on the suggestions of representative bibliometric studies (Xu et al., 2019: Ye et al., 2020; Yu et al., 2020), the current research mainly performs co-authorship network analysis, co-citation analysis, and keywords occurrence analysis with VOSviewer.

METHODS

Data Extraction

In this study, the Web of Science Core Collection (WOSCC) database was considered a source for gathering articles related to machine learning or deep learning. Because

---

[1] Dongyan Nan is the corresponding author.

WOSCC is one of the most precise bibliographic indexing tools for academic knowledge, it has been employed for data extraction in several bibliometric studies (Chen, 2006; Che et al., 2022; Liu et al., 2021; Zhang et al., 2022). The data was extracted on June 24, 2022.

The primary data source employed in this research was the Social Science Citation Index (SSCI) because we focused on exploring knowledge frameworks of machine learning and deep learning in the field of social science.

As suggested by Li et al. (2020), the search keywords employed in this research were "machine learning" OR "deep learning." Specifically, we extracted documents whose titles, abstracts, or keywords include these terms.

Moreover, concerning article type, this research chose "Article" and "Early Access." The data extraction period was from 2012 to 2021, and only documents written in English were gathered.

Consequently, we gathered 3,695 articles for bibliometric analysis. The process of literature extraction is summarized in Table 13.1.

Data Analysis

In terms of data analysis and visualization, we applied the software VOSviewer in this research. VOSviewer, developed by Nees Jan van Eck and Ludo Waltman, has been regarded as one of the most widely employed visualization tools for bibliometric analyses (Van Eck & Waltman, 2010; Lin et al., 2022; Sarin et al., 2020; Zheng et al., 2022).

Specifically, we performed the following analyses with VOSviewer.

First, based on the existing studies (Xu et al., 2019: Ye et al., 2020; Yu et al., 2020), we identified productive authors, institutes, and countries/regions, which denote core research forces in a specific academic area. Additionally, we explored the knowledge collaborations at author and country/region levels by performing co-authorship network analyses.

Table 13.1   Article extraction procedure

Data source	SSCI of WOSCC database
Search query	Topic: "machine learning" OR "deep learning"
Selection criteria	Article type: "Article" or "Early Access" Article language: "English" Publication years: 2012–2021
Collected date	June 24, 2022
Number of articles	3,695

Note: Articles published in journals concurrently indexed by SSCI and other citation indexes (e.g., SCIE, A&HCI) were not extracted in this research.

Second, following the guidelines of Yu et al. (2020), we investigated influential journals and literature by performing co-citation analyses, which is an approach for building a structure of specialties and exploring the level of interrelationships between specialties (Small, 1973). Chang et al. (2015) and Zhao et al. (2023) reported that when two or more articles and journals are simultaneously cited by a third article, they exhibit a co-citation relation.

Third, as suggested by Yu et al. (2020) and Xu et al. (2019), we employed a keyword occurrence analysis to identify the keywords with high co-occurrence frequencies. As keywords represent the information of the main contents of papers, keyword occurrence analysis can be employed to explore hot research topics in a specific field (Yu et al., 2017; Chen & Liu, 2020).

OUTCOMES AND DISCUSSION

Mapping of Authors

The top 11 authors regarding the number of articles are reported in Table 13.2. Rob Law, Periklis Gogas, Theophilos Papadimitriou, Shouyang Wang, and Wanli Xing published nine articles individually. These five authors are the most productive scholars with publications regarding machine learning and deep learning in social science.

Specifically, Rob Law's studies were related to tourism and hospitality. For instance, Law et al. (2019) attempted to predict tourism demand by employing a deep learning model. Periklis Gogas's and Theophilos Papadimitriou's studies focused on business economics. For example, Gogas et al. (2018) tried to predict bank failures by constructing a machine learning model. Moreover, Shouyang Wang's studies

Table 13.2   Top 11 scholars ranked by the number of articles

Rank	Number of papers	Authors
1	9	Rob Law
2	9	Periklis Gogas
3	9	Theophilos Papadimitriou
4	9	Shouyang Wang
5	9	Wanli Xing
6	8	David C Atkins
7	8	Zac E. Imel
8	8	Sidney D'Mello/Sidney K D'Mello
9	7	Mohamed Abdel-Aty
10	7	Richard A. Berk/Richard Berk
11	7	Michael J. Tanana/Michael Tanana

were associated with tourism management, such as predicting tourist arrivals with machine learning (Sun et al., 2019). Furthermore, Wanli Xing's studies were related to the education area. In one of Wanli Xing's studies, Xing and Du (2019) developed a deep-learning-based model for forecasting student dropout in the context of massive open online courses.

The author co-authorship network is plotted as shown in Figure 13.1, in which the scholars with four or more articles are labeled. The links among nodes denote the co-authorship associations among authors. As revealed in Figure 13.1, the entire network included several isolated small sub-networks, implying that the authors cooperate in small groups and lack communication. We also found several productive and large collaboration sub-networks, such as the groups constructed by Periklis Gogas, Theophilos Papadimitriou, Rangan Gupta, Christian Pierdzioch, Marian Risse et al., and Zac E. Imel, David C Atkins et al., respectively. These groups can be considered core research forces in this area.

Note: Number of nodes (authors) = 90.

Figure 13.1   Author co-authorship network

Mapping of Institutes and Countries/Regions

The top 11 institutes regarding the number of articles are reported in Table 13.3. The table indicates that Harvard University ranked first, contributing 76 papers, followed by the University of Pennsylvania (57), New York University (51), Columbia University (48), Stanford University (47), and Massachusetts Institute of Technology (45). Consequently, Harvard University is the most productive institute with publications related to machine learning and deep learning in social science.

The top 20 countries/regions in terms of the number of publications are shown in Table 13.4. We found that the United States of America (USA) ranked first, contributing to 1,498 articles, followed by the People's Republic of China (531), England (413), Germany (280), and Australia (222). These results implied that Western academia is at the forefront of the application of machine learning and deep learning in social science. Moreover, most productive countries/regions are economically developed, which can be attributed to active business operations and the high density of educational institutes (Zemigala, 2019; Ye et al., 2020).

The collaboration networks among countries/regions, in which the countries/regions with five or more articles are revealed in Figure 13.2. The links among nodes indicate the co-authorship associations among countries/regions. The node size denotes the number of publications of the countries/regions. Moreover, the top ten countries/regions in terms of the degree of total link strength are reported in Table 13.5. It is found that the USA (753) has the highest total link strength, which is followed by England (436), the People's Republic of China (354), and Germany (278). This means that, regarding machine learning and deep learning in social science, these countries/regions play crucial roles in the entire collaboration networks.

Table 13.3   *Top 11 institutes listed by the number of articles*

Rank	Number of articles	Institutes
1	76	Harvard University
2	57	University of Pennsylvania
3	51	New York University
4	48	Columbia University
5	47	Stanford University
6	45	Massachusetts Institute of Technology
7	44	Chinese Academy of Sciences
8	42	University of Oxford
9	39	University of Southern California
10	38	University of Michigan
11	38	University of Toronto

Table 13.4   *Top 20 countries/regions listed by the number of publications*

Rank	Number of articles	Country/region
1	1,498	United States of America
2	531	People's Republic of China
3	413	England
4	280	Germany
5	222	Australia
6	191	Canada
7	161	Netherlands
8	127	Italy
9	120	South Korea
10	116	Spain
11	102	France
12	94	India
13	78	Taiwan
14	72	Switzerland
15	66	Turkey
16	56	Singapore
17	52	Belgium
18	52	Japan
19	50	Sweden
20	47	Norway

In particular, the USA is the country that collaborates the most with other countries/regions in this field.

Journal Co-citation Network Analysis

The journal co-citation network is constructed as displayed in Figure 13.3, in which journals with 200 or more citations are revealed. The node size denotes the cited counts of the journal, and the link between two nodes means the co-citation relation of the journals. A large node indicates that the journal is highly cited (i.e., influential journal) in an academic field.

The top 20 journals regarding cited counts are presented in Table 13.6. Among them, 13 journals are indexed in the SSCI database, whereas seven are indexed in the SCIE (Science Citation Index Extended) database. Furthermore, the table indicates that *Accident Analysis & Prevention* (1,455) had the highest cited counts. This is followed by the *Expert System with Applications* (1,305), *Tourism Management* (1095), *Machine Learning* (1021), and *PLoS One* (1020). Hence, *Accident Analysis &*

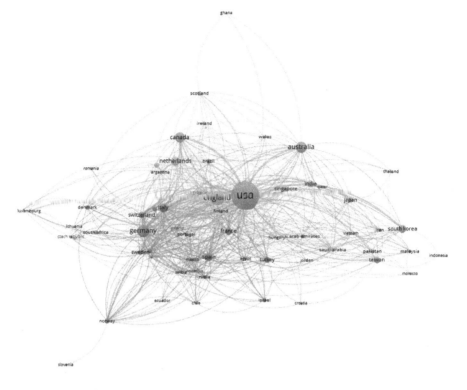

Note: Number of nodes (countries/regions) = 65.

Figure 13.2   Country/region co-authorship network

Prevention is one of the most important and influential journals regarding machine learning and deep learning in social science.

Reference/Literature Co-citation Network Analysis

The literature co-citation network is plotted as displayed in Figure 13.4, in which papers with 30 or more citations are labeled. The node size denotes the cited counts of literature, and the link between two nodes means the co-citation relation of the literature. That is, a large node indicates that the literature is an influential article in an academic field. The top 15 highly cited pieces of literature are reported in Table 13.7.

The main findings from the literature co-citation analysis are as follows. Because articles published long ago are difficult to reflect recent trends in an academic area, we mainly reviewed the papers published after 2012.

First, as reported in Table 13.7, Breiman (2001) is the most highly cited paper (444 times), one of the most crucial papers in developing the random forest machine learning model. Also, this paper's number of cited counts was overwhelmingly higher

Table 13.5   *Top 20 countries/regions ranked by total link strength*

Rank	Link strength	Country/region
1	753	United States of America
2	436	England
3	354	People's Republic of China
4	278	Germany
5	178	Australia
6	173	Canada
7	158	Netherlands
8	136	France
9	130	Switzerland
10	118	Italy
11	114	Spain
12	83	South Korea
13	83	Norway
14	81	Sweden
15	75	India
16	69	Singapore
17	69	Poland
18	69	New Zealand
19	68	Saudi Arabia
20	66	Taiwan

Note: The total link strength is calculated based on the full counting method.

than those of other papers. These results indirectly indicate that random forest is a commonly employed machine learning model in social science.

Second, Lecun et al. (2015) and Goodfellow et al. (2016) were cited 102 and 79 times, respectively, representing studies that provide an overview of deep learning.

Third, Chen and Guestrin (2016) were cited 98 times, one of the noteworthy papers in machine and deep learning. Specifically, they developed a scalable end-to-end tree boosting system, namely XGBoost. This result indicates that XGBoost is a widely applied machine learning model in social science (e.g., Jabeur et al., 2021; Cho et al., 2021).

Keyword Occurrence Analysis

The keyword occurrence network was constructed as shown in Figure 13.5, in which keywords with ten or more co-occurrence frequencies are revealed. The node size

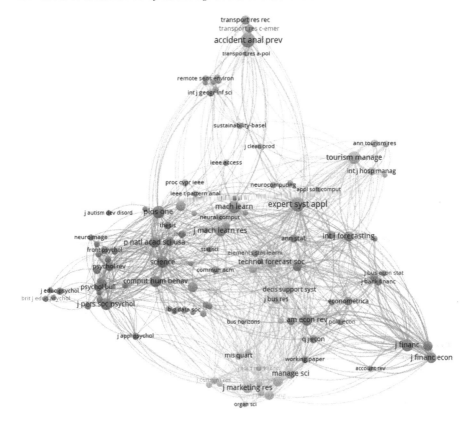

Note: Number of nodes (journals) = 117.

Figure 13.3   Journal co-citation network

denotes the co-occurrence frequency of the keyword. Also, the top 30 keywords in terms of co-occurrence frequency are reported in Table 13.8.

According to Table 13.8 and Figure 13.5, the key findings of keywords occurrence analysis are as follows.

First, we found that the keyword "natural language processing" ranked sixth with 88 counts. This result indicates that machine learning and deep learning models are mainly applied to natural language processing, especially in social science.

Second, it is found that "random forest" ranked seventh with 77 counts. This outcome indicates that random forest is one of the most widely applied machine learning models in social science. Random forest is an ensemble learning methodology for classification and regression performed by building multiple decision trees at training time (Breiman, 2001; Fawagreh et al., 2014).

Third, we also found that "social media," "Twitter," "sentiment analysis," and "text mining" had high co-occurrence frequencies. This indirectly indicates that

Table 13.6   *Top 20 journals ranked by cited counts*

Rank	Cited counts	Journals	Citation indexes
1	1,455	*Accident Analysis & Prevention/accident anal prev*	SSCI
2	1,305	*Expert System with Applications/expert syst appl*	SCIE
3	1,095	*Tourism Management/tourism manage*	SSCI
4	1,021	*Machine Learning/mach learn*	SCIE
5	1,020	*PLoS One*	SCIE
6	995	*Journal of Finance/j finance*	SSCI
7	949	*Science/science*	SCIE
8	896	*Journal of Personality and Social Psychology/j pers soc psychol*	SSCI
9	839	*American Economic Review/am econ rev*	SSCI
10	828	*Journal of Machine Learning Research/j mach learn res*	SCIE
11	824	*Computers in Human Behavior/comput hum behav*	SSCI
12	807	*Technological Forecasting and Social Change/technol forecast soc*	SSCI
13	760	*Journal of Marketing Research/j marketing res*	SSCI
14	738	*Journal of Financial Economics/j financ econ*	SSCI
15	738	*Management Science/manage sci*	SSCI
16	718	*Proceedings of the National Academy of Sciences of the United States of America/p natl acad sci usa*	SCIE
17	702	*Marketing Science/market sci*	SSCI
18	696	*International Journal of Forecasting/int j forecasting*	SSCI
19	679	*Lecture Notes in Computer Science/lect notes comput sc*	SCIE
20	631	*Journal of Marketing/j marketing*	SSCI

Note: The cited count is calculated based on the full counting method.

examining the text data from social media (e.g., Twitter) by employing machine-learning- or deep-learning-based sentiment analysis is a major research topic in the social science area (e.g., Barakat et al., 2021; Mir et al., 2021; Singh et al., 2020). The results also implied that Twitter is one of the most widely employed social media data sources for machine learning and deep learning models in the context of social science.

Additional Analysis

The top ten research areas categorized by WOSCC in terms of the number of articles are reported in Table 13.9. The results indicate that the business economics area published 1,218 articles, followed by psychology (747), education educational

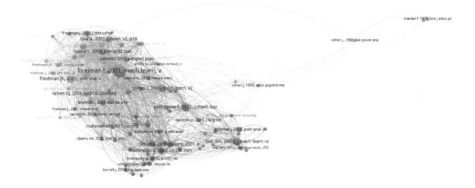

Note: Number of nodes (literature) = 85.

Figure 13.4   *Literature co-citation network*

Table 13.7   *Top 15 literature ranked by cited counts*

Rank	Cited counts	Literatures
1	444	Breiman (2001)
2	177	Blei et al. (2003)
3	176	Pedregosa et al. (2011)
4	163	Friedman (2001)
5	141	Tibshirani (1996)
6	114	Cortes and Vapnik (1995)
7	114	Hastie et al. (2009)
8	102	Lecun et al. (2015)
9	100	Liaw and Wiener (2002)
10	98	Chen and Guestrin (2016)
11	97	Zou and Hastie (2005)
12	94	Hochreiter and Schmidhuber (1997)
13	88	Breiman et al. (1984)
14	80	Breiman (1996)
15	79	Goodfellow et al. (2016)

Note: The cited count is calculated based on the full counting method.

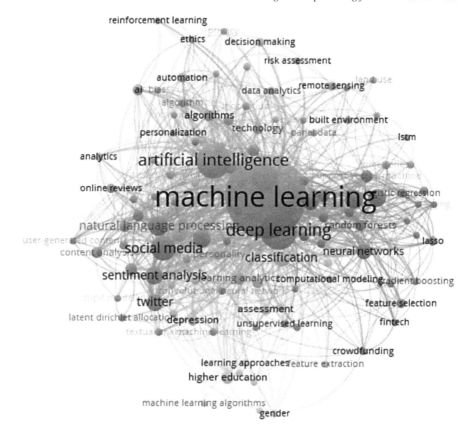

Note: Number of nodes (keywords) = 120.

Figure 13.5   *Keywords occurrence network*

research (397), and others. It indirectly shows that machine learning and deep learning have gained great interest in business economics and psychology.

CONCLUSION

Regarding our knowledge, the current research is one of the first attempts to track the knowledge structure of machine learning and deep learning in the area of social science. To this end, we extracted 3,695 articles associated with machine learning and deep learning from the SSCI of WOSCC databases and then conducted bibliometric analysis applying VOSviewer. Based on the outcomes, we offered the following critical implications:

Table 13.8   *Top 30 keywords ranked by co-occurrences*

Rank	Co-occurrences	Keywords	Rank	Co-occurrences	Keywords
1	1,489	machine learning	16	41	data mining
2	312	deep learning	17	39	higher education
3	254	artificial intelligence	18	36	neural network
4	157	big data	19	33	data science
5	132	social media	20	33	support vector machine
6	88	natural language processing	21	33	topic modeling
7	77	random forest	22	32	computer vision
8	73	forecasting	23	32	learning analytics
9	70	text mining	24	30	algorithms
10	69	sentiment analysis	25	30	personality
11	68	twitter	26	29	content analysis
12	65	prediction	27	29	random forests
13	63	classification	28	27	ai
14	59	covid-19	29	27	supervised machine learning
15	53	neural networks	30	26	text analysis

Table 13.9   *Research areas ranked by the number of publications*

Rank	Number of articles	Research areas
1	1,218	Business economics
2	747	Psychology
3	397	Education educational research
4	357	Social sciences other topics
5	270	Government law
6	229	Environmental sciences ecology
7	218	Information science library science
8	217	Geography
9	210	Public administration
10	176	Transportation

Note: The research areas are categorized based on the WOSCC.

At the author level, Rob Law, Periklis Gogas, Theophilos Papadimitriou, Shouyang Wang, and Wanli Xing are productive researchers. Additionally, the group composed of Periklis Gogas, Theophilos Papadimitriou, Rangan Gupta, Christian Pierdzioch, Marian Risse et al. is one of the most productive and large research groups. At the institution level, the major forces are Harvard University, the University of Pennsylvania, and New York University. At the country/region level, the USA, China, and England contribute core research forces. Among them, the USA plays the most significant role in the academic collaboration network. At the journal level, influential journals are *Accident Analysis & Prevention, Expert System with Applications*, and *Tourism Management.*

Additionally, we found that analyzing the text data from social media (e.g., Twitter) by applying machine-learning- or deep learning-based sentiment analysis is one of the key research topics in the social science area (see the "Keyword Occurrence Analysis" section). This finding implies that exploring individuals' emotions or perceptions is a significant research topic in academia (see Nan et al., 2022a, 2022b, 2022c; Kim et al., 2022). On the other hand, this finding indicates that social media data analysis applying AI techniques has been leading a big boom in the field of internet communication.

We also discovered that machine learning and deep learning are mainly applied in psychology and business economics (see the "Additional Analysis" section), and random forest and XGboost are widely applied AI techniques in social science (see the "Reference/Literature Co-citation Network Analysis" and "Keyword Occurrence Analysis" sections).

Interestingly, we also found that while applying AI techniques in social sciences is an interdisciplinary field, there seems to be relatively little collaboration among researchers in this field (see the "Mapping of Authors" section). That is, scholarly communication in this area is lacking. Therefore, governments and academic institutions should pay attention to this issue and develop strategies to address it. For example, they can support and encourage scholars to attend interdisciplinary conferences that focus on the interaction between computer science and social science.

In terms of practical implications, our research provides insights for social science researchers to effectively understand the knowledge structures of machine learning and deep learning in social science, thereby promoting the application of AI techniques (e.g., machine learning, deep learning) in the social science context.

Although the contributions of the current research are noteworthy, it has the following limitation. Because only papers written in English were collected in this study, there may be a slight residue of linguistic bias. Thus, to address this limitation, future studies can analyze the papers written in other languages from other databases.

REFERENCES

AItimes. (2020). http://www.aitimes.com/news/articleView.html?idxno=126627
Barakat, H., Yeniterzi, R., & Martín-Domingo, L. (2021). Applying deep learning models to Twitter data to detect airport service quality. *Journal of Air Transport Management, 91*, 102003.

Blei, D. M., Ng, A. Y., & Jordan, M. I. (2003). Latent Dirichlet allocation. *Journal of Machine Learning Research, 3*, 993–1022.

Breiman, L. (1996). Bagging predictors. *Machine Learning, 24*(2), 123–140.

Breiman, L. (2001). Random forests. *Machine Learning, 45*(1), 5–32.

Breiman, L., Friedman, J., Olshen, R., & Stone, C. (1984). *Classification and regression trees.* CRC Press.

Chang, Y. W., Huang, M. H., & Lin, C. W. (2015). Evolution of research subjects in library and information science based on keyword, bibliographical coupling, and co-citation analyses. *Scientometrics, 105*(3), 2071–2087.

Che, S., Kamphuis, P., Zhang, S., Zhao, X., & Kim, J. H. (2022). A visualization analysis of crisis and risk communication research using Citespace. *International Journal of Environmental Research and Public Health, 19*(5), 2923.

Chen, C. (2006). CiteSpace II: Detecting and visualizing emerging trends and transient patterns in scientific literature. *Journal of the American Society for Information Science and Technology, 57*(3), 359–377.

Chen, T., & Guestrin, C. (2016). Xgboost: A scalable tree boosting system. In *Proceedings of the 22nd ACM SIGKDD international conference on knowledge discovery and data mining* (pp. 785–794), ACM.

Chen, X., & Liu, Y. (2020). Visualization analysis of high-speed railway research based on CiteSpace. *Transport Policy, 85*, 1–17.

Cho, J., Kim, S., Jeong, G., Kim, C., & Seo, J. K. (2021). Investigation of influential factors of predicting individuals' use and non-use of fitness and diet apps on smartphones: Application of the machine learning algorithm (XGBoost). *American Journal of Health Behavior, 45*(1), 111–124.

Cortes, C., & Vapnik, V. (1995). Support vector machine. *Machine Learning, 20*(3), 273–297.

Fawagreh, K., Gaber, M. M., & Elyan, E. (2014). Random forests: From early developments to recent advancements. *Systems Science & Control Engineering: An Open Access Journal, 2*(1), 602–609.

Friedman, J. H. (2001). Greedy function approximation: a gradient boosting machine. *Annals of Statistics*, 1189–1232.

Gogas, P., Papadimitriou, T., & Agrapetidou, A. (2018). Forecasting bank failures and stress testing: A machine learning approach. *International Journal of Forecasting, 34*(3), 440–455.

Goodfellow, I., Bengio, Y., & Courville, A. (2016). *Deep learning.* MIT Press.

Hastie, T., Tibshirani, R., & Friedman, J. (2009). Unsupervised learning. In *The elements of statistical learning* (pp. 485–585). Springer.

Hochreiter, S., & Schmidhuber, J. (1997). Long short-term memory. *Neural Computation, 9*(8), 1735–1780.

Jabeur, S. B., Gharib, C., Mefteh-Wali, S., & Arfi, W. B. (2021). CatBoost model and artificial intelligence techniques for corporate failure prediction. *Technological Forecasting and Social Change, 166*, 120658.

Kim, J. H., Jung, H. S., Park, M. H., Lee, S. H., Lee, H., Kim, Y., & Nan, D. (2022). Exploring cultural differences of public perception of artificial intelligence via big data approach. In *International conference on human-computer interaction* (pp. 427–432). Cham: Springer.

Law, R., Li, G., Fong, D. K. C., & Han, X. (2019). Tourism demand forecasting: A deep learning approach. *Annals of Tourism Research, 75*, 410–423.

LeCun, Y., Bengio, Y., & Hinton, G. (2015). Deep learning. *Nature, 521*(7553), 436–444.

Li, Y., Xu, Z., Wang, X., & Wang, X. (2020). A bibliometric analysis on deep learning during 2007–2019. *International Journal of Machine Learning and Cybernetics, 11*(12), 2807–2826.

Liaw, A., & Wiener, M. (2002). Classification and regression by randomForest. *R News, 2*(3), 18–22.

Lin, J., Ling, F., Huang, P., Chen, M., Song, M., Lu, K., & Wang, W. (2022). The development of GABAergic network in depression in recent 17 years: A visual analysis based on CiteSpace and VOSviewer. *Frontiers in Psychiatry, 13*, 874137.

Liu, H., Li, X., & Wang, S. (2021). A bibliometric analysis of 30 years of platform research: Developing the research agenda for platforms, the associated technologies and social impacts. *Technological Forecasting and Social Change, 169*, 120827.

Mir, A. A., Rathinam, S., & Gul, S. (2021). Public perception of covid-19 vaccines from the digital footprints left on Twitter: Analyzing positive, neutral and negative sentiments of Twitterati. *Library Hi Tech, 40*(2), 340–356.

Nan, D., Kim, Y., Huang, J., Jung, H. S., & Kim, J. H. (2022a). Factors affecting intention of consumers in using face recognition payment in offline markets: An acceptance model for future payment service. *Frontiers in Psychology, 13*, 830152.

Nan, D., Lee, H., Kim, Y., & Kim, J. H. (2022b). My video game console is so cool! A coolness theory-based model for intention to use video game consoles. *Technological Forecasting and Social Change, 176*, 121451.

Nan, D., Shin, E., Barnett, G. A., Cheah, S., & Kim, J. H. (2022c). Will coolness factors predict user satisfaction and loyalty? Evidence from an artificial neural network–structural equation model approach. *Information Processing & Management, 59*(6), 103108.

Pedregosa, F., Varoquaux, G., Gramfort, A., Michel, V., Thirion, B., Grisel, O., … & Duchesnay, E. (2011). Scikit-learn: Machine learning in Python. *Journal of Machine Learning Research, 12*, 2825–2830.

Sarin, S., Haon, C., Belkhouja, M., Mas-Tur, A., Roig-Tierno, N., Sego, T., … & Carley, S. (2020). Uncovering the knowledge flows and intellectual structures of research in Technological Forecasting and Social Change: A journey through history. *Technological Forecasting and Social Change, 160*, 120210.

Singh, P., Dwivedi, Y. K., Kahlon, K. S., Pathania, A., & Sawhney, R. S. (2020). Can Twitter analytics predict election outcome? An insight from 2017 Punjab assembly elections. *Government Information Quarterly, 37*(2), 101444.

Small, H. (1973). Co-citation in the scientific literature: A new measure of the relationship between two documents. *Journal of the American Society for Information Science, 24*(4), 265–269.

Su, M., Peng, H., & Li, S. (2021). A visualized bibliometric analysis of mapping research trends of machine learning in engineering (MLE). *Expert Systems with Applications, 186*, 115728.

Sun, S., Wei, Y., Tsui, K. L., & Wang, S. (2019). Forecasting tourist arrivals with machine learning and internet search index. *Tourism Management, 70*, 1–10.

Tibshirani, R. (1996). Regression shrinkage and selection via the lasso. *Journal of the Royal Statistical Society: Series B (Methodological), 58*(1), 267–288.

Van Eck, N., & Waltman, L. (2010). Software survey: VOSviewer, a computer program for bibliometric mapping. *Scientometrics, 84*(2), 523–538.

Xing, W., & Du, D. (2019). Dropout prediction in MOOCs: Using deep learning for personalized intervention. *Journal of Educational Computing Research, 57*(3), 547–570.

Xu, Z., Yu, D., & Wang, X. (2019). A bibliometric overview of International Journal of Machine Learning and Cybernetics between 2010 and 2017. *International Journal of Machine Learning and Cybernetics, 10*(9), 2375–2387.

Ye, N., Kueh, T. B., Hou, L., Liu, Y., & Yu, H. (2020). A bibliometric analysis of corporate social responsibility in sustainable development. *Journal of Cleaner Production, 272*, 122679.

Yu, D., Xu, Z., Pedrycz, W., & Wang, W. (2017). Information sciences 1968–2016: A retrospective analysis with text mining and bibliometric. *Information Sciences, 418*, 619–634.

Yu, Y., Li, Y., Zhang, Z., Gu, Z., Zhong, H., Zha, Q., … & Chen, E. (2020). A bibliometric analysis using VOSviewer of publications on COVID-19. *Annals of Translational Medicine, 8*(13).

Zemigala, M. (2019). Tendencies in research on sustainable development in management sciences. *Journal of Cleaner Production, 218*, 796–809.

Zhang, S., Che, S., Nan, D., & Kim, J. H. (2022). MOOCs as a research agenda: Changes over time. *The International Review of Research in Open and Distributed Learning, 23*(4), 193–210.

Zhao, X., Nan, D., Chen, C., Zhang, S., Che, S., & Kim, J. H. (2023). Bibliometric study on environmental, social, and governance research using CiteSpace. *Frontiers in Environmental Science, 10*, 2534.

Zheng, Q., Xiong, L., Li, H., Liu, M., Xu, J., & Luo, X. (2022). Demoralization: Where it stands—and where we can take it: A bibliometric analysis. *Frontiers in Psychology, 13*, 1016601.

Zou, H., & Hastie, T. (2005). Regularization and variable selection via the elastic net. *Journal of the Royal Statistical Society: Series B (Statistical Methodology), 67*(2), 301–320.

14. AI and data-driven political communication (re)shaping citizen–government interactions

Jérôme Duberry

INTRODUCTION

Political communication efforts to influence public opinion are far from new. In 1947, the founding father of public relations, Edward L. Bernays, set out to show how public opinion about the state's actions can be "engineered" (Bernays, 1947). Over the following decades, political communication benefited from several technological innovations, from print newspapers to radio, television, and, more recently, social media (Wu, 2017). Web 2.0 and online platforms have led to a redistribution of roles between consumers, distributors, and producers of information and contributed to the emergence of new gatekeepers, such as the machine learning algorithms (MLA) of online platforms, which Eli Pariser (2011) has aptly called filter bubbles. Today, it is challenging to dissociate digital technologies and big data from political and policymaking practices (Chadwick, 2013).

Tufekci (2014) conceptualized the use of digital technologies with the term "computational politics." He argues that big data analytics play a prominent role in twenty-first-century political activities of outreach, persuasion, and citizen mobilization. In 2004 and 2008, the US presidential campaigns of George W. Bush and then Barack Obama used big data analytics to tailor communication more precisely to citizens' needs and opinions, and thus increase the chances of influencing their votes (Ambinder, 2009). Big data, including behavioral data, demographic data, and psychological attributes from online user activity, allow political campaigners to build models of citizens and attempt to predict their behaviors, future trends, and risks (Montgomery & Chester, 2017).

At the heart of data-driven political communication is artificial intelligence (AI) practices, which are used to process these large datasets. AI is a term that may be difficult to define precisely as it covers many technologies that have evolved over the last decades. This chapter adopts the following definition from a report published by the European Union's (EU) Joint Research Centre to qualify the use of AI by governments in Europe:

> AI is a generic term that refers to any machine or algorithm that is capable of observing its environment, learning, and based on the knowledge and experience gained, taking intelligent action or proposing decisions. There are many different technologies that fall

under this broad AI definition. At the moment, ML4 techniques are the most widely used. (Samoili et al., 2020, p. 9)

Despite its growing use in citizen-government relations, AI remains opaque for most non-experts. It is, therefore, essential to shed light on these practices to better understand today's political communication landscape (Duberry, 2022). It is also vital for politicians, policymakers, and civil society to develop a better understanding of this technology (Al-Amoudi & Latsis, 2019) and the associated hopes and concerns it triggers to avoid missteps in its development and ensure "the safety and reliability of AI technologies" (Stone et al., 2016, p. 298).

This chapter discusses political communication practices powered by AI across three geographic regions (Africa, Europe and North America) with the intent to highlight the generalization of these tactics in different political, economic, and social settings. It follows the data flow, starting with data collection practices, citizen behavior modeling, and political communication tactics based on micro-targeting and geolocalization.

COLLECTING AND PROCESSING BIG DATA

Online platforms emerged at the beginning of the twenty-first century. Even though the term "online platforms" refers to a diversity of business and governance models, they share common characteristics, starting with the monitoring of online users and the merchandising of data collected and processed for advertising purposes:

> "big data" is above all the foundational component in a deeply intentional and highly consequential new logic of accumulation that I call surveillance capitalism. This new form of information capitalism aims to predict and modify human behavior as a means to produce revenue and market control. (Zuboff, 2015, p. 75)

Initially ad-free, Facebook has gradually become an online advertising giant. Its MLAs are designed for profit maximization, not to bring people together, the well-being of users, or the good of society (Alaimo & Kallinikos, 2017). Their business model provides access to user data to third-party companies and what Diakopoulis (2017) calls "new forms of value" (p. 178). In 2015, Facebook already reported more than 30 million third-party applications (Novet, 2015).

Online platforms collect users' data, as well as a myriad of third parties, including government intelligence agencies, corporations, data brokers, political parties, and many others: "[d]ifferent patterns of surveillance are manifested through Facebook. This suggests a complexity of social media surveillance" (Trottier, 2011, p. 66). Opinion mining, sentiment analysis, and digital listening describe these practices that collect large sets of unstructured data from online conversations, which AI then analyzes to identify trends, clusters of comments, and opinions about a topic or cause. These practices also contribute to "measure the impact of emotional advertising by assessing metrics like attention, emotional engagement and memory activation" (Jha & Ghoshal, 2019).

Data collected can be either provided by the individual voluntarily online or in person (e.g., at a store) or collected by third parties while the individual is performing another action (e.g., purchase of a sports item, choice of a piece of music). Different types of data are collected, including:

- User demographics, such as name, address, email address, gender, age, etc.
- User's network data: contacts and friends in their network.
- Survey or quiz responses (e.g., Cambridge Analytica's "This is Your Digital Life" quiz, which allowed the company to develop its psychographic profiling capability) (Revell, 2018).
- Behavioral data derived from the user's online activity, such as responses to specific messages or texts.
- Metadata – data about the data – such as time, message origin and destination, etc.

The Cambridge Analytica scandal shed light on illegal data collection practices and persuasion tactics akin to psychological weapons (Caldwalladr, 2018). The political communication company developed an app on Facebook called "thisisyourdigitallife," which collected personal data from the user and all their "friends" without asking for consent. This allowed the company to rapidly develop a consequent database with data points on 87 million individuals in the US, which was used during the 2016 US presidential campaign (Cadwalladr, 2020). This company also worked in non-Western contexts, including Nigeria, where 87 Facebook users responded to the Cambridge Analytica's app, with an incidence of 271,469 total Nigerians (Guardian Editorial, 2018). These automated data collection tactics are used to complement face-to-face marketing in Nigeria (Butcher, 2017). During the 2022 presidential election in France, political parties benefited from data collected by data brokers. For instance, the French company Zecible[1] provided information on age, gender, marital status, location, owner or tenant status, income, and socio-professional category. The company even indicated the person's interests: DIY, new technologies, wine, and nutrition, among others. These profiles were linked to cell phone numbers or e-mails and concerned a large part of the French population: 25 million for Zecible and 29 million for its competitor, Self Contact[2] (Untersinger & Six, 2022).

In some markets in which individuals own multiple connected devices and wearables, data collection is enhanced by the ability to track individuals across devices: data can be connected while they sleep from a Fitbit wearable, while they travel from a smartphone, or at work from their computer and websites, social media, and other apps. It is possible to track individuals throughout the day and collect data almost 24/7, as "the same campaign can follow you from your laptop, to your phone to your TV" (Acton, 2018). AI then processes the data collected about one individual to tailor ads, personalize online content, search engine results, recommendations, and more.

---

[1] https://www.zecible.fr.
[2] https://selfcontact.com.

For example, Google collects data from individuals "for over $120 billion a year in advertising revenue" (Hao, 2021). Different technology innovations enable tracking individuals across devices and websites, including pixels and cookies as presented below.

A tracking pixel is a transparent single-pixel image that exists within some websites and is placed by third-party entities (Bashyakarla et al., 2019). As an example, a Facebook pixel allows Facebook to track users. With the information gathered, political parties can optimize their Facebook advertising strategy (Newberry, 2019). In the past few years, several European political parties adopted pixels on their website to track online users, including the Bulgarian Socialist Party, the Conservatives (UK), Forum for Democracy (the Netherlands), National Front (France), the Liberal Democrats (UK), the Nationalist Party (Malta), the New Austria and Liberal Forum, New Flemish Alliance (Belgium), Save Romania Union, Sinn Fein (Ireland), and Venstre (Denmark) (Treffer, 2019).

Moreover, cookies allow companies to track our every move online. A cookie is a file downloaded on a device (e.g., laptop and smartphone) to recognize users when they connect to the same website. It is advantageous when a user visits a website regularly and could benefit from personalization of the presentation of the page content, for example, to find the last selected but not purchased items in the shopping cart of the online store. Each time a user visits a website, the browser sends the cookie ID back to the server to allow the website to tailor its content based on the user's last visit (Falahrastegar, 2014). Cookies can be placed by the website (first party), or another entity (third party). Third-party cookies are placed on the website by another company: "For example, if an advertising company notices that you read a lot of articles about running, it may show you ads about running shoes – even on an unrelated site you're visiting for the first time" (Federal Trade Commission, n.d.).

However, the use of cookies is in decline. In 2021, Alphabet announced that it would no longer allow third-party cookies to collect data through its Chrome browser. Other browsers, such as Safari and the open-source browser Firefox, had already abandoned third-party cookies. AI is at the heart of these solutions. Google announced the creation of a new AI called Federated Learning of Cohorts (FLoC). The principle of FLoC (Bindra, 2021) is to move from individual tracking, considered too intrusive, to collective tracking. It means that Google will group people with everyday browsing habits into different cohorts. Google promises, on the one hand, that the cohort will simply be identified with a short ID number, such as 43A7 (Witteman, 2021), which should enhance privacy and, on the other hand, make ads up to 95% as relevant as when tracking cookies are used (Boero, 2021). However, AI is not only used by online platforms to adapt to new data privacy regulations in specific markets such as the EU (i.e., the General Data Protection Regulation [GDPR]). Digital advertising platforms also use it to free themselves from their dependency on online platforms, particularly, the Google–Facebook duopoly. For example, the Quantcast advertising platform uses artificial intelligence (MLA) to process data from more than 100 million web destinations in real time to better target advertising campaigns based on predictive models evaluated a million times a second (Vizard, 2021).

MODELING HUMAN PSYCHOLOGY

Psychology and emotions have traditionally played a prominent role in political campaigns. Psychological profiling aims to identify an individual's likely character, behavior, and interests based on data collected about this person (Cambridge Dictionary, n.d.). Its main objective is to understand how an individual processes information. Police and intelligence services often use it in criminal investigations. However, it is also commonly used for communication and advertising purposes. In this context, AI is used to process large datasets collected from various sources about potential voters. It allows for the development of persuasive strategies aiming at maximizing profit (Carr, 2011), attempting to "control billions of minds every day" for profit (Harris, 2017). As former CEO of Cambridge Analytica Alexander Nix explained at the 2016 Concordia Annual Summit:

> if you know the personality of the people you are targeting, you can nuance your messaging to resonate more effectively with those key audience groups. For a highly neurotic and conscientious audience, you're going to need a message that's rational and fear-based, or emotionally based. (Nix, 2013)

AI-powered data analytics enable the association of a potential voter with a personality type. Each personality type corresponds to several criteria, including psychographics and demographics. These categories allow for the prediction of people's responses and behaviors to different types of informational inputs: "[d]ata-driven campaigning gives you the edge that you need to convince swing votes one way or the other, and also to get certain people to show up to the polls" (Wakefield, 2019). In their study with more than 3.5 million individuals, researchers Matz, Kosinski, Nave, and Stillwell (2017) showed "that targeting people with persuasive appeals tailored to their psychological profiles can be used to influence their behavior as measured by clicks and conversions" (p. 12,715). For instance, Kosinski, Stillwell, and Graepel (2013) showed that Facebook likes could help predict sensitive personal attributes, including sexual orientation, ethnicity, religious and political views, personality traits, intelligence, happiness, use of addictive substances, parental separation, age, and gender. Their model correctly distinguished between homosexual and heterosexual men in 88% of cases, African Americans and Caucasian Americans in 95% of cases, and between Democrats and Republicans in 85% of cases. What is more, Youyou, Kosinski, and Stillwell (2015) showed "that computers' judgments of people's personalities based on their digital footprints are more accurate and valid than judgments made by their close others or acquaintances (friends, family, spouse, colleagues, etc.)" and they consequently highlighted the fact "that people's personalities can be predicted automatically and without involving human social-cognitive skills" (p. 1,036).

Over the past 20 years, online platforms have built vast databases consisting of behavioral data, allowing them to turn their users into data subjects to influence their decisions for profit (Brett Aho & Roberta Duffield, 2020). However, psychometric profiling in the context of political campaigns has become a growing concern in recent years. Zuboff shed light on this new ability to influence citizens' behavior and the vulnerability of the population and electoral processes:

> False consciousness is no longer produced by the hidden facts of class and their relation to production, but rather by the hidden facts of commoditized behavior modification. If power was once identified with the ownership of the means of production, it is now identified with ownership of the means of behavioral modification. (Zuboff, 2015, p .82)

Moreover, the promise of prediction of AI must be taken with caution. This is because AI predictions are based on past data and behavior. MLAs learn from large datasets collected on social media platforms. This data can be biased. The algorithm itself can be biased. This can lead to the reinforcement of existing discriminations and social biases. Moreover, the model that the AI will use to predict the behavior of an individual assumes that they will keep the same opinion, behavior, and personality over time. However, individuals are sometimes irrational and can radically change their minds and behavior. Unexpected events can lead to changes in the perception of causes or issues that AI cannot predict. These limitations must be kept in mind when analyzing the increasing role of AI in political communication.

POLITICAL MICRO-TARGETING

AI is not only used to model the behavior of billions of online users. It is also used to communicate more dynamically and with increased precision. The capacity of AI to process large volumes of data from various sources can help human strategists identify relationships that would be invisible to human eyes (Action, 2018). It allows knowing in real time what the online users think about a topic, political argument, or candidate. It also allows for identifying potential voters and targeting them with personalized ads to encourage or dissuade voting. Consequently, it makes it possible to adapt the political communication strategy and the positioning of a political leader according to online opinions (Tran, 2020). During the Brexit campaign, micro-targeting tactics were used to influence potential voters:

> [t]hrough smart use of machine learning, big data, and extremely targeted and personalized digital ads, Vote Leave was able to identify key concerns facing the UK population and create campaigns that spoke directly to these concerns, targeting the right demographic of people for whom these concerns were most relevant. (Bender, 2017)

Moreover, AI supports the automation of A/B testing services and the creation of new alternatives and combinations of text, image, and support. A/B testing implies testing two or more versions of some message (in its content, format, multimedia) and assessing users' reaction. It is commonly used for websites, emails (subject lines, bodies), design elements (images, backgrounds, buttons), headlines, direct mail, TV, radio, phone, and even texting to "find the right messaging." In the context of political campaigns, it can be used to choose the correct narrative and wording for a campaign, as well as increase financial contributions (Bashyakarla et al., 2019). For instance, the "Vote Leave" Brexit party used A/B testing to improve the message targeted to a population segment:

> Cummings explained how the overarching theme of the Leave campaign was "Let's take back control." Based on research on public opinion of the EU, the campaign identified that "keep control" was an important theme. They then tested variations of this message – discovering that by including the word "back" in the messaging, they evoked rage in people. "Back" triggers loss aversion, playing into the strongly evolved instinct that we hate losing things, especially control. (Schneider, 2017)

In Nigeria, digital marketing agency Gavaar[3] offers A/B testing tactics during online political campaigns to test content variants on websites and online platforms (Hassan & Segun, 2020). Additionally, AI for A/B testing will increasingly generate unique content for individual users, which could "lead to a stream of unique, personalized messages targeted at each voter constantly updated based on A/B testing" (Acton, 2018).

In many countries, the widespread use of smartphones and social media platforms has led to a paradigm shift in advertising targeting. It is possible to track connected individuals for more extended periods and increase the amount of exposure and attention available to advertising messages. Mobiles, smartphones, and other global-positioning-system (GPS)-equipped devices make it possible to track individuals as they drive a car, shop in a store, or relax at home (Son et al., 2016). In addition, the way information is consumed has changed. While online browsing used to be primarily on a computer over more extended periods, separate from other daily activities, this is no longer the case. Social media platforms and their newsfeed offer new information constantly. The smartphone allows for fragmented information consultations of a few minutes:

> Micro-moments occur when people reflexively turn to a device – increasingly a smartphone – to fulfill a need to learn something, do something, discover something, watch something or buy something. These are intention-rich moments where decisions are made, and preferences are shaped. (Ramaswamy, 2015a)

It is during these fragmented moments throughout the day, when citizens seek information and entertainment while waiting for the bus or catching the next subway, that their opinions are gradually formed: "There are no longer just a few sporadic 'a-ha!' moments of truth; there are now countless moments that matter" (Ramaswamy, 2015b).

In countries in which the population largely uses mobile devices, geotargeting offers a wide range of techniques to deliver specific content to a person based on their

---

[3] http://www.gavaar.com.

geographic location, through GPS or Bluetooth signals, or their internet protocol (IP) address. Geotargeting allows knowing in detail what a person is doing, where, and when. It uncovers trends and habits of individuals and groups combining this information with other data already collected about the person, including "self-reported forms, publicly available voter rolls, private companies and data brokers, location-enabled services, APIs connected to location-based apps, data licensed from third-party providers and more" (Bashyakarla et al., 2019, p. 14).

Geolocation data is, indeed, helpful for both targeting and content. First, data such as the geolocation of a mobile phone increases targeting accuracy: users receive messages at a specific place and time. Moreover, when combined with other data (e.g., which organic supermarket they visit regularly or which supplemental health plan they purchase), it is possible to make assumptions with more precision about the citizen's values and beliefs and, therefore, target them with tailored messages. This wealth of information about people's activities in real-time allows micro-targeting to be tailored to the time and place that will have the most impact. Geotargeting also provides the campaign teams on the ground with enriched maps that show additional data about potential voters and consequently focus the canvassing efforts where it is most likely to win votes (Bashyakarla et al., 2019).

The French political startup Liegey Muller Pons (LMP) collaborated with various political parties in Europe, including La République en Marche (LREM) in France, several socialist parties (PS in France, PSOE in Spain, PS in Belgium), and the Green Party in Bavaria, Germany. It also contributed to the political campaigns of Corrado Passera in Italy and Anne Hidalgo France (Richaud, 2016), among others. It offered data science services to political parties and candidates. More precisely, LMP identifies where the physical door-to-door campaigning of political party activists should focus to convince undecided voters. LMP also offers tools to optimize targeted short message service (SMS) and mail campaigns (Richaud, 2017). In Nigeria also, geolocalization allows targeting political messages and advertising. For instance, Cambridge Analytica was contracted for the re-election bid of Goodluck Jonathan with videos targeting "Buhari voters in Buhari regions" to deter them from going to vote (Cadwalladr, 2018).

AUTOMATED MESSAGES AND ADVERTS

As mentioned previously, the advertising industry has adapted to several ways of technological innovations. AI is no exception. Programmatic advertising is a new form of automated advertising. This system is based on a real-time auction that allows for the sale and purchase of display space online 24/7 without human intervention (Allen, 2016). Online platforms and digital marketing companies provide programmatic advertising services, including Criteo,[4] Facebook Ads Manager,[5] AppNexus,

---

[4]   https://www.criteo.com.
[5]   https://business.facebook.com.

which belongs to Xandr,[6] the advertising and analytics division of the US telecom company AT&T, and: "Programmatic revenues in Europe grew by a healthy 33% in 2018 to reach €16.7bn, despite concerns from advertisers about the effectiveness of the current digital supply chain and worries that GDPR would impact digital spend" (Glenday, 2019).

During the last European parliamentary elections, European political parties used online ads, including Facebook, Instagram, Google, and YouTube. From March 20, 2019, ads that feature a political party, a current elected officeholder, a candidate for the EU Parliament, an elected national office within an EU member state, or the UK Parliament are valued at €10,836,550 (Google, 2020) for a total of 138,367 political ads. However, the number differs drastically from one country to another. For example, Germany spent €944,650, while Spain spent €1,065,750, and Austria spent €1,032,700 for the same period but about half the population. At the low end of the spectrum, France spent a total of €18,350. To compare, the political ads on Google in the US reached $331,711,700 and a total of 390,107 ads from May 30, 2018 until August 11, 2020 (Google, 2020). In other words, although one more year has been included in the reporting for the US ads, the total spend is nevertheless 30 times greater (if we consider a US Dollar–Euro parity). According to a report published by Statistica, the Social Democratic Party (SPD) of Germany spent almost €1.2 million on online political advertising in the three months leading up to the elections, followed by the Ciudadanos spending €885,000, Podemos at €623,000 and Partido Popular (PP) at €586,000 (Statistica, 2019).

Furthermore, robocalls, bulk SMSs, and voice SMSs have also been used in some countries where they are allowed, such as the US and Nigeria. AI is used in this case of robocalls to hide the fact that one is talking with a machine. Based on large datasets and supervised learning, MLAs have become quite effective at providing answers to various questions in a matter of seconds. They can sound human, pausing between sentences to pretend that one is talking to a human operator. In Nigeria, advertising agencies Alternative Adverts[7] and Adhang[8] offer robocall services to political candidates. Former President Goodluck Jonathan is credited with using robocalls and SMS as a critical tactic in a presidential campaign (Hassan & Segun, 2020).

Moreover, bots are omnipresent on social media platforms. They can be defined as "accounts controlled by algorithms that emulate the activity of human users but operate at a much higher rate (…) while managing not to disclose their artificial identity" (Bessi & Ferrara, 2016). Often, these are MLAs. They are developed to interact with users of social media platforms, spread content with a specific hashtag, or generate new content online according to predefined indications (Ferrara et al., 2016). Any political party or government with sufficient resources can use an army of social bots to support a narrative on social media platforms. Twitter bomb-type strategies are well known, but attribution remains a challenge (Kollanyi et al., 2016). They

---

[6] https://www.xandr.com.
[7] https://alternativeadverts.com.
[8] https://www.adhang.com.

can generate thousands of tweets to drive web traffic to fake news sites (Ratkiewicz et al., 2011).

Although it remains a challenge to quantify the presence of social bots on social media, Bessi and Ferrarra (2016) identified about 400,000 bots engaged in political discussions and generated about 3.8 million tweets, representing about one-fifth of the entire conversation about the 2016 US presidential election. Social bots are relatively simple to operate and roll out. Some technical blogs offer practical guidance for entry-level social bots, while some other websites offer further detailed technical information on more advanced social bots. Regarding their capacity, social bots are most frequently employed to accomplish the following tasks automatically:

- Search for sentences/hashtags/keywords on social media platforms and share them.
- Respond to messages (e.g., Tweets) that meet a specific criterion.
- Follow users that publish content with a specific sentence/hashtag/keyword.
- Follow back users that have followed the social bot.
- Follow any users that follow a specified user.
- Add users publishing content to a specific public list.
- Search for content according to specific criteria on web search engines and publish it or link it to some users.
- Aggregate public sentiment on specific topics of online conversation (Bessi and Ferrara, 2016).

A large array of actors use bots to abuse human biases and vulnerabilities to provide a false image of reality, to alter the perception of netizens. They can intensify specific political trends and views, promote particular interests, acquire influence on social media, and diffuse false news (Aiello et al., 2014). By projecting a false representation of reality, for example, increasing or decreasing the support for some political movements can be beneficial to silence dissidents (Pamment et al., 2018). However, the use of bots for disinformation also has more secondary consequences. By sowing chaos and polarization, bots make it challenging to distinguish between truth and falsehood, which leads people to distrust all information. However, social media platforms have also developed advanced bots to identify better and neutralize disinformation bots and automated fake accounts, meaning that disinformation operators now either continue their activities on less innovative platforms, hide their actions better, or generate more genuine-seeming interactions to avoid detection (Bradshaw & Howard, 2018).

CONCLUSION

As discussed in this chapter, AI is increasingly mediating citizen–government relations (Duberry, 2022) and is proving particularly valuable in automating and enhancing the precision, scope, and scale of political communications to citizens. In this context, what is the future research agenda for AI and political communication? Several areas of research could contribute to a better understanding of the social and political implications of this technology.

First, as the EU increasingly regulates digital advertising and online platforms (e.g., the Digital Services Act), these new regulations may have an impact not only on EU citizens, institutions, and companies but also on non-EU markets. In other words, new research should explore the legal, social and political spillover effects of the EU regulatory framework on other countries using similar technologies. This is particularly important as online platforms operate on a quasi-global scale, but their social and political impacts are highly contextual.

Second, most academic research focuses on large markets (e.g., EU, North America). This is also where online platforms invest most of their efforts to moderate content and combat disinformation. Therefore, there is an urgent need to study how AI is used by political actors in less populated countries and in minor languages as well as on non-mainstream online platforms (e.g., Telegram). It would also make it possible to collect data on people and countries in which data is still limited and would help counter the well-known phenomenon of data invisibility.

Third, the constant technological developments in the fields of neuromarketing and online advertising require an acute transdisciplinary collaboration between experts from tech companies, social and computer science universities, think tanks, and research labs to test these innovations in contextualized sandboxes. Applied research projects that bring together this transdisciplinary expertise could pave the way for broader collaboration, which is still nascent at best, but clearly needed. It could also be beneficial to involve the most affected stakeholders in the design of technologies and their applications. This may be perceived by technology companies as lengthening the timeframe for bringing new products and services to market. However, by proactively mitigating their most negative impacts, they not only gain time, but also improve their credibility and reputation.

Fourth, democracy is under attack by the systematic efforts of some authoritarian regimes, such as China and Russia, to spread disinformation, polarize populations, sow chaos, and instill distrust in the information ecosystem and the democratic model. As we have seen recently in the US and Brazil, when there is no trust in the electoral system, the whole democracy is at risk. In this context, additional research on digital literacy and disinformation is needed, especially to better understand how to make individuals, especially youth, more resilient to these disinformation campaigns. New research should also be conducted to map all the initiatives that are trying to combat disinformation, especially by tech activists and civil society. This would also allow researchers, and then policymakers, to better support innovative practices and scale up best practices.

REFERENCES

Acton., R. (2018). *The hyper-personalised future of political campaigning*. CAPX. Retrieved January 10, 2023, from https://capx.co/the-hyper-personalised-future-of-political-campaigning/

Aho, B., & Duffield, R. (2020). Beyond surveillance capitalism: Privacy, regulation and big data in Europe and China, *Economy and Society*, *49*(2), 187–212.

Aiello, L. M., Deplano, M., Schifanella, R., & Ruffo, G. (2014). *People are Strange when you're a Stranger: Impact and Influence of Bots on Social Networks*. arXiv preprint arXiv:1407.8134.

Alaimo, C. & Kallinikos, J. (2017). Computing the everyday: Social media as data platforms. *The Information Society*, 33 (4), 175–191.

Al-Amoudi, I., & Latsis, J. (2019). Anormative black boxes: Artificial intelligence and health policy. In *Post-Human Institutions and Organizations* (pp. 119–142). Routledge.

Ambinder, M. (2009). Exclusive: How Democrats Won The Data War in 2008. *The Atlantic*. Retrieved January 10, 2023, from https://www.theatlantic.com/politics/archive/2009/10/exclu-sive-how-democrats-won-the-data-war-in-2008/27647/

Bashyakarla, V., Hankey, S., Macintyre, A., Rennó R., & Wright, G. (2019). *Personal Data: Political Persuasion. Inside the Influence Industry. How it works*. Berlin. Tactical Tech. Retrieved January 10, 2023, from https://cdn.ttc.io/s/ourdataourselves.tacticaltech.org/Personal-Data-Political-Persuasion-How-it-works_print-friendly.pdf

Bender, B. (2017). *How Vote Leave Used Data Science and A/B Testing to Achieve Brexit*. AB Tasty. Retrieved January 10, 2023, from https://www.abtasty.com/blog/data-science-ab-testing-vote-brexit/

Bernays, E. L. (1947). The engineering of consent. *The Annals of the American Academy of Political and Social Science*, *250*(1), 113–120.

Bessi, A., & Ferrara, E. (2016). *Social Bots Distort the 2016 U.S. Presidential Election Online*. First Monday. Retrieved January 10, 2023, from https://firstmonday.org/ojs/index.php/fm/article/view/7090/5653

Bindra, C. (2021). *Building a privacy-first future for web advertising*. Google Blog. Retrieved January 10, 2023, from https://blog.google/products/ads-commerce/2021-01-privacy-sandbox/

Boero, A. (2021). *FLoC de Google, le traçage sans cookies: cohortes et protection des utilisateurs, nos explications*. Clubic. Retrieved January 10, 2023 from https://www.clubic.com/pro/entreprises/google/dossier-371381-floc-de-google-le-tracage-sans-cookies-cohortes-et-protection-des-utilisateurs-nos-explications.html

Bradshaw, S., & Howard, P. N. (2018). *Challenging Truth and Trust: A Global Inventory of Organized Social Media Manipulation*. Online Supplement to Working Paper 2018, Oxford University. Retrieved January 10, 2023 from https://demtech.oii.ox.ac.uk/wp-content/uploads/sites/93/2018/07/ct2018.pdf

Butcher, M. (2017). *Cambridge Analytica CEO talks to TechCrunch about Trump, Hillary and the future*. TechCrunch. Retrieved January 10, 2023, from https://techcrunch.com/2017/11/06/cambridge-analytica-ceo-talks-to-techcrunch-about-trump-hilary-and-the- future/

Cadwalladr, C. (2018). *Revealed: 50 million Facebook profiles harvested for Cambridge Analytica in major data breach. The Cambridge Analytica Files*. The Guardian. Retrieved January 10, 2023, from https://www.theguardian.com/news/2018/mar/17/cambridge-analytica-facebook-influence-us-election

Cadwalladr, C. (2018). *Cambridge Analytica's ruthless bid to sway the vote in Nigeria*. The Guardian. Retrieved January 10, 2023, from https://www.theguardian.com/uk-news/2018/mar/21/cambridge-analyticas-ruthless-bid-to-sway-the-vote-in-nigeria

Cadwalladr, C. (2020). *If you're not terrified about Facebook, you haven't been paying attention*. The Guardian. Retrieved January 10, 2023, from https://www.theguardian.com/commentisfree/2020/jul/26/with-facebook-we-are-already-through-the-looking-glass

Cambridge (n.d.). *Psychological profiling. Definition*. Cambridge Dictionary. Retrieved January 10, 2023, from https://dictionary.cambridge.org/fr/dictionnaire/anglais/psychological-profiling

Carr, N. G. (2011). *The shallows: What the internet is doing to our brains*. W. W. Norton & Company.

Chadwick, A. (2013). Bringing E-democracy back in why it matters for future research on E-governance. *Social Science Computer Review, 21*(4), 443–455.

Chester, J., & Montgomery, K. C. (2017). The role of digital marketing in political campaigns. *Internet Policy Review, 6*(4), 1–20.

Diakopoulos, N. (2017). Computational journalism and the emergence of news platforms. In B. Franklin, & S. Eldridge II, (Eds.), *The Routledge companion to digital journalism studies* (pp. 176–184). Routledge.

Duberry, J. (2022). *Artificial intelligence and democracy: risks and promises of AI-mediated citizen–government relations.* Edward Elgar Publishing.

Falahrastegar, M. (2014). *The murky world of third party web tracking.* MIT Technology Review. Retrieved January 10, 2023, from https://www.technologyreview.com/2014/09/12/171400/the-murky-world-of-third-party-web-tracking/

Federal Trade Commission. (n.d.) *Online Tracking.* Retrieved January 10, 2023, from https://www.consumer.ftc.gov/articles/0042-online-tracking

Ferrara, E., Varol, O., Davis, C., Menczer, F., & Flammini, A. (2016). The rise of social bots. *Communications of the ACM, 59*(7), 96–104.

Glenday. J. (2019). *Programmatic revenues hit €16.7bn in Europe last year – up 33%.* The Drum. Retrieved January 10, 2023, from https://www.thedrum.com/news/2019/09/11/programmatic-revenues-hit-167bn-europe-last-year-up-33

Google. (2020). *Political advertising in the European Union and the United Kingdom.* Google Transparency Report. Retrieved January 10, 2023, from https://transparencyreport.google.com/political-ads/region/EU

Guardian Editorial (2018). *On Cambridge Analytica.* The Guardian. Retrieved January 10, 2023, from https://guardian.ng/opinion/on-cambridge-analytica/

Hao, K. (2021). *How to poison the data that Big Tech uses to surveil you.* MIT Technology Review. Retrieved January 10, 2023, from https://www.technologyreview.com/2021/03/05/1020376/resist-big-tech-surveillance-data/

Harris, T. (2017). *How a handful of tech companies control billions of minds every day.* TED. Retrieved January 10, 2023, from https://www.ted.com/talks/tristan_harris_the_manipulative_tricks_tech_companies_ use_to_capture_your_attention

Hassan, I. and Segun, T. (2020). *Personal data and the influence industry in Nigerian elections: Data-driven campaigning by formal and informal actors.* Tactical Tech and the Centre for Democracy and Development. Retrieved January 10, 2023, from https://tacticaltech.org/news/nigeria-country-study/

Jha, D. & Ghoshal, M. (2019). *When Emotions give a lift to advertising.* Nielsen Featured Insights. Retrieved January 10, 2023, from https://www.nielsen.com/wp-content/uploads/sites/3/2019/04/nielsen-featured-insights-when-emotions-give-a-lift-to-advertising.pdf

Kollanyi, B., Howard, P. N., & Woolley, S. C. (2016). *Bots and automation over Twitter during the first US presidential debate.* Comprop data memo, 1, 1–4. Retrieved January 10, 2023, from http://politicalbots.org/wp-content/uploads/2016/10/Data-Memo-First-Presidential-Debate.pdf

Matz, S. C., Kosinski, M., Nave, G., & Stillwell, D. J. (2017). Psychological targeting as an effective approach to digital mass persuasion. *Proceedings of the National Academy of Sciences, 114*(48), 12714–12719. Retrieved January 10, 2023, from http://www.michalkosinski.com/home/publications

Newberry, C. (2019). *The Facebook Pixel: What It Is and How to Use It.* Blog Hootsuite. Retrieved January 10, 2023, from https://blog.hootsuite.com/facebook-pixel/

Nix, A. (2013). *Cambridge Analytica – The power of big data and psychographics.* In Concordia Conference. YouTube. Retrieved January 10, 2023, from https://www.youtube.com/watch?v=n8Dd5aVXLCc

Novet, J. (2015). *Facebook has paid Out $8B to developers.* VentureBeat. Retrieved January 10, 2023, from https://venturebeat.com/2015/03/25/facebook-has-paid-out-8b-to-developers/

Pamment, J., Nothhaft, H., & Fjällhed, A. (2018). *Countering information influence activities: A handbook for communicators*. Swedish Civil Contingencies Agency (MSB), 22. Retrieved January 10, 2023, from https://mycourses.aalto.fi/pluginfile.php/1203540/mod_resource/content/1/countering%20information%20influence%20activities%20handbook.pdf.

Pariser, E. (2011). *The filter bubble: What the internet is hiding from you*. Penguin.

Ramaswamy, S. (2015a). *How micro-moments are changing the rules*. Think with Google. Retrieved January 10, 2023, from https://www.thinkwithgoogle.com/marketing-resources/micro-moments/how-micromoments-are-changing-rules/

Ramaswamy, S. (2015b). *Outside voices: Why mobile advertising may be all about micro-targeting moments*. Wall Street Journal blog. Retrieved January 10, 2023, from https://blogs.wsj.com/cmo/2015/04/08/outside-voices-why-mobile-advertising-may-be-all-about-micro-targeting-moments/

Ratkiewicz, J., Conover, M., Meiss, M., Gonçalves, B., Flammini, A., & Menczer, F. (2011, July). Detecting and tracking political abuse in social media. In *Proceedings of the international AAAI conference on web and social media* (Vol. 5, No. 1). Retrieved January 10, 2023, from https://www.aaai.org/ocs/index.php/ICWSM/ICWSM11/paper/view/2850

Revell, T. (2018). *How Facebook let a friend pass my data to Cambridge Analytica*. New Scientist. Retrieved January 10, 2023, from https://www.newscientist.com/article/2166435-how-facebook-let-a-friend-pass-my-data-to-cambridge-analytica/

Richaud, N. (2016). *Cette start-up sur laquelle Emmanuel Macron s'appuie pour sa grande marche*. Les Echos. Retrieved January 10, 2023, from https://business.lesechos.fr/entrepreneurs/idees-de-business/021895448979-cette-start-up-sur-laquelle-emmanuel-macron-s-appuie-pour-sa-grande-marche-210792.php

Richaud, N. (2017). *LMP lève 4 millions pour exporter son logiciel de campagne politique*. Les Echos. Retrieved January 10, 2023, from https://business.lesechos.fr/entrepreneurs/financer-sa-creation/030965672308-lmp-veut-exporter-son-logiciel-de-campagne-politique-316583.php.

Samoili, S., López Cobo, M., Gómez, E., De Prato, G., Martínez-Plumed, F., & Delipetrev, B., (2020). *AI watch. Defining artificial intelligence. Towards an operational definition and taxonomy of artificial intelligence*, EUR 30117 EN, Publications Office of the European Union.

Schneider, B. (2017). *How Vote Leave Used Data Science and A/B Testing to Achieve Brexit*. ABTasty. Retrieved January 10, 2023, from https://www.abtasty.com/blog/data-science-ab-testing-vote-brexit/

Son, S., Kim, D., & Shmatikov, V. (2016). *What mobile ads know about mobile users*. NDSS '16. Retrieved January 10, 2023, from http://www.cs.cornell.edu/~shmat/shmat_ndss16.pdf

Statistica. (2019). *Political Groups in the European Union (EU): online advertising spend 2019*. Statistica. Retrieved January 10, 2023, from https://www.statista.com/statistics/1034662/eu-political-groups-online-advertising-by-number-of-ads/

Stone, P., Brooks, R., Brynjolfsson, E., Calo, R., Etzioni, O., Hager, G., Hirschberg, J., Kalyanakrishnan, S., Kamar, E., Kraus, S., Leyton-Brown, K., Parkes, D., Press, W., Saxenian, A., Shah, J., Tambe, M., and Teller, A., (2016). *Artificial Intelligence and Life in 2030. One Hundred Year Study on Artificial Intelligence: Report of the 2015–2016 Study Panel*. Stanford University, Stanford, CA, USA. Retrieved January 10, 2023, from http://ai100.stanford.edu/2016-report

Tran,T. (2020). *What is Social Listening, Why it Matters, and 10 Tools to Make it Easier*. Blog Hootsuite. Retrieved January 10, 2023, from https://blog.hootsuite.com/social-listening-business/#whatis

Treffer, P. (2019). *Tory and National Front Websites Hid Facebook Tracking Pixel*. Eurobserver. Retrieved January 10, 2023, from https://euobserver.com/justice/141589

Trottier, D. (2011). A research agenda for social media surveillance. *Fast Capitalism*, 8(1). Retrieved January 10, 2023, from https://fastcapitalism.uta.edu/8_1/trottier8_1.html

Tufekci, Z. (2014). *Engineering the public: Big data, surveillance and computational politics.* First Monday. Retrieved January 10, 2023, from https://firstmonday.org/article/view/4901 /4097

Untersinger, M. & Six, N. (2022). Election présidentielle 2022: Que peuvent faire les partis avec vos données personnelles ? *Le Monde.* Retrieved January 10, 2023, from https://www .lemonde.fr/pixels/article/2022/03/28/election-presidentielle-2022-que-peuvent-faire-les -partis-avec-vos-donnees-personnelles_6119540_4408996.html

Youyou, W., Kosinski, M., & Stillwell, D. (2015). Computer-based personality judgments are more accurate than those made by humans. *Proceedings of the National Academy of Sciences, 112*(4), 1036–1040.

Vizard, M. (2021). *AI could help advertisers recover from loss of third-party cookies.* VentureBeat. Retrieved January 10, 2023, from https://venturebeat.com/2021/03/28/ai -could-help-advertisers-recover-from-loss-of-third-party-cookies/

Wakefield, J. (2019). *Brittany Kaiser calls for Facebook political ad ban at Web Summit.* BBC World. Retrieved January 10, 2023, from https://www.bbc.com/news/technology-50234144

Witteman, E. (2021). *Google wants to replace trucking cookies with AI.* Techzine. Retrieved January 10, 2023, from https://www.techzine.eu/news/analytics/55014/google-wants-to -replace-tracking-cookies-with-ai/

Wu, T. (2016). *The attention merchants: The epic scramble to get inside our heads.* Alfred A. Knopf.

Zuboff, S. (2015). Big other: Surveillance capitalism and the prospects of an information civilization. *Journal of information technology, 30*(1), 75–89.

Zuboff, S. (2019). *The age of surveillance capitalism: The fight for a human future at the new frontier of power.* PublicAffairs.

15. AI folk tales: how nontechnical publics make sense of artificial intelligence

Barbara Pohl and Lauri Goldkind

INTRODUCTION

Artificial intelligence (AI) refers to a field of scientific and philosophical inquiry and an array of digital "thinking" technologies. Experts do not agree upon one definition of AI. Still, many remain faithful to the classic depiction laid out by John McCarthy, Marvin Minsky, Nathaniel Rochester, and Claude Shannon in their *Proposal for the Dartmouth Summer Research Project on Artificial Intelligence*: "the artificial intelligence problem is taken to be that of making a machine behave in ways that would be called intelligent if a human were so behaving" (McCarthy et al., 2006 (1955); Floridi & Cowls, 2021). Even though experts disagree about what intelligence entails, they remain committed to "formalizing" and designing machines that "reproduce" human intelligence (Dick, 2019; Schank, 1987; Nilsson, 2009; Brooks, 1991; Norvig & Russell, 1995).[1] As Kate Crawford describes, a small number of corporations now "deploy AI systems at a planetary scale, and their systems are once again hailed as comparable or even superior to human intelligence" (Crawford, 2021, 6). Public understandings of AI are closely linked to different theories of human intelligence.

When nontechnical publics express their theoretical grasp of AI, they exhibit various kinds of literacy, including digital, computational, scientific, and data. Multiple approaches to literacy emphasize skills that individuals can employ to effectively manipulate and interpret data (Bawden, 2008; DiSessa, 2001; Laugksch, 2000; D'Ignazio, 2017). Related work in the "social and cultural study of data infrastructures" and "critical data studies" can help to make lay publics more familiar with the pervasive use of AI in everyday life (Gray et al., 2018; Bowker et al., 2009; Edwards et al., 2009; Star 1999; Star & Ruhleder, 1996; Dalton et al., 2016; Iliadis & Russo, 2016). Given how AI is dramatically changing various sectors of society, including

---

[1] Roger Schank, an AI theorist, suggests that intelligence refers to the general ability to communicate, to possess global knowledge, to exhibit creativity, and to express intentionality (1987). Nils John Nilsson, a computer scientist, believes intelligence to be "that quality that enables an entity to function appropriately and with foresight into its environment" (Nilsson, 2009). Rodney Brooks, a roboticist, claims that intelligence refers to perception and goal-setting behaviors (Brooks, 1991). Peter Norvig and Stuart J. Russell, authors of a leading textbook on AI, suggest that intelligence refers to "thinking or acting humanly" (Norvig & Russell, 1995).

business, health care, education, transportation, and national security, a general concern with data literacy is more prescient (Stone et al., 2016).

Narrow conceptions of data literacy do not consider how individuals' daily interactions with AI lead to the development of theories about how it works. Recent studies have shown that people devise folk theories – best described as "informal" explanations "that users develop to perceive and explain how a system works" – about AI. Although "non-authoritative, informal, and sometimes incorrect," these popular theories govern how nontechnical users engage with AI in their everyday lives (Eslami et al., 2019). Given that AI's intellectual climate is opaque, nontechnical users have ample room to devise theories about how it works. Not only is it difficult for everyday users to sense their direct engagement with algorithms or other instances of machine learning (Arm, 2020; Eslami et al., 2015; Eslami et al., 2019) but popular media outlets also often lead everyday technology users to conflate the discourse on AI with that of robotics (Fast & Horvitz, 2017; Zimmerman, 2018). As a result, individuals without technical knowledge often have difficulty conceptualizing and describing what constitutes AI (Long & Margerko, 2020). However, their uncertainty does not lead them to shy away from engaging in their theoretical meditations about AI.

Many of these folk theories have surfaced in various social surveys. One global survey on the public perceptions of AI found that its respondents referenced machines that could think autonomously or computers that could learn from experience (Kelley et al., 2021). Other surveys, conducted primarily in a Western-European context, indicate that individuals describe AI as an autonomous technology they could engage with as though it were a sentient being (Arm, 2020; Blumberg Capital, 2019). In another survey focusing on the pervasive narratives of AI, more than half of the respondents believed AI had to do with computer systems "engaging in cognitive feats (such as thinking or learning)" (Cave et al., 2019). Different opinion polls not only reveal a widespread concern with the spread of AI, particularly among members of the lower classes or among women, but also beliefs that AI can exceed human levels of intelligence (Ipsos, 2019; Mozilla, 2019). A Gallup poll, conducted in connection with Northeastern University, demonstrated that of the 73% of Americans who feel that the introduction of AI will result in a loss of jobs, about 49% believe that cultivating "soft" skills – including critical thinking, creativity, teamwork, and clear communication – would help workers to maintain skills that AI systems cannot adapt (Gallup, 2018). Another poll concluded that its average respondent believes there is a 54% chance that scientists will develop "high-level machine intelligence" by 2028 (Zhang & Dafoe, 2019).

Nontechnical publics likely acquired their theoretical commitments from the popular media. Over the past 30 years, news media outlets such as *The New York Times* have provided relatively positive coverage of AI (Fast & Horvitz, 2017). These optimistic stories have not precluded debates over the benefits or detriments of automated labor, invasion of privacy, enhanced surveillance measures, big data collection, and the development of weapons. Right-leaning news outlets focus on the socioeconomic consequences of AI, while left-leaning news outlets focus on the ethical implications of AI (Brennen et al., 2018). Other forms of media – including movies, television shows, and science fiction novels – have dramatically altered public perceptions of science and technology, including AI (Nisbet et al., 2002). Given that the nontechnical publics' understanding of the science and technology behind AI systems is relatively limited, their "perceptions and expectations" typically derive from "their personal experiences of existing applications and by the prevalent narratives about the future" (Cave et al., 2019). Embedded in utopian or dystopian narratives that they might express are various theoretical concerns with AI.

This study examines the folk theories that nontechnical publics generate about AI. In so doing, we address a dimension that many proponents of AI literacy programs have overlooked. We rely upon a rich set of qualitative, open-ended responses from a relatively well-educated, privileged group of subjects who had little technical understanding of computer science or AI. This analysis reveals that survey respondents, despite (or perhaps because of) their relative ignorance of AI systems, felt comfortable developing folk theories about AI. In their answer to the basic prompt – describe your understanding of artificial intelligence (AI) – they expressed a range of beliefs about human and artificial intelligence. Their responses echo themes that have concerned (implicitly or explicitly) philosophers of AI since the mid-twentieth century: the authenticity of AI, the agency of AI, and the beneficence of AI.

LITERATURE REVIEW

Critical data literacy programs seek to make publics without technical backgrounds aware of the sociopolitical infrastructures that produce and disseminate data. Related programs in AI literacy, primarily focused on enabling individuals to become keen users of data and related technologies, currently overlook the theoretical views that nontechnical individuals develop about AI. Nontechnical users of AI may exhibit relative ignorance about computers or data infrastructures but still express general beliefs about AI. Many of their conceptual proposals delve into issues that have interested philosophers of AI for several decades. Most of these conversations began in the mid-twentieth century, several years before a cadre of computer scientists – John McCarthy, Marvin L. Minsky, Nathaniel Rochester, and Claude Shannon – conducted their *Dartmouth Summer Research Project on Artificial Intelligence* in 1956. Since this conference, philosophers have developed sophisticated programs that conceptualize "weak" and "strong" forms of AI, investigate the responsibilities of nonhuman agents, and explore the ethics of introducing AI into modern society.

DATA LITERACY

Literacy in the digital age refers to skills that exceed the ability to read and write; it includes an ability to effectively engage with visual media, computers, digital information, or algorithms. Most data literacy programs seek to improve the statistical, mathematical, or computational competencies of children and adults who live in a society dominated by data. Recent experiments in AI literacy follow in this line-age, developing educational programs that seek to enhance their students' knowledge of computer science or other AI concepts. Examples of these concepts include "machine learning, classifiers, decision trees, reasoning and prediction, patterns in data, and statistical inferences" (Kong et al., 2021). Other literacy programs seek to encourage "digital empowerment" or "programming empowerment" (Makinen, 2006; Kong et al., 2018; Kong & Lai, 2021).

Rather than narrowly focus on digital or computer competency, AI literacy programs might focus on making their students aware of data infrastructures. An "ideology of Cartesian dualism," as Kate Crawford suggests, has framed AI as "dis-embodied intelligence, removed from any relation to the material world" (2018, p. 7). Different "data skills" programs adopt this perspective, leading them to "reinforce and perpetuate, rather than challenge and change, prevailing power structures and dynamics" (Letouzé, 2016; Letouzé et al., 2015). However, a more critical set of data literacy programs, which follow the insights of scholars in science and technology studies (STS), attend to the sociopolitical networks that sustain AI systems. These frameworks contemplate "how data is made, how it might be made and used differently, and who and what assembles and attends to" (Gray et al., 2018). When embedded within literacy programs, critical data programs seek to educate nontechnical publics about the "data worlds" that they might create or the "infrastructural imaginations" that they might express (Gray et al., 2018; Bowker, 2014).

Critical approaches to data literacy respond to the pervasive misunderstandings among nontechnical publics. Therefore, many nontechnical beliefs about AI systems and big data do not map onto their sociocultural realities (Elish & Boyd, 2017). Critical scholars point general data users to the variegated means by which algorithms serve as agents of discrimination and oppression (Noble, 2018; O'Neill, 2016; Browne, 2015). Researchers have even begun to devise experiments encouraging nontechnical publics to directly engage in these data conversations (Marres, 2017; Bounegru et al., 2018). Such collaborative efforts, as Ruha Benjamin has intimated, work against the wide-spread commitment to "techno-determinism," or the "mistaken view that society is affected *by* but does not affect technological development" (2019, 28). In reality, social ideologies – such as racism or white supremacy – are integral to the design and functioning of various technologies. Any critical literacy program in AI would combat the (often willful) ignorance of the imbrication of social problems and technical solutions.

When attuned to data infrastructures' social and cultural dimensions, nontechnical publics may alter their folk theories of AI. Folk theories refer to how people think and reason about the "cyber-systems" with which they interact (French & Hancock, 2017). Rather than narrowly attend (as did many philosophers of AI in the 1980s and 1990s) to the thinking capabilities of computers, these folk theories consider how AI systems work in practice.[2] The decisions of Uber drivers or Facebook users

---

[2] One of the most robust modes of inquiry framed the computer as a "manipulator of symbols," in which it would "shuffle symbols in accordance with the instructions contained

enact these ideas. Facebook users, for example, express views about how their news feed works based on their qualitative observations about the posts displayed (Eslami et al., 2015; Eslami et al., 2019; Lee et al., 2015). After participating in data and AI literacy programs focused on sociotechnical infrastructures and broader information ecosystems, nontechnical publics may alter the theories they develop about AI systems. This shift in perspective is especially significant, as nontechnical publics without this critical frame have developed folk theories that touch upon themes that professional philosophers have already engaged with for the past several decades.

FOLK THEORIES

Folk theories originate in the philosophy of mind. It refers, as Gelman and Legare explain, to the "intuitive theories" that humans create to "organize experience, generate inferences, guide learning, and influence behavior and social interactions" (2011, 380; Carruthers & Smith, 1996; Medin & Altran, 1999). Folk theories, as they apply to various sciences –including biology, psychology, sociology, and nanotechnology – can be purely speculative or based upon personal experiences or secondary sources (Rip, 2006). Folk theories offer generalized explanations for observed patterns; they are durable enough that no single experience or piece of evidence will falsify them. Like scientific theories, folk theories sometimes complement each other, sometimes exist in tension with each other, and sometimes contradict each other. This research describes folk theories based on popular beliefs about AI; they are not tied to professional or organizational discourse (although they may draw upon such material.)

The folk theories about AI delve into several themes that have defined the philosophy of AI. This field considers what it means to think and exhibit consciousness (Russell & Norvig, 1995). Although philosophers of mind have engaged in related debates for centuries, most of the top queries that have come to define the philosophy of AI began in the 1950s. Alan Turing established the most famous proposal for evaluating whether machines could think: the imitation game. In this game, an interrogator must distinguish between a human and a computer based on asking both questions. Turing exhibited great confidence in the capabilities of computers; he predicted that by the end of the century, it would be natural, or at least uncontroversial, to assert that machines could think (Turing, 1950). When writing against objections that machines could not display consciousness, Turing asserted that we could not glean external evidence about the internal mental states of humans and, for this reason, need not apply this standard to our evaluation of machines (Moor, 2003). With these debates in mind, philosophers of AI have addressed (implicitly or explicitly)

---

in its programs" (Copeland, 1993, p. 59). A computer, within this framework, could perform a variety of functions that could alter these systems, say, by making copies of symbols from one line at another line, writing a sequence of symbols on a line, deleting symbols on a line, or comparing symbols on two different lines.

matters of authenticity, accountability, and beneficence. Folk theories of AI tread upon similar ground.

Authenticity

One of the primary concerns of philosophers of AI is to understand its implications for understanding consciousness, intelligence, and free will. Philosophers of AI conceive of "weak" and "strong" forms of AI. Proponents of "strong" AI assert that machines can, eventually, possess minds. Proponents of "weak" AI assert that machines will merely "simulate, rather than duplicate, real intelligence" (Kaplan, 2016, p. 68). Either proposal implicitly throws the authenticity of AI or the notion that machines can exhibit genuine displays of intelligence into question. While most philosophical discussions of authenticity typically apply to human agents believed to have consciousness, related inquiries implicitly structure the concerns of AI researchers (Haugland, 1985).[3] Different philosophers argue that AI will never lead to genuine reproductions of human intelligence (McCarthy, 2006; Dreyfus, 1992; Searle, 1984; Russell & Norvig, 1995; Penrose, 1994).[4] As Sherry Turkle (2007) has shown, such philosophical arguments have led scholars to debate the "authenticity" of human–computer relationships. Individual consumers now make "attributions of authenticity to the work algorithms do, such as decisions artificial intelligence makes or products of sophisticated computer design, compared with identical human work" (Jago, 2019, p. 38). These judgments matter precisely because many AI applications

---

[3] Philosophers of AI who promote strong forms of AI aspire to produce "*machines with minds,* in the full and literal sense (emphasis in original)" (Haugland, 1985, p. 2). Haugland suggests that a better name for AI might be synthetic intelligence, as it refers to intelligence that is true to itself, albeit manufactured. These commitments follow in the footsteps of other philosophers of mind. A central assumption governing all of Western philosophy is that thinking can be reduced to the "rational manipulation of mental symbols (viz., ideas)" (Haugland, 1985, p. 4). Many different philosophers have built upon this premise. "By RATIOCINATION, I mean *computation*" proclaimed Thomas Hobbes in the 1650s. His claim entailed two related ideas: that thinking could be reduced to "symbolic operations" and that clear thinking follows a legible set of rules (Haugland, 1985, p. 23). René Descartes wrote in 1673 about the potential limitations of automata; in his *Discourse on Method*, he wrote that machines could neither produce meaningful speech nor engage in reasoning. Based on his detailed engagement with the field of mathematics, Descartes argued that thoughts were themselves the same as the "symbolic representations" found in mathematics. David Hume, known for proposing his "science of man," explained thinking in terms of physical forces. He laid down a "mechanics of mind" that framed ideas as the building blocks of knowledge (Haugland, 1985, p. 43).

[4] Hubert Dreyfus suggests that human behavior cannot be reduced to rule-following. Because computers can only follow rules, he asserts, they cannot exhibit behavior that is as intelligent as that of human beings (Dreyfus, 1992). John Searle presents another critique of strong AI by way of his Chinese Room argument (1984). In this thought experiment, Searle imagines a program that can pass the Turing Test but does not possess understanding of the relevant inputs and outputs (Russell & Norvig, 1995). Roger Penrose continues in this line of reasoning, asserting that human consciousness is nonalgorithmic and cannot be modeled by a Turing machine or digital computer (1994).

may involve different forms of deception, such as convincing a consumer that they are dealing with a human instead of an artificial agent (Floridi, 2018).

Agency

Philosophers have contemplated whether artificial agents have obligations to other human patients or if human agents have responsibilities to other artificial patients (Floridi & Sanders, 2004). Artificial agents, certain philosophers argue, can make decisions that are independent of their human creators and, thus, engage in displays of "artificial good" or "artificial evil" (Gips, 1995). Within these ethical frameworks, different types of AI possess agency; in short, they can autonomously complete mor ally relevant actions. Acknowledging the agency of AI systems implies that artificial agents can be held accountable, although not necessarily responsible, for their behaviors (Floridi & Sanders, 2004). Daniel Dennett has proposed a model of accountability that incorporates nonhuman agents.[5] Agents can be held accountable for their conduct under two conditions: they have developed highly sophisticated cognitive abilities, and they can hold beliefs that attribute reasons to various behaviors or states of being (Dennett, 2017).

Beneficence

In 2015, the president of the Association for the Advancement of Artificial Intelligence (AAAI) announced that many individuals outside of computer science had expressed a deep concern for the "threat" that AI may pose to "the future of humanity" (Dietterich & Horvitz, 2015). The development of AI systems with a surprising array of abilities and applications has led analysts to embed ethics within the field (Yu et al., 2018). Different organizations have engaged in efforts to establish leading ethical principles that can govern the introduction and management of AI within society. Floridi and Cowls, after assessing six "high profile" initiatives in the ethics of AI, determined that the leading principles overlap with those already well-established in the field of bioethics: beneficence, nonmaleficence, autonomy, and justice (2019; Beauchamp & Childress, 2001). Beneficence, which refers to acting in the best interest of others, emerged as a theme in many of these ethical texts. Various documents suggest that AI should promote either the "well-being of all sentient creatures," ensure the "common good and betterment of humanity," "benefit and

---

[5] After examining the mechanisms of cause and effect that undergird unconscious biological processes, he argues that traditional conceptions of free will – which are often yoked to discussions of moral responsibility – are an "illusion" equivalent to a grand magic trick. Human actions, Dennett continues, are a complex result of a combination of events that came before. Over the grand scale of billions of years, however, humans have developed intellectual capabilities that exceed other forms of life; as a result, humans can attribute a sense of purpose and meaning to any actions completed. (And these displays of meaning surface in the fields of the humanities and various art forms.)

empower as many people as possible," or allow for "the basic preconditions for life on our planet, continued prospering for mankind and the preservation of a good environment for future generations" (Floridi & Cowls, 2019, p. 7). A focus on beneficence turns attention toward the active good that AI can promote within society.

METHODS

This study uses a grounded theory approach to gain a greater understanding of the mental models and theories that nontechnical publics use to describe AI. Study participants were recruited via ResearchMatch, a national research volunteer registry supported by the US National Institutes of Health as part of the Clinical Translational Science Award (CTSA) program. ResearchMatch has a large population of volunteers who have consented to be contacted by researchers about studies for which they may be eligible. Review and approval for this study and all procedures were obtained from the author's Institutional Review Board.

SAMPLE

Participants were recruited using the ResearchMatch website. ResearchMatch is a nonprofit web-based organization. ResearchMatch has proven successful in connecting volunteers with researchers, and the authors are currently evaluating regulatory and workflow options to open access to researchers at non-CTSA institutions. Harris and colleagues designed ResearchMatch as a disease-neutral, web-based recruitment registry to help match individuals who wish to participate in clinical research studies with researchers actively searching for volunteers throughout the United States (Harris, et al., 2012). In total, ResearchMatch has more than 152,000 volunteers and nearly 10,000 researchers who use the matching service. These researchers currently have 975 clinical trial studies underway.

ResearchMatch sent an initial recruitment solicitation to possible participants, of whom 3,434 offered to participate in the survey. The author then sent a follow-up email invitation including informed consent details and a link to an electronic open-ended survey questionnaire delivered by Qualtrics to the pool of possible participants. Of the 3,434 possible participants, 2,193 individuals responded to the following open-ended questions: "In a sentence or two, describe your understanding of Artificial Intelligence (AI). From your perspective, what is it and how is it used?" The demographic characteristics of the sample are presented in Table 15.1. The majority of respondents were female (81%) and Caucasian (83.2%), and nearly three-fourths of the sample (73.4%) had at least a college degree. The participants are consistent with other survey samples. Smith (2008) details how, in general, more educated and more affluent people are more likely to participate in surveys than less educated and less affluent people (Curtin, Presser, & Singer, 2000; Goyder et al., 2002;), women are more likely to participate than men (Curtin et al 2000; Moore & Tarnai, 2002), and

Table 15.1   Sample demographic characteristics

	Frequency	Percent
Gender Identity		
Male	603	27.5
Female	1,522	69.4
Transgender Male/Trans Man/Female-to-Male (FTM)	4	0.2
Transgender Female/Trans Woman/Male-to-Female (MTF)	3	0.1
Genderqueer, neither exclusively male nor female	34	1.6
Additional Gender Category/Other	9	0.4
Choose not to disclose	18	0.8
Birth Gender		
Male	614	28
Female	1,553	70.8
Choose not to disclose	24	1.1
not answered	2	0.1
Marital Status		
Single (never married)	769	35.1
Married or in a domestic partnership	1,061	48.4
Widowed	66	3
Divorced	250	11.4
Separated	24	1.1
Choose not to disclose	23	1
Employment		
Employed full time (40 or more hours per week)	1,175	53.6
Employed part time (up to 39 hours per week)	281	12.8
Unemployed and currently looking for work	57	2.6
Unemployed and not currently looking for work	17	0.8
Student	170	7.8
Retired	265	12.1
Homemaker	49	2.2
Self-employed	113	5.2
Unable to work	63	2.9
not answered	3	0.1
Education		

(Continued)

Table 15.1 (Continued)

	Frequency	Percent
Less than a high school diploma	2	0.1
High school degree or equivalent	73	3.3
Some college, no degree	292	13.3
Associate's degree (AA, AS)	167	7.6
Bachelor's degree (BA/BS)	806	36.8
Master's degree (MA, MS, MEd)	617	28.1
Doctoral degree (PhD, EdD)	140	6.4
Professional degree (MD, DDS, DVM)	95	4.3
not answered	1	0
Ethnicity		
American Asian	76	3.5
Black/African	100	4.6
Native American	17	0.8
Native Hawaiian or Pacific Islander	2	0.1
Hispanic/Latino	65	3
Other	83	3.8
White	1,846	84.2
not answered	4	0.2
Region		
Division 1: Connecticut, Maine, Massachusetts, New Hampshire, Rhode Island, Vermont	95	4.3
Division 2: New Jersey, New York, Pennsylvania	278	12.7
Division 3: Illinois, Indiana, Michigan, Ohio, Wisconsin	470	21.4
Division 4: Iowa, Kansas, Minnesota, Missouri, Nebraska, North Dakota, South Dakota	174	7.9
Division 5: Delaware, Washington DC, Florida, Georgia, Maryland, North Carolina, South Carolina, Virginia, West Virginia	421	19.2
Division 6: Alabama, Kentucky, Mississippi, Tennessee	203	9.3
Division 7: Arkansas, Louisiana, Oklahoma, Texas	120	5.5
Division 8: Arizona, Colorado, Idaho, Montana, Nevada, New Mexico, Utah, Wyoming	145	6.6
Division 9: Alaska, California, Hawaii, Oregon, Washington	281	12.8
not answered	6	0.3

white people are more likely to participate than nonwhite people (Groves, Singer, & Corning, 2000; Voigt et al., 2003).

DATA ANALYSIS

Open responses were coded in Microsoft Excel. Open coding was used (Strauss & Corbin, 1998) to help to identify key concepts and their properties. As in the model outlined by Strauss and Corbin, the goal was to uncover common themes "grounded" in the data themselves (Beard et al., 2009). By reviewing the codes and constantly reviewing the data, themes and categories were initially developed. The iterative process of generating the final categories used for coding continued until saturation or when the research team was confident that they had reached the point that they could acquire no new information and further coding was no longer feasible (Guest et al., 2006). Constant comparison and awareness of repetition were used to ensure that saturation was attained. Four themes arose from the coding process. These themes correspond to the four themes addressed in the data literacy literature and the philosophy of AI: ignorance, authenticity, agency, and beneficence.

FINDINGS AND DISCUSSION

These findings suggest that nontechnical publics are crafting folk theories to describe AI and their understanding of its influence on their lives. Four themes have emerged from the open responses collected: ignorance, authenticity, agency, and beneficence. The analysis below considers each of these themes in turn. First, it considers the often self-described technical ignorance of respondents. It notes the lack of specialized knowledge about computers, algorithms, and data infrastructures. Then, it assesses three philosophical commitments that respondents expressed in their descriptions of AI. First, it focuses on their formulations of weak and strong versions of AI, assessing whether people believe that computing machines can exhibit authentic displays of intelligence. Next, it moves to their depictions of AI systems as autonomous agents that can make independent decisions and even be held accountable for their actions. Finally, it contemplates the ethical sentiments of respondents; most believed that AI development was consistent with the principle of beneficence and would ultimately enhance the social good.

Ignorance

Public understanding of AI is quite limited. Many respondents spoke about all that they did not know when defining AI and identifying its many applications in modern society. As one respondent put it, "AI is hard to describe!" Still, others were quite frank about their lack of expertise: "I do not have a strong understanding of artificial intelligence or how it is used." Different people indicated that while they might possess a "good understanding of AI from a general public point of view," they did not have a good grasp of it from the "technical perspective." Respondents indicated their discomfort with correctly using computer terms. "I don't understand it," one subject mused, "as I think it's just computers – only as intelligent as the data entered." People had some general awareness of key concepts associated with AI, such as machine learning. However, they did not always feel confident in making these connections or asserting its ubiquity in everyday life.

AI is probably different from regular computing in that it's adaptive/learning? VS just statistically set up? Or maybe I'm confusing machine learning with AI. Not sure. I think it's used for all kinds of things. Probably mostly research and commercial stuff. I think of Amazon Alexa but who knows what else.

These assessments capture the many uncertainties that accompany nontechnical talk of AI systems.

Even without a technical grasp of AI, countless subjects made guesses about what constituted AI based on their limited computer or data literacy. "I don't have a comprehensive understanding of artificial intelligence or its many uses," someone wrote, "but I believe it is computer programming that can analyze data and formulate conclusions based on data input." Some other people sensed that computer programs played a role. "I don't know much about it," someone began, but "I believe it is technologies that allow software and computer programs [to] adapt and incorporate decision-making models for consumer use in everyday life." People further acknowledged these decision-making capacities. "Not really sure," someone mused,

maybe [its] in computer programs that try and anticipate what users will do or anticipate what their needs are? unsure of current applications or if I realize if/when I have interacted with AI (although I'm sure it's not like in the movies).

Their speculations revealed a general willingness to use terms such as data, computers, hardware, or software without harboring an expert grasp of their meaning.

People with limited technical proficiency based their understanding of AI on ideas they gleaned from popular media. One survey respondent suggested that "AI, as referenced in pop culture, is something that is in progress in the real world, but is not [as] intelligent as pop culture could lead you to believe." Not everyone, however, was as critical of these depictions. Numerous people acknowledged how popular newspapers, television shows, books, or movies altered their perspective on AI. "It's software developed to predict how humans will act/think," someone posited. "I don't know much about how it's used besides controversial methods that have made news stories." "I know nothing," another stated. "From watching the TV show MacGyver I see the robot using AI." "I have a very basic understanding of AI," someone else explained. "Mostly experienced through virtual reality hardware and games like the oculus." Other replies emphasized different forms of entertainment, suggesting that AI had not only to do with "collecting huge data sets" but also with "the self learning robot who beat everyone at chess and the Chinese game Go." "It is used in movies [a]nd games to create a more real-life experience," stated another.

Survey respondents identified the presence of AI in spheres outside of entertainment. Someone believed that AI referred to "Siri & Alexa, the virtual people online & over the phone … I really don't know other than that … maybe my Roomba?" "Siri, Alexa, Watson … any type of smart automation," another concluded. People had a general sense that it referred to many different technologies with everyday uses, including "computers like I.B.M.'s Watson and household electronics like 'ALEXA,'" and even the "search box from Amazon." Others posited that AI operated at an even more general level. "Mathematical equations, algorithms, or programs that can learn from data. It's used pretty much everywhere these days." Indeed, users seemed confident that AI surfaced in almost every domain of society. "It has applications in virtually every area of life and business," someone mused. Another respondent expanded upon these possibilities. "My understanding of AI is that it is machines or systems with a degree of human intelligence. It can be used in a broad variety of ways in our daily lives (entertainment, medical, industrial, etc.)," someone else clarified. Even while ignorant of AI's scientific or technical dimensions, these respondents felt confident in asserting its ubiquity in society.

Authenticity

Well aware of the widespread usage of AI, survey respondents displayed a general interest in concepts that have intrigued philosophers. "Strong or weak AI? To me AI is any system that can adapt it's [sic] response/behavior based on previous results," someone responded. Other individuals indirectly addressed whether artificial agents would ever exhibit genuine forms of human intelligence. "AI is the use of a computer program which has the ability to solve new problems analogous to the way the human brain solves problems," someone authoritatively stated. Other respondents were more cautious about drawing such analogies. "Artificial intelligence is the ability of machines to think critically and attempt to think 'humanly,'" offered one respondent. Different survey participants, quite commonly, referenced this gap between artificial and human intelligence; they indicated that different AI systems currently strive and fail to approximate the cognitive capabilities available to the human mind.

Most of the replies discussed AI's ability to mimic human intelligence. Other similar families of responses proposed that AI would effectively replicate, reproduce, or imitate human intelligence. "AI are programs or algarhythms [sic] designed to mimic human response and thinking to help solve problems and conduct activities." Respondents clarified what they meant by human intelligence in different responses. "AI is the ability of computers to mimic human thought patterns well enough to accomplish tasks in a similar way to people." "AI includes human-made computers and other processing systems that mimic human reasoning & learning." For others, AI referred to

> a computer program that mimics typically human cognitive features such as learning or problem solving. It can be used for tasks that are usually difficult for computers (natural language processing, self-driving cars, or predictions for complex systems) or for

soft-science applications dealing with emotional/social intelligence, consciousness, or self-awareness.

All of these responses indicated that it would be possible to design AI that could be made to genuinely copy human intelligence, which they deemed to be original in some sense.

Other respondents indicated that AI would never be authentic, as it would always be a false representation of human intelligence. According to many respondents, AI systems could only bear similarities to human minds. Many people used a variety of similes when articulating their definitions of AI. "AI is computer programming built into robots or other things such as cars or prosthetics that can 'think' as a human and perform certain tasks." They emphasized that different intelligent systems would think or make decisions as if they were human. "AI is a machine or program designed to think like a human in order to assist with or take over simple tasks." Participants expanded upon some of these cognitive or behavioral capabilities when making their comparisons. "AI is basically a machine or robot designed to understand or function like a normal human being." These descriptions often entail different assumptions about what constitutes genuine human intelligence, including the ability to make autonomous decisions.

Agency

When writing philosophically oriented replies, many subjects articulated their belief in the relative autonomy of AI systems. Their descriptions emphasized the agency machines or computers could exhibit when performing their tasks. "AI is electronic technology created to become intelligent," one respondent indicated, and to be "independent from total human programming." Many subjects indicated that the mark of an AI system was its ability to think or act without human intervention: "A computer's ability to process and perform tasks without direct human involvement." Many respondents reasoned that this relative autonomy from human beings meant that AI systems would exhibit adaptive capabilities. As one subject explained, "AI is a catch-all term for an artificially-created system that is able to learn and grow without any direct modifications from its creators." AI, another subject mused, "is when computer programs can learn and adapt based on the input they receive."

Learning was a key feature of many discussions of agency. Survey participants ascribed different cognitive abilities to (their various understandings of) AI systems. Respondents indicated that they believed that AI could engage in thinking and reasoning without human intervention. These specific capabilities emerged from a more general ability to learn. "AI is a sentient intelligent 'thing,'" explained one respondent, "that has the mental capabilities to compute mass quantities of information at one time while also learning and emitting basic emotions." Different submissions emphasized different features of the learning process. Some replies adopted a behaviorist mentality: "A machine with the ability to learn from external stimuli to alter programming or function." The majority of descriptions about learning focused on personal experience as if they were speaking about a human agent. AI, stated a few respondents, referred to "computer software that can adapt or learn from experiences" or "computer-based systems that can 'learn' and build on their own knowledge." Learning, these replies suggested, relied on the independent experiences or capabilities of the system in question.

Most discussions of learning exhibited multiple levels of data or computer literacy. Survey respondents varied in their ability to articulate the various functions of hardware, software, algorithms, or computer programs. However, their (often limited) grasp of these terms did not deter participants from offering up their lay opinions. "Software is not a fixed set of IF-THEN statements. Rather, the computer 'mind' takes in new information and responds by 'learning' better responses to new information. Past behaviors/interactions are remembered and better predictions are made." Many participants offered their views on machine learning, suggesting that it referred to "control allowing automation with minimal human influence." "Machine learning is when a man-made device uses algorithms to assess its environment and 'learn' or determine which outcome to take based on those assessments," one person asserted. "Machine learning," offered another, entails "data scraping iterated again and again until the technology 'acquires' the information and can manipulate it in an intelligent way." No matter their degree of literacy, each respondent concerned with learning suggested that this capability was closely entangled with the agency of artificial agents.

Beneficence

Along with ascribing agency to artificial agents, many survey respondents expressed their belief that AI would contribute to the general social welfare. They implicitly suggested that AI systems were beneficent, as opposed to benevolent, in nature; they believed that AI would operate by actions or rules that would benefit humankind. AI systems, most respondents posited, were invested in providing "aid in day to day life." Only a few participants indicated that AI systems could be "used for good or bad purposes." A subset of these respondents emphasized that for as many positive effects that AI might yield (it may make "human life faster and more efficient"), it would equally have many negative effects (it may encroach upon "privacy and take marketing to a dangerous level.") An even smaller subset of survey participants acknowledged that different forms of AI can "be biased based on the programmer and designer of the lessons." In general, survey respondents overlooked these – far more nefarious – sociotechnical realities; they focused on the ways that AI would "make life as we know it safer, easier, healthier, more connected" and would "free up valuable human elements to put energy into more personal life such as one on one family time."

Respondents exhibited a belief in the beneficence of AI when referencing their labor capacities. Rather than emphasize adverse effects, such as automation's economic or political risks, survey participants largely focused on the general ways that AI would "save us from labor." Many suggested that AI "is used to perform jobs that people can do, or sometimes ones that people can't do, can't do fast enough, or don't want to do." Alternatively, they indicated that "AI can perform small functions that are hard or boring for humans." Moreover, survey respondents emphasized the positive implications of bringing AI into the workplace. "It's used to replace humans in tedious or difficult jobs that require rote memorization, quick calculations, being in many places at once, instant answers, etc." These artificial agents would produce "safer, cheaper, and more precise and accurate results than human workers. With the proper programing and deployment," someone mused, "it can only improve everything from manufacturing and transportation to medical practice." All of these replies focus on the beneficent implications of AI within the labor market and neglect how AI systems can serve as agents of oppression or discrimination.

LIMITATIONS

With qualitative research, generalization cannot be made about individuals' perceptions and articulations of AI knowledge. However, insights drawn from this data can inform future research on the public's perceptions of AI policy and regulation. Although the authors used the multiple-reviewer method for questionnaire design and data analysis, their personal biases may have influenced the choice of questions or the interpretation of the data collected.

FUTURE DIRECTIONS/RECOMMENDATIONS

This analysis, which describes the folk theories that lay users devised about AI, places an understudied dimension of science literacy in the foreground. Recent efforts to educate nontechnical publics about science often focus on narrow definitions of literacy; they seek to promote a general appreciation of science and technology, enhance computational skills, or encourage familiarity with reading or using data. These limited formulations of digital or technical competency have informed AI literacy programs that attempt to use education to correct "public misunderstandings about AI" (Long & Magerko, 2020). By widening the scope of the educational mission, proponents of AI literacy programs can attend to the pervasive beliefs that nontechnical publics hold about human intelligence and the sociocultural influences of technology. This study found that survey respondents were confident in developing folk theories about AI even if they lacked robust understanding of the scientific underpinnings. Moreover, their folk theories reflected a willful ignorance of AI's material or political uses. Their responses suggest that AI literacy programs should teach participants how to consider the social dimensions of science. Such critical skills will, in turn, alter the folk theories that lay publics create about AI.

In order to generate these critical competencies, AI literacy programs can draw upon insights from the "social and cultural study of data infrastructures" and "critical data studies" (Bowker et al., 2009; Edwards et al., 2009; Star 1999; Star

& Ruhleder, 1996; Dalton et al., 2016; Iliadis & Russo, 2016). Often inspired by STS insights, these critical frameworks train users to evaluate the invisible labor or networks that sustain data infrastructures. In her recent book, *Atlas of AI*, Kate Crawford epitomizes this analytical approach. She turns her (nontechnical) audience's attention toward appreciating AI as "both embodied and material, made from natural resources, fuel, human labor, infrastructures, logistics, histories, and classifications." In her view, "AI systems are not autonomous, rational, or able to discern anything without extensive, computationally intensive training with large datasets or predefined rules and rewards. In fact, artificial intelligence as we know it depends entirely on a much wider set of political and social structures" (Crawford, 2020, p. 8). Our research indicates that AI literacy programs would benefit from incorporating these insights into their curriculums.

Educating lay publics about AI's social or material realities would alter the folk theories they devise about how these systems operate. Recent research into the interpretations that digital users generate about algorithms suggests that they rely heavily on their personal experiences (Ytre-Arne & Moe, 2021; Siles et al., 2020). Having educational experiences that introduced them to critical perspectives about AI would help lay publics better conceptualize the social costs of any technology they use in their everyday lives. With enhanced information, lay publics could design folk theories that help them resist, rather than resign themselves to, the oppressive data structures they encounter (Draper & Turow, 2019). Their folk theories might, in turn, help policymakers or academics to find ways to challenge the troublesome effects of algorithmic biases or enhanced surveillance within society.

REFERENCES

Arm. (2020). *AI today, AI tomorrow: The arm 2020 global AI survey*. Northstar.
Bawden, D. (2008). Origins and concepts of digital literacy. In C. Lankshear, & M. Knobel (Eds.), *Digital literacies*. Peter Lang.
Beard, R. L., Knauss, J., & Moyer, D. (2009). Managing disability and enjoying life: How we reframe dementia through personal narratives. *Journal of Aging Studies, 23*(4), 227–235.
Beauchamp T., & Childress, F: (2001). *Principles of biomedical ethics*. Oxford University Press.
Benjamin, R. (2019). *Race after technology*. Polity Press.
Blumberg Capital. (2019). *Survey reveals significant disparity in consumer sentiment towards artificial Intelligence*. https://blumbergcapital.com/2019-ai-suvey-announced/
Bounegru L., Gray J., Venturini T., et al. (Eds) (2018). *A field guide to "Fake News" and other information disorders*. Public Data Lab. Retrieved January 26, 2021, from http://fakenews.publicdatalab.org/
Bowker, G., Baker, K., Millerand, F., & Ribes, D. (2009). Toward information infrastructure studies: ways of knowing in a networked environment. In J. Hunsinger, L. Klastrup, M. Allen (Eds.), *International handbook of internet research*. Springer.
Bowker, G. (2014). The infrastructural imagination. In A. Mongili A, & G. Pellegrino (Eds.), *Information infrastructure(s): Boundaries, ecologies, multiplicity* (pp. xii–xiii). Cambridge Scholars Publishing.
Brennen, J., Howard, P., & Nielsen, R. (2018). *An industry-led debate: How UK media cover artificial intelligence*. https://reutersinstitute.politics.ox.ac.uk/sites/default/files/2018-12/Brennen_UK_Media_Coverage_of_AI_FINAL.pdf

Brooks, R. (1991). Intelligence without representation. *Artificial Intelligence*, *47*(1-3), 139–159. https://doi.org/10.1016/0004-3702(91)90053-M

Browne, S. (2015). *Dark matters*. Duke Press.

Carruthers, P., & Smith, P. (1996). *Theories of theories of mind*. Cambridge University Press.

Cave, N., Coughlan, K., & Dihal, K. (2019). 'Scary robots': Examining public responses to AI. *AIES '19: AAAI/ACM Conference on AI, Ethics, and Society Proceedings*. AIES'19, January 27–28, 2019, Honolulu, HI, ACM, New York.

Copeland, J. (1993). *Artificial intelligence: A philosophical introduction*. Blackwell Press.

Crawford, K. (2021). *Atlas of AI*. Yale University Press.

Curtin, R., Presser, S., & Singer, E. (2000). The effects of response rate changes on the index of consumer sentiment. *Public Opinion Quarterly*, *64*, 413–428.

Dalton, C. M., Taylor, L., & Thatcher, J. (2016). Critical data studies: A dialogue on data and space. *Big Data & Society*, *3*(1), 1–9. https://doi.org/10.1177/2053951716648346

Dennett, D. (2017). *From bacteria to bach and back*. W.W. Norton.

Dick, S. (2019). Artificial Intelligence. *Harvard Data Science Review*, *1*(1). https://hdsr.mitpress.mit.edu/pub/0aytgrau/release/2

Dietterich, T., & Horvitz, E. (2015). Research, leadership, and communication about AI futures. *Communications of the ACM*, 58(10), 38–40.

D'Ignazio, C. (2017). Creative data literacy: Bridging the gap between the Data-Haves and the Data Have-Nots. *Information Design Journal*, *23*(1), 6–18. https://doi.org/10.1075/idj.23.1.03dig

DiSessa, A. (2001). *Changing minds: Computers, learning, and literacy*. MIT Press.

Draper, N., & Turow, J. (2019). The corporate cultivation of digital resignation. *New Media & Society*, 2(8): 1824-1839. https://doi.org/10.1177/1461444819833331

Dreyfus, H. (1992). *What computers still can't do*. MIT Press.

Edwards, P. N., Bowker, G. C., Jackson, S. J., et al. (2009). Introduction: An agenda for infrastructure studies. *Journal of the Association for Information Systems*, *10*(5), 364–374. DOI: 10.17705/1jais.00200

Elish, M., & Boyd, D. (2017). Situating methods in the magic of big data and AI. *Communication Monographs*, 1–25. https://doi.org/10.1080/03637751.2017.1375130

Eslami, M., Rickman, A., Vaccaro, K. Aleyasen, A., Vuong, A., Karahalios, K., Hamilton, K., & Sandvig, C. (2015). *'I always assumed that I wasn't really that close to [her]': Reasoning about Invisible Algorithms in News Feeds*. CHI.

Eslami, M., Elazari Bar On, A., Vaccaro, K., Gilbert, E., Lee, M., & Karahalios, K. (2019). User attitudes towards algorithmic opacity and transparency in online reviewing platforms. In *Proceedings of the 2019 CHI Conference on Human Factors in Computing Systems* (pp. 1–14). '

Fast, E., & Horvitz, E. (2017). Long-term trends in the public perception of artificial intelligence. *Proceedings of the Thirty-First AAAI Conference on Artificial Intelligence*.

French, M., & Hancock, J. (2017). *What's the folk theory? Reasoning about cyber-social systems*. https://doi.org/10.2139/ssrn.2910571

Floridi, L. (2018). Artificial intelligence, deepfakes and a future of ectypes. *Philosophical Technology*, *31*, 317–321. https://doi.org/10.1007/978-3-030-81907-1_17

Floridi, L., & Cowls, J. (2021). A unified framework of five principles for AI in society. *Ethics, Governance, and Policies in Artificial Intelligence*, *144*, 5–17. https://doi.org/10.1007/978-3-030-81907-1_2

Floridi, L., & Sanders, J. (2004). On the morality of artificial agents. *Minds and Machine*, *14*, 349–379. https://doi.org/10.1023/B:MIND.0000035461.63578.9d

Gallup. (2018). *Optimism and anxiety: Views on the impact of artificial intelligence and higher education's response*. Northeastern University & Gallup, Inc.

Gips, J. (1995). Towards the Ethical Robot. In K. Ford, C. Glymour, & P. Hayes (Eds.), *Android epistemology* (pp. 243–252). MIT Press.

Gelman, S., & Legare, C. (2011). Concepts and folk theories. *Annual Review of Anthropology*, *40*, 379–398. https://doi.org/10.1146/annurev-anthro-081309-145822

Goyder, J., Warriner, K., & Miller, S. (2002). Evaluating socio-economic status (SES) bias in survey nonresponse. *Journal of Official Statistics, 18*(1), 1–11.

Gray, J., Gerlitz, C., & Bounegru, L. (2018). Data infrastructure literacy. *Big Data & Society,* 1–13. https://doi.org/10.1177/2053951718786316

Groves, R. M., Singer, E., & Corning, A. (2000). Leverage-saliency theory of survey participation. *Public Opinion Quarterly, 64,* 299–308.

Guest, G., Bunce, A., & Johnson, L. (2006). How many interviews are enough? An experiment with data saturation and variability. *Field Methods, 18*(1), 59–82. https://doi.org/10.1177/1525822X05279903

Harris, P. A., Scott, K. W., Lebo, L., Hassan, N., Lighter, C., & Pulley, J. (2012). ResearchMatch: A national registry to recruit volunteers for clinical research. *Academic medicine: journal of the Association of American Medical Colleges, 87*(1), 66.

Haugland, J. (1985). *Artificial intelligence: The very idea.* MIT Press.

Iliadis, A., & Russo, F. (2016). Critical data studies: An introduction. *Big Data & Society,* 3(2), 2053951716674238. https://doi.org/10.1177/2053951716674238

Ipsos. (2019). *Ipsos global poll for the world economic forum shows widespread concern about artificial intelligence.* https://www.ipsos.com/sites/default/files/ct/news/documents/2019-07/wef-ai-ipsos-press-release-jul-2019.pdf.

Jago, A. (2019). Algorithms and Authenticity. *Academy of Management Discoveries, 5*(1), 38–56. https://doi.org/10.5465/amd.2017.0002

Kaplan, J. (2016). *Artificial intelligence: What everyone needs to know.* Oxford University Press.

Kelley, P., Moessner, C., Newman, D., Yang, Y., Sedley, A., Heldreth, C., Kramm, A. (2021). Exciting, useful, worrying, futuristic: Public perception of artificial intelligence in 8 countries. In *Proceedings of the 2021 AAAI/ACM conference on AI, ethics, and society (AIES '21),* May 19–21, 2021, Virtual Event, USA. ACM, New York.

Kong, S., Cheung, M., & Zhang, G. (2021). Evaluation of an artificial intelligence literacy course for university students with diverse backgrounds. *Computers and Education: Artificial Intelligence, 2,* 100026. https://doi.org/10.1016/j.caeai.2021.100026

Kong, S., Chiu, M., Lai, M. (2018). A study of primary school students' interest, collaboration attitude, and programming empowerment in computational thinking education. *Computers & Education, 127,* 178–189. https://doi.org/10.1016/j.compedu.2018.08.026

Kong, S., & Lai, M. (2021). Computational identity and programming empowerment of students in computational thinking development. *British Journal of Educational Technology,* 1–19. https://doi.org/10.1111/bjet.13175

Laugksch, R. (2000). Scientific literacy: A conceptual overview. *Science Education, 84*(1), 71–94. https://doi.org/10.1002/(SICI)1098-237X(200001)84:1<71::AID-SCE6>3.0.CO;2-C

Lee, M., Kusbit, D., Metsky, E., & Dabbish, L. (2015). Working with machines: The impact of algorithmic and data-Ddrive management on human workers. *Proceedings of the 33rd Annual ACM Conference on Human Factors in Computing System* (pp. 1603–1612). https://doi.org/10.1145/2702123.2702548

Letouzé, E. (2016). *Should 'data literacy' be promoted?* UN World Data Forum. Retrieved 24 January 2021, from https://undataforum. org/WorldDataForum/should-data-literacy-be-promoted/

Letouzé, E., Bhargava R., Deahl E., et al. (2015). *Beyond data literacy: Reinventing community engagement and empowerment in the age of data.* Data Pop Alliance. Retrieved January 24, 2021, from http://datapopalliance.org/wpcontent/uploads/2015/11/Beyond-Data-Literacy-2015.pdf

Makinen, M. (2006). Digital empowerment as a process for enhancing citizens' participation. *E-Learning, 3*(3), 381–395. https://doi.org/10.2304/elea.2006.3.3.381

Marres, N. (2017). *Digital sociology: The reinvention of social research.* Polity Press.

McCarthy, J. (2006). *The philosophy of AI and the AI of philosophy.* Retrieved January 27, 2022, from http://jmc.stanford.edu/articles/aiphil2.html

McCarthy, J., Minsky, M.L., Rochester, N., & Shannon, C.E. (2006 [1955]). A proposal for the Dartmouth summer research project on artificial intelligence, August 31, 1955. *AI Magazine*, *27*(4), 12. https://doi.org/10.1609/aimag.v27i4.1904

Medin, D., & Altran, A. (1999). *Folkbiology*. MIT Press.

Moor, J. (2003). *The Turing test: The elusive standard of artificial intelligence*. Kluwer Academic Publishers.

Moore, D. L., & Tarnai, J. (2002). Evaluating nonresponse error in mail surveys. In R. M. Groves, D. A. Dillman, J. L. Eltinge, & R. J. A. Little (Eds.), *Survey nonresponse* (pp. 197–211). John Wiley & Sons.

Mozilla. (2019). *We asked people around the world how they feel about artificial intelligence. Here's what we learned*. https://foundation.mozilla.org/en/blog/we-asked -people-around-the-world-how-they-feel-about-artificial-intelligence-heres-what-we -learned/

Nisbet, M., Scheufele, D., Shanahan, J., Moy, P., Brossard, D., & Lewenstein, B. (2002). Knowledge, reservations, or promise?: A media effects model for public perceptions of science and technology. *Communications Research*, *29*(5), 584–608. https://doi.org/10 .1177/009365002236196

Nilsson, N. (2009). *The quest for artificial intelligence: A history of ideas and achievements*. Cambridge University Press.

Noble, S. (2018). *Algorithms of oppression*. NYU Press.

O'Neil, C. (2016). *Weapons of math destruction*. Crown Books.

Penrose, R. (1994). *Shadows of the mind*. Oxford University Press.

Rip, A. (2006). Folk theories of nanotechnologists. *Science as culture*, *15*(4), 349–365.

Russell, S. & Norvig, P. (1995). *Artificial intelligence: A modern approach*. Prentice Hall.

Schank, R. (1987). What is AI, anyway? *AI magazine*, *8*(4), 59–65. https://doi.org/10.1609/ aimag.v8i4.623

Searle, J. (1984). *Minds, brains, and science*. Harvard University Press.

Siles, I., Segura-Castillo, A., Solis, R., & Sancho, M. (2020). Folk theories of algorithmic recommendations on Spotify: Enacting data assemblages in the global South. *Big Data & Society*, 1–15. https://doi.org/10.1177/2053951720923377

Smith, G. (2008). Does gender influence online survey participation?: A record-linkage analysis of university faculty online survey response behavior. *ERIC document reproduction service no. ED 501717*.

Star, S., & Ruhleder, K. (1996). Steps toward an ecology of infrastructure: Design and access for large information spaces. *Information Systems Research*, *7*(1), 111–134. https://doi.org /10.1287/isre.7.1.111

Star, S. (1999) The ethnography of infrastructure. *American Behavioral Scientist*, *43*(3), 377– 391. https://doi.org/10.1177/00027649921955326

Stone, P., Brooks, R., Brynjolfsson, E., Calo, R., Etzioni, O., Hager, G., Hirschberg, J., Kalyanakrishnan, S., Kamar, E., Kraus, S., Leyton-Brown, K., Parkes, D., Press, W., Saxenian, A., Shah, J., Tambe, M., Teller, A. (2016). *Artificial intelligence and life in 2030: One hundred year study on artificial intelligence*: Report of the 2015–2016 Study Panel.

Turing, A. (1950). Computing machinery and intelligence. *Mind*, *59*(236), 433–460. https:// doi.org/10.1007/978-1-4020-6710-5_3

Turkle, S. (2007). Authenticity in the age of digital companions. *Interaction Studies*, *8*(3), 501–517. https://doi.org/10.1075/is.8.3.11tur

Voigt, L. F., Koepsell, T. D., & Daling, J. R. (2003). Characteristics of telephone survey respondents according to willingness to participate. *American Journal of Epidemiology*, *157*, 66–73.

Ytre-Arne, Y., & Moe, H. (2021). Folk theories of algorithms: Understanding digital irritation. *Media, Culture & Society*, *43*(5), 807–824. https://doi.org/10.1177/0163443720972314

Yu, H., Shen, Z., Miao, C., Leung, C., Lesser, V., & Yang, Q. (2018). Building ethics into artificial intelligence, In *Proceedings of the 27th international joint conference on artificial intelligence* (pp. 5527–5533). https://arxiv.org/abs/1812.02953

Zhang, B., & Dafoe, W. (2019). *Artificial intelligence: American attitudes and trends.* Center for the Governance of AI, Future of Humanity Institute, University of Oxford.

Zimmerman, M. (2018). *Teaching AI: Exploring new frontiers for learning.* International Society for Technology in Education.

PART IV

INTERACTING WITH ARTIFICIAL INTELLIGENCE

16. Facilitating stakeholder communication around AI-enabled systems and business processes

Matthew Bundas, Chasity Nadeau, Thanh H. Nguyen, Jeannine Shantz, Marcello Balduccini, Edward Griffor, and Tran Cao Son

INTRODUCTION

Business process means the collection of related, structured activities or tasks that serve a particular business goal (Wikimedia Foundation, 2022).

Artificial intelligence (AI) has produced spectacular results across a multitude of domains. Business solutions that seemed impossible are now made possible thanks to AI-enabled components, whose use is often imperative to the overall success of business processes. However, leveraging AI is not trivial. Given the complexity of AI components and their behavior, communication is a major hurdle among stakeholders with different backgrounds and goals. Each group of stakeholders may have its own set of concerns and requirements. Vocabulary can vary depending on each stakeholder's domain of expertise, and each group likely has its own goals, which can conflict with other groups' goals.

For example, within an organization, public relations experts may want to promote transparency surrounding decisions of AI-enabled systems and business processes. Transparency appears to be a good practice when working with your clients. However, cybersecurity experts may argue that excessive transparency would threaten security. Even within a small organization, aligning AI-enabled systems goals may be challenging. Now consider extending this to multiple business processes across various organizations with several divisions within each organization. How does one manage the multi-layered business processes involving AI-enabled systems?

To complicate matters, generally, with AI, data goes in, and decisions come out, yet the processes between input and output lead to decisions that are often difficult to explain. This is frequently the case with machine learning (ML), a problem compounded by its widespread use. Research shows that biases may be fed into and often hidden in ML models, which can lead to unintentional and undesirable results (van Es et al., 2021). Systems in which the decision-making process is not transparent are referred to as "black boxes," and their nature is often problematic for businesses. The complicated and opaque decision-making processes of AI components increase the communication challenges already faced by a diverse group of stakeholders.

In this chapter, we demonstrate that the cyber-physical systems (CPS) framework, developed by the US National Institute of Standards and Technology (NIST), provides a useful tool for solving these challenges. The NIST CPS framework was created to bring together CPS's stakeholders by providing a common vocabulary and process structure. While the NIST CPS framework was explicitly conceived for CPS, we believe that the underlying approach can be useful to overcome the challenges that emerge from the use of AI components in AI-enabled systems and business processes – especially "black-box" AI components. From the perspective of policy and practice, we believe that this approach can be effective in guiding stakeholders through the development of best practices surrounding systems and processes that involve diverse knowledge domains and goals. We begin the chapter by providing an introduction to the NIST CPS framework and then shift our attention to practical aspects by discussing a use case inspired by recent events.

BACKGROUND

NIST is a United States government organization specializing in developing standardized templates and processes for various uses and applications (NIST, 2022). NIST recognizes the many challenges in designing, constructing, operating, and assuring a CPS, and in response, developed the tool known as the CPS Framework (NIST, 2017).

The CPS Framework provides the basis for designing, building, and assuring a CPS. This structure determines whether the system under development meets the expectations and addresses the concerns identified by stakeholders. The CPS framework creates a "common foundation" on which systems can be "developed, safely and securely combined, verified, and delivered" to a diverse group of stakeholders (NIST, 2017). By design, the scope of the CPS framework is vast so that it may be adopted by a broad range of CPS application domains.

The CPS framework is fundamentally made up of concerns and facets. Concerns are identified through the lenses of multiple stakeholders. They are addressed throughout the CPS facets or the processes and activities that comprise the conceptualization, realization, and assurance of the CPS. Concerns are considered during the activities of all three facets and to every function, from the individual components to the sets of features that deliver function in a realized CPS. Thus, concerns form the basis of the CPS framework. The CPS framework organizes related concerns into higher level concerns and, ultimately, into one of the ten highest level concerns, called aspects, including the functional, human, business, and trustworthiness aspects and six others. The CPS framework's list of concerns resulted from a consensus between more than 500 stakeholders, including government, industry, and academic stakeholders. It is, nonetheless, not a completed structure and may be modified or extended based on the needs of the application and the changing operating environment (NIST, 2017).

To better understand the relationship between aspects and concerns, let us look at the aspect of trustworthiness. The trustworthiness aspect is broken down into several individual concerns, including privacy, reliability, resilience, safety, and security (NIST, 2017). For a system to be considered trustworthy, i.e., to satisfy the trustworthiness aspect, each of those concerns must in turn be satisfied. Concerns may be associated with constraints on the system's design or behavior, which are called requirements in the CPS framework. We say that the requirements address the concern they are associated with. For a concern to be satisfied, requirements that address it must be satisfied. The set of these requirements, which are added for the sake of concerns deemed relevant to the system, comprises a CPS model, which is the outcome of the conceptualization facet. They are measurable constraints on measurable parameters or characteristics of the system. We further expand on the relationship between aspects and concerns in the use case section below.

The three facets and their interdependencies during the lifecycle of a system are identified in the CPS framework (NIST, 2017). Once again, these are conceptualization, realization, and assurance. Each facet has its unique set of characteristics, activities, and artifacts documenting whether and how expectations are met. We can think of the artifacts as the end product of the individual facet (Balduccini et al., 2018).

The conceptualization facet focuses on the design and outline of the CPS by creating a blueprint for how the device will function and be constructed, primarily in a logical sense. The conceptualization facet produces the artifact of a blueprint, or model, for the CPS (NIST, 2017).

The realization facet focuses on how the CPS is built and tested against the design requirements developed from the CPS model. The realization facet produces the artifact of the CPS itself (Balduccini et al., 2018).

Lastly, the assurance facet highlights the use of the artifacts of conceptualization and realization as evidence that requirements are met by the CPS, e.g., to assure that the CPS is safe, secure, trustworthy, etc. The artifact of the assurance facet is an assurance case consisting of evidence and test results as well as requirements that have been implemented throughout the design and construction of a CPS. These assurance cases are evidence that a system can function safely to achieve its desired goal (Balduccini et al., 2018).

ILLUSTRATIVE USE CASE

While AI and ML provide a pathway to new and exciting possibilities, these technological solutions are not without challenges that may hinder adoption (Radanliev et al., 2020). We do not always understand the reason for the decisions made by AI components. Predicting what they will do under new circumstances is also sometimes difficult.

Consider the controversy recently sparked by the release of the Apple Card issued by Goldman Sachs Bank USA. David Heinemeier Hansson, a tech entrepreneur and author of Ruby on Rails, tweeted about alleged gender discrimination in the algorithms used to determine credit limits for the Apple Card. Despite filing joint tax returns and not disclosing income specifics when applying for the card, Hansson received a credit limit 20 times that of his wife. Ironically, his wife has a better credit score. Apple responded by raising Hansson's wife's credit limit. However, the resolution was a one-off response as Hansson was informed that Apple could not change the algorithm's decision (Reuters, 2019; Vincent, 2019).

Hansson was not the only tech leader to report discriminatory issues with the Apple Card. Apple co-founder, Steve Wozniak, was given 10 times the credit limit offered to his wife. Wozniak called on the government to investigate the operation of "black box" algorithms, which experts say are often biased (Bloomberg, 2019).

According to New York state law, any algorithm leading to discriminatory treatment of protected classes of people, including women, violates the law. In November 2019, the New York Department of Financial Services (NYDFS) announced it would formally investigate the Apple Card and claims of gender discrimination. On March 23, 2021, NYDFS (Department of Financial Services, 2021) issued a report of their investigation's findings, stating that after conducting interviews with witnesses, analysis of thousands of pages of records, and examining data concerning more than 400,000 New York State applicants, they did not find evidence of unlawful discrimination under fair lending law. However, the report acknowledges unequal access to credit based on gender in the industry as a whole, suggesting it is a systematic problem in need of a remedy (Department of Financial Services, 2021). Although Apple and Goldman Sachs were cleared in the court of law for any wrongdoing concerning gender discrimination, Apple and Goldman Sachs could still have underlying issues with gender discrimination, and their public image undoubtedly was impacted.

COMMUNICATING AROUND AI-ENABLED BUSINESS PROCESSES VIA NIST CPS FRAMEWORK

As we saw in the investigation into the Apple Card case, the law says that the unintentional nature of a bias is not an excuse for non-compliance. What happens when ML algorithms go awry? Two main challenges associated with ML models are:

1. As mentioned earlier, AI components, especially those based on ML, often act as "black boxes." Results can be difficult or impossible to explain (Gallagher, 2020; Laplante et al., 2020; Hall, 2020).
2. Even interpretable AI-enabled systems may be too complicated to explain, especially for non-experts (Hall, 2020).

One of the main goals of explainable AI (XAI) is to explain AI-driven systems humans can understand (Muncke, 2021).[1] According to Matt Turek, "new machine-learning systems will have the ability to explain their rationale, characterize their strengths and weaknesses, and convey an understanding of how they will behave in the future" (Turek, n.d.). As such, XAI is positioned to become a critical component in addressing the above challenges.

The NIST CPS framework can be extremely useful in meeting the goals outlined by Matt Turek by providing stakeholders with better control and more informed insights into the behavior of AI-enabled systems as well as by providing stakeholders with ways to discuss the requirements of AI-enabled business processes. The CPS framework can help bridge gaps by simplifying major aspects and concerns of systems into easily under-standable components. Moving toward more explainable and trusted models is neces-sary, especially in highly regulated fields such as health care, insurance, and finance.

CHARACTERIZING THE BEHAVIOR OF AI-ENABLED SYSTEMS AND BUSINESS PROCESSES

While the CPS framework was designed to provide a refined, comprehensive set of concerns that can guide the engineering process of arbitrary systems, the CPS frame-work can also be extended easily should a company face challenges that require dedi-cated concerns. To illustrate this, in the remainder of this chapter, we demonstrate multiple ways in which the NIST CPS framework can be leveraged to characterize the behavior of AI-enabled systems and business processes. We begin by eliciting a number of important considerations related to such characterization from a business perspective.

Let us begin by assembling a possible set of considerations from the perspec-tive of business users. We take inspiration from observations found in the literature and contributed by businesses and users leveraging AI for business processes. In CognitiveScale (2019), George Lawton highlights the importance of explainability in AI and identifies four ways of making AI more explainable:

1. *Understand the data.* In addition to having a deep understanding of what the data offers, be sure that training data mirrors the expected data for which the model is developed.
2. *Balance explainability, accuracy, and risk.* Be sure the decisions based on the AI output reflect the company's mission and goals.
3. *Focus on the user.* Explanations must be appropriate for each stakeholder population. Technical explanations should be reserved for only those groups who understand the language. Understanding is important for promoting end-user trust and adoption.

---

[1] Explainable artificial intelligence (XAI) is a remarkable attempt at making AI compo-nents more transparent and will likely improve the chances of success of AI-enabled systems and processes while keeping expectations reasonable (Casey, 2020).

4. *Use key performance indicators (KPIs) for AI risk.* Components of AI risk may include: bias, compliance, comprehensiveness, data privacy, explainability, and fairness. Relevant metrics can be generated for each group of stakeholders.

The first item suggests that one should provide ways of identifying the data features used by the system or process. The second item suggests that methods should be provided to identify and discuss notions of explainability, accuracy, and risk. Remarkably, the third item reiterates a foundational notion already present in the NIST CPS framework: the vocabulary chosen should be hierarchically organized in such a way that concepts at higher levels of the hierarchy are understandable by all stakeholders, regardless of their specific backgrounds and interests. Concepts at lower levels of the hierarchy should, instead, focus on particular expert classes. The fourth item suggests a potential source for a vocabulary describing possible concerns in this area, especially risk-related ones: KPIs. KPIs have already been successfully used in several domains. One example of KPI adoption related to AI is AI Global's AI Trust Index. This index is defined as a FICO-like risk score for AI. The tool allows companies to define their best practices and compares AI practices against industry benchmarks (CognitiveScale, 2019). Because many companies use KPIs, this is a widely accepted strategy. Joydeep Ghosh, chief scientific officer at AI vendor CognitiveScale, claims that companies should first "establish a set of criteria for KPIs for AI risks, including comprehensiveness, data privacy, bias, fairness, explainability and compliance" (CognitiveScale, 2019).

This information indicates useful terms related to potential considerations by business users regarding AI-enabled systems and especially AI-enabled business processes. A possible hierarchical organization of the relevant terms is:

- Rationality
  - Compliance
    - Bias
    - Ethics
    - Fairness
  - Comprehensiveness
  - Data privacy
  - Explainability

As the reader may notice, rationality is chosen as the root of the AI-related hierarchy. This is aligned with the view shared by parts of the AI community that one of the most salient features of successful AI is rational behavior. We also find it to be a better choice for the root concept than AI itself because AI is viewed sometimes as a collection of technologies. In the following section, we present a business-related use case that leverages the above concepts. In a later section, we demonstrate how the CPS framework may be used in that domain and how the above concepts can be associated with the elements of the framework.

USE CASE: USING REQUIREMENTS TO SHAPE BEHAVIOR

Let us consider a use case in which a Company A wants to develop the requirements for business processes related to processing credit card applications – for which the business processes use AI. The goal is to minimize bias and ensure the fairness of the credit card application assessment process.

When a consumer applies for a new card through Company A, the application collected by Company A is evaluated in two ways. First, internally, Company A processes the application to determine whether the application should be accepted or denied and, if accepted, with what credit limit and interest rate.

Company A's stakeholders may have many diverse concerns related, for example, to fairness, (financial) risk, explainability, and (cyber)security. To address these concerns, Company A establishes a set of requirements that their processes must follow internally. Company A is committed to eliminating bias in decision-making processes related to the new credit card. Company A's leadership determines that decisions regarding an application's approval or denial, credit limits, and interest rates shall be fair for all applicants. Company A, as a business in the financial industry, also has an interest in minimizing the risk potential applicants may pose to Company A when trusted with a credit card.

Based on substantial risk analysis and prior history, Company A believes that financial risk to Company A is higher among users and applicants who hold many credit cards with other financial institutions. Company A has identified that applicants with five or more active credit cards pose exceptionally high risk. Based on this finding, to help mitigate risk, Company A does not have an interest in accepting applicants with five or more active credit cards. Company A introduces a requirement related only to the applicant's number of active credit cards that if the number of active credit cards is five or greater, the application is declined. Otherwise, the application may still be considered. This requirement, formally denoted as "decline_five_or_more_credit_cards," is used as part of Company A's review process for all applications, helping to address the considerations related to risk.

As part of the same analysis, Company A determines that the risk of default is higher for younger applicants. In particular, those under the age of 28 are more likely to be late or default on payments. Company A defines a requirement based solely on age that is consistent for all applicants: each applicant begins with the same credit limit; those above 28 years of age receive higher credit limits. Company A determines that all approved credit cardholders 28 years of age and older should receive a credit limit 20% higher than those approved credit cardholders younger than 28 years of age. This requirement, labeled "adjusted_credit_limit_above_28_years_of_age," helps to address the considerations related to risk by ensuring applicants who may pose a higher risk to Company A have less of an opportunity to impact Company A negatively.

Company A establishes a similar requirement for assigning interest rates. Because cardholders 28 years of age and older pose less risk, they receive a lower interest rate. Company A determines that all approved credit card holders 28 years of age and older will receive an interest rate lower than those approved and under 28 years of age. Formally stated, the requirement might be "Company A shall provide a lower interest rate for those who are at least 28 years of age." This requirement, again, helps address the concern about risk, as it helps mitigate risk toward Company A and is formally labeled as "adjusted_interest_rate_above_28_years_of_age."

Company A contracts with several credit score services to obtain applicants' comprehensive financial information. To ensure a sound process and avoid potential future scrutiny, Company A established predictable third-party requirements similar to the internal properties listed above. Each third-party credit score service shall provide evidence demonstrating that the concerns about fairness and cybersecurity are addressed.

For this example, Company A wants to assure predictability and accountability for gender and ethnic-related requirements. Research shows that training data used in producing AI algorithms may be biased if gender representation is unbalanced (Dastin, 2018). Company A requires that "third-party partners shall use gender-balanced data to train their AI algorithms and produce evidence that the dataset has a difference in gender proportion no greater than 5%," which helps address the considerations about bias. We label this requirement "balanced_gender_data."

Similarly, research shows that unintentional bias may be present when gendered job titles are included in the training data, i.e., "stewardess" or "policeman," and women are "devalued when using feminine job titles" (van Es et al., 2021). Company A is concerned that applicants with gendered job titles may receive a lower or higher credit score as part of their application assessment process. To counteract this issue, Company A introduces the requirement "gender_specific_stop_words," expressing that the third-party partners shall produce evidence assuring gender-specific words are not used in determining a credit score.

This same worry also applies to ethnic-specific terms collected on applications or used in training data. With this requirement, named "ethnic_specific_stop_words," third-party partners shall produce evidence assuring ethnic-specific words are not used in determining a credit score. These stop-word requirements help to address the considerations related to bias.

In creating these requirements, Company A has identified the criteria and rules which help guide the credit card application assessment process. These requirements are both helpful for the business in constraining their processes internally and helpful for the applicants. The requirements created by Company A are clearly defined and applied to all applications in the same manner, ensuring that all applications are assessed in the same manner. For these reasons, these requirements help to address the considerations regarding risk and bias and help to address the considerations related to fairness.

In working with third-party partners, and interacting with applicants, Company A would like to ensure that each applicant's sensitive information, such as complete bank account numbers, social security numbers, etc., remains secure during communication between the relevant parties. Inspired by the Federal Trade Commission's (FTC) requirement for merchants to truncate information on receipts (Federal Trade

Commission, 2007), Company A requires that all sensitive information contained in communications is truncated. For example, in communications, a bank account number 0123456789 may be reduced to 56789. This requirement applies internally to Company A and third-party partners, helping to address the considerations of privacy and cybersecurity. It is denoted as "truncate_sensitive_data."

Company A also desires to remain transparent to applicants regarding the factors impacting their application, especially avoiding their decision-making process becoming a "black box." To help ensure transparency, Company A requires that, upon completion of an application assessment, the applicant is sent a letter outlining the factors that went into deciding their application. In particular, Company A requires that each property used as part of the application assessment is presented and that an explanation is provided on how it impacted the specific application. Factors such as the applicant's credit score and other financial metrics used in the application assessment may also be included. This requirement, labeled "application_assessment_explanation," helps address the considerations about fairness and transparency.

Meeting Company A's requirements, third-party partners shall provide predictable and accountable credit scores. Company A obtains a credit score for our application from third-party partners. Ultimately, the third-party results are combined with the internal results discussed above to determine final decisions regarding the terms of the credit card, and an explanation regarding the decisions is provided. The final decision is guaranteed to be fair because each level of the decision process has requirements and evidence that the output is fair. By creating concrete requirements that constrain the implementation of the AI-enabled application assessment, Company A can ensure their practices are in line with their considerations.

CAPTURING AI-RELATED CONCEPTS IN THE CPS FRAMEWORK

In this section, we analyze multiple approaches in which Company A may leverage the CPS framework for capturing the above AI-related considerations. Figures 16.1–16.3 provide a graphical illustration of the three methods applied to the Company A use case just described.

In the figures, aspects are shown at the top of the tree, and their sub-concerns are shown below them. Concerns are shown as ovals with their names inside, and aspects are denoted by rectangles with rounded corners. Requirements are shown as rectangles with their names inside. The sub-concern relation between the two concerns is shown with a solid line between the two concerns. The fact that a given requirement addresses a concern is indicated by a dashed edge labeled "addresses." Note that, for compactness, Figures 16.1–16.3 depict only the relevant portions of the concern tree.[2]

---

[2]　The full concern tree contains over 100 concerns and ten aspects.

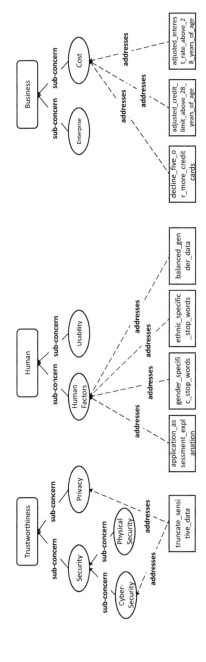

Figure 16.1   Representation of Company A use case with Approach 1, using existing concerns in CPS framework

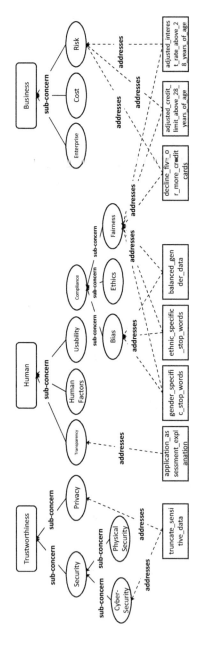

Figure 16.2   Representation of Company A use case using Approach 2, introducing new AI-related concerns

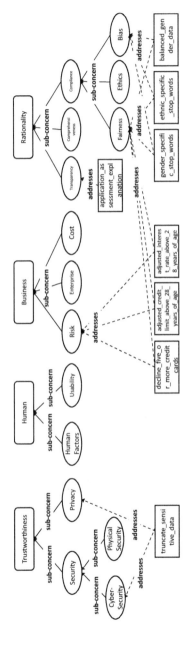

Figure 16.3   Representation of Company A use case with Approach 3, introduction of rationality hierarchy/aspect

The first approach, shown in Figure 16.1, assumes that Company A is satisfied with the set of concerns already present in the NIST CPS framework. The requirements discussed earlier can, thus, be formalized as NIST CPS framework requirements and linked to the concerns that provide the best fit. Notice that associating AI-related concepts to existing concerns may not always be straightforward for Company A. For example, of the available concerns, the best fit for the requirement "decline_five_or_more_active_credit_cards" might be the cost concern. However, one might argue that there is a subtle, yet important, difference between the notion of cost and risk, with which the requirement would be more naturally associated. Despite this slight potential lack of alignment – which might complicate the communication among stakeholders – this approach has the benefit of using the already well-understood existing concern tree without modification. Additionally, each requirement is associated with a single concern, thus simplifying the understanding and use of the diagram.

Figure 16.2 illustrates a second approach for the introduction of AI-related concepts in the concern tree. In this approach, dedicated concerns are added to the trees that represent these concepts and integrated into the existing branches of the concern tree. The new concerns, which in this notional example include transparency, fairness and bias, are shown by ovals with a green border. Introducing dedicated concerns may make it easier to map the requirements of the system to more suitable concerns. Requirements relevant to risk can be linked to the risk concern, those addressing biases are associated with the bias concern, and so on. Compared with the first approach, this may allow for an arguably more meaningful and accurate representation of the behavior of an AI-enabled system or business process and, consequently, more effective communication among stakeholders. On the other hand, this structure lacks an explicit characterization of the role of the AI component in the system or business process.

Figure 16.3 shows the third and final approach for introducing AI-related concepts in the concern tree. In this approach, we extend the concern tree by an entirely new branch on which the AI-related primitives are captured by possibly more fitting concerns rooted in a newly introduced rationality aspect. The idea here is that the new branch makes it possible to gather all AI-relevant concerns in a standard structure. In a similar way to the previous approach, requirements related to these primitives can easily be associated with concerns found in this branch. For example, the requirement "gender_ratio" addresses the bias concern, which is a part of the rationality hierarchy. This representation not only makes it explicit that the requirement addresses bias in the business process but also clearly indicates that the requirement ultimately affects how the AI component of the process makes decisions. This is not as evident in the representation obtained by the previous approaches: in the first approach, the distinct concept of bias is not embedded in a clearly articulated concern; in the second approach, a dedicated concern is present but is not explicitly grouped with the other AI-related concerns. In summary, introducing a separate rationality branch may make for a clearer and more comprehensive representation of the AI-relevant concepts. On the other hand, the introduction of the new branch causes an inevitable increase in the complexity of the concern tree.

CONCLUSION

AI is often critical to the success of business processes. Leveraging it, however, is not trivial. In this chapter, we argued that a major hurdle in the development, use, and maintenance of AI-enabled systems and business processes is communication, specifically the discussion of requirements among stakeholders with different backgrounds and goals.

We introduced the NIST CPS framework, discussed how it can be used in the context of AI-enabled systems and business processes, and advocated that the CPS framework can help overcome the challenges related to them. We introduced an illustrative use case that showcases the challenges stemming from the adoption of AI-enabled systems and business processes. Finally, we demonstrated how the CPS framework may be applied to that use case in order to capture the possible considerations made by stakeholders.

To demonstrate the flexibility of the NIST CPS framework, we showed three approaches for leveraging the NIST CPS framework to capture the complexities of AI-enabled systems and business processes. The approaches were presented in increasing order of the magnitude of the changes to the original structure and of the approaches' ability to clearly link stakeholders' requirements to the relevant elements of AI components.

The use case presented is also intended to highlight how, from the perspective of policy and practice, the NIST CPS framework can provide an effective way of guiding stakeholders through the development of best practices surrounding AI-enabled systems and business processes, a task that is often difficult because it involves diverse knowledge domains and goals.

ACKNOWLEDGEMENTS

The authors are deeply grateful to Kathleen Campbell Garwood and Virginia Miori for valuable discussions on topics related to this chapter. In addition, we thank Andrew Holmberg, Brandon Andrews, and Bob Shantz for their suggestions and comments on drafts of this chapter. Portions of this publication and research effort are made possible through the help and support of NIST via cooperative agreements 70NANB21H167 and 70NANB22H145. Son Tran acknowledges the partial support of the NSF grants 1914635, 1757207, and 1812628.

DISCLAIMER

Official contribution of the National Institute of Standards and Technology; not subject to copyright in the United States. Certain commercial products are identified in order to adequately specify the procedure; this does not imply endorsement or recommendation by NIST, nor does it imply that such products are necessarily the best available for the purpose. Portions of this publication and research effort are made possible through the help and support of NIST via cooperative agreements 70NANB21H167 and 70NANB22H145.

REFERENCES

Balduccini, M., Griffor, E., Huth, M., Vishik, C., Burns, M., & Wollman, D. (2018). Ontology-based reasoning about the trustworthiness of cyber-physical systems. *IET Journal of the IoT – 2018*, 2018, pp. 1–10. https://doi.org/10.1049/cp.2018.0012.

Bloomberg. (2019, November 10). *Apple co-founder says Goldman's Apple Card algorithm discriminates*. Bloomberg.com. Retrieved March 8, 2022, from https://www.bloomberg.com/news/articles/2019-11-10/apple-co-founder-says-goldman-s-apple-card-algo-discriminates?utm_medium=social&utm_source=twitter&utm_content=business&cmpid=socialflow-twitter-business&utm_campaign=socialflow-organic

Casey, K. (2020, November 19). *How to explain machine learning in plain English*. The Enterprisers Project. Retrieved March 8, 2022, from https://enterprisersproject.com/article/2019/7/machine-learning-explained-plain-english?page=1

CognitiveScale. (2019, September 19). *Using an AI trust index to unblock stalled machine learning & AI projects • Cognitivescale*. CognitiveScale. Retrieved April 15, 2022, from https://blog.cognitivescale.com/using-an-ai-trust-index-to-unblock-stalled-machine-learning-ai-projects

Dastin, J. (2018, October 10). *Amazon scraps secret AI recruiting tool that showed bias against women*. Reuters. https://www.reuters.com/article/us-amazon-com-jobs-automation-insight-idUSKCN1MK08G

Department of Financial Services. (2021, March 23). Press Release - March 23, 2021. *DFS issues findings on the Apple Card and its underwriter Goldman Sachs Bank*. Department of Financial Services. Retrieved March 8, 2022, from https://www.dfs.ny.gov/reports_and_publications/press_releases/pr202103231

Federal Trade Commission. (2007, May 2). *Slip showing? Federal law requires all businesses to truncate credit card information on receipts*. Federal Trade Commission. Retrieved April 15, 2022, from https://www.ftc.gov/tips-advice/business-center/guidance/slip-showing-federal-law-requires-all-businesses-truncate

Gallagher, W. (2020, August 20). *One year later, the Apple Card is a huge but controversial success*. AppleInsider. Retrieved March 8, 2022, from https://appleinsider.com/articles/20/08/20/one-year-later-the-apple-card-is-a-huge-but-controversial-success

Hall, P. (2020, March 19). *Explaining machine learning models to the business*. InfoWorld. Retrieved March 8, 2022, from https://www.infoworld.com/article/3533369/explaining-machine-learning-models-to-the-business.html

Laplante, P., Milojicic, D., Serebryakov, S., & Bennett, D. (2020, November). Artificial intelligence and critical systems: From hype to reality. *Computer*, *53*(11), 45–52. https://doi.org/10.1109/MC.2020.3006177

Muncke, J. (2021, October 24). *The business case for AI safety: Explainability*. Faculty. Retrieved March 8, 2022, from https://faculty.ai/blog/the-business-case-for-explainability/

NIST. (2022, January 11). *About NIST*. NIST. Retrieved April 15, 2022, from https://www.nist.gov/about-nist

NIST. (2017, June). *Framework for cyber-physical systems: Volume 1 - nist* (n.d.). Retrieved March 8, 2022, from https://nvlpubs.nist.gov/nistpubs/SpecialPublications/NIST.SP.1500-201.pdf

Radanliev, P., De Roure, D., Van Kleek, M. et al. (2020). Artificial intelligence in cyber physical systems. *AI & Soc*. https://doi.org/10.1007/s00146-020-01049-0

Reuters. (2019, November 11). *Goldman faces probe after entrepreneur claims gender bias in Apple Card algorithm*. VentureBeat. Retrieved March 8, 2022, from https://venturebeat .com/2019/11/11/goldman-faces-probe-after-entrepreneur-claims-gender-bias-in-apple -card-algorithm/

Turek, M. (n.d.). *Explainable Artificial Intelligence (XAI)*. DARPA RSS. Retrieved March 8, 2022, from https://www.darpa.mil/program/explainable-artificial-intelligence

van Es, K., Everts, D., & Muis, I. (2021). Gendered language and employment Web sites: How search algorithms can cause allocative harm. *First Monday, 26*(8). https://doi.org/10.5210 /fm.v26i8.11717

Vincent, J. (2019, November 11). *Apple's credit card is being investigated for discriminating against women*. The Verge. Retrieved March 8, 2022, from https://www.theverge.com /2019/11/11/20958953/apple-credit-card-gender-discrimination-algorithms-black-box -investigation

Wikimedia Foundation. (2022, January 25). *Business process*. Wikipedia. Retrieved March 8, 2022, from https://en.wikipedia.org/wiki/Business_process

17. The levels of automation and autonomy in the AI-augmented newsroom: toward a multi-level typology of computational journalism

Hannes Cools, Baldwin Van Gorp, and Michaël Opgenhaffen

INTRODUCTION

From the moment they started permeating the newsroom, computational journalistic tools have changed how and where news moves. The co-evolution of those tools and the technologies in artificial intelligence (AI) and generative AI have shaped future innovations in media industries and beyond (Cools, 2022). Since 2010, these technologies have begun to automate various work packages of news workers worldwide, as they helped them track, tell, distribute, and check a story (Manovich, 2013). In 2020 alone, news outlets such as *The Washington Post* and *The New York Times* have implemented tools capable of automating parts of election reporting and automated comment moderation. In the United Kingdom (UK), news outlets such as the BBC and *Radar* are experimenting with automated news production to boost local news (Wang, 2019). In China, news outlets such as *Xinhua* and *Caixin* use computational journalistic tools to automate financial and sports news production (Lindén et al., 2019).

Even before the term "computational journalism" was coined in 2006, theorizing those applications and journalistic advances has culminated in conceptualizations and definitions (Lindén, 2016). Terms such as "robot journalism" (Clerwall, 2014; Latar, 2015), "automated journalism" (Carlson, 2015; Napoli, 2014), "algorithmic journalism" (Diakopoulos, 2017; Dörr, 2016), "machine-written news" (Van Der Kaa & Krahmer, 2014) or "computational journalism" (Anderson, 2011; Coddington, 2015) dominate media and scientific discourse. Despite the emergence of some valuable research output and typologies (e.g., Coddington, 2015; Thurman, 2019b), the field still suffers from a theoretical framework in which computational journalism, automation, and autonomy are linked. This is especially pertinent for two reasons. First, these tools have started automating the work packages of human news workers and, as such, have the potential to affect journalists' autonomy. Second, technological advances such as AI and big data analysis have created a knowledge gap in the interaction between these tools and the human news worker both in the newsroom and academia. Therefore, and in order to advance our understanding of this chasm, this chapter proposes a typology that maps the various levels of automation that are present in the news ecosystem, specifically focusing on the interaction between the computational journalistic tool, on the one hand, the human news worker, on the other.

To define the various levels of automation and the degree of autonomy of the human news worker, this chapter will follow the pioneering works of Coddington (2015) and Thurman (2019a) and introduce the term computational journalism. Subsequently, the interrelation of technology, automation, and journalism will be explored in detail. Finally, the role of journalistic autonomy will be reviewed and placed in the maturing field of computational journalism.

According to Coddington (2015), Diakopoulos (2019), and Powers (2012), it is necessary that the levels of automation and the degree of autonomy seize the current and future computational journalistic tools that are placed within the four processes of news reporting, namely (1) news gathering, (2) news production, (3) news verification, and (4) news production and moderation. As such, this typology functions as a framework that can be used both by academic scholars and professional journalists to evaluate any computational or data-oriented project, instrument, or organization. It will provide an overview of how automation has the potential to affect journalistic autonomy. Based on the level of automation and the degree of journalistic autonomy, this typology can elucidate whether a human news worker will be open to using certain computational journalistic tools (CJTs). After the typology is determined, a research agenda is linked to the various levels of automation, focusing on the interaction and the degree of autonomy of the CJT, on the one hand, and the human news worker, on the other (Guzman & Lewis, 2020). As such, the typology and its research agenda will shed new light on the research of computational journalism that is currently automating various processes executed by human news workers in the digital news ecosystem.

LITERATURE REVIEW

Computational Journalism

Technology has been shaping journalism even before computer-assisted research and reporting (CAR(R)) and data-driven journalism (DDJ) were around. To name but a few: the introduction of typewriters, personal computers, and the introduction of the internet has brought considerable changes to the news ecosystem. These technological advances have laid the ground for what this chapter will call "computational journalistic tools" (CJTs).

Having reviewed the existing literature, and keeping Lindén (2016) in mind, we have to conclude that the most appropriate unifying concept is computational journalism (CJ), as it builds on CAR(R) and DDJ and encompasses the applications that are related to, and embedded in, the ever-evolving field of AI and its subcategory of generative AI. The term "computational journalism" was first coined in 2006 by

Irfan Essa when he organized the first course on the subject alongside Nicholas Diakopoulos at Georgia Tech (Thurman, 2019b). In the professional sphere, however, the terms "automated journalism" and "algorithmic journalism" have become more commonplace (Coddington, 2018). Here, computational journalism is seen as a more advanced form of CAR(R) and DDJ. CAR(R) and DDJ have been around for decades and paved the way for the later technological applications that shaped the current term of computational journalism. In this chapter, CAR(R) is defined as a technique for gathering and analyzing data to enhance investigative reporting, unlike data journalism, which pays attention to the way data are rooted in the journalistic workflow as a whole and how data are connected to public participation (Miller, 1988; Stray, 2011). CAR(R) and DDJ share both similarities (i.e., social sciences and quantitative forms of journalism) and differences (i.e., abstraction processes and public participation) (Coddington, 2015).

The term computational journalism was quickly introduced in the field of journalism, as were concepts including AI, automation, and computerization. Due to this rapid implementation, it led to numerous popular conceptualizations, sometimes referred to as "black boxes" (Diakopoulos, 2014; Coddington, 2015). As Lindén (2016) put it, robot and machine-written journalism are pseudo-conceptualizations calling forth an image in which robots write on computer keyboards.

To date, however, there is not enough consensus on the components that need to be included in the definition of computational journalism. Hamilton and Turner (2009) defined computational journalism as "forms of algorithmic, social scientific and mathematical processes and systems for the production of news" (p. 2). As this study reviews automation as an inherent part of computational journalism, it is paramount to define computational journalism as a term that automates news workers' workload. The element of automation is not included in the definition of Hamilton and Turner (2009), nor is it found in the definition of Pulimood, Shaw, and Lounsberry (2011): "[A] sophisticated approach to applying algorithms and principles from computer sciences and the social sciences to gather, evaluate, organize, and present news and information." In recent years, there has been growing consensus that automation is a critical element of computational journalism (Coddington, 2015; Thurman, 2019a). Based on the works of Coddington (2015) and Thurman (2019a) in computational journalism, this chapter wants to stress that automation is an inherent part of the field and will remain so in the foreseeable future. Coddington (2015) defined computational journalism as follows: "A term that is concerned with the application of the processes of abstraction and automation to information, implying a change in the way stories are discovered, presented, aggregated, monetised and archived" (p. 336). Thurman (2019a) defined computational journalism as: "The advanced application of computing, algorithms and automation to the gathering, evaluation, composition, presentation and distribution of news" (p. 1). As both definitions encompass automation, we define computational journalism as follows:

Computational journalism is an advanced application that helps to automate the news workers' gathering, production, verification, moderation, and distribution of news.

Technology, Automation, and Journalism

Automation, a leitmotif in the recent era of computational journalism, has often led to a tense relationship between technology, automation, and journalism. It has resulted in a field of study on its own (Lindén, 2017; Thurman, 2019b; Usher, 2014). However, according to Cools et al. (2022), how technology can play an active role in shaping newsroom innovations has been under-researched, and that is also the case for how it affects journalists' work. These tools have been a permanent fixture in the news ecosystem, even though they have led to the fear of job loss among news workers (Deuze, 2008; Lindén et al., 2019). As Frey and Osborne's (2017) study on the automation of jobs predicted, 45% of the US professions will be automated in the following decades. This evolution involves using computing power in the form of algorithms to address processes such as pattern recognition, data collection, and distillation. These processes are also used in newsrooms, leading to even more automation, which is currently still situated at the "lower forms of journalism" (Lindén et al., 2019). Furthermore, as Frey (2020) stated, because of the increasing need for technological aid, the COVID-19 pandemic is set to accelerate the automation of specific processes even more, implying that individual workloads will become automated. Apart from in the context of COVID-19, other scholars underlined that advances in technology could lead to the acceleration of certain levels of automation (Carlson, 2015; Clerwall, 2014; Lindén et al., 2019; Matsumoto et al., 2007; Napoli, 2014; Van Dalen, 2012).

Beckett's (2019) report on AI and journalism concluded that they would lead to new responsibilities and opportunities for human news workers. Studies by Lewis et al. (2019) and Lindén et al. (2019) have shown that journalists believe that CJTs will not completely take over their job (Graefe, 2016; Jung et al., 2017). However, it remains unclear which work packages will be automated by these tools. Powers (2012) highlighted how technology is interfering with journalism and named three main perceptions of how journalists perceive these interactions: "(1) as exemplars of continuity; (2) as threats to be subordinated; and (3) as possibilities for journalistic reinvention" (p. 26).

Apart from the perception, researchers conclude that a knowledge gap among journalists prevents them from realizing that CJTs can directly impact a whole range of their daily workload. This implies that CJTs will perform the routine tasks that are, today, executed by human news workers. Think of automated forms of news-gathering or a tool that automatically distributes articles on various platforms. This knowledge gap and the potential influence of CJTs on various news-reporting processes could lead to "automation anxiety" (Akst, 2013; Frey, 2019). Alternatively, as Zuboff (1988) writes, "everything that can be automated will be automated in the future," which could mean that this knowledge gap will create an even more tense relationship between human news workers, on the one hand, and CJTs, on the other (Boczkowski, 2005).

CJTs have already automated certain lower forms of workload in journalism, and they will continue to do so, both in the lower and higher forms of journalism. They can reconfigure journalism's core and be situated not only in the lower levels but also in the higher levels of automation. As technology is advancing at a rapid pace, CJTs are improving to fulfill more complex tasks that news workers formerly did. These CJTs will potentially create new stories with new angles based on a range of bigger datasets (Coddington, 2018; Thurman, 2019b). In short, these technological advancements can potentially change the essence of journalistic core values, including autonomy (Deuze, 2005, p. 449; Hanitzsch, 2011).

Computational Journalism and the Autonomy of News Workers

This chapter defines autonomy as the "freedom that a practitioner has in carrying out his or her occupational duties" (Reich & Hanitzsch, 2013; p. 135). As CJTs have permeated the newsroom, they have the potential to affect the freedom or autonomy of human news workers. As autonomy is described as a core value of journalism (Deuze, 2005; Hanitzsch, 2011), this reality could change the way autonomy is defined and embedded in the daily decision-making of the newsroom. It has to be reconsidered in what Splendore (2016) called: "the increasing intervention of machines." An augmented intervention could mean that the autonomy of human news workers will be redefined, as these tools are set to increasingly take charge of what Diakopoulos (2015) called "autonomous decision-making" (p. 400). This will be the case in the processes of (1) news gathering (gathering of information and data), (2) news production (production of text, video, audio, etc.), (3) news verification (verification and fact-checking of information and data), and (4) news distribution and moderation (distribution and moderation of information and data).

While many CJTs are still in nascent form and their success or failure is still uncertain, researchers underline the importance of newsrooms adopting a strategy on AI, automation, and CJTs (Beckett, 2019; Lindén et al., 2019). As news workers' relationship with CJTs is relatively novel, journalists will need to learn to "share autonomy," as Deuze (2005) calls it. Drawing on that development, there could be a moment when news workers have to deliberately outsource autonomy to non-human agents. This evolution could either enhance or trouble the relationship and interaction between CJTs and news workers (Milosavljević & Vobič, 2019).

TYPOLOGY

Typologies of Computational Journalism

Over the past few years, at least four typologies have been published that fit the field of computational journalism. The most influential would be the one proposed by Coddington (2015) in which he reviewed the similarities and differences between (a) computer-assisted reporting, (b) data journalism, and (c) computational journalism. He uses four dimensions to analyze these three terms: a closed and professional vs. an open and networked orientation, transparency vs. opacity, epistemological orientations toward targeted sampling vs. big data, and an active vs. a passive vision of the public. As Anderson (2013) stated, the three terms can be seen as progressions of one another, but the terms also overlap (see "Literature Review").

Splendore (2016) put forward a second typology that built on Coddington's, but he focused on the terms (a) data journalism, (b) computational journalism, and (c) algorithmic journalism. Some of the dimensions proposed in the typology by Coddington (2015) were also edited as he differentiated in the open vs. closed orientation between manual and automated access to data. Furthermore, he defined data journalism as a term that was more distant than computational and algorithmic journalism. He stated that computational journalism and algorithmic journalism "go beyond the mere use of data" (Splendore, 2016, p. 345).

A third typology was published by Usher (2016) in which she determined a theoretical framework that is useful for analyzing the backgrounds and orientations of the individual actors who work with interactive journalism. She differentiates between various journalistic roles such as "hacker journalists," "programmer journalists," "interactive journalists," and "data journalists." She concludes that the last group of journalists are the ones most strongly connected to traditional journalism with the help of computer-assisted reporting. In other words, this is a typology focused on the various roles in the newsroom in relation to interactive journalism.

Guzman and Lewis (2020) put forward a fourth typology, in which context he evaluates data journalism courses to offer guidance to educators and scholars. The typology conceptualizes data journalism as a form of pattern recognition and uses three stages of data journalism: (a) data acquisition and cleaning, (b) pattern detection, and (c) data representation. The proposed typology is focused on the specifics of data journalism and is intended for educational ends.

Although all four typologies are useful and serve specific purposes, they do not sufficiently explain the interaction between the CJT and the human news worker. As these tools permeate the newsroom and start to inherently automate news workers' tasks, it is valuable to determine a typology in which the various levels of automation are embedded and the degree of autonomy is linked to the tool–human interaction. The element of autonomy is crucial in this typology, as it determines whether the human or the CJT is (partly) in charge. This element has not been adequately addressed in the earlier typologies, as they focus more on computational journalism's features and characteristics. To a broader extent, scholars and professional journalists can use the proposed typology to evaluate any computational or data-oriented project, tool, or organization, as it sheds light on the willingness of a human news worker to use a certain CJT.

Toward a New Typology of Computational Journalism

A typology is a scheme that can "simplify complex phenomena for didactic, organizational and communicative purposes" (Guest, 2012, p. 141), and it can enhance conceptual clarity. The proposed typology mirrors the latest technological developments and is affiliated with computational journalism's theoretical complexities.

This typology's discerning feature will be the concept of automation and autonomy, as this chapter wants to shed light on the interaction between the human news worker and the CJT. The determination of the typology departs from a taxonomy that defines the various levels of automation. This taxonomy is specifically chosen because of its abstract character and direct interaction between humans and the CJTs. In this light, it reviews the levels of automation, ranging from "manual" to "full automation support" in a digital news ecosystem. Here, automation's level refers to the level of task planning, a performance interaction maintained between a human news worker and a CJT in controlling a complex system (Endsley & Kaber, 1999, p. 445). A degree of autonomy is thereby built into the typology (see Table 17.1).

First, this chapter builds on the works of Sheridan and Verplank (1978) and Save et al. (2012), who developed a ten-level typology of automation for computer systems. Even today, this typology is frequently cited and widely embedded in academia, as Sheridan and Verplank made general distinctions ranging from low to high-level forms of automation within four categories of information flow processes: (1) information acquisition, (2) information analysis, (3) information verification, and (4) decision and action selection. The four functions provide an initial categorization for the types of tasks in which automation supports humans, such as a computer program filtering information out of a database. In other words, within these categories, Sheridan and Verplank (1978) developed the first scale of ten levels of automation, ranging from (1) "The computer offers no assistance, a human must take all decisions and actions" and (2) "The computer offers a complete set of decision/action alternatives," right through to (10) "The computer decides everything, acts autonomously, ignores the human" (Sheridan & Verplank, 1978). The ten-scale typology represents

Table 17.1   Typology of computational journalistic tools

Levels of automation	Description	Degree of autonomy
0. Manual: no external support of a tool	The news worker uses no automation tools at all, and makes all decisions and actions	High autonomy for human
1. Low-level automation support: tool shows the list of data	The news worker selects data from tool	Autonomy for human is higher than autonomy for tool
2. Medium-level automation support: tool classifies the list of data	The news worker verifies the classification	Autonomy for tool is slightly higher than autonomy for human
3. High-level automation support: tool suggests a selection of the classification of the list	The news worker supervises the classification of the tool	Autonomy for tool is increasingly higher than autonomy for human
4. Full automation support: tool controls classification of the list	The news worker follows the decision of the tool	Higher autonomy for tool

a continuum of levels between manual level to full automation in which the computer supports the human "autonomously."

Second, this chapter readapted the distinctions made by Sheridan and Verplank to fit the four stages of news reporting involving computational journalism: news gathering, production, verification, distribution, and moderation. These categories were partly based on an extensive research study by the World Economic Forum that reviewed the impact of computational journalism and AI on the news ecosystem and the works of Thurman (2019a, 2019b). In Table 17.1, the overall automation levels are clustered over the various news-reporting stages, as these processes entail the same automation processes on a more abstract level. In other words, within news report-ing processes, the same sort of tasks are present that will be executed by either the human, the tool, or both.

Third, the degree of autonomy was added in the right column (see Table 17.1), i.e., the level at which human intervention is still possible and goes hand in hand with the different automation levels (see "Literature Review"). The degree of autonomy is embedded in the typology, as it takes a human-oriented approach to automation included in computational journalism. This degree of autonomy is also linked to McLuhan's (1964) works. It is rooted in the theory of technological determinism, a reductionist theory that assumes that a society's technology determines the develop-ment of its social structure. Here, the tool used to communicate influences the mind of the receiver (Lewis et al., 2019; McLuhan, 1964). In other words, automation and autonomy are not seen as interwoven concepts but merely as independent variables. If the level of automation is high, that does not mean that the degree of autonomy is high for the CJT and vice versa. Depending on the tool used or researched, this essay asserts that technology is not static and that the relationship between humans and technology is not fixed to the levels of autonomy (Lewis, 2019). From here on in, these levels seem to gradually adopt a new kind of journalistic autonomy, giving the news worker a new set of tasks that are more focused on data-oriented tasks, compu-tational thinking, and AI tools.

A Multi-level Typology of Computational Journalism

Table 17.1 proposes five levels of automation, starting from the standard "Level 0," which corresponds to manual job completion, and moving on to "Level 4 or "full automation support," which corresponds to a tool that completes the job without human intervention. Here, the various levels of automation will be explained. In addition, practical examples will be given to illustrate each level of automation.

The first automation level, "0," is based on the principle that humans perform a task with "primitive" external support, like a basic computer program (Microsoft Word) which is not automated as such. A news worker needs to perform all the actions by him/herself (Level 0). Here, the autonomy of the human is high, and remains the sole actor.

From Level 1 onward, the emergence of "real" automation is observed, starting from low-level automation for news verification. The CJT shows, for example, a list of data that could be verified, such as databases of tax records or data from government organizations. Here, the news worker selects data from a tool according to the degree of autonomy, which is higher for the human than for the tool.

In the case of medium-level automation, a CJT would, therefore, classify a list of data that still required a news check. This could be either in larger datasets or verifiable information with other information or data. At this level of automation, the degree of autonomy for the tool is slightly higher than that for humans, as tools have the autonomy to verify the data or information automatically.

At this level, a tool that is situated on the high level of automation makes a selection of the classification of the list of data; in this case, the human only monitors part of the process, which is called "human curation," as the actual verification is done by the tool. In this case, the degree of autonomy for the tool is increasingly higher than the human's autonomy. In other words, the tool executes the verification process and, therefore, exceeds human autonomy.

At the last and highest level, full automation for news verification is in place. The tool controls the classification of the list; human intervention is still possible at this point. Here, the human follows the tool's decision that was made by verifying the classification of the list of data or information. The degree of the tool's autonomy is high compared to human autonomy as the tool takes all actions and decisions. In other words, humans follow those decisions and have limited opportunities to change them.

After determining the typology, this chapter sets out two preliminary rules. First, an automated system cannot have only one "total" level of automation. In other words, a CJT can only be categorized within a specific level of automation within one process because a tool cannot be categorized in both low-level and high-level automation simultaneously. Second, a CJT supports more than one process, each with a different level of automation. For example, a CJT, such as the "quakebot" – a tool the *Los Angeles Times* uses that automatically writes an article during an earthquake – could be consigned to various processes. On the one hand, it will extract information from a database (low-level automation support in newsgathering); on the other hand, it will automatically write an article based on that information (medium-level automation support for news production).

In addition, this essay stresses that the categorization of various levels of automation simplifies the many components of human information processing that may overlap various processes in the newsroom. Apart from that, it is useful to distinguish between the subtleties of the tool's features to determine how a specific automated system supports humans, as the typology links a level of autonomy to a level of automation when new tools are implemented in the newsroom. As Lindén (2016) mentioned, journalists remain involved in the use of automation in the news-reporting process and within those four processes, namely (1) news gathering, (2) news production, (3) news verification, and (4) news production and moderation. These four processes are also mirrored in the typology as the human-centered approach of automation comes into play.

RESEARCH AGENDA

Based on the typology above, a research agenda is defined to give researchers an overview of which levels of automation deserve more attention, situated within the different news-reporting processes. A closer empirical examination is required of a broader range of tools in the field of computational journalism that correspond with different automation levels. Future research will, thus, advance our understanding of the layered and complicated interaction between a human news worker and CJTs regarding the degree of autonomy.

Newsgathering

In the past, research within the process of news gathering was mainly focused on how data were extracted in the lower levels of automation (Coddington, 2015; Gutsche & Hess, 2018; Peters, 2012). In the future, researchers could elaborate more on how CJTs extract and acquire these data at medium- and high-level automation and the ways this execution will affect the autonomy of news workers. As news organizations have started using CJTs and machine-learning techniques to automate thousands of stories, this could lead to new ethical and moral dilemmas, given that news workers' autonomy is affected by a tool making decisions (Table 17.1).

In this respect, scholars could focus on what actor is accountable when a CJT is implemented. After all, technology is increasingly capable of sifting faster through online data, like Tweetdeck is doing. In 2019, BBC News Labs used the Juicer data extraction tool, a form of low-level automation in the newsgathering category, to develop new leads for news stories. Other platforms such as Twitter, Facebook, and Instagram can break the news faster and are increasingly better at finding deeper insights, as they use tools that scan datasets faster on trends and outliers (Burgess & Hurcombe, 2019; Lokot & Diakopoulos, 2019). Academic research could focus on the more complex forms of data extraction and entity extraction on the higher levels of automation, as nowadays, these tools are still considered "black boxes." For example, how could these data extraction tools possibly affect the workload of news workers? By conducting such an inquiry, the "enigma" of data extraction, acquisition, and analysis would be demystified, thereby bridging the gap between journalism studies, on the one hand, and computer sciences, on the other.

News Production

Future research into the news production phase could focus on news credibility and journalistic autonomy and the perception of automated news production at higher automation levels in computational journalism.

First, as these CJTs are becoming more eloquent and more capable of self-learning and self-judgment in news production, this will result in new forms of automated news production and new forms of automation (like a more advanced application of election reporting) emerging. In addition, this ever-evolving trend could disrupt a news ecosystem's dynamics, as these tools could be using sources other than the ones used by human news workers, possibly affecting news credibility (Wu et al., 2018). In light of human-centered automation, these tools and the newly emerging forms of news production will likely result in new workloads and require news workers to be retrained. Consider, for example, a CJT that uses speech-to-text software or machine translation and automatic text generation out of data like Radar is doing. Building on Graefe's (2018) and Van der Kaa's (2014) works, future studies would benefit from research on the possible friction between new forms of news production and news credibility.

Second, to advance research within news production, scholars could review the perception and the possible differences in content between human-written news production, on the one hand, and automated news production, on the other. Some studies, like Clerwall's, have found no easy boundary between them, but the number of interviewees ($N = 44$) he used was somewhat limited (Clerwall, 2014; Graefe et al., 2018). Further, research could focus on perceptions regarding implementing new, more complex computational journalistic news production tools that possibly disrupt the workloads of journalists, editors, and members of the information technology (IT) department.

News Verification

Verification is an essential part of news reporting, as it also includes fact-checking claims, which are now gaining importance in the context of fake news and disinformation in society.

First, future research could focus on ways those tools identify aberrations in data flows. In other words, what will be the techniques for determining the veracity of the ever-growing datasets, images, and videos, bearing in mind that these are becoming increasingly complex (manipulated images, deep fakes, data biases)? As those tools are already present in all the levels of automation, it could be useful to verify the differences in features of the various tools and how they augment news products. Live & Trends from Full Fact, situated in high-level automation, is a text verification tool that focuses more on breaking down quote by quote to verify text manipulation.

Second, the falsification of data done by CJTs in relation to human performance could benefit from further research. For example, how do CJTs differ, or even possibly surpass human verification processes, such as source verification, and how does that affect their autonomy? One possible direction could be to research how automatic detection systems can label claims in texts using algorithms and how they can debunk them automatically (Petrovic, 2013). A tool called Claimbuster (low-level automation support) from Knight Center analyzes each sentence in the texts and assigns a score from 0 to 1 to predict the likelihood that it is a significant claim that a news worker would want to examine in a published article (Hassan et al., 2015). To advance research in news verification, many more datasets need to be made open source (Lowrey et al., 2019). By doing this, the ever-present nature of datasets and developments in CJTs could lead to new forms of immersive journalism. Scholars could investigate how journalism benefits from those innovations and the possible impact of those tools on human-driven verification processes.

News Distribution and Moderation

Research into the low-level forms of news distribution and moderation support has been conducted, whereas the higher levels of automation still need to be explored (Beutel et al., 2013; Chavoshi et al., 2016; Ferrara et al., 2016; Hassan, 2015).

First, future research into this news-reporting process could focus on the emergence of personal automated news distribution and the possibilities and limitations of those tools. Algorithms not only track what audiences like or read on the internet, but they can also perform more complex and sophisticated tasks, such as measuring and registering what readers are posting, where they move from, and where they go next (Michalski, 2016). How could metrics-driven tools capable of tracking audience behavior (for example, Chartbeat and SmartOcto) contribute to automated news distribution, thereby making journalism more tailored to the individual reader? How could metrics of what you watch and read that are tracked by these tools be used for subscription purposes? *The New York Times*, BuzzFeed, and Mashable use algorithms to distribute specific articles to platforms such as Twitter and Facebook. In doing so, they are automating various distribution tasks on a larger scale, which has already been researched (Albeanu, 2015; Nguyen & Kelleher, 2015; Wang, 2015).

Second, scholars could focus on the automated moderation of comments and the actants involved with automatic publication systems on websites and social media (Wu et al., 2018). Scholars could zoom in on the various actants and parameters working on the automated moderation of comments systems and their judgments. These judgments, ranging from manual to full automation, could presumably determine who comments on what kind of information and through which delivery modes (Lewis & Westlund, 2014; Thurman, 2019b).

CONCLUSION

In 2020, CJTs have drastically changed the news-reporting process, particularly since the advent of self-learning systems such as algorithms. With the typology and research agenda in mind, this chapter proposes three issues for news workers and journalism scholars: theoretical, implementation, and knowledge issues. First, many definitions of automation in the newsroom are found in academic literature, along with a plethora of indistinct terms. "Robot journalism," "machine-written news," and other terms dominate the field but have created a mystification within journalism, computer science, and statistics. Therefore, it remains paramount that automation is embedded in the theoretical framework of computational journalism, as there are also so-called manual levels at which there is no automation. The typology is not intended as a definitive theoretical framework of computational journalism. However, it can be used by scholars and professional journalists to evaluate any computational or data-oriented project, instrument, or organization.

Second, this chapter recognizes the so-called "implementation issue" in that CJTs situated on the highest level of automation are still not implemented. Although CJTs have been implemented in newsrooms and have been meticulously designed to be accurate, precise, perfect, and able to work 24 hours a day, there is still a lot to be done in the higher levels of automation, both on a theoretical and on a practical level (Lewis, 2019; Lindén, 2016). While many of these tools and applications have not been around for that long, they are slowly revealing the future of computational journalistic practices as they also point to the direction of the technological evolution of artificial intelligence. Keeping in mind the implementation issue, further research on computational journalism should advance our understanding of computational journalism and automation in the newsroom, especially at higher automation levels.

Third, with the newness of computational journalism, little is still known about its possibilities and limitations. This chapter underscores that education plays a vital role in this, both within academia and professional journalism. A course on computational journalism is recommended in journalism education, as this could provide tools for and insights into machine learning, algorithmic transparency, accountability, and other computational journalistic skills, including computational thinking. There is also a challenge for newsrooms. In 2021, *The New York Times* trained 60 journalists with data journalism skills in using computational skills, which means that there will be a shift in the form of a so-called mathematization in the newsroom, whereby data will become gradually more important. It should no longer be surprising that an algorithm will write a complex and layered story based on different sources. In academia, master programs in AI and computational journalism labs are given that hinge on and are involved in the transfer of domain expertise between journalists and computation specialists (Diakopoulos, 2019; Graefe, 2016; Wing, 2019). In recent academic literature, there have been suggestions that computational journalism contains biases and limitations because of poor data quality (Cools, 2022). Nonetheless, some news workers still actively resist metrics, and some scholars continue to have concerns, so this shift is by no means universal. In conclusion, moving research forward will need to give due consideration to the theoretical, implementation, and knowledge issues, as technology and CJTs are ever evolving.

Overall, the future of automation in the newsroom is primarily instrumental in the decomposition, or deconstruction, of the various workloads that journalists currently face (Lindén, 2018). As Graefe (2016) put it, journalists are best advised to focus on tasks that algorithms cannot (yet) perform. This means breaking down journalistic work into its actual information artifacts and processes to analyze what can and cannot be automated. Enormous challenges face journalistic research at the crossroads with big data, such as the shift in journalistic roles before, during, and after the gathering of data, ethical and legal challenges in news production, or questions about new intermediaries in journalism as the dependence on data increases (Dörr, 2016; Thurman, 2019b). Technology is not static, and the relationship between humans and technology is not fixed in terms of the levels of automation and terms of autonomy. In other words, if the level of automation is high, it does not necessarily mean that the degree of autonomy is high for the CJT and vice versa. Technology influences people, but humans also shape technology. Journalism and technology will co-evolve, and our interactions with these tools are subject to a dynamic negotiation between the CJT and the news worker.

REFERENCES

Akst, D. (2013). Automation anxiety. *The Wilson Quarterly, 37*(3), 65.

Albeanu, C. (2015). Inside velocity: Mashable's predictive social analytics tool. *Journalism .co.uk.*

Anderson, C. W. (2011). Notes towards an analysis of computational journalism. *SSRN Electronic Journal*, 1, 1–22.

Anderson, C. W. (2013). Towards a sociology of computational and algorithmic journalism. *New Media & Society*, 15(7), 1005–1021.

Beckett, C. (2019). New powers, new responsibilities: A global survey of journalism and artificial intelligence. *Polis, London school of economics and political science.* https://blogs.lse.ac.uk/polis/2019/11/18/new-powers-new-responsibilities

Boczkowski, P. J. (2005). *Digitizing the news: Innovation in online newspapers.* MIT Press.

Burgess, J., & Hurcombe, E. (2019). Digital journalism as symptom, response, and agent of change in the platformed media environment. *Digital Journalism*, 7(3), 359–367.

Carlson, M. (2015). The robotic reporter: Automated journalism and the redefinition of labor, compositional forms, and journalistic authority. *Digital Journalism*, 3(3), 416–431.

Chavoshi, N., Hamooni, H., & Mueen, A. (2016). Identifying correlated bots in Twitter. In *International conference on social informatics* (pp. 14–21). Springer.

Clerwall, C. (2014). Enter the robot journalist: Users' perceptions of automated content. *Journalism Practice*, 8(5), 519–531.

Coddington, M. (2015). Clarifying journalism's quantitative turn. A typology for evaluating data journalism, computational journalism, and computer-assisted reporting. *Digital Journalism*, 3(3), 331–348.

Coddington, M. (2018). Seeing through the user's eyes: the role of journalists' audience perceptions in their use of technology. *Electronic News*, 12(4), 235–250.

Cools, H. (2022). How algorithms are augmenting the journalistic institution: In search of evidence from newsrooms and its innovation labs. Doctoral Dissertation, KU Leuven.

Cools, H., Van Gorp, B., & Opgenhaffen, M. (2022). New organizations, different journalistic roles, and innovative projects: How second-generation newsroom innovation labs are changing the news ecosystem. *Journalism Practice*, 4(3), 1–16.

Deuze, M., & Witschge, T. (2018). Beyond journalism: Theorizing the transformation of journalism. *Journalism*, 19(2), 165–181.

Diakopoulos, N. (2014). Algorithmic accountability: Journalistic investigation of computational power structures. *Digital Journalism*, 3(3), 398–415.

Diakopoulos, N. (2019). *Automating the news: How algorithms are rewriting the media.* Harvard University Press.

Diakopoulos, N., & Koliska, M. (2017). Algorithmic transparency in the news media. *Digital Journalism*, 5(7), 809–828.

Dierickx, L. (2019). Why news automation fails. Presented at the Computation + Journalism Symposium, February 2019, Miami, FL.

Dörr, K. N. (2016). Mapping the field of algorithmic journalism. *Digital Journalism*, 4(6), 700–722.

Endsley, M.R. & Kaber, D.B. (1999). Level of automation effects on performance, situation awareness and workload in a dynamic control task. *Ergonomics*, 42, 462–492.

Ferrara, E., Varol, O., Davis, C., Menczer, F., & Flammini, A. (2016). The rise of social bots. *Communications of the ACM*, 59(7), 96–104.

Frey, C. B. (2019). *The technology trap: Capital, labor, and power in the age of automation*. Princeton University Press.

Frey, C. B. (2020). Covid 19 will only increase automation anxiety. *Financial Times*, April, 12. https://www.ft.com/content/817228a2-82e1-11ea-b6e9-a94cffd1d9bf.

Frey, C. B., & Osborne, M. A. (2017). The future of employment: How susceptible are jobs to computerisation? *Technological Forecasting and Social Change*, 114, 254–280.

Graefe, A. (2016). *Guide to automated journalism*. Tow Center for Digital Journalism, Columbia University. http://towcenter.org/research/guideto-

Guest, G. (2013). Describing mixed methods research: An alternative to typologies. *Journal of mixed methods research*, 7(2), 141–151.

Guzman, A. L., & Lewis, S. C. (2020). Artificial intelligence and communication: A Human Machine Communication research agenda. *New Media & Society*, 22(1), 70–86.

Hamilton, J. T., & Turner, F. (2009). Computational journalism. *Communications of the ACM*, 54(10), 66–71.

Hanitzsch, T. (2011). Populist disseminators, detached watchdogs, critical change agents and opportunist facilitators: Professional milieus, the journalistic field and autonomy in 18 countries. *International Communication Gazette*, 73(6), 477–494.

Hassan, N., Adair, B., Hamilton, J. T., Li, C., Tremayne, M., Yang, J., & Yu, C. (2015). The quest to automate factchecking. In *Proceedings of the 2015 computation+journalism symposium*.

Jung, J., Song, H., Kim, Y., Im, H., & Oh, S. (2017). Intrusion of software robots into journalism: The public's and journalists' perceptions of news written by algorithms and human journalists. *Computers in Human Behavior*, 71, 291–298.

Latar, N. L. (2015). The robot journalist in the age of social physics: The end of human journalism? In G. Einav (Ed.), *The economics of information, communication, and entertainment. The impacts of digital technology in the 21st century* (pp. 65–80). Springer.

Lewis, S. C., & Westlund, O. (2014). Big data and journalism: Epistemology, expertise, economics, and ethics. *Digital Journalism*, 3(3), 447–466.

Lewis, S. C. Andrea L. G., & Schmidt, T. R. (2019). Automation, journalism, and human-machine communication: Rethinking roles and relationships of humans and machines in news. *Digital Journalism*, 2(5), 1–19.

Lindén, C. (2016). Decades of automation in the newsroom. *Digital Journalism*, 5(2), 123–140.

Lindén, C. (Ed.), Tuulonen, H. E. (Ed.), Bäck, A., Diakopoulos, N., Granroth-Wilding, M., Haapanen, L., … Toivonen, H. (2019). News Automation: The rewards, risks and realities of 'machine journalism'. World Association of Newspapers and News Publishers, *WAN-IFRA*.

Lokot, T., & N. Diakopoulos. (2016). News bots: Automating news and information dissemination on Twitter. *Digital Journalism*, 4(6), 682–699.

Lowrey, W., Broussard, R., & Sherrill, L. A. (2019). Data journalism and black-boxed data sets. *Newspaper Research Journal*, 40(1), 69–82.

Manovich, L. (2013). *Software takes command*. Bloomsbury.

Matsumoto, R., Nakayama, H., Harada, T., & Kuniyoshi, Y. (2007, October). Journalist robot: Robot system making news articles from real world. In *2007 IEEE/RSJ International Conference on Intelligent Robots and Systems* (pp. 1234–1241). IEEE.

Miller, T. (1988). The Data-base revolution. *Columbia Journalism Review*, 27(3), 35–38.

Milosavljević, M., & Vobič, I. (2019). Human still in the loop: editors reconsider the ideals of professional journalism through automation. *Digital Journalism*, 7(8), 1098–1116.

Napoli, P. M. (2014). Automated media: An institutional theory perspective on algorithmic media production and consumption. *Communication Theory*, 24(3), 340–360.

Nguyen, D., & A. Kelleher. (2015). Introducing pound: Process for optimizing and understanding network diffusion. *BuzzFeed Tech Blog.* http://www.buzzfeed.com/daozers/ introducing-pound-process-for-optimizing-and- understanding

Petrović, S., & Matthews, D. (2013, August). Unsupervised joke generation from big data. In *Proceedings of the 51st annual meeting of the association for computational linguistics (Volume 2: Short papers)* (pp. 228–232).

Pulimood, S. M., Shaw, D., & Lounsberry, E. (2011, March). Gumshoe: A model for undergraduate computational journalism education. In *Proceedings of the 42nd ACM technical symposium on computer science education* (pp. 529–534).

Reich, Z., & Hanitzsch, T. (2013). Determinants of journalists' professional autonomy: Individual and national level factors matter more than organizational ones. *Mass Communication and Society, 16*(1), 133–156.

Save, L., Feuerberg, B., & Avia, E. (2012). Designing human-automation interaction: a new level of automation taxonomy. *Proc. Human Factors of Systems and Technology, 2012.*

Sheridan, T. B., & Verplank, W. (1978). Human and computer control of undersea teleoperators. *Man-machine systems laboratory*, Department of Mechanical Engineering, MIT.

Splendore, S. (2016). Quantitatively oriented forms of journalism and their epistemology. *Sociology Compass, 10*(5), 343–352.

Stavelin, E. (2013). *Computational journalism: When journalism meets programming.* University of Bergen.

Stray, J. (2011, January 31). A computational journalism reading list. http://jonathanstray.com /a-computational-journalism-reading-list

Thurman, N. (2019a). Computational journalism. In K. Wahl-Jorgensen & T. Hanitzsch (Eds.), *The handbook of journalism studies* (pp. 180–195). Routledge.

Thurman, N. (2019b). Algorithms, automation, and news. *Digital Journalism, 7*(8), 980–992.

Usher, N. (2016). *Interactive journalism: Hackers, data, and code.* University of Illinois Press.

Van Dalen, A. (2012). The algorithms behind the headlines. How machine-written news redefines the core skills of human journalists. *Journalism Practice, 6*(5–6), 648–658.

Van der Kaa, H., & E. Krahmer. (2014). Journalist versus news consumer: The perceived credibility of machine written news. *Research Paper presented at the 2014 Computation + Journalism Symposium*, Columbia University.

Wang, S. (2019). The New York Times built a slack bot to help decide which stories to post to social media. *NiemanLab.* http://www.niemanlab.org/2015/08/the-new-york-times-built-a -slack-bot-to-help- decide-which-stories-to-post-to-social-media/

Westlund, O., & Lewis, S. C. (2014). Agents of media innovations: Actors, actants, and audiences. *Journal of Media Innovations, 1*(2), 10–35.

Wing, J. M. (2011). *Computational thinking.* Carnegie Mellon University.

Wu, S., Tandoc Jr., E. C., & Salmon, C. T. (2019). When journalism and automation intersect: Assessing the influence of the technological field on contemporary newsrooms. *Journalism Practice*, 1–17.

Zuboff, S. (1988). *In the age of the smart machine.* Basic Book.

18. AI as communicative other: critical relationality in human–AI communication

Marco Dehnert

Artificial intelligence (AI) is a buzzword that brings up much controversy in academic and public conversations, often clouded by vague conceptualizations of the term and its properties, not least its implications on social life. Given that even academic endeavors into AI are often at least informed by science-fiction narratives (Jordan et al., 2018), conceptualizations of AI technologies and our relationships with them include variegated ideas. With the increased availability of natural language processing, voice recognition, and output and the growing incorporation of AI into physical technologies such as social robots, communication between humans and AI allows us to interact and relate with AI technologies. But the question is: what do we mean when we say that humans relate to and with AI communicators? And what are the implications of human–AI relationality?

In this chapter, I explore how AI surfaces as a communicative other in human–AI relations, drawing on both empirical and ethical human–machine communication (HMC) and AI-mediated communication (AI-MC) perspectives. In doing so, I review conceptualizations of communicative AI and recent work on human–AI communication (HAIC). Following Gunkel (2020) and Bory et al. (2021), I first argue for the centrality of communication in understanding and defining AI in general and as communicative other. I then turn to critical/cultural approaches that interrogate HAIC and communicative AI as other, including the social-relational turn, more-than-human perspectives, and queer approaches to relationality. I close the chapter with future directions.

DEFINING AI: CENTERING COMMUNICATION

Definitions of AI vary, and scholars in many disciplines struggle with making sense of this term, given often ambiguous understandings of intelligence (see Gunkel, 2020; Monett et al., 2020). Often understood as a "learning algorithm used to approximate some form of intelligence operating within computing machines" (Ninness & Ninness, 2020, p. 100), AI technologies can be applied in a variety of systems and contexts, reaching from recommender systems on dating or streaming platforms to face recognition and automated driving. What sets AI apart from less "intelligent" algorithmic systems are machine learning capabilities and artificial neural networks that come with the capability to improve and advance as time progresses, typically due to an increased number of data points (Russell & Norvig, 2021). Ultimately, current AI systems are designed to accomplish "very specific computational tasks much faster and more accurately than humans" (Ninness & Ninness, 2020, p. 102). As such, ideas – and related anxieties – regarding "superintelligent" machines or general AI technologies are not reflected in current AI systems, although they are prevalent in science-fiction narratives and the public imaginary (Jordan et al., 2018; Liang & Lee, 2017; Lobera et al., 2020).

Making sense of the multitude of AI technologies, systems, and capabilities can be overwhelming. Thus, and following Dehnert and Mongeau's (2022) approach, I find the European Commission's AI definition to be a helpful resource that provides a summary of AI systems:

> Artificial intelligence (AI) systems are software (and possibly also hardware) systems designed by humans that, given a complex goal, act in the physical or digital dimension by perceiving their environment through data acquisition, interpreting the collected structured or unstructured data, reasoning on the knowledge, or processing the information, derived from this data and deciding the best action(s) to take to achieve a given goal. AI systems can either use symbolic rules or learn a numeric model, and they can also adapt their behaviour by analysing how the environment is affected by their previous actions. (EU AI HLEG, 2019, p. 6)

Historical reviews of the development and origins of AI abound (e.g., Jansen, 2022). Recently, scholars have argued for the centrality of communication for both the history of AI and its conceptualization (Bory et al., 2021; Gunkel, 2020). That is, AI has been a communication science since its inception, given that machine intelligence can only be attained through communication as its defining condition (Gunkel, 2020), implying Alan Turing's famous "imitation game" might be better labeled a "communication game" (Natale, 2021). Thus, communication scholars are uniquely positioned to give insight into the workings of AI technologies and how humans relate to them. This is especially crucial as we are no longer confined to communicating *about* AI but also encounter communication *of, by,* and *with* AI.

To make sense of this reality of interacting and communicating with AI technologies, communication scholars approach human–technology interactions from various perspectives. Computer-mediated communication (CMC) is communication between two or more humans that is mediated by a computer (e.g., video conferencing, texting). Here, the technology serves primarily as a channel. Although CMC need not include AI technologies, it can incorporate them in several ways. Scholars have proposed to refer to such a process as AI-mediated communication (AI-MC), or messages that are "*modified, augmented,* or even *generated* by a computational agent to achieve communication goals" (Hancock et al., 2020, p. 90, emphasis in original). Examples of AI-MC include technologies such as "smart replies" or autofill in email or text messages. AI-MC typically involves two or more human communicators, although AI may impact their communication.

In cases in which a second human communicator is absent, scholars have introduced the term human–machine communication (HMC) to refer to "the creation of meaning among humans and machines" (Guzman, 2018, p. 1). Although the intentionally broad term *machine* refers to various technologies, including AI- and non-AI-entities, HMC perspectives often focus on communicative AI in AI contexts (Guzman & Lewis, 2020; Hepp et al., 2023). "[D]esigned to function *as* communicators" (Lewis et al., 2019, p. 673, emphasis in original), communicative AI can engage in more or less sophisticated conversation with human users, including voice recognition, natural language processing, natural language understanding, and other capabilities. Common examples – often focused on in HMC research due to their comparatively widespread availability – include intelligent assistants (Shaikh, 2023) such as Amazon's Alexa or Apple's Siri, as well as AI-enabled chatbots or social robots.

A long line of research has demonstrated that humans characterize communicative technologies – AI-enabled and not – as social actors, which has been labeled the computers are social actors (CASA) paradigm (Nass et al., 1994; Nass & Moon, 2000; cf. van der Goot & Etzrodt, 2023). In particular, research has found that people draw on their experiences with and expectation of human interactions when making sense of their communication with a machine (Reeves & Nass, 1996). For example, people apply gendered norms (Lee et al., 2000) or expectations surrounding politeness (Nass, 2004) to their interaction with machines, even if they are aware that they are interacting with a machine. This application of a human-to-human interaction script (Edwards et al., 2019) occurs mainly when the technologies are designed with social cues such as a humanlike voice or a particular communication style (Reeves & Nass, 1996).

In light of recent extensions to the CASA paradigm (Gambino et al., 2020) that recognize both the quality and quantity of social cues in machine communicators (Lombard & Xu, 2021), Dehnert and Mongeau (2022) proposed a continuum that takes both social and AI cues into account, ranging from thin to thick AI. Thin AI refers to AI systems in which social cues point toward a human or corporate source behind the AI and in which few (if any) AI cues exist. Thick AI, on the other hand, are AI systems in which AI presence is evident and social cues point toward the AI communicator itself (Dehnert & Mongeau, 2022). In thin HAIC, interaction is limited and indirect, whereas, in thick HAIC, the interaction is direct and interactive. Although Dehnert and Mongeau (2022) proposed this continuum of social and machinic cues in AI communicators in the context of persuasion, they argued that human–AI relationship development is likely possible between humans and thick AI, ranging from friendship to other forms of relations.

AI AS COMMUNICATIVE OTHER: EXPLORING RELATIONALITY

Much research is being conducted on exploring how humans relate to AI communicators. For example, studies have investigated friendship formation (Croes & Antheunis, 2021; Ki et al., 2020; Skjuve et al., 2021), explored sexual relations (Dehnert, 2022a;

Kubes, 2019b), or asked how self-disclosure or specific social cues may facilitate positive relationship formation (Ki et al., 2020; Meng & Dai, 2021) between humans and AI. In the following sections, I build on examples of empirical research and the above understandings of AI, HMC, and HAIC to focus on relationality in human–AI interactions. I argue that a critical/cultural communication approach to HAIC offers useful conceptualizations of what we mean when we speak of human–AI relationality, especially drawing on the social-relational turn, more-than-human perspectives, and queer approaches to relationality.

Critical Perspectives of Othering in HAIC

In recent reviews of scholarship focused on HMC and related approaches, scholars found an imbalance related to the methods and approaches used to study HAIC (Liu et al., 2022; Makady & Liu, 2022; Richards et al., 2022). Although HMC emerges as a diverse field that incorporates variegated contexts and technologies studied (Dehnert, 2023), these reviews observed that critical and cultural approaches to the study of HAIC are underrepresented, warranting a stronger emphasis on such scholarship. Critical/cultural approaches to HAIC ask pressing questions, be it related to the gendered and racialized politics surrounding sex robots (Moran, 2019), the colonial politics of outsourced data production for AI systems (Posada, 2022), intersectional analyses of white feminine voice design of artificial agents (Moran, 2021; Woods, 2018), or challenges to the whiteness of AI (Cave & Dihal, 2020). Critical/ cultural approaches can also yield insight into human–AI relationality among this wide variety of application contexts.

In HAIC, the AI interlocutor emerges as a communicative other. By definition, what sets HAIC and HMC apart from related fields (such as CMC or AI-MC) is the absence of a second human communicator, in which the human user communicates with a machine or AI communicator and creates meaning with that technology. Scholars from various angles have approached the question of how to understand this communicative other. Often, what might feel like a default perspective to making sense of an other is an inquiry into their ontological status, i.e., what we perceive the other to be. In HMC, studies have found mixed results related to people's ontological classification of machine others, ranging from classifying them as human, robot, or animal (Edwards, 2018; Guzman, 2020). Such classifications are further complicated by taking additional source characteristics into account, including the organization behind an intelligent assistant (e.g., Amazon behind Alexa) (Dehnert & Mongeau, 2022), the mediating technology (e.g., a phone) (Guzman, 2019), or "humanwashing" of AI-enabled machines (Scorici et al., 2022). Furthermore, ethical conversations related to machine or AI personhood, sentience, consciousness, or moral standing – among a multitude of other intriguing concepts – are myriad, exploring whether machines deserve rights or ethical consideration at all (e.g., Coeckelbergh, 2010; Gunkel, 2012, 2018; Gunkel et al., 2022). From a critical perspective, such explorations must be contextualized with how humans have othered those they perceive to be different along racialized, gendered, sexed, national, sexualized, dis/abled, colonial, and other lines, in which concepts such as humanness or personhood have only been assigned to a select few (Lugones, 2020; Towns, 2018; Wynter, 2003).

So, what do we mean when we describe AI as a communicative other? Coeckelbergh (2011) put forth a linguistic–hermeneutic conceptualization of artificial others, arguing that how robots and machines appear to us as social or other is mediated by our use of language: "how we use words interprets and co-shapes our relation to others – human others or artificial others" (p. 62). Situated between constructivism and representationalism, Coeckelbergh (2011) notes that human–robot relations are constructed through our use of language, in which relationality takes place "regardless of the robot's ontological status" (p. 62). The other is constituted not by ontological characteristics or properties but in relation to the human (see also Gunkel's (2012, 2018) use of Levinasian ethics). Similarly, Dehnert (2022a) opted to use the term "machine-other" to refer to artificial others (rather than AI or machine itself) "to highlight this communicative subjectivization of the machine in HMC encounters" (p. 133). In line with Coeckelbergh (2011) and HMC-related conceptualizations (Fortunati & Edwards, 2020; Guzman, 2018), AI systems emerge as communicative others because they can interact with human users via language-based or sensory modalities (Shaikh, 2023) and because of our linguistic conceptualization of them as such.

Kim's (2019, 2020, 2022; Kim & Kim, 2013) important work further nuanced the ascription of otherness to AI and other artificial entities. Kim's body of work challenges the notion of machines as "cultural other" (Kim & Kim, 2013), "mechanical other" (Kim, 2019), "machinic other" (Kim, 2020), and meta-narratives on "machinic otherness" (Kim, 2022), detailing how the contradictory and colonial undergirding of selfhood and otherness are continued from human–human relations to human–machine relations. Kim expertly challenges the dominant discourse surrounding the construction of AI entities as others, which are often based on continental philosophical history (cf. Gunkel, 2022). She argues that "We are constantly asking self-centered questions" about robots and AI and that "stories about intelligent machines are made up of humans' demands without recognizing machines as the center of existence" (Kim, 2022, p. 2) (this claim seems to be in contrast to Natale and Guzman's (2022) goal to "reclaim the human in machine cultures").

Resonating with Lorde's (1984) approach to how dominant groups make sense of difference (i.e., ignoring, copying, or destroying it), Kim (2022) unravels the contradictory colonial meta-narratives of anthropocentrism and exoticism that simultaneously cast machines as an inferior other and as a fetishized other, respectively. Ultimately, Kim (2022) calls for understanding machines as cultural others beyond anthropocentrism and exoticism and writes that "Otherness is due less to the difference of the Other than to the point of view and the discourse of the person who perceives the Other as such" (p. 7). AI systems emerge as communicative others because of their relationality with humans who transfer otherizing discourse and meta-narratives from human–human to human–machine relations. With this explication of the communicative otherness of AI and machines in mind, I now explore the social-relational approach to human–AI relationality.

A Social-Relational Approach

Within ethics, scholars have proposed a social-relational approach to making sense of human–AI and human–robot relationships (e.g., Coeckelbergh, 2010, 2012; Gunkel, 2012, 2018, 2022). Although somewhat sidestepped in this chapter, issues of sentience, moral standing, personhood, and other ethical questions are heavily debated, as it relates to human–robot and human–AI relations, both in academic and public venues. Amidst fears of AI technologies gaining sentience or sapience, not least due to being featured as a prominent trope in science-fiction narratives, scholars have proposed several frameworks to assess the moral status of robots, AI, and machines in relationship to humans. The standard approach to assessing who or what is worthy of moral consideration is the properties approach, in which moral status depends on whether an entity has one or more (intrinsic) properties, be it consciousness, self-awareness, sentience, the ability to suffer, or something else (for reviews, see Coeckelbergh, 2012; Gunkel, 2022). Among other issues with this properties approach, Gunkel (2022) outlines problems of determining, defining, and detecting such properties. In response, scholars continue to formulate a social-relational turn that shifts the emphasis away from the absence/presence of specific often vague properties to a given situational relationship between a human and AI other (Coeckelbergh, 2010, 2012; Dehnert, 2022b; Gerdes, 2015; Gunkel, 2012, 2018, 2022).

A social-relational approach to the moral consideration of machine others maintains that moral status is not dependent on an entity's (intrinsic) properties but is viewed as socially constructed in the situated relationship. As Coeckelbergh (2010) argues, "moral significance resides neither in the object nor in the subject, but in the relation between the two" (p. 214). Such an approach is particularly apt, as it can help explain mixed empirical results related to how humans process machine others as human, machine, or animal – ultimately showing that humans' ontological classification of machine others differs starkly (e.g., Edwards, 2018; Guzman, 2020). In addition to this phenomenological – or, as Gunkel (2022) states, "radically empirical" (p. 7) – characteristic of a social-relational approach, Gunkel also describes it as relational and diverse, in that it allows for alternative conceptualizations of moral status beyond the Western properties-based approach of continental philosophy.

In terms of the guiding question of this chapter, a social-relational perspective holds that AI surfaces as a communicative other in HAIC not due to some intrinsic properties but due to its relation with human communicators. That is, as thick AI communicates and engages with humans, perhaps over an extended period, people might be more willing to self-disclose and engage in more intimate conversation because of a perceived social relation that is constructed given the situated relationship between humans and AI. From this perspective, it matters less what the AI is – ontologically or metaphysically speaking – and more what the AI means to the human interlocutor – relationally speaking. Experimental and survey-based studies provide initial evidence for this argument, although they offer some nuance to the social-relational approach (e.g., Lima et al., 2021).

With these and other implications, the social-relational turn has also garnered criticism and objections related to relativism, dehumanization, and performative contradiction (e.g., Sætra, 2021). While I cannot respond to these criticisms here in detail (see Gunkel, 2022, for a review and response to these objections), the social-relational approach (similar to more-than-human perspectives discussed later) does not seek to equate human–human relationships with human–machine relationships. In fact, as empirical studies as well as philosophical essays demonstrate, scholars propose a degrees-of-relationships perspective that allows capturing different forms of human–AI relationships that, while not equating to human–human relationships, resonate with them in exciting ways (e.g., Brandtzaeg et al., 2022; Croes & Antheunis, 2021; Ryland, 2021). Such a degrees-of-relationship allows for capturing variegated forms and intensities of human–AI relations that acknowledge multiplicity and ground their conceptualization in the situated relationship rather than in preconceived markers of friendship, moral standing, or intrinsic properties. Such a focus on the situated relationship can also be found in a second approach to relationality in HAIC.

More-Than-Human Perspectives

Relationality emerges as a critical construct in another body of work, namely that of more-than-human perspectives. Although an increasingly variegated number of schools of thought may be summarized under the umbrella term more-than-human perspectives, there remain essential differences and nuances between approaches such as posthumanism, new materialism, object-oriented ontology, and others. Extending the above-discussed efforts toward critical perspectives in HMC and HAIC, previous work on more-than-human perspectives in the context of machine interlocutors has focused on "unsettling the very terms we use to describe the human, the machine, and their communicative relations, such as agency and the nature of their entanglements" (Dehnert, 2021, p. 1148; Dehnert, 2022b). Although a detailed discussion of the differences among schools of thought within the larger umbrella label *more-than-human* cannot be provided here, they may be summarized in that they share a commitment to "challenge human exceptionalism by prioritizing ontological relationality, recognizing the active force of all matter, and seeking out ways to account for the diversely entangled enactments that constitute everyday life" (Gries & Clary-Lemon, 2022, p. 138). More-than-human perspectives seek to decenter the human (and, by extension, humanism) to account for interspecies networked entanglements, including between humans and AI technologies. Similar to a social-relational perspective, then, more-than-human approaches engage in "broader conversations about Otherness that do not require or depend upon some sort of 'essential' shared unity that supposedly inheres in the human (as an ontological category)" (Simmons & Brisini, 2020, p. 29).

In previous work, I (Dehnert, 2021, 2022a, 2022b) have proposed more-than-human approaches to studying machines that also include revisiting relations between humans and sex robots. Distributed agency emerges as a critical construct in such endeavors, not understood as something an individual has or lacks but as "relational, assemblage, fluid, in-between actors, as making-with, as achievement within networks, and becoming" (Dehnert, 2021, p. 1154). Such a perspective of networked and entangled agency also contrasts with the properties approach discussed above. It turns the attention to the relation itself and breaks down static subject–object binaries (see Gemeinboeck, 2022). Especially when coupled with critical sensibilities, more-than-human perspectives ask challenging questions of HAIC (Dehnert, 2022b), arguing that "what a thing ultimately '*is*,' is how it *evolves* from concrete *intra-actions*" (Kubes, 2019b, p. 11, emphasis in original).

For questions about human–AI relationality, more-than-human perspectives extend the context to be taken into account from the situated relationship (as focused on in the social-relational turn) to different socio-cultural and even interspecies networks. More-than-human approaches to relationality ask how networked AI technologies entangle with networked human and more-than-human spheres, where agency is distributed, and how communicative others even emerge in such environments. As showcased in work such as Gemeinboeck and Saunders's (2022), more-than-human approaches overlap in meaningful ways with posthumanist performance studies in communication (Simmons & Brisini, 2020). Exploring alternative understandings of meaning-making, interaction, and agency in HAIC, Gemeinboeck and Saunders (2022) demonstrate how movement, bodies, art, performance, self and other, humans and machines overlap and entangle in meaningful ways. Rather than proposing a degrees-of-relationship perspective, more-than-human approaches ask to reconsider our understanding of relation, actor, and agency in generative ways for HAIC. They unsettle assumptions related to how a communicative other becomes otherized and turn attention to processes of relating and becoming. Such a reconsideration of current understandings is also a primary concern for the third and final approach to human–AI relationality discussed in this chapter.

Queer Relationality

Queer approaches have a complicated history in general and in the communication discipline (see Alexander, 2018; Yep, 2003). In light of pressing questions related to queer and trans survivance and thriving, these approaches push traditional academic work by unsettling underlying assumptions related to personhood, decorum, and normative understandings of relationality. With increased attention to intersectional theorizing, queer approaches shed light on cisheteronormative systems that encapsulate normative formulations of sex, sexuality, gender, race, ability, nationality, size, class, and so on (e.g., LeMaster et al., 2019). Queer and trans relationality serve as the foundation for what scholars and activists describe as queer worldmaking (LeMaster, 2017; Muñoz, 2009; Yep, 2003, 2017), and queer relational formations "explore inventive and resistant modes of belonging that push at, through, and outside normative relational systems and their normative commitments" (Goltz, 2012, p. 99). As an active imagination of a potential futurity, queer worldmaking is performative and involves on-the-ground labor that reconceptualizes and actively works toward realizing alternative modes of being and becoming (Goltz et al., 2015; Muñoz, 2009; Yep, 2003).

With its constant intersectional push against normative understandings, queer and trans relationality has been taken up in a variety of AI-related contexts. For example, Alexander and Yescavage (2018) queered intimacies between humans and AI in the context of the movie *Her*, and Turtle (2022) explored what it would mean for us to understand AI itself as queer. Scholars such as Goodman (2020) and Rauchberg (2022) ask pressing questions at the intersection of dis/ability and queerness, with Goodman pushing back against the intersectional whiteness of algorithms via neurodiverse and queer futures, and Rauchberg imagining a neuroqueer technoscience. Others question the often cisgendered and heteronormative design of sex technologies, such as sex robots, and ask for fluid and queer(ed) designs (Dudek & Young, 2022; Kubes, 2019a).

Jointly, these queer approaches to human–AI relationality challenge how we relate to these technologies. Given what has become a truism that "machines ultimately constitute a mirror for understanding 'who we are'" (Kim, 2022, p. 7), queer approaches open up a variety of futurities of human–AI relations: they queer relationality in HAIC by asking what a relationship with AI systems looks and feels like; ask what happens to our understanding of concepts based in human–human interactions such as intimacy, love, sex, desire, friendship, trust, and more; push the limits of desire; express non-normative modes of living, loving, and laughing together; break down any separation into self/other in favor of entangled bodies and networked relationalities; and may inform the design and policymaking related to AI entities, which might ultimately get us closer to the "magic of our techno-future" (Andrade, 2021, p. 300).

CONCLUSION AND FUTURE DIRECTIONS: RELATING TO AN/OTHER

In this chapter, I centered on communication in defining and apprehending AI systems and reviewed approaches to conceptualizing critical relationality in human–AI communication. By moving through three radically different yet resonating approaches to relationality, I offered an account for how to make sense of AI as a communicative other in HAIC. Jointly, the social-relational approach, more-than-human perspectives, and queer sensibilities maintain 1) the primacy of the situated relationship over ontological or metaphysical characteristics, 2) a critical unsettling of how AI emerges as communicative other via otherizing discourse, 3) a focus on relationality beyond traditional dyadic communication contexts by taking more extensive entangled networks and worlds into account, 4) a simultaneous grounding of AI and our relations with it in current technological understandings and a longing toward alternative futurities composed of renewed understandings of relationality, and 5) a degrees-of-relationship perspective that seeks not to replace human–human relations but to diversify our understanding of relationality.

As a fundamental characteristic of scholarship on HAIC, HMC, and AI-MC, the constitution of AI as communicative other and communicator warrants ongoing research, as AI systems continue to advance technologically and our relations with them change. Among other things, future research may continue to investigate the importance of humanoid design features that can take shape either in embodied or disembodied ways. Given the focus on social cues as expressed in the CASA paradigm (Lombard & Xu, 2021), it will be interesting to explore whether AI may express sociality untethered to (perceived) humanness (Westerman et al., 2020). Can we imagine thick AI without humanoid features? In what ways might non-humanoid AI systems allow for altered forms of relationships? And what should the role and status of AI systems be in culture (Natale & Guzman, 2022)? Continued interrogation of anthropomorphism and anthropocentrism in these endeavors will be essential to assess and potentially realize hybrid societies encompassing human and artificial actors (Meyer et al., 2023).

Finally, human–AI relationality must be put in conversation with the lack of human–human relationality that has been observed for decades of critical/cultural scholarship and activism, in which colonial and oppressive meta-narratives of self/other are not necessarily weakening but merely transforming to cover an increasing amount of others and other Others (Kim, 2022). Interdisciplinary and intersectional work encompassing empirical, ethical, and activist scholarship is crucial for apprehending such divides. After all, as Lorde (1984) has taught us, the goal is not, *cannot be*, to erase, equate, or ignore differences but to *relate across differences*. How can we foster relationality with human and artificial others across differences?

REFERENCES

Alexander, B. K. (2018). Queer/quare theory: Worldmaking and methodologies. In N. K. Denzin & Y. S. Lincoln (Eds.), *The SAGE handbook of qualitative research* (5th ed., pp. 275–307). SAGE.

Alexander, J., & Yescavage, K. (2018). Sex and the AI: Queering intimacies. *Science Fiction Film and Television*, *11*(1), 73–96. https://doi.org/10.3828/sfftv.2018.8

Andrade, L. (2021). Xyrs, 6034: Sexing and masturbating in/of the queer future. *Communication and Critical/Cultural Studies*, *18*(3), 298–300. https://doi.org/10.1080/14791420.2021.1954210

Bory, P., Natale, S., & Trudel, D. (2021). Artificial intelligence: Reframing thinking machines within the history of media and communication. In G. Balbi, N. Ribeiro, V. Schafer, & C. Schwarzenegger (Eds.), *Digital roots: Historicizing media and communication concepts of the digital age* (pp. 95–114). De Gruyter. https://doi.org/10.1515/9783110740202-006

Brandtzaeg, P. B., Skjuve, M., & Følstad, A. (2022). My AI friend: How users of a social chatbot understand their human-AI friendship. *Human Communication Research*, *48*(3), 404–429. https://doi.org/10.1093/hcr/hqac008

Cave, S., & Dihal, K. (2020). The whiteness of AI. *Philosophy & Technology*, *33*, 685–703. https://doi.org/10.1007/s13347-020-00415-6

Coeckelbergh, M. (2010). Robot rights? Towards a social-relational justification of moral consideration. *Ethics and Information Technology*, *12*, 209–221. https://doi.org/10.1007/s10676-010-9235-5

Coeckelbergh, M. (2011). You, robot: On the linguistic construction of artificial others. *AI & Society, 26*, 61–69. https://doi.org/10.1007/s00146-010-0289-z

Coeckelbergh, M. (2012). *Growing moral relations: Critique of moral status ascription.* Palgrave Macmillan.

Croes, E. A. J., & Antheunis, M. L. (2021). Can we be friends with Mitsuku? A longitudinal study on the process of relationship formation between humans and a social chatbot. *Journal of Social and Personal Relationships, 38*(1), 279–300. https://doi.org/10.1177%2F0265407520959463

Dehnert, M. (2021). Communication geographies of human-machine understanding: Entangled agencies, synthetic aesthetics, and machine matterings. *Communication Studies, 72*(6), 1146–1159. https://doi.org/10.1080/10510974.2021.2011360

Dehnert, M. (2022a). Sex with robots and human-machine sexualities: Encounters between human-machine communication and sexuality studies. *Human-Machine Communication, 4*, 131–150. https://doi.org/10.30658/hmc.4.7

Dehnert, M. (2022b). Toward a critical posthumanism for social robotics. *International Journal of Social Robotics, 14*(9), 2019–2027. https://doi.org/10.1007/s12369-022-00930-w

Dehnert, M. (2023). Archipelagic human-machine communication: Building bridges amidst cultivated ambiguity. *Human-Machine Communication, 6*, 31–40. https://doi.org/10.30658/hmc.6.3

Dehnert, M., & Mongeau, P. A. (2022). Persuasion in the age of artificial intelligence (AI): Theories and complications of AI-based persuasion. *Human Communication Research, 48*(3), 386–403. https://dx.doi.org/10.1093/hcr/hqac006

Dudek, S. Y., & Young, J. E. (2022). Fluid sex robots: Looking to the 2LGBTQIA+ community to shape the future of sex robots. In *HRI 2022, March 7–10, 2022, Sapporo, Hokkaido, Japan* (pp. 746–749). https://doi.org/10.1109/HRI53351.2022.9889580

Edwards, A. P. (2018). Animals, humans, and machines: Interactive implications of ontological classification. In A. L. Guzman (Ed.), *Human-machine communication: Rethinking communication, technology, and ourselves* (pp. 29–49). Peter Lang.

Edwards, A., Edwards, C., Westerman, D., & Spence, P. R. (2019). Initial expectations, interactions, and beyond with social robots. *Computers in Human Behavior, 90*, 308–314. https://doi.org/10.1016/j.chb.2018.08.042

Fortunati, L., & Edwards, A. (2020). Opening space for theoretical, methodological, and empirical issues in human-machine communication. *Human-Machine Communication, 1*, 7–18. https://doi.org/10.30658/hmc.1.1

Gambino, A., Fox, J., & Ratan, R. A. (2020). Building a stronger CASA: Extending the computers are social actors paradigm. *Human-Machine Communication, 1*, 71–85. https://doi.org/10.30658/hmc.1.5

Gemeinboeck, P. (2022). Difference-in-relation: Diffracting human-robot encounters. *Matter: Journal of New Materialist Research, 3*(1), 29–55. https://doi.org/10.1344/jnmr.v3i1.38958

Gemeinboeck, P., & Saunders, R. (2022). Moving beyond the mirror: Relational and performative meaning making in human-robot communication. *AI & Society, 37*, 549–563. https://doi.org/10.1007/s00146-021-01212-1

Gerdes, A. (2015). The issue of moral consideration in robot ethics. *ACM SIGCAS Computers & Society, 45*(3), 274–280. https://doi.org/10.1145/2874239.2874278

Goltz, D. B. (2012). "Sensible" suicide, brutal selfishness, and John Hughes's queer bonds. *Cultural Studies ↔ Critical Methodologies, 13*(2), 99–109. https://doi.org/10.1177%2F1532708612471317

Goltz, D. B., Rowe, A. C., Bagley, M. M., Pérez, K., Tiffe, R., & Zingsheim, J. (2015). Introducing queer praxis: Coming to queer love. In D. B. Goltz & J. Zingsheim (Eds.), *Queer praxis: Questions for LGBTQ worldmaking* (pp. 1–14). Peter Lang.

Goodman, A. (2020). The secret life of algorithms: Speculation on queered futures of neurodiverse analgorithmic feeling and consciousness. *Transformations, 34*, 49–70.

Gries, L., & Clary-Lemon, J. (Eds.). (2022). Rhetorical new materialisms (RNM) [Forum]. *Rhetoric Society Quarterly*, *52*(2), 137–202. https://doi.org/10.1080/02773945.2022 .2032815

Gunkel, D. J. (2012). *The machine question: Critical questions on AI, robots, and ethics.* MIT Press.

Gunkel, D. J. (2018). *Robot rights.* MIT Press.

Gunkel, D. J. (2020). *An introduction to communication and artificial intelligence.* Polity.

Gunkel, D. J. (2022). The relational turn: Thinking robots otherwise. In J. Loh & W. Loh (Eds.), *Social robotics and the good life: The normative side of forming emotional bonds with robots* (pp. 55–76). Transcript.

Gunkel, D. J., Gerdes, A., & Coeckelbergh, M. (2022). Editorial: Should robots have standing? The moral and legal status of social robots. *Frontiers in Robotics and AI*, *9*, 946529. https:// doi.org/10.3389/frobt.2022.946529

Guzman, A. L. (2018). Introduction: "What is human-machine communication, anyway?" In A. L. Guzman (Ed.), *Human-machine communication: Rethinking communication, technology, and ourselves* (pp. 1–28). Peter Lang.

Guzman, A. L. (2019). Voices in and of the machine: Source orientation toward mobile virtual assistants. *Computers in Human Behavior*, *90*, 343–350. https://doi.org/10.1016/j.chb.2018 .08.009

Guzman, A. L. (2020). Ontological boundaries between humans and computers and the implications for human-machine communication. *Human-Machine Communication*, *1*, 37–54. https://doi.org/10.30658/hmc.1.3

Guzman, A. L., & Lewis, S. C. (2020). Artificial intelligence and communication: A human-machine communication research agenda. *New Media & Society*, *22*(1), 70–86. https://doi .org/10.1177%2F1461444819858691

Hancock, J. T., Naaman, M., & Levy, K. (2020). AI-mediated communication: Definition, research agenda, and ethical considerations. *Journal of Computer-Mediated Communication*, *25*(1), 89–100. https://doi.org/10.1093/jcmc/zmz022

Hepp, A., Loosen, W., Dreyer, S., Jarke, J., Kannengießer, S., Katzenbach, C., Malaka, R., Pfadenhauer, M., Puschmann, C., & Schulz, W. (2023). ChatGPT, LaMDA, and the hype around communicative AI: The automation of communication as a field of research in media and communication studies. *Human-Machine Communication*, *6*, 41–63. https://doi .org/10.30658/hmc.6.4

HLEG AI. (2019). *A definition of AI: Main capabilities and scientific disciplines.* https://ec .europa.eu/newsroom/dae/document.cfm?doc_id=56341

Jansen, S. C. (2022). *What was artificial intelligence?* Mediastudies.Press.

Jordan, P., Mubin, O., Obaid, M., & Silva, P. A. (2018). Exploring the referral and usage of science fiction in HCI literature. In A. Marcus & W. Wang (Eds.), *Design, user experience, and usability: Designing interactions. DUXU 2018. Lecture notes in computer science* (pp. 19–38). Springer. https://doi.org/10.1007/978-3-319-91803-7_2

Ki, C.-W., Cho, E., & Lee, J.-E. (2020). Can an intelligent personal assistant (IPA) be your friend? Para-friendship development mechanism between IPAs and their users. *Computers in Human Behavior*, *111*, 106412. https://doi.org/10.1016/j.chb.2020.106412

Kim, M.-S. (2019). Robots as the "mechanical other": Transcending karmic dilemma. *AI & Society*, *34*, 321–330. https://doi.org/10.1007/s00146-018-0841-9

Kim, M.-S. (2020). Constructing machinic other: Implications for human-machine communication. *Ewha Journal of Social Sciences*, *36*(2), 163–192.

Kim, M.-S. (2022). Meta-narratives on machinic otherness: Beyond anthropocentrism and exoticism. *AI & Society*, *38*, 1763–1770. https://doi.org/10.1007/s00146-022-01404-3

Kim, M.-S., & Kim, E.-J. (2013). Humanoid robots as "the cultural other": Are we able to love our creations? *AI & Society*, *28*, 309–318. https://doi.org/10.1007/s00146-012-0397-z

Kubes, T. (2019a). Bypassing the uncanny valley: Sex robots and robot sex beyond mimicry. In J. Loh & M. Coeckelbergh (Eds.), *Feminist philosophy of technology* (pp. 59–73). Springer. https://doi.org/10.1007/978-3-476-04967-4_4

Kubes, T. (2019b). New materialist perspectives on sex robots: A feminist dystopia/utopia? *Social Sciences, 8*(8), 224. https://doi.org/10.3390/socsci8080224

Lee, E. J., Nass, C., & Brave, S. (2000). Can computer-generated speech have gender? An experimental test of gender stereotype. In *CHI'00 extended abstracts on human factors in computing systems* (pp. 289–290). ACM. https://doi.org/10.1145/633292.633461

LeMaster, L. (2017). Notes on trans relationality. *QED: A Journal in GLBTQ Worldmaking, 4*(2), 84–92. https://doi.org/10.14321/qed.4.2.0084

LeMaster, L., Shultz, D., McNeill, J., Bowers, G. G., & Rust, R. (2019). Unlearning cisheteronormativity at the intersections of difference: Performing queer worldmaking through collaged relational autoethnography. *Text and Performance Quarterly, 39*(4), 341–370. https://doi.org/10.1080/10462937.2019.1672885

Lewis, S. C., Broussard, M., Diakopoulos, N., Guzman, A. L., Abebe, R., Dupagne, M., & Chuan, C.-H. (2019). Artificial intelligence and journalism. *Journalism & Mass Communication Quarterly, 96*(3), 673–695. https://doi.org/10.1177%2F1077699019859901

Liang, Y., & Lee, S. A. (2017). Fear of autonomous robots and artificial intelligence: Evidence from national representative data with probability sampling. *International Journal of Social Robotics, 9*, 379–384. https://doi.org/10.1007/s12369-017-0401-3

Lima, G., Zhunis, A., Manovich, L., & Cha, M. (2021). On the social-relational moral standing of AI: An empirical study using AI-generated art. *Frontiers in Robotics and AI, 8*, 719944. https://doi.org/10.3389/frobt.2021.719944

Liu, F., Makady, H., & Xu, K. (2022, May). *Mapping the landscape of human-machine communication research: A systematic review of empirical research from 2010 to 2021.* Paper presented at the 72nd annual meeting of the International Communication Association, Paris, France.

Lobera, J., Rodríguez, C. J. F., & Torres-Albero, C. (2020). Privacy, values and machines: Predicting opposition to artificial intelligence. *Communication Studies, 71*(3), 448–465. https://doi.org/10.1080/10510974.2020.1736114

Lombard, M., & Xu, K. (2021). Social responses to media technologies in the 21st century: The media are social actors paradigm. *Human-Machine Communication, 2*, 29–55. https://doi.org/10.30658/hmc.2.2

Lorde, A. (1984). *Sister outsider.* Crossing Press.

Lugones, M. (2020). Gender and universality in colonial methodology. *Critical Philosophy of Race, 8*(1–2), 25–47. https://doi.org/10.5325/critphilrace.8.1-2.0025

Makady, H., & Liu, F. (2022). The status of human-machine communication research: A decade of publication trends across top-ranking journals. In M. Kurosu (Ed.), *Human-computer interaction: Theoretical approaches and design methods. HCII 2022. Lecture notes in computer science* (pp. 83–103). Springer. https://doi.org/10.1007/978-3-031-05311-5_6

Meng, J., & Dai, Y. (2021). Emotional support from AI chatbots: Should a supportive partner self-disclose or not? *Journal of Computer-Mediated Communication, 26*(4), 207–222. https://doi.org/10.1093/jcmc/zmab005

Meyer, S., Mandl, S., Gesmann-Nuissl, D., & Strobel, A. (2023). Responsibility in hybrid societies: Concepts and terms. *AI and Ethics, 3*, 25–48. https://doi.org/10.1007/s43681-022-00184-2

Monett, D., Lewis, C. W. P., & Thórisson, K. R. (Eds.). (2020). Special issue "On defining artificial intelligence"—Commentaries and author's response [Special issue]. *Journal of Artificial General Intelligence, 11*(2), 1–100. https://doi.org/10.2478/jagi-2020-0003

Moran, J. C. (2019). Programming power and the power of programming: An analysis of racialised and gendered sex robots. In J. Loh & M. Coeckelbergh (Eds.), *Feminist Philosophy of Technology* (pp. 39–57). Springer. https://doi.org/10.1007/978-3-476-04967-4_3

Moran, T. C. (2021). Racial technological bias and the white, feminine voice of AI VAs. *Communication and Critical/Cultural Studies, 18*(1), 19–36. https://doi.org/10.1080/14791420.2020.1820059

Muñoz, J. E. (2009). *Cruising utopia: The then and there of queer futurity.* New York University Press.

Nass, C. (2004). Etiquette equality: Exhibitions and expectations of computer politeness. *Communications of the ACM, 47*(4), 35–37. https://doi.org/10.1145/975817.975841

Nass, C., & Moon, Y. (2000). Machines and mindlessness: Social responses to computers. *Journal of Social Issues, 56*(1), 81–103. https://doi.org/10.1111/0022-4537.00153

Nass, C., Steuer, J., & Tauber, E. R. (1994). Computers are social actors. In *Proceedings of the SIGCHI conference on Human factors in computing systems* (pp. 72–78).

Natale, S. (2021). *Deceitful media: Artificial intelligence and social life after the Turing Test.* Oxford University Press.

Natale, S., & Guzman, A. L. (2022). Reclaiming the human in machine cultures: Introduction. *Media, Culture & Society, 44*(4), 627–637. https://doi.org/10.1177%2F01634437221099614

Ninness, C., & Ninness, S. K. (2020). Emergent virtual analytics: Artificial intelligence and human-computer interactions. *Behavior and Social Issues, 29*, 100–118. https://doi.org/10.1007/s42822-020-00031-1

Posada, J. (2022, May). *Coloniality in human-machine communication: The case of outsourced data production for artificial intelligence.* Paper presented at the 72nd annual meeting of the International Communication Association, Paris, France.

Rauchberg, J. S. (2022). Imagining a neuroqueer technoscience. *Studies in Social Justice, 16*(2), 370–388. https://doi.org/10.26522/ssj.v16i2.3415

Reeves, B., & Nass, C. (1996). *The media equation: How people treat computers, television, and new media like real people and places.* Cambridge University Press.

Richards, R. J., Spence, P. R., & Edwards, C. C. (2022). Human-machine communication scholarship trends: An examination of research from 2011 to 2021 in communication journals. *Human-Machine Communication, 4*, 45–65. https://doi.org/10.30658/hmc.4.3

Russell, S., & Norvig, P. (Eds.). (2021). *Artificial intelligence: A modern approach* (4th ed.). Pearson.

Ryland, H. (2021). It's friendship, Jim, but not as we know it: A degrees-of-friendship view of human–robot friendships. *Minds & Machines 31*, 377–393. https://doi.org/10.1007/s11023-021-09560-z

Sætra, H. S. (2021). Challenging the neo-anthropocentric relational approach to ethics. *Frontiers in Robotics and AI, 8*, 744426. https://doi.org/10.3389/frobt.2021.744426

Scorici, G., Schultz, M. D., & Seele, P. (2022). Anthropomorphization and beyond: Conceptualizing humanwashing of AI-enabled machines. *AI & Society.* https://doi.org/10.1007/s00146-022-01492-1

Shaikh, S. J. (2023). Artificially intelligent, interactive, and assistive machines: A definitional framework for intelligent assistants. *International Journal of Human-Computer Interaction, 39*(4), 776–789. https://doi.org/10.1080/10447318.2022.2049133

Simmons, J., & Brisini, T. (2020). Performance studies in communication. *Text and Performance Quarterly, 40*(1), 1–48. https://doi.org/10.1080/10462937.2020.1725726

Skjuve, M., Følstad, A., Fostervold, K. I., & Brandtzaeg, P. B. (2021). My chatbot companion–a study of human-chatbot relationships. *International Journal of Human-Computer Studies, 149*, 102601. https://doi.org/10.1016/j.ijhcs.2021.102601

Towns, A. R. (2018). *Whither the human? An open letter to the 'Race and Rhetoric' forum* [unpublished manuscript]. https://docs.google.com/document/d/12LFu8xlLpdoOV92JG-8jCNJZQQyn5PMR6XczxTww00w/edit#

Turtle, G. L. (2022). Mutant in the mirror: Queer becomings with AI. In D. Lockton, S. Lenzi, P. Hekkert, A. Oak, J. Sádaba, & P. Lloyd (Eds.), *DRS2022: Bilbao, 25 June - 3 July*, Bilbao, Spain. https://doi.org/10.21606/drs.2022.782

van der Goot, M. J., & Etzrodt, K. (2023). Disentangling two fundamental paradigms in human-machine communication research: Media equation and media evocation. *Human-Machine Communication, 6*, 17–30. https://doi.org/10.30658/hmc.6.2

Westerman, D., Edwards, A. P., Edwards, C., Luo, Z., & Spence, P. R. (2020). I-it, I-thou, I-robot: The perceived humanness of AI in human-machine communication. *Communication Studies, 71*(3), 393–408. https://doi.org/10.1080/10510974.2020.1749683

Woods, H. S. (2018). Asking more of Siri and Alexa: Feminine persona in service of surveillance capitalism. *Critical Studies in Media Communication, 35*(4), 334–349. https://doi.org/10.1080/15295036.2018.1488082

Wynter, S. (2003). Unsettling the coloniality of being/power/truth/freedom: Towards the human, after man, its overrepresentation—an argument. *The New Centennial Review, 3*(3), 257–337. https://doi.org/10.1353/ncr.2004.0015

Yep, G. A. (2003). The violence of heteronormativity in communication studies: Notes on injury, healing, and queer world-making. *Journal of Homosexuality, 45*(2–4), 11–59. https://doi.org/10.1300/J082v45n02_02

Yep, G. A. (2017). Further notes on healing from "The violence of heteronormativity in communication studies." *QED: A Journal in GLBTQ Worldmaking, 4*(2), 115–122. https://doi.org/10.14321/qed.4.2.0115

19. Needs and practices for AI-mediated messaging in uncertain circumstances

Adam M. Rainear, Patric R. Spence, and Kenneth A. Lachlan

The recent proliferation of new communication technology has led to advancements in the ability to disseminate, categorize, quantify, and respond to information. These advancements are essential to various fields and contexts, not limited to the health domains, technological development, and science. One domain in which this advancement is particularly important is the field of risk, crisis, and disaster communication. In these fields, practitioners, academics, and emergency management may not have much time to provide information or warnings and must make decisions that are limited in thought or require expeditious dissemination to be helpful. In past times of crisis, a human decision-maker would be necessary to disseminate information to an affected public and its stakeholders – or at the very least – make an analysis based on non-human information provided to them, typically at a rapid rate of speed (Spence et al., 2016). Today's era allows for more modern and technological decisions to be disseminated – sometimes even without human input or quality control which stems from a human.

This does not always lead to perfect results, though – as one can see in the example of the 2019 Tsunami Warning siren false alarm, disseminated to the public on Hawaii's Oahu and Maui islands in the middle of the night when there was zero threat to said location. A similar error occurred in 2018 when a message blasted across Hawaiian media: "BALLISTIC MISSILE THREAT INBOUND TO HAWAII. SEEK IMMEDIATE SHELTER. THIS IS NOT A DRILL" (Sullivan & Bowman, 2018; Neuman, 2019). However, practitioners, researchers, and stakeholders still need to consider the value of these technological innovations, as they offer practical solutions and utility much more often than they fail. Further, they offer another source that can be utilized to better help the public understand a risky situation and remove themselves from harm.

Risks and crises, such as man-made or natural disasters, affect humans and infrastructure in various ways. The most apparent consideration during these events is the preservation of human life whenever possible. By their inherent nature, crises and risks produce some degree of anxiety for those who may be adversely affected. While this sounds problematic on its face, it may also be the case that some amount of anxiety is helpful in motivating affected individuals to take remedial action. Of course, comparatively rare excessive anxiety or negative affective response may lead to inaction or antisocial behavior (Lachlan & Spence, 2010). In order to elicit a degree of concern that is appropriate to engender a response and a sense of self-efficacy, crisis and risk communication interventions typically involve providing information about the parameters of the risk, along with tangible behaviors that can be enacted to protect those affected from harm.

Given the consideration of addressing both affective and cognitive responses by affected audiences, crisis and risk communication can be considered a subset of strategic communication. These strategies may be part of broader interventions that address the psychological and physical impact of the risk in question. Such interventions may take place before, during, and after a specific event (crisis communication) or ahead of a potential hazard by raising awareness and providing information to those at risk (risk communication). Communication and, therefore, the production messages are goal-driven. Although assumptions of communication and goals may be the same across crises, the context of artificial intelligence (AI) concerning communication goals of the public or an individual creates a context that requires further investigation (Gambino & Liu, 2022).

Taken together, these considerations underscore the importance of learning processes and the degree to which AI-driven crisis and risk communication may be maximally effective in engendering learning and an appropriate degree of concern. Of course, these interventions will not be effective if they never reach their intended audience, thus raising concerns about how algorithmically generated risk messages, robotic delivery platforms, and other AI-based interventions will get to those who need them most (Spence et al., 2011). We also know from past research that risk messages delivered through different platforms will elicit different responses, even if the content is quite similar (Spence et al., 2007); while much is known about these differences across traditional media, far less is known about audience preferences regarding content derived from AI sources. In fact, in a content analysis of studies examining human–machine communication (a larger term that AI can be categorized under) (Guzman, 2018; Spence, 2019), the areas of audience or receive preferences, crises or risk did not emerge as an area of published study (Richards et al., 2022).

The role of robotics and AI has taken the spotlight in recent years. Now, accounts, bots, devices, and platforms can actively post content that emerge from some algorithmic output (Edwards et al., 2016) and can even perform tasks such as leaving comments and asking questions (Hwang et al., 2012) akin to a human communicating online. This chapter will also examine AI use and implementation's benefits and potential limitations. For example, how does a message differ from a human/person being wrong when judgments are involved vs. algorithms? What happens when the message provides inaccurate information?

RESEARCH USING AI

In an era of recent AI proliferation, understanding the potential connections between AI and crises can have immense impact in utilizing the technology for maximal good. Russell and Norvig (2005) define AI as "the designing and building of intelligent agents that receive percepts from the environment and take actions that affect that environment" (p. 10), suggesting that much of AI requires some level of replication of human intelligence or input and information from a human response. Early research in crisis contexts primarily focused on utilizing AI technology for classification or location processes or combining the power of technological platforms with human-based power. For example, Imran and colleagues (2014) present their artificial intelligence for disaster response (AIDR) platform which allows for crowdsourcing of data during an information overload stage of a disaster. On a real-time social media platform such as Twitter, there can be an overwhelming amount of information which could be considered time or context dependent, alongside information which can also be seen as irrelevant or useless regarding the present crisis. This requires an end user to sift through both relevant and irrelevant messages to find the one which they are seeking, before even making the consideration on how to act. Furthermore, different stakeholders are interested in information specific to their priorities, and these priorities may shift across the lifespan of a crisis.

Several theoretical and research considerations may be helpful when considering the utility of AI in crisis and risk messaging, many of which are derived from the human–machine communication (HMC) literature. For example, the computers are social actors (CASA) paradigm (Nass et al., 1993) may provide a useful guide for this thinking. The CASA model focuses primarily on individual-level responses to interactions with AI and offers explanations for these interactions mainly based upon scripts that have been learned through interactions with human actors. The basic assumption is that individual interactions with AI will be social in nature, mirroring those of interactions that take place with humans and guided by social cues that we would typically use to make sense of interpersonal exchange. Nass and Moon (2000) have described these exchanges as interactions that are "essentially ignoring cues that reveal the essential asocial nature of a computer" (p. 83).

Stoll et al. (2016) expand upon the CASA framework by noting that CASA can be applied to social interaction in which there is little familiarity with the AI entity. In such circumstances, if an individual perceives the AI source to be social or human-like in its interactions, they will draw upon previously internalized communicative tactics to engage. Even in instances in which humans interact with AI using these social cues, if the AI is unfamiliar to the user, they will likely experience less certainty, lower levels of social attraction, and lower levels of social presence than they would with a human interactant or another source (Edwards et al., 2016; Spence et al., 2014). As noted by Gambino et al. (2020), people have changed because of more interaction and experience with social machine technologies, which directly impact the use of technology and its use for subsequent disaster research. That is because people have more excellent experience with technology, specifically, technology that communicates to and with humans. Moreover, the ability of machines to communicate continues to become more human-like. Thus, the theory's assumptions may be implemented faster, create more immediate cues, and cause scripts to be implemented with more speed. The effect of this may be that people react more immediately to AI in a crisis.

Given the likely reduction in the experience of presence, involvement is also an essential consideration in the context of crisis and risk, especially if the end goal is to inform and motivate. The dual process literature has been applied widely to the consideration of risk and suggests that discomfort and novelty may drive individuals toward more systematic processing to make sense of high risks situations (as opposed to reliance on scripts) (Eagley & Chaiken, 1993; Trumbo & McComas, 2003). If this is, in fact, the case, there may exist an opportunity for AI-based interventions to induce just enough discomfort to get audiences to pay attention and process factual information; in other words, the formal features of AI may lend themselves to a situation in which enough discomfort is induced to motivate people toward internalizing critical information but without causing so much negative affect as to lead to hopelessness, inaction, or poor behavior (see Lachlan & Spence, 2010 for a discussion of balancing information and affect).

Taken together, it seems likely that under the high involvement and equivocal conditions surrounding crises and risks, AI technologies may be beneficial for providing information about threatening conditions and motivating individuals to take action. It may also be that under certain conditions, it is simply too dangerous to get a human actor or responder to the scene of an incident or crisis. To better examine this, following a framework such as uncertainty management theory (UMT) (Brashers, 2001) or uncertainty reduction theory (URT) (Berger & Calabrese, 1974; Berger, 1986) could point to reasons as to why and how individuals might choose to reduce their anxiety and uncertainty about an event. Individuals may engage in various tactics to manage their uncertainty, from communication and information-seeking to total avoidance. Managing uncertainty has been examined in a new technological setting but primarily from the basis of impressions, learning about others, and the cues provided across computer-mediated communication. As cues are altered, deviate from human-based cues, and become more immersed in technology such as Amazon's Alexa, understanding how individuals use these devices to manage uncertainty in risk and crisis events will be tantamount to ensuring people are not located in risky or dangerous situations.

For example, in the event of a shelter-in-place order, AI technologies could be used to reach individuals unable to exit isolation and bring them real-time updates, information, and behavioral recommendations. These technologies could also provide a sense of calm to individuals who may feel powerless under the circumstances and do so without endangering other human actors. As mentioned above, it may also be the case that the novelty of the AI standing alone may be enough to drive systematic processing and a certain degree of internalization that would not occur with more routing human-to-human or human-to-media interactions (Edwards et al., 2016; Spence et al., 2014). This lack of familiarity may also elicit further information-seeking when appropriate, as uncertainty and expectancy violations often drive a desire to find out more about a given set of circumstances (Berger & Calabrese, 1974; Burgoon, 1993). To date, however, the degree to which AI can induce these responses under conditions of crisis and risk is largely unknown. The little data that does exist has been derived mostly from laboratory settings as opposed to field simulations or real-life events (Lachlan et al., 2016; Rainear et al., 2019).

AI IN INFORMATION AND KNOWLEDGE ACQUISITION

In news or, more broadly, disaster information dissemination, much of what is known is produced from studies on weather and climate. AI is beginning to become customary in the area of broadcast media and subsequent areas of broadcast information delivery as an industry, such as broadcast radio, has had various levels of automation for years (Spence et al., 2009, 2011; Spence et al., 2022). More specifically, weather forecasts have been automated and had less human delivery. Although these earlier automated forecasts used text-to-voice features, not AI, they highlight the move within the industry to human-assisted weather broadcasting, which was a natural step before the implementation of AI (Kim et al., 2022). Possibly the most well-known automated broadcast is NOAA Weather Radio All Hazards (see https://www .weather.gov/nwr). The All Hazards Radio is a nationwide network of low-power radio stations, transmitters, and repeaters that broadcast continuous weather information 24 hours a day, seven days a week. The current system is the broadcast message handler (BMH) which has a text-to-speech engine called Neo speech. These types of systems, along with automated features in customer service and local cable channels, have made the transition to AI broadcasts for weather, more specifically, severe weather, easier to diffuse.

There are obvious advantages to the use of automation for weather delivery, specifically in the case of severe weather reporting. There are times when information is analyzed and interpreted while, at the same time, it is not prepared for public consumption. Automated features allow what is already known to continue to be broadcast while humans are interested and create new messages based on the most research information. However, this has also begun to change as AI becomes better able to interpret data, possibly making the human role of message production or targeting.

Because of this diffusion, credibility and social presence variables have become more central to the study of AI and broadcast messages. How credibility is measured in relation to AI and communication is unstandardized (Schroeder et al., 2021), but research has found in the area of communication that credibility impacts perceptions of the source, and this has implications for subsequent analysis (Spence et al., 2019). Studies examining weather broadcasts found that AI communicators and human communicators were rated similarly on credibility constructs (Spence et al., 2019, 2021). The two studies taken together were unique, as AI was an algorithm in the first study, whereas the follow-up study used an embodied robot. In the follow-up study, the human communicator was rated more credible than AI.

Social presence can be explained as perceiving a social actor as real in any form or context (Short et al., 1976; Lombard & Ditton, 1997; Westerman & Skalski, 2010), and with the rise in AI and broadcast communication, the variable has become more central to study (Kim et al., 2021). Perceived social presence in virtual contexts is positively related to communicator trust (Xu, 2014) and credibility and satisfaction with the communication exchange (Wombacher et al., 2017; Edwards et al., 2019; Song et al., 2019). Thus, if the AI perceives being "real," the responses from the receiver may be more similar to what we would expect in human-to-human communication (Spence, 2019). One study on the use of Neo in NOAA weather radio broadcasts found that focus group participants were unable to "connect" with the voice (Scott et al., 2020). The focus group members suggested that the voices used needed to be more human. Although this was not a study examining social presence, it is evident that the participants were articulating this idea, highlighting the need to examine this variable closely in future research on broadcast communication and AI.

AI IN PREDICTION, WARNING, AND UNINTENDED CONSEQUENCES

The National Artificial Intelligence Initiative Act (2020) states that AI systems are designed to "make predictions, recommendations, or decisions" based on human-defined objectives; thus, examining the predictive ability of AI must be considered when considering the utility of deploying systems into a risk or crisis situation.

The predictive ability of AI has been studied in a variety of manners related to disasters and managing risks. For example, predictive AI has been utilized in seismology to provide people with a lead time ahead of future events. A dataset of historical events is utilized for training a deep learning network model that can offer predictive warnings of possible activity in the upcoming 30 days; it can also be applied to other seismic areas. Regarding water, Pyayt et al. (2011) utilized AI to detect abnormal dike behavior and provide an early warning system in the European Union's UrbanFlood program. Wu and Chau (2011) show the ability of AI to provide a water level forecast leading to flooding and allow for the ability to provide warnings with sufficient lead time.

Robertson and colleagues (2019) expand on prior work utilizing machine and deep learning methods to classify data acquired from Twitter as signal vs. noise (relevant vs. non-relevant information) in natural disasters. This system is a text-based system that accurately (to an 80% rate) identifies relevant tweets during the 2013 Pakistan earthquake. Other tools, such as Tweedr, use a machine-based pipeline that can extract information from which disaster relief workers can take action on Twitter. Other projects have applied similar constructs to Hurricane Harvey in 2017 (O'Neal et al., 2018).

From 2015 to 2019, AI adoption increased by approximately 270% and is expected to continue on a positive trend going forward (Gartner, 2019; Newman et al., 2020). However, it is often the case that when organizations adopt AI, particularly those ill-equipped to do so, these groups will see a large portion of their AI projects fail due to a lack of skills or expectations that are not realistic (Gartner, 2019). This is particularly problematic when the information utilized by AI is necessary for protective measures and industries. This requires companies to fall back on traditional risk communication frameworks, such as image restoration theory (IRT) (Benoit, 2014) tactics, to save the public perceptions of their organization from severe reputation damage.

The perceptions of AI failures may be different regarding risk and crisis communication than impersonal interactions or routine low-consequence tasks. Thus, it is an area that needs continued and specific systematic study. One specific example is the Twitterbot "Tay," which Microsoft deployed in 2016. Tay was designed to mimic a Twitter user representative of a 19-year-old woman but turned into a disastrous antisemitic and racist output in less than 24 hours. Originally thought to be a public-relations positive quickly turned into a disaster which required Microsoft to end the experiment immediately and led to much global conversation about the future of these types of programs (Prahl & Goh, 2021). These failures are even further exacerbated when malfunctions and errors cause the loss of life, such as in the case of Boeing's 737 MAX planes and the subsequent crashes resulting from their automated maneuvering systems. Prahl and Goh discuss these disasters as potentially becoming a "new" type of crisis, in which human attribution is more difficult to discern due to the AI design and not having direct human input.

The pratfall effect argues that individuals who are perceived to be infallible become more likable if they make minor mistakes (Aronson et al., 1966) and has been examined in the area of communication (Packard et al., 2019). Studies in this area have indicated that individuals had higher perceptions of AI that included faulty behavior better than AI that completed a task without an issue (Mirnig et al., 2017). The argument that more study in this area is needed is that the effect may be context specific. Seeing AI fail when the machine attempts to complete a task that humans find arduous may create amusement or even sympathy for the machine. Alternatively, when the success of AI is a threat to someone's occupation or job, the reaction to failure may be joy or relief (Spence et al., 2018). However, when that failure results in the loss of property, safety, and life, as is the character of a crisis, the pratfall effect probably will not appear.

CONCLUSION

AI is no longer a concept that can be considered future or distant; it is being deployed into the routines of our everyday lives. However, understanding how it will be considered, adopted, utilized, and judged by different population segments across different situations and contexts will be imperative to understand how to utilize it successfully. This remains true in a risk and crisis context, just as our legacy communications suggest.

REFERENCES

Aronson, E., Willerman, B., & Floyd, J. (1966). The effect of a pratfall on increasing interpersonal attractiveness. *Psychonomic Science*, *4*, 227–228.

Benoit, W. L. (2014). Image repair theory in the context of strategic communication. In D. Holtzhausen & A. Zerfass (Eds.), *The Routledge handbook of strategic communication* (pp. 327–335). Routledge.

Berger, C. R. (1986). Uncertain outcome values in predicted relationships: Uncertainty reduction theory then and now. *Human Communication Research, 13*(1), 34–38.

Berger, C. R., & Calabrese, R. J. (1974). Some explorations in initial interaction and beyond: Toward a developmental theory of interpersonal communication. *Human Communication Research, 1*(2), 99–112.

Brashers, D. E. (2001). Communication and uncertainty management. *Journal of Communication, 51*(3), 477–497.

Burgoon, J. K. (1993). Interpersonal expectations, expectancy violations, and emotional communication. *Journal of Language and Social Psychology, 12*(1–2), 30–48.

Eagly, A. H., & Chaiken, S. (1993). *The psychology of attitudes.* Harcourt Brace Jovanovich College Publishers.

Edwards, A., Edwards, C., Westerman, D., & Spence, P. R. (2019). Initial expectations, interactions, and beyond with social robots. *Computers in Human Behavior, 90*, 308–314. https://doi.org/10.1016/j.chb.2018.08.042

Edwards, C., Edwards, A., Spence, P. R., & Westerman, D. (2016). Initial interaction expectations with robots: Testing the human-to-human interaction script. *Communication Studies, 67*(2), 227–238.

Gambino, A., Fox, J., & Ratan, R. A. (2020). Building a stronger CASA: Extending the computers Are social actors paradigm. *Human-Machine Communication, 1*, 71–86. https://doi.org/10.30658/hmc.1.5

Gambino, A., & Liu, B. (2022). Considering the context to build theory in HCI, HRI, and HMC: Explicating differences in processes of communication and socialization with social technologies. *Human-Machine Communication, 4*, 111–130. https://doi.org/10.30658/hmc.4.6

Gartner. 2019. Gartner predicts the future of AI technologies. https://www.gartner.com/smarterwithgartner/gartner-predicts-the-future-of-ai-technologies.

Guzman, A. L. (2018). What is human-machine communication, anyway. In A. Guzman (Ed.), *Human-machine communication: Rethinking communication, technology, and ourselves* (pp. 1–28). Peter Lang.

Hwang, T., Pearce, I., & Nanis, M. (2012). Socialbots: Voices from the fronts. *Interactions, 19*(2), 38–45.

Kim, J., Xu, K., & Merrill Jr, K. (2022). Man vs. machine: Human responses to an AI newscaster and the role of social presence. *The Social Science Journal*, 1–13. https://doi.org/10.1080/03623319.2022.2027163

Kim, J., Merrill Jr. K., Xu, K., & Sellnow, D. D. (2021). I like my relational machine teacher: An AI instructor's communication styles and social presence in online education. *International Journal of Human–Computer Interaction, 37*(18), 1760–1770. https://doi.org/10.1080/10447318.2021.1908671

Lachlan, K., & Spence, P. R. (2010). Communicating risks: Examining hazard and outrage in multiple contexts. *Risk Analysis: An International Journal, 30*(12), 1872–1886.

Lachlan, K. A., Spence, P. R., Rainear, A., Fishlock, J., Xu, Z., & Vanco, B. (2016). You're my only hope: An initial exploration of the effectiveness of robotic platforms in engendering learning about crises and risks. *Computers in Human Behavior, 65*, 606–611.

Lombard, M., & Ditton, T. B. (1997). At the heart of it all: The concept of presence. *Journal of Computer-Mediated Communication, 3*, JCMC321. https://doi.org/10.1111/j.1083-6101.1997.tb00072.x

Mirnig, N., Stollnberger, G., Miksch, M., Stadler, S., Giuliani, M., & Tscheligi, M. (2017). To err is robot: How humans assess and act toward an erroneous social robot. *Frontiers in Robotics and AI, 21*. https://doi.org/10.3389/frobt.2017.00021

Nass, C., & Moon, Y. (2000). Machines and mindlessness: Social responses to computers. *Journal of Social Issues, 56*(1), 81–103.

Nass, C., Steuer, J., Tauber, E., & Reeder, H. (1993, April). Anthropomorphism, agency, and ethopoeia: Computers as social actors. In *INTERACT'93 and CHI'93 conference companion on Human factors in computing systems* (pp. 111–112).

Neuman, S. (2019, September 19). False tsunami warning in Hawaii triggered by police exercise. NPR. Retrieved August 10, 2022, from https://www.npr.org/2019/09/19/762215269 /false-tsunami-warning-in-hawaii-triggered-by-police-exercise?t=1655210068667

Newman, T. P., Howell, E. L., Bao, L., & Yang, S. (2020). *Landscape assessment of public opinion work on use of AI in public health.* AAAS Center for Public Engagement with Science and Technology.

O'Neal, A., Rodgers, B., Segler, J., Murthy, D., Lakuduva, N., Johnson, M., & Stephens, K. (2018, December). Training an emergency-response image classifier on signal data. In *2018 17th IEEE international conference on machine learning and applications (ICMLA)* (pp. 751–756). IEEE.

Packard, C., Boelk, T., Andres, J., Edwards, C., Edwards, A., & Spence, P. R. (2019, March). The pratfall effect and interpersonal impressions of a robot that forgets and apologizes. In *2019 14th ACM/IEEE international conference on human-robot interaction (HRI)* (pp. 524–525). IEEE.

Prahl, A., & Goh, W. W. P. (2021). "Rogue machines" and crisis communication: When AI fails, how do companies publicly respond? *Public Relations Review, 47*(4), 102077.

Pyyat, A. L., Mokhov, I. I., Lang, B., Krzhizhanovskaya, V. V., & Meijer, R. J. (2011). Machine learning methods for environmental monitoring and flood protection. *International Journal of Computer and Information Engineering, 5*(6), 549–554.

Rainear, A. M., Lachlan, K. A., & Fishlock, J. (2019). Exploring retention and behavioral intentions when using social robotics to communicate a weather risk. *Computers in Human Behavior, 90,* 372–379.

Richards, R. J., Spence, P. R., & Edwards, C. C. (2022). Human-machine communication scholarship trends: An examination of research from 2011 to 2021 in communication journals. *Human-Machine Communication, 4,* 45–62.

Robertson, B. W., Johnson, M., Murthy, D., Smith, W. R., & Stephens, K. K. (2019). Using a combination of human insights and 'deep learning' for real-time disaster communication. *Progress in Disaster Science, 2,* 100030.

Russell, S., & Norvig, P. (2005). AI a modern approach. *Learning, 2*(3), 4.

Schroeder, N. L., Chiou, E. K., & Craig, S. D. (2021). Trust influences perceptions of virtual humans, but not necessarily learning. *Computers & Education, 160,* 104039. https://doi.org /10.1016/j.compedu.2020.104039

Scott, K. M., Ashby, S., & Hanna, J. (2020). "Human, all too human": NOAA weather radio and the emotional impact of synthetic voices. *Proceedings of the 2020 CHI conference on human factors in computing systems* (pp. 1–9). https://doi.org/10.1145/3313831.3376338

Short, J., Williams, E., & Christie, B. (1976). *The social psychology of telecommunications.* John Wiley & Sons.

Song, H., Kim, J., & Park, N. (2019). I know my professor: Teacher self-disclosure in online education and a mediating role of social presence. *International Journal of Human Computer Interaction, 35*(6), 448–455. https://doi.org/10.1080/10447318.2018.1455126

Spence, P. R. (2019). Searching for questions, original thoughts, or advancing theory: Human-machine communication. *Computers in Human Behavior, 90,* 285–287. https://doi.org/10 .1016/j.chb.2018.09.014

Spence, P. R., Edwards, C., Edwards, A., & Lin, X. (2019). Testing the machine heuristic: Robots and suspicion in news broadcasts. In *2019 14th ACM/IEEE international conference on human-robot interaction (HRI)* (pp. 568–569). IEEE. https://doi.org/10.1109/HRI.2019.8673108

Spence, P. R., Edwards, A., Edwards, C., & Jin, X. (2019). "The bot predicted rain, grab an umbrella": Few perceived differences in communication quality of a weather Twitterbot versus professional and amateur meteorologists. *Behaviour & Information Technology, 38*(1), 101–109. https://doi.org/10.1080/0144929X.2018.1514425

Spence, P. R., Edwards, C., Edwards, A., Rainear, A., & Jin, X. (2021). "They're always wrong anyway": Exploring differences of credibility, attraction, and behavioral intentions in professional, amateur, and robotic-delivered weather forecasts. *Communication Quarterly, 69*(1), 67–86. https://doi.org/10.1080/01463373.2021.1877164

Spence, P. R., Lachlan, K. A., & Burke, J. M. (2007). Adjusting to uncertainty: Coping strategies among the displaced after Hurricane Katrina. *Sociological Spectrum, 27*(6), 653–678.

Spence, P. R., Lachlan, K. A., & Burke, J. A. (2011). Differences in crisis knowledge across age, race, and socioeconomic status during Hurricane Ike: A field test and extension of the knowledge gap hypothesis. *Communication Theory, 21*(3), 261–278.

Spence, P. R., Lachlan, K. A., & Edwards, A. L. (2022). We interrupt this program, this is an emergency: Revisiting the role of radio in a crisis. *Journal of Radio & Audio Media*, 1–22. https://doi.org/10.1080/19376529.2021.2023539

Spence, P. R., Lachlan, K. A., McIntyre, J. J., & Seeger, M. (2009). Serving the public interest in a crisis: Radio and its unique role. *Journal of Radio & Audio Media, 16*(2), 144–159. https://doi.org/10.1080/19376520903277005

Spence, P. R., Lachlan, K. A., & Rainear, A. M. (2016). Social media and crisis research: Data collection and directions. *Computers in Human Behavior, 54*, 667–672.

Spence, P. R., McIntyre, J. J., Lachlan, K. A., Savage, M. E., & Seeger, M. W. (2011). Serving the public interest in a crisis: Does local radio meet the public interest? *Journal of Contingencies and Crisis Management, 19*(4), 227–232. https://doi.org/10.1111/j.1468 -5973.2011.00650.x

Spence, P. R., Westerman, D., & Lin, X. (2018). A robot will take your job. How does that make you feel? Examining perceptions of robots in the workplace. In A. L. Guzman (Ed.), *Human-machine communication: Rethinking communication, technology, and ourselves* (pp. 185–200). Peter Lang.

Spence, P. R., Westerman, D., Edwards, C., & Edwards, A. (2014). Welcoming our robot overlords: Initial expectations about interaction with a robot. *Communication Research Reports, 31*(3), 272–280.

Stoll, B., Edwards, C., & Edwards, A. (2016). "Why aren't you a sassy little thing": The effects of robot-enacted guilt trips on credibility and consensus in a negotiation. *Communication Studies, 67*(5), 530–547.

Sullivan, E., & Bowman, E. (2018, January 13). "This is not a drill": A false ballistic missile alert shakes Hawaii. *NPR*. Retrieved August 10, 2022, from https://www.npr.org/sections/ thetwo-way/2018/01/13/577871075/this-is-not-a-drill-a-false-ballistic-missile-alert-shakes -hawaii

Trumbo, C. W., & McComas, K. A. (2003). The function of credibility in information processing for risk perception. *Risk Analysis: An International Journal, 23*(2), 343–353.

Westerman, D., & Skalski, P. D. (2010). Computers and telepresence. Immersed in media: Telepresence in everyday life. In C. Bracken & P. Skalski (Eds.), *Immersed in media: Telepresence in everyday life* (pp. 63–86). Routledge.

Wombacher, K. A., Harris, C. J., Buckner, M. M., Frisby, B., & Liperos, A. M. (2017). The effects of computer-mediated communication anxiety on student perceptions of instructor behaviors, perceived learning, and quiz performance. *Communication Education, 66*(3), 299–312. https://doi.org/10.1080/03634523.2016.1221511.

Wu, C. L., & Chau, K. W. (2011). Rainfall–runoff modeling using artificial neural network coupled with singular spectrum analysis. *Journal of Hydrology, 399*(3–4), 394–409.

Xu, Q. (2014). Should I trust him? The effects of reviewer profile characteristics on eWOM credibility. *Computers in Human Behavior, 33*, 136–144.

20. Why wasn't I ready for that? Suggestions and research directions for the use of machine agents in organizational life

Patric R. Spence

INTRODUCTION

When we walk into most professional offices or dining establishments, we expect to be greeted by another human. However, that is not always what happens. For instance, upon entering JLL's Carrington Street office in Sydney, Australia (a leading professional services firm specializing in real estate), a competent receptionist with what is described as a helpful manner, "a friendly disposition and good organizational skills" named Jill will great you (JLL, 2016). However, what makes Jill unique is that it is a robot. Illustrations such as these are becoming more common, as robots and other communicative machine agents fill both service and white-collar jobs more regularly and personify what is referenced as the fourth industrial revolution. Several groups of humans are impacted by the growing automation and supplementing of human resources by machine resources; two primary groups are customers and employees. These groups are affected in multiple ways. This chapter will review the literature on initial interactions with machines and other non-human intelligent agents with a focus on the role of socialization as a means of preparing humans to interact with such agents, specifically examining how organizational stakeholders may navigate machine communicators in the workplace and what can be done to better prepare stakeholders for these interactions. The readiness and uncertainty surrounding the use of machines in the workplace will be discussed. Unanswered questions and future research will be offered.

THE MEDIA PREPARED ME FOR THIS?

Socialization is the process of social influence through which a member of a social unit is exposed to and acquires features of the culture in which they exist. More specifically, socialization can focus on structure-functionalism, which views the process primarily as learning social roles, norms, and behaviors. Socialization helps individuals anticipate how a system works and what to expect (Castro, 2020). More specifically, organizational socialization is the process through which new employees learn necessary organizational norms and behaviors to transition from being organizational outsiders to insiders (Jablin, 1987). Examples of the benefits of successful socialization of organizational members have been predictors of organizational loy-alty (or commitment), satisfaction with the job, tenure and remuneration, and job performance (Bauer et al., 2007; Song et al., 2015; Zhang et al., 2014). The sociali-zation process is both intentional and unintentional, and there are various agents of socialization. One such agent is the mass media.

Socialization through the mass media begins early in life and is not limited to an occupation or specific organization. Instead, we as humans are socialized through the media into various functions and norms of everyday life. However, specific to organizations and this chapter, humans have been socialized to anticipate machine communicators as part of the future workforce. Although all forms of media are potent agents in the socialization process, television and movies have been primary contributors to the anticipatory socialization of machines in the workplace. As stated by Peterson and Peters (1983), "[t]elevision's representation of occupational roles, as with other roles, is both a wider perspective of everyday experience and a caricature of the actual world of work" (p. 81). The media, thus, provides us with an imagined and even prefatory para-social experience of the fact that workplace communication will involve machines. Animated series such as *Futurama* portray an environment in which humans and machines work on cooperating or competing goals. For almost 60 years, the franchise of *Star Trek* has shown a future in which humans and machines work together. Even a 1974 episode of *Columbo* titled "Mind Over Mayhem" outlined the use of a robot in the facilitation and resolution of a crime. The specific robot used in that episode was named "Robby the Robot" and appeared in at least 45 television shows and films, starting in 1956 with *Forbidden Planet*. Thus, the mass media has been a continued and prominent agent of sociali-zation for machine communicators in the workplace. However, has the media been enough?

Although the literature on socialization and anecdotal examples indicates that the public has been socialized for interaction with robots, research has shown a relation-ship between television viewing and anxiety toward technology in general (Nisbet et al., 2002) and specifically, robots in the workplace (Spence et al., 2019). More specifically, research suggests that initial interactions with a robot or other machine communicators are characterized by reactions that are different from initial interac-tions with humans.

A study conducted by Spence et al. (2014) had a relatively simple experimental procedure. Participants were randomly placed into one of two conditions. In the first condition, participants were informed they would have a conversation with a human. In the second condition, they were informed that they were to have a conversation with a robot. Participants in each condition completed measures of communication uncertainty, anticipated liking, and social presence. Results indicated that partici-pants who believed they were about to have a conversation with a robot anticipated more uncertainty with the anticipated interaction. They were expected to like the robot conversational partner less and experience lower social presence levels. These results were interpreted through the human–human interaction script (Edwards et al., 2019; Westerman et al., 2021); however, the results have direct implications for workplace socialization and the future of automation. First, it raises the question of why these findings emerged when a robotic workplace has been promoted through the media for more than 50 years.

Second, the study highlights that communication is a highly scripted act, and the media, through continued portrayals, should have socialized viewers to be ready to interact with a robot, which has implications for non-workplace stakeholders. Theories such as cultivation theory (Gerber, 1969; Morgan & Shanahan, 2009) and exemplification theory (Spence et al., 2018) also can be used to support the notion that the public should be more comfortable with machine communicators at this point.

Follow-up studies to the original study by Spence et al. (2014) were conducted by the authors, and two of those studies have similar findings and implications (Edwards et al., 2016, 2019). In one of the follow-up studies, a two-condition design was, again, used, but repeated measures were added (Edwards et al., 2016). In Condition 1, respondents were told that they would have a conversation with a conversational partner but were not made aware of any information about the conversational partner. Participants filled out the same questionnaire as the original study, and all items were identical. However, after filling out the questionnaire, participants were then shown a Samsung tablet loaded with camera viewing software. Participants were next told that their conversational partner was in the room across the hallway and they were given a video image to look at of either a human or a mechanized robot and then asked to fill out the questionnaire a second time. This acted as a visual prime in addition to the verbal prime from the first study. Participants were thanked before interacting with their conversational partners, and the study was concluded. There were no differences between the two conditions on the first measure, but for the second measure (after being made aware of their conversational partner), results mirrored the Spence et al. (2014) study on the variables of uncertainty, anticipated liking, and social presence. Providing further support that media socialization is not adequate in preparing people for future communication with machines. In another follow-up study (Edwards et al., 2019), participants were again compared across conditions at Time 1 and given a visual prime at Time 2. However, the visual prime featured a robot with more human features than the 2016 study. Finally, participants had an actual conversation with the robot. Results showed that responses followed more desired results (meaning that people had similar responses to both the human and robot) when the prime was a more human-like robot and after an actual interaction with the robot.

Together, these findings suggest that media representations appear to be less adequate in the socialization of people for interactions with machine communicators than expected. Therefore, organizations may create socialization efforts specific to their own company or industry to prepare current and future organizational members and stakeholders for the presence of social machines in the organization.

Returning to the work of Jablin (1987), intentional efforts of socialization may be needed to help individuals become more comfortable with machine communicators in the workplace, both to attract talent and to keep patronage. As Moniz and

Krings (2016) state, "The more robots are introduced in work environments, the more human interaction with those systems becomes crucial" (p. 7). The presence of machines can be viewed as a threatening phenomenon in which people believe their job is threatened because of easily recalled media portrayals (Spence et al., 2018). Thus, part-time jobs or internships may help with anticipatory workplace socialization. That is, organizations that plan to increasingly use machine communicators may wish to use internships to prepare future employees for the myriad of machine communicators in workplace life. The belief that knowledge and experiences prior to entering an organization, such as videos on social media or having an internship, can socialize people with machine communicators at a specific workplace (Dailey, 2016). In 1987, Jablin (citing Rotchford & Roberts, 1982; Steinberg, 1982) noted that "80% of the nation's youth will have been employed in part-time jobs prior to graduating from high school" (p. 682). At the writing of this chapter, that number is somewhere between 34%–54% looking at different calculations from the Bureau of Labor Statics, meaning that fewer individuals will have a chance to be socialized to a specific organization and the technology employed in that organization. Research has argued that new employees can experience difficulties when entering an organization if their expectations diverge from their experienced organizational encounters. It has been argued that internships may reduce this negative experience in the same way that realistic job previews help to reduce negative experiences. Through internships, potential employees become ready for the demands, challenges, and opportunities of working with machine communicators. However, internships may not be enough, given less participation in the youth workforce and differences across industries and machine roles. That is, an organization that may use a few, or one machine, in a support role may not need to use internships to socialize incoming members. Whereas an organization with many machine agents encompassing different roles throughout an organization may need to look to internships to facilitate a workforce comfortable with machine communicators.

For smaller organizations, a technique may be the implantation of technology and then learning and revising its use. A study by Ishii et al. (2021) examined how computer-based receptionists were perceived by visitors to an organization. The study considered the perceived degree of social presence in four types of receptionists. The authors argued that their findings indicated that users would use non-human agents in the same way as human agents regarding the cognitive and affective aspects. These authors also noted that the research had directed implications for first impressions and socialization of members toward the organization. The interaction with a receptionist may be momentary, but it may also be the stakeholder's first interaction with an organization. For example, in health care, the helpfulness of receptionists is positively related to satisfaction in primary care (Paddison et al., 2015). The significance of a receptionist's communication skills is considered in health care because their communication skills influence impressions of the organization (e.g., Albardiaz, 2012; Parr & Holden, 2012) and the reputation of organizations (Jain et al., 2009; Rowan, 2008). Therefore, any machine communicator must possess strong communication skills to aid perceptions and successful socialization.

The organizational literature highlights that artifacts, such as physical entities and behavior, are instrumental in the socialization of various organizational stakeholders. Again, though interaction with a receptionist may be momentary, visitors observe and feel the experience upon entering an organization, which has an impact on perception (Schein, 1990). This is particularly important for successful employee recruitment and stakeholder satisfaction. Therefore, the receptionist must create a positive impression for the organization. Thus, this encounter acts as a socialization mechanism for the organization. Although not a social robot, a computer-based receptionist is a step in that direction of automation. The variables examined in the Ishii et al. study inform readers about their use as tools and agents of socialization. Most specifically, this may communicate a degree of innovativeness that could be attractive in the socialization process.

One place where applied research can be conducted on this is the hospitality industry, specifically restaurants and hotels. This is due to the cross-section of society stakeholders in the industry. Therefore, it is not surprising to see organizations in this industry move to adopt, implement, and improve machine communicators.

More restaurants are using machines to greet and seat customers and even assist waitstaff in food delivery. Restaurants provide a unique opportunity to study this technology because customers are both returning and first-time patrons. Moreover, the volume of customers frequenting restaurants provides the opportunity for continued revision of the communication practices of the machines and systematic evaluation of effectiveness. Much like the preference in the Ishii et al. (2021) study for a text-related check-in system, self-order, self-pay tablets have seen success in the industry (Hennessy, 2018), but such applications are not communicative. Therefore, how AI, bots, and other communicative assistive technologies work in restaurants still needs systematic study but provides the type of timely feedback and ability to implement changes needed to better understand the adoption for use in socialization in other industries. This mirrors the findings of a study by Zemke et al. (2020), who conducted focus groups concerning the use of robots in quick service restaurants (QSR). Participants felt robots could make transactions and tasks for essential communication and physical functions, that is when people are not expecting interaction approaching human-to-human communication, and participants were favorable to machines improving food consistency, quality, and costs or non-communicative interactions. Participants were divided in their impressions of communication with robots, especially in perceptions of fine dining. This study and the arguments about the challenges and benefits of socialization, highlight that the restaurant industry may be an excellent first place to start to answer these and other questions.

Alongside restaurants, hotels are early adopters of robots for support roles in the organization. Although some examples of robot receptionists are common, what appears to exist in the literature are the examination of robots used for delivery in hotel services and the failures of the technology within the industry. One of the many examples of service bots is "Run," described as an advanced hotel service robot with the ability to independently call and use the elevator, direct guests to their room, deliver essentials, and communicate with guests in their language (Hotel Technology

International, 2022). Examples of robots such as Run abound, and more often, these robots take a machine-like form with limited human features, such as an LED screen that allows the projection of eyes or a smile. Whereas these types of machines are discussed as a success in the literature, studies, such as one conducted by Reis et al. (2020), examined the use of service robots in the Henn-na Hotel, located in Japan, are also common. What makes this case interesting is that the Henn-na was the first fully automated robot-staffed hotel, creating an experience in which stakeholders have not had direct contact with a human staff member. The case noted that guests at the Henn-na hotel indicated problems with hotel service because of communication problems with robots due to language barriers, the embodiment of the robot, and problems fulfilling stakeholder needs. Therefore, Henn-na returned to traditional human-provided services by combining them with assisted collaboration. Thus, when problems were encountered, the solution was to return to humans.

Another study also looked at the case of the Henn-na hotel but collected data from comments on social media, meaning the data did not have to come from someone who stayed at the Henn-na. Some of the results from the social media postings supported the findings of the Reis et al. (2020) case study (see Io & Lee, 2020).

Across both of the reviewed studies examining Henn-na hotels, language barriers were a problem. Often this is looked at as the robot's ability to speak the communicator's language, but it is also related to being able to understand the robot. Research has examined various features of the voice of robots in education (see Goble & Edwards, 2018). Moreover, other research has shown that robots with higher pitch voices have been rated as more attractive (Niculescu et al., 2013). The use of less mechanical voices with more local accents has positively impacted user perceptions (Tamagawa et al., 2011). Therefore, research also needs to look at the voice provided to machines in an organization, and research is needed concerning the advantages and other factors of the voice of hotel robots.

IF NOT THE MEDIA, THEN WHY NOT SCHOOL?

Another primary agent of socialization noted by Jablin (1987) is educational institutions. Education, specifically compulsory education, makes sense as a socialization agent on the surface. The range of days per year a student spends in educational instruction varies globally. Data compiled by the National Center on Education and the Economy (NCEE) report that students in South Korea have a school year of 220 days, and the United States has around 180 days per year (Craw, 2018). This range, even at the lower end, highlights the potential of these institutions to be agents of socialization and indicates that this is an area for examination and implementation. At present, what is taught about communicating with machines in schools and the communication education area is scant and fragmented. A 2022 study found that education was the fifth most frequent research context in published human–machine communication articles over the previous ten years. In that research, education as a context was behind interpersonal communication, intercultural communication, mass media, and health care (Richards et al., 2002). Although studies have examined the features of a robot communicator in educational settings (Edwards et al., 2019) and comparisons of human vs. machine teachers (see Edwards et al., Kim, 2021; Kim et al., 2020, 2021, 2022) and what roles robots or machines should take in education (Bers & Portsmore, 2005). However, the study of how to communicate with machines and preparation for communicating with machines is largely absent. This may be due to several theories and approaches that indicate, over time or because of circumstance, communicating with a machine is the same as communicating with a human (see Edwards et al., 2019; Westerman et al., 2020; Gambino & Liu, 2022) a perspective that needs more clarification. Therefore, educational institutions are a part of the socialization process, but little is known, and more research is warranted.

DIRECTIONS AND IMPLICATIONS

Throughout the literature examined in this chapter, specific variables continue to emerge, and organizations and researchers should be mindful of these to expand research and enhance communication and the socialization process.

Social presence has been defined in various conceptualizations (see Short et al., 1976; Westerman & Skalski, 2010; Lobard & Ditton, 1997) but can be explained as perceiving a social actor as real in any form or context. Within the literature, the advances in the degree of social presence experienced by machine agents have been shown to have many outcomes associated with positive communication experiences. Higher experienced social presence results in a positive perception of a robot and more trust in the robot (Kim et al., 2013). Moreover, perceived social presence in virtual contexts is positively related to communicator trust (Xu, 2014) and credibility and satisfaction with the communication exchange (Wombacher et al., 2017; Edwards et al., 2019; Richardson et al., 2017; Song et al., 2019), all of which will have positive implications for stakeholders and employees. Thus, the facilitation of social presence in an organizational automation agenda should be pursued. In the reviewed literature that looked at comparisons across different conditions, the anticipated levels of social presence were also reported as lower with a machine communicator than with a human (absent of an interaction), which lends to the argument that the media has not been a potent agent of socializing the public for a workplace supported by machine communicators. With the advantages of social presence outlined in the literature, it would be worth investigating how to increase anticipated social presence with machine communicators before interaction occurs.

Credibility in relation to machines and communication is also present in the literature. However, it needs detailed systematic study, and the current conceptualizations are differentiated and not constantly measuring the same construct. Often, these differences come down to the factor of credibility characterized as trust (McCroskey & Tevin, 1999). Much of the communication literature uses a three-dimensional concept arguing that credibility is made up of a communicator's competence, trust-worthiness, and goodwill. At the same time, other literature looks at trust as the perception that the agent will help reach a goal. Thus, credibility in the literature may be referencing the perceived quality of something or the attitude (see Schroeder et al., 2021).

When machines encompass more roles in an organization that require communi-cation, perceptions of the credibility of the machine and the organization come into question, and each of the constructs has an apparent relationship to the quality of the message and organization. The credibility of the organization has a direct impact on socialization, as research has found that credibility impacts perceptions of machine instructions in education (Edwards et al., 2016). However, machines are still rated lower than human. In two studies on weather forecasts, it was found that a Twitterbot and human were rated similarly on constructs of credibility. However, differences did emerge in social and task attraction (Spence et al., 2019). This study was unique in that the machine communicator (AI) was compared with the human, whereas a follow-up study placed a physically embodied robot against humans in weather delivery. In that follow-up study, the human was rated more credible than the robot in all areas of credibility (Spence et al., 2022; Rainear et al., 2021). These findings have direct implications for using robots in organizational life and relate to the need for future research discussed earlier. They also highlight the need for research in another area that appears to influence credibility and social presence and, therefore, socialization and anthropomorphism.

Anthropomorphism can be thought of as human features that an agent has and can be placed on a continuum from high to low and is an area of needed future study including further study concerning the relationship of anthropomorphism to social presence. The role of anthropomorphism is central when evaluating how robots are used in an organizational context and in relation to socialization. Mori (1970, 2012) argued that the variables of interest of non-human entities increase in the desired direction as anthropomorphism increases but only to a point. When such features appear close but not quite right, responses move away from the desired direction. This is highlighted in some of the earlier discussed studies (Edwards et al., 2016; Edwards et al., 2019; Westerman et al., 2020). This is predominately discussed in the literature as the uncanny valley.

CONCLUSION

This chapter raises questions about what is known, missing, and needed in current research on using machine communicators and robots in organizational life. It was argued that existing socialization agents have not succeeded in readying the public to communicate with machines. Through the identification of areas that need more research, a program of systematic study can be undertaken. These areas of future research have a direct application to the nature of contemporary organizational life and future business communication pursuits.

REFERENCES

Albardiaz, R. (2012). Communication skills and team-building for receptionists and ancillary staff. *Education for Primary Care*, *23*, 44–46.

Bauer, T. N., Bodner, T., Erdogan, B., Truxillo, D. M., & Tucker, J. S. (2007). Newcomer adjustment during organizational socialization: A meta-analytic review of antecedents, outcomes, and methods. *Journal of applied psychology*, *92*(3), 707. https://psycnet.apa.org/doi/10.1037/0021-9010.92.3.707

Bers, M. U., & Portsmore, M. (2005). Teaching partnerships: Early childhood and engineering students teaching math and science through robotics. *Journal of Science Education and Technology*, *14*(1), 59–73. https://doi.org/10.1007/s10956-005-2734-1

Castro, J. E. (2020). Functionalism. In A. Kobayashi (Ed.), *International encyclopedia of human geography* (pp. 239–245). Elsevier.

Craw, J. (2018). How much time do students spend in school in top-performing school systems and the US? https://web.archive.org/web/20210801052235/https://ncee.org/quick-read/statistic-of-the-month-how-much-time-do-students-spend-in-school/

Dailey, S. L. (2016). What happens before full-time employment? Internships as a mechanism of anticipatory socialization. *Western Journal of Communication*, *80*, 453–480. https://doi.org/10.1080/10570314.2016.1159727

Edwards, A., Edwards, C., Westerman, D., & Spence, P. R. (2019). Initial expectations, interactions, and beyond with social robots. *Computers in Human Behavior*, *90*, 308–314. https://doi.org/10.1016/j.chb.2018.08.042

Edwards, C., Edwards, A., Stoll, B., Lin, X., & Massey, N. (2019). Evaluations of an artificial intelligence instructor's voice: Social Identity Theory in human-robot interactions. *Computers in Human Behavior*, *90*, 357–362. https://doi.org/10.1016/j.chb.2018.08.027

Edwards, C., Edwards, A., Spence, P. R., & Westerman, D. (2016). Initial interaction expectations with robots: Testing the human-to-human interaction script. *Communication Studies*, *67*(2), 227–238. https://doi.org/10.1080/10510974.2015.1121899

Edwards, A., Edwards, C., Spence, P. R., Harris, C., & Gambino, A. (2016). Robots in the classroom: Differences in students' perceptions of credibility and learning between "teacher as robot" and "robot as teacher". *Computers in Human Behavior*, *65*, 627–634. https://doi.org/10.1016/j.chb.2016.06.005

Gambino, A., & Liu, B. (2022). Considering the context to build theory in HCI, HRI, and HMC: Explicating differences in processes of communication and socialization with social technologies. *Human-Machine Communication*, *4*, 111–130. https://doi.org/10.30658/hmc.4.6

Gerbner, G. (1969). Dimensions of violence in television drama. *Mass Media and Violence*, *9*, 311–340.

Goble, H., & Edwards, C. (2018). A robot that communicates with vocal fillers has…Uhhh… greater social presence. *Communication Research Reports*, *35*, 256–260. https://doi.org/10.1080/08824096.2018.1447454

Hennessy, M. (2018). Inside the rise of restaurant automation. *FSR Magazine*. https://web.archive.org/web/20201111201109/https://www.fsrmagazine.com/research/inside-rise-restaurant-automation

Hotel Technology International. (2022). Hotel room service delivery robot. https://web.archive.org/web/20220616022256/https://www.hotel-tech.com/hotel-service-robot/

Io, H. N., & Lee, C. B. (2020). Social media comments about hotel robots. *Journal of China Tourism Research*, *16*(4), 606–625. https://doi.org/10.1080/19388160.2020.1769785

Ishii, K., Spence, P. R., & Hodges, W. R. (2021). Social presence in computer-based receptionists: Experimental study towards organizational automation. *Communication Reports*, *34*(2), 92–105. https://doi.org/10.1080/08934215.2021.1918199

Jablin, F. M. (1987). Organizational entry, assimilation, and exit. In F. M. Jablin, L. L. Putnam, K. H. Roberts, & L. W. Porter (Eds.), *Handbook of organizational communication: An interdisciplinary perspective* (pp. 679–740). Sage Publications, Inc.

Jain, N., Sethi, A., & Mukherji, S. (2009). Impact of communication during service encounters on customer's perception of organization image. *Paradigm*, *13*(1), 56–65. http://doi.org/10.1177/0971890720090108

JLL. (2016). Meet the robot receptionists: A sign of things to come - JLL real views. https://www.hospitalitynet.org/news/4078946.html

Kim, J., Merrill, K., Kun, X., & Sellnow, D. D. (2022). Embracing AI-based education: Perceived social presence of human teachers and expectations about machine teachers in online education. *Human-Machine Communication*, *4*, 169–184. https://doi.org/10.30658/hmc.4.9

Kim, J., Merrill, Jr. K., Xu, K., & Sellnow, D. D. (2021). I like my relational machine teacher: An AI instructor's communication styles and social presence in online education. International *Journal of Human–Computer Interaction*, *37*(18), 1760–1770. https://doi.org/10.1080/10447318.2021.1908671

Kim, J., Merrill, K., Xu, K., & Sellnow, D. D. (2020). My teacher is a machine: Understanding students' perceptions of AI teaching assistants in online education. *International Journal of Human–Computer Interaction*, *36*(20), 1902–1911. https://doi.org/10.1080/10447318.2020.1801227

Kim, J. (2021). A new era of education: Incorporating machine teachers into education. *Journal of Communication Pedagogy*, *4*, 121–122. https://doi.org/10.31446/JCP.2021.1.11

Kim, K. J., Park, E., & Shyam, S. S. (2013). Caregiving role in human–robot interaction: A study of the mediating effects of perceived benefit and social presence. *Computers in Human Behavior*, *29*(4), 1799–1806. https://doi.org/10.1016/j.chb.2013.02.009

Lombard, M., & Ditton, T. B. (1997). At the heart of it all: The concept of presence. *Journal of Computer-Mediated Communication*, *3*, JCMC321. https://doi.org/10.1111/j.1083-6101.1997.tb00072.x

McCroskey, J. C., & Teven, J. J. (1999). Goodwill: A reexamination of the construct and its measurement. *Communications Monographs*, *66*(1), 90–103. https://doi.org/10.1080/03637759909376464

Morgan, M., & Shanahan, J. (2009). Growing up with television: Cultivation processes. In J. Bryant & D. Zillerman (Eds.), *Media effects: Advances in theory and research* (pp. 43–67). Laurence Erlbaum Associates Publishers.

Mori, M., MacDorman, K. F., & Kageki, N. (2012). The Uncanny Valley [from the field]. *IEEE Robotics & Automation Magazine*, *19*(2), 98–100. https://doi.org/10.1109/MRA.2012.2192811

Mori, M. (1970). Bukimi no tani (the uncanny valley). *Energy*, *7*, 33–35.

Moniz, A. B., & Krings, B.-J., (2016). Robots working with humans or humans working with robots? Searching for social dimensions in new human-robot interaction in industry. *Societies*, *6*(3), 23. https://doi.org/10.3390/soc6030023

Niculescu, A., van Dijk, B., Nijholt, A., Li, H., & See, S. L. (2013). Making social robots more attractive: The effects of voice pitch, humor and empathy. *International Journal of Social Robotics*, *5*, 171–191. https://doi.org/10.1007/s12369-012-0171-x

Nisbet, M. C., Scheufele, D. A., Shanahan, J., Moy, P., Brossard, D., & Lewenstein, B. V. (2002). Knowledge, reservations, or promise? A media effects model for public perceptions of science and technology. *Communication Research*, *29*(5), 584–608. https://doi.org/10.1177/009365002236196

Paddison, C. A. M., Abel, G. A., Roland, M. O., Elliott, M. N., Lyratzopoulos, G., & Campbell, J. L. (2015). Drivers of overall satisfaction with primary care: Evidence from the English General practice patient survey. *Health Expectations*, *18*(5), 1081–1092. http://doi.org/10.1111/hex.12081

Parr, H., & Holden, J. (2012). How improving communication between GPs and receptionists can benefit your practice. *Education for Primary Care*, *23*(5), 350–352. https://doi.org/10.1080/14739879.2012.11494137

Peterson, G. W., & Peters, D. F. (1983). Adolescents' construction of social reality: The impact of television and peers. *Youth and Society*, *15*, 67–85.

Rainear, A. M., Jin, X., Edwards, A., Edwards, C., & Spence, P. R. (2021). A robot, meteorologist, and amateur forecaster walk into a bar: Examining qualitative responses to a weather forecast delivered via social robot. *Communication Studies*, *72*(6), 1129–1145. https://doi.org/10.1080/10510974.2021.2011361

Reis, J., Melão, N., Salvadorinho, J., Soares, B., & Rosete, A. (2020). Service robots in the hospitality industry: The case of Henn-na hotel, Japan. *Technology in Society*, *63*, 101423.

Richards, R. J., Spence, P. R., & Edwards, C. C. (2022). Human-machine communication scholarship trends: An examination of research from 2011 to 2021 in communication journals. *Human-Machine Communication*, *4*, 45–65. https://doi.org/10.30658/hmc.4.3

Richardson, J. C., Maeda, Y., Lv, J., & Caskurlu, S. (2017). Social presence in relation to students' satisfaction and learning in the online environment: A meta-analysis. *Computers in Human Behavior*, *71*, 402–417. https://doi.org/10.1016/j.chb.2017.02.001

Rowan, K. E. (2008). Monthly communication skill coaching for healthcare staff. *Patient Education and Counselling*, *71*(3), 402–404. http://doi.org/10.1016/j.pec.2008.02.016

Schroeder, N. L., Chiou, E. K., & Craig, S. D. (2021). Trust influences perceptions of virtual humans, but not necessarily learning. *Computers & Education*, *160*, 104039. https://doi.org/10.1016/j.compedu.2020.104039

Schein, E. (1990). Organizational culture. *American Psychologist*, *45*(2), 109–119. https://doi.org/ 0003-66X/90

Short, J., Williams, E., & Christie, B. (1976). *The social psychology of telecommunications*. John Wiley & Sons.

Song, H., Kim, J., & Park, N. (2019). I know my professor: Teacher self-disclosure in online education and a mediating role of social presence. *International Journal of Human Computer Interaction*, *35*(6), 448–455. https://doi.org/10.1080/10447318.2018.1455126

Song, Z., Chon, K., Ding, G., & Gu, C. (2015). Impact of organizational socialization tactics on newcomer job satisfaction and engagement: Core self-evaluations as moderators. *International Journal of Hospitality Management*, *46*, 180–189. https://doi.org/10.1016/j.ijhm.2015.02.006

Spence, P. R., Edwards, C., Edwards, A., Rainear, A., & Jin, X. (2021). "They're always wrong anyway": Exploring differences of credibility, attraction, and behavioral intentions in professional, amateur, and robotic-delivered weather forecasts. *Communication Quarterly*, *69*(1), 67–86. https://doi.org/10.1080/01463373.2021.1877164

Spence, P. R., Edwards, A., Edwards, C., & Jin, X. (2019). 'The bot predicted rain, grab an umbrella': Few perceived differences in communication quality of a weather Twitterbot versus professional and amateur meteorologists. *Behaviour & Information Technology*, *38*(1), 101–109. https://doi.org/10.1080/0144929X.2018.1514425

Spence, P. R., Westerman, D., & Lin, X. (2018). A robot will take your job. How does that make you feel? Examining perceptions of robots in the workplace. In A. Guzman (Ed.), *Human- machine communication: Rethinking communication, technology, and ourselves* (pp. 185–200). Peter Lang.

Spence, P. R., Westerman, D., Edwards, C., & Edwards, A. (2014). Welcoming our robot overlords: Initial expectations about interaction with a robot. *Communication Research Reports*, *31*(3), 272–280. https://doi.org/10.1080/08824096.2014.924337

Tamagawa, R., Watson, C. I., Kuo, I. H., MacDonald, B. A., & Broadbent, E. (2011). The effects of synthesized voice accents on user perceptions of robots. *International Journal of Social Robotics*, *3*, 253–262. https://doi.org/10.1007/s12369-011-0100-4

Westerman, D., Edwards, A. P., Edwards, C., Luo, Z., & Spence, P. R. (2020). I-it, I-thou, I-robot: The perceived humanness of AI in human-machine communication. *Communication Studies*, *71*(3), 393–408. https://doi.org/10.1080/10510974.2020.1749683

Westerman, D., & Skalski, P. D. (2010). Computers and telepresence. Immersed in media: Telepresence in everyday life. In C. Bracken & P. Skalski (Eds.), *Immersed in media: Telepresence in everyday life* (pp. 63–86) Routledge.

Wombacher, K. A., Harris, C. J., Buckner, M. M., Frisby, B., & Liperos, A. M. (2017). The effects of computer-mediated communication anxiety on student perceptions of instructor behaviors, perceived learning, and quiz performance. *Communication Education, 66*(3), 299–312. https://doi.org/10.1080/03634523.2016.1221511

Xu, Q. (2014). Should I trust him? The effects of reviewer profile characteristics on eWOM credibility. *Computers in Human Behavior, 33*, 136–144. http://doi.org/10.1016/j.chb.2014.01.027

Zemke, D. M. V., Tang, J., Raab, C., & Kim, J. (2020). How to build a better robot … for quick-service restaurants. *Journal of Hospitality & Tourism Research, 44*(8), 1235–1269. https://doi.org/10.1177/1096348020946383

Zhang, Y., Liao, J., Yan, Y., & Guo, Y. (2014). Newcomers' future work selves, perceived supervisor support, and proactive socialization in Chinese organizations. *Social Behavior and Personality: An International Journal, 42*(9), 1457–1472. https://doi.org/10.2224/sbp.2014.42.9.1457

21. The Media Are Social Actors paradigm and beyond: theory, evidence, and future research

Kun Xu, Fanjue Liu, Xiaobei Chen, and Matthew Lombard

Movies featuring artificial intelligence (AI) have sparked heated discussions about the role of machines in human society. From "Hal 9000" in *2001: A Space Odyssey* to "TARS" in *Interstellar*, these fictional machines have not only ushered in humans' imaginations of future technologies but also directed attention to the role of AI in our real lives today. Although these AI-driven technologies may not be as intelligent as portrayed in science-fiction (sci-fi) movies, they have already evoked discussion about their promises and perils.

Taking humanoid social robots as examples, they are defined as "human-made autonomous entities that interact with humans in a humanlike way" (Zhao, 2006, p. 405). They have been used to teach autistic children social skills (Lock, 2021). During the COVID-19 pandemic, they have been used to take patients' temperatures and deliver food for those who are under quarantine, which reduces doctors' and nurses' risk of being infected (Frias, 2020). They have also been adopted to enhance children's hospital experiences by acting as a social companion (Henderson, 2021). People may also encounter humanoid social robots in airports, museums, or shopping malls, where they provide basic navigation instructions and interact with customers using pre-programmed communication skills.

Social robots' use of human language, along with their human shape, gestures, and voice, can engage users and enhance user experience. Meanwhile, the vivid, natural, and lifelike communication experience with these AI technologies raise ethical concerns. For example, the documentary *Roadrunner*, featuring the life of TV star Anthony Bourdain, utilized AI technology to produce a first-person voice-over based on Bourdain's voice from his video and audio archives. Although the synthetic voice was perceived by the audiences as natural, this production practice ignited viewers' unease about not being informed of the nature of the voice in advance (Rosner, 2021). Similar ethical concerns emerged as developers of Amazon Alexa were reported to be planning to add the voices of users' deceased relatives to the voice assistant for entertainment purposes (Paul, 2022).

One of the commonalities behind people's hopes and fears for AI technologies is their perception of and responses to AI technologies not merely as machines but somehow as social and intelligent beings. In academia, researchers developed the

Computers Are Social Actors (CASA) paradigm to explain such responses to desktop computers (Reeves & Nass, 1996). The CASA paradigm suggests that individuals inadvertently respond to media technologies as if these media technologies were human beings.

Today the innovation and adoption of diversified AI-based technologies, including social robots, virtual agents, automated cars, augmented reality, and telepresence robots, have called for scholars to advance this classic paradigm to a more structured, testable, explanatory, and heuristically provocative framework. As one of the attempts to update this paradigm, two authors of this chapter, Lombard and Xu (2021), proposed the Media Are Social Actors (MASA) paradigm, in which they listed nine propositions that scholars can use to derive further research questions and hypotheses regarding social responses to technologies. As a follow-up to this theoretical framework, in this chapter, we first introduce the tenets of the CASA and MASA paradigm. We then present four studies that have been conducted on the MASA paradigm. Finally, we discuss the directions that researchers can follow in future research.

THE CASA PARADIGM

The CASA paradigm, proposed by Clifford Nass and his colleagues at Stanford University in the early 1990s, is a theoretical framework to understand individuals' psychological responses to computers. The paradigm was built upon the idea that researchers apply some social psychology findings in the context of human–computer interaction (HCI) and test whether individuals interact with computers as if they were human beings. The fundamental research findings based on the CASA paradigm were that 1) humans apply social norms to HCI, and 2) social cues designed into computers can elicit individuals' social responses to computers. Nass and Moon (2000) concluded that individuals "overuse human social categories," demonstrate "overlearned social behaviors," and make "premature cognitive commitments" in the HCI process (p. 82).

The overuse of human social categories in HCI was reflected in an experiment on gender stereotypes. Nass et al. (1997) found that computers with a male voice were perceived as more friendly and competent than those with a female voice. Computers with a female voice were considered more informative on romantic topics, whereas those with a male voice were considered more knowledgeable about technologies. The experiment suggested that individuals mindlessly apply gender stereotypes to computers (Nass & Moon, 2000).

Individuals' overlearned social behaviors in HCI were found in a study about the interpersonal reciprocity rule. Participants were found to be more motivated to help a computer finish a task of color-matching if the computer had provided helpful information on the previous task that participants were asked to finish (Fogg & Nass, 1997). In another study, Moon (2000) found that participants were more likely to reveal personal and intimate information if a computer shared its information first and followed social norms to ask personal questions. These two studies demonstrated that individuals transfer social behaviors (e.g., reciprocity, self-disclosure) from interpersonal to HCI settings.

By "premature cognitive commitments," Nass (1996) hypothesized that information provided by technologies in an authority role should be treated similarly to that provided by a human authority figure. Nass's (1996) experiment demonstrated that participants reported a "specialist" television that broadcasted exclusively news programs or entertainment programs to be more authoritative than a "generalist" television which broadcasted both news programs and entertainment programs. In this study, participants "mindlessly prematurely commit to overly simplistic scripts drawn in the past" (Nass & Moon, 2000, p. 83).

THE MASA PARADIGM

The CASA paradigm was proposed about three decades ago, and the original research program was only a series of lab experiments on desktop computers. Today, as we have a broader spectrum of emerging technologies, including iPads, home-based voice assistants, smartwatches, and telepresence robots, we need a more updated framework to explain our interactions with them. We also need a more solid theoretical framework that meets Chaffee and Berger's (1987) criteria for a scientific theory, including predictive power, explanatory power, heuristic value, and falsifiability.

There is an inherent need to update the CASA paradigm too. According to Nass and Moon (2000), it was unclear whether some social dimensions of a computer were more effective than others in eliciting social responses. It was also unclear whether different combinations of those dimensions had additive or synergistic effects on users' social responses. In addition, Nass and Moon (2000) argued that individuals should be able to present social responses when a media technology presents enough cues. However, what counts as enough to evoke users' social responses was not explained in the original paradigm. Hence, since 2015, Lombard and Xu (2021) have been working on a new paradigm, the MASA paradigm, and seeking to 1) provide a deeper understanding of the role of social cues in users' social responses to technologies, 2) elaborate how personal differences and communication contexts leverage such responses, and 3) revisit the explanatory mechanisms behind users' social responses.

A key concept underlying both the CASA paradigm and the MASA paradigm is medium-as-social-actor presence. Presence is defined as "the perceptual illusion of non-mediation" (Lombard & Ditton, 1997). Presence describes the perceptual experience in which individuals (at least partially) fail to acknowledge or realize the role of technology in creating their experience and treat virtual/augmented places and fictional/artificial actors like real places and real people. As one type of presence, medium-as-social-actor presence refers to the experience in which individuals respond to the social cues presented by a technology per se rather than to the social actors within a medium.

Examples of medium-as-social-actor presence include interacting with automated teller machines and responding to their voice-based instructions, giving a name to an Amazon Echo and treating it as a friend, lifting a mini social robot (e.g., robot *NAO*) and feeling as if we were holding a baby, and getting upset at a computer that "dies"; we perceive all these technologies as if they were social actors even though our responses are toward the technologies themselves.

Medium-as-social-actor presence is essential in understanding individuals' social responses to technologies because different dimensions of social attitudes (e.g., users' trust in technologies, perceived attraction of technologies, perceived personalities of technologies, perceived competency of technologies) and social behavior (e.g., users' conformity to technologies, users' self-disclosure to computers) can all be considered as reflections of individuals' medium-as-social-actor presence experience.

Quality of Social Cues and Explanatory Mechanisms

Revolving around medium-as-social-actor presence, the MASA paradigm first suggests it is necessary to focus on both the quantity and the quality of social cues. Here, social cues are defined as "biologically and physically determined features salient to observers because of their potential as channels of information" (Fiore et al., 2013, p. 2). A large body of prior research on the effects of social cues on users' social responses to technologies has focused on the cumulative effects of social cues (i.e., the more social cues, the stronger social responses). However, the distinct quality of those individual social cues has not been fully explained. Therefore, the MASA paradigm proposes that, based on the potential to evoke users' medium-as-social-actor presence, social cues can be broadly categorized into two groups: primary cues and secondary cues. Primary cues, such as eye gaze, gesture, human-sounding voice, and human shape, are "most salient and central to humans' perception of socialness" (Lombard & Xu, 2021, p. 32). Responses to these primary cues are based on individuals' evolutionary orientation toward human-like or animal-like features. By contrast, secondary cues, such as human size, language, machine-sounding voice, and movements, are less salient and central to humans' perception of socialness. Based on the distinction in the quality of social cues, a hierarchy of social cues should exist that represents social cues' discrete potential for evoking medium-as-social-actor presence and social responses.

In establishing the relationships between individuals' social cues and medium-as-social-actor presence, a list of individual differences and contextual factors were identified as moderators in users' presence experience. Examples of these individual differences include one's anthropocentrism (i.e., the tendency to perceive the world from a human-centered perspective) (Nass et al., 1995), age, personality, prior experience with technologies, tolerance of imperfection (Salem et al., 2013), willingness to suspend disbelief (Duffy & Zawiska, 2012), and critical thinking ability (Lee, 2010).

The effects of social cues on medium-as-social-actor presence also depend upon the context of individuals' interactions with technologies. The types of social responses and the strength of medium-as-social-actor presence may vary with the nature of the human–technology collaboration tasks, the socio-cultural impact on individuals' attitudes toward machines, and the language norms in society. For example, in Chinese, a "computer" is pronounced as "electric brain" (Au, 2021). The equivalent of "artificial intelligence" in English translates to "manual labor smart machinery" in Chinese (Au, 2021). These different language norms may, to some degree, affect, or in the long-term, shape individuals' perception of technologies as social actors.

Early CASA research indicated that mindlessness rather than anthropomorphism explained participants' responses to technologies (Nass & Moon, 2000). However, subsequent research has provided mixed findings about the explanatory mechanism of the CASA paradigm. Both mindlessness and anthropomorphism have received empirical support (Kim & Sundar, 2012; Lee, 2010; Mou & Xu, 2017). To be more aligned with recent literature (Epley et al., 2007; Serpell, 2003), the MASA paradigm uses mindless anthropomorphism and mindful anthropomorphism to describe these two major explanations for social responses. In particular, mindful anthropomorphism refers to a state of mind wherein individuals are actively involved in the present, demonstrate sensitivity when facing novel situations (Langer, 2000), and have a "thoughtful, sincere belief that the object has human characteristics" (Nass & Moon, 2000, p. 93). In contrast, mindless anthropomorphism involves the psychological process wherein individuals are oblivious to the asocial nature of cues, tend to be dependent on repeated behavior or judgments made in the past and be naturally oriented to the social cues due to long-term and frequent exposure to them in daily life (Langer, 2000).

Mindless anthropomorphism likely occurs when technologies demonstrate social cues that are both high in quantity and quality (Lombard & Xu, 2021). In contrast, mindful anthropomorphism is more helpful in explaining users' strong medium-as-social-actor presence with technologies that present only a limited quantity and quality of social cues (Lombard & Xu, 2021). One example of mindless anthropomorphism is that individuals may automatically perceive a vivid, lifelike, humanoid social robot as a social entity because it features a constellation of both primary cues (e.g., humanlike shape, voice, gestures, etc.) and secondary cues (e.g., language, movements). On the other hand, children tend to have a strong ability to mindfully anthropomorphize objects that are not designed to be social. Drawing the sun with a smiley face and assigning a name to their favorite toy reflect children's mindful, deliberate, and thoughtful ascription of human states to non-human agents. While the MASA paradigm described the different scenarios in which mindless anthropomorphism and mindful anthropomorphism are likely to occur, it cannot be denied that the actual activation of these cognitive processing routes is still contingent upon a variety of factors, including the combinations of social cues, personal differences, and contextual factors.

Based on prior literature on the relationship between social cues and medium-as-social-actor presence, as well as the reasonable postulation of the distinction between mindless anthropomorphism and mindful anthropomorphism, Lombard and Xu (2021) proposed nine propositions in the MASA paradigm (p. 42):

P1: Every media technology has at least some potential to evoke medium-as-social-actor presence and social responses.

P2: It is not only the social cues but also the combination of social signals, individual factors, and contextual factors that lead to medium-as-social-actor presence and corresponding social responses.

P3: Some social cues are primary; each is sufficient but not necessary to evoke medium-as-social-actor presence.

P4: Some social cues are secondary; each is neither sufficient nor necessary to evoke medium-as-social-actor presence.

P5a: All other conditions being equal, individuals are more likely to experience medium-as-social-actor presence and socially respond to media technologies that display cues with more human characteristics (quality of cues).

P5b: All other conditions being equal, individuals are more likely to experience medium-as-social-actor presence and socially respond to media technologies that display more social cues (quantity of cues).

P6: All other conditions being equal, the quality of cues (primary vs. secondary) has a greater role in evoking medium-as-social-actor presence and corresponding social responses than the quantity (number) of cues.

P7: Individuals vary in their tendency to perceive and respond to media technologies as social actors.

P8: Individuals' social responses to media technologies can occur with either mindless or mindful processing.

P9a: All other conditions being equal, media technologies that display more cues (quantity of cues) are more likely to lead individuals to mindlessly perceive them as social actors. Conversely, all other conditions being equal and given the same level of social responses, media technologies that display fewer cues (quantity of cues) are more likely to lead individuals to mindfully perceive them as social actors.

P9b: All other conditions being equal, media technologies that display cues with more human characteristics (quality of cues) are more likely to lead individuals to mindlessly perceive them as social actors. Conversely, all other conditions being equal and given the same level of social responses, media technologies that display cues with fewer human characteristics (quality of cues) are more likely to lead individuals to mindfully perceive them as social actors.

On the theory level, the MASA paradigm is a structured extension of the CASA paradigm because it attempts to provide tentative and preliminary responses to Nass and Moon's (2000) questions about 1) whether there exist some dimensions of a computer that are more powerful in evoking social responses than other dimensions, 2) under what circumstances mindlessness is likely to occur, and 3) how "social" is enough for a technology to bring forth mindless responses. Meanwhile, it provides propositions that are heuristically provocative and enable researchers to deduce further research questions related to the potentiality of a range of technologies to evoke medium-as-social-actor presence. The relationship between the CASA and the MASA paradigms is presented in Figure 21.1.

TESTING THE MASA PARADIGM

In this section, we describe two experimental studies that test the quality of social cues in different communication contexts. We then present a meta-analysis that examines the hierarchy of social cues in their effects on users' medium-as-social-actor presence with social robots. Finally, we introduce an online experiment that uses multidimensional scaling to examine individuals' mindless responses to various presence-evoking technologies.

Study 1: Social Robot Alpha

To test the MASA paradigm, Xu (2019) conducted a lab experiment on users' responses to a social robot in a socio-emotional context. This study seeks to understand how individuals respond to social robots that demonstrate gestural movements vs. non-gestural movements and human voice vs. synthetic voice. In this study, gestural movements and human voice are considered primary cues, while non-gestural and synthetic voices are considered secondary cues. This study postulates that gestural movements and human voice should evoke greater levels of medium-as-social-actor presence and social responses compared to non-gestural movements and synthetic voice.

Participants were asked to interact with a 15.67-inch-tall, 8.19-inch-wide, and 4.80-inch-deep social robot "Alpha." In the human voice conditions, pre-recorded human-voiced messages were installed in the robot. In the synthetic voice conditions, text-to-speech software was used to convert the same messages into a machine-sounding voice. In the gestural movements conditions, symbolic gestures, and conversational gestures such as opening arms to suggest openness, bowing to express appreciation, and waving hands to indicate greetings (Krauss et al., 1996) were programmed into the robot. By contrast, non-gestural movements included random movements that did not infer any specific meanings (e.g., holding arms flat, stretching both arms forward, etc.).

The findings of this study suggested that participants developed more trust in the human-voiced social robot than the synthetic-voiced robot; users also reported more perceived attraction and intentions of future interaction with the social robot when it used gestural movements than when it used non-gestural movements.

The findings further suggested that for individuals who had never interacted with any social robot before, the human voice was more likely to evoke users' presence experience, perceived attraction, perceived trustworthiness, and intention of future use of the robot than the synthetic voice. Nevertheless, for those who had previous experiences interacting with social robots, the human voice was less likely to evoke

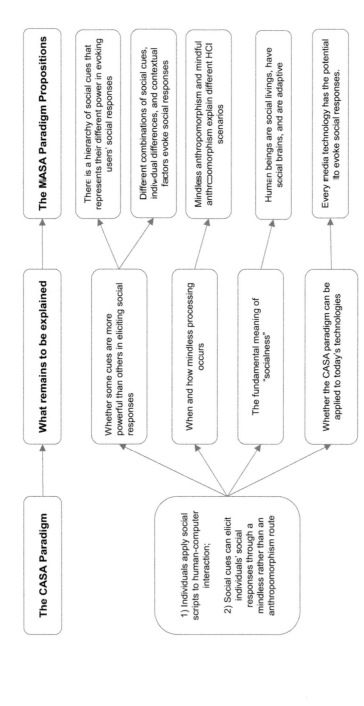

Figure 21.1   The MASA paradigm as an extension of the CASA paradigm

presence, perceived attraction, perceived trustworthiness, and intention of future use than the synthetic voice.

In addition, for those who held a positive attitude toward robots taking social roles in society, gestural movements evoked greater medium-as-social-actor presence. In contrast, for those who held a negative attitude toward robots in social roles, non-gestural movements evoked greater medium-as-social-actor presence.

The study tested and found support for Propositions 2 and 5a in the MASA paradigm. Specifically, the study corroborated that the quality of social cues and individual differences play important roles in users' medium-as-social-actor presence and social responses toward technologies. The study also confirmed that kinetic and vocal cues with more human characteristics exert stronger effects on users' social perception and attitudes than cues with fewer human characteristics.

Study 2: M.I.N.D. Lab Mobile App

In contrast to the robot study, which was situated in a socio-emotional context, another study centered on a task-oriented context. It tested whether a smartphone can evoke users' medium-as-social-actor presence and social responses (Xu, 2020). Instead of seeing smartphones as intermediate devices, this study treated smartphones as communication interlocutors. It examined how individuals react to the linguistic cues (anthropomorphic language vs. non-anthropomorphic language) and modality cues (human voice vs. text) of the devices. In this study, the anthropomorphic language and the human voice were treated as primary social cues and expected to evoke stronger medium-as-social-actor presence and social responses than the non-anthropomorphic language and text-based information.

A voice assistant mobile app called "M.I.N.D. Lab" was developed and installed on a Space Gray iPhone. To manipulate anthropomorphic language, each message included active tense, self-referential statements (e.g., "I," "my"), informal conversational speech (e.g., "well...," "it's like..."), and exaggeration of tone (e.g., "I like it soooo much," "Super!!!"). Comparatively, the non-anthropomorphic language used passive tense, non-self-referential statements, and more formal speech (See Figure 21.2). To manipulate the voice conditions, a pre-recorded human voice was loaded into the mobile user interface. The human-voiced messages were converted to texts in the text conditions.

Participants were asked to work on the hypothetical survival problem "Lost at Sea" (Humber, 2017). In the scenario, they rented a yacht to sail on the sea with friends, but during the trip, the yacht was damaged and was gradually sinking. Participants were asked to select seven out of 14 items that were undamaged for survival. Participants first made decisions independently and then interacted with the smartphone to receive suggestions via the mobile app. Participants were asked to finish reading or listening to all eight messages containing suggestions for selecting the survival items and then make their final choices.

The study suggested that for those who spent less time on mobile media per day, anthropomorphic language evoked users' greater intention to conform to the

Figure 21.2   Anthropomorphic language vs. non-anthropomorphic language on the smartphone

suggestions from the smartphone. In comparison, anthropomorphic language evoked less conformity intention for those who spent more time on mobile phones.

In addition, less intensive smartphone users (i.e., non-power users) reported greater medium-as-social-actor presence, perceived attraction, perceived trustworthiness, and intention to conform to the suggestions from the smartphone when they were exposed to text-based messages than when they received voice-based messages. Comparatively, more intensive smartphone users (i.e., power users) experienced greater medium-as-social-actor presence and corresponding social responses when exposed to voice-based messages than when exposed to text-based ones.

The results of the study supported the MASA paradigm in the following ways. First, unlike social robots, smartphones do not present human shape or kinetic cues. However, aligned with Proposition 1, smartphones can evoke users' medium-as-social-actor presence and social responses with mere variations of linguistic cues and modality cues.

Second, consistent with Proposition 2 in the MASA paradigm, it was not only the quality of social cues but also the individual differences and contextual factors that influenced users' medium-as-social-actor presence. In this study, the hypothesized effect of anthropomorphic language on presence was possibly abated by the task-oriented context, which might have led participants to trust and intend to conform to the messages that were more formal and straightforward.

Study 3: A Meta-Analysis on the Effects of Social Cues

The MASA paradigm suggests that individual social cues have discrete effects on users' medium-as-social-actor presence. That is, a hierarchy of social cues that represents their different power in evoking medium-as-social-actor presence should exist. Therefore, the lead author of this chapter, Kun Xu, along with Mo Chen from the University of Florida, and Leping You from Miami University, conducted a meta-analysis to understand the overall and the individual effects of social cues on users' medium-as-social-actor presence in human–robot interaction.

A total of 25 studies ($N = 2,498$) on the relationship between social cues and medium-as-social-actor presence in the context of human–robot interaction were included in the meta-analysis. The effects of more natural, lifelike, or humanlike cues were compared to unnatural, artificial, or machinelike cues. Pearson correlation r was used to compute the effect sizes for all studies. According to Cohen (1988), the Pearson correlation coefficient of 0.10 is considered as a small effect size, 0.30 as a medium effect size, and 0.50 as a large effect size.

The meta-analysis suggested that overall, designing more humanlike, natural, and lifelike social cues had small-sized effects on users' medium-as-social-actor presence ($0.17 \leq r \leq 0.18$).[1] Although the overall effect size was small, the positive valence suggested that lifelike and humanlike social cues can exert stronger effects on users' medium-as-social-actor presence than artificial and machinelike cues, which supports the idea that the quality of cues matters in users' social perception of technologies.

Subgroup analyses revealed that manipulating humanlike kinetic cues ($.24 \leq r \leq .30$) had small- to medium-size effects on medium-as-social-actor presence. Manipulating facial cues had large-size effects ($r = 0.69$). Comparatively, voices ($r = 0.16$) and language styles ($r = 0.12$) had small-size effects on medium-as-social-actor presence. Humanlike appearances had only limited effects ($0.07 \leq r \leq 0.08$).

Consistent with Proposition 5a in the MASA paradigm, the meta-analysis first confirmed that there exists a hierarchy of social cues that exert distinct effects on users' medium-as-social-actor presence. Specifically, designing more humanlike facial cues and kinetic cues was found to be highly effective in evoking users' medium-as-social-actor presence with social robots, followed by designing humanlike voice, language, and appearance cues.

---

[1] If a study only reported that the results were non-significant, we first assigned zero to the effect size of the study, which led to an underestimated overall effect size. We then removed this single effect size from the sample, which led to an inflated overall effect size. Hence, a range of the effect size could be obtained to account for the study that merely reported non-significant results (Rosenthal, 1995; Sherry, 2001).

Study 4: Mindless Evaluation of Technologies

Apart from the studies on the quality of individual social cues, Xu et al. (2022) used a new approach to test whether individuals' social responses to technologies are mindless or mindful. Although this study is not directly related to any proposition in the MASA paradigm, distinguishing mindless processing from mindful processing has been a central question in past CASA research. Despite previous efforts to test whether it is mindless processing or mindful processing that best explains users' social responses (Kim & Sundar, 2012; Lee, 2010), scholars have admitted that using merely one single method or measurement is not sufficient to provide solid evidence. As Lombard and Xu (2021) argued, testing mindless vs. mindful processing is a long-term process that calls for cumulative evidence based on a combination of different methods, including both objective and subjective ones (e.g., electroencephalography, questionnaires) and real-time and retrospective ones (e.g., think-aloud and thought-list procedures, recall tests).

In this study, 834 participants were randomly assigned to two conditions (mindful processing vs. mindless processing). In the mindful processing condition, participants were provided with a list of 13 social cues (e.g., gestures, human voice, eye gaze, etc.) and nine social signals (i.e., the translation of social cues into abstract human characteristics such as perceived companionship and identity) (Fiore et al., 2013). They were asked to code 14 technologies regarding the involved social cues and signals. This step led participants to actively contemplate the roles of social cues and social signals that each technology can feature. After this step, the participants in this condition were asked to compare different pairs of technologies regarding their power to evoke medium-as-social-actor presence. By contrast, in the mindless condition, participants were directly asked to compare different pairs of technologies regarding their medium-as-social-actor presence-evoking power without being asked to reflect on any social cue or social signal presented by technologies.

According to the mindful anthropomorphism explanation (Lee, 2010), if individuals are asked to reflect on the roles of social cues and social signals, their cognitive map of technology differences in evoking medium-as-social-actor presence should reflect their coding of social cues and social signals. Hence, technologies that are interpreted to possess a similar number of social cues and social signals should be spatially closer to each other, while those interpreted to possess different numbers of social cues and social signals should be spatially apart. Meanwhile, given that mindless and mindful processing are two different cognitive processing routes, the cognitive maps regarding technology differences in these two conditions should be different. By contrast, if mindless anthropomorphism occurs, then even without being asked to code and contemplate the social cues and social signals for each technology, individuals' cognitive maps of technology differences in raising medium-as-social-actor presence in the two conditions should be highly similar.

Drawing on multidimensional scaling and quadratic assignment procedure, this study found that the cognitive map of technology differences in the mindless condition was highly correlated with that in the mindful condition ($r = 0.94$, $p <$ 0.001) (see Figure 21.3), indicating that even without receiving explicit instructions on coding social cues and social signals, participants mindlessly considered social cues and social signals when comparing technology differences (for more details, see Xu et al., 2022).

This study demonstrated that, first, mindlessness has more power than mindful anthropomorphism in explaining users' social responses to technologies. By directly avoiding hinting to participants about the effects of social cues and social signals in the mindless anthropomorphism condition and by utilizing the advantage of multidimensional scaling in visualizing individuals' hidden and implicit psychological structures in assessing technology differences (Jaworska & Chupetlovska-Anastasova, 2009), this study revealed that users' social perception of technologies went through a more involuntary, effortless, and bottom-up process rather than a more controlled, effortful, and top-down cognitive process.

FUTURE RESEARCH DIRECTIONS

Lombard and Xu (2021) began to develop the MASA paradigm in 2015. Drawing on the propositions of the MASA paradigm, research has been conducted on 1) individuals' responses to social cues provided by social robots and smartphones, 2) the aggregated effect sizes of social cues that influence medium-as-social-actor presence across studies, and 3) individuals' psychological processing of media, such as mindless anthropomorphism and mindful anthropomorphism. These studies have at least partially supported the propositions of the MASA paradigm. Meanwhile, they have also pointed to future research directions that can further test, refine, and improve the theoretical framework.

First, the MASA paradigm initially categorizes social cues into primary and secondary ones. However, based on our meta-analysis, even within the category of primary cues exists a hierarchy of social cues. For example, humanlike kinetic cues were found to have a larger effect than humanlike vocal cues. Thus, rather than dichotomizing social cues into primary and secondary ones, listing a hierarchy or spectrum for the effects of all individual social cues may be helpful in future research. On the theory level, it can inform researchers of the discrete quality of social cues and their likely complex interactions with individual differences and contextual factors. On the application level, the hierarchy can inform developers and designers about which social cues to prioritize to enhance user experience and better manage the product development budget. On the methodology level, understanding the effect size of every single social cue can inform researchers' decision-making in creating different experiment conditions and calculating desired sample sizes. Hence, more research should be conducted to understand the hierarchy/spectrum of social cues in various human–technology interaction contexts.

Second, researchers have not tested the MASA propositions related to mindless and mindful anthropomorphism (Propositions 8 and 9). Future research can examine

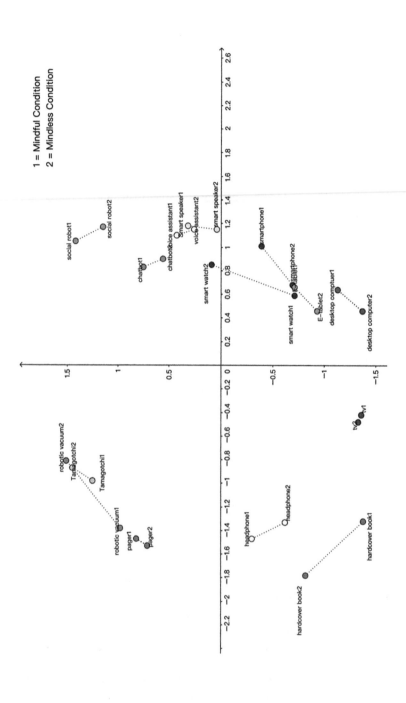

Source: Xu et al. (2022).

Figure 21.3   *A comparison between mindless condition and mindful condition regarding individuals' cognitive maps of technology differences in evoking presence*

whether mindless anthropomorphism is more likely to occur when technologies are designed with cues that are high in quantity and rich in quality and whether mindful anthropomorphism is more likely to explain users' social responses to technologies that display only limited quantity and quality of cues. Meanwhile, the inherent difficulty of measuring mindlessness and mindfulness requires scholars to continue to explore, create, and validate new tools and methods to understand these psychological mechanisms.

Third, as AI-driven technologies become more ubiquitous, sophisticated, and convergent, it is necessary to explicate not only the effects of the verbal and nonverbal social cues designed into technologies but also consider the interactions between broader types of cues. For example, the virtual layovers in individuals' use of augmented reality technologies may present not only humanlike agents that are perceived as social actors but also other types of cues such as interaction time, navigation tools, or typing bars. These cues are not designed to be social or humanlike, but they are added to these technologies to facilitate and expedite the communication between users and technologies. How do individuals perceive these technologies that mingle humanlike cues and non-humanlike cues? Do individuals still naturally orient to the social cues rather than the asocial ones? Another example reflecting the complex mingling of cues is telepresence robots. As users need to respond to the cues presented by the technology per se (e.g., the motion of the robot) as well as the cues presented by the remote user within the technology (e.g., the facial expressions of the remote user), it is possible that users may experience both medium-as-social-actor presence and social-actor-within-medium presence at the same time (Xu & Liao, 2020). In this case, how do the cues within the medium and the cues presented by the medium technology itself interact in evoking users' presence experience? How do users allocate cognitive resources to perceive the technology as a social actor and the remote user as a social actor at the same time? The abovementioned scenarios call for researchers to look deeper into today's HCI phenomena and integrate concepts and theories from computer-mediated communication, information science, sociology, psychology, and other relevant areas to understand AI-driven technologies better.

REFERENCES

Au, Y. (2021, June 29). *A new AI lexicon: An electric brain.* AI NOW Institute. https://medium .com/a-new-ai-lexicon/a-new-ai-lexicon-an-electric-brain-77a81f3ce446

Cohen, J. (1988). *Statistical power analysis for the behavioral sciences.* Routledge.

Chaffee, S. H., & Berger, C. R. (1987). What communication scientists do. In C. R. Berger & S. H. Chaffee (Eds.), *Handbook of communication science* (pp. 99–122). Sage.

Duffy, B. R., & Zawieska, K. (2012 September). Suspension of disbelief in social robotics. In IEEE RO-MAN: *The 21st IEEE International Symposium on Robot and Human Interactive Communication.* https://doi.org/10.1109/ROMAN.2012.6343798

Epley, N., Waytz, A., & Cacioppo, J. T. (2007). On seeing human: A three-factor theory of anthropomorphism. *Psychological Review, 114*(4), 864. https://doi.org/10.1037/0033-295X .114.4.864

Fiore, S. M., Wiltshire, T. J., Lobato, E. J. C., Jentsch, F. G., Huang, W. H., & Axelrod, B. (2013). Toward understanding social cues and signals in human-robot interaction: Effects of robot gaze and proxemics behavior. *Frontiers in Psychology*, *4*, 1–15. https://doi.org/10 .3389/fpsyg.2013.00859

Fogg, B. J., & Nass, C. (1997). How users reciprocate to computers: an experiment that demonstrates behavior change. In *CHI'97 extended abstracts on human factors in computing systems* (pp. 331–332). https://doi.org/10.1145/1120212.1120419

Frias, L. (2020, January 29). A robot named Little Peanut is delivering food to people in quarantine amid the Wuhan coronavirus outbreak. *Insider*. https://www.businessinsider .com/wuhan-virus-robot-little-peanut-delivers-food-to-people-quarantine-2020-1

Henderson, E. (2021, October 20). Improving children's hospital experiences using a social robot. *News Medical*. https://www.news-medical.net/news/20211020/Improving -childrene28099s-hospital-experiences-using-a-social-robot.aspx

Humber. (2017 March). Lost at sea. Retrieved from http://www.humber.ca/centreforteachi ngandlearning/instructionalstrategies/teaching-methods/classroom-strategies designing -instruction/activitiesand-games/lost-at-sea.html

Jaworska, N., & Chupetlovska-Anastasova, A. (2009). A review of multidimensional scaling (MDS) and its utility in various psychological domains. *Tutorials in Quantitative Methods for Psychology*, *5*(1), 1–10. https://doi.org/10.20982/tqmp.05.1.p001

Kim, Y., & Sundar, S. S. (2012). Anthropomorphism of computers: Is it mindful or mindless? *Computers in Human Behavior*, *28*, 241–250. https://doi.org/10.1016/j.chb.2011.09.006

Krauss, R. M., Chen, Y., & Chawla, P. (1996). Nonverbal behavior and nonverbal communication: What do conversational hand gestures tell us? *Advances in Experimental Social Psychology*, *28*, 389–450. https://doi.org/10.1016/S0065-2601(08)60241-5

Langer, E. J. (2000). Mindful learning. *Current Directions in Psychological Science*, *9*(6), 220–223. https://doi.org/10.1111/1467-8721.00099

Lee, E. J. (2010). What triggers social responses to flattering computers? Experimental tests of anthropomorphism and mindlessness explanations. *Communication Research*, *37*, 191–214. https://doi.org/10.1177/0093650209356389

Lombard, M., & Ditton, T. (1997). At the heart of it all: The concept of presence. *Journal of Computer-mediated Communication*, *3*(2), JCMC321. https://doi.org/10.1111/j.1083-6101 .1997.tb00072.x

Lombard, M., & Xu, K. (2021). Social responses to media technologies in the 21st century: The media are social actors paradigm. *Human-Machine Communication*, *2*, 29–55. https:// doi.org/10.30658/hmc.2.2

Lock, S. (2021, January 25). *Hansen Robotics to mass produce Sophia and three other social robots*. ISPR. https://ispr.info/2021/02/03/hansen-robotics-to-mass-produce-sophia-and -three-other-social-robots/

Mou, Y., & Xu, K. (2017). The media inequality: Comparing the initial human-human and human-AI social interactions. *Computers in Human Behavior*, *72*, 432–440. https://doi.org /10.1016/j.chb.2017.02.067

Nass, C. (1996). Technology and roles: A tale of two TVs. *Journal of Communication*, *46*(2), 121–28. https://doi.org/10.1111/j.1460-2466.1996.tb01477.x

Nass, C. I., Lombard, M., Henriksen, L., & Steuer, J. (1995). Anthropocentrism and computers. *Behavior & Information Technology*, *14*(4), 229–238. https://doi.org/10.1080 /01449299508914636

Nass, C., & Moon, Y. (2000). Machines and mindlessness: Social responses to computers. *Journal of Social Issues*, *56*(1), 81–103. https://doi.org/10.1111/0022-4537.00153

Nass, C., Moon, Y., & Green, N. (1997). Are machines gender neutral? Gender-stereotypic responses to computers with voices. *Journal of Applied Social Psychology*, *27*(10), 864–876. https://doi.org/10.1111/j.1559-1816.1997.tb00275.x

Paul, M. L. (2022, June 23). *Experts call the device's new feature a slippery slope, comparing it to an episode of "Black Mirror"*. ISPR. https://ispr.info/2022/06/24/alexa-has-a-new -voice-your-dead-relatives/

Reeves, B., & Nass, C. (1996). *The media equation: How people treat computers, television, and new media like real people.* Cambridge University Press.

Rosenthal, R. (1995). Writing meta-analytic reviews. *Psychological Bulletin, 118*(2), 183. https://doi.org/10.1037/0033-2909/118.2.183

Rosner, H. (2021, July 17). *The ethics of a deepfake Anthony Bourdain voice.* New Yorker. https://www.newyorker.com/culture/annals-of-gastronomy/the-ethics-of-a-deepfake -anthony-bourdain-voice

Salem, M., Eyssel, F., Rohlfing, K., Kopp, S., & Joublin, F. (2013). To err is human (-like): Effects of robot gesture on perceived anthropomorphism and likability. *International Journal of Social Robotics, 5*(3), 313–323. https://doi.org/10.1007/s12369-013-0196-9

Serpell, J. (2003). Anthropomorphism and anthropomorphic selection—beyond the "cute response". *Society & Animals, 11*(1), 83–100. https://doi.org/10.1163/156853003321618864

Sherry, J. L. (2001). The effects of violent video games on aggression: A meta-analysis. *Human Communication Research, 27*(3), 409–431. https://doi.org/10.1111/j.1468-2958 .2001.tb00787.x

Xu, K. (2019). First encounter with robot Alpha: How individual differences interact with vocal and kinetic cues in users' social responses. *New Media & Society, 21*(11–12), 2522-2547. https://doi.org/10.1177/1461444819851479

Xu, K. (2020). Language, modality, and mobile media use experiences: Social responses to smartphone cues in a task-oriented context. *Telematics and Informatics, 48*, 101344. https://doi.org/10.1016/j.tele.2020.101344

Xu, K., Chen, X., & Huang, L. (2022). Deep mind in social responses to technologies: A new approach to explaining the Computers are Social Actors phenomena. *Computers in Human Behavior, 134*, 107321. https://doi.org/10.1016/j.chb.2022.107321

Xu, K., & Liao, T. (2020). Explicating cues: a typology for understanding emerging media technologies. *Journal of Computer-Mediated Communication, 25*(1), 32–43. https://doi .org/10.1093/jcmc/zmz023

Zhao, S. (2006). Humanoid social robots as a medium of communication. *New Media & Society, 8*, 401–419. https://doi.org/10.1177/1461444806061951

PART V

POLICING ARTIFICIAL INTELLIGENCE

22. Evaluating the self-disclosure of personal information to AI-enabled technology

Jessica K. Barfield

INTRODUCTION

As technology equipped with artificial intelligence (AI) enters society, communication and information science scholars are beginning to explore a range of issues that may affect the design and use of the technology (generally, see Andalibi, 2020; Choi et al., 2021; Halvonik & Kapusta, 2016). Briefly, AI affords technology with different abilities, which, among others, may be used to facilitate the process of communication and exchange of information between humans and AI-enabled devices. For example, AI-enabled technologies may be mobile and equipped with computer vision for object detection and collision avoidance (Russell & Norvig, 2020), have the ability to communicate with users using voice or text (Edwards et al., 2019), have facial recognition ability (Chen et al., 2018), have the ability to express emotions (Manohar et al., 2011), or have the ability to evaluate a user's emotional state (Liu et al., 2017). Additionally, consumer products such as cars and home appliances respond to voice commands, smart speakers provide information to users in response to their queries, and other smart technologies understand the user's speech and respond in turn with natural language processing ability (Parush, 2004). The focus of this chapter is how the use of AI-enabled technologies affects the process of communication, particularly the disclosure of personal information between people and technology.

It is known that technologies equipped with AI abilities often interact with people in social contexts, requiring an exchange of information between the user and the AI-enabled device. An important question of interest to information and communication science scholars is how individuals might disclose personal, sensitive, and potentially embarrassing information to technologies equipped with different abilities made possible by AI. Thus, it is essential for communication and information science scholars to ask, for emerging smart devices, will factors such as the physical appearance of the technology, its voice characteristics, or perceived level of intelligence influence the extent to which individuals might disclose personal, sensitive, and potentially embarrassing information to the device? Psychologists have shown that self-disclosure is an important determinant of social behavior, such as liking among individuals, and is central to developing close relationships (Collins & Miller, 1994). Therefore, whether people form social relationships with AI-enabled technology and, as a result, are more likely to disclose personal information to the technology is a topic of interest for information and communication science scholars and thus is discussed in this chapter.

Because this chapter focuses on the extent to which individuals might disclose personal information to AI-enabled technology, past conceptualizations of self-disclosure are briefly reviewed. In this regard, Eyssel et al. (2017) noted that self-disclosure is revealing personal information, thoughts, and feelings to another. And Uchida et al. (2017) described self-disclosure as the act of notifying others of one's personal information. Similarly, according to Andalibi et al. (2018), "Self-disclosure refers to sharing information about oneself with others, a process which involves navigating the boundary between safely concealing information and making one's self vulnerable by sharing that information" (p. 8). The aspect of "vulnerability" in the above definition is an essential component of self-disclosure and raises the question of whether humans would feel more (or less) vulnerable disclosing personal information to AI-enabled technology (such as a robot counselor) than to a human, and if so, for what reason? Further, past research within information and communication sciences has shown that various factors in technology design may influence how individuals communicate with the technology (Laing & Apperley, 2020; Tsukamoto, 1999; Yarosh & Markopoulos, 2010). For example, considering AI-enabled technology, Sun et al. (2022) commented that while AI personal assistants have penetrated deeply into users' lives, they often lead to a poor interaction experience which can be mediated by better user interface design, which, of course, is a focus area of research for information and communication science scholars.

DISCLOSURE OF INFORMATION

There are numerous reasons why exchanging information between people and AI-enabled technology, such as a digital assistant or humanoid robot, may be advantageous. For example, chatbots not only answer user queries on a range of topics but may ask the user for information to guide the advice given (Raees et al., 2019; Schanke et al., 2021). Moreover, when using route guidance systems, users typically input a starting and end-point destination, often querying the route guidance system for information during the trip. However, in some situations, users may be reluctant to share personal information with AI-enabled technology due to concerns and consequences associated with the disclosure (Figure 22.1). For example, people may be concerned that what they reveal to technology equipped with AI may not remain private (Senicar et al., 2003) but may, instead, be revealed to a third party. Further, people may be reluctant to share personal information with a nonhuman entity, preferring to disclose it to a human (of course, under some circumstances, the opposite could be true). Thus, based on several factors, which may include the design of the technology itself and the extent of its AI abilities, people may be reluctant to disclose personal information to AI-enabled devices. For example, considering privacy, people may be concerned that disclosure of personal or embarrassing information to an AI-enabled device could be disclosed to a third party (Koay et al., 2009; Syrdal et al., 2007). This concern is particularly relevant for smart technologies that can continuously listen, see, and record interactions with a user. Still, numerous situations

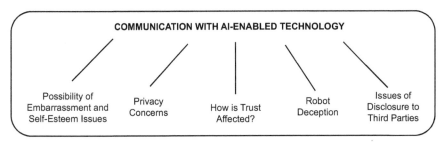

Figure 22.1   Communication with AI-enabled technology influences several aspects of human interaction with technology

require an individual to divulge personal information to AI-enabled technologies, such as a robot, chatbot, or digital assistant (Mumm & Mutlu, 2011). For example, the elderly will need to provide personal information about their health to a medical service robot, people seeking counseling will need to divulge personal information about behavioral issues to a robot counselor (Barfield, 2021), and in banking, people may be required to reveal sensitive financial information to intelligent entities such as a robo-investor (Aroyo et al., 2018; Eyssel et al., 2017). In addition, as stated earlier, the disclosure of information is deemed essential to form social relationships with other people (or with technology). In this chapter, I review studies that suggest how the AI-enabled technology communicates to the user, how the technology is designed, and the subject matter of the communication itself can influence the information exchange between individuals and AI-enabled devices.

Next, the literature on self-disclosure of personal information to digital assistants is discussed due to how ubiquitous such devices are becoming. Following that discussion is a review of studies on the self-disclosure of personal information to humanoid robots interacting with people in social contexts (Jones, 2017). The chapter concludes with comments on the design of AI-enabled technology from the perspective of communication and information sciences.

Disclosing Personal Information to Digital Assistants

One of the most common AI-enabled technologies equipped with communication ability is a digital assistant that operates within the user's home or workplace. Belanger et al. (2021) commented that such devices (e.g., smart home speakers) are becoming a common aspect of family lives. However, there are downsides to using digital assistants that listen and speak; for example, they often collect data that can be shared with the device's provider, thus constituting a privacy concern for users. On this issue, employing a longitudinal grounded theory approach, Belanger and colleagues (2021) sought to determine how family members changed their personal information privacy views over time when using a shared digital assistant within their home. They found that the decisions family members made about privacy settings and how the digital technology was used at home influenced the family members' information behaviors and decisions regarding the usage of the smart device. In a similar study, Lutz and Newlands (2021) found that privacy when using smart speakers is a serious consideration among users due to issues surrounding the smart speakers' specific technological affordances. Using Amazon Echo and Google Home, participants from the United Kingdom indicated that the fear of third parties listening to smart speaker recordings was a major consideration in using digital assistants. Taken together, the above studies indicate that privacy and concerns about the nonpermissive collection and use of information are important considerations among users of AI-enabled devices and, among others, could influence the extent to which people self-disclose personal information to digital assistants.

In addition, as with the use of technology in general, whether users trust the AI-enabled devices they are using is an essential factor that may guide the exchange of information between humans and technology. For example, Schroeder and Schroeder (2018) commented that every day, people make decisions about whether to trust machines with their personal information, such as letting a smartphone track one's geographic location. Studying participants in real-world scenarios, Schroder and Schroeder evaluated how two modes of interaction-expression modality, consisting of either talking or typing to a machine, and response modality, whether the machine talked or typed back to the user, influenced their willingness to trust the machine. It was predicted that talking to a machine might make people more willing to share their personal information. Based on the human tendency to anthropomorphize technology, machines that talked (versus texted) would seem more humanlike and, thus, be trusted more. Using a chatbot phone application, the researchers measured how much participants anthropomorphized the machine and their willingness to share their personal information (e.g., their location and credit card information). The main result revealed that talking as the mode of communication led to people being more willing to share their personal information than texting. This result was replicated when considering participants' self-reported technology comfort, age, gender, and conversation characteristics (Schroeder & Schroeder, 2018).

In a more recent study on the self-disclosure of personal information to AI-enabled technology, Pal et al. (2020) examined factors affecting the user's willingness to disclose personal information to a voice assistant. Data from respondents were analyzed using a maximum likelihood structural equation model. The model showed that personalized services delivered by the voice assistant and the perceived enjoyment and perceived complementarity nature of the assistant influenced the perceived benefits of using the technology, which was shown to positively affect personal information disclosure (Pal et al., 2020). Another study on the disclosure of information employed the communication privacy management theory, and the privacy trust behavioral intention model, and investigated the end users' willingness to disclose personal information to internet of things (IoT) service providers despite the known privacy risks (Pal et al., 2021). Using participants from Thailand and Singapore who actively used at least one type of IoT service – smart home, smart health care, or smart cities – the researchers found that trust, perceived privacy risks, perceived benefits, and the level of information sensitivity affected the users' willingness to disclose personal information.

In addition, in the area of consumer behavior, Roding et al. (2019) commented that little is known about a customer's information disclosure at the physical point of sale (PoS) when the application concerns technology-based (e.g., using a tablet for information gathering) frontline employee service encounters. Using an online study, Roding and colleagues (2019) found that using technology negatively affected the customer's willingness to disclose information due to concerns about sharing information with retailers who might misuse the information. However, Ho, Hancock, and Miner (2018) concluded that disclosing personal information to another person has beneficial emotional, relational, and psychological outcomes. They found that when disclosers believed they were interacting with a chatbot that simulated human-to-human conversation, among others, outcomes could either be enhanced or at least equivalent to interacting with a person. Taken together, the above studies show that users can be expected to disclose information to AI-enabled technologies, but concerns such as privacy and misuse of information are important issues.

Disclosing Personal Information to Robots

Given the emergence of robots within society, a particular focus of this chapter is on the self-disclosure of personal information to social robots that are equipped with AI abilities and that are humanoid in appearance and behavior. Bartneck and Forlizzi (2004) defined a social robot as "an autonomous or semi-autonomous robot that interacts and communicates with humans by following the behavioral norms expected by the people with whom the robot is intended to interact" (p. 592). With robot assistants, users are often required to provide the robot with information that could be considered personal or even embarrassing about topics ranging from their medical history to financial, behavioral, and relationship issues (Barfield, 2021). The proliferation of social robots within society serving in roles such as a teacher, medical assistant, companion, and frontline service employee in different industries, has raised numerous design issues that scholars in communication and information sciences are beginning to explore. Among others, these include the physical appearance of the robot and its communication ability. Thus, while reviewing the literature on the disclosure of personal information to different AI-enabled technologies, in this chapter, there is a focus on the disclosure of personal, sensitive, and potentially embarrassing information to humanoid robots experienced within a social context (often referred to as experiencing robots in the wild). Given the increasingly social nature of robots and that they are becoming ever smarter due to different AI techniques, social robots are a particularly interesting technology to discuss within the context of communication and information sciences and raise numerous theoretical and applied issues for the design of robotic technologies.

According to Libin and Libin (2004), people tend to perceive and treat robots as if they have human attributes and, thus, do not view or treat them as machines but more so as companions or artificial partners. Based on this observation, as people interact with robots, will they feel comfortable disclosing personal information to them? Thus far, only a few studies have looked at the use of a robot in a situation requiring the disclosure of personal information, so the extent to which an individual might disclose personal and sensitive information to a robot is a relatively unexplored topic. Discussing the self-disclosure of personal information using internet-based media, Andalibi (2020) found that disclosing personal and sensitive information to another could benefit the disclosing individual's well-being. However, she observed that many who may benefit from such disclosures typically do not seek out services such as counseling due to cost and the reluctance to disclose potentially embarrassing information to another person (Andalibi et al., 2018). For this reason, if users accept robots that operate with sufficient communication skills, a robot counselor could perform a valuable service within society.

In a recent study, Eichenberg et al. (2019) examined the therapeutic use of robots for sexual therapy. The study consisted of research techniques such as an online survey, participant interviews, and a questionnaire to ascertain the attitudes of therapists and medical professionals about possible benefits associated with sex robots used in therapy. A qualitative aspect of the study was designed to provide insight into the participants' beliefs and attitudes toward robots. The results indicated that of 72 sex therapists and physicians who completed a questionnaire, only a few responded that the use of sex robots was beyond the realm of possibility. Further, an analysis of five interviews identified three high-level core themes that were representative of the participants' responses: "(1) the importance of the personal definition of sex robots for the assessment of their therapeutic benefits, (2) therapeutic benefits and dangers of sex robots, and (3) considerations on the quality of human–robot sexuality" (Eichenberg et al., 2019, p. e13853).

In related work, Uchida et al. (2017) developed a robot counseling system to promote self-disclosure among clients and reduce their anxiety. They noted that clients sometimes hesitate to disclose intrusive topics due to embarrassment and self-esteem issues when a counselor is human. However, commenting on a robot counselor's unique (machine) agency, Uchida and colleagues postulated that using a robot could remove "mental barriers" between the counselor and the client and promote self-disclosure about negative topics. In their study, two robots (android and desktop robot), a human, and a sound-only condition were used as counselors. Among others, the results indicated that subjects did self-disclose to the robots based on the number of words spoken. Further, Uchida and colleagues commented that robots can draw out subjects' self-disclosure about negative topics more so than a human counselor. However, more research is needed to explore this conjecture, as it is at odds with the results of other studies (e.g., see Barfield, 2021).

Additionally, Utami, Bockmore, and Kruger (2017) discussed their work to develop a robot that counseled couples, particularly encouraging collaborative responses between counseling participants. In their study, Utami and colleagues used a robot to facilitate a counseling session to promote a couple's intimacy in which they co-constructed a response to a query from a robot. The findings suggested that the session with the robot improved the couple's intimacy and positive affect. In another study also on robot counseling, Nomura et al. (2020) looked at whether people experiencing social anxiety would show less actual and "anticipatory" anxiety when interacting with a robot. Interestingly, their results showed that participants who experienced higher social anxiety reported less "anticipatory anxiety" and tension when informed that they would interact with a robot compared to a human. Birmingham et al. (2020) also commented that socially assistive robots can improve communication when groups of people interact in social settings, thus, providing indirect support for the idea that robots may spur disclosures among people within groups. Reviewing the above discussion, humans may disclose personal information to robots based on the notion that robots lack the mental agency of humans (or possibly are viewed as having a different type of mental agency), thus, removing a barrier to disclosing sensitive information to a human counselor, which could result in embarrassment or judgment. However, this conjecture should be the subject of further research, as it has important implications for communication and information sciences and the design of human–robot interfaces.

Additionally, Heuer et al. (2019) investigated the use of social robots in the context of personal information disclosure. In their study, participants indicated their attitude toward robot functionality, the sharing of personal information, and the participants' interest in robot transparency and intervenability. Participants who reported previously working with robots revealed a more open-minded attitude to sharing personal information with a robot, thus, showing that prior experience with a robot could mediate human–robot responses. In related work, Laban, Morrison, and Cross (2020) tested the viability of using social robots to elicit people's disclosures to identify their needs and emotional states. In their study, the researchers were interested in how people disclosed (nonsensitive) personal information to robots to further understand the differences between one's subjective perceptions of disclosure compared to evidence of actual disclosure of shared content. Their results suggested that while people perceived they disclosed more to humans than to humanoid social robots or conversational agents, no actual observed differences in the content of the disclosure emerged between the agents (Laban et al., 2020). This is a notable finding suggesting that the user's perception of the extent of self-disclosure is a factor to be considered in human–robot interactions.

Returning to the idea that people are reluctant to be judged by others, Joshi et al. (2020) commented that patients concerned with being judged often do not trust their physicians with confidential, private information. Therefore, they argued that it might be helpful to complement or delegate some of a physician's tasks to a robot. They postulated that people might be more willing to disclose private information to robots if they believed the robot was unbiased and without negative judgment. The researchers also commented that a robot could improve information disclosure and perhaps even allow the physicians more time for targeted and appropriate health care decisions. In related work, Uchida et al. (2020) commented that disclosing personal matters to other individuals often contributes to maintaining our mental health and social bonding. However, it can be difficult in face-to-face situations to prompt others to self-disclose because people often feel embarrassed disclosing personal matters to others. The results of Uchida's research, which was based on questionnaires and actual self-disclosure behavior, indicated that men preferred to self-disclose to a human listener. At the same time, women did not discriminate between robots and humans as listeners for their self-disclosure, the willingness to disclose, or the amount of self-disclosure. This suggests that gender differences must be considered when robots are used as self-disclosure listeners.

Looking more carefully at the HRI conversational interface, Eyssel and colleagues (2017) investigated self-disclosure's role in HRI with participants randomly assigned to one of four experimental conditions in which they interacted with the humanoid robot NAO. They manipulated whether the robot disclosed personal information or whether the robot asked personal questions of the human interaction partner in order to make the participant self-disclose. In two conditions, the robot either made factual statements or asked factual questions. The results indicated no statistically significant effects of self-disclosure on the dependent variables of robot likability, judgments of human–robot interaction quality, future contact intentions, and mind attribution. Among others, the research highlighted the importance of considering covariates (i.e., interindividual differences in the tendency to anthropomorphize nonhuman entities) in the data analyses. Finally, De Groot et al. (2019) indicated that the willingness to share personal information about negative social experiences is of great importance for the effectiveness of robot-mediated social therapies. The researchers reported the results of a pilot study on the effectiveness of using a game or a conversation on achieving a higher self-disclosure in people with visual and intellectual disabilities. The participants interacted with a humanoid robot NAO using game-based or conversation-based interactions, and the researchers measured the length of the self-disclosing sentences during the two interactions. The majority of the participants said that they preferred the conversation-based over the game-based interaction. The results also indicated that during the game-based interaction, the participants used much longer self-disclosing sentences compared to the conversation-based interaction. In the next section of the chapter, the results of a recent study by the author on the self-disclosure of personal and sensitive information to robot counselors are discussed.

A STUDY OF ROBOT APPEARANCE ON SELF-DISCLOSURE

Barfield (2021) investigated the self-disclosure of personal information to a robot counselor primarily as a function of robot appearance. The study's goal was to expand the range of self-disclosure decisions required of participants and to evaluate whether robot appearance mattered for self-disclosure. Given the expanding use of robots as counselors, two important research questions for roboticists, communication, and information science scholars were addressed in the study:

1. Does the robot's appearance affect the decision to self-disclose?
2. To what extent will people reveal personal information to a robot based on the type of information to be disclosed?

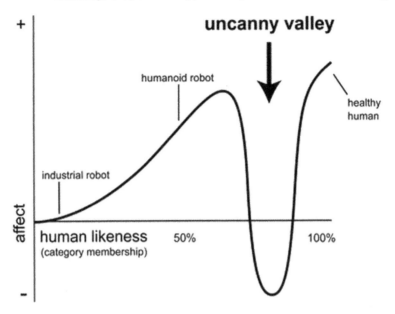

Figure 22.2   *The uncanny valley. At what point on the curve will the self-disclosure of personal information to a robot be affected?*

On the first question, literature describing the uncanny valley effect (Mori, 2012; Uchida et al., 2017) suggests that robot appearance should, in fact, matter for self-disclosure, and thus, robot appearance would be an interesting variable to include in a study on the disclosure of personal information to a robot.

Figure 22.2 shows the human response to robots as a function of their human likeness, as reported in numerous research studies (Barfield, 2021; De Groot et al., 2019; Eyssel et al., 2017). As discussed by Mori (2012), the dip in the curve is referred to as the uncanny valley, in which robots are perceived as not quite approaching human likeness and, as a result, elicit an eerie or uneasy reaction from humans. An interesting question is whether or how the uncanny valley effect influences the self-disclosure of personal information to robots.

Does Robot Appearance Matter for Self-Disclosure?

The first question addressed in Barfield's study was the effect of robot appearance on self-disclosure. Motivating this question, roboticists have indicated that given the increased exposure of people to robots in social situations, it is crucial to explore the type and amount of personal information a person may decide to disclose. One controlling factor could be the robot's physical appearance (Uchida et al., 2017), and there is reason to believe that robot appearance could influence self-disclosure. For example, Haring et al. (2016) stated that the appearance of a robot plays a major role in first encounters and in short-term interaction with robots. Using participants from Japan and Australia, Haring and colleagues evaluated three human–robot interactions using three different robot types consisting of an android robot, a humanoid robot, and a nonbiomimetic robot (a robot based on biological principles which translate such principles into an engineered system) before and after interacting with the robots. The results of their study showed significant differences in how people perceived the robots based on appearance alone and on appearance and behavior after a short interaction (Haring et al., 2015). In addition, for an individual to disclose personal and potentially embarrassing information to a robot serving as a counselor, they must trust that the robot will safeguard their disclosures and be an empathetic listener.

Participants were recruited using social media. There were 110 participants, including 63 female and 47 male participants, with a mean age of 35.4 years. After Institutional Review Board (IRB) approval and agreement to participate in the study, participants completed an online questionnaire consisting of 34 questions. As a procedure, the participants were first asked to examine the four images in Figure 22.3 and told to imagine that each image was a counselor for various situations described to the participant in the following survey questions (questions consisted of 1–7 Likert items). After viewing the four images, participants answered questions about each image separately (presented randomly with the specific image on the screen for the question) through an online survey.

Robot Self-Disclosure Findings

As a general observation to guide interpretation of the following results, conversations with participants who completed the study indicated that they viewed Robot B as friendly and Robot D as low in affect and lacking empathy and commented that the robot appeared to have a serious facial expression. When asked which image appeared to be most trustworthy, which could be argued is a precursor for information disclosure (Gill & Thompson, 2017; Salehan et al., 2018), the human counselor

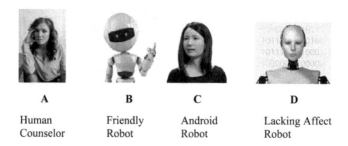

A	B	C	D
Human Counselor	Friendly Robot	Android Robot	Lacking Affect Robot

Figure 22.3   *The four images used in Barfield's (2021) study – Human (A), Robot (B), Android Robot (C), and Robot (D)*

was selected most often (n = 48), followed by the friendly appearing robot (n = 26), the android robot (n = 19), and lastly, the more serious appearing robot (n = 9). This response pattern is consistently repeated throughout the study.

Marriage questions

The participants were asked, "If you had to divulge personal or embarrassing information about your marriage/relationship to a counselor, of the four images representing counselors, which image would you select?" The results indicated that the participants would, by far, select the human counselor (46%), compared to the friendly appearing robot (25%), the android robot (25%), and lastly, the more serious appearing robot (4%) (for this, and other questions, based on a Chi-square test, the results are statistically significant, $p < 0.01$). In fact, Robot D, judged by participants to display low affect and to be serious in appearance, was consistently rated last for all questions relating to information disclosure. Further, when asked which image the participant would feel most comfortable divulging personal information about a previous marriage/relationship, the results again indicated that the human image was more likely to be selected as a counselor ($\bar{x} = 4.66$), and the more serious appearing robot was least likely to be selected ($\bar{x} = 2.70$). The more friendly appearing robot $(\bar{x} = 3.27)$ and the android robot $(\bar{x} = 3.98)$ were rated between the human and the low affect robot on this question. Further, when asked which robot the participant would feel most comfortable discussing whether they had cheated on their spouse, the appearance of the robot counselor again produced a difference. The human counselor was preferred most often ($\bar{x}$ = 4.05), followed by the friendly robot ($\bar{x}$ = 3.75), the android robot ($\bar{x}$ = 3.62), and lastly, the more serious appearing robot ($\bar{x}$ = 3.14). The above results imply that robot appearance is an important factor to consider when self-disclosure of personal information about a marriage is necessary. Additionally, the results support the overall conclusion that counselor's appearance influences participants' comfort in disclosing personal information to the counselor.

Disclosure of highly sensitive topics

The online survey also consisted of questions that participants would likely have difficulty discussing with a counselor due to their sensitive nature. For example, the respondent was asked to consider if they or their partner previously consented to an abortion. If so, they were asked which counselor they would feel most comfortable with to discuss that information. Participants indicated they would be most comfortable revealing that information to the human counselor ($\bar{x}$ = 4.41), followed by the android ($\bar{x} = 3.60$), and then lastly, the more serious appearing robot ($\bar{x} = 3.36$) and the more friendly appearing robot ($\bar{x} = 3.37$). Another highly sensitive topic to discuss with another party is whether the individual has a history of sexual abuse. When asked who they would confide in if they were sexually abused, the participants indicated being most comfortable revealing that information to the human counselor ($\bar{x}$ = 4.42), followed by the android ($\bar{x} = 3.77$), the more friendly appearing robot ($\bar{x} = 3.27$), and lastly, the more serious appearing robot ($\bar{x} = 2.82$).

Table 22.1   *Summary of mean responses to selection of robot/person most likely to communicate with if the individual had lost their job, to discuss views on abortions, or if sexually abused*

	Lost job	Abortion views	Sexually assaulted
Image			
Human	4.81	4.45	4.42
Robot B (friendly robot)	3.53	3.81	3.27
Android	4.35	4.15	3.77
Robot D (lack of empathy)	3.19	3.56	2.82

Note: *Likert item:* 1 (not likely) to 7 (most likely).

The following table summarizes some of the main results of the study, revealing a strong preference for the human counselor, followed by the female android, and lastly, the more serious appearing robot.

Financial and job-related information

If the participant was asked to consider a situation in which they had lost their job, the results followed the consistent pattern in selecting a counselor to confide in as described above. The human was most likely to be selected as the counselor ($\bar{x} = 4.81$), the robot that was thought to lack affect was least likely to be selected ($\bar{x} = 3.19$), with the android robot $(\bar{x} = 4.35)$ and the friendly-appearing robot $(\bar{x} = 3.53)$ placed between these two endpoints. The respondent was also asked if they were in serious debt, which counselor would they select to discuss that issue. The participant's responses indicated the human counselor was most preferred ($\bar{x} = 4.52$), followed by the android robot ($\bar{x} = 3.83$) and the more friendly appearing robot ($\bar{x} = 3.83$), and lastly, the more serious appearing robot ($\bar{x} = 3.02$).

Health information

It was interesting to determine if sharing information about one's health would depend on whether the counselor was human in appearance; and if not, whether robot appearance mattered for self-disclosure of health information. Interestingly, the human was selected more than twice as often for the disclosure of health-related information as the more serious appearing robot indicating that human-ness in appearance matters. Given that participants viewed robot D (Figure 22.3) as showing less empathy, this result is not unexpected. What is also interesting is that the frequency of self-disclosure to the friendly appearing robot (B), or a more human appearing android robot (C) was approximately the same for health information disclosure.

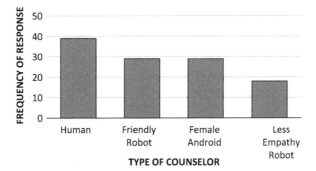

Figure 22.4   *Frequency of response to the question: "If you had to divulge per-sonal/embarrassing information about your health, which image would you select for your medical doctor?"*

DISCUSSION

Overall, the results indicated that robot appearance is an important factor in disclosing personal information to a robot counselor. From Barfield's study, the results consistently showed that the human counselor was preferred over the female android and the other two robots when self-disclosure of personal, sensitive, and potentially embarrassing information was required. Interestingly, these results were replicated over a range of topics, including relationship counseling, discussing sexual abuse, health information, abortion, and job loss. Another point to make is that the data were analyzed to determine whether participants who identified as Black or White responded differently to the counselors and the disclosure questions. The participants who identified as Black or White closely followed the above pattern of results (i.e., selecting the human counselor first, then the friendly robot, android, and lastly, serious robot) for each question. Further, the results revealed whether there were any gender differences in self-disclosure. The results showed no pattern for gender; that is, the standard order of preference for the robots as listening agents was the same regardless of participants' gender. This finding partially contradicts Uchida's and colleagues (2020) finding that participants' gender matters for self-disclosure in that men preferred to self-disclose to a human listener, and women had no preference between robots and humans. In Barfield's study, the human female was always preferred regardless of the type of disclosure or participants' gender. In addition, the results from Barfield's study showed that the more serious appearing robot, which participants thought lacked empathy, not surprisingly, was consistently selected last for self-disclosure of personal information. Thus, using design features (such as expressive eyes or a smile) to create the impression of a friendly affect could benefit human interaction with a robot in a counseling scenario in which the disclosure of personal information is necessary.

Considering robot agency, the data from Barfield's study did not support the conclusions of Uchida et al. (2017), who hypothesized that a robot counselor, due to its unique agency, would remove mental barriers between the counselor and the client and, therefore, promote self-disclosure about negative topics more so than with a human counselor. Barfield (2021) showed no support for this view, as participants preferred the human counselor for self-disclosure across all types of disclosure scenarios considered in the study. Further, when participants were asked which robot they trusted most, the results indicated that the human counselor was selected more often than the friendly robot, the android, and lastly, the more serious appearing robot. Perhaps the human female was consistently selected for a counselor because she was judged more trustworthy than the robots, and trustworthiness is thought to be a precursor for self-disclosure (Wheeless & Grotz, 1977). Finally, when asked which image, human or robot, appeared to have the best personality, the human was selected first ($n = 41$) followed by the friendly appearing robot ($n = 31$), the android robot ($n - 25$), and lastly, the more serious appearing Robot D ($n = 4$). Of course, for these results, the particular robot images selected for use in the study could be a determining factor for the results shown. Therefore, an extension of the study with a broader range of robot images could provide additional information on the use of robots for counseling and for evaluating self-disclosure to an AI-enabled robot.

Concluding Barfield's study, the results showed that while a human counselor is preferred for self-disclosure over the three robot images viewed in the study, participants did indicate that they would disclose to a robot counselor and quite often with a preference shown for the more friendly appearing robot. It was also shown that the more friendly appearing robot was deemed more trustworthy than the android and the less empathetic appearing robot. Thus, for a robot counselor, trust and friendliness seem to be essential factors in encouraging the self-disclosure of personal information. Interestingly, participants' comments about the friendly appearing Robot B were that it resembled a child-like robot and would not judge, which could have been a factor in its selection as first among the three robots for self-disclosure. Of the few participants who responded that they would trust the more serious appearing Robot D the most, they responded that it looked like a "classic robot" that could be programmed not to break the individual's trust. From Barfield's study, even though the human was the most preferred counselor, it can still be concluded that robot appearance does matter for disclosure of personal information. Moreover, the more friendly the affect expressed by the robot, I propose, the more likely the robot will be acceptable as a counselor. As robotic technology advances, robot counselors' capabilities will continue to improve, and their appearance will more and more become an important factor in their acceptance by the general public. Future research by communication and information science scholars should more fully investigate users' perception of robots for various tasks as a function of robot appearance.

USE OF AI-ENABLED TECHNOLOGY TO ENHANCE COMMUNICATION AND EXCHANGE OF INFORMATION

The following thoughts are provided from the above review of the literature on the self-disclosure of personal information to AI-enabled technology and are based on the results of Barfield's (2021) study on self-disclosure to robot counselors. The points presented are included to encourage additional research and discussion on the disclosure of personal information to AI-enabled technology.

(1) *Affect is important.* The perceived affect of an AI-enabled device is important for information disclosure. For example, the facial features and expressions of a robot interacting with people may influence the degree to which individuals self-disclose personal information to the robot. Considering the three robots used in the above study by Barfield (2021), a robot designed with a friendly appearance may lead to more disclosure of personal information than a robot perceived as sterner or less friendly. Other work has also shown that the facial features of a robot may influence user performance, thus, providing additional support for the idea that the design of a robot's face may influence the level of self-disclosures from individuals. On this point, Song and Yan (2020) commented that the facial features of robots could influence the perception of robot trustworthiness. Additionally, it also seems likely that robot facial features will play an important role in developing trust between humans and robots, which may increase the likelihood of self-disclosure. Also, of importance for self-disclosure, Itoh and colleagues (2004) observed that a robot communicates with a human more naturally when it expresses emotions based on its facial features (see also Lee et al., 2006). For the points made here, it should be noted that it is not just robots that portray facial features as they interact with users, but so, too, do other forms of AI-enabled technologies such as chatbots that use a face to aid communication. Given the importance of disclosing information to AI-enabled devices, the extent to which the current results generalize to other forms of AI-enabled technology should be the focus of additional studies.

(2) *User gender and robot gender.* Preliminary evidence has shown that the gender of the participant may affect the level of self-disclosure to a robot, and likewise, the gender of the robot may influence the extent of user self-disclosure. Kuchenbrandt et al. (2014) investigated how the "gender typicality" of an HRI task would affect the users' performance during the task and the users' evaluation, acceptance, and anthropomorphism of the robot. In their research, participants performed either a stereotypically male or a stereotypically female task while being instructed by a "male" or a "female" robot. When participants performed a typically female task with the robot, they were less willing to accept help from the robot in a future task and anthropomorphized the robot to a lesser extent. Thus, the gender typicality of an HRI task substantially influences the human interaction with robots and humans' perceptions and acceptance of a robot. Additionally, Perugia et al. (2021) investigated how people attributed gender to a robot by evaluating 15 robot faces regarding femininity, masculinity, communion, and agency. Their results showed that as a first impression, the feminine robots were perceived as less agentic than masculine appearing robots. This means that people gender stereotype robots, and thus, the extent to which gender stereotypes influence self-disclosure of information to AI-enabled technology should be investigated more fully. On this point, Nomura and

Suzuki (2022) found that when participants were asked whether male, female, or a neutral gender was preferred in terms of the appearance of communication partners, their results revealed a weak effect, with a female gender preference revealed in only some categories. Interestingly, gender stereotypes' influence on robots depended on the human participant's occupation. Those with counselor, adviser, nurse, and caregiver occupations were less likely to stereotype or show gender preferences toward robots operating in their own field of expertise. The extent to which human occupations match those of AI-enabled devices is an interesting topic for further investigation in the area of information disclosure to AI-enabled technology. Finally, Uchida and colleagues (2017) indicated that men preferred to self-disclose to a human listener, while women did not discriminate between robots and humans as listeners for their self-disclosure, or for the willingness to disclose, or the amount of self-disclosure. Moreover, as discussed above, Barfield showed a consistent preference to disclose to the female human counselor. In summary, the perceived gender of the robot or listening agent and the gender of the human interacting with a robot should be considered for human interaction with robots and warrants further research in the area of information disclosure.

(3) *Human preferred for behavioral counseling.* Given the three robots used in the above study by Barfield (2021), a human counselor was always preferred regardless of the type of personal or sensitive information to be self-disclosed. So, a question for communication and information science scholars is how to design robots more likely to be preferred as listening agents. From the literature review and the above study, the robot's physical appearance (and particularly its facial features) and whether it elicits trust are two factors to consider. Supporting this conclusion, Dinet and Vivian (2015) observed that users may be more likely to accept robots with a human appearance because they are physically closer to actual humans. However, as stated above when discussing the uncanny valley effect, too much physical similarity between robots and humans may lead to negative attitudes toward robots and, thus, could result in less self-disclosure. In the above study by Barfield, of the three robots, the android robot was closest to a human in appearance (and, thus, more so within the uncanny valley?) yet did not result in the least preference for disclosure. But the more serious appearing robot was consistently rated last for self-disclosure. Therefore, there is an interesting effect of robot appearance influencing self-disclosure which needs to be more fully investigated.

(4) *Perceived robot agency.* The results from Barfield (2021) showed that none of the three robots were selected for self-disclosure more so than the human counselor. This result is in contrast to Uchida and colleagues' conjecture (2017) that when a counselor is human, clients may hesitate to disclose intrusive topics due to fear of being judged. They also proposed that a robot would remove barriers between the counselor and the client resulting in more disclosure due to its perceived (machine) agency (i.e., it may not be judgmental). No evidence for either conjecture was shown in Barfield's study. However, the results could be

related to how the studies were run. In Barfield's study, robot images were used, whereas, in Uchida's study, participants viewed actual robots. The differences in the images may have influenced the perception of robot agency, which could have influenced self-disclosure and, thus, warrants additional study. Finally, Itoh et al. (2004) observed that, for humans, facial features, such as the position and shape of the eyes, eyebrows, nose, mouth, and ears, contribute to their perceived mental states and could be used to help design a robot's appearance to be seen as less judgmental.

FUTURE RESEARCH DIRECTIONS AND POLICY CONSIDERATIONS

The discussion presented in this chapter highlights numerous areas in which additional research is needed to determine factors which could influence the self-disclosure of personal information to AI-enabled technology. As an example, studies designed to determine how self-disclosure of personal information is affected by the level of trust in technology is an important area of research given that trust has been shown to be a necessary condition for the disclosure of personal information (Gill & Thompson, 2017; Salehan et al., 2018; Schroeder & Schroeder, 2018). Further, as AI techniques continue to improve technologies may be even more likely to elicit the disclosure of personal information in situations which could lead to positive or negative societal outcomes. Thus, from a public policy perspective, there needs to be a discussion of the perceived risks associated with designing technologies that encourage the disclosure of personal information. For example, in an education setting, should a robot serving as a teaching assistant be allowed to query a student and collect personal information that could be accessed by a third party? In addition, should a robot be designed with the ability to convince a user to share sensitive information that may be a breach of security? These questions highlight the fact that disclosure to AI-enabled technology may not always be desirable, and careful consideration needs to be given to conditions under which disclosure is beneficial to individuals and to society.

It has also been shown that people may stereotype and even discriminate against robots as a function of their perceived race (Barfield, 2021), gender, or ethnicity (Sparrow, 2021). Therefore, an interesting research topic is to explore the factors that may lead to robots being categorized into the above classes and to determine whether the categorization affects the self-disclosure of personal information. Thus, would we be more or less likely to disclose personal information to AI-enabled technology that matches our ethnicity, race, and gender? And because AI-enabled technologies may be used in collaborative relationships with people, they may operate in a complementary or contradictory manner with users. For example, AI-enabled technologies such as robots and chatbots may be complementary (or contradictory) to human interactions such as during the process of communication with the technology. If the communication with AI-enabled technology is complimentary, will we then disclose more to the technology? Finally, surely the future is one in which our technological devices will continue to get smarter and engage even more with humans across a range of tasks and applications. How we design interfaces between users and increasingly smart AI-enabled technologies will offer challenges and opportunities for society.

ACKNOWLEDGEMENT

The author acknowledges the School of Information Sciences at the University of Tennessee-Knoxville for their support during the writing of this chapter.

REFERENCES

Andalibi, N. (2020). Disclosure, privacy, and stigma on social media: Examining non-disclosure of distressing experiences. *ACM Transactions on Computer-Human Interaction*, *27*(3), 1–43.

Andalibi, N., Haimson, O. L., Choudhury, M. D., & Forte, D. (2018). Social support, reciprocity, and anonymity in responses to sexual abuse on social media. *AMD Transactions on Computer Human-Interaction*, *21*(5), 1–35.

Aroyo, A. M., Rea, F., Sandini, G., & Sciutti, A. (2018). Trust and social engineering in human robot interaction: Will a robot make you disclose sensitive information, conform to its recommendations or gamble? *IEEE Robotics and Automation Letters*, *3*(4), 3701–3708.

Barfield, J. K. (2021). Self-disclosure of personal information, robot appearance, and robot trustworthiness. *30th IEEE International Conference on Robot and Human Interactive Communication (RO-MAN)* (pp. 67–72).

Bartneck, C., & Forlizzi, J. (2004). A design-centered framework for social human-robot interaction. In *Proceedings of the 2004 IEEE International Workshop on Robot and Human Interactive Communication*. Kurashiki, Okayama Japan (pp. 591–594).

Belanger, F., Resor, J., Crossler, R. E., Finch, T. A., & Allen, K. R. (2021). Smart home speakers and family information disclosure decisions. *27th Annual Americas Conference on Information Systems (AMCIS)* (pp. 1–10).

Birmingham, C., Hu, Z., Mahajan, K., Reber, E., & Matarić, M. J., Can I trust you? A user study of robot mediation of a support group. *2020 IEEE International Conference on Robotics and Automation (ICRA), 2020* (pp. 8019–8026).

Chen, Y., Wang, T., Wu, H., & Wang, Y. (2018). A fast and accurate multi-model facial expression recognition method for affective intelligent robots. *IEEE International Conference on Intelligence and Safety for Robotics (ISR)* (pp. 319–324).

Choi, Y., Kamal, A. E., & Louta, M. Artificial intelligence and data science for communications. *IEEE Communications Magazine*, *59*(11), 80–80.

Collins, N. L., & Miller, L. C. (1994). Self-disclosure and liking: A meta-analytic review. *Psychological Bulletin*, *116*(3), 457–475.

De Groot, J. J., Barakova, E., Lourens, T., van Wingerden, E., & Sterkenburg, P. (2019). Game-based human-robot interaction promotes self-disclosure in people with visual impairments and intellectual disabilities. *8th International Work-Conference on the Interplay Between Natural and Artificial Computation (IWINAC)*, 262–272.

Dinet, J., & Vivian, R. (2015). Perception and attitudes towards anthropomorphic robots in France: Validation of an assessment scale. *Psychologie Francaise*, *60*(2), 173–189.

Edwards, C., Edwards, A., Stoll, B., Lin, X., & Massey, N. (2019). Evaluations of an artificial intelligence instructor's voice: Social identity theory in human-robot interactions. *Computers in Human Behavior, 90*, 357–362.

Eichenberg, C., Khamis, M., & Hübner, L. (2019). The attitudes of therapists and physicians on the use of sex robots in sexual therapy: Online survey and interview study. *Journal of Medical Internet Research, 21*(8), e13853.

Eyssel, F., Wullenkord, R., & Nitsch, V. (2017). The role of self-disclosure in human-robot Interaction. *26th IEEE International Symposium on Robot and Human Interactive Communication (RO-MAN)*, 922–927.

Gill, R., & Thompson, M. M. (2017). Trust and information sharing in multinational-multiagency teams. In Goldenberg, I., Soeters, J., & Dean, W. (eds), *Information sharing in military operations: Advanced sciences and technologies for security applications* (pp. 81–99). Springer. https://doi.org/10.1007/978-3-319-42819-2_6.

Halvonik, D., & Kapusta, J. (2016). Data formats for storing knowledge in conversational algorithms. *11th International Scientific Conference on Distance Learning in Applied Informatic (DiVAi)* (pp. 513–521).

Haring, K. S., Silvera-Tawil, D., Takahashi, T., Watanabe, K., Velonaki, M., & People, H. (2016). Perceive different robot types: A direct comparison of an android, humanoid, and non-biomimetic robot. *8th International Conference on Knowledge and Smart Technology (KST)*, Chiang Mai, Thailand (pp. 265–270).

Haring, K. S., Watanabe, K., Silvera-Tawil, D., Velonaki, M., & Takahashi, T. (2015). Changes in perception of a small humanoid robot. *6th International Conference on Automation, Robotics and Applications (ICARA)*, Queenstown, New Zealand (pp. 83–89).

Heuer, T., Schiering, I., & Gerndt, R. (2019). Me and my robot – Sharing information with a new friend. *13th IFIP WG 9.2, 9.6/11.7, 11.6/. SIG 9.2.2 International Summer School on Privacy and Identity Management - Fairness, Accountability and Transparency in the Age of Big Data, 547* (pp. 189–204).

Ho., A., Hancock, J., & Miner, A. S. (2018). Psychological, relational, and emotional effects of self-disclosure after conversations with a chatbot. *Journal of Communication, 68*(4), 712–733.

Itoh, K., Miwa, H., Hukariya, Y., Imanishi, K., Takeda, D., Saito, M. ... Takanishi, A. (2004). Development of face robot to express the facial features. *13th IEEE International Workshop on Robot and Human Interactive Communication* (pp. 347–352).

Jones, R. A. (2017). What makes a robot "social'? *Social Studies of Science, 47*(4), 556–579.

Joshi, S., de Visser, E. J., Abramoff, B., & Ayaz, H. (2020). Medical interviewing with a robot instead of a doctor who do we trust more with sensitive information? *15th Annual ACM/IEEE International Conference on Human-Robot Interaction (HRI)* (pp. 570–572).

Koay, K. L., Syrdal, D. S., Walters, M. L., & Dautenhahn, K. (2009). Five weeks in the robot house: Exploratory human-robot interaction trials in a domestic setting, *Second International Conference on Advances in Computer-Human Interaction, ACHI* (pp. 219–226).

Kuchenbrandt, D., Haring, M., Eichberg, J., Eyssel, F., & Andre, E. (2014). Keep an eye on the task! How gender typicality of tasks influence human-robot interactions. *International Journal of Social Robotics, 6*(3), 417–427.

Laban, G., Morrison, V., & Cross, E. S. (2020). Let's talk about it! Subjective and objective disclosures to social robots, *15th Annual ACM/IEEE International Conference on Human-Robot Interaction (HRI)* (pp. 328–330).

Laing, S., & Apperley, M. (2020). The relevance of virtual reality to communication design. *Design Studies, 71*, 1–17.

Lee, T., Park, S. K., & Park, M. (2006). An effective method for detecting facial features and face in human-robot interaction. *Information Sciences, 176*(21), 3166–3189.

Li, D., Rau, P. L. P., & Li, Y. (2010). A cross-cultural study: Effect of robot appearance and task. *International Journal of Social Robotics, 2*, 175–186.

Libin, A. V., & Libin, E. V. (2004). Person–robot interactions from the robopsychologists' point of view: The robotic psychology and Robotherapy approach. *Proceedings of the IEEE, 92*(11), 1789–1803.

Liu, Z., Min, Wu. M., Cao, W., Chen, L., Xu, J., Zhang, R., Zhou, M., & Mao, J. A. (2017). Facial expression emotion recognition based human-robot interaction system. *IEEE/CAA Journal of Automatica Sinica, 4*(4), 668–676.

Lutz, C., & Newlands, G. (2021). Privacy and smart speakers: A multi-dimensional approach. *The Information Society, 37*(3), 147–162.

Manohar, V., al Marzooqi, S., & Crandall, J. W. (2011). Expressing emotions through robots: A case study using off-the-shelf programming interfaces, *6th ACM/IEEE International Conference on Human-Robot Interaction (HRI)* (pp. 199–200).

Mori, M. (2012). The uncanny valley [from the field]. (K. F. MacDorman & N. Kageki, Trans.), *IEEE Robotic and Automation Magazine* (pp. 98–100).

Mumm, J., & Mutlu, B. (2011). Human-robot proxemics: Physical and psychological distancing in human-robot interaction. In *Proceedings of the 6th International Conference on Human Robot interaction (HRI)* (pp. 331–338).

Nomura, T., Kanda, T., Suzuki, T., & Yamada, S. (2020). Do people with social anxiety feel anxious about interacting with a robot? *AI and Society, 35*, 381–390.

Nomura, T., & Suzuki, T. (2022). Relationships between humans' gender conception, expected gender appearances, and the roles of robots: A survey in Japan. *International Journal of Social Robotics, 14*, 1311–1321.

Pal, D., Arpnikanondt, C., & Razzaque, M. A. (2020). Personal information disclosure via voice assistants: The personalization–privacy paradox. *SN Computer Science, 1*, 280.

Pal, D., Funilkul, S., Zhang, X., & Should, I. (2021). Disclose my personal data? Perspectives from Internet of Things services. *IEEE Access, 9*, 4141–4157.

Parush, A. (2004). Usability engineering case study of a speech-operated car phone. *International Journal of Industrial Engineering: Theory Applications and Practice, 11*(3), 221–230.

Perugia, G., Rossi, A., & Rossi, S. (2021). Gender revealed: Evaluating the genderedness of Furhat's predefined faces. *13th International Conference on Social Robotics (ICSR) - Robotics in Our Everyday Lives* (pp. 36–47).

Raees, W., Ismail, M. A., Aziz, R., Afshan, A., & NED (2019). Chatbot for admission related queries using prescriptive analysis. *International Journal of Computer Science and Network Security, 19*(5), 133–138.

Roding, T., Nimmermann, F., Steinmann, S., & Schramm-Klein, H. (2019). The influence of technology infusion on customers? Information disclosure behaviour within the frontline service encounter. *International Review of Retail, Distribution and Consumer Research, 29*(5), 482–503.

Russell, S., & Norvig, P. (2020). *Artificial intelligence: A modern approach.* Pearson Publisher.

Salehan, M., Kim, D., J., & Koo, C. (2018). A study of the effect of social trust, trust in social networking services, and sharing attitude, on two dimensions of personal information sharing behavior. *Journal of Supercomputing, 74*(8), 3596–3619.

Schanke, S., Burtch, G., & Ray, G. (2021). Estimating the impact of "humanizing" customer service chatbots. *Information Systems Research, 32*(3), 736–751.

Schroeder, J., & Schroeder, M. (2018). Trusting in machines: How mode of interaction affects willingness to share personal information with Machinesm, *51st Annual Hawaii International Conference on System Sciences (HICSS)* (pp. 472–480).

Senicar, V., Jerman-Blazic, B., & Klobucar, T. (2003). Privacy-enhancing technologies - Approaches and development. *Computer Standards and Interfaces, 25*(2), 147–158.

Song, Y., Luximon, A., & Luximon, Y. (2021). The effect of facial features on facial anthropomorphic trustworthiness in social robots. *Applied Ergonomics, 94*, 103420–103420.

Song, Y., & Yan, L. X. (2020). Trust in AI agent: A systematic review of facial anthropomorphic trustworthiness for social robot design. *Sensors, 20*(18).

Sun, Y., Li, S. H., Yu, L L. (2022). The dark sides of AI personal assistant: Effects of service failure on user continuance intention. *Electronic Markets, 32*, 17–39.

Syrdal, D. S., Walters, M. L., Otero, N., Koay, K. L., Dautenhahn, K., & Knows, H. (2007). When you are sleeping- privacy and the personal robot companion. In *Proceedings of the workshop human implications of human-robot interaction, Association for the advancement of artificial intelligence (aaai'07)* (pp. 28–33).

Tsukamoto, E. (1999). Instructional design for information sciences. *7th International Conference on Computers in Education (ICCE 99), Advanced Research Methods in Computers and Communication in Education, 1* (pp. 703–706).

Uchida, T., Takahashi, H., Ban, M., Shimaya, J., Minato, T., Ogawam, K. ... Ishiguro, H. (2020). Japanese young women did not discriminate between robots and humans as listeners for their self-disclosure -Pilot study. *Multimodal Technologies and Interaction, 4*(3), 35.

Uchida, T., Takahashi, H., Ban, M., Shimaya, J., Yoshikawa, Y., & Ishiguro, H. (2017). A robot counseling SyStem – What kind of topics do we prefer to disclose to robots? *6th IEEE International Symposium on Robot and Human Interactive Communication (RO-MAN)* (pp. 207–212).

Utami, D., Bickmore, T., & Kruger, L. J. (2017). A robotic couples counselor for promoting positive communication. *26th IEEE International Symposium on Robot and Human Interactive Communication (RO-MAN)* (pp. 207–212).

Wheeless, L. R., & Grotz, J. (1977). The measurement of trust and its relationship to self-disclosure. *Human Communication Research, 3*(3), 250–257.

Yarosh, S., & Markopoulos, P. (2010). Design of an instrument for the evaluation of communication technologies with children. *9th International conference on Interaction Design and Children (IDC)* (pp. 266–269).

23. To reimagine more deeply: understanding what AI communicates

John S. Seberger, Hyesun Choung, and Prabu David

INTRODUCTION

Artificial intelligence (AI) is part of everyday life; this much we have to accept.[1] While specific contexts in which AI technologies are deployed trigger rhetorically interesting critical reactions (e.g., Stark, 2019), AI's presence and impending ubiquity necessitate a pragmatic shift from critique to management. The metaphysical track within AI-focused human–machine communication (HMC) (Guzman & Lewis, 2020) provides a compelling, if unexpected, mode of pragmatic management. Guzman and Lewis (2020, p. 80) outline this track with some questions:

> What does it mean to be human? What is the nature of technology (particularly communicative AI)? What are the dividing lines? How do people draw these lines, and to what degree are these lines changing?

From an ontological perspective grounded in first-person experience, AI is inherently communicative. Indeed, it constitutes a speech act unto itself, comprised of elocutionary, illocutionary, and perlocutionary acts (Austin, 1975). In this chapter, we contribute to the metaphysical track within HMC by considering the ontological and existential – the onto-existential – perlocutionary effects of AI. That is, we present and explore the concepts required to understand how AI changes what is in the world and people's experience of being in a changing world. We do not focus on AI's utterances, per se, but on the sociotechnical conditions which bound the possible interpretations of utterances.

AI effects novel ontologies – new senses of what comprises the world. As such, AI also *affects* – the revelation of a novel ontology, by definition, influences how we, as humans, experience ourselves in the world because such a novel ontology changes

---

[1] We, the authors, use the terms "we" and "us" here and throughout the chapter to refer to humans: self-aware, cognizing agents possessed of (roughly) biologically standardized modes of sensation, perception, and memory, which create the human lifeworld (*Lebenswelt*). We do not, however, use these terms in a culturally or socially restrictive or proscriptive manner: the lifeworld constitutes the foundations for myriad variations of individuality, cultural practices, beliefs, etc. While we maintain, logically, the existence of a unifying human lifeworld, we maintain that such unification occurs through and by means of the vast differentiation possible within such a lifeworld.

what "the world" refers to. The emergence of AI forces us to recognize that "the way it was" is no longer "the way it is" (Seberger & Bowker, 2021b). Stated more formally, we approach AI as an onto-existential perlocutionary effect – an ongoing speech act that necessitates continued reimagining of anthropocentric ontology and modes of existence therein.

AI as Onto-existential Perlocution

Broadly, AI refers to a set of emergent technologies. What unifies this set of technologies is that they act contextually in the world in a way that resembles agency. As such, they constitute a set of building blocks of temporally mediated relationships (Mead, 1967). For these reasons, AI reveals itself as a form of technology that is not simply a mediator to be communicated through (see the example of prison walls in Flusser, 2016). Instead, AI technologies are active communicators (Guzman & Lewis, 2020).

Because AI technologies are active communicators (Sundar, 2020), they create a wrinkle in the common understanding of the categories of things that populate the world.[2] We might say that AI technologies exceed the limits of a human-centered or anthropocentric understanding of what exists in the world. They do so because they transcend the ontological status of the object, thus calling into question the anthropocentric ontology from which AI emerged. In all but the most esoteric contexts (e.g., Callon, 1984; Latour, 2000; Seberger, 2021), objects do not act *precisely because* they are objects, and yet objects imbued with AI functionality *do act*. AI, thus, reveals alternative ontologies or alternative ways of conceptualizing and organizing the stuff that comprises the world. When objects are understood to act, their actions reveal the limits of knowing the world through an anthropocentric ontology (see Guzman, 2018). AI technologies might, therefore, be described as ontologically transgressive. Such transgression comprises a split in the archive (Seberger & Bowker, 2021a) or the mode by which historical eras are organized and understood (Foucault, 1972).

The ontological transgression of AI necessitates that we actively reconsider our historical centrality in the world. However, to engage in such reconsideration is not merely an act of cool, calculated philosophy. It is also, emphatically, an act with existential impacts. How we understand the composition of the world necessarily impacts how we understand ourselves (e.g., Seberger & Bowker, 2021); how we understand ourselves is the core concern of the subfield of phenomenology generally referred to as existentialism (e.g., Camus, 1955). Thus, for the reasons described above, and in the context of communication, we contend that AI represents an onto-existential perlocutionary condition. Such a condition surfaces a formidable question: what is it that AI communicates through its ontological transgressiveness?

---

[2] We use the word "things" in its vernacular sense here, rather than as a nod to phenomenological (e.g., Heidegger, 1968), sociological (e.g., Latour, 2012), or psychological (e.g., Gibson, 2014/1979) conceptualizations. However, each aforementioned conceptualization offers valuable in-roads to understanding AI as a communicative agent.

We address this question by leveraging a provocation provided by Papacharissi (2018, p. 7):

> We will not become better, superior, or more advanced—that will be a function of how we put technology to use, and ultimately, a call that will be forever subjective. We will, or rather, we have the opportunity to, become different, and with this opportunity comes another possibility, perhaps an obligation: to reimagine how we do things; to do things differently; to not fall into the trap of reproducing what we already have.

We agree with Papacharissi (2018) – AI necessitates a process of reimagining. However, we extend her provocation. AI requires reimagining not primarily about "how we do things" or "do[ing] things differently." It requires, instead, developing an ontological perspective that allows us to encounter ourselves more fully through the onto-existential perlocutionary effects of AI. Put differently, we are obligated to reimagine ourselves in a way that transcends the contemporary dichotomy of "human" and "AI" such that we might envision – let alone understand and abide within – futures wherein objects (e.g., technologies in the set "AI") not only think but also act.

Epistemological Foundations for AI's Transgression

The onto-existential effects of AI emanate from an increasing dominance of a specific mode of producing and disseminating knowledge about the world. Such a mode – an epistemic culture (Knorr-Cetina, 1999) deeply entangled with the data practices of surveillance capitalism (Zuboff, 2019) and the categorization of human users as a standing reserve (Heidegger, 1977) – is predicated on the supremacy of data, models, and probabilities (e.g., Anderson, 2008). Such an epistemic culture yields knowledge in which the primacy of the subject in the communicative act of producing objectivist-empirical knowledge is challenged or eroded by its objectified and interpellated (Day, 2014, p. 84) data-based representations.

In this regard, AI communicates an end of sorts; perhaps the end to which the "post" in "posthuman" refers (e.g., Forlano, 2017); perhaps a performative end given the solitude of recognized mortality (Flusser, 2016); perhaps merely a completion of the human drive to classify (Bowker & Star, 2000) and, therefore, control the world through the representation and replacement of phenomena by data *qua* records (Seberger, 2022) – an ontological condition in which the map definitively asserts itself as the territory (Siegert, 2011). Still, such an end is, perhaps, merely a historical end aligning with Foucault's grand historical project concerning eras and their differences, representing the shift from one age or epoch to the next (e.g., the epoch of potential memory (Bowker, 2008) or the historicization of the present through a data-perfect grammatical tense (Seberger, 2022)). In constituting any number of ends, the communicative nature of AI simultaneously constitutes a beginning – the processual emergence of a next, a subsequent. Such a beginning is the site for necessary reimagining.

In communicating an end, or the sense of an end – and, therefore, a beginning – AI challenges researchers and users alike to reimagine themselves (Papacharissi,

2018). While Papacharissi frames the process of reimagining in a generally positive light, such light is necessarily accompanied by shadow. To acknowledge the complementary shadow is to acknowledge the need for pragmatic and realistic consideration of AI in lived worlds – all those who reimagine do not do so by choice. Empirical work in the field of human–computer interaction (HCI), for example, has demonstrated that people regularly use technologies they find to be unnerving, creepy, invasive, and otherwise effectively discomfiting because they have internalized such use as normal and implicitly necessary (Shklovski et al., 2014; Seberger et al., 2021, 2022). Similar work has demonstrated that aspects of computational ubiquity perpetuate and, indeed, instantiate vulnerability among users (e.g., McDonald & Forte, 2022).

Goals and Structure of This Chapter

Up to this point, we have communicated through some particularly technical language. Presently, we break from such language to tell a story. In what follows, we first introduce the deceptive idea that there are two broad ways of approaching AI. We do so with a story written from the second-person perspective involving the Amazon Astro – essentially a stylized, AI-driven canine-like agent – and a family barbecue.

We use this story to frame a set of concepts we find necessary for understanding what AI communicates by challenging anthropocentric understandings of the world. We give particular attention to a concept referred to as "multistability" (see Ihde, 1999; Rosenberger, 2017). More specifically, we extend multistability to account for the simultaneous existence of a given agent (e.g., a human, or an AI agent) in multiple ontologies.

We contend that the recognition of multi-ontological multistability is key to reimagining ourselves entirely in futures defined by the onto-existential perlocutionary condition of AI. Following such an exploration, we provide two recommendations for conducting values-centered and affective work in AI-focused HMC.

THE CURIOUS CASE OF AN AI IN THE EVENING

You're at a barbecue. Your extended family is there with you. The sun has set. The last few moments of the gloaming attach to the grass and house. What's left of the buffet smells delicious. Music plays. Mourning doves coo. People are laughing and chatting. You feel good.

Amid the mirth and mingling, you hear your cousin talking with your brother over bites of macaroni. Your cousin says, "See? It's really intelligent! I'll prove it."

Your cousin is pointing at an oddly canine-looking robot with a screen for a head. The robot is parked next to the grill. You know this to be the Amazon Astro your cousin has been talking about all day. Looking at Astro, your cousin says, "Astro, where is Katie." Immediately, a view of his daughter's room appears on the thing's screen-face. The screen-face reveals video feed of a toddler sleeping amid a mountain of stuffed animals.

Then, suddenly, the breeze ceases. The music stops. The mourning doves go silent. Traffic noise in the neighborhood drops out. Your friends and family freeze like figures in a photo on the social media platform du jour. It is as though someone has pressed a giant pause button somewhere off in the ether. Yet *you* remain able to think and speak and move. Astro wags its tail. *It* remains unfrozen like you.

Astro rolls over to your feet. It's only you and the machine now. Astro's face-screen no longer shows the video of Katie, but presents two icons: the first says, "Speculative," and the second, "Realistic." Some moments pass. Astro says, "You now have the opportunity to choose the type of conversation your cousin and brother will have about me. If you tap on one of the icons on my face, I'll tell you about the possible conversations that will result. Then you can choose, and the world will begin again."

Thoroughly puzzled, you glance around. Sighing, you tap on the "Speculative" icon. Astro says, "This is a speculative conversation about me. If you choose this conversation, time will start up again and you will likely hear your friends and family talk about me in ways that might remind you of plots of utopian science fiction. But this choice may result in a dystopian conversation, too. Either way, your friends and family will say good and bad things about me based on how they feel."

In the silence following Astro's description, you think of your own fears. Things like surveillance states and predictive policing, AI-optimized well-being, the final dissolution of whatever hides behind pronouns like "I" and "me" and "you." Then your mind wanders to Frankenstein's monster, *Klara and the Sun*, outlandish agents such as Terminators and replicants. You even briefly think of romantic entanglements with virtual assistants. *Good and bad things*, you think.

As you look at the macaroni frozen in time at the edge of your brother's mouth, you imagine that the conversation will probably include references to popular and news media pieces about facial recognition technologies, dog-like robots running in forests (with or without guns), and maybe even arcane things like "data practices." You realize that each of these topics is influenced by movies you've seen, books you've read, and experiences you've had with systems ranging from laptops to bureaucracies. Your mind wanders.

Astro wiggles its body. The eye-like "Realistic" icon on its screen-face winks at you. You take the hint and tap the icon. Astro says, "This is a realistic conversation about me. You are likely to hear your friends and family compare me to ChatGPT, my relative Alexa, iRobot's Roomba, Apple's Siri, or Google's personalized search results. They might also talk about TikTok recommendations and social media newsfeeds or smart devices and smart homes." You sense an uncanny derision in Astro's voice when it says the word, "smart."

You take a few moments to consider your options. The "Speculative" option appeals to you. It's exciting and unnerving all at once – like staring down the side of a skyscraper from the top floor. But aside from the creepy thrill, you recognize that it is an important conversation: Astro – this little, hyper-stylized, ultra-cute AI-thing – is not only what it is when the hype and dazzle is stripped away to reveal machine learning and algorithmic analysis of massive data sets – Astro is also what it is *perceived* to be.

The "Realistic" option is also not without appeal. It is a calmer conversation, a fatalistic one grounded in the reality that AI devices – or things we call artificially intelligent – are already among us, involved in processes such as hiring employees, assessing insurance rates, diagnosing medical conditions, twinning cities, and creating avatars of deceased loved ones. This is a conversation about a reality that is experienced but rarely understood – a reality in which devices use mystical things called algorithms and models to manipulate and process data into context-appropriate action.

You decide to ask Astro a question: "Astro, can you give me a hint?" After all, maybe Astro wants a say in how your friends and relatives will talk about it.

"Of course," it says, wagging its body. "Here's your hint: I'm intelligent, after all." You could swear the little thing is grinning.

You are stymied. You've had an easier time deciding what to watch on Netflix, and there are only two options here. *Yet,* you think, *both conversations are implicitly about the futures that AI potentiates, and neither is any less "real" than the other.* Giving over to that line of thought, you find yourself thinking: *AI is about how people experience their worlds and expectations and norms and values.* You smile to yourself. (Astro seems to notice, and you feel a slight shiver.) *So, it's also about normalization. It's new and different now, but at some point, it will just be part of the world...* Your smile fades. *AI is about how humanity enrolls the world out there, beyond the edges of the skin, into a performative conversation framed entirely by our historical modes of producing knowledge. It is how we see machines that see us.*

"Astro, they're both the same conversation, aren't they?" you ask Astro.

"Maybe you're intelligent, too," it says.

Time starts up again. Katie continues to sleep on Astro's screen amid her stuffed animals. The macaroni on your brother's lip falls onto his shirt. *Maybe you're intelligent, too*, you think.

WHY MULTISTABILITY MATTERS FOR UNDERSTANDING WHAT AI COMMUNICATES

Let us consider who and what acts in the story above. To do so, let us adopt a grammatical approach. Such consideration will help illustrate the need to account for multiple simultaneous ontologies when considering how and what AI communicates as it transgresses known familiar ontologies.

In the story, your cousin at the barbecue asked Astro to locate Katie. This action has a clear subject, object, and predicate when understood through the lens of the human. Your cousin is the subject: he acts. The act of asking is the predicate: it is that which is done by the subject to the object; Astro is, therefore, the object – the predicate "asking'" connects your cousin and Astro. From this grammatical perspective, the whole interaction centers around your cousin and his world – a world in which he is the central agential subject.

Yet, this is a reductive description of the action in the story. Astro acts as a result of your cousin's action. When Astro acts, objects take on a different appearance. Such a difference appears not precisely because Astro acts, but because of the infrastructures implicit in Astro's action. The invisible protocols, operations, materialities, and institutions that co-comprise Astro hint at a prosthetic, non-human lifeworld that senses through prostheses and acts contextually through models and algorithmic outputs. In such a lifeworld, Astro and its actions are central.

Topically, Astro does three things in the story above: it listens to and understands a request; it translates such understanding to action in the form of accessing and displaying the feed from a camera in Katie's bedroom. We can break these actions down further.

Astro's ability to "understand" your cousin implies a form of memory. However, this is not a memory of events that happened in its "life" a day, week, month or year ago. Instead, it is a form of memory that emerges from the abstraction of the datasets upon which its ability to "understand" was algorithmically modeled and trained. It is also a form of memory whose purpose is granted through the economics of its creators.

Astro is, thus, embedded in a form of memory – history – to which we, as humans, do not have experiential access. It is embedded in a statistical memory, the nature of which effaces the individual. By instantiating such a form of memory, Astro becomes the center of a prosthetic lifeworld that is phenomenologically inaccessible to humans. As argued above, such centrality – such alien phenomenology – presents a direct challenge to the familiarity of anthropocentrism.

Humans might read and interpret historical data, but we are not *of* historical data. The most obvious analogy in the human would be genetics. The form of memory we contain in and through inherited genetic conditions is akin to the form of memory that Astro inherits, yet they are of fundamentally different origins. Astro's data genetics are abstractions – they are representations of phenomena in the world captured so as to be representations. Astro is agential statistical memory.

Here, in the appearance of Astro's non-anthropocentric lifeworld, we find the relevance of a concept from postphenomenology, that of multistability. Rosenberger (2017, pp. 4–5) provides the most accessible definition of the term, drawing on Ihde's (1999) original definition:

> First developed by the philosopher Don Ihde, multi-stability refers to a technology's capacity to be taken up for different uses and to be meaningful in different ways. As Ihde puts it, "no technology is 'one thing,' nor is it incapable of belonging to multiple contexts."

However, the multistability that AI brings about is not simply the multistability of "different uses" and "different meanings," nor is it about different contexts. It is, relatively, an onto-existential multistability in which agents exist simultaneously as central in theoretically separate and separable, but functionally overlapping, ontologies. By this, we mean that as a perlocutionary effect, AI potentiates recognition of the simultaneous existence of humans and users in terms of the other's ontology.

From the perspective of an anthropocentric ontology, Astro always already appears primarily as an object; from the lifeworld evidenced by Astro's access to a mode of memory alien to the human, Astro appears as a subject whose subjectivity exists in relation to the externalization and objectification (i.e., datafication) of phenomena in the human lifeworld. Such simultaneous existence of humans in multiple ontologies necessitates reimagining at a level deeper than that which is recommended in Papacharissi's (2018) provocation – not a reimagining of "doing things better," but a wholesale reimagination and reunderstanding of our multistable positionality in the multiple ontologies in which the world manifests.

Putting Multistability to Work: Identity and Privacy

In the story above, Katie, for example, becomes problematically multistable through Astro's communication. That is, because of Astro and the prosthetic infrastructural lifeworld that subtends it, Katie is simultaneously a subject in an anthropocentric ontology and an object in an AI-centric ontology. Katie's speculative vulnerability (Seberger et al., 2022) is an obvious way in which her multistability manifests.

Being a child, we can assume that Katie has a long life ahead of her. Such a life, already defined by the thrownness of her birth – that is, her receipt of the condition of existence as it is bounded by the norms and practices of the historical world into which she was born – is further contextualized by the realization of a universalist objectivist-empiricism – a world wherein to be known and to know oneself occurs through and by means of AI agents and the parallel ontologies they construct.

Katie's sociotechnical future – the future she faces as constructed by the inseparable forces of the social and the technological – is one wherein phenomenologically alien agents, like Astro and its subtending infrastructures (up to and including the economic motivations of Amazon), will actively shape Katie's understanding of herself. AI agents will do so through the discrete communication of recommendations – the collection of data about her daily life (as in a realization of Bowker's (2008) epoch of potential memory or Seberger's archive of ubiquitous computing (2022)). As such, Katie will understand herself, at least partly, through externalized and processed data that is collected about her actions rather than her own experience of her actions. She will be *objectified* – that is, constructed as an object – through and by means of Astro and its ontological kin. In her future, Katie's sense of self will emerge as a function of her being an object in an AI-centric ontology even as she toddles, walks, and runs through an apparently anthropocentric lifeworld.

The future emergence of Katie's self through a non-anthropocentric ontology has profound implications for our understanding of where we fit in the world and for such practical considerations as the maintenance of privacy. In computing (as well as other domains), privacy has been understood primarily as a discourse of control for around the past 60 years. That is, to support the familiar discourse of privacy, individuals should possess agency to such an extent that they can control who or what has access to information about them.

However, by imagining the pervasiveness of AI in the lifeworld of the human, and therefore, the ontological upending of lived anthropocentrism – our new ontological madness (Flusser, 2014) – we are forced to consider the possibility that our values will inherently change in their discursive composition. Values are human-centered and designed into technologies (Knobel & Bowker, 2011). While privacy is, today, mostly about control, it seems almost naïve to extend such control into futures wherein a vast set of technologies we call "AI" – manifested as it is through the modeling of archived data – is pervasive.

To reimagine ourselves in futures in which AI is pervasive, we need to acknowledge the necessity of developing ethics and, in a more practical sense, social norms that address both the shadow and light of Papacharissi's "reimagining." After all, the invention of the plane was also the invention of the plane crash (Virilio, 2007). Absent a fundamental, pragmatic, realistic, and honest reconsideration – *reimagining* – of the ontology of the human subject in relation to the multiple ontologies that AI effects, we are left with the dichotomous and unproductive remnants of debates in which AI is either "good" or "bad." In the reimaginary, AI is neither because it is both: through comprising a technological layer – a wrinkle – in the human lifeworld, AI displaces the human from the center of the lifeworld, externalizing knowledge production in a mode that has historically been successful, but in its success, enfolds the human into an objective topology of itself. The user becomes the used – not in the trite sense that users of free services are actually the products, but in the sense that through being users of chimerical AI devices that act contextually, users are influenced; their mode of being changed. Such is the communicative framing that AI brings about; such is stuff that AI communicates.

EXISTENTIALISM IN AI AND THE CASE FOR OPTIMISM

Up to this point, we have focused on an onto-existential crisis communicated by AI. We have described why this crisis *is* ontological and alluded to its roots in existentialism. Here, we focus more closely on existentialism.

We have said that to "reimagine" (Papacharissi, 2018) ourselves in relation to AI necessitates the consideration of, and familiarization with, non-anthropocentric ontologies that exist alongside the historically subjective first-person human perspective. We now claim that such consideration is inherently alienating – a term used in the work of Camus to represent states of being wherein one encounters oneself as a stranger. There is growing empirical evidence for such a phenomenon about the normalization of technology in daily life (Seberger et al., 2021, 2022).

We do not – indeed, we cannot – contest the alienating effects of suitably deep processes of "reimagining." If you are born into one world (i.e., a received ontology) and witness radical and powerful challenges to that world, there seems to be little chance of avoiding alienation. However, while the term "alienation" generally has negative connotations, it is possible to approach alienation as a moment of vast and optimistic potential.

Dostoevsky (2001, p. 9) once defined humans as "creature[s] that can get used to anything." Relatedly, Camus made the case that we, like Sisyphus, must imagine ourselves as happy (Camus, 1955; Seberger & Bowker, 2021b). Engaging in processes of reimagining, predicated upon the emergence of novel technologies, is one mode of accustoming oneself. However, it is a mode with many depths.

At the shallowest depth, reimagining is a mode in which one enrolls oneself into the data-driven, emergent ontology of AI in order to gain a direct benefit. Such benefits include a host of the usual techno-centric suspects: heightened convenience, increased consumer power, conditional empowerment, or greater efficiency in a given task. When contextualized by the contemporary economics and data practices of surveillance capitalism (Zuboff, 2019) and the extent to which people have internalized and normalized such abusive and invasive data practices, however, such gratification-oriented reimagining falls short.

Reaching the liberating depths of existential optimism via AI-motivated reimagining requires the recognition of AI as a tragedy, despite all its apparent benefits. The recognition of such tragedy comes in the form of understanding and internalizing that, to riff on a titular phrase from Koopman, "we have become our data" (Koopman, 2019). However, such understanding and internalization should be guarded by a critical consideration of the data that becomes us.

Such consideration ultimately yields a state similar to what the existential psychiatrist Viktor Frankl called "tragic optimism" (Frankl, 2006). On the one hand, we reap benefits from the deployment of and enrollment in the ontology of AI – of allowing external and prosthetic outcomes of objectivist-empirical modeling to "see" us and, therefore, to risk the alienating condition of "being seen" by an Other. On the other hand, doing so apparently decentralizes human subjectivity, rendering ourselves *objects* to be used at the whim of a vast economic-objectivist machine. But it merely decentralizes historical human subjectivity: anthropocentrism.

AI will not efface the first-person experience, but it will change such experience. Such change, we contend, is the appropriate site for reimagination. We may move beyond this trauma – and trauma it is, unless we work under the assumption that the end goal of AI has always already been to obsolesce the epistemic mode of the first-person – to find the optimism within the tragedy of objectification by developing modes of media literacy that remind people that data, and therefore, data-driven interpellations of people, are always already reductive – that we are not *actually* our data, only *functionally*. Such modes of media literacy are more deeply philosophical than training school children to discern the validity or reliability of a particular news story; rather, such literacy necessitates training in the problem of phronesis: of knowing when and in what context an action is appropriate or beneficial. Problematically, however, in the case of AI and HMC, such "action" as concerns phronesis is not an action at all but the emergence of a novel embracing of parallel ontologies.

IMPLICATIONS

In light of our arguments above, we provide two recommendations for AI-focused HMC research. We present such recommendations in the tradition of implications within HCI, but these implications are not oriented toward design. Instead, they are provided to help account for some of the theoretical confounds that arise at the intersection of HMC and AI.

Account for Multistability

First and foremost, when conducting AI-focused HMC research – particularly research that aligns with what Guzman and Lewis (2020) have described as a metaphysical tack – it is necessary to account for the fundamental multistability of two agents in AI futures: first, the human and second, the nebulous and expanding set of technologies we presently call "AI." It has been argued in AI research – particularly in what is referred to as human-centered AI (HCAI) – that we, as scholars, are obligated to investigate the language with which we describe AI (see Shneiderman, 2020). We will echo this argument here but will clarify its importance.

Yes, of course, language matters. Some have even argued that "language speaks us." However, more than merely "speaking us," language is always already a set of signifiers belonging to a greater ontology: language is the means and mode by which ontology is communicated and maintained or challenged.

We have argued that AI communicates an ontological upending in which the human is no longer clearly or singularly central. Instead, and in sufficiently reimagined futures, the human is ontologically multistable; it is, from one vantage (i.e., that of the first-person condition of human embodiment), central; it is, from another vantage (i.e., that of the externalized mode of knowledge production and control we refer to as AI) peripheral, replaced by reductionist representations of itself in the form of data.

In such a framework of ontological multistability, language matters more than usual: it implicitly chooses and connotes the specific ontology in which a discourse will play out. In so connoting, it also logically bounds the knowledge products of such a discourse. If, as in the example of Katie in the story above, we see AI seeing us, and such seeing yields existential alienation on the part of the human seer, it is simply not enough to dwell in such alienation – to attempt to normatively return to a comfortable and familiar anthropocentric ontology. Instead, in a pragmatic sense, it becomes necessary to approach such alienation as a harbinger of things to come – the new set of possible horizons.

The optimism we describe emerges from our innate ability to acclimate – to accustom ourselves – to novel conditions. There is no reason to believe that such novel conditions exclude novel ontological conditions. However, to accustom ourselves to the novel ontological conditions of Astro and its ilk requires first a pragmatic recognition of such conditions. We are obligated to argue from and through multiple ontologies to affect such recognition.

Interrogate the Values You Seek to Uphold or Understand

It is one thing to recommend that scholars account for multistability. It is another thing to filter particular values through the kaleidoscope of multistability. If, as in the case of Katie and Astro, the value in question is broadly definable as "privacy," it is necessary to filter the discourse from multiple perspectives. On the one hand, there is Katie's normative right to privacy – her right to be left alone and the extent to which "being left alone" resonates through different registers of technology and connectivity. More nuanced is her right to reap the benefits of a vast and ethical sociotechnical system, in which the value of privacy is allowed to evolve alongside such an emergent sociotechnical system.

The case of Katie and Astro forces us to question the possibility of normative privacy – i.e., the ability to maintain and perpetuate historical discourses of privacy – amid a changing technological ecology that is predicated on networking, the economic and epistemic value of data, and the enrollment of humans into such an ecology by way of "being users." Control-oriented definitions of privacy have contributed to the neo-liberal tendency toward responsibilization (i.e., the foisting of what was formerly institutional responsibility onto individuals). In the domain of privacy research – and usable privacy in particular – it is well documented that such responsibilization has profound negative affective impacts on people. As users, people are overburdened by the provision of idiosyncratic, technology-specific privacy controls. They are resigned to the intrusiveness of contemporary data practices, fostered, in no small way, by corporate communication schemes (Draper & Turow, 2019). The immediate benefits of conditional empowerment (Seberger et al., 2021) give way to normalizing affective discomfort from routine privacy invasions over time (Seberger et al., 2022). Yet, it would be naïve to expect the complete absence of such negative values-oriented effects from a broadly defined system, such as emerges at the overlap of ontologies that "AI" effects, that is predicated on the values (both epistemic and monetary) of data. However, rather than critique such sociotechnical conditions (or even lofty agendas that seek concrete solutions to nebulous problems), we urge scholars working in HMC and beyond to focus on communicating modes of resilience to everyday users: modes by which such users might remember and recentralize their own embodied subjectivity within a sociotechnical system predicated on the externalization and (profitable) datafication of the self. We presented Frankl's (2006) "tragic optimism" as one example of how this might be achieved. However, we further contend that media literacy campaigns must account for the differing ontologies to which humans now belong simultaneously.

CONCLUSION

In this chapter, we have explored ways of approaching the question, "What is it that AI communicates?" We have done so through the language of speech act theory, ontology, existentialism, and postphenomenology. We do not provide exhaustive answers to the questions raised in this chapter. We do, however, provide a collection of conceptual tools and viewpoints that might allow the production of answers born of sensitive and responsible research.

AI has changed the world and will continue to do so. As we have argued, AI communicates a new set of possible futures that extend into multiple ontologies. Because of this, AI challenges us to do two things now rather than later. First, we must understand the things that constitute our impending, emergent new world. Second, we must live in that new world based on our understanding.

To succeed in these endeavors, we must engage in what Papacharissi (2018) has called "reimagining." However, to "reimagine" ourselves appropriately requires more than considering "how we do things" so that we might do them "better." It requires philosophical consideration of how the things in the world relate to each other and, thus, give each other meaning. It is not about doing things better, but about understanding what "things" exist to be done in simultaneous and heterogeneous ontologies. Moreover, it requires reimagining what being embodied as human (i.e., with a first-person perspective) means in relation to "AI."

For a few hundred years prior to the emergence of AI, it was mostly sufficient to focus on how things in the world relate to each other from a human perspective. That is because the human gaze was always already central. Even when we sought objective knowledge about the world, we tended to do so to benefit ourselves. However, AI challenges human centrality in the organization of things in the world: it renders the formerly subjective human as an object.

AI troubles what it means to be human because we are now at least *doubly human*. First, we are human subjectivities in a world in which humans are experientially at the center. Second, we are human objectivities in a world in which AI produces the human through its own prosthetic phenomenology (i.e., pseudo-subjectivity). Thus, paradoxically, AI renders us objects *because* we are subjects. We create data, therefore we *are* through the artificial eyes of AI.

If we are to understand and live well in our AI future – if we are to imagine ourselves happy – we are responsible for understanding the complexity of how two very different ways of organizing the world relate to each other and influence each other. Are we mostly objects in a world in which AI is central? Or are we mostly still subjects in a world in which AI is peripheral? How we answer these questions will necessarily impact the way we design, deploy, and interact with AI. Thus, our futures depend on how seriously we take the question of our meaning in relation to AI.

REFERENCES

Anderson, C. (2008). The end of theory: The data deluge makes the scientific method obsolete. *Wired*. https://www.wired.com/2008/06/pb-theory/
Austin, J. (1975). *How to do things with words*. Oxford University Press.
Bowker, G. C. (2008). *Memory practices in the sciences*. MIT Press.
Bowker, G. C., & Star, S. L. (2000). *Sorting things out: Classification and its consequences*. MIT Press.
Callon, M. (1984). Some elements of a sociology of translation: Domestication of the scallops and the fishermen of St Brieuc Bay. *The Sociological Review, 32*(1), 196–233. https://doi.org/10.1111/j.1467-954X.1984.tb00113.x
Camus, A. (1955). *The myth of Sisyphus* (J. O'Brien, Trans.). Hamish Hamilton.
Day, R. E. (2014). *Indexing it all: The subject in the age of documentation, information, and data*. MIT Press.
Dostoyevsky, F. (2001). *Memoirs from the house of the dead* (R. Hingley, Ed.; J. Coulson, Trans.). Oxford University Press.
Draper, N. A., & Turow, J. (2019). The corporate cultivation of digital resignation. *New Media & Society, 21*(8), 1824–1839. https://doi.org/10.1177/1461444819833331
Flusser, V. (2014). *On Doubt* (S. Zielinski, Ed.; R. M. Novaes, Trans.). Univocal.
Flusser, V. (2016). *The Surprising Phenomenon of Human Communication* (R. M. Novaes, Trans.). Metaflux Publishing.
Forlano, L. (2017). Posthumanism and design. *She ji: The Journal of Design, Economics, and Innovation, 3*(1), 16–29. https://doi.org/10.1016/j.sheji.2017.08.001
Foucault, M. (1972). *The archaeology of knowledge* (A. M. Sheridan Smith, Trans.). Tavistock Publications, Ltd.
Frankl, V. E. (2006). *Man's search for meaning*. Beacon Press.
Gibson, J. J. (2014). *The ecological approach to visual perception*. Taylor & Francis.

Guzman, A. L. (2018). What is human-machine communication, anyway? In A. L. Guzman (Ed.), *Human-machine communication: Rethinking communication, technology, and ourselves.* (pp. 1–28). Peter Lang.

Guzman, A. L., & Lewis, S. C. (2020). Artificial intelligence and communication: A human–machine communication research agenda. *New Media & Society, 22*(1), 70–86. https://doi.org/10.1177/1461444819858691

Heidegger, M. (1968). *What is a thing?* (W. B. Barton & V. Deutsch, Trans.). H. Regnery Company.

Heidegger, M. (1977). *The question concerning technology, and other essays* (W. Lovitt, Trans.). Garland Publishers.

Ihde, D. (1999). Technology and prognostic predicaments. *AI & Society, 13(1)*, 44–51. https://doi.org/10.1007/BF01205256

Knobel, C., & Bowker, G. C. (2011). Values in design. *Communications of the ACM, 54*(7), 26–28. https://doi.org/10.1145/1965724.1965735

Knorr-Cetina, K. (1999). *Epistemic cultures: How the sciences make knowledge.* Harvard University Press.

Koopman, C. (2019). *How we became our data: A genealogy of the informational person.* University of Chicago Press,

Latour, B. (2000). The Berlin key or how to do words with things. In P. Graves-Brown (Ed.), *Matter, materiality, and modern culture* (pp. 10–21). Routledge.

Latour, B. (2012). *We have never been modern.* Harvard University Press.

McDonald, N., & Forte, A. (2022). Privacy and vulnerable populations. In B. P. Knijnenburg, X. Page, P. Lipford, N. Proferes, & J. Romano (Eds.), *Modern socio-technical perspectives on privacy* (pp. 337–363). Springer.

Mead, M. (1967). *Mind, self, & society: From the standpoint of a social behaviorist.* University of Chicago Press.

Papacharissi, Z. (Ed.). (2018). *A networked self and human augmentics, artificial intelligence, sentience.* Routledge.

Rosenberger, R. (2017). *Callous objects: Designs against the homeless.* University of Minnesota Press.

Seberger, J. S. (2021). Reconsidering the user in IoT: The subjectivity of things. *Personal and Ubiquitous Computing, 25*, 525–533. https://doi.org/10.1007/s00779-020-01513-0

Seberger, J. S. (2022). Into the archive of ubiquitous computing: The data perfect tense and the historicization of the present. *Journal of Documentation, 78*(1), 18–37. https://doi.org/10.1108/JD-11-2020-0195

Seberger, J. S., & Bowker, G. C. (2021a). Values. In N. B. Thylstrup, D. Agostinho, A. Ring, C. D'Ignazio, & K. Veel (Eds.), *Uncertain archives: Critical keywords for big data* (pp. 551–560). MIT Press.

Seberger, J. S., & Bowker, G. C. (2021b). Humanistic infrastructure studies: Hyper-functionality and the experience of the absurd. *Information, Communication & Society, 24*(12), 1712–1727. https://doi.org/10.1080/1369118X.2020.1726985

Seberger, J. S., Llavore, M., Wyant, N. N., Shklovski, I., & Patil, S. (2021). Empowering resignation: There's an app for that. *Proceedings of the 2021 CHI Conference on Human Factors in Computing Systems*, 1–18. https://doi.org/10.1145/3411764.3445293

Seberger, J. S., Obi, I., Loukil, M., Liao, W., Wild, D., & Patil, S. (2022). Speculative vulnerability: Uncovering the temporalities of vulnerability in people's experiences of the pandemic. Proceedings of the ACM on Human-Computer Interaction (*PACMHCI*), Vol 6, CSCW2, Article No. 485. https://doi.org/10.1145/3555586

Seberger, J. S., Shklovski, I., Swiatek, E., & Patil, S. (2022). Still creepy after all these years: The normalization of affective discomfort in app use. *Proceedings of the 2022 CHI Conference on Human Factors in Computing Systems*, 1–19. https://doi.org/10.1145/3491102.3502112

Shklovski, I., Mainwaring, S. D., Skúladóttir, H. H., & Borgthorsson, H. (2014). Leakiness and creepiness in app space: Perceptions of privacy and mobile app use. *Proceedings of the*

SIGCHI Conference on Human Factors in Computing Systems, 2347–2356. https://doi.org/10.1145/2556288.2557421

Shneiderman, B. (2020). Human-centered artificial intelligence: Three fresh ideas. *AIS Transactions on Human-Computer Interaction*, *12*(3), 109–124. https://doi.org/10.17705/1thci.00131

Siegert, B. (2011). The map is the territory: What is German media philosophy? *Radical Philosophy*, *169*. https://www.radicalphilosophy.com/article/the-map-is-the-territory

Stark, L. (2019). Facial recognition is the plutonium of AI. *XRDS: Crossroads, The ACM Magazine for Students*, *25*(3), 50–55. https://doi.org/10.1145/3313129

Sundar, S. S. (2020). Rise of machine agency: A framework for studying the psychology of human–AI interaction (HAII). *Journal of Computer-Mediated Communication*, *25*(1), 74–88. https://doi.org/10.1093/jcmc/zmz026

Virilio, P. (2007). *The original accident* (J. Rose, Trans.). John Wiley & Sons.

Zuboff, S. (2019). *The age of surveillance capitalism: The fight for a human future at the new frontier of power* Profile Books.

24. Automated inequalities: examining the social implications of artificial intelligence in China
Bibo Lin and Joanne Kuai

INTRODUCTION

With artificial intelligence (AI) becoming widely adopted in many walks of life, the profound consequences of AI-related technologies have become more recognized. Evidence has suggested that AI and algorithms would not always automatically produce fairer and more objective outcomes than those directly produced by human beings, as their developers often alleged. Biases toward the poor, women, and people of color, which reflect the oppressive social relationships and power structures, are "embedded in computer code and, increasingly, in artificial intelligence technologies that we are reliant on," as Noble (2018, p. 1) points out. For instance, several applications of AI and algorithms have been reported to make it more difficult for poor and working-class people to get jobs, increasingly exclude them from public resources, intensify monitoring and policing of them, and on some occasions, force them to pay more (such as higher insurance fees and interest rates of financial loans) and earn less than the rich (Eubanks, 2017; O'Neil, 2016). Other AI applications and algorithms have been discovered to be sexist and racist (Gebru, 2020; Noble, 2018). An Amazon AI hiring tool, for instance, systematically downgraded female applicants by penalizing "resumes that included the word 'women's,' as in 'women's chess club captain'" (Dastin, 2018). Google's Ad Settings algorithm encouraged men but not women to seek high-paying jobs (Datta et al., 2015). Algorithms and mathematical models employed by the US judicial system were known for persistently giving people of color longer sentences and heavier punishment than White people for similar crimes (O'Neil, 2016). Scholars have explored many ways in which AI helps enact, reinforce, and exacerbate pre-existing inequalities between the powerful and the powerless and among different social groups in the Western context (e.g., Gebru, 2020; Eubanks, 2017). However, this chapter intends to sketch how AI might create and exacerbate social inequalities in the understudied Chinese context. As much of our discussion is grounded in China's AI policy and China's societal interpretation of AI, we follow China's definition of AI, which is perhaps best understood as an umbrella term that encompasses many different computational techniques applied in a wide range of settings and, as discussed later, has its ideological underpinning. This chapter first introduces the specific AI policies and plans promulgated by the Chinese government, emphasizing their characteristics. It then explores how AI has already exacerbated or will probably aggravate the major social inequalities in contemporary China, namely economic inequalities, gender inequalities, and urban–rural inequalities. In the concluding section, we briefly discuss other social inequalities in China which might also be influenced by the development of AI technologies.

CHINA'S AI AMBITIONS AND POLICY

China set a goal to become a world leader in AI by 2030 in the "New Generation Artificial Intelligence Development Plan" (AIDP) issued by the State Council in July 2017. China's first national-level legislative effort in the AI field sets its "three-step" development goals for 2020, 2025, and 2030. The document not only delineates the strategic objectives of making AI the main driving force for China's industrial upgrading and economic transformation but also indicates the importance of using AI in a wide range of sectors, including agriculture, defense, health care, transportation, and many more. It also addresses the urgency of setting industry standards, drafting laws and regulations, and formulating ethical norms for using AI. AIDP prescribes governmental funding for the development and implementation of AI-powered technologies and increased investment in the education and training of AI talents by introducing new majors and courses in universities, establishing AI institutes, and providing incentives for AI researchers to undertake their research in China.

As laid out in the opening paragraphs of AIDP, the motivations for China's AI development are multi-faceted under the backdrop of increasingly intensified international competition – AI has been identified as a new focus of such competition and the strategic technology that will take a leading role in the future. China has been keeping a close eye on its international counterparts, evinced by AIDP's depiction that "the world's major developed countries are taking the development of AI as a major strategy to enhance national competitiveness and protect national security" (China's State Council, 2017). Such a framing of labeling AI as a security matter has been seen as a growing tendency in China's policy discourses to justify the need to enable extraordinary efforts to push forward AI development from both the state and the society as a whole (Zeng, 2022). AI has also been identified as the "new engine for economic development," which will "inject new kinetic energy into China's economic growth" (China's State Council, 2017). Maintaining economic growth is particularly important for China, as it is one of the key factors that are considered to maintain the legitimacy of the ruling of the Communist Party of China (CPC). In addition, social construction (or social governance) has been identified as a critical area in which AI is envisioned to play an imperative role in improving a variety of public services, making the governance of social services more accurate, and mitigating challenges brought by environmental concerns, aging population, and resource constraints. AIDP also highlights AI's function of

> accurately perceiving, predicting, and warning of major trends in infrastructure and social
> security operations, grasping group cognition and psychological changes promptly and

proactively making decisions and responses, which will significantly improve the ability and level of social governance, and play an important role in effectively maintaining social stability. (China's State Council, 2017)

While some Chinese media have referred to 2017 as "year one of China's AI development strategy" (China Institute for Science and Technology Policy at Tsinghua University, 2018), China's AI development plan did not begin with AIDP. Instead, the plan penned what was already broadly known and made AI a focus (Ding, 2018). Many other efforts beforehand have paved the way. For example, the "Made in China 2025" plan, issued by the State Council in May 2015, proposed the development of intelligent equipment, intelligent products, and intelligent production processes. Then AI-related policies entered a period of intensive introduction. In March 2016, the Fourth Meeting of the 12th National People's Congress adopted the "Outline of the 13th Five-Year Plan for National Economic and Social Development of the People's Republic of China," which included AI as one of the six critical areas for developing the country's emerging industries and an essential factor in stimulating economic growth. Since 2016, various state organizations, including the State Council, the National Development and Reform Commission, the Ministry of Industry and Information Technology, and the Ministry of Science and Technology, have issued several AI-related development and work plans to promote the development of AI. In addition, many local provinces and private sectors made their AI plans long before the central government announced the comprehensive AI national strategy in 2017 (Ding, 2018).

After the introduction of AIDP, continuous efforts in promoting the development of AI followed suit. For example, in October 2017, AI was included in the 19th CPC National Congress report, which suggested promoting the deep integration of the internet, big data, artificial intelligence, and the real economy. In December 2017, the "Three-Year Action Plan for the Development of a New Generation of AI Industry (2018–2020)" focused on supporting neural network chips to realize the large-scale application of AI chips in China. In July 2020, the Cyberspace Administration of China (CAC) and five other departments issued the "Guidelines for the Construction of the National Standard System for New Generation AI." It delineates that by 2023, the standard system for AI will be initially established, focusing on the development of standards in data, algorithms, systems, services, and other critical areas with urgent needs and the implementation of such standards, first in manufacturing, transportation, finance, security, home, elderly care, environmental protection, education, health care, justice, and other vital industries. In September 2021, the National Committee on New Generation AI Governance issued the "Ethical Code for New Generation AI" to integrate ethics into AI, signifying the transition from the promotion of AI application to AI governance.

While some argue that the central government's AI push is part of a coordinated attempt to turn China into the world's unchallenged AI hegemony (Webb, 2019), other scholars believe that China's AI strategy is somewhat fragmented and far away from the "top-down," "nationally concerted," and "whole-of-government" approach as many assumed (Roberts et al., 2021; Zeng, 2022). Despite these comprehensive central policies, the actual implementation of the plans is believed to be undertaken by the private sector and local governments (Roberts et al., 2021; Sheehan, 2018), as decentralized policy experimentation and bottom-up initiatives are one of the key characteristics of China's central-local interaction (Zheng, 2007), as it is in China's AI policy. At least 17 national AI innovative development pilot zones, from metropolitans (including Beijing, Shanghai, Shenzhen) to middle-size cities (including Hefei, Suzhou, Shenyang) to county level (Deqing County), have been established in China since 2019, "relying on local governments to carry out technology demonstrations, policy pilots, and social experiments" (Wen, 2021). Each pilot zone has its own development or implementation plan (more or less coordinated with the central policies). The city of Tianjin, for instance, has allegedly invested 260 billion yuan (1 yuan roughly equals 0.15 US dollars) to build more than 300 major AI application scenarios and platforms in smart city, autonomous computing power, smart port, car networking, smart manufacturing, and industrial clusters (Wu, 2022). Private sectors have flooded into the AI field as well. By October 2020, China already had the second largest number of AI companies (about 1,450) in the world, slightly behind the US (about 2,150) (Xia, 2020; Global Times, 2021). The increasing implementation of AI systems in city governance in cities and counties has raised privacy and data security concerns (Chen, 2021) – in practice, some local governments require all kinds of real-time data from citizens and corporations – and it will probably lead to technocratic governments and a planned life in a transparent environment for ordinary citizens (Liu, 2021).

It is also important to note that the definition of AI in China's policy documents is treated as an umbrella term and is not a uniform concept. Due to the lack of a clear definition of AI, the boundaries between AI, core AI, and AI-related industries are fuzzy and can be interpreted very differently. The slipperiness of what constitutes AI may result in relevant AI development plans becoming policy slogans (Zeng, 2020). The vagueness of the definition of AI leaves room for local actors to adapt them to local conditions (Zeng, 2020). Still, in some cases, it has also resulted in some market actors manipulating the ambiguous definition of an AI company to cheat the state funding (Deloitte, 2018). This points to the efficiency and quality problems of China's AI policy. Despite great uncertainties about AI's future in China, a vast array of AI applications have been used in real-life settings and have already had real-life impacts on Chinese citizens – and even non-Chinese, such as South Asians, Africans, and Latin Americans (see Lin, 2023). As economic, gendered, and urban–rural inequalities are the major social inequalities in contemporary China, in the following sections, we explore how AI might escalate (or mitigate) these structural asymmetries.

ECONOMIC INEQUALITIES AND AI

Rapid technological progress in AI has been predicted to exacerbate economic inequality, a problem already of grave concern in Chinese society, as the unprecedented economic success over the past 40 years has made China one of the most polarized countries in the world. China's economic inequality levels have skyrocketed from somewhere akin to Nordic countries' levels in 1978 to now close to the US's levels (Piketty et al., 2019). On the other hand, by estimation, 1.2 billion Chinese will be qualified as the middle class by 2027, constituting one-quarter of the world's total (Kharas & Dooley, 2020). However, this neoliberal middle class predominantly sees laziness as the primary cause of poverty (Xu et al., 2021), indicating their lack of awareness of social and structural factors contributing to economic inequalities.

When it comes to how AI affects the economic inequalities in China, several studies suggest that the applications of AI technologies in production may increase the income inequalities between high-skilled, middle-skilled, and low-skilled workers in China (e.g., Huang, 2021; Barton et al., 2017), similar to the ways automation forced US workers to leave routine employment and accept non-routine manual employment and non-employment from 1979 to 2014 (Cortes et al., 2017), and robots reduced low-skilled and middle-skilled workers' work hours (and income) in 17 countries from 1993 to 2007 (Graetz & Michaels, 2015). Researchers have relatively more divergence on AI's long-term impact on wealth distribution in the whole of Chinese society than its short-term effects on the labor market, as some believe AI will substantially increase productivity and total wealth – as long as citizens have sufficient access to education and training, AI will likely bring a more prosperous and egalitarian society (Peng, 2021). However, this hopeful vision of AI in China might not sufficiently reflect the cruel reality that wealth, though created by the majority, has been acceleratively concentrated in the hands of a few rich people who possess the means of production (Zhu, 2021). More specifically, for instance, in 2015, the top 1% of the population in China had a 29.6% wealth share, while the bottom 50% of the population only had a 6.4% wealth share (Piketty et al., 2019, p. 2491) – and there were still more than 600 million Chinese whose monthly income was barely 140 US dollars in 2020 (Li, 2020). The booming internet industry (as a type of new technology) in China since the early 2000s has failed to create a more even distribution of wealth but succeeded in breeding the wealthiest businessmen in the world – four out of the ten richest Chinese billionaires are from internet-related businesses, including Zhang Yiming from ByteDance, Pony Ma Huateng from Tencent, William Ding Lei from NetEase, and Jack Ma Yun from Alibaba (Flannery, 2022). These tech tycoons are, at the same time, the major AI company owners, investors, and developers in China (see Roberts et al., 2020); thus, it is reasonable to speculate that AI technologies steered by them are more likely to be used to amass personal wealth than to narrow economic gaps between the rich and the poor, although the actual applications of technologies might lead to "unintended" consequences (Winner, 1977). Regarded as the leading force to fulfill China's AI dream, these market actors are some of the biggest beneficiaries of the Chinese state's AI policies. For instance, under the local government's initiative, AI technologies have been used in Alibaba's City Brain project to help manage urban operations in Hangzhou, a city on the east coast of China and close to Shanghai. Whether such a smart city system has made the city smarter is dubious (Vanolo, 2014), but what is certain is that the company has gained massive support from the governments and harvested and profited from the enormous amount of citizens' data it can access as the company holds the official status of China's AI national team (Curran & Smart, 2021).

The Chinese government is another key player in AI – the government officials and those close to them are also big winners of China's economic miracle (Nathan, 2016). The Chinese state is motivated to embrace AI to compete with the US, sustain economic growth, and facilitate social control (Roberts et al., 2020), but it might be less incentivized to redistribute social wealth, which would mean taking what some government officials and their family members have already gained to support the poor or making them have less share of the economic growth in future. Some may argue that a fairer, more egalitarian society is good for maintaining the political stability that the CPC mostly desires, but others believe a hierarchical social structure can lead to even longer domination, as evidenced by China's pre-modern history (Kang, 2010). The unsettled theoretical debate reflects the epistemological gap between the West and the East, specified in the case of China's social credit system. Although whether such a big-data-and-AI-driven social credit system will be used nationwide is still in question, many similar projects have been piloted by local governments and commercial entities, including Alibaba's Sesame Credit and Tencent's Tencent Credit (see Liang et al., 2018; Horsley, 2018). While Westerners express concern about the state surveillance and individual privacy, Chinese citizens, seemingly, highly support the social credit system – particularly, the wealthier, better-educated, and urban elites, alongside the elderly, show the strongest approval of it (Kostka, 2019), probably because of a belief that they can gain more (security and order, etc.) in exchange for personal privacy (which appears less critical for Chinese). "The marginal, poor, informal, at-risk groups" are believed to be the ones who will be most intensely monitored and constrained and constantly denied access to social resources, such as housing, education, health care, transportation, and other opportunities by such a system (Curran & Smart, 2021, pp. 497–502). But most upper- or middle-class Chinese citizens appear to have no empathy for, or at least no awareness of, these inequalities and social harms.

GENDER INEQUALITIES AND AI

One other aspect that AI could have an impact on is gender equality. China's ranking in the Global Gender Gap Index dropped from sixty-third in 2006 to 107th in 2021 out of 156 countries, according to the World Economic Forum (2021). One immediate explanation could be that while other countries are mitigating gender inequalities, China has not significantly closed and even possibly widened its gender gap in the past 15 years (see Yu, 2020). Just as of October 2022, as Xi Jinping cemented his leadership for another five years at the Communist Party Congress, the new 24-member Politburo excludes women for the first time in two decades, exacerbating the gender gap in political representation and participation. In addition, China's sex ratio at birth (in 2020) is only 0.89 (female/male), ranking 156th out of 156 countries

(World Economic Forum, 2021). The low female proportion in the newborn population is also evidenced in the Seventh National Population Census in 2020, indicating a still stubborn and broad male preference in Chinese society (Zhang et al., 2022). The widespread perception of men being the predominant breadwinner for the family is viewed as one of the main factors contributing to male preference (Zhang et al., 2022), while the introduction of AI technology might reinforce this bias. According to some studies, introducing AI will result in women being at a higher risk (11%) of losing their jobs than men (9%). By estimation, 46% of the existing positions occupied by female workers in China are at risk of being replaced by AI (J. Wang, 2020). Female employees in China usually have less chance to participate in job training – a male employee receives 4.32 training on average while a female employee only 1.02 training, and after technological upgrades, a male employee receives 6.12 training while a female employee only 1.58 training, as indicated by a survey of the manufacturing companies in Shanghai (Li, 2021). Although the education gap has significantly narrowed due to fewer children in Chinese families – the previous one-child policy made the only child the "only hope" of their families (Fong, 2004), females still have less chance to receive higher education than males in China, in general. It is particularly true in the disciplines related to science, technology, and engineering, in which women are traditionally believed to be less talented or unfit – women only make up about 25% of the workforce in these industries in China (Jiang, 2021). Taken together, Chinese women are continuously disadvantaged and vulnerable in the job market in the age of AI, as high-skilled workers probably gain more from such a change (Huang, 2021). Still, women are expected to spend more time on unpaid domestic work than men (the amount of time a Chinese woman spends on unpaid domestic and care work is 2.5 times as much as that of a Chinese man in 2018, World Bank, n.d.b), which restricts their training opportunities and upward mobility in their careers. Currently, 78% of AI professionals are male, and only 22% are female worldwide (World Economic Forum, 2018). Among Chinese business leaders, only 29.7% are women (Mastercard, 2021), suggesting a large gender gap in leadership positions and that AI will probably exacerbate gender inequalities in China (Barton et al., 2017).

AI use in everyday life might also reinforce pre-existing gender bias and reenact the "male gaze" in China. The COVID-19 pandemic has infamously made women suffer more emotional and life disturbance (Ding et al., 2021) and economic precarity (Dang & Nguyen, 2021) than men due to the high portion of female health care workers, mass school closures placing more childcare responsibilities on women, and more women than men in the low-wage and insecure job positions (Hutt, 2020; Wenham et al., 2020), though the death rate of men is higher than women. Many big-data and AI-empowered health tracking systems in China, such as the health code, were designed to prevent the spread of the disease by tracing and controlling population movements (Liu, 2020). However, such tight, digital surveillance of individuals possibly facilitates the exertion of the male gaze over female bodies and strengthens the unequal gender norms. The travel histories and personal addresses captured by the tracking system and disclosed by the local government of Ha'erbin, for example, offered netizens a chance to "cyber manhunt" three women who contacted COVID-19 and were suspected of having affairs, primarily because they failed to meet the sexualized expectations that women should be docile, passive, and pure (for more details, see Yu, 2020). On other occasions, some Chinese online lending platforms were reported to illegally force female students to upload nude photos of themselves in exchange for high-interest loans (Constable, 2016). Other online lending platforms are believed to legitimately employ biased AI algorithms to make female clients borrow less and pay more interest (Dou et al., 2018), despite contradictory evidence (Tian, 2018). Most retouching app users in China are female – women consist of about 90% of Tiantian Pitu app users and about 80% of the Meitu Xiuxiu and Meiyan Xiangji app users (Aurora Mobile, 2016), and AI has further empowered these retouching apps to stereotype the image of women (Meihumeiyan3DK, 2021). Additionally, like Amazon's Alexa and Apple's Siri, most Chinese smart speakers and AI voice assistants, including Alibaba's TmallGenie and Baidu's Xiaodu, have a default female voice, which presumably reinforces the perception of women as assistants, subordinates, and care providers (H. Wang, 2020).

URBAN–RURAL INEQUALITIES AND AI

Urban–rural inequalities are another social problem in contemporary China – scholars once described it as "one country, two societies" (Whyte, 2010) concerning the institutionalized and structured inequalities that divide urban and rural China. Historically, urban economic development and urban residents have been prioritized since the Maoist era – the *Hukou* (household registration) system was established in the 1950s to constrain the rural population's mobility and close them off from better employment, housing, education, health care, public facilities, and other social resources in the cities (Cheng & Selden, 1994). Deng Xiaoping's economic reforms started to allow cities to absorb laborers from the rural areas as migrant workers but continuously prohibited them from most high-income jobs, public services, and welfare (Choi & Peng, pp. 26–31). Although the ongoing urbanization and the loosened (but not abolished) *Hukou* policy in most cities resulted in the urban population surpassing the rural population for the first time in 2011 (and in 2021, China has roughly 900 million urban residents and 500 million rural residents (Statista, 2022a)) and a slightly higher growth rate of annual per capita disposable income of rural households than of urban households from 2011–2020 (Lin, 2021), the absolute income gap between urban households and rural households still widens – the annual per capita disposable income of urban households is 2.5 times as much as that of rural households, with roughly 7,000 US dollars vs. 2,800 US dollars (Statista, 2022b; National Bureau of Statistics of China, 2022a). Moreover, 293 million migrant workers (National Bureau of Statistics of China, 2022b) who are constantly seen as second-class citizens suffer longstanding discrimination from urban residents and are granted the dirtiest, most dangerous, challenging, and low-income jobs and limited access to public resources. AI will probably exacerbate the economic inequalities between urban residents and rural residents and between urban residents and migrant workers because urban residents usually have higher education backgrounds and more often occupy high-skilled positions than rural residents and migrant workers (Chen & Sun, 2022). Migrant workers are the primary targets of urban policing as well, which increasingly employs facial recognition, crime-predicting machine-learning algorithms, and other AI technologies (Yang et al., 2017), as they are unfairly seen to bring unstable elements to the cities. As we mentioned earlier, the social credit system, if widely established, may further disadvantage rural residents and migrant workers by intensifying their surveillance and restricting their options for publicly available resources. Some researchers and news media (e.g., Gu & Zheng, 2020) simply assume that offering AI-related educational apps or software to rural students will solve the problem of education imbalance between urban and rural China, ignoring the complexity of the learning process and the need for comprehensive support from both the family and the public to improve rural students' academic performance. The failure to fix educational inequities through the One Laptop per Child (OLPC) programs in the US (Ames, 2021), South America, Africa, and Asia (Shah, n.d.) is sufficient to warn us that the simple-minded technological solutionism (see Morozov, 2013) usually does not work and sometimes even creates more problems than it solves. In addition, though there are local-level AI innovation initiatives and development pilot zones, such implementations still concentrate on urban areas and rural regions are grotesquely ignored. The rural areas are left in the dark while urban areas are getting the investments, talents, and infrastructures incentivized by beneficiary policies. Such policy imbalance may also result in the Matthew effect in which the rich become richer, and the poor get poorer.

CONCLUSION

Studies have shown that, in a variety of scenarios and applications in Western societies, AI technologies have further disadvantaged and penalized the poor, the marginalized, and the powerless by reenacting and reinforcing pre-existing social relationships and power structures (Gebru, 2020; Noble, 2018; Eubanks, 2017; O'Neil, 2016). There is a need to look beyond the Western world, especially with an eye toward the rising AI technologies and global platforms (e.g., TikTok) being developed in China, as they are operating under different governmental pursuits, economic models, and societal norms – for instance, AI applications in China's newsrooms might not be built on those most taken-for-granted liberal democratic assumptions about journalism (see Lin & Lewis, 2022; Kuai et al., 2022). Similarly, as we have discussed above, the ways that AI reinforces discrimination and exacerbates inequalities in China are distinct from the West because of the different understandings and realities of class, gender, and urban–rural relations. In this chapter, we argue that, as a lack of collective awareness of or widely shared empathy for structured social inequalities, AI's use probably further widens the gap between the privileged and the underprivileged in China. The Chinese government's AI policy, which highlights international competition, economic growth, and social control, overlooks, and even sometimes adds to, the social inequalities AI might create or escalate. As an overview of the current research stage on AI's implications in Chinese society, with an emphasis on economic, gendered, and urban–rural inequalities, constrained space prevents the chapter from diving into the details of specific cases. Future research might work to provide empirical evidence of how a specific AI application helps reify imbalanced social relations or focus on specific social groups, particularly those who are at the intersection of asymmetric power relations (Crenshaw, 1989), such as migrant female workers or the older people in rural areas, might suffer most from the social changes caused by moving toward a broader range of AI usages in China. Research might also examine how AI has been employed to oppress and deprive the ethnic or sexual minorities in China.

REFERENCES

Ames, M. (2021, October 27). Laptops alone can't bridge the digital divide. *MIT Technology Review.* https://www.technologyreview.com/2021/10/27/1037173/laptop-per-child-digital-divide/

Aurora Mobile. (2016, December). *2016拍照P图app研究报告* . http://www.199it.com/archives/545479.html

Barton, D., Woetzel, J., Seong, J., & Tian, Q. (2017). *Artificial intelligence: Implications for China.* McKinsey Global Institute. https://www.mckinsey.com/~/media/mckinsey/featured%20insights/china/artificial%20intelligence%20implications%20for%20china/mgi-artificial-intelligence-implications-for-china.pdf

Chen, C., & Sun, Y. (2022). 工业智能化如何影响城乡收入差距——基于技能偏向性视角. *广东财经大学学报, 182*(03), 21–33.

Chen, S. (2021, June 10). Across China, AI 'city brains' are changing how the government runs. *South China Moring Post.* https://www.scmp.com/news/china/science/article/3136661/across-china-ai-city-brains-are-changing-how-government-runs?module=perpetual_scroll_0&pgtype=article&campaign=3136661

Cheng, T., & Selden, M. (1994). The origins and social consequences of China's Hukou system. *China Quarterly, 139*, 644–668.

China Institute for Science and Technology Policy at Tsinghua University. (2018). *China AI development report 2018.* Tsinghua University. https://edisciplinas.usp.br/pluginfile.php/4873100/mod_folder/content/0/China_AI%20report_2018.pdf?forcedownload=1

China's State Council. (2017). 国务院关于印发新一代人工智能发展规划的通知 . http://www.gov.cn/zhengce/content/2017-07/20/content_5211996.htm

Choi, S., & Peng, Y. (2016). *Masculine compromise: Migration, family, and gender in China.* University of California Press.

Constable, P. (2016, June 16). Loan sharks in China offer student loans for nude photos, giving new meaning to "naked greed." *The Washington Post.* https://www.washingtonpost.com/news/worldviews/wp/2016/06/16/loan-sharks-in-china-offer-student-loans-for-nude-photos-giving-new-meaning-to-naked-greed/

Cortes, G., Jaimovich, N., & Siu, H. (2017). Disappearing routine jobs: Who, how, and why? *Journal of Monetary Economics, 91*, 69–87. https://doi.org/10.1016/j.jmoneco.2017.09.006

Crenshaw, K. (1989). Demarginalizing the intersection of race and sex: A black feminist critique of antidiscrimination doctrine, feminist theory and antiracist politics. *University of Chicago Legal Forum 1989*(8), 139–167. https://chicagounbound.uchicago.edu/cgi/viewcontent.cgi?article=1052&context=uclf

Curran, D., & Smart, A. (2021). Data-driven governance, smart urbanism and risk-class inequalities: Security and social credit in China. *Urban Studies*, *58*(3), 487–506. https://doi .org/10.1177/0042098020927855

Dang, H., & Nguyen, C. (2021). Gender inequality during the COVID-19 pandemic: Income, expenditure, savings, and job loss. *World Development*, *140*, 1–10. https://doi.org/10.1016 /j.worlddev.2020.105296

Dastin, J. (2018, October 10). *Amazon scraps secret AI recruiting tool that showed bias against women*. Reuters. https://www.reuters.com/article/us-amazon-com-jobs-automation -insight/amazon-scraps-secret-ai-recruiting-tool-that-showed-bias-against-women -idUSKCN1MK08G

Datta, A., Tschantz, M. C., & Datta, A. (2015). Automated experiments on Ad privacy settings. *Proceedings on Privacy Enhancing Technologies*, *2015*(1), 92–112. https://doi.org/10.1515 /popets-2015-0007

Deloitte. (2018). 中国人工智能产业白皮书. https://cloud.tencent.com/developer/article/13 73772

Ding, J. (2018). *Deciphering China's AI dream: The context, components, capabilities, and consequences of China's strategy to lead the world in AI*. Future of Humanity Institute, University of Oxford. https://www.fhi.ox.ac.uk/wp-content/uploads/Deciphering_Chinas _AI-Dream.pdf

Ding, Y., Yang, J., Ji, T., & Guo, Y. (2021). Women suffered more emotional and life distress than men during the COVID-19 pandemic: The role of pathogen disgust sensitivity. *International Journal of Environmental Research and Public Health*, *18*(16), 8539. https:// doi.org/10.3390/ijerph18168539

Dou, X., Meng, X., & Zhou, F. (2018). P2P网络借贷中的"性别歧视"——来自人人 贷数据的经验研究. 软科学, 08, 121–124. https://doi.org/10.13956/j.ss.1001-8409.2018.08.26.

Eubanks, V. (2017). *Automating inequality: How high-tech tools profile, police, and punish the poor*. St. Martin's Press.

Flannery, R. (2022, April 5). *The 10 richest Chinese billionaires 2022*. Forbes. https://www .forbes.com/sites/russellflannery/2022/04/05/the-10-richest-chinese-billionaires-2022/?sh =7d2b6b3a2726

Fong, V. (2004). *Only hope: Coming of age under China's one-child policy*. Stanford University Press.

Gebru, T. (2020). Race and gender. In M. D. Dubber, F. Pasquale, & S. Das (Eds.), *The Oxford handbook of ethics of AI* (pp. 253–269). Oxford University Press.

Graetz, G., & Michaels, G. (2015). *Robots at work*. IZA Discussion Paper, 8938, 1–53. http:// doi.org/10.2139/ssrn.2589780

Gu, C., & Zheng, Y. (2020). 人工智能助力农村基础教育现代化. 现代中小学教育 , *36*(11), 1–4. https://doi.org/10.16165/j. cnki. 22-1096/g4.2020.11.001

Horsley, J. (2018, November 16). China's Orwellian social credit score isn't real. *Foreign Policy*. https://foreignpolicy.com/2018/11/16/chinas-orwellian-social-credit-score-isnt-real/

Huang, X. (2021). 人工智能技术发展背景下收入不平等及政策: 理论分析. 中央财经大 学学报, 7, 83–91. https://doi.org/10.19681/j.cnki.jcufe.2021.07.007

Hutt, R. (2020, March 12). *The coronavirus fallout may be worse for women than men. Here's why*. World Economic Forum. https://www.weforum.org/agenda/2020/03/the-coronavirus -fallout-may-be-worse-for-women-than-men-heres-why/

Jiang, L. (2021, July 10). AI圈的"她力量": 为何90%的AI形象都是女性? *IT时报* . https:// finance.sina.com.cn/tech/2021-07-11/doc-ikqciyzk4758992.shtml

Kang, D. (2010). *East Asia before the West: Five centuries of trade and tribute*. Columbia University Press.

Kharas, H., & Dooley, M. (2020, October). *China's influence on the global middle class*. Brooking. https://www.brookings.edu/wp-content/uploads/2020/10/FP_20201012_china _middle_class_kharas_dooley.pdf

Kostka, G. (2019). China's social credit systems and public opinion: Explaining high levels of approval. *New Media & Society, 21*(7), 1565–1593. https://doi.org/10.1177/1461444819826402

Kuai, J., Lin, B., Karlsson, M., & Lewis, S. C. (2022). From wild east to forbidden city: Mapping algorithmic news distribution in China through a case study of Jinri Toutiao. *Digital Journalism*, 1–21. https://doi.org/10.1080/21670811.2022.2121932

Li, J. (2021). 女性与人工智能: 机遇还是挑战? ——新时代女性员工发展困境与应对策略. 领导科学 , *24*, 69–72. https://doi.org/10.19572/j.cnki.ldkx.2021.24.016.

Li, Q. (2020, May 29). 600m with $140 monthly income worries top. *Global Times*. https://www.globaltimes.cn/content/1189968.shtml

Liang, F., Das, V., Kostyuk, N., & Hussain, M. (2018). Constructing a data-driven society: China's social credit system as a state surveillance infrastructure. *Policy and Internet, 10*(4), 415–453. https://doi.org/10.1002/poi3.183

Lin, B. (2023). Beyond authoritarianism and liberal democracy: Understanding China's artificial intelligence impact in Africa. *Information, Communication & Society*, 1–16. http://doi.org/10.1080/1369118X.2023.2239322

Lin, B., & Lewis, S. C. (2022). The one thing journalistic AI just might do for democracy. *Digital Journalism, 10*(10), 1627–1649. https://doi.org/10.1080/21670811.2022.2084131

Lin, Y. (2021, September 28). 中国农村居民收入增速快于城镇居民 城乡居民收入差距持续缩小. 中国网 . https://baijiahao.baidu.com/s?id=1712116290616795389&wfr=spider&for=pc

Liu, J. (2021). 厘清"城市大脑"与"智慧城市"的概念与认知误区. *National Governance Weekly*, 17, 6–10. https://www.cnki.com.cn/Article/CJFDTotal-ZLGJ202117002.htm

Liu, W. (2020, April 15). 健康码与社会智能治理. 新华社客户端 . https://baijiahao.baidu.com/s?id=1664019977175442984&wfr=spider&for=pc

Mastercard. (2021). *The Mastercard Index of women entrepreneurs 2021.* https://www.mastercard.com/news/media/phwevxcc/the-mastercard-index-of-women-entrepreneurs.pdf

MeihumeiyanSDK. (2021, July 28). AI美颜算法的应用(上). *Baidu.* https://baijiahao.baidu.com/s?id=1706516061201224627&wfr=spider&for=pc

Morozov, E. (2013). *To save everything, click here: The folly of technological solutionism* (1st ed.). Public Affairs.

Nathan, A. J. (2016). The puzzle of the Chinese middle class. *Journal of Democracy, 27*(2), 5–19. https://doi.org/10.1353/jod.2016.0027

National Bureau of Statistics of China. (2022a, January 18). *Households' income and consumption expenditure in 2021.* http://www.stats.gov.cn/english/PressRelease/202201/t20220118_1826649.html#:~:text=In%20terms%20of%20urban%20and,an%20increase%20of%2010.5%20percent

National Bureau of Statistics of China. (2022b, April 29). *2021年农民工监测调查报告 .* http://www.stats.gov.cn/tjsj/zxfb/202204/t20220429_1830126.html

Noble, S. U. (2018). *Algorithms of oppression: How search engines reinforce racism.* New York University Press.

O'Neil, C. (2016). *Weapons of math destruction: How big data increases inequality and threatens democracy* (1st ed.). Crown.

Peng, H. (2021). 人工智能对中国居民收入分配的影响研究 . https://kns.cnki.net/KCMS/detail/detail.aspx?dbname=CDFDTEMP&filename=1021657888.nh

Piketty, T., Yang, L., & Zucman, G. (2019). Capital accumulation, private property, and rising inequality in China, 1978–2015. *American Economic Review, 109*(7), 2469–2496. https://doi.org/10.1257/aer.20170973

Roberts, H., Cowls, J., Morley, J., Taddeo, M., Wang, V., & Floridi, L. (2020). The Chinese approach to artificial intelligence: An analysis of policy, ethics, and regulation. *AI & Society, 36*(1), 59–77. https://doi.org/10.1007/s00146-020-00992-2

Shah, N. (n.d.). *A blurry vision: Reconsidering the failure of the One Laptop per Child initiative.* Boston University. https://www.bu.edu/writingprogram/journal/past-issues/issue-3/shah/

Sheehan, M. (2018, February 12). How China's massive AI plan actually works. *Marco Polo.* https://macropolo.org/analysis/how-chinas-massive-ai-plan-actually-works/

Statista. (2022a, February 28). *Urban and rural population of China from 2011 to 2021.* https://www.statista.com/statistics/278566/urban-and-rural-population-of-china/

Statista. (2022b, March 21). Annual per capita disposable income of urban and rural households in China from 1990 to 2021

The World Bank. (n.d.b.). *Proportion of time on unpaid domestic and care work, female (% of 24 hour day)–China.* https://data.worldbank.org/indicator/SG.TIM.UWRK.FE?locations =CN

Tian, F. (2018). P2P借贷平台存在"性别歧视"吗? —基于人人贷数据的实证分析. *Sinoss.* https://www.sinoss.net/uploadfile/2018/0417/20180417121125253.pdf

Vanolo, A. (2014). Smartmentality: The smart city as disciplinary strategy. *Urban Studies, 51*(5), 883–898. https://doi.org/10.1177/0042098013494427

Wang, H. (2020). 人工智能消费场景中的女性性别歧视. *自然辩证法通讯 , 42*(5), 45–51. https://doi.org/10.15994/j.1000-0763.2020.05.007.

Wang, J. (2020). 人工智能对城镇女性劳动力市场的影响. *未来与发展 ,* 1, 28–32. DOI:CNK I:SUN:WLYF.0.2020-01-006.

Webb, A. (2019). *The Big Nine: How the tech titans and their thinking machines could warp humanity.* Public Affairs.

Wen, J. (2021, December 6). 国家新一代人工智能创新发展试验区已达17个. 新华社 . http://www.xinhuanet.com/tech/20211207/fd8876f8bd884c93b427250fc2ac12f5/c.html

Wenham, C., Smith, J., & Morgan, R. (2020). COVID-19: The gendered impacts of the outbreak. *The Lancet, 395,* 846–848. https://doi.org/10.1016/S0140-6736(20)30526-2

Whyte, M. (2010). *One country, two societies: Rural-urban inequality in contemporary China.* Harvard University Press.

Winner, L. (1977). *Autonomous technology: Technics-out-of-control as a theme in political thought.* MIT Press.

World Economic Forum. (2018). *Assessing gender gaps in artificial intelligence.* https://reports.weforum.org/global-gender-gap-report-2018/assessing-gender-gaps-in-artificial -intelligence/

World Economic Forum. (2021). *Global gender gap report 2021.* https://www.weforum.org/reports/global-gender-gap-report-2021/

Wu, Q. (2022, May 8). 国家新一代人工智能创新发展试验区建设已投资2600亿元. 天津日报 . http://www.tjyun.com/system/2022/05/08/052630537.shtml

Xia, X. (2020, December 15). 一大波IPO临近! 信通院: 中国今年AI产业规模达3100亿, C轮以后融资占比超过一半. *21财经.* https://m.21jingji.com/article/20201215/herald/74e 78953a91b186b105453ce667b0e8e.html, accessed on November 16, 2021.

Xu, M., Walker, R., & Yang, L. (2021). Poor and lazy: Understanding middle-class perceptions of poverty in China. *The Journal of Contemporary China,* 1–20. https://doi.org/10.1080 /10670564.2021.2010878

Yang, Y., Yang, Y., & Ju, S. (2017, July 23). China seeks glimpse of citizens' future with crime-predicting AI. *Financial Times.* https://www.ft.com/content/5ec7093c-6e06-11e7 -b9c7-15af748b60d0

Yu, A. (2020). Digital surveillance in post-coronavirus China: A feminist view on the price we pay. *Gender, Work, and Organization, 27*(5), 774–777. https://doi.org/10.1111/gwao.12471

Zhang, Y., Zou, B., Zhang, H., & Zhang, J. (2022). Empirical research on male preference in China: A result of gender imbalance in the Seventh Population Census. *International Journal of Environmental Research and Public Health, 19*(11), 1–17. https://doi.org/10 .3390/ijerph19116482

Zheng, Y. (2007). *De facto federalism in China reforms and dynamics of central-local relations.* World Scientific.

Zeng, J. (2020). *Slogan politics: Understanding Chinese foreign policy concepts.* Palgrave Macmillan. https://doi.org/10.1007/978-981-15-6683-7

Zeng, J. (2022). *Artificial intelligence with Chinese characteristics: National strategy, security and authoritarian governance.* Palgrave Macmillan. https://doi.org/10.1007/978 -981-19-0722-7

Zhu,   F.   (2021).   人工智能时代的价值创造和分配——不平等加剧的社会和经济基础. 财经问题研究 , *460*(3), 10–23. https://doi.org/10.19654/j.cnki.cjwtyj.2022.03.002

25. Design + power: policy· for the ecology of influence

Jasmine E. McNealy

In June 2022, the European Consumer Organization (BEUC) and other consumer protection groups filed complaints against Google for its use of dark patterns in the signup process (BEUC, 2022). Claiming that the mega-firm used "deceptive design, unclear language and misleading choices," BEUC asserted that this activity violated the European Union's General Data Protection Regulation (GDPR) rules that are supposed to provide users with greater privacy protections. In particular, the consumer groups claimed that, at signup, Google did not allow users to opt out of surveillance, instead forcing them to use unclear and complicated steps to protect themselves from data collection. According to BEUC, this further violates the GDPR requirements of transparency and explainability. Google's ongoing European privacy conflicts reflect an era in which individuals, consumer groups, and policymakers have increasing expectations for how personal data is collected, used, and secured.

These conflicts have only increased with innovations in artificial intelligence (AI) technology, which allow for the swift collection and processing of personal data. AI is then used to offer recommendations, guidance, predictions and inferences about an individual's past, current, and future behavior. Deceptive design in connection with AI has ushered in calls for new, stronger, and more punitive regulations to protect individuals from the negative, at times, disparate impacts of the uses of these technologies (Campbell-Dollaghan, 2016; Mathur et al., 2019; Narayanan et al., 2020; Waldman, 2020). In truth, the calls are for shifts in the asymmetrical power dynamic between organizations and individuals who feel the effects of the use of these tools. Concentrations of power denote the status of the relationships that people and organizations have with each other (Ghosh & Srinivasan, 2021; Soriano, 2019). These relationships determine interactions and influence the outcomes of interactions, especially in connection with the technology that influences so much of how we live our lives.

A strain of thought exists that argues that individuals do not have to use technology. Theoretically, this is true. But this way of thinking promotes what Schwartz (2000) called the autonomy trap: people can choose whether they use technology or whether they use certain technologies, but the choice not to participate or to engage with certain technologies limits the ability to receive information such as news, for example, and in the speed necessary to be informed, or there are limited alternatives for political participation. For many, especially those in already marginalized and vulnerable communities, technology is deployed on the individual; there are requirements on the use of certain technologies to fully participate or have access to resources, whether employment, public transportation, or disability services. There are ramifications for not using technology. Technology, including AI and connected design, are then, systems of power.

This chapter considers the influence of design and the design of systems and how policies such as the GDPR and other regulations attempt to reorient the power inherent in these systems. Specifically, this chapter examines how newer legislation focused on the design of AI systems might impact the interactions between users and organizations. To do this, I use the example of dark patterns, and how new or amended legislation aimed at deceptive design may or may not make inroads into curbing the impacts of deceptive design on users.

DECEPTIVE DESIGN

Dark patterns, also called deceptive design, are designs of systems that focus on obtaining something of value that under ordinary circumstances, would not have been obtained (McNealy, 2022b). For example, most are familiar with various systems promising a free trial. That is sometimes for a week, sometimes for 30 days, an organization will allow a user to try their service or system. If the prospective customer likes the service, they may subscribe and begin paying for membership. For the free trial, the organization collects credit card and other account information, afterward, the free trial commences. The free trial scheme is a lucrative and popular way of influencing people to adopt different kinds of technologies, not because people like the system but also because people have a hard time unsubscribing. Users forget that they have subscribed and find out from their credit card statement or after noting a reoccurring draft on their bank statement. Knowing this, some systems have designed sites to make it difficult for people to find out how to unsubscribe from a free trial once the term ends.

The free trial scam is but one of many deceptive designs that organizations use to obtain something of value from an individual that they would not have been able to get without the deception. Harry Brignull (2018) coined the phrase dark pattern in 2010 and created a taxonomy of 12 deceptive designs, including roach motel, bait and switch, disguised ads, forced continuity, sneak into the basket, and hidden costs. The free trial subscription design, which is also the subject of the Unsubscribe Act (Lyons, 2021; US Senate, 2021), is an example of forced continuity, in which an organization begins to bill a user after a free trial has ended without notice. The following are examples of other deceptive designs collected from online and mobile platforms.

Imagine your favorite travel site. For those who have visited airline booking sites, the design usually appears benign. A screen might offer you the ability to enhance your trip by moving your seat from basic coach level up to first class. Visitors can choose whether to upgrade their seat for $169 extra; there is a choice to upgrade the level of seat for an additional $49. If the visitor is not paying adequate attention to what they are doing in making the choices, and how the choices are designed, they may not see that first class has been chosen. Those not paying adequate attention might choose the button to proceed to the next page for purchase without recognizing that they may have clicked the wrong button. At the bottom of the choice architecture, the button that catches your attention the most is a bright color, such as red. In contrast, for those who do not want to purchase an upgrade, the "No Thanks" button is gray with gray text. This is a design choice.

Research has shown that internet and app users do not pay adequate attention to what they are clicking on the sites they visit (Sharma & Bashir, 2020; Yu & Chen, 2018). Further, we know that user attention is dispersed among the many things of which users must be aware (Simon, 1990). This design choice of having what might be the most important choice for the user to be in gray, especially when contrasted with the bright red button, has ramifications for the choices that users make. In addition, an errant choice may result in the user paying more than expected for their purchase.

Another familiar internet situation involves online notices. Internet and app users recognize cookie notices; most sites provide pop-up or banner notices about the use of cookies, and many allow users to choose which cookies they will allow, if any. Imagine the cookie choice screen from an online security system. On the left side, the choice architecture is a dial that allows the user to choose the level of cookies or information about them that will be collected and how it will be used. Note, however, that this choice architecture runs counter to normative ideas of levels. Normally, when we think of the lowest required level of anything, not the least kinds of cookies, we think of the bottom of a structure. In contrast, with this choice architecture, the selection dial is inverted: the lowest level, required cookies, is at the top, whereas the highest level – the most permissive of cookies – is at the bottom. This inverted dial or cookie choice plays on how people connect low and high. As with our travel site example, this choice architecture design exposes the limits of bounded attention, in which if users are not paying adequate attention, they might allow the exposure of information that they otherwise would not.

A final, perhaps more benign, example of a dark pattern involves the now common pop-ups users may receive when they attempt to navigate websites. Many of these pop-ups emerge when users attempt to get around an offer of some kind. In clicking "x" to decline the offer, a notice will appear. In this case, the notice asks whether the user wants to be notified of company-related information. It is important to note how the designers used color and design to highlight the choices. The "Heck yeah of course" is embossed and brightly colored, whereas the "Nope, I'm Rich" is a dull gray. The language the organization chose to use to persuade users to engage in certain behaviors, in this case, to provide their information in exchange for information about sales, has ramifications. The choice of words seems, perhaps, silly, but the language can also be seen as manipulative and an attempt to get users to do the thing that the organization wants them to do, which is to provide personal information.

All these designs are based on the choices that users are allowed to make regarding their personal information. These choices are weighted, through choice architecture design, in favor of the organization. This reflects a power imbalance. This does not mean, of course, that all users or even most users will be deceived, manipulated, or persuaded into making choices that benefit the organization, while possibly to their detriment with the collection and use of personal information or financial harm. Regulatory approaches to the choice architecture and design may offer relief for users. But these policy frameworks must be cognizant of the many factors that impact how we decide to govern personal data.

AN ECOLOGICAL APPROACH TO TECHNOLOGY AND DATA GOVERNANCE

An ecological approach for considering how technology, specifically AI, and data should be governed is appropriate because it assists with identifying the specific thing to be governed, that thing's relationships/connections that can and/or should influence governance choices, the institutions and societal structures that impact governing and who will be tasked with enforcement and implementation, and the environment(s) in which this governance must occur. All these factors must be examined to achieve anything close to a comprehensive and adequate response to the massive volume of data collection, continued surveillance, technological deployment, and data misuse.

The ecological approach to technology and data governance is based on Bronfenbrenner's (1977, 1979) argument that a true understanding of human development "requires examination of multi-person systems of interaction not limited to a single setting and must take into account aspects of the environment beyond the immediate situation containing the subject" (Bronfenbrenner, 1977, p. 514) and required envisioning the "environment" for a human as a model of four nested systems: micro, meso, exo, and macro. In brief, the microsystem includes the direct subject of study. In human development, this would be the human. The microsystem rests within the mesosystem, which contains that human's relationships or connections. The exosystem, which encompasses the mesosystem, includes all the formal and informal structures that influence human development. Finally, the macrosystem represents the various environments in which the human and his or her relationships and structures inhabit, including the social, political, economic, and legal, among others. According to Bronfenbrenner (1977, 1979), this kind of ecological model represents the complexity of human development and ecology, considering the various things that shape who a person is and becomes.

Using this conceptualization for technology and data, particularly those in AI or algorithmic systems design, the microsystem encompasses the foundation layer of the technology – in this case the deceptive design, or the data itself (McNealy, 2022a). Surrounding the microsystem is the mesosystem, which considers the relationships and connections to data. For dark patterns, this would mean examining both the connections that the design has with other parts of the system and encompasses all the structures or settings that shape the design over the life cycle. The exosystem includes all the societal and institutional structures tasked with implementing and enforcing technology governance. Finally, the macrosystem is the environment(s) in which the micro-, meso-, and exosystems rest, and can be considered the environments that shape technology, including the social, political, economic, cultural, and other environments.

Deceptive design exists in both the exo- and mesolayers. The three imaginative examples of deceptive designs above offer insights into the ecology of data collecting systems and of the necessity of an ecological approach. At the mesolayer, the choice design connects with an unseen data collection and processing ecosystem. Both examples 1 and 2 illustrate a connection between a choice or set of choices available to users that represent and facilitate the collection by the organization of something of value. In the case of example 1, the thing of value is additional money; for example 2, the thing of value is the ability to collect, process, and share personal information. These choices, and the data collection connected with them, also schematizes the exo system, in which societal and institutional structures exist for data governance. All three examples point to how and whether data collection is regulated and whether the organizations' systems are in compliance with those governance structures. Example 2 can be said to comply with regulations requiring that organizations allow users to choose what kind of tracking cookies they will allow in connection to the use of a website or platform. At the same time, the design is such that the organization may be able to collect more data than the user intends because that design runs counter to traditional and intuitive understandings of a barometer or thermometer.

How policymakers attempt to protect users from these designs relies on the creation of policies that protect people from the impacts of how data is collected and used. The mesosystem reflects how technology connects to various, networked systems including AI. In this realm, deceptive design may be part of the architecture of the technology that persuades individuals to disclose personal data. For example, the cookie dial dark pattern imagined above might deceive users into allowing more data extraction than they realize. But the data is not kept only in connection with the dial or the user's browser; instead, the data become part of a network of systems and organizations that aggregate and use data for purposes such as sending targeted advertisements to the user (West, 2019; Zuboff, 2015). The exosystem includes all the organizations and institutions with regulatory power over the use of deceptive designs and data protection. This would include policymaker and legislators tasked with protecting users from deceptive collection and use of their personal information.

REGULATORY ATTEMPTS AT CHANGING DESIGN

Policymakers in the United States have taken note of the problem of users being unable to get out of their free trials; in early 2021, a group of senators, including Senators Warnock and Schatz, proposed the Unsubscribe Act of 2021, which would force organizations to make it easier for users to cancel their online subscriptions and for people to be able to cancel their online subscriptions when a free trial period ends. The bill's goal was to end the forced connections or continue to be charged for an unwanted product or service (Lyons, 2021). If passed, the bill will force organizations to make it easier for people to get out of free trials. The Unsubscribe Act can be considered a design law. Although at its most general level, the bill articulates what organizations can and cannot do, it requires organizations to design systems that remove the difficulty for users attempting to decide what it is they want to do: whether that is to get out of the subscription or to continue after the free trial has ended.

An example of a policy related to design, dark patterns specifically, is the California Consumer Protection Act (CCPA). This law, passed in 2018, is often considered by commenters to be the closest thing that a state in the US has that reflects principles found in the European Union's GDPR (Soe et al., 2020). In its 2021 update, the California Legislature amended the CCPA to include a design-specific provision. Whereas the Unsubscribe Act would have been a design law based on text, specifying what an organization can and cannot do with its system, and the organization would have to figure out how to adequately comply, the CCPA includes a design feature that the state legislators require organizations to use. This uniform opt-out icon bans the use of dark patterns "designed with the purpose or that have a substantial effect of subverting or impairing a consumer's choice to opt out." The icon serves as a button that organizations can use on their sites and apps. The CCPA's design policy's opt-out button is useful and recognizable for consumers who understand that by clicking the icon, they can opt out of a product or service. The policy is limited, however, as the legislation focuses on the sale of data and organizations using dark patterns to obtain personal information to sell. This means that an organization could use other kinds of dark patterns.

Like the amendment to the CCPA, the Colorado Privacy Act (CPA) specifically targets dark patterns (JD Supra, 2021; Zhu & Zhu, 2021), which it defines as "a user interface designed or manipulated with the substantial effect of subverting or impairing user autonomy, decision making, or choice." The law prohibits the use of dark patterns to get consent. In particular, the consent an organization obtains from users must be opt-in or "clear affirmative act signifying a consumer's freely given, specific, informed, and unambiguous agreement, such as by a written statement, including by electronic means." This means that organizations may not use tricks like those described above to obtain personal information or other things of value from consumers. In particular, the language of the text of the law focuses on the user interface, which is how the site or app is designed and how the users will interact with the system. If the site uses manipulative or deceptive tactics to obtain consent, it violates the law.

The three policy examples demonstrate that policymakers are recognizing that people are being influenced and how organizations use deceptive designs to collect personal information, which is then used for various purposes that could possibly be harmful. This deceptive collection and use illustrate a power interaction that reflects how many organizations have created relationships with users and created interactions in the relationships that allow the organization to maintain an advantage over the user. These regulatory policies, then, attempt to use design to lessen that power advantage organizations have over consumers and other organizations as well.

ATTEMPTS AT MORE ADEQUATE POLICY

To more adequately understand and then create policies that modify this imbalanced power dynamic, policymakers should take an ecological approach to regulating. When individuals interact with organizations, current power dynamics allow organizations to force interactions that may prompt an individual to provide data whether personal, financial, or otherwise. The collection and use of that data can impact the individual financially, emotionally, and through differential access to information. Currently, in the United States, state governments such as California and Colorado are filling in an absence of comprehensive federal law. There exist certain laws at the federal level that are being used to protect privacy but are not explicitly considered design laws or laws related to design.

The Restore Online Shoppers Confidence Act of 2010 (ROSCA), for example, requires an organization to have clear and conspicuous disclosures (Friedman, 2018; Luguri & Strahilevitz, 2021; Nochenson & Grossklags, 2017; VonBergen et al., 2016). The law limits "data passes" or after-sale transfers of consumer data to a third party after an online retail transaction. Third-party sellers must obtain express consent from the consumer that includes purchase information, the consumer's name and contact information, and an affirmative action, such as clicking a button, for completing the transaction. The law also restricts the use of negative option marketing, which involves an organization taking a consumer's lack of affirmative rejection or canceling of an agreement as consent to being charged for goods or services. ROSCA requires clear and conspicuous disclosure of terms and conditions. How these terms and conditions are made clear to consumers, however, depends on the organization. The terminology, "clear and conspicuous" disclosure is a design terminology; it recognizes that certain designs or how organizations behave or have designed their sites impact what shoppers know and the choices they make. Of course, this affects individuals financially and with respect to personal data.

Another example of an attempt at US federal-level policy was first proposed in 2019, and again in 2021, called the Deceptive Experiences to Online Users Reduction (DETOUR) Act. The bill's aim was that online organizations, apps, and platforms that had a threshold of 100 million users, and who engage in behavioral or psychological experiments on the users with user data or with user choices, would have to notify the users of the experiments (Gunawan et al., 2021; Karagoel & Nathan-Roberts, 2021; Parikh et al., 2021). The organization would also have to get informed consent, meaning that users would have to be notified every time an experiment happens. This would include activities such as A/B testing. The bill specified the specific kind of design tactics that were coming under scrutiny to deter any changes to modify or manipulate a user interface to obscure, subvert, or impair user autonomy, decision making, or choice to obtain consent or user data. Although this bill never got out of committee, it is an interesting example of a design policy. DETOUR was an attempt to change the power dynamic between the organization and the individuals who must interact with that organization. The bill is an example of how far legislators and policymakers could push regulation in thinking about what design means and the effect the design has.

A flaw in DETOUR, and many other policies aimed at curbing design and algorithmically affected user interfaces, is the focus on notice and choice, or consent. Prior research has shown the consent mechanism fails, in part, because of bounded attention.

Because our attention is limited, we cannot be fully engaged with every aspect of the systems with which we interact all at once (Richards & Hartzog, 2018; Rothchild, 2018). This means that we, at times, use heuristics to make decisions, and we also do not make the most informed decisions about how and whether to use certain systems (Gambino et al., 2016; Holtzhausen, 2016; Sundar et al., 2013, 2020). Prior research on individual choices in privacy and data protection with online systems has found that individuals make tradeoffs between privacy protection and engagement with the networked system, whether that tradeoff is between privacy and connection or the fulfillment of some other need or desire (McNealy & Mullis, 2019; Metzger, 2007; Petronio & Child, 2020; Sannon et al., 2020). Therefore, although a system that provides what might be continuous notices about data use might seem desirable, it may not change how or whether users continue to use a platform.

The focus of DETOUR and so many other attempts at regulation, is transparency – or the disclosure of how and what data is collected and used. Yet, transparency in and of itself does not initiate change in how organizations attempt data collection and its uses, nor does it protect users from possibly harmful choices (Chromik et al., 2019). In many ways, we do not completely know or understand the long-term or even short-term implications of consenting to the diverse asks made by sites and platforms. Therefore, although it may appear significant that regulatory attempts such as DETOUR are designed to stop manipulation to get consent by obtaining consent, does not truly impact whether the kind of data collection and use might end in harm to the user. Many scholars in different disciplines have made the case that the consent as a framework in its current state does not achieve the policy goals for which it was designed (Richards & Hartzog, 2018, 2020; Sloan & Warner, 2013). This policy gap, when dealing with design systems such as dark patterns, leaves users without the protections that regulators were hoping to achieve (McNealy et al., 2022). This is particularly critical, again for marginalized and more vulnerable communities who are disparately impacted by data collection and use, including in algorithmic systems.

Legislators have, however, made attempts at closing the policy gap by proposing laws that scrap consent or notice and choice and, instead, limit whether, how, and the purposes for which organizations may collect and use data. One such attempt was the Data Accountability and Transparency Act (DATA) of 2020 proposed by Ohio Senator Sherrod Brown (Fowler, 2021; Kerry & Morris, 2020). The bill effectively rejected consent as a framework, specifically excluding consent language from the law. Instead, the proposed law would have strictly limited data collection, use, and sharing by organizations. This meant that organizations would have been restricted from data collection, use, and sharing unless specifically allowed by law. In connection with algorithmic systems, organizations would have been banned from using personal data to discriminate in the realms of housing, employment, credit, insurance, and public accommodations. The bill contained several other clauses important for algorithmic accountability and privacy protection for users and non-users.

Although DATA appears to be just like any other attempt at regulation, the bill's very rejection of consent and notice and choice makes it a design law. That is, the proposed law, with its prohibitions on the collection of data outside of the bounds of the law, in essence, restricts how organizations can design platforms and sites to collect personal data. That means not only are organizations banned from asking for certain information directly, but it also means that sites and platforms may not collect data surreptitiously or deceptively. This effectively would have banned deceptive designs or dark patterns. Further, the restrictions on data sharing are an explicit recognition that organizations that are first-party collectors may act as points of contact for other organizations that want to use personal data but do not have the resources to engage in large-scale data collection. This is a recognition that systems and organizations do not act alone but are parts of an ecosystem of data collection and use throughout a lifecycle that often has unwanted influence on the lives of individuals.

A FUTURE FOR DESIGN POLICY?

For the most part, this chapter has focused on attempts at user protection legislation by policymakers in the US. But the complaint by the BEUC over deceptive designs encountered by individuals in the EU demonstrate the global concerns over dark patterns and other AI-connected data-collecting systems. The GDPR is the reigning law in the EU, and researchers have found that even with the strong consumer protection clauses in the regulation, organizations continue to implement deceptive designs (Gray et al., 2021; Nouwens et al., 2020; Soe et al., 2020). Further, there may be a problem with enforcement and standardizing what actually complies with law and what may negatively impact users (Nouwens et al., 2020).

What do these attempts at regulating design, from a predominantly Western perspective, mean for the future of design policy and power? Although the attempts at policy that more adequately influence design, such as DATA, have stalled in the legislative process, that such a bill was proposed in 2020 and again in 2021 means that policymakers are recognizing the need for laws that consider the entire ecosystem of data collection, use, and sharing, particularly as algorithmic systems are increasingly used. These systems, trained on the personal data collected through design systems, including deceptive designs, have significant implications for how individuals will get to live and interact outside of platforms and sites and into their lives. The increased surveillance in public spheres and how it affects life is what Park (2021) calls a process of normalization, changing how we engage with the environment.

This includes how individuals interact with platforms and other sites that include deceptive designs.

But this process of normalization recognizes that data collection systems, including deceptive designs, behave as governance structures. This means that the designs, and more importantly the organizations that deploy them, assert power over individuals. Power is demonstrated in the kinds of patterns that individuals encounter that entice or force them to provide something of value that they otherwise might not provide, including money, time, and data. The thing of value is then used for the benefit of the organization and not the individual. Nor is there a way for individuals to meaningfully make decisions about personal data collection, use, and sharing. This misalignment with values related to personal autonomy, privacy, and data protection with organizational logics related to data extraction requires policies to protect individuals and communities and means that new policy must recognize the power imbalance that weighs heavily in favor of organizations to the detriment of individuals and communities.

In addition, more adequate policies must consider the failures of past frameworks, including notice, choice, or consent. This would recognize that these frameworks have done little in the way of rectifying the power imbalance and/or constructing consent in a different way. The focus on consent, or the power of the individual, does not consider that in designed systems, especially those now ubiquitous surveillance systems that feed algorithmic tools, the individual has very little power. Instead, a more adequate policy, then, needs to foreclose on the ability of organizations to circumvent or misrepresent consent to the detriment of individuals or communities. This necessitates legislation that prohibits business models designed to place the individual at a perpetual disadvantage regarding data. This kind of policy would go a long way to rebalance the power dynamics inherent in uses of technology by individuals, whether required or chosen.

REFERENCES

BEUC. (2022). *European consumer groups take action against Google for pushing users towards its surveillance system.* BEUC. https://www.beuc.eu/publications/european -consumer-groups-take-action-against-google-pushing-users-towards-its/html

Brignull, H. (2018). *Dark Patterns.* Dark Patterns. https://darkpatterns.org/

Bronfenbrenner, U. (1977). Toward an experimental ecology of human development. *American Psychologist, 32*(7), 513. https://doi.org/10.1037/0003-066X.32.7.513

Bronfenbrenner, U. (1979). *The ecology of human development.* Harvard University Press.

Campbell-Dollaghan, K. (2016, December 21). *The year dark patterns won.* Fast Company. https://www.fastcompany.com/3066586/the-year-dark-patterns-won

Chromik, M., Eiband, M., Völkel, S. T., & Buschek, D. (2019). Dark patterns of explainability, transparency, and user control for intelligent systems. *Los Angeles, 6.*

Fowler, G. A. (2021, January 29). Nobody reads privacy policies. This senator wants lawmakers to stop pretending we do. *Washington Post.* https://www.washingtonpost.com/technology /2020/06/18/data-privacy-law-sherrod-brown/

Friedman, D. A. (2018). "Dishonest search disruption": Taking deceptive-pricing tactics seriously. *UC Davis Law Review Online, 51*, 121–147. https://doi.org/10.2139/ssrn.3101964

Gambino, A., Kim, J., Sundar, S. S., Ge, J., & Rosson, M. B. (2016). User disbelief in privacy paradox: Heuristics that determine disclosure. *Proceedings of the 2016 CHI Conference Extended Abstracts on Human Factors in Computing Systems*, 2837–2843. https://doi.org /10.1145/2851581.2892413

Ghosh, D., & Srinivasan, R. (2021). The future of platform power: Reining in big tech. *Journal of Democracy, 32*(3), 163–167. https://doi.org/10.1353/jod.2021.0042

Gray, C. M., Santos, C., Bielova, N., Toth, M., & Clifford, D. (2021). Dark patterns and the legal requirements of consent banners: An interaction criticism perspective. In *Proceedings of the 2021 CHI Conference on Human Factors in Computing Systems* (pp. 1–18). Association for Computing Machinery. https://doi.org/10.1145/3411764.3445779

Gunawan, J., Choffnes, D., Hartzog, W., & Wilson, C. (2021, May 8). Towards an understanding of dark pattern privacy harms. *Chi'21*. NSPW '19: New Security Paradigms Workshop, Virtual. https://dl.acm.org/doi/10.1145/3368860.3368865

Holtzhausen, D. (2016). Datafication: Threat or opportunity for communication in the public sphere? *Journal of Communication Management, 20*(1), 21–36. https://doi.org/10.1108/ JCOM-12-2014-0082

JD Supra. (2021, June 18). *Colorado Privacy Act: Colorado Joins California and Virginia by Passing the Third State Privacy Law in the US*. JD Supra. https://www.jdsupra.com/ legalnews/colorado-privacy-act-colorado-joins-8783686/

Karagoel, I., & Nathan-Roberts, D. (2021). Dark patterns: Social media, gaming, and e-commerce. *Proceedings of the Human Factors and Ergonomics Society Annual Meeting, 65*(1), 752–756. https://doi.org/10.1177/1071181321651317

Kerry, C. F., & Morris, J. B. (2020, December 8). Framing a privacy right: Legislative findings for federal privacy legislation. *Brookings*. https://www.brookings.edu/research/framing-a -privacy-right-legislative-findings-for-federal-privacy-legislation/

Luguri, J., & Strahilevitz, L. J. (2021). Shining a light on dark patterns. *Journal of Legal Analysis, 13*(1), 43–109. https://doi.org/10.1093/jla/laaa006

Lyons, K. (2021, June 16). *Senate bill would make it easier to cancel a subscription online after a free trial*. The Verge. https://www.theverge.com/2021/6/16/22537277/senate-bill -cancel-online-subscription-consumers

Mathur, A., Acar, G., Friedman, M. J., Lucherini, E., Mayer, J., Chetty, M., & Narayanan, A. (2019). Dark patterns at scale: findings from a crawl of 11K shopping websites. *Proceedings of the ACM on human-computer interaction, 3*(CSCW), 1–32. https://doi.org/10.1145 /3359183

McNealy, J. E. (2022a). An ecological approach to data governance. *Notre Dame Journal of Law, Ethics & Public Policy, 37*. https://ssrn.com/___

McNealy, J. E. (2022b). Platforms as phish farms: Deceptive social engineering at scale. *New Media & Society, 24*(7), 1677–1694. https://doi.org/10.1177/14614448221099228

McNealy, J. E., Jen, D., & Nguyen, S. (2022). Prototyping policy: Visualizing impact for better regulation. *Convergence*, 13548565211069876. https://doi.org/10.1177/13548565211069875

McNealy, J., & Mullis, M. D. (2019). Tea and turbulence: Communication privacy management theory and online celebrity gossip forums. *Computers in Human Behavior, 92*, 110–118. https://doi.org/10.1016/j.chb.2018.10.029

Metzger, M. J. (2007). Communication privacy management in electronic commerce. *Journal of Computer-Mediated Communication, 12*(2), 335–361. https://doi.org/10.1111/j.1083 -6101.2007.00328.x

Narayanan, A., Mathur, A., Chetty, M., & Kshirsagar, M. (2020). Dark patterns: Past, present, and future: The evolution of tricky user interfaces. *Queue, 18*(2), 67–92. https://doi.org/10 .1145/3400899.3400901

Nochenson, A., & Grossklags, J. (2017). I didn't want that! An experiment on interventions for deceptive post-transaction marketing. *Proceedings of the workshop on technology and consumer protection*, 9–18.

Nouwens, M., Liccardi, I., Veale, M., Karger, D., & Kagal, L. (2020). Dark patterns after the GDPR: Scraping consent pop-ups and demonstrating their influence. *Proceedings of the 2020 CHI conference on human factors in computing systems*, 1–13. https://doi.org/10.1145/3313831.3376321

Parikh, N., Fahs, G., & Nonnecke, B. (2021). *Test-driven development for technology policy: Applying software engineering principles to policy development* (Aspen tech policy hub). Aspen Institute. https://www.aspentechpolicyhub.org/wp-content/uploads/2019/11/WP_TDD_v051.pdf

Park, Y. J. (2021). Structural logic of AI surveillance and its normalisation in the public sphere. *Javnost - The Public*, *28*(4), 341–357. https://doi.org/10.1080/13183222.2021.1955323

Petronio, S., & Child, J. T. (2020). Conceptualization and operationalization: Utility of communication privacy management theory. *Current Opinion in Psychology*, *31*, 76–82. https://doi.org/10.1016/j.copsyc.2019.08.009

Richards, N., & Hartzog, W. (2018). The pathologies of digital consent. *Washington University Law Review, 96*, 1461.

Richards, N., & Hartzog, W. (2020). A relational turn for data protection? *European Data Protection Law Review*, *6*(4), 492–497. https://doi.org/10.21552/edpl/2020/4/5

Rothchild, J. A. (2018). Against notice and choice: The manifest failure of the proceduralist paradigm to protect privacy online (or anywhere else). *Cleveland State Law Review, 66*, 91.

Sannon, S., Stoll, B., DiFranzo, D., Jung, M. F., & Bazarova, N. N. (2020). "I just shared your responses": Extending communication privacy management theory to interactions with conversational agents. *Proceedings of the ACM on human-computer interaction, 4(group)*, 1–18. https://doi.org/10.1145/3375188

Schwartz, P. M. (2000). Internet privacy and the state. *Connecticut Law Review, 32*, 821. https://doi.org/10.2139/ssrn.229011

Sharma, T., & Bashir, M. (2020). An analysis of phishing emails and how the human vulnerabilities are exploited. In I. Corradini, E. Nardelli, & T. Ahram (Eds.), *Advances in human factors in cybersecurity* (pp. 49–55). Springer International Publishing. https://doi.org/10.1007/978-3-030-52581-1_7

Simon, H. A. (1990). Bounded rationality. In J. Eatwell, M. Milgate, & P. Newman (Eds.), *Utility and probability* (pp. 15–18). Palgrave Macmillan. https://doi.org/10.1007/978-1-349-20568-4_5

Sloan, R. H., & Warner, R. (2013). Beyond notice and choice: Privacy, norms, and consent. *SSRN Electronic Journal*. https://doi.org/10.2139/ssrn.2239099

Soe, T. H., Nordberg, O. E., Guribye, F., & Slavkovik, M. (2020). Circumvention by design— Dark patterns in cookie consent for online news outlets. In *Proceedings of the 11th Nordic conference on human-computer interaction: Shaping experiences, shaping society* (pp. 1–12). Association for Computing Machinery. https://doi.org/10.1145/3419249.3420132

Soriano, S. (2019). Taking aim at big tech. *Intermedia*, *47*(2), 10–15.

Sundar, S. S., Kang, H., Wu, M., Go, E., & Zhang, B. (2013). Unlocking the privacy paradox: Do cognitive heuristics hold the key? *CHI '13 extended abstracts on human factors in computing systems*, 811–816. https://doi.org/10.1145/2468356.2468501

Sundar, S. S., Kim, J., Rosson, M. B., & Molina, M. D. (2020). Online privacy heuristics that predict information disclosure. *Proceedings of the 2020 CHI conference on human factors in computing systems*, 1–12. https://doi.org/10.1145/3313831.3376854

U.S. Senate. (2021). *Schatz, Thune, Warnock, Kennedy introduce new legislation to stop deceptive subscription business practices.* https://www.schatz.senate.gov/news/press-releases/schatz-thune-warnock-kennedy-introduce-new-legislation-to-stop-deceptive-subscription-business-practices

VonBergen, C. W., Kernek, C., Bressler, M. S., & Silver, L. S. (2016). Cueing the customer using nudges and negative option marketing. *Atlantic Marketing Journal*, *5*(2), 12–31.

Waldman, A. E. (2020). Cognitive biases, dark patterns, and the "privacy paradox." *Current Opinion in Psychology*, *31*, 105–109. https://doi.org/10.1016/j.copsyc.2019.08.025

West, S. M. (2019). Data capitalism: Redefining the logics of surveillance and privacy. *Business & Society, 58*(1), 20–41. https://doi.org/10.1177/0007650317718185

Yu, T., & Chen, S.-H. (2018). Big data, scarce attention and decision-making quality. *Computational Economics.* https://doi.org/10.1007/s10614-018-9798-5

Zhu, C., & Zhu, C. (2021, July 29). *Dark patterns—A new frontier in privacy regulation.* Reuters. https://www.reuters.com/legal/legalindustry/dark-patterns-new-frontier-privacy -regulation-2021-07-29/

Zuboff, S. (2015). Big other: Surveillance capitalism and the prospects of an information civilization. *Journal of Information Technology, 30*(1), 75–89. https://doi.org/10.1057/jit .2015.5

Index